澳门基金会
※
北京外国语大学
中国海外汉学研究中心
※
大象出版社

合作项目

卫三畏文集
Selected Works of Samuel Wells Williams

卫三畏在东亚——美日所藏资料选编

Samuel W. Williams in East Asia: Selected Archives from the United States and Japan

（卷下）

陶德民　编

中原出版传媒集团
大地传媒
大象出版社
·郑州·

第4部分

天津缔约与北京驻节

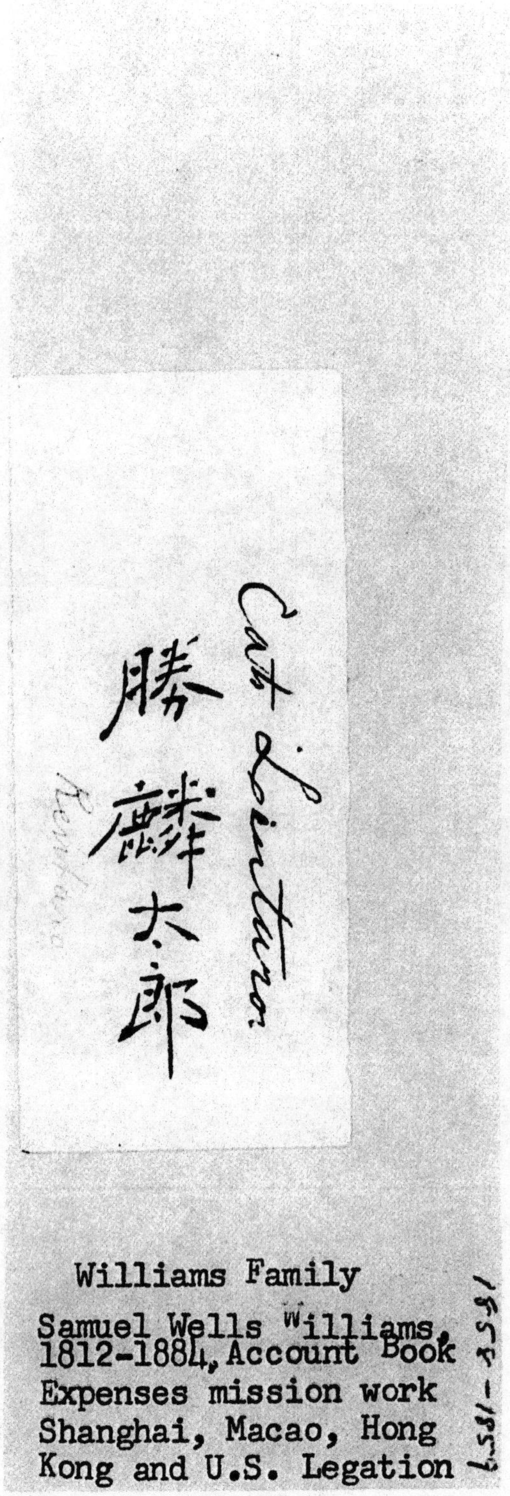
勝麟太郎
Cats Lintaro
Rintaro
Williams Family
Samuel Wells Williams,
1812-1884, Account Book
Expenses mission work
Shanghai, Macao, Hong
Kong and U.S. Legation
1853-1857

NOTICE FROM CHIN TO THE FOREIGN OFFICIALS AT CANTON.

A respectful communication. It has has been my uniform and strong desire to cultivate friendly relations with my neighbors, and to have kind thoughts towards them. I have often received communications inquiring about what regulations might be established, but the pressing and varied engagements and affairs connected with the army on the north of the city has left no leisure to see you and confer on such matters; and the distance between us has been such as unluckily to prevent my learning your views.

At this juncture the rising of our soldiers has caused the traders to flee and move away, and merchandize to be stopped, and trade to be impeded, for which I am truly most sorry, but for which I now see no remedy. You are well aware that latterly, officers and rapacious rulers in Canton province of every rank have been exacting to enrich themselves, treating merchants from the provinces with no respect or good faith, and looking upon the common people as bandits or personal enemies. The traders and inhabitants have suffered these grievous injuries, and the robbers have ventured upon outrageous acts, so that the suffering country and harassed people have never been afflicted to such a pitch. Not long ago in the neighborhood of Canton, in the villages of Si-wá, Tieh-kau, Chá-táu, Si-tsun, Kin-kí, and others, these unprincipled soldiers, under pretense of expelling our forces, assaulted and carried off the people and their property, burning their houses, and even going so far as to cut off the ears of men and women, old and young, that they might claim a reward for their valor, and then tumbling the bodies into fish-ponds and ditches.

Such inhuman cruelty can never be forgiven. Whoever has heard the tale is aroused at it, as are all who have seen the sight, affected to tears. And still amid all the calamities of war ensuent upon these excesses, they are using their power to harass the people and contrive how to enrich themselves, until now both gods and men are indignant, and heaven and earth can no longer endure them. I have been impelled by my indignation and great anger to do something, and have raised my patriotic troops, swearing that I will exterminate the rascally horde and save the people, as one would snatch persons from fire or water, or cut down one found hanging.

Wherever my own troops are stationed, they do not molest or rob, but the avocations of the fields and market-places are continued as usual. At this moment, in the districts of Tung-kwán, Tsang-ching, Shun-teh, Tsingyuen, Hwá, Tsung-hwá and Sán-shwui, as also in the other prefectures of Sháu-king, Lo-ting, Káu-chau, Sháu-chau, Lien-chau, Hwui-chau and Cháu-chau, I hear a general report that a junction is to take place for coöperation; as probably your countrymen have both heard and seen the same. Furthermore, as you and we, the people of Canton, have had friendly acquaintance for many generations, and have esteemed just advantage in our mutual intercourse; it is proper that we should have the same enemies and purposes, and not cast off our former compact. Recently, I have heard that you do not despise us, and stupid as I am, I have been often desirous of learning your views, to which I shall give the most serious attention. If you would grant this extraordinary token of your regard, it would hang on my ear like a drop, and be engraven on my heart.

At present I have merely made a temporary movement with a detachment from the great camp at Fuhshan to this movable camp at Sin-tsau, here to await a personal conference with you, when we can not only establish good commercial regulations, but also devise an excellent plan to exterminate these flagitious and cruel officers, and thus restore trade to its usual channels, bringing back peace and quiet to the general joy of all. This would not only be a substantial benefit to the people of this province, but merchants of all western countries would be deeply indebted for such an act of favor. If therefore you will be good enough to intimate beforehand the day when you will come, I will have everything here made clean and ready, awaiting your coming, for which I stand on tiptoe most earnestly desiring. For this purpose I have sent this, hoping that your joy and security may be as perfect as you desire.

Chin Hien-liáng,
Generalissimo of the patriot troops of Canton province.

Kiáh-yin year, eighth moon, tenth day (Oct. 1st, 1854)

錄致總理衙門照會稿

照會事、照得吳淞口攔江沙一案、本年三月二十六日接准
貴親王來文、當經本大臣以
南洋通商大臣所派委員於此事未免多有誤會、
容繪具圖說送呈、等因、先行照復在案、厥後已將圖式
繪就、曾經派委漢文正使梅携指
貴署呈遞、
大臣閱覽、随承函云所見各節、俟復備文照會前來、
再為核議各等語、今本大臣將所繪圖式兩件、送呈
貴親王祈為查閱、至
南洋大臣所云黃浦口外水底積沙、可謂天設之險、防由
海入蘇松等處要道、口內有炮台對設東西兩岸等語、
此節依本大臣所見、恐係悞將內沙外沙牽混、蓋所欲設
法挑濬之地段、實係內沙、而內沙本距炮台較遠、須已入
口經過炮台後、方至其地、設有外來之敵船意欲入口、此段
內沙、終無扶助炮台之力、希
覽各圖、足可為證、是此段積沙以為險要之說、似可無
須置議、查
南洋大臣叙及天津辦法、乃吳淞口內沙、實與大沽炮台
海面對積外沙、難以並論、即使情形無不相同、僅此項防
禦之備、似亦難以足恃、總之欲籌海防以及保全內河、非賴於
水師興事、尚無實濟、今
貴國漸次已具水師規模、各國旁觀無不慣懷、而慣懷之中、
毫無疑忌之念、誠如
南洋大臣所謂自各國通商以來、外國未嘗阻修武備也、況多
年以來本國大臣等屢向
總署商勸、欲
中國妥籌自護自固之計、諒此必在
貴親王記憶之中、矧思
貴國現在製造戰船式類、匪但外商輪船必望疏濬水道、且
不久
貴國兵船更欲挑挖該處積沙、以便出入駛行、又有所言近
日洋輪船身較昔尤大、以致吃水更深、此語頗見誠然、但船
身愈大噸數愈多、船鈔因之愈增、且大小輪船比年加衆、
貴國更得利益、至從前本大臣函商此事、有云者以為
該處積沙若已挑濬、嗣後難保輪船增大、吃水更深勢
迫從新開挖、必致再需經費等語、試問誠如所慮、何難
先行訂明、庶免日後異辭、惟以目下情形而論、又念濬沙
經費甚屬有限、其宜為今日輪船計議之處、固不待
言、再查
南洋大臣所謂民船設奔洪不設攔淺、若於海口驟
添中洪之險、則避之惟恐不及等語、然內地大小各船
向來多在該處小洲以北河汊取道、而洋商所請挖濬之
段、實在小洲之南、各不相防、至意謂近來彼處舟楫較
前難通之故、在積沙者少、實在洋船漸次增大者多、此

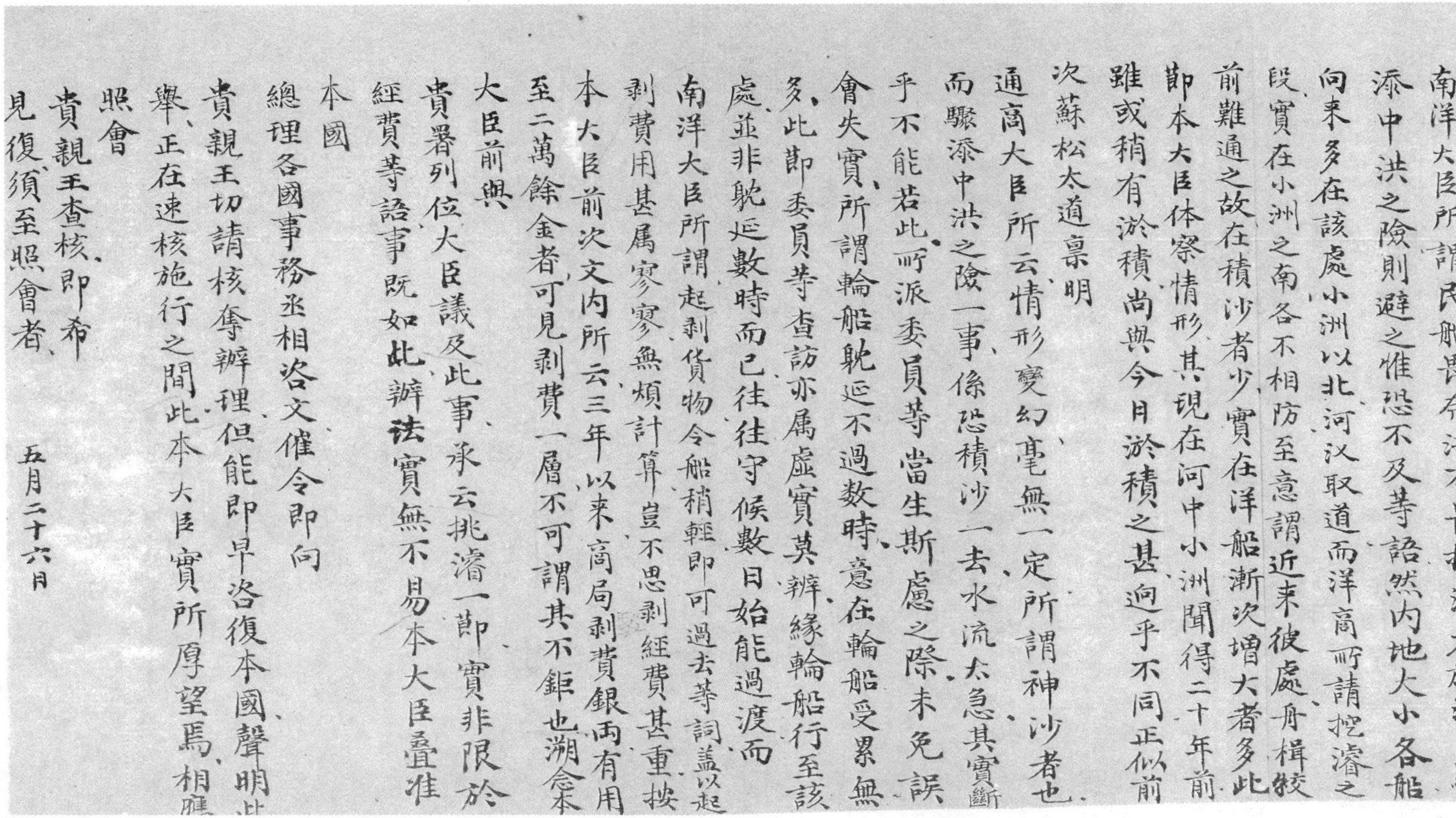
南洋大臣所謂民船畏奔洪不畏擱淺若於海口驟
添中洪之險則避之惟恐不及等語然內地大小各船
向來多在該處小洲以北河汊取道而洋商所請挖濬之
段實在小洲之南各不相防至意謂近來彼處舟楫較
前難通之故在積沙者少實在洋船漸次增大者多此
節本大臣体察情形其現在河中小洲聞得二十年前
雖或稍有淤積尚與今日淤積之甚迥乎不同正似前
次蘇松太道稟明
通商大臣所云情形變幻毫無一定所謂神沙者也
而驟添中洪之險一事係恐積沙一去水流太急其實斷
乎不能若此所派委員等當生斯慮之際未免誤
會失實所謂輪船耽延不過數時意在輪船受累無
多此節委員等查訪亦屬虛實莫辨緣輪船行至該
處並非耽延數時而已往往守候數日始能過渡而
南洋大臣所謂起剝貨物令船稍輕即可過去等詞蓋以起
剝費用甚屬寥寥無煩計算豈不思剝經費甚重按
本大臣前次文內所云三年以來商局剝費銀兩有用
至二萬餘金者可見剝費一層不可謂其不鉅也溯念本
大臣前與
貴署列位大臣議及此事承云挑濬一節實非限於
經費等語事既如此辦法實無不易本大臣疊准
本國
總理各國事務丞相咨文催令即向
貴親王切請核奪辦理但能即早咨復本國聲明此
舉正在速核施行之間此本大臣實所厚望焉相應
照會
貴親王查核即希
見復須至照會者

五月二十六日

第八條

耶穌基督聖教又名天主教原為行善嗣後中国於安分傳教習教之人當一體矜恤保護不可欺侮凌虐亦不可於安分之人禁其傳習若大美俄国人有由通商處所進內地傳教者領事官与內地沿海邊地方官按照定額酌定額數查驗執照果係良民即行盖用圖記畫押放行以便稽查

Copy of the Toleration article in the Russian Treaty with alterations suiting it to the American Treaty.

第廿九款

耶穌基督聖教又名天主教原為勸人行善欲人
施諸已者亦如是施於人嗣後所有安分傳教習
教之人當一體矜卹保護不可欺侮凌虐凡有遵
照教規聚集祈禱分散聖書者他人毋得騷擾

These slips of Chinese refer to the discussion respecting toleration of Christianity. See 40 &c & 51 ff.

第三十一款

耶穌基督聖教（亦名天主教）原為行善嗣後 中國於安分傳教習教之人當
一體矜恤保護不可欺侮凌虐亦不可於安分之人禁其傳習若
大美國人有由通商處所進內地傳教者領事官與內地沿海
地方官酌定額數查驗執照果係良民蓋用圖記放行以便稽
查

耶穌基督聖教亦名天主教原為行善嗣後中國於安分傳教習教
之人並當一體矜恤保護不可于安分傳習之人欺侮凌虐若 大美
國人有由通商地方傳教者領事官與沿海地方官酌定額數
查驗執照果係良民畫押放行以憑稽查

逕啓者傳教一款請照送來底稿繕寫查（原五月初七日呈交 法大人來函書回的）
貴國傳教向來攜眷貿易与他國傳教者迥不
相同若入內地斷不准攜眷貿易況俄國內地
二字亦必另改否則又須會議有悞定期矣專
此佈達即候
晚佳　立候回音以便繕寫
衛
丁　二位大人閣下

第廿九款
耶穌基督聖教原為行善嗣後中國於安分傳
教習教之人當一體矜恤保護不可欺侮凌虐
若大合衆國人只須在通商處所行道領事
官与該處地方官酌定額數查驗執照以便
稽查

廷霞者、頃閱
華翰、當經稟明、現奉
列大人面諭、倘除進內地三字、則不若將此款不列條約
之內、全行刪去、免阻[illegible]翌午互易、務希
覆函、俾得繕至
尊處、將條約謄正後、請即攜來、敝寓、先行較對、致
下午六點鐘可以互換、專此覆達、並頌
曉安、
知名恕具　初七日

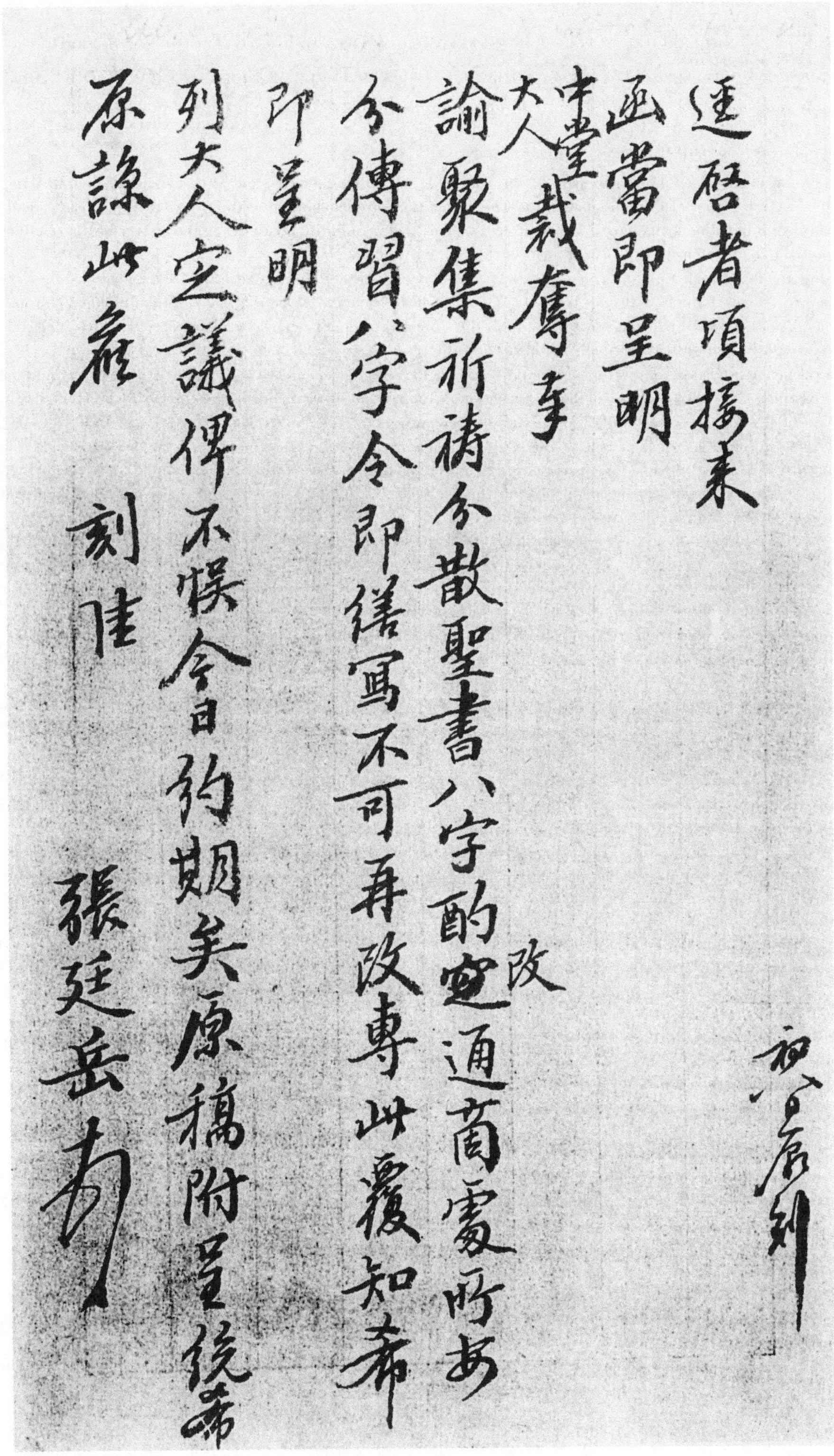
初八日辰刻
逕啓者頃接來
函當即呈明
中堂裁奪奉
大人諭聚集祈禱分散聖書八字酌改通商處所安
分傳習八字令即繕寫不可再改專此覆知希
即呈明
列大人定議俾不誤今日約期矣原稿附呈統希
原諒此覆　刻佳　張廷岳頓

A LETTER TO THE ARCHBISHOP OF CANTERBURY FROM THE BISHOP OF VICTORIA, IN REVIEW OF THE RECENT CHINESE TREATIES AS AFFECTING THE PROSPECTS OF CHRISTIANITY IN THE EAST.

SHANGHAE, CHINA, *October 18th*, 1858.

MY LORD ARCHBISHOP,

WITHIN a few hundred yards of the spot from which I now write, and at this same moment of time, Lord Elgin and the Chinese High Imperial Commissioners are negotiating the supplemental articles of the Treaty of Peace; and the last acts will soon be consummated of a diplomacy which (it is expected) will inaugurate a new era in the history of the relations of Western Christendom with the population and Government of the Chinese Empire.

In taking a general review of the recent treaties formed by Western Powers with China, I may state at the very outset that I regard the provisions of the new British treaty (so far as we have been able to gain a knowledge of the details from semi-official authority here) as eminently calculated to encourage the Church at home to new and enlarged Missionary efforts, and to arouse the Christian youth of Britain to a more adequate and prompt response to the demand for additional labourers.

Various concurrent circumstances during the present year have served to smooth the course of diplomacy, and to render the Imperial Government of China more disposed to accede to all the reasonable demands of the British Plenipotentiary.

It was no slight advantage to Lord Elgin that the representatives of the four Great Powers of Britain, France, Russia and the United States all combined in a joint naval demonstration on the Chinese Coast, and in a contemporaneous transmission of their demands to Peking. When the Anglo-French expedition advanced to the Mouth of the Peiho, the two non-belligerent Powers appeared also on the scene, and as neutral parties anticipated the British and French in their negotiations at Teentsin. It is understood that the Russian Envoy gave opportune warning to the Chinese officials of the grave emergency which had arisen. The fact had been notorious among the Chinese that Russia herself was but lately involved in a deadly war with Britain and France; and the representations of the Russian Envoy hence derived additional force. Count Putiatine plainly intimated to the Chinese the irresistible power of the Anglo-French squadron on their coast, and the inevitable ruin to the Manchow Tartar dynasty which must result from a blind and obstinate persistence in their past course.

The representations of the American Minister afforded too the same testimony confirmed by a second non-belligerent and neutral Power, as to the magnitude of the impending peril and the hopelessness of further resistance to the demands of the British and French.

The sequel is well known. Warlike operations of brief duration, but of decisive effect, prepared the way for the definitive negotiation of a treaty. At Teentsin, on the level high-road to Peking and within 70 miles of the capital, the terms of peace were signed, by the British on June 26th, and by the French on the following day.

Each of the four successive Treaties of 1858 has been a further step in advance beyond previous concessions to foreigners.

The Russian Ambassador who signed a Treaty on June 13th gained for the Russo-Greek Missionaries long established at Peking the right of free ingress to all the other parts of the empire.

The American Minister in his Treaty concluded five days later obtained beyond this a slight addition to the commercial ports along the coast. But he has the higher distinction of being the first to obtain by the open stipulations of treaty an honourable mention of the beneficent character of the Christian religion, and a renewed pledge of universal toleration for Native converts throughout the Chinese empire.

It has been reserved for Lord Elgin to achieve a still more prominent act in the annals of Oriental Diplomacy. In addition to the concession acquired by the Minister of the United States, he gained also for foreigners of every class, and by implication for our Missionaries also, the right of unlimited access into the interior of the country, and has thus thrown down the last barriers which interrupted our free intercourse with every part of China.

The VIII and IX clauses of Lord Elgin's Treaty comprise the main points which have reference to our extended privileges in respect to Missions.

The former of these two Articles is in substance, and almost in words, identical with that previously negotiated on behalf of the United States by Mr. Reed; and its terms are honourable to both the British and the American officials who had the moral decision to press its admission into the Treaty. The "*religion of Jesus*" (the Chinese term for "Protestant Christianity") is for the first time distinctly mentioned in these Treaties, in conjunction with and in priority to the "*religion of the Lord of Heaven*" (the old term for the Roman Catholic form of the Christian religion"). I have reason for believing that the favourable mention of Christianity contains (at least in the wording of the American version) an exact quotation of the Chinese text in the New Testament of the golden law of universal positive Christian duty in "doing unto others as we would they should do unto us." This same extensive law of well doing has been long current among the Chinese sages in its *negative* form:—"*Abstain from* doing unto others what you would that they should *not* do unto you." It seems to be taken (according to the best foreign Sinologues) from an old Commentator on the Confucian Classics who flourished subsequently to the Christian era; and its currency even in a diluted negative form may have been but the transference of the universal moral law of relative duty, borrowed in meaning, but lowered in extent, from the Gospel narrative of our Lord's teaching.

As this VIII. Article stands (presumptively) in the British and American Treaties, its favourable recognition of the Christian religion is highly important: "The doctrine of Jesus, and the doctrine of the Lord of Heaven, teach the practice of virtue and "the treatment of others as ourselves. Henceforth all teachers or professors of it shall, one and all, be protected. No man "peaceably following his calling without offence shall be in the least oppressed or hindered by the Chinese authorities."

The IX. Article is that which peculiarly belongs to Lord Elgin's Treaty, and comprises those general concessions of locomotion and residence in the interior which (if its provisions be carried out and administered by Consular representatives possessing the requisite moral and mental qualifications for their responsible posts) hold out to Protestant Missionaries the prospect of extended opportunities in new and more favourable spheres of Missionary usefulness. They will henceforth be able, under the reasonable regulation of a moderate passport system, to penetrate into the interior and to establish stations in localities remote from the disturbing influences of mercantile positions on the sea-board.

I have reason to believe that the provisions of the French Treaty signed by Baron Gros the day after the English Treaty are almost identical with those of the latter, with one addition which, although unimportant at first sight, may nevertheless be hereafter fraught with consequences of serious moment. In addition to toleration of the Christian religion, protection of the Native converts, and unlimited access for the Roman-Catholic Missionaries into the interior, Baron Gros has also stipulated that whatever in past times has been decreed by the Chinese Government against the "religion of the Lord of Heaven" shall henceforth be null and void.

I know some intelligent observers of passing events, well versed in the history of Jesuit Missions in China, who are filled with anxious apprehension lest under the cover of this retrospective clause there may be a latent purpose on the part of the Roman-Catholic Missionaries to revive dormant claims to the property confiscated at various times of old in different parts of the empire, and especially the site of their former Cathedral at Peking. The instance of a similar demand not long ago preferred at Ningpo, and the recovery through French influence of valuable property and Mission-sites in the heart of that city, lend some plausibility to this view. Such recent experience suggests the fear lest here, as elsewhere over the waters of the broad Pacific, French diplomacy, having no commercial interests to foster, may busy itself in efforts to sustain the cause of the Propaganda,—a French Protectorate of Native Romanist converts be gradually established on this Continent,—and a powerful French ecclesiastico-political organization in favour of Romish Missions in China be one of the results of an Anglo-French alliance and joint-intervention in the affairs of the East.

It is to be noted that in the passport-regulations it is stipulated that foreigners shall not visit Nanking or other places occupied by the Insurgents I think this to be as fair and favourable a solution of the difficulties caused by the Insurrection as we might reasonably expect. Non-intervention in the civil convulsions of China was clearly the course for a British statesman to pursue. In the view of the decrepitude, cruelty and corruption of the Manchow Tartar dynasty, to have propped up such a Power by a forcible intervention of foreign arms against the Taeping Movement at Nanking, would be an act manifestly at variance with the sound dictates of expediency and right. On the other hand, there is too much uncertainty as to the present developments and tendencies of the Insurgent cause to authorize on the part of British Christians the wish that, under any circumstances, an armed external interposition should be exercised on their behalf. After five years and a half in occupation of Nanking—without the advantage of foreign spiritual instructors—with some, possibly all, the more hopeful class of Leaders removed from the scene—with all the elements of human depravity diffused among that pent-up motley host of semi-pagan Iconoclasts, constrained by rigorous severity to maintain an outward show of asceticism, and to memorize the established and half-understood forms of Prayer,—it is too much to expect that, under such exceptional circumstances, good has been more potential than evil amongst the multitude, and that its earlier promise has not been followed by degeneracy and decay.

In the earlier stages of the Taeping Movement five years ago, the entrance of Protestant Missionaries among them at Nanking might have turned the tide in the right direction and given a sounder character to their practice and belief. As it is, we must patiently abide the issue, moderating excessive hopes and repressing undue despondency and fear. However much a nearer view of the Rebel Movement may hereafter repel our minds, it must at the same time be remembered that doubtless in the hands of Providence it will have accomplished a good result. It will have laid bare the weak hold which Budhism has upon the masses of the Chinese people. It will have scattered broad-cast through the interior the seeds of Scriptural knowledge in the portions of the Christian Bible authoritatively published by the Chief at Nanking. It will have shown how Christian truths circulated in the Taeping manifestos and books, even when diluted with a mixture of pagan ideas, have nevertheless proved their innate strength in shaking the fabric of idolatry and preparing the way for a purer faith. If truth, when deformed and caricatured, has been thus effective in demolishing error, what may not be hoped for from the unimpeded circulation of the Holy Scriptures and the zealous preaching of Protestant Missionaries through the length and breadth of the land?

One serious question arising out of our relations with the Chinese appears to have been excluded from all mention or allusion in the published Articles of Treaty. So far as we can judge on the spot (the text of the British treaty not having yet been officially made known to the foreign community in China) the Opium-question has been ignored or kept out of sight; but it is difficult to think that this topic can have been altogether excluded from past discussions, or that in the pending negotiation of a Tariff in the Supplemental Articles of Treaty here at Shanghae Lord Elgin will continue to exclude the subject from a positive and final settlement.

I would mention in terms of the deepest respect the name of a British Plenipotentiary, who has won so distinguished a place in public estimation by his highly successful career. I fully believe in the benevolent highmindedness, which has actuated him in his difficult and honourable course in China. I know by friendly conversation and by private correspondence the mode of solution which *on the whole* he deems best for terminating a great and admitted evil. I know too that some of the most intelligent and zealous Missionaries labouring for the welfare of the Chinese, wearied and perplexed by the view of the sad collateral effects of a smuggling system almost virtually legalized by the indifference or the corruption of the local mandarins, have deemed it expedient to succumb to an unavoidable evil, and to limit and check by the regulations of a legalized Custom-house tariff the spread of a moral mischief now utterly beyond control.

I confess that it is with mingled pity and shame that I contemplate the affecting spectacle of a pagan Government, almost powerless in the means of resistance and feeble in the arts of war, thus humiliated, weakened and overpowered; and the top-stone thus finally set on the pillar of our own inconsistency and disgrace, as a people placed in the vanguard of Christian nations in our dealings with this race. The year in which this monument may possibly be erected in commemoration of the final act in the series of wrongs perpetrated on the millions of China, will singularly enough he marked also by the extinction and corporate death of the East India Company. Our Anglo-Indian revenue from the growth of the poppy has been the chief plea and prop of the Opium-smuggling trade in China. What we failed to relinquish on the ground of Christian principle, will probably be wrung from us by the defensive action of the Chinese Government itself. The eventual withdrawal of the Imperial prohibition against growing Opium in the eighteen provinces has been a remedy long available and within reach. Embarrassed and overcome in the long contest with Native and foreign contrabandists, it is not improbable that the Chinese Imperial Government may at length have submitted to a termination of the struggle,—an addition to the impoverished Exchequer in the shape of a regulated tariff-duty be preferred to the continued prevalence of a lawless smuggling of the prohibited drug along the sea-board,—and Opium at last be recognized among the legally-permitted indigenous produce of China.

It is satisfactory to know that both in the British and in the American Treaties lately concluded with the Japanese an Article exists expressly prohibiting the importation of Opium; and that thus by the humane policy of Christian negotiators Japan, hitherto exempt from this form of intemperance, will in all probability be saved from one class of evils which has resulted from our intercourse with China. Unprecedented privileges have been recently granted to Christian Missionaries within the newly opened ports of Japan.

It is right that the friends of Christian Missions on both sides of the Atlantic should know how much they are preeminently indebted for the Christian element in the wording of the treaties, to the hearty zeal, sympathy and co-operation of His Excellency W. B. Reed, ably seconded by his Secretary of Legation and his Interpreter, Dr. Williams and Revd. W. A. P. Martin,—names well known in connexion with the Missionary work in China.

The wider opening of these Eastern regions to Missionary labour is an animating topic on which I could glowingly enlarge, as a call to more adequate efforts on the part of our own Church. But I confess, my Lord, that I have gathered lessons of moderate expectation from the fruitlessness of my past appeals for help. In the tenth year of my Episcopate I behold but few signs of any great and sustained movement of our Church for the evangelization of the Chinese race, or for our entrance upon the recent Missionary openings in Japan. My dear and valued fellow-labourers sent out to the China Mission, do but scantily fill up the breaches made in the ranks of our Church by disease and death. But six Church of England Missionary clergy are spread along the stations on this extended coast, of whom two have been only six months in the country. It is indeed a satisfactory result to my mind to see chaplaincies instituted in the Chinese cities, and the British communities supplied with the means of grace. I rejoice also in the increasing number of labourers in connexion with other Protestant Missionary bodies, and the marked success which in some cases has resulted from their attempts. But as to Missions of our Church among the Chinese, after fourteen years since my first landing on these shores, I still see (with the one exception of the Church Missionary station of Ningpo) but little progress made and but inconsiderable results achieved. I feel no despondency as to the certain final success of our work as the cause of God himself. I am sustained by the assurance that God is working out His purposes of mercy and love to our race in these passing events of the East;—that this our fallen world shall one day become a temple worthy of its holy and beneficent Creator;—and that this vast pagan empire, now an exile from the great community of Christian nations, shall hereafter participate in the promised outpouring of God's Spirit upon all flesh, and in the predicted blessedness of the renewed earth "in which dwelleth righteousness." But I deplore the want of an adequate supply of labourers to enter upon these fields "white unto the harvest";—men suited by mental habit and by bodily strength for this peculiar Mission;—men whose faith has been long strengthened by secret prayer, and whose love to Christ has been long watered by the heavenly dew of spiritual communion with God;—men, willing to forego (if needful) the comforts of domestic life, and ready to yield to the possible requirements of a "present necessity" in being free and unfettered by family-ties in their itinerancy in the interior from place to place. Once more I reiterate the appeal to the Church at home:—"The harvest truly is great, but the labourers are few." Once more I appeal to British Christians that while India is claiming her meed of Missionary sympathy and evangelistic help in this her day of trial, China may not be overlooked or forgotten in their prayers, nor her 400 millions receive less than her due amount of consideration and thought in the counsels and deliberations of our Church of England Missionary Committees.

My Lord, my pen grows weary and my theme becomes diffusive. I know by experience the mental sickness of hope long deferred. In my own person I can do but little beyond sounding the trumpet and leading others to the conflict. The goal of middle life scarce gained, I am experiencing the effects of climate on a shattered frame, and the infirmities of advancing years. In the early afternoon of my course, the shades of evening are prematurely falling and lengthening around me. Once again I appeal to my younger fellow-soldiers of Christ that they desert not the standard of the Cross unfurled in the far East, nor allow a standard-bearer to fall unsupported and unsustained in this Mission battle-field.

I remain,

My Lord Archbishop,

Your Grace's most obedient humble servant,

G. VICTORIA.

Formerly Rev. Geo. Smith, Missionary of the Church Miss. Soc. Now Bishop at Hongkong. He is a good man

S. W. Williams らの日本宣教勧告書翰

鈴　木　　武

1. はじめに

1853（嘉永6）年7月と翌年（安政元）年2月の2回にわたって日本に来航したペリー提督の日本語通訳として活躍した Samuel Wells Williams, 1858（安政5）年6月日米通商条約締結の場であるアメリカ軍艦 Powhattan 号附牧師 Henry Wood, およびアメリカ Episcopal Church 派の上海駐在宣教師 Edward W. Syle ら三名の日本へのキリスト教宣教勧告書翰は日本 Protestant 宣教史上に大きな役割を果したばかりでなく，日本近代史の展開に極めて重要な係りあいを持つものであった。彼等の宣教勧告書翰は実際にキリスト教伝道に携わる者の目からみた，キリスト教伝道をめぐる日本の諸状況を伝える貴重な情報でもあり，アメリカ Protestant 各派が人格，識見ともに秀れた宣教師を日本に派遣する直接あるいは間接的動機となったことはよく知られているところである。勧告書翰が書かれた翌年の1859（安政6）年5月には Episcopal の John Liggins, 6月には立教大学創設者 C. M. Williams が長崎に到着。同年10月には Presbyterian の J. C. Hepburn 夫妻，11月には Reformed の S. R. Brown と D. B. Simons 等が横浜に，G. H. F. Verbeck が長崎に上陸し本格的に社会事業・教育事業を通じてキリスト教伝道が開始され，幕末から明治にかけての政治的・社会的転換期の混乱の中に秀れた Protestant 宣教師によってもたらされた Protestantism は，その伝道方法として力を入れた社会・教育事業を通じて日本の近代思想の形成に深い影響を及ぼしたことは多言を要さないところである。かように彼らの宣教勧告書翰のあげた成果についてはよく知られているのであるが，それら書翰の内容についてはこれまであまり知られていないようである。宣教勧告書翰のうち S. W. Williams と H. Wood の二通は1964年アメリカ New Jersey 州の New Brunswick Theological Seminary より高谷道男氏に送られた同校図書館所蔵の各種資料を収めたマイクロフィルムの中から見つかったもので，これら二通の書翰をここに紹介したい。なおこれら書翰には損傷，部分的なインクの薄れ，各人の筆跡にみられる独特の僻，表現等解読に困難，ないしは不明の箇所が少なからずあったこと，また E. W. Syle のものは見当らなかったことを附記しておきたい。

2. 勧告書翰について

これら書翰がどのような事情で出されたものであるかについて S. W. Williams は次のように述べている。(*)

"I was much impressed with what Mr. Donker Curtius, the Dutch envoy, who had just signed a treaty, then said: that the Japanese officials had told him they were ready to allow foreigners all trading privileges if a way could be found to keep opium and Christianity out of the country. There were also then at Nagasaki [on the Minnesota], Rev. Mr. Syle and Chaplain Henry Wood, and we three agreed to write to the directors of the Episocopal, Reformed, and Presbyterian Mission Boards, urging them to appoint missionaries for Japan who could teach the people what true Christianity was. Within the coming year we all had the pleasure of meeting the agents of these three societies in Shanghai."

彼らがショックを受けたのは幕府高官がアヘンとキリスト教の流入を防ぐ方途がわかれば，すべての外国人に貿易上の特権を与える用意がある，と Curtius に明言した，と云われたことである。そこで彼らは相談して Episcopal, Reformed, Presbyterian の各本部へ書翰を送り，真のキリスト教を日本人に伝道するため宣教師を急ぎ派遣するよう要請することで意見が一致した，ということである。この情報を聞いたのは Williams が Syle らと共に中国駐在アメリカ公使 W. B. Reed の長崎への休暇旅行に随行して1858年9月20日軍艦 Minnesota 号で上海から長崎に入港し，22日出島のオランダ商館を表敬訪問した際のことであった。Syle はこの旅行について

"A continued weakness of my throat, which renders it useless for public speaking, seems to justify my leaving Shanghai for a season, and availing

S. W. Williams らの日本宣教勧告書翰

myself of a very favorable opportunity for visiting Japan. My brethren of the mission consent to my doing so,. . . . "

と云っているが，Williams との今回の旅行の真の目的はこの後がきに (**)

After reflecting a good deal on the circumstances of my recent trip to Japan, I cannot come to any other conclusion than that it is a matter of simple, straight-forward duty on the part of our Church to begin the good work there at once, ...

とあることから覗えるようにキリスト教伝道調査のための日本訪問であった。当時のキリスト教をめぐる日本の状況は，安政年間に締結された諸条約――日蘭追加条約，日蘭修好通商航海条約，日米修好通商条約等の中にキリスト教関係条項が盛られ，「踏絵」の撤廃をはじめとして徐々に禁教解除の方向に向いつつあった。しかしこれも諸外国の外交的圧力によるもので，幕府として歓迎すべきことではなかったので，Curtius が幕府高官の言明と称するものは当然あり得るものであろう。しかし，キリスト教宣教師である彼らの前でオランダ商館長としての Curtius が殊さらに幕府要路の言葉を持ち出した背景には，オランダが略2世紀半にもわたるキリスト教抜きの日本との独占的通商関係がアメリカ，ロシア等に破られつつある，という現実と，後に紹介する H. Wood の勧告書翰の中にみられるように，イギリス・フランス・アメリカ等の東洋における政治的・経済的進出と相互補完的に遂行されてきた面もあるキリスト教布教への悪感情，といったものがあったものと思われる。Curtius の発言は Williams と Syle の長崎訪問がキリスト教伝道のための調査であることを意識していた上でのものであることは充分に考えられるところであるが，反面彼らもまたオランダ商館と日本との歴史的関係からして伝道のため利用しなければならない難関であることを理解したものと思われる。それ故にこそオランダにMother Church を持つ Reformed Dutch Church にオランダ商館に伝道活動に協力させるよう要請する書翰を「真のキリスト教を日本人に伝道するため」という名目の下に送らざるを得なかったのである。

注 (*) "Life and Letters of Dr. S. Wells Williams" p. 284

(**) Spirit of Missions vol. 24 "Narrative of Rev. Mr. Syle's Visit to

Japan"

3. **S. W. Williams の勧告書翰**

書翰の宛先の Thomas De Witt 師は1791年 New York 州 Kingston 生まれ。Union College, New Brunswick Theological Seminary 卒業。当時は New York City の Collegiate Church 牧師。The Christian Intelligencer 編集者。30年間 New York Historical Society 副会長を勤めた。歴史関係著書多数。

U. S. S. "Minnesota",

Nagasaki, Sept. 30, 1858

Rev. T. De Witt DD:

Dear Sir:

I have learned that Rev. H. Wood, the chaplain of the "Powhattan" now in this harbor, has written to G. Bethune, recommending the establishment of a mission of the Reformed Dutch Church at this port, partly to preach in Dutch to the merchants and seamen from Holland residing here and chiefly to commence missionary operations among the natives. *The treaty* (1) between the United States and Japan goes into operation with *those* (2) made by the Dutch, English and Russian plenipotentiaries, next year in July; and though I do not know the provisions of any of these treaties in detail, I have learned enough to encourage the formation of missions in some of the ports *then* to be opened to foreign intercourse as soon as they can be established.

後で紹介する H. Wood の書翰の冒頭にもあるように，彼はすでに前年の1857年の夏にアメリカ Reformed Dutch Church の Bethune 師に，出島在住のオランダ商人や船員にオランダ語で説教するためと，日本人に対して伝道活動を始めるために，長崎で Reformed Dutch Church の Mission 設立を勧告する書翰を送っている。キリスト教については日米修好条約の第八条に詳細な規定がある。要するに「踏絵」の廃止が確認され，日米人は互いに信教の自由を尊重し，米国人は居留地において礼拝及び礼拝堂の建設が認められる，というもので，これによってキリスト教の日本での伝道の第一歩が踏み出されることになった。

注 (1) 日米修好通商条約。1858年7月29日神奈川沖に碇泊中の米軍艦 Powhattan 号上で締結された。

(2) 同年8月（陰暦）日米修好通商条約に準拠してイギリス，オランダ，ロシア三国と，同年10月フランスとの間に調印された修好通商条約。

The Japanese government has shown some readiness to introduce the arts and improvements of western nations in ship-building, steam-machinery, medical science, and surgery, and have begun the erection of a large engine shop at this port. The officers here are desirous to have their assistants learn English, and the expectation of trade induces the shopkeepers to pcik up all the words they can learn; so that it will not be amiss to assist them at first in learning to speak and write it correctly. The missionary could I suppose easily find pupils who were appointed by their authorities to acquaint themselves with the English language, and make an engagement for a year or two that while he taught them English, he should have all the assistance he needed in learning Japanese. At the end of two years he would probably be able to preach intelligibly, by which time his experience would guide him as to the best measures in promoting his objects. If a medical man was joined with him, who could not only show the practical benevolence of Christianity by healing those around him, but also teach the rudiments of medicine and surgery to a few natives while learning their language himself, the probable success and comfort of the whole mission would be increased.

幕府は工業技術・医学の導入のため，商人は貿易上の必要から英語修得をのぞんでいるので，宣教師は彼らに英語を1，2年教えていれば，その間に日本語を習うことができ，日本語で伝道することが可能である，として英語教授を日本でのキリスト教伝道の第1歩と考えている。また医師が宣教師と共にあって病人の治療に奉仕すればキリスト教の実践的な慈善を示すことができ，且つ日本語を習っている間に，日本人に内科と外科の初歩を教えることができ，Mission の成功は疑いない，としている。

The Japanese have no doubt a dread of Christianity, for they remember the struggle they had to expel the Roman Catholics and destroy their converts two centuries ago; and *the Dutch commissioner here,* (*) *when he was negotiating his treaty last July,* (**) *was urged to introduce a clause making opium and Christianity contraband.* If, therefore, at the beginning of a mission it can present some of its practical effects so that the authorities and people can then perceive and receive them, this dislike will not be so likely to frustrate the higher and better objects it has in view, while its members are learning the language and making the acquaintance of the people. If the missionary to Nagasaki can talk Dutch, the Factory here will be able to give him a reason for living in the place by employing him as its preacher; and there is not likely to be any serious difficulty in learning the language. The Commissioner himself, Mr. Donker Curtius, has shown me a grammar which he has written, lately printed in Holland. A small printing office exists in Desima, where books are printed at the expense of the Japanese, chiefly phrase books & vocabularies, so that a printing office would soon be desirable, furnished with Japanese & Chinese type.

日本人はキリスト教を怖れていて，オランダ商館長 Curtius は条約交渉中にアヘンとキリスト教を禁制にする条項を差し込むことを押しつけられた，と Williams は伝えている。これは彼の云う通りで，1856（安政3）年7月 Curtius は幕府に条約の追加を申し入れたが，その中に日本在留外人のキリスト教信奉を認めること，「踏絵」を廃止すること等が含まれていた。幕府は「踏絵」廃止の代償としてアヘンおよびキリスト教伝播防止に関する条項を条約中に含めることを企図したが，日露追加条約とのかね合いの関係で撤回することを余儀なくされたものである。日本人のキリスト教への恐怖心を払拭するために為すべきことは，幕府当局者にも民衆にも必要にして且つ受け入れられる実際効果のあるもの——英語教授と医療奉仕であり，特に英語教授は相互理解を深める最も適切なもの

S. W. Williams らの日本宣教勧告書翰

と彼は考えている。長崎へ来る宣教師でオランダ語が話せれば，商館はその者を援助するであろう，と彼は極めて楽観的な見通しを述べているが，Wood の書翰によれば，商館長 Curtius によって宣教師も英語教師も受け入れを拒否された。

次いで彼は印刷所の設置を要望しているが，これは彼が1833年10月，21歳でキリスト教禁制下の中国に渡り，印刷技術をもって Mission Press で働き，また中国における宗教活動を中心とする情報機関の "Chinese Repository" に執筆したり，編集主任として活躍した経歴を持つ故であり，高度な文化水準にある異教徒にキリスト教を滲透させてゆく手段として，彼は印刷出版物を最も重視しているからであろう。

注 （*） the Dutch Commission here とあるのは1852年来日した長崎出島のオランダ商館長 Jan Hendrick Donker Curtius のこと。

（**） 日蘭追加条約。

I hope the Dutch Reformed Church will *see its way clear* to send one or two chosen men to this new field of mission labor, so that they can be on the spot soon after the treaties go into effect. It may be worth while to ascertain from the Hague whether the government intends to send out a chaplain, and get a letter to this effect to its commissioner here, if there is no design. Such a position may be preferable as rendering it unneccessary to open a school to teach English, but there are objections of more weight against connecting missions with government, and government control. Of the two, the opening of a school is preferable, and the Japanese governor, when asked, said he would be glad to have an American come to Nagasaki to teach English to the Japanese.

彼は日本との条約が発効すれば直ちに伝道のための諸活動を展開してゆくためオランダの Reformed Church が宣教師を派遣するよう希望している。これはキリスト教伝道に関してオランダ商館の後援を期待してのことであって，彼はそのためにはオランダ政府が商館付き牧師を派遣する意図があるかどうか，ハーグの Reformed Church から確めるのも無益なことではない，としてオランダ政府の協力をも期待するが，しかし彼は，その場合オランダとしては英語を教える学校を開設することには協力しかねるであろうし，また Mission が政府と結びついたり，政府の監督を受けることには大きな反対もある，ということも考えている。そうすると他に伝道の方途といえば，先に彼が述べているように，宣教師が日本人に受け入れられるような実際的効果のある英語教授，医療奉仕等の活動に従うことによって日本人のキリスト教に対する恐怖心や偏見を取除きつつ，併せて日本語を修得し，徐々にキリスト教の伝道を具体化してゆく方が得策で，しかも英語教授は長崎奉行の要請に応えることでもあり，この要請に応じることによって今後のキリスト教伝道に何らかの展望が拓けることを期待したもので，そのため彼は英語学校の開設を強く望んだものであろう。

The expenses of living here would not be greater I think than at Amoy, but there would be incipient expenses of building, which would require an outlay of perhaps 4000 dollars for a house and land at first with the salary for the first year. If two persons come, one of them had better be married, though until a settlement be made the lady might remain at Shanghai. The first European lady whom I have heard of coming here and succeeding in getting a residence in Japan, died shortly since from the hardships of ship-wreck, and now there is none in the country. But there will be no objections to families living at the ports, especially this.

I need hardly enter into any arguments to show the desirableness of the American churches beginning the work now opening for them in this land, but it seems to me that the fields offers special inducements to your Mission board, which has now, I believe, only the Amoy & Ascot missions to support, & may be looking over the world to find good localities for beginning others. The remarkable readiness of the Japanese to learn of foreigners is probably stimulated by the hope of benefiting themselves; and this desire will I hope be gratified to its fullest and best degree; but they will not desire of themselves to learn the humbling doctrines of the crop. It is enough to know

S. W. Williams らの日本宣教勧告書翰

that access to them is open, I hope, to stir up some converts to that cross to come here and make known the truth, the way & the life, if by any means he can save some. The town of Nagasaki contains about 60,000 inhabitans, and there are numerous villages within the limits of the governor's jurisdiction, where foreigners can go, a population large enough to engage the lifelong labors of many men. He may confidently trust that the same Almighty Power which has inclined the hearts of the rulers of this land to alter their prohibitions respecting foreign intercourse, and allow their subjects to receive & trade with their fellowmen from abroad, will further the designs and labors of his servants to make known His Word in obedience to his command — all these openings being but preliminary to those designs and those labors which will carry out His purposes of mercy towards all men.

Williams は伝道上のことだけでなく，宣教師が来日した場合の生活費，住居等の実生活の面にまで細い配慮を示している。それは伝道のための基本的条件だからである。未知の異教徒の中でこのような日常の生活に関する情報こそ，実は各派本部が宣教師を派遣する上で最も重要なものであろう。彼はまた日本における伝道上の利点をいくつか挙げたり，宣教師の日本伝道の使命感に訴えたりして Reformed 派の関心を惹くことに努めている。

The labors of missionaries in China have done something to assist those who may begin the work of evangelization in Japan, by preparing dictionaries and making a laudation of the Scriptures. The Japanese have incorporated Chinese characters into their own written language in such a manner that a knowledge of Chinese will be indispensable to the missionary; but this will enable him to present truth to them thro' a medium they are already somewhat acquainted with, while he is learning their spoken and written languages. The Dutch, also, have prepared Dictionaries for their own use and that of the Japanese, which will be useful to your missionaries, if they understand Dutch. The Bible has yet to be translated, and much work is to be done among these islanders. I pray the Lord of the harvest to send forth laborers into his harvest; for though it looks like the prophet's valley of dry bones now, to the eye of Him who sees the end from the beginning, it is the harvest of souls.

I cannot doubt that from the great revival which has blessed all your churches in America, many missionaries, will come forth. Select a company, and say to them that there are much people in Japan to be taught and the way is opening, and God calls them with an encouraging voice to go up and declare his word, for he will go with them. The wonderful outpouring, the wonderful openings here of China and Japan, fully 450 millions of sinful, ignorant, idolators therein, are meant, one cannot doubt, to fit into each other; and the converts in America must leave their homes and sanctuaries then to come hither to make new ones.

I am Very respectfully Yours

S. Wells Williams

I inclose a catholic minded letter lately published by the Bishop of Victoria respecting missions in the Oriental world, and a newly prepared list of the missionaries hitherto sent to the Chinese.

日本より約50年前に始まった中国への Protestant の伝道は，日本における伝道に大いに役立ったのである。それは中国に派遣された宣教師—— Robert Morrison, W. H. Medhurst, Karl Gutzlaff, E. C. Bridgman 等によって中国文の著書や翻訳書，辞書等が数多く出版されていたからである。これらはキリスト教関係のものに限らず，歴史・地理・医学・科学等各分野の諸学問約800種類あり，その中から当時100種類以上の書籍が清国より輸入され，宣教師達はキリスト教禁制下にあっても，これら書籍によって間接的に伝道を行っていたのである。

S. W. Williams らの日本宣教勧告書翰

4. **Henry Wood の勧告書翰**

書翰の宛先は Reformed Dutch 派の George Washington Bethune 師である。同師は Dickinson College 及び Princeton Theological Seminary 卒業。Reformed 派の指導的人物で学者・神学者・詩人としても著名である。

Hong Kong China 30 Nov. 1858

Rev. Dr. Bethune

Dear Sir,

Since the date of *the letter I wrote you last summer* relating to Japan & the implanting of Christianity there, we have made a special visit to these beautiful islands, where unexpected opportunities were presented for mingling with the Japanese & studying their character, their habits, their institutions, & the present attitude of mind, in regard to intercourse with foreigners.

The main object however before my mind was, to learn what reception Christianity would probably meet with, if reintroduced, & the best method of introducing it — we returned from Shanghai to Nagasaki, Japan, for the sake of health, having been attacked with cholera in Shanghai & left several men there, & spent the entire month of Sep. & Oct. in Nagasaki, when we returned to Shanghai, & from Shanghai came down here.

Wood が日本でのキリスト教伝道に関して Bethune 師に宛てた書翰はこれで二回目ということになる。彼もまた Williams, Syle らの長崎来航の目的と同じで，日本人のキリスト教受容の問題とその伝道の方法に関する調査である。

Nagasaki is a city containing at least 100,000 inhabitants & is finely located on a Bay, 5 miles back from the Sea, with a line of mountains on each side, rising from 1500 to 2000 ft high with every inch mantled with green, here Christianity had its strong hold, its holy city — its Jerusalem, in the days of Catholic Missions, when it contained churches, seminaries & hospitals, a printing press, & 40,000 christians here, too, Christianity expired after a long struggle with persecution, & I succeeded in finding the very prison in which its last detected christians about 1700 A. D. were confined & died, & the "Martyr's Hill," long since forgotten, on which thousands had been burned at the stake, or died on the cross, or been hewn in pieces & cast into the waters of the bay immediately below—the city is regularly laid out, the streets being generally wide & paved, & crossing each other at right angles....I never saw a brawl in the street or out of these, I never heard an angry or threatening word, & never saw two individuals in a quarrel, or an instance of drunkenness, or show of an act of dishonesty, though the people love *saki*, a kind of beer made from rice in its form & in another an intoxicating distillation of rice, but they never drink it by day, reserving it for the night & these private houses when the labors of the day are ended, there is doubtless a vast amount of licentiousness, as in all the East, while the courtesy & politeness & amiable disposition of the people are most admirable & unlike to any thing I ever saw. The little artificial island of Desim, built on a Coral reef & containing only 3 acres, is separated from the City of N. by a bed 3 or 4 rods wide which is covered with water, only when the tide is in, & joined to the town by a single bridge....the whole island being surrounded by a wall, having 2 gates....one on the wharf & the other at the bridge, which are closed & guarded after sun set, this is the entire foothold gained by the Dutch in about 220 yrs. & here they exist in character & morals & aims & spirit as they did in the beginning, sometimes reduced to 8 or 10 in number & sometimes rising to 50 & never under that figure, they have lived like as in a prison, though voluntarily such, for the sake of gain, for they have had the exculsive European commerce with Japan for this long period, & I am pained & ashamed to say it, but every one who has been here knows it, they have lived not only as the heathen, but as the brutes, & worse, than the brutes. A European woman never touched this island since the Dutch had it, until one arrived here in a Dutch vessel & was wrecked at the entrance of the Bay & the Capt's wife being rescued & brought here to die, was buried without any religious observance or decency, but every man from the Governor downward, has one or more Japanese young women, who lives in his house & with whom he cohabits in the sight of all the world & with the most umblushing impenitence, the whole island indeed is but one vast hot-bed of licentiousness in its most revolting forms.... the Governor actually making a contract with the Japanese government for a supply of as many women as they might want, this I know to be true & so do all the officers of our ship; been naturally & indeed inevitably his petty colony, have now as ever during these 220 yrs abandoned Christianity practically if not formally, observing no Sabbath, having no minister, no church, & no public worship or social in any form whatever; I could never get sight even of a Bible or a Testament or any religious book whatever, nor have they ever inculcated one Christian doctrine in the Japanese mind or given them any christian knowledge, or left one single trace of christian influence of any sort. They have occupied this little post so long & been the only accredited friends & representatives of Christianity with the Japanese government & the Japanese empire, embracing a population estimated at 30,000,000 & even 40,000,000 — a glorious & rare opportunity was providentially given them to civilize, elevate & christianize the most interesting & hopeful nation on the face of the globe, instead of which, they have only lived to obstruct & disgrace Christianity & put the heathen to shame by their vices. All this they have done for this long period with impurity & boldness, because in their deep seclusion & isolation the eyes of the civilized & christian world did not fall upon them & their iniquities were not revealed. Such have been the Dutch in Japan & such they are now.

ここで長崎の人口，地理的位置，人々の生活，キリスト教徒殉難の歴史等について述べている。次に出島の外観，構造に触れ，出島に居住するオランダ人を彼は激しく非難する。——オランダ人は220年間にもわたり独占的に日本と通商関係を維持してきたが，その間教会も牧師も持たず，キリスト教徒として従うべき宗教上の掟に全く無縁な生活を送ってきた。オランダ人は3千万から4千万と見積られる人口を抱えた日本の唯一の正式な友人であり，キリスト教国の代表として日本にキリスト教を広める絶好の立場にありながら，彼等のやったことと云えば逆にキリスト教を妨害し，卑しめただけである——と。これもキリスト教宣教師としての立場からみた出島のオランダ人の一つの側面であろう。キリスト教禁制政策をとる幕府とキリスト教国オランダが正式な通商関係を維持してゆくためには当然キリスト教抜きでなければならなかったのもまたオランダ人のもう一つの側面である。

Upon the returning the third time to N.— Sep. 14th, the Governor sent an official on board our ship, requesting that the commodor would allow & designate some one to instruct a class of young men, his interpretors; in the English language or any useful branch of knowledge, the offer was made to me & gladly accepted & for 2 whole months I went into the town every day, Sundays excepted, & in a fine room appropriated in one of the bazars taught nine most interesting young men from 20 to 27 years of age, orthography, Spelling, Reading, Grammar & Writing, with some lessons in Arithmetic, Astronomy, Geography & History & Nat. Philosophy. The proficiency they made was to me truly astounding....some things they learnt at a glance & some almost by intuition, & at the close of the two months when I was obliged to leave them, they could write a handsome hand & read common English lessons intelligently & pronounce the words accurately & write out exercises for the most part correctly in Grammar & Spelling. Such uniform & docility could not be exceeded, or the gratitude they expressed in the most touching language & manner. They requested me to remain among them & teach them more thoroughly & extensively. The Governor often sent his officials to inspect my school & more frequently sent his thanks. I was highly gratified as well as surprised to learn from my scholars that the *Lieutenant Governor* himself a young man of bright intellect & progressive ideas was learning English from my scholars! I called upon him & found this to be the fact & I gave him several English books suitable for a learner & yet having more or less Christian instruction, which he accepted with thanks & requested me to procure more, I also gave all I could obtain, which was a pretty good supply to my scholars, enjoining it upon them that they should teach others, which they promised to do.

Wood は長崎奉行の依頼を受けて英語の正字法，綴字法，読み方，文法，書き方から算術，天文学，地理，歴史，物理学に至るまで20才から27才の９名のオランダ通辞の青年達に教えたのである。Syle はこの授業風景をみて，

It seems that the authorities here have not enough to provide their own English-speaking interpreters: six young men, all bright and intelligent looking, are attached in this capacity to the Governor's staff. This afternoon, I saw most of them gathered round the Rev. Mr. Wood, chaplain of the "Powhattan," who has been invited to become their instructor during his stay in the port.

と述べ，青年６名としている。９名ないし６名の青年の名は不明であるが，その中の１名はおそらく(*) Syle の９月24日の記録(**)にみられる Nalabyash Disayemon（楢林栄左衛門）と思われる。青年達は極めて熱心に Wood の指導を受け上達も早かった，という。奉行所青年通辞に英語を教えることによって長崎奉行所首脳へのアプローチは成功し，多少ともキリストの教えの入った英語学習書物を贈呈するなど伝道のための下地づくりにも成功しつつあることを報告している。

注（＊）Spirit of Missions Vol. 24; Narrative of Rev. Mr. Syle's visit to Japan.

(**) 同上

All these books, or nearly all, contained also beautiful lessons of a Christian character & some full statement of Christian doctrine. Still the young men were very glad to receive them. But my object was higher & accordingly I waited & watched for opportunities to explain & discuss *Christian subjects*, which were soon offered by the words which they wished me to explain or by subjects they proposed. Thus I again & again unfolded the whole Christian system & the Bible history & even exposed the inutility & absurdity of idols & idol worship, which they listened to with interest & respect & seemed even to approve. Some disn. memories of Christian doctrine seemed to flit & linger about them & one had a dim idea of a resurrection & another when I uttered the word Christ, exclaimed interrogatively "*Jesus Christ?*"It seemed vastly important to continue the instruction & increase the number of scholars, as the interpreters again & again requested near the close of my labors, there fore I called upon the Lieutenant Governor & asked him if he would like to have me send to America & obtain a young man to come out as teacher & take my place & continue the school? He seemed evidently pleased with the proposal but said he must consult with others & then would inform me. I suppose he would be obliged, to refer the matter to Jeddo according to Japanese usage.

Wood は英語の授業を通じてキリスト教について青年達を啓蒙，つまり初歩的な伝道を行っていた。彼は云う——私は単に英語を教えるだけでなく，もっと高い望みを持っておりました。私はキリスト教の問題を説明したり討論したりする機会を探しもとめていたのです。……私は何べんも繰りかえし全キリスト教の体系や聖書の歴史を説明し，果ては偶像崇拝の無意味，無用論を展開しさえしたのです。……日米，日蘭条約においてキリスト教条項が加えられたといっても，未だ宣教師はその属する居留地の外で民衆に伝道することは認められてはいなかった。しかし Wood は幕府——長崎奉行所が外交貿易面で加

S. W. Williams らの日本宣教勧告書翰

速度的に増大した英語修得の必要性に乗じて，英語教授を極めて有効なキリスト教伝道のかくれミノに利用していたのである。彼はこの間接的伝道方法の有効性を感じ，2カ月の任期の終った後も英語学校の存続と発展を図り，アメリカより英語教師を招く許可を奉行所に求めるなど積極的な動きをみせている。

I next called upon the Dutch Governor Dunker Curtius, & respectfully asked him if he would not be pleased to have a young gentleman & teacher speaking his own language, having his own blood & belonging to the same church, the American Dutch Reformed, sent out from N. Y. at the expense of others or his own, & take my place instructing the Japanese young men in English & other branches & at the same time master the Japanese language himself.... he should not come out as a Minister or a Missionary but simply as a teacher (& wait the indications of Providence & good sense for his course of whose (?)) 'til he had acquired the language which would be quite fully 2 years. At the mere naming of the subject he flew into a violent passion, rising from his chair & walking the room, violently throwing his arms, declaring that Missionaries always had done more mischief than good to the heathen, that he believed the rebellion & massacre in India were owing to them & that even a teacher could not be trusted, for when an opportunity presented, he would be introducing Christian ideas again, & again he furiously declared he would give no countenance whatever to the introduction of a teacher, while he held missionaries in terror. But teacher Missionaries would only make the mischief to the Japanese. We must wait 'til they come to *us* for our religion, & when they saw it, they would understand its superiority to their own & embrace it. But nothing, nothing should be attempted 'til then, I replied that his views seemed to be in conflict with those of the Author of Christianity, as He commended his deciples to carry to all nations; & besides as the Dutch had waited here for 220 years & done nothing, he would respectfully ask if it was not about time to think of making a beginning? He became only the more angry & repeated his violent denunciation of missionaries & his determination to oppose their introduction into Japan. I then left him with sadness of heart for I had hoped that he, at least would welcome an intelligent & agreeable young gentleman who would enliven & interest their dull society & with whom from nationality, religion & language they would freely sympathize & he with them in turn. The whole opposition comes from the infamous life led by this handful Dutchmen, the Governor not excepted, who would be compelled to abandon their master vice or flee the island upon the arrival of a missionary or teacher hinc lacryma.

次いで Wood はオランダ商館長 D. Curtius を訪ね，ここでも英語教師の受け入れを要請している。但しここではオランダ系でオランダ語も話せる，オランダ Reformed Church と同系の American Dutch Reformed に属する一青年教師を，としてオランダ商館が受け入れ易いよう配慮している。Williams は書翰の中で

If the missionary to Nagasaki can talk Dutch, the Factory here will be able to give him a reason for living in the place by employing him a its preacher; ....

と云っているが，前にも述べたように，これは非常にあまい見通しで，Curtius は宣教師そのものを嫌っていたのである。Wood は前年にも長崎へ来ており，出島の商館とキリスト教との関係や，Curtius の人柄についてはよく知っていたものと思われる。それ故 Wood は宣教師としてではなく，単に英語教師として出島に来ることを認めてもらいたい，と要請しているのである。それは，彼は Williams と違って実際に通辞の青年達に英語を教えた体験を通じ，英語教師としての立場でも充分に伝道の目的を果しうる，と考えたからに他ならない。しかし Curtius はこの要請を激しく拒絶する。——キリスト教宣教師というものは異教徒に対して常に悪いことばかりしている。インドで起った反乱や虐殺(*)も皆，宣教師の仕業であり，単に英語教師といっても信用できない。機会があれば

S. W. Williams らの日本宣教勧告書翰

キリスト教を持ち出すに決っている——というのがその理由である。この拒絶に対して Wood は Curtius が全面的に反対するのは，出島のひとつかみのオランダ人が送っている恥ずべき生活から発しているもので，商館長もまた例外ではない，と非難を加えている。

注 (*) インド・Sepoy の反乱。

The Japanese have the best feelings towards the Americans & would believe teachers & missionaries from there sooner than any other nation. They have an idea as my young men often expressed it, that the American language is universal, with the opening of commerce therefore they see the importance of a knowledge of the English language.

彼の目には日本人はアメリカ人に好意的で，素直に教師や宣教師を信じる国民である，と映っている。また，日本人は英語は国際語で貿易等商取引の面で非常に有利であることを知っている，という指摘は，前掲の Williams 書翰の中にみられる指摘と同様である。

Now my dear Sir, forgive this long letter dictated simply by the object proposed—*the restoration of Christianity to Japan.* Nagasaki is an important point. The city is destined from its commercial position to become very populated.... another New York & also influential, instantly there will be a rush there & indeed it has already begun. Nothing can be expected from the Dutch but bitter opposition 'til an influence is brought to bear upon them *from home.* I doubt not they would make false representations to the Japanese government, if missionaries or teachers should come & kindle up again the fires of persecutions as their ancestors did against the Jesuits. The Governor however it should be said in justice to the rest would be the main instigator. I therefore beg respectfully & deferentially to suggest that *your Church*(*) immediately make a representation of the case to the mother church of Holland & urge it to send out a minister for the colony; & as soon as one appears in Nagasaki, opposition will die away; the Dutch colonists & their *Governor* will be compelled to abandon the prostitutes they keep & outwardly at least to live decently & not outrage the christian name & doctrine in sight of the Japanese. Then teachers & missionaries can come without hindrance.... be received with respect & when they have mastered the language, kindle up the fires of Christianity in the very place where nearly two centuries and a half ago they were extinguished at the stake. Great changes are coming over Japan & rapidly. A more interesting & hopeful case does not exist in the world, & should they be enlightened & christianized, it cannot be told what changes would come over the whole Eastern world.

The Japanese differ from the Chinese.... in better natural affections & for greater logical powers .... they can reason & feel the force of an argument & obey it. I beg you my dear friend to press this matter upon your honored church, in which the greatest revival originated of which I read with joy at this rising of the sun for Japan, or Niphon, as I am told in the native language; "Sun rising" & in cooperation with the Western church in Holland establish schools in Desima & Nagasaki; & then let the teachers become preachers & the gospel trumpet be heard again on the hill & mountain tops of these beautiful islands. Your church cannot 〔?〕(**) a more promising or honorable a work. But all must be done kindly & justly, that the old suspicions & prejudices may not be awakened. For myself if Providence permitted, I should above all things, like to go back & strike my last stroke there.

I am with the highest respect & much affection,

Truly & ever your brother,

Henry Wood

Rev. G. W. Bethune D. D.

長崎がキリスト教伝道に重要な地点だとしているのは，貿易港として栄える大都市であること，中国経由で来日する Protestant 各派宣教師にとって地理的に中国に近いこと，等である。キリスト教伝道上の重要拠点ともいうべき長崎の地にあって，同じキリスト教

S. W. Williams らの日本宣教勧告書翰

国でありながらキリスト教伝道に対して，商館長をはじめとするオランダ人の妨害を排除する対策として彼は G. W. Bethune 師に直ちにこの実情をオランダの Mother Church に告げ，出島に牧師を派遣するよう説得してもらいたい，と訴えている。一人でも牧師が派遣されれば妨害もなくなるであろうし，商館長も他の出島在住オランダ人もその恥ずべき生活を清算せざるを得ず，日本人の前でキリスト教を踏みにじるようなことはしないであろう，と云っている。彼はまた日本について，今や偉大な変化が急速に日本に起りつつあり，もし日本がキリスト教の光に教化されれば，東アジア全体にどんな<偉大な>変化がもたらされるかは全く自明のことだ，として，そのために Bethune 師の教会(*)がオランダの教会と協力して学校を設立し，この優れた資質を持つ日本人を導くよう強く要請している。

注（*） 当時 Rev. G. W. Bethune は Reformed Dutch 派の Church on the Heights の牧師。

（**） 2語消滅。

おわりに

S. W. Williams と H. Wood 両名の書翰はそれぞれ Reformed Dutch Church 派の指導的人物である De Witt 師と Bethune 師とに宛てたものである。これら二通の書翰に共通しているものは Protestant 伝道に長崎出島のオランダ商館の後援を強く期待している点である。後援というのは宣教師，あるいは英語教師——Wood の書翰中で D. Curtius の云う teacher missionary——の受入である。商館に受入れさせるため，半ば政治的圧力をかけることさえ考えていることは書翰の中にみられるところである。彼らがそれ程までにオランダ商館の後援を求めているのは，キリスト教伝道が禁じられている日本において Protestant は伝道の足がかりとなるものがなかった，という事情によるものであろう。そこでアメリカ Protestant 各派が盛んに伝道活動を行っている中国（清国）と近接している長崎において，略2世紀半にわたって徳川幕府と通商関係を維持し，確固とした足場を築いているオランダ商館に，同じキリスト教国の意識をもってアプローチを試みたものである。この試みは失敗したものの，それがこれら書翰を書かしめた要因であり，これら書翰が送られた翌年に入ると，Protestant 各派は日本 Protestant 伝道史に，あるいは日本英学史，キリスト教教育史に大きな足跡を残した，秀れた宣教師を日本へ派遣することになったのである。

E. W. Syle の書翰が手に入らなかったことは誠に残念なことであった。Syle のものがあれば Williams の勧告書翰が出されるに至った事情の記述を或る程度はっきりと跡づけることができたと思われる。しかし勧告書翰の存在を伝える記述が，書翰を書いた本人であれば，特にその信憑性を疑う必要もないかも知れない。Williams の記述によれば三人は Episcopal, Reformed, Presbyterian の各本部に勧告書翰を送ることになっているのであるが，紹介した Williams と Wood のものは二通とも Reformed 宛である。このことからすれば三人は各々の宗派の本部へ書翰を送ったのではなく，三人は各本部全部に送ったことになる。もしこれが事実とすれば，Episcopal にも Presbyterian にも三人の書翰が送られている訳で，これらの追求も今後の課題としたい。

（本稿は昭和49年11月大阪市で行なわれた第11回日本英学史学会大会で口頭発表した原稿に加筆したものである）

Mission Work in ~~China~~ Japan ①

When travelers visit a region or a city, they seek an eminence from which to get a wide view of the whole at once. So we can turn aside to go up into this mount, and it is our own fault if we do not get a wide view of God's work among the nations, and see the pivot on which it turns, the Governor's action on the machinery.

Disorganizing power of divine truth on systems of religious error and fiscal oppression

The results of its progress not always considered

Good work does not always or altogether produce good results; irritates enemies, causes new powers to energize their opposition

"I came to bring a sword" applies in ways we cannot perceive; the sword seems now to be sheathed

Examples of Christian nations have already worked out problems for pagan nations in government; they need not go thro' the same ordeal. Pym, Luther, Washington

Different races have been regarded as different species, but when truth brings out its just results then we better understand Micah's prophecy (4:1) that the Mt. of the H of the Ld. shall be established in the top of the Mts & exalted above the hills, & people shall flow unto it

(2)

Japan a good instance of this overruling of a race. Shutting it up when its life was in danger by Romish power, which w. give it neither truth, liberty or Bible. That power had neither mercy, knowledge, nor religion in its gift. The mission efforts of that time were nearly all indigenous. Persecutions not uncaused by converts. "So long as the sun shall shine or warm the earth, let no Christian be so bold as to come to Japan; and let all know that the king of Spain himself, or the Christian's God, or the great God of all, if he violate this law shall pay for it with his head." "In 1858, only keep out Xty & opium"

This expulsion doubtless saved the nation's life; and 1639 to 1853 furnished new elements in the world's progress, Protestant power, new ideas as to conscience, national rights, missions, and intercourse, making it safe for Japan to allow all she had forbidden.

Mission work wonderfully blessed; proof to my mind of God's ripening plan. In 1837. I wrote Because one attempt has failed, shall all future endeavors cease? The rejection of the men, tho' painful, may be the best thing for them & for us. If they had been received.. & we quietly dismissed, our means for doing them good, & their country thro' them, would have been taken out of our hands. In this view of the case let us not abandon this nation, but by making the best use of the men we have get better prepared to do them permanent good; and "by & by as Otokitchi says, we will try again." Otho. T Harris

It was not best then. The Annual Report of the A B C F M for 1838, commenting on that expedition and its results says, in effect "It is not lost; it is something to have attracted the attention & the prayers of God's people to that insular empire." No steamers then; U. S. had not the control of the Pacific slope; Japan not learned her own position; civil war which ended the divided govt., wd. have maintained it in the Tokugawa family, or a fiercer conflict ended it

We must not think that all these preliminary things touch the human hearts of the Japanese wedded to their rites, customs, sins, and good works. Their advance in knowledge fits them for receiving divine truth. But their willingness to receive Xty stirs up opposite instructors.

"Had I time I wd tell you at some length of the obstacles to Xn work wh. we find in some of the newly arrived profs in the Impl. Coll. Profs Morse & Fenelosa are delivering popular lectures to large auds on scientific subjects, & omit no opps. to assail Xty, &

America led the rest of the world in its intercourse with the Empire of the Rising Sun. It was the U. S. that made the first treaty with it [in 1854] it was that republic which made the first treaty for regulating the intercourse of Am. citizens within the empire of Japan; it was the U S which made the first treaty of amity & commerce; and in none of these do we find as cunning devices of diplomatic imposition as have since been inaugurated by later diplomats. The course of Am. diplomacy was appreciated then, is appreciated now, & will be in the future. After the first treaty had been signed, & the sincerity of Am. friendship confided in by the Jap. authorities, as was the case, it w. have been comparatively easy to impose any stipulation which might ultimately destroy the prosperity of the empire upon those who hardly knew what a treaty meant. But U S did not attempt such an unjust policy against a people enfeebled by long isolation from the family of nations, & the suicidal policy of the Tokugawa despotism. The friendly & conscientious course of the U S in dealing with Japan in those days cannot be overestimated socially as well as professionally seek to lead away men from the paths of morality. Morse of Cornell tells the Jap., that their morality is fully equal to that of any other nation, our own among them; no body is now worth listening to who believes X^ty, or denies Darwin's doctrines of development. Prof Fenollosa, his protege, usually lectures in this way on Sunday; one Sunday he told 500 natives, "No intelligent man who knows the facts believes the special creation of man & the world. X^ns say that God created man perfect, but that he sinned & hence the race degenerated; but this is only held by those who to support the absurd idea that X^t came to save men". This absurdity he then showed up, & maintained that man who rose from a brute, must have been himself one at first, with no ideas of religion morality or God. The Buddhists appreciate these attacks on X^ty & are doing all they can to help them. ~~Influence of T Harris~~

But "By their fruits ye shall know them". Also John. He that believeth &c.

All this only 20 years since I wrote the letters from Nagasaki to the Ref. & Dutch Boards, because Dr Anderson had declined then to enter on the field

V. Recd by W.H.T. Nov. Mr. DeWitt

Washington, Nov. 3. 1860

Hon. Lewis Cass,
Secretary of State.

Sir,

By the terms of the Convention made at Shanghai, Nov. 8, 1858, between the American and Chinese Ministers, the sum of 500,000 taels was agreed upon as the amount to be paid by the Chinese government for all claims upon it on account of losses sustained by American citizens. The commission to investigate these claims admitted a total of about 490,000 dollars, as the sum to be paid those citizens for their losses out of the proceeds of the debentures issued by the customs authorities in payment of the total amount named in the Convention. Two instalments have been already paid to the claimants, amounting to nearly 60 per cent. on their awards, and there is a reasonable prospect that the remainder will be liquidated during the year 1862. When these claims have been paid, there will remain the sum of a little more than 200,000 dollars in the hands of the United States' authorities in China, and subject to their direction.

The disposition to be made of this surplus has perhaps already engaged your attention, but I would respectfully ~~suggest~~ it that it be used as a fund for establishing a school of a high rank in China, where the natives of that empire can be taught the languages and science of western countries, under the tuition of of competent men, with the object of making them serviceable to their own countrymen and government. Such an application of this money will commend itself to the Chinese people, who are familiar with literary institutions; and my acquaintance with schools established by foreigners in China assures me that they are appreciated, and that there will be no lack of pupils to attend such a one as is here proposed. The whole design of the school can be made known to the Chinese authorities, and they will attach importance to a plan which comes before them with the sanction of the American minister.

I am unable to enter into details respecting the constitution of such a seminary, nor am I certain which would be the best port to locate it. The money could be invested under the direction of trustees living in China; and the American minister to that country, the consul at the place, and the instructors of the institution, with such other suitable persons resident there, could be constituted a board of management. After the necessary buildings to accommodate two foreign instructors and about fifty pupils are erected, I estimate the permanent income would be at least ten thousand dollars annually; and this would defray their charges, and the general expenses of the establishment. The experience already obtained would guide in the conduct of this institution, and I apprehend no serious obstacle would arise in carrying out the design with economy, wisdom, and efficiency. Of the benefits likely to accrue to the Chinese from the results of such a school, conducted by able teachers, I need not

~~here~~

here enlarge, the object of this communication is simply to bring the founding of it to your favorable notice by giving an outline of the way in which this surplus can ~~thus be applied~~.

I have the honor to be, Sir,

Your obedient Servant

S. Wells Williams

S. Wells Williams

Care of

Olyphant's Sons

& Co.

48 South St.

New York

Sec. [illegible]

[illegible]

[of 3rd Novr 1860]

[illegible] C. L. Roberts'

[illegible] of 16th Febr 1860 [illegible]

[illegible] of Chinese [illegible]

on file

Washington, November 3, 1860

Hon. Lewis Cass,
Secretary of State

Sir,

By the terms of the Convention made at Shanghai, November 8, 1858, between the American and Chinese Ministers, the sum of 500,000 taels was agreed upon as the amount to be paid by the Chinese government for all claims upon it on account of losses sustained by American citizens. The commission to investigate these claims admitted a total of about $400,000, as the sum to be paid the citizens for their losses out of the proceeds of the debentures issued by the customs authorities in payment of the total amount named in the Convention. Two installments have already been paid to the claimants, amounting to nearly 60% on their awards, and there is a reasonable prospect that the remainder will be liquidated during the year 1862. When these claims have been paid, there will remain the sum of a little more than $200,000 in the hands of the United States' authorities in China, and subject to their direction.

The disposition to be made of this surplus has perhaps already engaged your attention, but I would respectfully suggest that it be used as a fund for establishing a school of a high rank in China, where the natives of that empire can be taught the languages and science of western countries, under the tuition of competent men, with the object of making them serviceable to their own countrymen and government. Such an application of this money will commend itself to the Chinese people, who are familiar with literary institutions; and my acquaintance with schools established by foreigners in China assures me that they are appreciated, and that there will be no lack of pupils to attend such a one as is here proposed. The whole design of the school can be made known to the Chinese authorities, and they will attach importance to a plan which comes before them with the sanction of the American minister.

I am unable to enter into details respecting the constitution of such a seminary, nor am I certain which would be the best port to locate it. The money could be invested under the direction of trustees living in China; and the American minister to that country, the consul at the place, and the instructors of the institution, with such other suitable persons **(????)** there, could be constituted a board of management. After the necessary buildings to accommodate two foreign instructors and about fifty pupils are erected, I estimate the permanent income would be at least $10,000 annually; and this would defray their charges, and the general expenses of the establishment. The experience already attained would guide in the conduct of this institution, and I apprehend no serious obstacle would arise in carrying out the design with economy, wisdom, and efficiency. Of the benefits likely to accrue to the Chinese from the results of such a school, conducted by able teachers, I need not here enlarge; the object of this communication is simply to bring the founding of it to your favorable notice by giving an outline of the way in which this surplus can best be applied.

I have the honor to be, Sir,
Your obedient servant
S.Wells Williams

第19卷第1期　　西昌学院学报·社会科学版　　Vol.19,NO.1
2007年3月　　Journal of Xichang College·Social Science Edition　　Mar.,2007

卫三畏与美国早期的对华退款兴学计划

金卫婷

(西华师范大学　历史文化学院，四川 南充 637000)

【摘　要】1858年中美签订赔偿条约，中国付给美国700，000美元损失赔偿费，所有的赔款付清后，还剩下二十多万美元余额。卫三畏提议用它在中国建一所学校，这是美国最早的退款兴学计划。该计划由于实施的条件不成熟而流产，但它表达了"用中国人的钱按美国方式教育中国优秀学生"的愿望，这种愿望对后来的庚子赔款兴学产生了重要影响。

【关键词】退款兴学；卫三畏；1858年赔款

【中图分类号】K207　【文献标识码】A　【文章编号】1673-1883(2007)01-0083-03

20世纪初美国向中国退还庚款余额，用于在中国广设学堂和资助中国学生赴美留学，史称"庚款兴学"。庚款兴学是中美关系史和中国留学史上令人瞩目的大事，很多学者对此已有研究。但对于美国最早的退款兴学计划和它的倡议人则鲜有人知，美国学者马丁(Martin R. Ring)认为，"对20世纪中美关系产生重大影响的庚款兴学无疑应归功于卫三畏和他早期的退款兴学计划"[1](P57)。本文试图追溯卫三畏及其退款兴学计划，以此作为美国实施庚款兴学的嚆矢。

一 卫三畏与1858年赔款

卫三畏(Samuel Wells Williams)是美国外交家、美国第一位汉学家。1812年9月21日生于纽约州犹提卡(Utica)，1833年6月，卫三畏作为美部会派到广州传教站的印刷工来到广州，协助裨治文编辑《中国丛报》，并负责《中国丛报》的印刷和发行。1855年卫三畏辞教会职，任美国驻华公使馆参赞兼中文翻译。1855-1876年的二十年中，卫三畏一直在美国驻华使馆工作，期间七次代理馆务。1877年辞职回国，受聘于美国耶鲁大学，成为第一位中国学教授。

卫三畏在中国工作生活长达四十三年，其中有二十年在美国驻华使馆任参赞。史学家李定一认为，在早期中美关系史上产生影响的传教士最重要的除伯驾及裨治文外，影响美国外交甚远的，应推卫三畏。"[2](P156)

1858年，卫三畏以美国驻华使馆头等参赞兼中文翻译的身份，参与了中美天津谈判和上海谈判。赔款问题是美国天津谈判的内容之一，该问题起源于《望厦条约》签订后。美侨利用《望厦条约》中有中国地方官有保护境内美国商民生命及财产不受伤害的责任等内容，对其在华财产意外损失向中国提出索赔要求。最先提出此种要求的是美国传教士罗孝全。1847年5月23日，罗孝全在广州东石角的教堂和住所失窃，向两江总督提出赔偿要求，美国领事为了扩大在华特权始终支持该项申诉，到1858年其损失连本带息共2,800美元。以罗孝全案为起始，美侨向中国提出了各种各样的索赔，其中数目最大的是1856年广州亚罗战争(Arrow War)期间美商遭受的火灾损失赔偿。[4](P249) 1856年10月至11月间，英国以亚罗事件为借口，炮击广州附近中国炮台，引起西关城外起火，美、法、英商馆被焚。事后西方舆论一口咬定是粤督叶名琛为报复而故意纵火，要求中国赔偿损失。中国一直拒绝美国的无理要求，但1858年前后的内忧外患，使清政府拟实行"以夷制夷"策略，欲拉拢美国，故在赔款问题上一方面坚持美国商民船货意外之损失，中国不能负责赔偿，但又表示，由于美国未助英国，可酌赔偿美商之损失，以示优渥。[5](P10-13)

1858年11月8日，中美通过上海谈判签订

收稿日期：2006-12-15
作者简介：金卫婷(1966-　)，女，汉族，湖南怀化人，西华师范大学历史文化学院2004级世界近现代史研究生。

《赔偿美商民损失专约》，规定：中国赔偿美国五十万两银，合735288美元，以清结历年至今在华美侨向中国提出的各种赔偿。"拟于咸丰九年正月初一起，由广东、福州、上海三港海关，将该银五十万两分别立单，颁给美国使臣所定应收之人领取；其三港该派之额数，现拟定：广东三十万两，上海十万两，福州十万两，以上款项于中国征美国出入口货税、船钞，以五分之一扣抵，言明作为清结历年至今中国赔偿美国各口商民之数"。[3](P142)

赔款条约签订后，由卫三畏具体负责赔款的处理。他制定了理赔程序，在进一步调查核实后，发现赔款数额远远超出美国商民实际损失。所有的赔偿仅付出489694.78美元，剩下二十多万美元余额。

二 退款兴学计划的提出

关于这笔赔款余额的处置，卫三畏首先提出把这笔钱退还中国，但中国表示不愿再谈此事。[1](P55)于是卫三畏设想用这笔钱在中国办一所西方式的学校，1860年11月他给国务卿卡斯写信建议将该款作为"在华建立一所高等学校的资金。"校名为"美华学院"(American—Chinese College in China)，"学校聘请合格的教师，指导中国学生学习西方各国的语言和科学，将他们培养成对于他们的同胞和政府有用的人才"；并招收美国学生，使之接受中国语文及中国知识训练，作为今后驻华的领事及外交官或从事在华经商等人之用。他预计这笔钱可建一所能容纳五十个学生的学校和维持两个外国教师的工资。1861年布坎南总统离任前夕卫三畏特地拜访华盛顿，再次提出该建议，但没有结果。布坎南总统解释说，"这笔钱的所有权属于中国政府，擅自挪用有碍公平，即使是用于某种中国人也许特别感兴趣的慈善活动"。[1](P55-57)

林肯总统上台后，卫三畏又通过美国驻华公使蒲安臣(Anson Burlingame)向国务卿西沃德提出退款办学的建议，认为中国缺乏对西方的了解，以此款在北京设一所学院，对中国的好处将更甚于美国。"我们比中国人自己更清楚他们需要这样一所学校，用西方的语言、科学和道德伦理来训练年轻人，"[6](P844)建议强调"目前各国正采取措施来帮助帝国的重要政治家们使帝国走上新的发展道路，美国人应该继续对此施加更大的影响；在北京建一所美国学院将对帝国政府维持和平与各省贸易产生持久的卓越的影响。"[6](P845)办学计划得到林肯总统和西沃德的支持，因国会反对而作罢。1885年，美国国会通过议案，将此款连本带息退还中国，中国驻美公使郑藻如在收到453400美元后，特代表中国政府向美国政府表示感谢。[7](P282)

卫三畏首倡用退款在华办学一是想利用办学扩大美国在华的影响。由于英国所冀求的商务贸易特权，在1858年及1860年的条约中，全部如愿以偿，其在华优势地位更加显赫。俄国在《瑷珲条约》及《北京条约》中，不折一兵一矢而获得黑龙江以北乌苏里江以东的广大土地，在华实力大大增强。美国虽实力远远不及他们，但对华贸易发展迅速，仅次于英国。自1850年以来，美国输华棉布占全部对华出口的比例均为80%以上，占美国全部棉布出口总额的30%以上，到1853年增长到40%。[8](P72)因此，美国极想发展其在华势力，在中国办一所美国学校既代表了一种美国势力，又可以通过办学对中国政府施加影响。"如果我们在北京有一所训练中国译员的学校，我们的影响将较现在远为深远。"二是现实的需要。美国驻华使馆缺少中文译员，美国领事在与中国官方交往时，往往求助于其在华传教士。"在一个我们拥有治外法权的国家，如果希望我们的才智能够胜任美国领事法庭对美国人和中国人之间的所有案件作出裁决，那么就要求具备一定的双方语言知识。在中国建一所学校可以为政府提供人选。"[6](P844)早在1846年，传教士伯驾代理驻华专使期间就给国务卿布坎南写信，建议办一所学校，由美国国务院挑选一些具有必要能力和资格的年轻人来华学习汉语，未引起美国政府的重视。实行外人监督中国海关制后，美国驻华公使竟然找不到一位能通汉语的美国人去担任美籍海关职位。英国在中国的14个条约港口设有译员，而美国仅在三个港口有译员。英国在华势力显赫，与"颇多英人能通中国语文，自易为中国政府所任用"有关。通过办学培养更多的美国译员，可以在中国市场的控制方面与英国竞争。中国也需要通悉外语的人才。直到第二次鸦片战争结束，中国没有一所政府开办的外语学校。《天津条约》规定外国公使驻京，中外直接交流已是必然。中英、中法《天津条约》规定两国交涉使用英语或法语，暂时附送中文，俟中国选派学生学习外语之后，即停附中文，各项文件若发生争持，均以英文或法文为准。开办语言学校也是中国的当务之急。在华办学可以教导中国人接受西方生活方式，帮助他们获得使其永远幸福的方法和事业。”。鉴于此，卫三畏认为用余款在中国建一所学校，选派中美优秀青年学习彼此的语言和文学是最有益于两国的事情。

三 退款兴学计划的失败原因及其影响

卫三畏的退款兴学计划最终流产，是因为美国缺乏实践这一计划的政治经济利益基础。从整体来看，19世纪末以前中美关系主要建立在商务贸易上，而中美经贸关系在美国整个对外经济关系中微不足道。虽然1844-1858年间，美国对中国的商务曾迅速发展，但从六十年代起直到1895年，一直在衰退。1860-1897年间美国同中国的贸易，从贸易总额的3%降低到不及2%。利益的微弱，使美国政府将中国视为未来发展需要的潜在市场加以占有，追求以最小的代价或不付出代价分享其他列强的特权，政府则尽可能避免直接卷入中国事物。事实上，19世纪60年代实施在华退款办学计划的政治经济时机远未成熟。当时正值美国内战前夕和内战期间，林肯总统全部精神贯注于内战，无暇顾及中国事务，国务卿西沃德忙于应付对欧洲的外交，对中国外交心有余而力不足。美国内战期间，中美间贸易额急剧下降：1860年中美进出口总值22,472,605美元，到1865年时，进出总值仅7,799,366美元，几乎锐减三分之二。这种情况下，美国对华关系只求保存现有既得权益，不再进取以图更多商务贸易特权，这也是美国国会否决卫三畏在华退款兴学计划的主要原因。1885年该款归还中国时，卫三畏的办学理想已无人再提。

卫三畏的退款兴学计划与美国政府对华根本目标并无二致，只是因为在美国的整体外交战略中，中国处于边缘的位置，当时美国在华的既有利益和潜在利益都不足以使美国政府对中国发生兴趣。退款兴学计划的意义在于它提前为美国设计了教育蓝图和通过文化渗透发展在华势力的独特途径，表达了“用中国人的钱按美国方式教育中国优秀学生的强烈愿望，”这种愿望保留下来，并最终形成了归还庚子赔款余额的条款。”[10](P416) 卫三畏倡议在华退款办学正是20世纪初美国退还庚款余额在华兴办清华学堂的先声。

注释及参考文献：

[1] Martin R. Ring Anson burlingame, S. Wells Williams and China, 1861 - 1870, Tulane University, ph. D., 1972.

[2]李定一．中美早期外交史［M］．北京大学出版社，1997.

[3]王铁崖．中外旧约章汇编：第一册［M］．北京：三联书店，1957.

[4]Te - long Tong: United States Diplomacy in China, 1844 - 1860，Washington University Press, 1964.

[5]咸丰朝筹办夷务始末：卷二十三［M］．中华书局，1964.

[6] FRUS 1862. Washington，Government Printing Ofice, 1863.

[7]泰勒·丹涅特．美国人在东亚［M］．姚曾译，中译本，北京：商务印书馆出版，1959.

[8]王玮．美国对亚太政策的演变（1776 - 1995）［M］山东人民出版社，1995.

[9]韩德．一种特殊关系形成——1914年前的美国与中国［M］．项立玲等译，复旦大学出版社，1993.

On Williams and His Plan of Using the Remission of Indemnity for a School

JIN Wei-ting

(*School of History and Culture, China West Normal University, Nanchong, Sichuan 637000*)

Abstract: According to the Sino-American indemnity treaty of 1858, China had settled upon the United States 700,000 dollars for fire damages. When all the claims were paid, it appeared that some 200,000 dollars of the indemnity would be left over. Williams conceived using that for a school in China and that was the earliest plan of using the remission of indemnity for a school. Due to lack of mature conditions, the plan failed. However, it demonstrated a good willing: using Chinese money to educate Chinese excellent students with American model. It had an important influence on the later Boxer indemnity scholarships.

Key words: Using the Remission of Indemnity for a School; Williams; The Indemnity of 1858

（责任编辑：张俊之）

British attack upon Canton in 1856, Mr. Reed undertook to support only with reluctance. He said:[36]

"The total amount of our pecuniary claims . . . never amounted to a million dollars, and did not at the beginning of the war amount to more than a fifth of that sum, for you will recollect the bulk of our claims are of recent occurrence, for loss of property at the factories, when the Chinese were defending their own soil, and for which they are only responsible on the un-Christian principle of English and American public law, that the assailed party always pays the damages."

However, so eminent an authority as John W. Foster remarked, many years later, that notwithstanding the various reductions of the claims, and the close examination to which they were finally subjected, "many of those allowed were of questionable validity in international law."[37]

The claims commissioners were Charles W. Bradley, American consul at Ningpo, and Oliver E. Roberts, lately of the customs service. They began their hearings at Macao, November 10, 1859, and the report was submitted to the American minister February 27, 1860. The entire amount of the awards totalled $489,694.78, thus leaving a balance of about $220,000 which, when paid by the Chinese customs authorities, was deposited in the Oriental Bank of Hongkong.* [38]

*While the final disposition of this surplus money was not settled until 1885 when, with some further deductions for claims subsequently allowed, the surplus and accumulated interest, amounting to $453,400, was returned to China by the act of Congress, it is of interest to note various proposals which were made in the interval for the disposition of this money. When S. Wells Williams was in Washington in 1860 he submitted to the Secretary of State an outline for the utilization of it in the establishment of an American-Chinese College in China in which Chinese students should be instructed in Western learning, and in which American students could receive such instruction as would fit them for positions in the consular, diplomatic, customs and commercial life of China. Anson Burlingame supported this proposition, and it seems to have met with the approval of President Lincoln. Congress, however, took no action on it. Another proposal was that the money should be used to build American consulates and a legation in China, but this was rejected on the ground that the money really belonged to China. However, the first money paid over for the purchase of the present legation in Peking was taken from this fund, though it was afterwards returned to the fund by order of the Secretary of State. Still another proposal was that the money be held as a fund out of which any claims arising in the future might be paid. This also was discarded on the ground that the Government of China ought always to be made to feel the direct responsibility for the settlement of any claims which might arise. The most notable proposal, of course, was that involving the creation of an American-Chinese College, for in it was clearly foreshadowed the system of 'indemnity students' for which provision was made at the time of the return of the Boxer Indemnity surplus nearly 50 years later.[39] The balance of the 1858 indemnity was returned by act of Congress in 1885, two years after the return of the Japanese indemnity.

OFFICE OF THE UNITED STATES
COMMISSIONERS OF CLAIMS IN CHINA,
MACAO, 16*th December*, 1859.

S. Wells Williams Esq. LL.D
Macao

SIR

We have to inform you that your Claims for indemnity on the Government of China have been examined by us, and we have allowed said Claims in full with three years interest at twelve per cent per annum, as per statement.

Principal Sum,	$ 7450.
Interest, ...	$ 2682.
Total award,	$ 10,132 —

We are,

Your obedient Servants,

C. W. Bradley.
O. E. Roberts

Commissioners of Claims.

List of items in claim of S. W. Williams

1 fourpost dble bedstead, curtains, mattrass & 2 pillows	30.00
2 feather pillows $4 – 1 toilet glass gilt frame $4	8.00
8 lacquered arm dining chairs $16 – 2 easy chairs $4	20.00
1 round satin wood table $10 – 1 lackered letter case $[illegible]	13.50
1 clothes horse, 2 spittoons & toilet set $7 – 1 rosewood dining table	27.00
2 sideboard tables $14 – 1 bamboo screen & 2 washbasins 4½	18.50
1 study lamp, 2 hanging lamps & hall lamp $7 – bath tub $8	15.00
70 yds matting $8 – 1 grasshopper couch $7 – tools & chest 30	45.00
6 Ningpo carved frames & 1 vase 12 – 2 punkas, chairs & bath 20	32.00
2 small stoves & set of fire irons 19 – 1 Microscope 20	39.00
2 office desks with additions $60 – 1 Map of the world 10	70.00
1 Mold for casting type 40 – 2 reams letter paper &c 6	46.00
3 Maps of China, 3 General Maps, & 4 of New Testament mounted	22.00
100 small stereotype pictures $50 – 30 of Scripture subjects 30	80.00
Collection of Chinese books $60 – Sundries in office 35	95.00
Mathematical instruments tape &c 9 – rattan partition basket, lamp	17.00
20 English Bibles 20 – 100 Manchu Testaments 150	170.00
30 vols. English books miscellaneous	45.00
1 font Japanese Long Primer	275.00
1 " Manchu Pica	300.00
20 Vols. Oriental Christian Spectator 30 – 18 Merchants Mag.	57.00
15 " Calcutta " Observer 20 – 1 porcelain kettle & padlock 4½	24.50
1 scale & balances 2½ – 150 coins of various nations 11½	14.00
2 teacaddies 4½ – Sundries in house, as water jars, monkey rack, coal, bookshelf, benches, 6 Chinese chairs, 4 tables, ladder, 4 blankets, 1 counterpane, screens, pots &c	80.50
Sundries in pantry, dishes, covers, trays, &c	6.00
3 folio MS. vols. of Japanese & Chinese Dict. lost at Room	75.00
1 MS. copy of Matthew in Japanese	25.00
Chinese type, small size, estimated at 6cts each	4000.00
Do Do large font, 20,000 types	1200.00
Do Do seal, running & other sorts	100.00
Expenses of saving part of furniture 100 – Newspapers 50	150.00
Rent of house 6 weeks $95 – Rooms & godown, built $355	450.00
	$ 7550

3 years interest [illegible] Total $[illegible]

There will remain of the 500,000 taels to be paid by the Chinese Govt. for the losses incurred by American citizens, after paying the total award of the Commissioners, defraying their expenses and salaries and compensating three compradores for their losses, about $170,000. The debentures for the whole amount have already been issued to the collectors of customs of Canton, Fuhchau & Shanghai, and may perhaps be cancelled by Dec. 1862. I suggest that this balance in the hands of the U.S. authorities, after all claims upon the original sum are paid off, be used as a fund for establishing a school or higher seminary of learning for the education of Chinese lads of good promise in the literature of their own and western countries. This application of this surplus can be stated to the highest Chinese authorities with the expectation of their approval; and it is highly probable that it will not be opposed, for such institutions fall in with their notions, and they regard the whole sum as under the control of the American authorities.

The income of the principal sum, after deducting the outlay for necessary buildings, would be about ten thousand dollars, which would suffice for the support of two foreign instructors and about fifty pupils. A school like that here proposed was started in Macao by foreign merchants in 1835, but failed for want of permanent funds, tho' it existed long enough to show that the project was not chimerical, nor the results unsatisfactory. The direction of this institution could be easily arranged as that was, and full reports of its operations might be annually made to the Chinese, as well as to the U. S. governments. The American minister to China, & the consul at the port where the seminary was located, and the leading American merchants there, might be constituted a board of management, which, from my experience, would, I think, be found quite trustworthy, in connection with the instructors to be selected; so that no doubt need be felt as to the judicious application of the money, or thoroughness of the instruction. Such a project as this would be creditable to the name of America among the Chinese; and what is still more important be doing them good by furnishing well educated men, whose knowledge of western science and power would amply repay their education by devoting it to the service of their own country. But it is not needful, here, to enlarge upon what would suggest itself to every

BIBLE SOCIETY RECORD,

CONTAINING

CORRESPONDENCE, RECEIPTS, ETC., OF THE AMERICAN BIBLE SOCIETY.

"THY WORD IS A LAMP UNTO MY FEET, AND A LIGHT UNTO MY PATH."

VOL. X. NEW YORK, JANUARY, 1865. NO. 1.

China.

There are several points in the following letter, from Hon. S. Wells Williams, in which the Board is seeking further information, and is therefore not fully prepared to determine its future action. But the letter contains so much that is interesting and excellent, that we doubt not it will be read with great pleasure:

PEKING, Sept. 28th, 1864.

MY DEAR SIR:—Your interesting and kind letter of July 2d has recently come to hand, and I have showed it to Rev. Mr. Blodget and Dr. Martin, who are both living in the city, and who will thus be able to act as members of your Bible Committee in this part of China in concert. China itself is so large a country, and the habits of its people differ so much in its various parts, that a plan of operations suitable in one region must be modified in another, that you need to have committees invested with discretionary powers. I think the results of ten years' labour in Bible distribution, through the present plan of confiding the work to missionaries at their several stations, will be quite as great and satisfactory as it would be by a special agent, who must needs still employ his missionary brethren to help him.

As to the Bible Society defraying part or all the expenses of missionary tours undertaken to distribute the Scriptures in the neighbourhood of the stations, there can be, I should think, only one opinion of its desirableness and propriety. At the present time, especially, such tours cannot probably be undertaken without such aid, owing to the straits for funds in all the mission boards; and with proper limitations and directions, I feel confident your great purpose would be greatly promoted, and your Record be furnished with very interesting narratives, throwing much light on the ability of the Chinese to understand the Word, and their disposition to receive it. Although so many years have elapsed since Protestant missions commenced in China, very little has yet been done to bring this Word into contact with the educated and the literati, who form the governing class. Doubtless, thousands of these men have read it somewhat, but it has not attracted much attention.

We are told that one of the evidences of Christ being He that should come, was that to the poor the gospel is preached; and experience shows that in a heathen country, like China, it is eminently suitable that it should be so, and for two or three reasons. Society in this country is more democratic and homogeneous than in any other Asiatic kingdom, and its ruling minds proceed from all conditions of life according to their talents and acquirements. Yet the fact is plain that only a small portion of the male adults in the population can read intelligently, even the simplest books in their own language, owing chiefly to the draft on their time to learn its complex characters, amid the imperious demands for earning their living. This, consequently, turns the whole of the really educated class into that part of society which has time and means to study and compete for office, only a few of whom succeed indeed in becoming officers, but all of whom become educated gentry, and take the lead of society in every village and city in the land; and not a few of them, too, petty oppressors and severe landlords in their own districts. They usually head all insurrections, and all the organizations formed against the government, deluding the people as Absalom did sometimes; at others directing the public sentiment and wrongs into such channels as they like, of a more peaceful and legitimate kind. The rebellion lately checked by the capture of Nanking, was started and guided by disappointed and ambitious literati; and during its whole progress, in fourteen years, not a single officer in the emperor's service joined it voluntarily. The struggle for Christianity is come between this proud and influential educated class and the advocates of truth, as the latter multiply; and it is plain that as the poor and uneducated classes receive the gospel, and live up to its requirements, they form a basis for the changes in society which begin as soon as an acknowledged want is felt; and those who demand it can show its reasonableness by their lives and teachings. The progress may be slow, and, if peaceable, it is likely to carry great masses of mind with it on that account. If, however, the educated classes first receive the gospel, they are far in advance of their countrymen, and could maintain their position by a greater stringency, and evolve, perhaps, a worse despotism than now exists; for power is too sweet to its possessors to be parted with from principle. Happily, in China, there is no hereditary aristocracy or state priestcraft to maintain organized class resistance to the truth; and I think its professors will experience only that persecution which error and hatred can incite against them among local communities and in families. It is to the great credit of Chinese notions of government that the welfare of the people is its highest object, and peace its best end and evidence.

The only difficulty in the way of your suggestion respecting Bible women, and its adoption everywhere at the station, is the almost utter absence of readers. Female education among the Chinese is too limited to expect to find Christian women among them who could go out as Bible readers, for a good while yet. After all, one of the very chiefest obstacles in the way of the progress of Bible and all other truth among the Chinese, is their own language, which now proves to be more and more beyond the reach of the working classes. At the age of twenty, if a man has little knowledge of the written language, it is almost certain that he never will find mind, time, and means, for its attainment. The solution of the question, whether to use phonetic instead of the present ideographic symbols to write the spoken language, or to elevate the people through their own characters, depends on causes beyond our present knowledge. I hope the characters will be maintained, as the least of the evils.

It is a blessed work to give a people like this the Scriptures, and to preach to them the hope that is in Christ the Saviour. The God of the Scriptures raised up Confucius in China about the time that he raised up Ezra in Persia, and gave him as the Teacher of Ten Thousand Ages to this people to set before them the highest system of worldly morals, and to show to the human race the highest condition of civilization those morals could produce. The experiment has been conducted 2,000 years, and is in full energy now, and exhibits the best results fallen man can educe from it. We live when the higher Revelation is coming in to take its place and elevate this people to its proper standing among the nations. When I saw Dr. Morrison, thirty years ago, in February, 1834, he felt that this coming in had commenced, though no church, no schools, no missions, had been organized among them; how much more can I rejoice, after thirty-one years of pleasant labour, to see all these in active operation from Canton to Peking. Happy, too, will they be who help to reap the present sowing.

Most truly yours,

S. Wells Williams.

美國弟請安臣卡放

貴親王呈上　聖經一套此經是西域各國至
其至王之書是以本國有賢德信士合成一
公會將貨利送於使天下萬國人民皆知經
書道理為重今代公會呈送
貴親王轉達
大皇帝御覽竊以是書原是米稽大國士庶
聖靈默示而作非世人私意則度而成書中
第一卷是夏朝時所著從言開闢之事歷
至下卷是漢朝時所著從見天下萬國底
是一根而出人在世間有五常之理身後有
福禍之分世界末日人類復生惟人靈魂永不
可滅　其神特遣其愛子耶穌降臨世間三
十三載甘心受苦為人贖罪俾悉信者享永
遠之福是知　其神造化天地萬物人之日
用飲食器物皆感謝　上天所賜之恩也謹
將　聖經呈上伏祈
笑納是幸

七月二十五日

[A. Burlingame]

[1867 Mar 25]

Peking

Mar 25th 1867

My dear Dr Williams

Please find
an order on Russell & Co.
for three hundred
dollars which I beg you to use for
missionary purposes at
your own discretion

ever Yours truly

Anson Burlingame.

大清國與
大美國於咸豐八年五月初八日即一千八百五十八年六月十八日議定和約後續增條
款
查從
大清國於咸豐八年五月初八日與
大美國定約之後因事有宜增條款之處是以
大清國
大皇帝特派
二品頂戴辦理中外交涉事務大臣志
欽差辦理中外交涉事務重任大臣蒲
二品頂戴辦理中外交涉事務大臣孫
大美國
大伯理璽天德特派
欽命總理各國事務大臣徐　各將所奉
諭旨互閲俱屬妥實議定條款開列於左

第一條

大清國
大皇帝按約准各國商民在指定通商口岸及水路洋面貿易行走之處推原約內該款之意並無將管轄地方水面之權一併議給嗣後如別國與美國或有失和或至爭戰該國官兵不得在中國轄境洋面及准外國人居住行走之處與美國人爭戰奪貨刼人美國或與別國失和亦不在中國境內洋面及准外國人居住行走之處有爭奪之事有別國在中國轄境先與美國擅起爭端不得因此條款禁美國自行保護再凡中國已經指准美國官民居住貿易之地及續有指准之地或別國人民在此地內有居住貿易等事除有約各國款內指明歸某國官管轄外皆仍歸中國地方
官管轄

第二條

嗣後如有於兩國貿易興旺之事中國欲於原定貿易章程之外與美國商民另開貿易行船利益之路皆由中國作主自定章程仍不得與原約之義相背如此辦理似與貿易所獲利益較爲安穩

第三條

大清國大皇帝可於大美國通商各口岸任便派領事官前往駐劄美國接待與英國俄國所派之領事官按照公法條約所定之規一體優待

第四條

原約第二十九款內載

耶穌基督聖教暨天主教有安分傳教習教之人當一體保護不可欺侮等語現在議定是美國人在中國不得因美國人民異教稍有欺侮淩虐嗣後中國人在美國亦不得因中國人民異教稍有屈抑苛待以昭公允至兩國人之墳墓均當一體鄭重保護不得傷毁

第五條

大清國與大美國切念民人前往各國或願常住入籍或隨時來往總聽其自便不得禁阻爲是現在兩國人民互相來往或遊歷或貿易或久居得以自由方有利益除兩國人民自願往來居住之外別有招致之法均非所准是以兩國許定條例除彼此自願往來外如有美國及中國人將中國人勉强帶往美國或運於別國若中國及美國人將美國人强勉帶往中國或運於別國均照例治罪

第六條

美國人民前往中國或經歷各處或常行居住中國總須按照相待最優之國所得經歷常住之利益俾美國人一體均沾中國人至美國或經歷各處或常行居住美國亦必按照相待最優之國所得經歷與常住之利益俾中國人一體均沾惟美國人在中國者不得因有此條卽時作爲中國人民中國人在美國者亦不得因有此條卽時作爲美國人民

第七條

嗣後中國人欲入美國大小官學學習各等文藝須照相待最優國之人民一體優待美國人欲入中國大小官學學習各等文藝亦照相待最優國之人民一體優待美國人可以在中國按約指准外國人居住地方設立學堂中國人

亦可在美國一體照辦

第八條

凡無故干預代謀別國內治之事美國向不以爲然至於中國之內治美國聲明並無干預之權及催問之意即如通
線鐵路各等機法於何時照何法因何情欲行製造總由中國
皇帝自主酌度辦理此意預已言明將來中國自欲製造各項機法向美國以及泰西各國借助襄理美國自願指准精練
工師前往並願勸別國一體相助中國自必妥爲保護其身家公平酧勞

以上續增各條現在
大清
大美各大臣同在華盛頓京師議定先爲畫押蓋印以昭憑信

大清同治七年六月初九日
大美一千八百六十八年七月二十八日

ADDITIONAL ARTICLES TO THE TREATY BETWEEN THE UNITED STATES OF AMERICA AND THE TA TSING EMPIRE, OF 18th OF JUNE, 1858.

WHEREAS, since the conclusion of the treaty between the United States of America and the Ta Tsing Empire (China) of the 18th of June, 1858, circumstances have arisen showing the necessity of additional articles thereto: the President of the United States and the August Sovereign of the Ta Tsing Empire have named for their Plenipotentiaries to wit the President of the United States of America, WILLIAM H. SEWARD, Secretary of State; and His Majesty the Emperor of China ANSON BURLINGAME, accredited as his Envoy Extraordinary and Minister Plenipotentiary, and CHIH-KANG, and SUN-CHIA-KU, of the second Chinese rank, associated high Envoys and Ministers of his said Majesty; and the said Plenipotentiaries, after having exchanged their full powers, found to be in due and proper form, have agreed upon the following articles:—

ART. I.

His Majesty the Emperor of China, being of the opinion that in making concessions to the citizens or subjects of foreign powers, of the privilege of residing on certain tracts of land, or resorting to certain waters of that Empire, for purposes of trade, he has by no means relinquished his right of eminent domain or dominion over the said lands and waters, hereby agrees that no such concession or grant shall be construed to give to any power or party, which may be at war with or hostile to the United States, the right to attack the citizens of the United States, or their property, within the said lands or waters: And the United States, for themselves, hereby agree to abstain from offensively attacking the citizens or subjects of any power or party, or their property, with which they may be at war, on any such tract of land or waters of the said Empire. But nothing in this article shall be construed to prevent the United States from resisting an attack by any hostile power or party upon their citizens or their property.

It is further agreed that if any right or interest in any tract of land in China has been, or shall hereafter be, granted by the Government of China to the United States or their citizens for purposes of trade or commerce,—that grant shall in no event be construed to divest the Chinese Authorities of their right of jurisdiction over persons and property within said tract of land except so far as the right may have been expressly relinquished by treaty.

ART. II.

The United States of America and His Majesty the Emperor of China, believing that the safety and prosperity of commerce will thereby best be promoted, agree that any privilege or immunity in respect to trade or navigation within the Chinese Dominions which may not have been stipulated for by treaty, shall be subject to the discretion of the Chinese Government, and may be regulated by it accordingly, but not in a manner or spirit incompatible with the Treaty Stipulations of the parties.

ART. III.

The Emperor of China shall have the right to appoint Consuls at ports of the United States, who shall enjoy the same privileges and immunities as those which are enjoyed by public law and treaty in the United States by the Consuls of Great Britain and Russia or either of them.

ART. IV.

The 29th article of the Treaty of the 18th of June, 1858, having stipulated for the exemption of Christian citizens of the United States and Chinese Converts from persecution in China on account of their faith; it is further agreed that citizens of the United States in China of every religious persuasion, and Chinese subjects in the United States, shall enjoy entire liberty of conscience, and shall be exempt from all disability or persecution on account of their religious faith or worship in either country. Cemeteries for sepulture of the dead, of whatever nativity or nationality, shall be held in respect and free from disturbance or profanation.

ART. V.

The United States of America and the Emperor of China, cordially recognize the inherent and inalienable right of man to change his home and allegiance, and also the mutual advantage of the free migration and emigration of their citizens and subjects respectively from the one country to the other for the purposes of curiosity, of trade, or as permanent residents. The high Contracting Parties therefore, join in reprobating any other than an entirely voluntary emigration for these purposes. They consequently agree to pass laws, making it a penal offense for a citizen of the United States, or a Chinese subject, to take Chinese subjects either to the United States or to any other foreign country; or for a Chinese subject or a citizen of the United States to take citizens of the United States to China, or to any other foreign country, without their free and voluntary consent respectively.

ART. VI.

Citizens of the United States visiting or residing in China, shall enjoy the same privileges, immunities, or exemptions in respect to travel or residence as may there be enjoyed by the citizens or subjects of the most favored nation. And, reciprocally, Chinese subjects visiting or residing in the United States, shall enjoy the same privileges, immunities, and exemptions in respect to travel or residence as may there be enjoyed by the citizens or subjects of the most favored nation. But nothing herein contained shall be held to confer naturalization upon citizens of the United States in China, nor upon the subjects of China in the United States.

ART. VII.

Citizens of the United States shall enjoy all the privileges of the public educational institutions under the control of the Government of China; and reciprocally Chinese subjects shall enjoy all the privileges of the public educational institutions under the control of the Government of the United States, which are enjoyed in the respective countries by the citizens or subjects of the most favored nation. The citizens of the United States may freely establish and maintain schools within the Empire of China at those places where foreigners are by treaty permitted to reside; and reciprocally, the Chinese subjects may enjoy the same privileges and immunities in the United States.

ART. VIII.

The United States, always disclaiming and discouraging all practices of unnecessary dictation and intervention by one nation in the affairs or domestic administration of another, do hereby freely disclaim and disavow any intention or right to intervene in the domestic administration of China in regard to the construction of railroads, telegraphs, or other material internal improvements. On the other hand His Majesty the Emperor of China, reserves to himself the right to decide the time and manner and circumstances of introducing such improvements within his dominions. With this mutual understanding it is agreed by the contracting parties that, if at any time hereafter, his Imperial Majesty shall determine to construct, or cause to be constructed, works of the character mentioned, within the Empire, and shall make application to the United States, or any other Western Power for facilities to carry out that policy, the United States will in that case designate or authorize suitable Engineers to be employed by the Chinese Government, and will recommend to other nations an equal compliance with such applications: the Chinese Government in that case protecting such Engineers in their persons and property, and paying them a reasonable compensation for their services.

In faith whereof, the respective Plenipotentiaries have signed this treaty and thereto affixed the seals of their arms.

Done at Washington, the 28th day of July, in the year of Our Lord one thousand eight hundred and sixty-eight.

L.S.	(Signed)	WILLIAM H. SEWARD,
	"	ANSON BURLINGAME,
L.S.	"	CHIH-KANG,
	"	SUN CHIA-KU.

PROCLAMATION.

Whereas, certain Additional Articles to the Treaty now in force between the United States of America and the Ta Tsing Empire, signed at Tientsin, June 18th, 1858, were negotiated and signed by the Plenipotentiaries of those nations at Washington on the 28th day of July, 1868; which Additional Articles have been ratified by the President of the United States, by and with the advice and consent of the Senate thereof, and by the Emperor of China; and the said Ratifications have this day been duly exchanged:—

Therefore, be it known that these eight Additional Articles, being of the same force and effect as the original Treaty, are now published for the general information and guidance of all whom it may concern; and I hereby call upon all citizens of the United States residing in or visiting this Empire, to regard them as equally valid, and thereby promote the amicable relations now existing between the two nations.

L. S.

Given under my Hand and Seal of Office at the Legation of the United States in PEKING, this twenty-third day of November, A.D. eighteen hundred and sixty-nine, and of the Independence of the United States, the ninety-fourth.

S. WELLS WILLIAMS,

Chargé d'Affaires ad interim of the United States.

美華合曆

同治十三年歲次甲戌

美正月		華十一月	美二月		華十二月	美三月		華正月
初一	4	十三	初一	禮拜	十五	初一	禮拜	十三
初二	5	十四	初二	1	十六	初二	1	十四
初三	6	十五	初三	2	十七	初三	2	十五
初四	禮拜	十六	初四	3	十八	初四	3	十六
初五	1	十七	初五	4	十九	初五	4	十七
初六	2	十八	初六	5	二十	初六	5	十八
初七	3	十九	初七	6	廿一	初七	6	十九
初八	4	二十	初八	禮拜	廿二	初八	禮拜	二十
初九	5	廿一	初九	1	廿三	初九	1	廿一
初十	6	廿二	初十	2	廿四	初十	2	廿二
十一	禮拜	廿三	十一	3	廿五	十一	3	廿三
十二	1	廿四	十二	4	廿六	十二	4	廿四
十三	2	廿五	十三	5	廿七	十三	5	廿五
十四	3	廿六	十四	6	廿八	十四	6	廿六
十五	4	廿七	十五	禮拜	廿九	十五	禮拜	廿七
十六	5	廿八	十六	1	三十	十六	1	廿八
十七	6	廿九	十七	2	正月初一	十七	2	廿九
十八	禮拜	十二月初一	十八	3	初二	十八	3	二月初一
十九	1	初二	十九	4	初三	十九	4	初二
二十	2	初三	二十	5	初四	二十	5	初三
廿一	3	初四	廿一	6	初五	廿一	6	初四
廿二	4	初五	廿二	禮拜	初六	廿二	禮拜	初五
廿三	5	初六	廿三	1	初七	廿三	1	初六
廿四	6	初七	廿四	2	初八	廿四	2	初七
廿五	禮拜	初八	廿五	3	初九	廿五	3	初八
廿六	1	初九	廿六	4	初十	廿六	4	初九
廿七	2	初十	廿七	5	十一	廿七	5	初十
廿八	3	十一	廿八	6	十二	廿八	6	十一
廿九	4	十二	○	○	○	廿九	禮拜	十二
三十	5	十三	○	○	○	三十	1	十三
卅一	6	十四	○	○	○	卅一	2	十四
十一月十八酉小寒		十二月初三午大寒	十二月十八卯立春		正月初三丑雨水	正月十八子驚蟄		二月初四丑春分

美四月		華二月	美五月		華三月	美六月		華四月
初一	3	十五	初一	5	十六	初一	1	十七
初二	4	十六	初二	6	十七	初二	2	十八
初三	5	十七	初三	禮拜	十八	初三	3	十九
初四	6	十八	初四	1	十九	初四	4	二十
初五	禮拜	十九	初五	2	二十	初五	5	廿一
初六	1	二十	初六	3	廿一	初六	6	廿二
初七	2	廿一	初七	4	廿二	初七	禮拜	廿三
初八	3	廿二	初八	5	廿三	初八	1	廿四
初九	4	廿三	初九	6	廿四	初九	2	廿五
初十	5	廿四	初十	禮拜	廿五	初十	3	廿六
十一	6	廿五	十一	1	廿六	十一	4	廿七
十二	禮拜	廿六	十二	2	廿七	十二	5	廿八
十三	1	廿七	十三	3	廿八	十三	6	廿九
十四	2	廿八	十四	4	廿九	十四	禮拜	五月初一
十五	3	廿九	十五	5	三十	十五	1	初二
十六	4	三月初一	十六	6	四月初一	十六	2	初三
十七	5	初二	十七	禮拜	初二	十七	3	初四
十八	6	初三	十八	1	初三	十八	4	初五
十九	禮拜	初四	十九	2	初四	十九	5	初六
二十	1	初五	二十	3	初五	二十	6	初七
廿一	2	初六	廿一	4	初六	廿一	禮拜	初八
廿二	3	初七	廿二	5	初七	廿二	1	初九
廿三	4	初八	廿三	6	初八	廿三	2	初十
廿四	5	初九	廿四	禮拜	初九	廿四	3	十一
廿五	6	初十	廿五	1	初十	廿五	4	十二
廿六	禮拜	十一	廿六	2	十一	廿六	5	十三
廿七	1	十二	廿七	3	十二	廿七	6	十四
廿八	2	十三	廿八	4	十三	廿八	禮拜	十五
廿九	3	十四	廿九	5	十四	廿九	1	十六
三十	4	十五	三十	6	十五	三十	2	十七
○	○	○	卅一	禮拜	十六	○	○	○
二月十九卯清明		三月初五未穀雨	三月廿一丑立夏		四月初六未小滿	四月廿二卯芒種		五月初八子夏至

美七月		華五月	美八月		華六月	美九月		華七月
初一	3	十八	初一	6	十九	初一	2	廿一
初二	4	十九	初二	禮拜	二十	初二	3	廿二
初三	5	二十	初三	1	廿一	初三	4	廿三
初四	6	廿一	初四	2	廿二	初四	5	廿四
初五	禮拜	廿二	初五	3	廿三	初五	6	廿五
初六	1	廿三	初六	4	廿四	初六	禮拜	廿六
初七	2	廿四	初七	5	廿五	初七	1	廿七
初八	3	廿五	初八	6	廿六	初八	2	廿八
初九	4	廿六	初九	禮拜	廿七	初九	3	廿九
初十	5	廿七	初十	1	廿八	初十	4	三十
十一	6	廿八	十一	2	廿九	十一	5	八月初一
十二	禮拜	廿九	十二	3	七月初一	十二	6	初二
十三	1	三十	十三	4	初二	十三	禮拜	初三
十四	2	六月初一	十四	5	初三	十四	1	初四
十五	3	初二	十五	6	初四	十五	2	初五
十六	4	初三	十六	禮拜	初五	十六	3	初六
十七	5	初四	十七	1	初六	十七	4	初七
十八	6	初五	十八	2	初七	十八	5	初八
十九	禮拜	初六	十九	3	初八	十九	6	初九
二十	1	初七	二十	4	初九	二十	禮拜	初十
廿一	2	初八	廿一	5	初十	廿一	1	十一
廿二	3	初九	廿二	6	十一	廿二	2	十二
廿三	4	初十	廿三	禮拜	十二	廿三	3	十三
廿四	5	十一	廿四	1	十三	廿四	4	十四
廿五	6	十二	廿五	2	十四	廿五	5	十五
廿六	禮拜	十三	廿六	3	十五	廿六	6	十六
廿七	1	十四	廿七	4	十六	廿七	禮拜	十七
廿八	2	十五	廿八	5	十七	廿八	1	十八
廿九	3	十六	廿九	6	十八	廿九	2	十九
三十	4	十七	三十	禮拜	十九	三十	3	二十
卅一	5	十八	卅一	1	二十	○	○	○
五月廿四申小暑		六月初十巳大暑	六月廿六丑立秋		七月十二申處暑	七月廿八卯白露		八月十三未秋分

美十月		華八月	美十一月		華九月	美十二月		華十月
初一	4	廿一	初一	禮拜	廿三	初一	2	廿三
初二	5	廿二	初二	1	廿四	初二	3	廿四
初三	6	廿三	初三	2	廿五	初三	4	廿五
初四	禮拜	廿四	初四	3	廿六	初四	5	廿六
初五	1	廿五	初五	4	廿七	初五	6	廿七
初六	2	廿六	初六	5	廿八	初六	禮拜	廿八
初七	3	廿七	初七	6	廿九	初七	1	廿九
初八	4	廿八	初八	禮拜	三十	初八	2	三十
初九	5	廿九	初九	1	十月初一	初九	3	十一月初一
初十	6	九月初一	初十	2	初二	初十	4	初二
十一	禮拜	初二	十一	3	初三	十一	5	初三
十二	1	初三	十二	4	初四	十二	6	初四
十三	2	初四	十三	5	初五	十三	禮拜	初五
十四	3	初五	十四	6	初六	十四	1	初六
十五	4	初六	十五	禮拜	初七	十五	2	初七
十六	5	初七	十六	1	初八	十六	3	初八
十七	6	初八	十七	2	初九	十七	4	初九
十八	禮拜	初九	十八	3	初十	十八	5	初十
十九	1	初十	十九	4	十一	十九	6	十一
二十	2	十一	二十	5	十二	二十	禮拜	十二
廿一	3	十二	廿一	6	十三	廿一	1	十三
廿二	4	十三	廿二	禮拜	十四	廿二	2	十四
廿三	5	十四	廿三	1	十五	廿三	3	十五
廿四	6	十五	廿四	2	十六	廿四	4	十六
廿五	禮拜	十六	廿五	3	十七	廿五	5	十七
廿六	1	十七	廿六	4	十八	廿六	6	十八
廿七	2	十八	廿七	5	十九	廿七	禮拜	十九
廿八	3	十九	廿八	6	二十	廿八	1	二十
廿九	4	二十	廿九	禮拜	廿一	廿九	2	廿一
三十	5	廿一	三十	1	廿二	三十	3	廿二
卅一	6	廿二	○	○	○	卅一	4	廿三
八月廿八戌寒露		九月十四亥霜降	九月廿九亥立冬		十月十四戌小雪	十月廿九未大雪		十一月十四辰冬至

Presbyterian Mission Press, Shanghai.

1874.

Double Calendar for 1874 in Chinese

大清欽命總理各國事務和碩恭親王
公文
大亞美理駕合衆國欽命駐劄中華便宜行事全權大臣文
當[illegible]

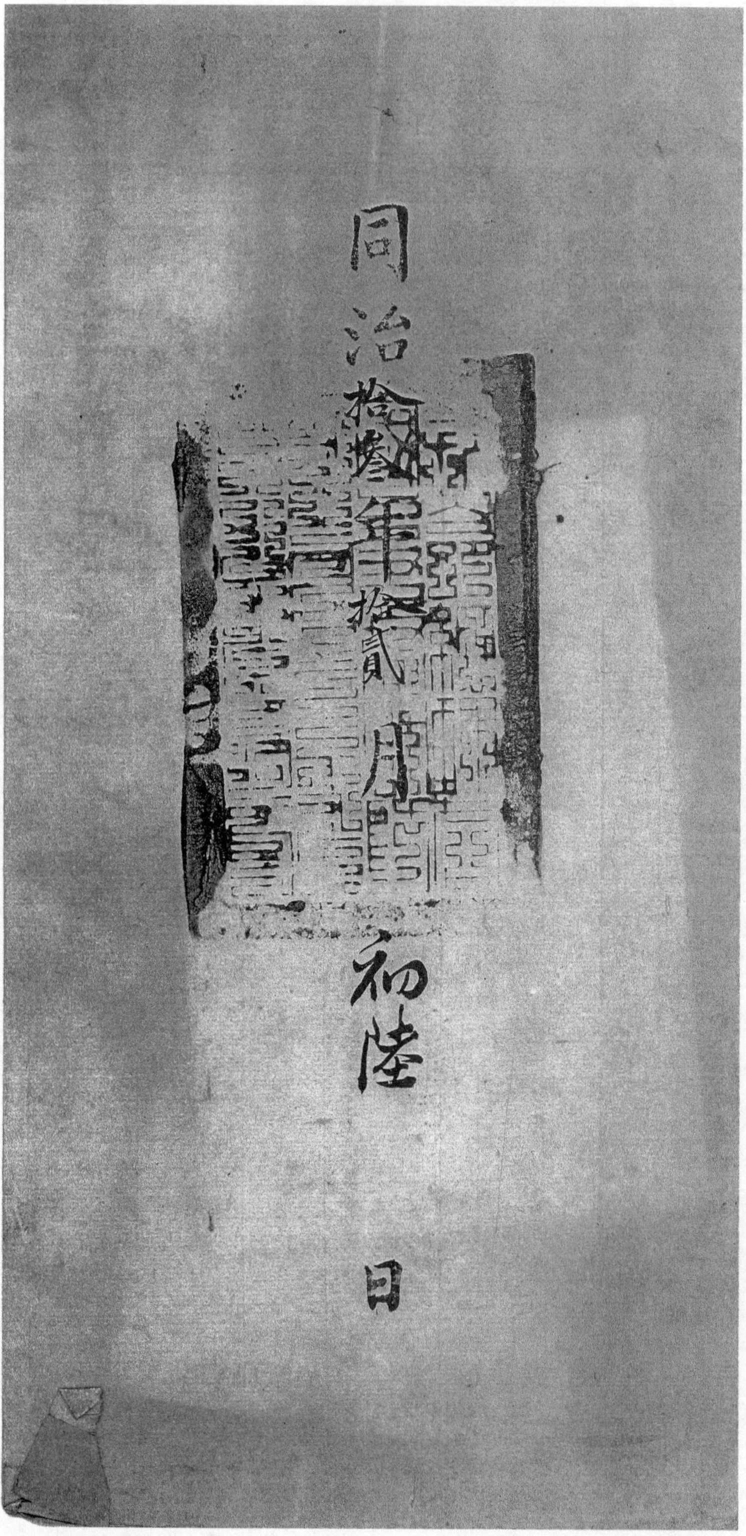

同治拾叁年拾贰月初陆日

美國駐華奉使大臣艾忭敏、奉
伯理璽天德旨、恭代賀
皇帝陛下、憶
貴國更睦悠久、願祝
陛下鴻祚無疆、遐齡永享、欣看
德政日新、藝翻素譜、且喜
陛下赤子、身蒞美國者、六萬餘人、技學均優、更比他
邦愈敦、益見兩國、永締堅固、彼此相交尤
重也、茲使臣恭呈為全權大臣之
國書、於
皇帝陛下、

Sire,

I am charged by the President, on receiving his appointment to reside near you, to present to Your Imperial Majesty ~~his great~~ ~~re~~ ~~the~~ ~~assur~~ his ~~congratulations~~ salutations, and to express his renewed assurance of the friendship entertained for China. ~~by~~ ~~Kinn~~ He hopes that your reign may be ~~greatly~~ ~~blessed~~ happy and long continued, and marked by constant advancement and prosperity in everything that will benefit the land and people.

He is pleased to know that more than sixty thousand of Your Majesty's subjects, who are now in the United States, are actively engaged in ~~quietly following~~ ~~their~~ their industrial pursuits and learning, and this fact gives my country a closer interest in this than any other can feel, and strengthens the bonds which have always existed to bring our two nations into amicable relations.

I have now the honor, Sire, to lay before you the letter which accredits me as Envoy Extraordinary & Minister Plenipotentiary at your Imperial Majesty's Court.

B. P. Avery's address at Audience Nov 29, 1874.
English + Chinese text.

INTERNATIONAL EXHIBITION
1876
PHILADELPHIA.

The Congress of the United States of America has provided for the holding of an Exhibition of Arts, Manufactures, and Products of the Soil and Mine. A proclamation by the President, issued July 4, 1873, announced the Exhibition and commended it to all nations.

Upon the nomination of the Governors of the States and Territories of the United States the President has appointed Commissioners to represent each State and Territory in the United States Centennial Commission. This Commission has been charged with the duty of perfecting and carrying out the plan for holding the Exhibition.

Its officers are:

President,	JOSEPH R. HAWLEY	Connecticut.
Vice-Presidents,	A. T. GOSHORN	Ohio.
	ORESTES CLEVELAND	New Jersey.
	WM. M. BYRD	Alabama.
	JOHN D. CREIGH	California.
	ROBERT LOWRY	Iowa.
	ROBERT MALLORY	Kentucky.
Director-General,	ALFRED T. GOSHORN	Ohio.
Secretary,	JOHN L. CAMPBELL	Indiana.
Executive Committee,	DANIEL J. MORRELL	Pennsylvania.
	ALFRED T. GOSHORN	Ohio.
	WALTER W. WOOD	Virginia.
	E. A. STRAW	New Hampshire.
	N. M. BECKWITH	New York.
	JAMES T. EARLE	Maryland.
	GEORGE H. CORLISS	Rhode Island.
	JOHN G. STEVENS	New Jersey.
	ALEXANDER R. BOTELER	West Virginia.
	RICHARD C. MCCORMICK	Arizona.
	LEWIS WALN SMITH	Georgia.
	JOHN LYNCH	Louisiana.
	JAMES BIRNEY	Michigan.

The Commissioners appointed by the Chinese Government to superintend the transmission of articles intended for the Centennial Exhibition are as follows:—

For the ports of Chefoo, Tientsin and Newchwang, EDWARD B. DREW, Commissioner of Customs at Chefoo.

For the ports of Shanghai, Ningpo, Chinkiang, Kewkiang and Hankow, GUSTAV DETRING, Commissioner of Customs at Ningpo.

For the ports of Foochow, Amoy, Tamsuy, Takow, Swatow, and Canton, CHARLES HANNEN, or *pro tem.* J. L. HAMMOND, Commissioner of Customs at Swatow.

大美國慶百年大會序

溯查歐羅巴各國開立賽奇公會肇始於英京倫敦次則法京巴理嗣此英法兩國迭相爲之後則澳京咈咭吶繼之二十年來凡設五次踵事增華幾於無美不具誠以此會萃萬寶之精英極天人之能事彰物采而振心思其法良其意美故各國循行不怠今合衆國由乾隆乙未開國定鼎至同治丙子三月值百載之週期特開賽奇之公會以爲傳祚無疆之慶溥請萬國各將人工物巧交相比賽一爲敦好篤誼二爲鼓才勵能三爲國與國相親民與民相睦永息讒慝之風各臻富强之業前由美國耆老會擬於丙子年開設賽奇會經

國家飭知總理衙門復轉飭各國使臣旋到駐中華京都使臣照會中華總理衙門嗣經　恭親王照覆業通飭南北洋通商大臣曉諭各省工匠商人百姓等周知俾有願賽者以備赴會並札總稅務司選派妥員前往會堂照料現暫派稅務司天津烟台牛庄三口派烟台之稅務司杜德維承管寧波上海鎮江九江漢口五口派駐甯波之稅務司德璀琳承管福州厦門淡水旗後汕頭廣州六口派駐稅務司漢南或暫派駐汕頭稅務司哈捫德承管如有中國工匠商人等擬寄發賽會一切奇珍寶物按照所派三口之稅務司員名寫交不誤如欲問各樣事件並欲寄之物件應由該三口之稅務司寄去茲准慶百年大會寄來擬定章程現均譯出漢英文字以便觀察

GENERAL REGULATIONS FOR FOREIGN EXHIBITORS.

Rule I. Duration of the Exhibition. The Exhibition will be held at Fairmount Park, in the City of Philadelphia, and will be opened on the 19th day of April, 1876, and closed on the 19th of October following.

慶百年大會各國通行章程二十五款

第一款爲賽奇公會起止期限

一丙子年係西歷一千八百七十六年在美國嘖哩吔嘖城開設萬國賽奇公會開會之日即自丙子年三月二十五日起至九月二十二日止

Rule II. Organization of exhibits. All governments have been invited to appoint Commissions, for the purpose of organizing their departments of the Exhibition. The Director-General should be notified of the appointment of such Foreign Commissions before January 1st, 1875.

Allotment of space. Full diagrams of the buildings and grounds will be furnished to the Foreign Commissions on or before February 1st, 1875, indicating the localities to be occupied by each nation, subject, however, to revision and readjustment.

Rule III. Applications for space. Applications for space, and negotiations relative thereto must be conducted with the Commission of the country to which the applicant belongs.

Rule IV. Foreign Commissions are requested to notify the Director-General, not later than May 1st, 1875, whether they desire any increase or diminution of the space offered them, and the amount.

Rule V. Before December 1st, 1875, the Foreign Commissions must furnish the Director-General with approximate plans, showing the manner of allotting the space assigned to them, and also with lists of their exhibitors, and other information necessary for the preparation of the Official Catalogue.

Custom-house regulations. Products brought into the United States, at the ports of Boston, New York, Philadelphia, Baltimore, Portland, Me., Port Huron, New Orleans, or San Francisco, intended for display at the International Exhibition, will be allowed to go forward to the Exhibition buildings under proper supervision of customs officers, without examination at such ports of original entry, and at the close of the Exhibition will be allowed to go forward to the port from which they are to be exported. No duties will be levied upon such goods, unless entered for consumption in the United States.

Rule VI. Delivery and removal of goods. The transportation, receiving, unpacking, and arranging of the products for exhibition will be at the expense of the exhibitor.

Rule VII. Reception of goods. The installation of heavy articles requiring special foundations or adjustment, should, by special arrangement, begin as soon as the progress of the work upon the buildings will permit. The general reception of articles at the Exhibition Buildings will commence on January 1st, 1876, and no articles will be admitted after March 31st, 1876.

Rule VIII. Forfeiture of space. Space assigned to Foreign Commissions and not occupied on the 1st, of April, 1876, will revert to the Director-General for re-assignment.

Rule IX. If products are not intended for competition, it must be so stated by the exhibitor; and they will be excluded from the examination by the International Juries.

第二款為各國派官員及各股各院圖式

一本國乘此誠請天下萬國各派官數員經理關係各國事務須將所派之員姓名先於本年十一月二十四日以前報明公會摠理司得知摠理司於十二月二十五日以前將公會堂內及分屬各院之圖式分與各國官員指明其地如何或所指之地大小有不合用之處後可變通

第三款為各國用地大小以定地式

一各國之民陳列賽物之所並其所應用地方之大小俱應通知本國官員商辦定其地式

第四款為定各股用地寬減之日期

一各國官員或欲寬其地或欲減其地應於乙亥年三月二十六日以前達知公會摠理司因後難改

第五款 為賽客進口出口之例

一乙亥年十一月初四日以前各國官員須將各國擺物之所之圖式並其賽客之姓名以及各物之件數一一寫清送與摠理司以便編排摠目所有賽會之珍奇物件於進口時海關驗明押送到會堂並不納稅俟會畢後本客如願將貨物在美國地方銷售應先納稅後發貨物如原物未售仍押回口岸概不納稅

第六欵為賽客應自出資

一運此物件到會堂接收開裝擺好在本股裏應歸賽客貨主出費錢

第七欵為賽堂接排物件之期

一或股中賽客有大而且重之機器須預備非常寬大非常堅固之地基應先與總理司商明樑式庶堂一建完即可為此機器預備地方收物件之限期即於乙亥年十二月初五日起丙子年二月初八日止此後不准入堂

第八欵為賽客償還空地

一丙子年二月初九日以後所有堂裏分定與各國擺物之所其中或有不用之空地摠理司可另與別人擺物

第九款為不願賽物之例

一所擺之物倘有本客不願賽者各客須早報明摠理司以便達知由各國所選察物定償之會不用察查

Rule X. Official Catalogue. An Official Catalogue will be published in four distinct versions,—viz., English, French, German, and Spanish. The sale of Catalogues is reserved to the Centennial Commission.

The ten departments of the classification which will determine the relative location of articles in the Exhibition,—except in such collective exhibitions as may receive special sanction,—and also the arrangement of names in the Catalogue, are as follows:

I. *Raw Materials—Mineral, Vegetable, and Animal.*
II. *Materials and Manufactures used for food, or in the Arts, the result of Extractive or Combining Processes.*
III. *Textile and Felted Fabrics; Apparel, Costumes, and Ornaments for the Person.*
IV. *Furniture and Manufactures of general use in construction and in dwellings.*
V. *Tools, Implements, Machines, and Processes.*
VI. *Motors and Transportation.*
VII. *Apparatus and Methods for the increase and diffusion of knowledge.*
VIII. *Engineering, Public Works, Architecture, etc.*
IX. *Plastic and Graphic Arts.*
X. *Objects illustrating efforts for the improvement of the Physical, Intellectual, and Moral Condition of Man.*

第十款爲賽物之目錄應分十部一賽奇會之摠理司須以英法德呂宋四國之語印於珍奇物件之摠目錄買此目錄惟屬慶百年大會經理所有各國物件載在目錄安放各所俱依總理司式樣分爲十部如左

一部 天然所生金石草木禽獸等物
二部 人用取法合法由天產物中而得之料物或爲各行手藝所用或爲人食
三部 織撚貨工並衣服首飾工以及各國古今穿戴制度
四部 製造房屋之工所需器具並家具什物各種
五部 琢磨織紡印鑄各樣工匠之機器並活造之樣式
六部 轉運所用各樣機法及運力造物之机
七部 使人學問增長普傳之妙法機器
八部 製造窰礦河濠橋殿等類工法
九部 技藝模式像畫賞心物件
十部 凡修身體長識見與禮仁各敎學之物件式法

所印摠目錄各股中雖按此十部分列如總理司如見有一大褀寶珍奇物件仍自歸一處

Rule XI. Foreign Commissions may publish Catalogues of their respective sections.

第十一款爲各國准自印目錄一總目錄之外准各國官員各印本國物件目錄

Rule XII. Charges and exemptions. Exhibitors will not be charged for space. A limited quantity of steam and water-power will be supplied gratuitously. The quantity of each will be settled definitively at the time of the allotments of space. Any power required by the exhibitor in excess of that allowed will be furnished by the Centennial Commission at a fixed price. Demands for such excess of power must also be settled at the time of the allotment of space.

第十二款爲股中有賃不賃之具一賽客不應出賃地之項所有爲賽客預備之汽力水力可按定額分與大小各股此定額須在分派各所時議定此外如再用汽力水力慶百年大會必按定價賣給賽客但在分派各所時告明

Rule XIII. Exhibitors must provide, at their own cost, all show-cases, shelving, counters, fittings etc., which they may require; and all counter-shafts, with their pulleys, belting, etc., for the transmission of power from the main shafts in the Machinery Hall. All arrangements of articles and decorations must be in conformity with the general plan adopted by the Director-General.

Special constructions of any kind, whether in the buildings or grounds, can only be made upon the written approval of the Director-General.

Responsibility for safety of goods. The Centennial Commission will take precautions for the safe preservation of all objects in the Exhibition; but it will in no way be responsible for damage or loss of any kind, or for accidents by fire or otherwise, however originating.

第十三款爲股中擺物之費擔保之具一賽客欲作排物之木架櫃鉤玻璃帳子等件並以本股中之汽力水力接到外邊之皮帶轆轤杠筩等物俱應自己出資置辦各股中安放物件妝飾一切俱應仿照總理司大圖之式無論在賽奇堂內或在外院欲蓋造大小之房屋須先告知總理司得有總理司允准之文憑方可各股中各國官員仍自擔保如有失壞損燒之處不與慶百年大會相干但會中亦必時刻小心防範務期合堂內無意外之虞

Rule XIV. Favorable facilities will be arranged by which exhibitors or Foreign Commissions may insure their own goods.

Foreign Commissions may employ watchmen of their own choice to guard their goods during the hours the exhibition is open to the public. Appointments of such watchmen will be subject to the approval of the Director-General.

第十四欵爲各官員雇人看防之例

一賽客如怕危險欲自己物件無失有擔保會允承保險保險之價無多可向伊講定得其保單各國官員如願雇人在白晝開堂時看守本股中之貨亦無不可須先將所雇之人姓名報於總理司候其允准

Rule XV. Exhibitors' agents. Foreign Commissions, or such agents as they may designate, shall be responsible for the receiving, unpacking, and arrangement of objects, as well as for their removal at the close of the Exhibition; but no person shall be permitted to act as such agent until he can give to the Director-General written evidence of his having been approved by the proper Commission.

第十五欵爲各官員能代派人收接物之例

一收開擺列各樣貨物並會完之後遷移裝運各樣貨物皆須各國官員或伊派人經管然須將所派之人姓名寫明先發給憑據以便總理司查考

Rule XVI. Each package must be addressed "To the Commission for [*Name of Country*], at the International Exhibition of 1876, Philadelphia, United States of America," and should have at least two labels affixed to different but not opposite sides of each case, and giving the following information:—

第十六欵爲寄發箱包封條式樣

一各國賽客欲寄發箱包等物到堂應先在箱包面上用英字寫云此箱送到美國嘖哩吔嘖城入慶百年賽奇堂請交本國官員收入中國賽客自當寫中國官員收入

Rule XVII. (1) The country from which it comes; (2) name or firm of the exhibitor; (3) residence of the exhibitor; (4) department to which objects belong; (5) total number of packages sent by that exhibitor; (6) serial number of that particular package.

第十七欵爲箱包上各封條詳細

一各國箱包等物至少應於箱之正面旁面釘帖詳細寫明條目須寫英字一寫國名二賽客姓名三賽客居住之城名四寄入何股何客五本客共寄箱隻若干六本箱第幾隻

Rule XVIII. Within each package should be a list of all objects it contains.

第十八款爲箱包內數目單

一各箱包內須裝物件數目單務寫英字

Rule XIX. If no authorized person is at hand to receive goods on their arrival at the Exhibition building, they will be removed without delay, and stored at the cost and risk of whomsoever it may concern.

第十九款爲貯物棧房之例

一各國官員須派人到賽堂收接本股箱包等物如貨物到堂無本股所派之人收接應另雇堂內夫役將貨物運入棧房寄存其運物等費並有損壞之處俱歸貨主自管

Rule XX. Excluded articles. Articles that are in any way dangerous or offensive, also patent medicines, nostrums, and empirical preparations whose ingredients are concealed, will not be admitted to the Exhibition.

第二十款爲不准入堂之物

一危險臭濁之物非出於正之藥材性味不明之丸散一概不准入堂

Rule XXI. The removal of goods will not be permitted prior to the close of the Exhibition.

第二十一款爲搬物有定期

一賽奇未畢總理司必不准各股搬出物件

Rule XXII. Reproduction of articles. Sketches, drawings, photographs, or other reproductions of articles exhibited, will only be allowed upon the joint assent of the exhibitor and the Director-General; but views of portions of the building may be made upon the Director-General's sanction.

第二十二款爲照繪之例

一堂內院內無論何物如有人願描畫寫繪照像須先請賽客並總理司俱各允准再行如有願照繪堂內外者須通知總理司再行

Rule XXIII. Removal of goods. Immediately after the close of the Exhibition, exhibitors shall remove their effects, and complete such removal before December 31, 1876. Goods then remaining will be removed by the Director-General and sold for expenses, or otherwise disposed of under the direction of the Centennial Commission.

第二十三款爲搬移貨物之期

一丙子年九月二十二日賽奇會期畢各國賽客即當自是日起搬移其貨架等物以十二月初三日爲度務必一律挪清或有貨物尚留股中任憑總理司吩咐遷去或爲花費而賣或任憑慶百年大會作何辦理

Rule XXIV. Acknowledgment of rules. Each person who becomes an exhibitor thereby acknowledges and undertakes to keep the rules and regulations established for the government of the Exhibition.

Special regulations will be issued concerning the exhibition of fine arts, the organization of international juries, awards of prizes, and sales of special articles within the buildings, and on other points not touched upon in these preliminary instructions.

第二十四款爲賽客應遵章程

一慶百年大會宣明此二十四條章程各國賽客既將貨物運入賽堂自然願意仔細遵其章程此外大會再特出章程論及何法安排各項寶玩由各國揀選察物定賞之會並賞賚之事堂內買小奇物件以及二十四條章程中未曾議到之事

Rule XXV. Communications concerning the Exhibition should be addressed to "The Director-General, International Exhibition, 1876, Philadelphia, Pa., U. S. A."

The Centennial Commission reserves the right to explain or amend these regulations, whenever it may be deemed necessary for the interests of the Exhibition.

A. T. GOSHORN,
Director-General.

JOHN L. CAMPBELL,
Secretary.

PHILADELPHIA, July 4, 1874.

第二十五款爲商辦變通章程

一以上章程如有不明不合之處必須本大會自己解說更改始於賽奇會有益此外無論欲問何事必須專函到大美國嘳哩吡嘳城賽奇會之總理司函面須寫英字

These sentences were arranged as an exercise in Chinese Composition. There are four sentences under each English example, & the student must analyze each of them which were not used in the Syllabic Dictionary

大雨如注可望豐年
甘雨時降無虞歉歲
雨下透了莊稼就有收成了
雨水足夠不怕再有荒年了

If the rains come, we may expect a good harvest.

資斧不足如何能去
旅費不周何以赴程
盤纏不夠用恐怕半路不能走
路費很少終究到不那了裏

If I have not money, how can I make the journey?

斯人心術紆曲
此人不甚直爽
那人的心裏灣灣曲曲
那人的肚子裏吐絲繞毫

This man has many crafty schemes.

只因感冒股肱微痛
稍中風寒四肢痠疼
因為着了涼胳膊骽兒都怪疼的
受了寒手脚屈伸不便了

Owing to his having caught cold, his limbs all ache greatly.

予之朋友真實無妄
吾之知交居心誠慤
他是我的至好狠老實的
他是我好友没一点兒虛假

My friend is a very upright man

夜間向其動靜
密處稽其舉止
暗地裏訪查他的去跡
冷不防窺探他的來踪

Look carefully after what he does at night

不用于秦猶用于楚
不利西南猶利東北
此處不留人還有留人處呢
這裏不能吃那裏還吃呢

If you don't want me, somebody else may.

貴体仍健
尊躬仍康
身子還是硬朗嗎
肢體照舊結實嗎

Are you still as vigorous as ever?

愚拙豈堪勝任
椎魯實以傾敗
莽戇之人那不能成事
冒失之人只會壞事

How can such a blundering dolt be trusted with affairs?

指物說價
物之所值
見了東西纔能說價錢
值多少錢還多少價

I can't tell what it is worth till I see it

我未失信
我無虛語
咱們的說話何曾含糊過
我們多偺撒謊謞過人

I have never violated my word

吾不信道塗之言
予豈受他人搖惑
我有主意不受旁人唆慫
我肚子裏有准頭誰能攛掇

I never trust to such vague rumors.

此事如何處置
斯事如何調停
有怎麼主意办理這件
有甚麼法子纔可以了結這事呢

How can we settle (or manage) this affair?

舊日何處傭工
前者何人僱爾
你從前給誰家作活呢
你一向伺候過甚麼人

Who has employed you lately?

爾意思我料中
爾肺腑我洞見
你的心路我没猜不着的
你的計策我早已看破了

I have understood your views
(or scheme) for some time.

天氣在春秋之間
無溽暑亦無嚴寒
這時候不狠冷也不狠熱
恰好似二八月的光景

The weather now is neither very hot nor very cold.

伊之名聲若何
彼之口碑奚似
他有甚麼好名兒
他有甚麼可稱讚的

What is his general re-putation!

竭力措辦
急速挪借
趁早去張羅罷
快些去凑對纔好

You had better go and borrow some money quickly

解組歸田
致仕旋里
多年作官退歸林下了
离了任回家去了

He has returned home after years of service

抱恙難支
因病廢事
病身子難以札挣
帶着病怎能彀出力

I cannot work when I am ill

此非崇論宏議
不是正言讜論
那裏是大方的話兒
豈是冠冕堂皇的話

This is not a very proper (or exalting) discussion

汝欲并日而營耶
汝欲事半功倍乎
你要一天作兩天的事嗎
你想作一天的勞苦収兩天的利息嗎

Do you intend to do two days' work in one?

坦衷直腸
直捷痛快
這是直心眼兒
没有彎子轉子

He is an honest straightforward man.

不必乘車
無須命駕
可以不用坐車
不必吽人套車了

I do not wish to go in a cart— It is not necessary to go in a cart.

竟夕不寐
通宵未眠
一夜没有睡着贍
終夜不能打个盹兒

I did not sleep any all night

其人乖戾不堪試用
彼不和平性難以指使
他脾氣狠大用他就壞事了
他素常執性誰還敢留他呢

He has such a perverse disposition that no one is willing to employ him.

先付定錢以免反悔
先給定銀始能憑信
給過定錢這買賣就算成了
下了定銀不怕他打趴了

Advance the earnest money, and the bargain is closed.

此價是貴是賤
此價是高是低
這個價錢值是不值
這個價兒上當不上當呢

Is the price dear or cheap?

此事甚覺詫異
此事十分蹊蹺
這事真奇怪的狠
這事真想不到的了

This is a very strange affair

舌尖鋒利
語言爭勝
不能饒人嘴裏
議論總要壓倒人

To get the better in an argument

器局不大方
其人太淺陋
沒見過世面的人
不是四海的朋友

He is a rustic and uneducated man

世界不豐富
財帛不寬裕
地皮兒真是太緊
錢財兒實在不方便

The times are unusually hard

腹中抑鬱難伸
常含不白之冤
滿肚子藏着委曲
心裏總是不痛快

I cannot easily make known all my troubles.

其人不識路徑
彼忽迷失大道
那个人轉了向兒了
他找不着大路了

That man has lost his way

幾分認真幾分將就
得寬容處且寬容
睜着一隻眼閉着一隻眼
可以包涵就包涵了

He is not very strict about little things, — He lets some things pass.

其人狙詐不測
彼有詭計多端
那个人真是賊鬼似的
他是賊鬼溜滑的

He has many rascally schemes.

鄉談難改
口音難轉
土音最不易懂
土話誰能曉得呢

This patois is hard to understand

柔不茹剛不吐
不欺貧不諂富
輭的不欺硬的不怕
不壓民不倚官

He is not oppressive to the weak, nor cringing to the strong.

巧言如簧
便佞之口
真是伶牙俐齒
不是笨嘴拙顋

A very eloquent, persuasive man

我自承當
不倚賴人
獨自擔當起來
何用靠託別人

I can manage this without help

心憂不能奮飛
恨不直上九霄
我只發愁不生翅髈
怕不能彀飛騰直上

I am too sad to be able to make merry.

以羨補不足
挹彼注茲
拆了東墻補西墻
富漢戲窮漢用

To supply one man's want with another man's abundance

愛子之心無所不至
親之憐子恩同罔極
疼愛兒子没到周不
愛惜親生不比尋常

A parent's loving heart follows its children wherever they are.

分位如天淵之隔
高卑似天壤之殊
天上地下差的很遠
一高一低迥然各別

As far apart as heaven and earth.

我难堪人折磨
誰能受他欺侮
我怎能當他的揉挫
有誰耐得他的凌虐

I cannot bear with his harshness

未嘗刻薄待人
全是厚道接物
不敢存着小人心腸
一味要孝君子的行為

I always mean to treat men well

名為愚忠亦奚有益
樸實有餘美中不足
十分老實𨚫是無用的別名
拙笨之亟能彀做甚麼呢

He is indeed a stupid fellow; of what use can he be?

畢竟直行不須由徑
豈容取巧捷足先登
照直道走心裏沒有彎曲
不抄近路是直心腸的

Let your way always be in the right path, nor ever go aside to error

無救計將安出
𨚫是獨力難支
缺少救兵甚麼法子
獨自個兒有何妙策呢

We are so short of strength, what way shall we take?

撫衷喪胆
內顧怯懦
心裏有些發㤼
覺着有些害怕

He is rather scared

愛人揄揚
喜人讚美
好戴個高帽子
最愛聽人的誇獎

He likes to have people praise him.

出言如見肺腑
吐語不容偽飾
說話怎能藏私呢
句句可以顯出實情

He lets all his feelings appear

譏誚之言詞
諷刺之談論
謔薄人的話頭
挖剳人的言語

To find fault with (or ridicule)
peoples words.

要一切妥貼
必事事精詳
攏總都要齊備
要四面齊八面整

I wish to have everything done
properly (or in its right time)

我諸貨買完
謂雜貨齊置
我一罟腦兒留下了
有一打躉兒全包圓

The whole lot is sold

末技藝果出衆
全才幹洵不凡
不本事真是出奇的
一能耐當真不小

His talents are above the average

名巨測難以取信
狙詐毫無把握
十詭計多端誰不疑惑
掉鬼弄神全没拿手

A very clever man is not soon trusted.

此蝇頭微利
乃針尖削鐵
直是一脚球錢
不够一壺醋錢

A very petty trade

欺哄吾耶
愚弄我歟
給我窟窿橋走嗎
要想胡弄我嗎

Are you not trying to take me in!

大德不計人過
海量無所不容
肚内可以撑船
包涵一切心中

Liberal men do not pick at peoples faults

執一不通断難處世
牢不可破寸步莫行
鑿死夘兒不能通行
一条道兒走到黑的

One who is so obstinate cannot manage men

言須有物切莫圓通
有公是非莫執兩端
話當决断不可以模棱
要有主意不可隨風倒

He whose words guide others must not himself be vacillating

但知明有王法不知幽有神刑
共見目前笞杖不曉死後沉淪
只見活人受罪那見死鬼帶枷
只怕活着不享福不怕死了去受罪

The sufferings of the living (or this world) are enough; who can tell what those of hades are!

莫中伊之計策
勿入他之陷阱
别落仇人的圈套
防着對頭的牢籠

Do not let him take you in

身長甚是躴躿
身高難鞠躬
他的身量幌杆似的
高大漢子躬不下腰

He is tall and thin, it is not easy for him to bend.

肝胆可託之僕
夙日深信之价
心腹的底下人
靠得住的跟役

A very trustworthy servant

此事無隱藏
此事無遮掩
一眼可以到底
十指全是漏縫

There can be no concealment in this business

情猶繾綣不忘
志仍紆迴莫舍
不能死心蹋地的
豈肯永不惦記呢

It is impossible to forget all this

此事恐無結局
斯釁豈易彌縫
這件事豈容了結
他豈肯善罷干休

How can such an act be passed over?

十分固執
太覺拘泥
一點兒也不活動
全是一味的發死

He is very obstinate

日用須儉勿奢
自奉從嗇莫豐
每天的費用不可信着意兒
見天的花消不可不打算盤

I must retrench my daily expenses.

時運不通心中抑鬱
事多掣肘五中焦燥
諸事不利没甚麽興頭
動輒得咎怎能有精神

If ones affairs do not prosper, they get all out of spirits

屢易春秋無建立
幾及半世名不稱
虛過年月一無所成就
一直到老没有一点出息

I am getting old and yet have done nothing of any note

及早悔罪猶未晚
一息尚存可贖愆
没到末日可望回頭
未入陰司不至無救

Do not delay repentance till you come to the end of life

忿懥之心時常抑之
有拂意来勿含怒色
心有不平壓制下去
事有可惱宜忍耐些

Restrain your temper when you have much to anger you

工夫以漸積而熟
學業以歷久而成
慢中可以生出巧来
要快反倒不能成功

Perfection comes only by practice

學古必細心推測
用力豈可不經心
念書不可囫圇讀過
講究書籍須要字句分明

When studying one must carefully get at the meaning

事不干己置之度外
與我無涉漠不關心
人家的事何必因操心
别人的夠當無庸理會

Do not trouble yourself about other peoples' affairs

畫餅充饑無濟于事
望空射雁究屬子虛
瓦匠没土打不起墻
巧婦無米煮不成粥

One can not accomplish anything without means

馬齒虛度五旬
賤齒已及半百
白白活了五十歲
業已過了半輩子

I have already reached the age of fifty

彼睚眦視我
他常怒目看我
他又瞪着眼瞧我
他又惡狠狠的瞪我

He looks at me very crossly

實在未會染指
真是净手拈香
没有沾一點兒光
没有聽着一個錢

I have not taken the least bonus (or bonus)

有些虛假難悉其詳
稍有不實莫見其隱
若不透澈説明怎麽知道細底
只是含糊其詞総測不透

If there is the least untruth, how is one to find out the real secret

土木之偶毫無知覺
性靈錮蔽心如木石
泥塑木雕蠢笨不靈似的
茅草塞住了心一味的是糊塗

He is stupid as a block, he comprehends nothing at all

養癰不治漸成大患
不除瘀血其症難痊
不治這毒越套越深了
由這瘡長着更加釁了

If that sore is not soon cleansed (or cured) it will grow worse

除惡不使滋滋
除賊必須欲盡
薅去草根怕再發出来
潑滅火焰怕再熇起来

If you can remove the cause, you need not again fear trouble

無勇如何得位
怯懦難以取榮
胆小不得將軍做
怕死不得挂帥印

With such a craven spirit, he will never be distinguished

去彼處幾次
往彼地幾遭
到那裏有幾磨兒
上那兒有幾輛了

How often have you been there?

甘步足下後塵
願隨閣下鞭鐙
情願作你的跟隨
懽喜受你的指使

I am very well pleased to be your scholar

長厚之輩
和平之度
厚道大方之人
心慈面善之人

A truly earnest & honest man

門公幾許門敬
閽人幾多門包
門丁要多少門規
門上得若干花消

What are the fees of the porter?

事當分任不能獨任
同勞共苦不甘偏勞
大衆的事單靠着我嗎
人家閒着我該當忙嗎

Are you going to put the duties of all on me?

自鄉移居城內
由郊遷至市井
打山上搬到家裏
起田野挪回鄉里

To move into the city from the country.

錙銖必較之人
此輩不遺餘利
是数星星的手
没便宜不幹的

A very particular and finical man

竢何日方可渡河
至幾時方可登岸
要等甚麼時候纔有擺渡
要等多咱纔能彀上岸

On what day will you cross the river?

在牀病不能起
寢疾展轉猶難
躺在炕上不能抽身
災病未除真是寸步難移

I am ill abed and cannot rise.

事甚幾密
事十分密
人不知鬼不覺
真是神出鬼没了

The affair is a close secret.

奢侈性成
夙不能儉
花慣錢收不住了
大手大脚的人

He spends money without stint

無計可施
無術調停
真是無可奈何
左右全是為難了

There seems to be no help for it.

出處同轍
内外通行
閉門造車出門合轍
自已過得去也叶人家過得去

To act always and everywhere alike proper

面含喜色
頗有笑容
滿臉堆下笑來
真是滿面春風

A pleasing manner and jolly face.

非君子類
乃小人黨
不是個正派人
全是些無賴子

He is not an honorable man

怨及于友
遷怒同儔
埋怨到別人
抱怨夥伴兒

To hate even those not concerned in it

不和平孰恭敬伊
性乖戾衆不欽佩
若發偃誰賓服他
鬧脾氣令人厭惡

With such a bad temper he gets everybody's ill-will.

实不通晓交易
未嘗夸过貿易
我不熟悉買賣的規矩
我做不慣經紀牙行的事情

I am not very well acquainted with trade

汝肯作保
爾願作中
你管保没錯兒嗎
你情願擔當起來嗎

Will you become security?

但望革面洗心
所期改絃更轍
指望着把不好心眼兒都改變了
盼望着洗手不幹了

I really hope that you will reform your evil courses

斯言不如我意
此語我不投緣
這些話全是不中聽的
這个言詞很不順我的耳

I do not like to hear such talk

妄人莫交
偽友莫託
那个人多詐來往不得
一味虛情假意靠不住的

Donot be intimate (or trust) with rascals

門外立一群人
路上集一起人
街上站着一干人呢
道上聚了一夥人呢

There is a crowd in the street

各日火食若干串
逐日薪水費幾兩
每天吃喝要用多少錢
見天的花消合多少銀子

How much are the daily expenses?

閣下做何生涯
老兄素務何業
領教你納有貴何幹
你您在那裏發財

What, Sir, is your occupation?

些須之費尚能應酬
大力包舉實難從命
小小的貼補不至于為難
時常的接濟如何行的了

I can, perhaps, help you a little for this once

衆口一詞汝仍不信耶
異口同音爾不以為然乎
大家都這麽説你還猶疑嗎
大夥兒同這樣説單是你各別嗎

Everybody says it is so, and why do you doubt it?

一年清俸若干
終年食俸幾多
四季的俸祿約摸多少
每歲的養廉攏共多少

About what sum is his yearly salary?

不過署事
暫行護理
替那个官办理公事
不過幫前任办事務

I am only temporarily doing duty for the officer

無術餬口
朝不謀夕
沒有法子治肚子
有了早頓沒有晚頓

I have no way of getting a living

夕陽欲下
晷影西沈
日頭太平西了
老爺兒快落了

The sun is going down

做事不甚仔細
辦事不大認真
這工夫全是撩草做的
作事情都是很含糊

You attend to your duties very carelessly

即刻為我取來
急速取來我用
馬上給我拿來纔好
我立等着就要用呢

Bring it for my use immediately

伊之罪名不至太重
彼雖得罪情有可原
他雖犯了法不是大罪呢
他的罪過是輕的呢

His crime is not very grievous

事已定局不必叮嚀
事無更改何庸多言
事已訂准了何用費好些話
不怕事有反覆絮叨幹甚麼

The matter is finished, and we need not discuss it any more.

近日閣下有何新聞
邇來吾兄有何新聞否
這程子你納聽見甚麼新樣兒的事哪
這些日子你有新聞没有

What news have you had recently?

君國大事我何敢干預
朝廷密事不敢稍參末議
皇上家的事我怎能曉得
國家的事百姓不敢説長道短

I dare not talk about the affairs of Government

只得方命
萬難依從
這个不能全由着你
這不能依你的吩咐

I can not comply with your wishes

工畢始付錢
不完工不付錢
作完了工纔能給錢
没有完工就不給錢

I will pay the money when the work is done

慮吾不清数目乎
畏吾將來有拖欠歟
怕我該下了賬老不還嗎
怕我賒借了後來坑騙人嗎

Are you afraid that I'll not pay the account?

喜看書不喜馳馬
好提筆不好揚鞭
看書比跑馬安逸多了
習文的比那耀武的強多了

I had rather study than race horses

甚辛苦須稍停
亟勞苦須休息
作活累的慌要喘喘氣兒
身上攞汗略歇一歇兒

It is best to rest awhile after such hard toil

欲往村莊閒游
想至郊外散步
要出去城逛逛了
要去閒逛鄉村的野景

I wish to take a ramble thro' the villages and hamlets

握手是禮兒
搭手是儀文
見面拉手是規矩
手拉手兒是過節

It is the custom to shake hands.

請君浮一大白
為君更進一杯
請你再喝一杯罷
勸你再照乾一盅

Please take another glass

屨敝須加縫紉
舄破宜再織補
鞋上該打個鞝子了
鞋要補一個補靪呢

This shoe needs to be patched

似曾與伊謀面
迥非素不相識
我和他面善的狠
這人不是生臉兒的

I am very well acquainted with him.

1

Copies of Dr. Williams dicty sent at.

Hongkong & Canton.
Revd. C. F. Preston.
" H. V. Noyes.
" B. C. Henry.
" A. P. Happer.
Dr. J. G. Kerr.
Revd. A. A. Roach.
" J. C. Chalmers.
" F. Hubrig.
" D. Goodman.
" R. H. Graves.
" J. Gibson
" J. C. Nevin.
" ~~J. [illegible]~~
" S. Whitehead.
" A. B. Williams.
Miss H. Noyes.
Revd. E. Faber.
" W. Dilthei.
" J. Nacken.
" W. Louis.
" E. J. Eitel.
" J. Piton.
" G. Reusch.
" W. Bellon.
" J. C. Edge.
" Bender.
" Ott.
" Goosman.

27
28

Foochow.
Dr. D. W. Osgood

Revd. J. Wolfe.
" S. L. Baldwin.
" J. E. Walker.
" John E. Mahood.
" S. F. Woodin.

6

Ningpo.
Revd. Dr. Knowlton.
" Goddard
" Dr Lord.
" Butler
" Leyenberger.
" Galpin.
" Bp. Russell.
" Moule.
" Valentine.
" Gretton.
Miss Lawrence.
Revd. Cormick.
" Stott
Mr. Jackson.
" Williamson.
" Meadows.
Revd. Gough.

17

Hankow.
Revd. G. John.
" A. Foster.
" J. Bryne.
" Hoyt.
" Hötting.

2

Hankow cont.

Revd Stricker.
" E. Judd.
" J. Cox.
" D. W. Brewer.
" D. Hill.
" J. Race
" W. Scarborough.
" E. P. Hardey.
" E. Dr. Mitchil.
Mr. Gün.
Mrs. Cox
Sold for $15.00. Sent by [illegible] at [illegible], & $6.00 pd by them, balance being pd in to Posey.

16.

Kiukiang.

Revd F. E. Hart.
" J. Ing.
" A. Stritmatter.
" A. Cook.
" J. Hykes.
" A. E. Cardwell.
Miss Lucy Hoag.
" Gertrude Howe.

8.

Chefoo.

Revd J. L. Nevius.
" MacIntyre.
Dr Henderson.
Revd Hartwell.
" Corbett.
" Williamson.
" Mateer.

Chefoo cont'd.

Revd Mills.
" Crawford.
" Richard.
" J. L. Whiting.
" Crossette.
" J. Ross.

13.

Taylor mission.

Dr A. H. Douthwaite.
Revd Rudland.
" E. Fiske.
" C. F. Fiske.
" J. McCarthy.
Miss Boyer.
Revd J. Donovan.
" Hy Taylor.
" F. Baller.
" C. H. Judd.
" J. H. Taylor.
" Bagnell.

12

Swatow.

Revd Geo Smith.
Dr Gauld.
Revd Mackenzie.
" Duffus.
" Partridge.
" W. Ashmore.
Miss Fielde.

7

3

Hangchow.		Presented.	
Revd Horston.		Mr. A. Wylie.	
" Helm.		Miss. H. Fay.	
" G. E. Moule.		Dr. J. C. Hepburn.	
" S. Dodd.		Mr. A. Gordon.	
" D. N. Lyon.		" J. L. Mateer.	
Dr. Galt.		Daily News. Review	6
Mr. G.W. Painter.			
Mrs Randolph.		Consigned.	
Revd Elwin.		Dr Williams	1
	9	" "	50
Amoy.		" "	15
Dr. Douglass.	5	C. A. Stanley	15
Shanghai & Soochow.		" " "	1
Revd Farnham.		Kelly & Co. up to Apr. 1st '75 & independent of copies sent out through them to Dr W. & for the Missionaries	129
" Fitch.		Trübner & Co	50
" Davis.		J. A. Leyenberger	1
" Thomson.		J. G. Kerr. 28 cops were sent him for missys on 19/8/74 & only 27 needed, other 1 sold for full price	
" DuBose		Sent him on 29/9/74	6
" Holt.		A. W. Loomis D.D.	1
" Barrett.		A. L. Bancroft & Co	1
" Allen.		Dr. Eitel. by request of Dr. W.	15
" Muirhead.		Wetmore & Co	5.
" Carpenter.		Sold at $15.00	21
" McClatchie.		P. Loureiro. Cost unbound	1
" Lambuth. (2 copies)		J. B. Tootal unbound	1
Miss Safford.			
Revd Whiting.	15		
Miscellaneous.			
Revd Ashmore. unbound			
" Hillman.			
" Pilcher.			
" McGregor. (Amoy)			
R. Gerstone	5		
Total No to Missionaries @ $16.00 = 140		Total Number sent out to date Apl 10th 1875	488

A SYLLABIC DICTIONARY

OF THE

CHINESE LANGUAGE,

ARRANGED ACCORDING TO THE

WU-FANG YUEN YIN,

WITH THE PRONUNCIATION OF THE CHARACTERS AS HEARD IN

Peking, Canton, Amoy, and Shanghai.

BY S. WELLS WILLIAMS, LL.D.

Shanghai:

AMERICAN PRESBYTERIAN MISSION PRESS, 1874.

COMPLETE IN ONE QUARTO VOLUME OF 1336 PAGES.

FOR SALE BY SCRIBNER, WELFORD & ARMSTRONG,

Nos. 743 and 745 Broadway, New York.

Price 30 Dollars nett.

A few copies of this work have recently been received from China, where it has been favorably noticed by students in the language, and has superseded all former dictionaries. It is believed that many of the colleges, seminaries, and literary institutions in the United States, will be desirous of procuring a copy for their public libraries, to place it where students can consult it. Scholars interested in Oriental Languages will also be glad to get this aid in their studies, and the presence of many thousands of Chinese in this country may likewise serve as an inducement to curious scholars to examine into the nature of their language in its spoken and written forms. It may also interest many others to learn that this book is the product of American scholarship and skill. The author has resided in China over forty years, and has been connected with the United States Legation as Secretary and Chinese Interpreter, for the past twenty years. The three fonts of Chinese type used in printing the book were mostly cut, and all cast at the Presbyterian Mission Press in Shanghai, where the stereotype plates were also made by native workmen taught in the establishment.

Instead of relying upon the usual channels for notices of new publications, it has been deemed best to append to this notice a few extracts from reviews, from which the design, arrangement, and execution of this Dictionary can be more fully understood, and send copies in this form to persons who are likely to be interested in such a publication.

Extracts from Reviews of the Syllabic Dictionary.

Note from SIR THOMAS F. WADE, K. C. B., H. B. M. Minister at Peking, and author of several works on the Chinese Language.

"I have seen enough of this Dictionary to justify the conviction I have uniformly expressed, that it will be a great advance on any former Chinese Dictionary yet published."

By REV. HENRY BLODGETT, D. D., for 22 years a Missionary to China, and one of the Translators of the New Version of the New Testament.

* * "In the year 1855, Dr. Williams being a layman, accepted the position, which he still holds, of Secretary of Legation to the United States Government in China. While discharging the duties of this office, he still found time for the prosecution of his literary labors. A new edition of the Commercial Guide, adapted to the changed relations of foreign nations with China, appeared in 1862. In 1863, as we are informed in the preface, he commenced the preparation of this Dictionary, which must be regarded as the great work of his life, and which, after eleven years of consecutive labor, and in the forty-first year of his residence in China, is now presented to the public.

"Dr. Williams did not come to this work as a fresh hand. His previous efforts, and especially his preparation of the Dictionary of the Canton Dialect, opened the way for a Dictionary of the general language; so that this, his latest work, is the ripe fruit of his life-long studies.

"The Dictionary comes to us in the form of a handsome quarto, bound in cloth and leather, containing 1336 pages, including the Preface, which has ten pages, and the Introduction, which has seventy-four pages.

"The Preface first refers to the fact that fifty-two years have elapsed since Morrison completed his Dictionary of the Chinese Language, and, after briefly noticing the labors of others in this department, passes on to give the considerations which prevailed with the author to undertake the present work. The design and general plan of the work are indicated, and acknowledgments are made of assistance derived from the labors of others.

"We learn from the Preface that the number of characters in the work is 12,527, of which 1,587 are duplicate forms; so that the number of articles is 10,940. Although the number of characters in the Chinese Language is above 40,000, yet the number in this Dictionary is deemed sufficient for all ordinary purposes.

"The Introduction contains eight sections. Section first treats of the Mandarin Dialect, as exhibited in the *Wu-fang Yuen Yin*, a very popular vocabulary of the Court Dialect, in use among the Chinese of the northern and central provinces. Dr. Williams here divides Chinese Dictionaries into three classes, and notes the fact that the oldest of them—the *'Rh Ya*, or Ready Guide,—is also the earliest philological work extant in any language, and was composed nearly three thousand years ago.

"It is well known that the Chinese language is monosyllabic, and that the number of the syllables employed in it is very small, only a partial and limited use being made of the vocal organs, while this poverty of sounds is compensated by the richness of the written symbols. We learn that, while in this dictionary the number of characters is 12,527, the number of syllables in the Mandarin Dialect is only 522; that the number in the Canton Dialect is 707; in the Fuhchau Dialect is 928; in the Amoy Dialect 846; in the Shanghai Dialect, 660. Each syllable in the Mandarin Dialect, owing to the tones, may be pronounced in four or five different ways; while in the other dialects, each syllable may, for the same reason, be pronounced in eight different ways.

"The second section relates to the system of Orthography by which these sounds may be represented in the Roman alphabet. Dr. Williams has made the first attempt to arrange a system applicable to all the dialects.

"The third section treats of the Aspirates: the fourth of the Tones; the fifth, prepared by Mr. Edkins, of the old Sounds of the Chinese characters—an interesting branch of investigation in its bearings on comparative philology, yet one in which it is difficult to reach satisfactory conclusions.

"Section sixth relates to the Range of the Dialects. The author had already mentioned the fact that the Mandarin Dialect is spoken throughout the region north of the YANG-TSE River and very extensively in the provinces south of it, except FUH-KIEN and KWANG-TUNG, to such an extent, in fact, as to make it the prevailing speech in sixteen of the eighteen provinces.

"Section seventh gives the 214 Radicals, which so greatly assist in determining the meaning of the Chinese characters, a knowledge of which lies at the basis of all successful study of the language.

"The eighth and last section treats of 1040 Primitives or Phonetics, which afford important aid in remembering the sounds of the characters. Each character may be divided into two parts—the Radical and the Primitive; to the first of which we look for some clue to the meaning; to the second for some aid, however slight it may be, in regard to the sound.

"In his definitions, the author's method is to group the principal meanings of the words together, and then to give examples of their use in particular instances, specifying frequently, at the close, special uses in the Canton or other dialects. The definitions are clear and copious—the Dictionary, in this respect, as also in the number of examples adduced under each character, greatly excelling those which have preceded it. The definitions are particularly valuable in the various departments of Natural Science, owing to the fondness of the author for such studies.

"We miss, indeed, that logical arrangement of the definitions, with examples under each head, which is found in dictionaries of the Latin and Greek languages. In truth, the Chinese language will not admit of such precision. Frequently, it is impossible to trace any connection between different significations of the same word; yet, even here, we may hope for improvement by more protracted study and careful analysis. * * *

"This Dictionary, as a whole, is a treasury of knowlege in regard to China and Chinese affairs; a treasury accumulated by many years of study both of Protestant and Roman Catholic missionaries. Well may its author, now the oldest resident in China of those from Western nations, as he looks back upon his past course, and especially upon the eleven years of toil in the completion of this dictionary, in which even every Chinese character has been written by his own pen, although at the same time he was discharging the onerous duties of his official position, in which frequently the combined functions of Minister, Secretary, Interpreter, and General Business Agent, have devolved upon himself alone—take a high degree of satisfaction in his completed work, and render humble thanks to the good Lord who has enabled him to bring it to a close. He now makes this new offering to promote every good interest of China in her intercourse with Western nations, and signifies his unabated love to the missionary work by placing the Dictionary within the reach of those engaged in it at but little more than one-third of its original cost."—*New York Observer, Nov.*, 1874.

By EDWARD C. TAINTOR, A. M., F. R. G. S., *Commissioner of Customs in the Chinese Government, in charge of the Statistical Department.*

"This long expected work is at last given to the large and increasing body of students of Chinese. How urgently it was needed, and what a saving of time and labor it is destined to effect for all those whose duties or occupations bring them into contact with any branch of Chinese literature, need not be described to such students here. Those who have, for years past, been driven to the necessity of extracting from a native teacher, often by a slow and painful process of questioning and cross-questioning, of *pi-fang* and illustrative examples, the exact shade of meaning of some new phrase, which is encountered in one's reading, and which in a majority of instances was not to be found in the previously existing helps of this kind, will hail the appearance of this work, calculated to abridge so much of this process, with the liveliest satisfaction. The reputation which its author had already earned in a section of the same field, in his Dictionary of the Canton Dialect, and the extended studies which it was known he was making, as a preparation for the present work, have led to the expectation that we should receive from his hands a great and valuable addition to our present stock of aids to the acquirement of Chinese; and however much the opinions of critics may differ on individual points, and whatever minor imperfections may be found to exist, we believe that the high expectations formed, are destined to be realized. * * *

"The real value of the Dictionary, however, is not to be estimated by any of the above features, but by that department of it, which far exceeds all the others in importance, the quality of its explanations and definitions; and here, we conceive, is the best test of the skill of a lexicographer to be found, *in giving the fullest meaning in the fewest words.* It is possible for almost any one, by means of a long paraphrase, to describe the import of a Chinese phrase; but an exact and full equivalent in English, comprised within the limits of a few words, is often not to be arrived at without patient and careful searching, and sometimes not even then. The *genius* of the two languages, the modes of thought and expression, are so diverse, that in many instances it is almost impossible to convey the force of a brief Chinese phrase in a proportionately brief English sentence; and this difficulty is aggravated by the frequent use in Chinese, of short proverbial expressions, involving an allusion to some historical event or popular legend, an exact translation of which into English would generally be unintelligible. As an instance of this use of proverbs, and at the same time to illustrate the appropriateness which characterizes the definitions of the new Dictionary, we select a single phrase, *ki hu chi shi*, the meaning of which, will perhaps be best understood, by applying it to the present position of the Japanese in their Formosan enterprise. The phrase is thus defined in Morrison's Dictionary:—"The state of a person who rides on a tiger, it is more dangerous to dismount than to remain on its back; to be so involved in a bad cause that retreat is certain ruin." Dr. Williams' definition is in these words:—"[in for it,] as when one rides a tiger; there's no backing down." Dr. Morrison uses thirty-five words, Dr. Williams, thirteen. Every one must recognize the superior aptness, point, and brevity, which mark the latter translation.

"The same terse, idiomatic, we may say epigrammatic method of expression, the application of which to the conversational style, is seen to such advantage in Mr. Wade's admirable translations from Chinese colloquial in the *Tzu Erh Chi*, is constantly to be met with. Errors in translation undoubtedly exist, and it is impossible that it should be otherwise in a work like this. * * *

"To have given to the world two such monuments of patient industry and research, as the *Middle Kingdom* and this new *Dictionary*, may well have satisfied a loftier ambition than their author boasts. The unassuming yet eloquent language of the last paragraph of the preface, discloses the high and unselfish motives which have actuated him throughout the forty years, during which he has been engaged in these pursuits; and if his own modesty would deter him from claiming with Horace,

Exegi monumentum ære perennius,

we may claim for him, that he has made, in these two works, contributions to a knowledge of China and the Chinese, which will secure for him a foremost place among those who have built up the stock of such knowledge, and the lasting gratitude of all those who benefit by their use."

—*North China Herald, Shanghai, October* 15, 1874.

By ALEXANDER WYLIE, *author of several works in the Chinese language, and others in English upon Chinese literature, and editor of the Chinese Recorder and Missionary Journal.*

"Probably the highest tribute of commendation we could pay to the above work, would be the simple publication of the title, unaccompanied by further remark. It has long been looked for, and many have been the inquiries as to when it would make its appearance. The name of Dr. Williams is a sufficient passport to its general admission into public favor. The student is here presented with the result of eleven years' labor, during the intervals of official duties of one of the most competent authoriteis in this department.

"Dr. Williams has no senior in the missionary field in China; and we almost envy the man who can look back through the vista of forty years' service, and thank God for the progress he has been permitted to see. Speaking of his literary labors, he remarks:—"The stimulus to past effort, and the hope that it would not be in vain, both sprang from the desire to aid the labors of those who are imparting truth in any branch to the sons of Han, especially those religious and scientific truths, whose acquisition and practice can alone Christianize and elevate them."

"A retrospect of some of the past efforts of the author in the same department, will show that the present volume is far from being the work of a novice. So early as 1844, he published "An English and Chinese Vocabulary in the Court Dialect." This was a very useful little book, and was eagerly sought after; but it has long been out of print. His "Tonic Dictionary of the Chinese Language in the Canton Dialect," published in 1856, was still more popular, and the few remaining copies are offered at greatly enhanced prices.

"The new work commends itself at first sight, by the attractive form of the page; but on a more mature examination, our first-sight prepossession is superseded by impressions of a higher order. Looking through the bulky volume we recognize the wide range of information which the author has made his own, in the course of his protracted residence in the Empire, and the careful hand that refuses to insert an erroneous definition, merely because it has been used by his predecessors. It is the fate of a conscientious lexicographer to be very much lost sight of behind his labors. The experience he may possess,—the time and trouble he spends in identifying a phrase,—or verifying a definition, the pains it may have cost to determine an etymology, to fix an orthography, or give a reliable decision as to the form of a character, the care he takes to point out the numerous synonyms and variants, as also to warn the student against incorrect forms and other tantalizing seductions;—all these are for the greater part invisible to the public, who only know or care about the result. On such points Dr. Williams has a right to be looked up to as an authority; and we venture to say that the volume before us, is one of the most important guides to the Chinese language and literature that has yet appeared; if indeed it is not entitled to the very first rank."—*Missionary Recorder and Journal, August*, 1874.

By WILLIAM F. MAYERS, Chinese Secretary to the British Legation at Peking.

"It is not always the excellence of the work under review that contributes most to the satisfaction of the critic. Where defects are to be pointed out, ignorance exposed, or baseless presumption chastised, the task is usually more congenial, it must be confessed, than when little else is to be done than to recount the merits of a literary achievement. It is not only that in the course of adverse criticism a superior judgment and a more profound erudition may be deftly displayed at the expense of the writer who is being called to account, but a reviewer's functions proverbially impose the duty of exposing whatever errors or deficiencies may characterize the work before him; and a suspicion of incompetency or partiality is easily entailed by the absence of critical fault-finding. Be this as it may, it is our province now to commend, in the latest contribution toward a knowledge of the Chinese language, a work to which a tribute of almost unqualified admiration must be accorded, and upon the advent of which every student of Chinese may be heartily congratulated. * * * *

"The author of this new Dictionary, which has cast all its predecessors into the shade, had too much practical experience of the Chinese language to aim at achieving an impossible degree of completeness or perfection. He was impressed with the conviction, no doubt, that with a language so chaotic, and a literature so immense as the Chinese, it can be given to no single individual—we may say to no single generation—to meet all, or nearly all the requirements which their study carries with it. No wholly satisfactory dictionary in even French and English, to say nothing of less familiar European tongues, has yet been produced, and it would be unreasonable indeed to imagine that for a language, the difficulties of which are incalculably greater, and the cultivation of which is still restricted within a narrow area, the required labor of classification and definition can be achieved for the present in more than a partial degree. What Dr. Williams has done has been to amplify his own previous work, and that of his predecessors to a very great extent, to increase and rectify very largely the definitions heretofore supplied for the individual Chinese characters, and to add plentifully to the list of illustrative and idiomatic phrases under each character, which in earlier dictionaries have been most unsatisfactorily represented. * *

"In respect of definitions, no one can compare a column of the new dictionary with a corresponding portion of any preceding work, without taking note of the great advance that has been made in the collection of phraseology, and in the fullness and accuracy of exegesis. We do not wish to be understood as implying that there is no room left for improvement in this respect. Apart from the technology of the language, which is as yet in an almost rudimentary stage of interpretation, the difficulty of finding absolutely exact equivalents for a vast proportion of Chinese characters and phrases, is one which can only be solved by a succession of laborious efforts, and by a very much larger development than the work of translation has yet attained to. * * * We do not look upon the new dictionary as the last word in Sinology, but we believe that we do not overrate it in assigning it as high a position with reference to Chinese study at the present day, as that which by common consent was assigned in its own generation to the work of Morrison. The groundwork has now been laid, and it remains for future architects to enlarge the structure by systematic additions transferred from the vast storehouses which lie ready to hand in the *P'ei Wăn Yun Fu*, and similar repertories of phraseology. The field, as Dr. Williams well observes in his modest preface, is too vast to be explored or exhausted by even many laborers; and we feel sure that no one who turns to the pages of his work for information and assistance will fail to appreciate at a high value the results of the present undertaking."
—*China Review, January*, 1875.

From W. P. GROENEVELDT, Secretary and Chinese Interpreter to the Netherlands Legation to China.

"When it became known, some time ago, that Dr. S. Wells Williams was preparing a new dictionary, every student of Chinese, well aware of the valuable services already rendered by that gentleman to the study of this language, looked impatiently forward to the publication of this work, in which he hoped to find something better able to meet his wants than the book he had formerly been using. * * * The result of his labors is such that the author has not only achieved what he proposed to do, but he has gone considerably beyond it. Surpassing all those before him, he has given us a dictionary better than any before existing."
—*China Review, March*, 1875.

THE CHINESE IMPERIAL FAMILY.

The following particulars respecting the Imperial family of China, in connection with the order of succession to the throne, may be found not without interest.

As is well known, the reigning Sovereign is eighth in direct line of descent from his ancestor the emperor She Tsu Chang Hwang Ti (Shun Che), who ascended the throne at the age of five in 1643, his reign being reckoned, however, according to the invariable Chinese usage, from the beginning of the following year, or Feb. 8th, 1644. The legendary progenitor of the Manchu chieftains who advanced, by successive steps, to the assumption of the imperial crown of China, bore, according to tradition, the surname Aisin Gioro, represented by the Chinese characters 愛新覺羅. The signification of the word *Aisin* is the same as that of the Chinese *Kin* 金, gold (or metal), and an identification is thus suggested with the dynastic title of the reputed ancestors of the Manchus, the Nü-chih Tartars, who reigned in northern China during the 12th and 13th centuries. The surname of their Imperial house was, however, Wan-yen 完顏. The word *Gioro* is said to be equivalent to the Chinese 氏 or family-stem. It is borne as a distinctive surname by every descendant of the founder of the present Imperial line, and it serves in particular as an appellation, prefixed to the personal name, for the more remote scions of the original stock. Actual descendants of Hien Tsu, the acknowledged founder of the family, (1583-1615), are designated *Tsung-shih* 宗室, in conformity with the usage adopted by earlier Chinese dynasties. In order to make the observations which are to follow, with reference to the various branches of the imperial lineage, more easily understood, it is necessary here to explain the further system of family nomenclature which has been adopted by the existing line. The foundations of this system were laid in the reign of the second emperor of the dynasty, Shêng Tsu Jên, (K'ang Hi), who gave to each of his twenty-four sons a personal name consisting of two characters, the first of which was Yin 胤—subsequently exchanged in writing, as a token of respect, for Yün 允—and the second compounded with the radical *she* 示 throughout, as 禔, 祺, and so on. His grandson, K'ien Lung, extended this practice into a system for perpetual application, ordaining that future generations deriving their descent from K'ang Hi should be successively designated by the following four characters, viz:

1. 永 Yung.
2. 綿 Mien.
3. 奕 Yih.
4. 載 Tsai.

Minute regulations were drawn up, and incorporated with the fundamental institutes of the dynasty, setting forth the manner in which both these characters and those employed for the second or individual half of each name, should be bestowed. In the 49th year of his reign (A.D. 1784), on the birth of a great-great-grandson, to whom the character Tsai consequently appertained, K'ien Lung decreed the addition of the character Fêng 奉 as the next in succession; but this character was dismissed from use by order of the emperor Tao Kwang. In the sixth year of the reign of this sovereign (1826), an addition to the number of characters appears to have been thought advisable (probably in order to avoid repetition as the list became exhausted), and ten characters were proposed for his Majesty's selection, out of which the following four were approved for future use, viz:—

5. 溥 P'u.
6. 毓 Yü.
7. 恒 Hêng.
8. 啟 K'i.

The Emperor Hien Fêng, again, saw fit to increase the list by the addition of four more characters. The *Peking Gazette* of the 9th June, 1857, contains a copy of a decree directing the chief officers of Government to draw up a list of four characters, to be submitted, together with the six remaining on record since 1826, when they were put on one side after the four above enumerated were chosen, for approval by his Majesty. A short time afterwards a further decree announced the fact that the following additional characters had been adopted from the list drawn up:

9. 燾 Tao.
10. 闓 K'ai.
11. 增 Tsêng.
12. 祺 K'i.

So much for the first of the two characters forming the compound name. The complementary part of the system of nomenclature is well illustrated by Dr. S. W. Williams, in his "Middle Kingdom" (vol. I., p. 310), in the following terms: "The members [of the imperial family] most nearly allied in blood, as sons, nephews, etc., are still further distinguished by having the second syllables of their names written in compound Chinese characters, whose radicals are alike; thus Kia K'ing and his brothers wrote their names with Yung (the fourth syllable in the above list) and under the radical *gem*; Tau Kwang and his brothers and cousins with Mien, and under the radical *heart*. This peculiarity is easily represented in the Chinese characters, but a comparison can be made in English with the supposed names of a family of sons, as Louis *Ed*ward, Louis *Ed*win, Louis *Ed*wy, Louis *Ed*gar, and so on."

The personal names, thus compounded, will be traced in the following list of the Sovereigns who have successively occupied the throne, whose historical or posthumous titles (廟號) and the titles of whose reigns (年號) are likewise given:—

Historical Title.	Title of Reign.	Period of Reign.	Personal Name.
1.—Shè Tsu Chang. 世祖章	Shun Che. 順治	1644-1661.	Fuh Lin. 福臨
2.—Shêng Tsu Jên. 聖祖仁	K'ang Hi. 康熙	1666-1722.	Hüan Yeh. 玄燁
3.—She Tsung Hien. 世宗憲	Yung Chêng. 雍正	1723-1735.	Yin Chên. 胤禛
4.—Kao Tsung Ch'un. 高宗純	K'ien Lung. 乾隆	1736-1795.	Hung Li. 弘曆
5. Jên Tsung Jui. 仁宗睿	Kia K'ing. 嘉慶	1796-1820.	Yung Yen. 永琰
6. Süan Tsung Ch'êng. 宣宗成	Tao Kwang. 道光	1821-1850.	Mien Ning. 綿寧
7. Wên Tsung Hien. 文宗顯	Hien Fêng. 咸豐	1851-1861.	Yih Chu. 奕詝
8. (The reigning Emperor)	T'ung Che. 同治	1862.	Tsai Ch'un. 載淳

The characters *Hwang Ti* 皇帝 (commonly rendered Emperor) follow, in practice, the three characters constituting the historical title, and a deceased sovereign, when not spoken of, colloquially though incorrectly, by the title of his reign, is designated by the *last* of the three characters in combination with the words *Hwang Ti*—*e.g.* Ch'êng Hwang Ti for the Emperor who reigned with the designation Tao Kwang.

Up to the period of the late Emperor (Hien Hwang Ti or Hien Fêng), no difficulty in regard to the succession presented itself in the Imperial line. Shun Che was the ninth son of his father, K'ang Hi the third of Shun Che; Yung Chêng the fourth of K'ang Hi; K'ien Lung the fourth of Yung Chêng; Kia K'ing the fifteenth of K'ien Lung; Tao Kwang the second of Kia K'ing; and Hien Fêng the fourth of the nine sons who were, in all, born to the Emperor Tao Kwang. The Emperor Hien Fêng, however, was without male issue for some years after he succeeded to the throne; and it was probably with a view to securing the dynastic succession that, about five years after his accession an adoptive heir was provided, in conformity with the national usage, to the eldest son of the emperor, a prince who had died at an early age many years before. On the 21st January 1855 it was decreed that Tsai Chung 載中, a *tsung-shih* or member of the imperial clan, be adopted (過繼) as son to the Prince above-mentioned, whose personal name was Yih Wei, and whose title was that of Prince of Yin Che (undeveloped wisdom.") The adopted heir was a son of the *tsung-shih* Yih Ki, a great grandson of the emperor K'ien Lung. By a subsequent decree, the second name of the youth thus adopted was changed from Chung to Che 治, bringing it into accord, as regards its radical (*water*) with that prescribed for the line which, by adoption, he had entered. As, however, the birth of a son (the present Emperor) to Hien Fêng, on the 27th April 1856, apparently assured the succession in the direct line, any prospects that may have been connected with Tsai Che were for the time being at an end. The heir apparent received, by decree dated the 13th June 1856, the name Tsai Ch'un 載淳; and by his father's decease on the 17th Aug. 1861, he became successor to the throne. His marriage on the 15th October 1872 and his assumption of the reins of government on the 23rd February 1873, are events fresh within the recollection of the public.

In view of the fact that, up to the present time, no issue has been vouchsafed to the young sovereign, attention has naturally been turned toward the condition of the imperial lineage; and the state of affairs in this respect can best be made clear by means of a genealogical table such as the following, commencing with the Emperor Kia K'ing. (The table will be found on next page.)

The point of first importance to be noted in the above Table is the fact that, in default of issue to the reigning sovereign, the direct line of Imperial devolution terminates with his person. His father, Hien Fêng, was one of nine brothers, however, of whom four are still living; and to a mind accustomed to the European order of succession, it might seem natural that in the event of the nephew's decease without issue, the uncles would inherit in the order of their seniority. This is inadmissible according to Chinese ideas. The especial attribute of a son and heir being that of keeping up the ancestral sacrifices, the maintenance of which are essential to the well-being of the spirits of the departed (who repay the benefit by assuring temporal rewards in return for the assiduity of their descendants), it is held essential that the heir be of a generation posterior to that of the individual deceased. Hence, in the Imperial family, following the succession of the eight characters used in their nomenclature, a Mien should have a Yih as adoptive heir, whenever necessary, a Yih a Tsai, and so forth. This rule is exemplified in the adoption, already mentioned, of Tsai Che as heir to the deceased elder-born of the emperor Tao Kwang, the prince Yih Wei.

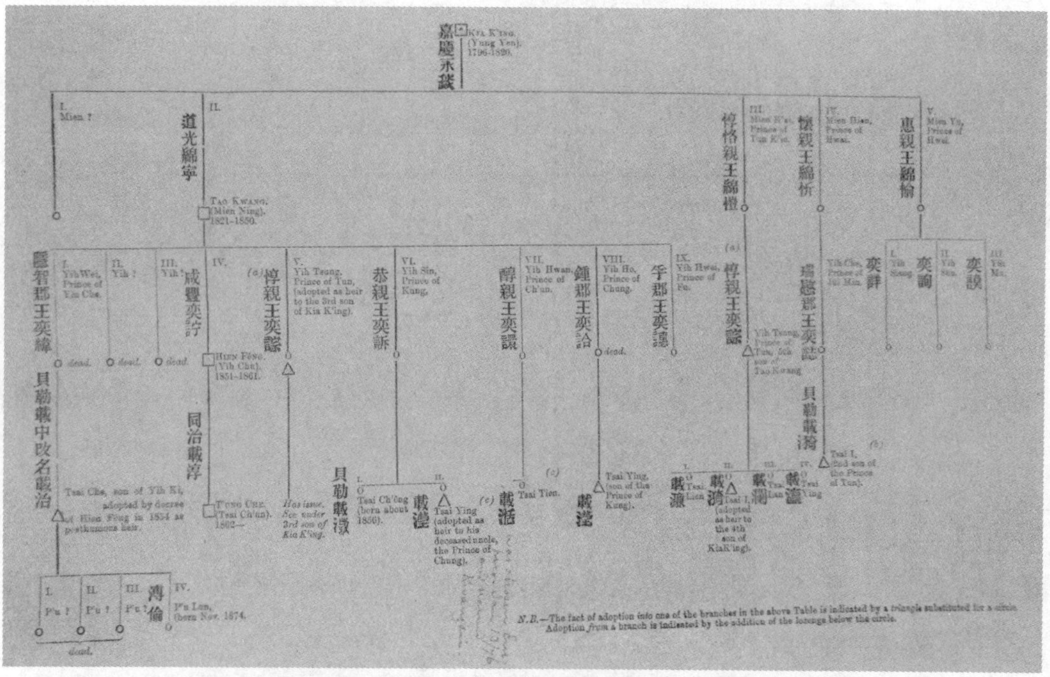
嘉慶永琰
Kia K'ing. (Yung Yen). 1796-1820.
I. Mien ?
II.
道光綿寧
Tao Kwang. (Mien Ning). 1821-1850.
III. Mien K'ai, Prince of Tun K'ui.
惇恪親王綿愷
IV. Prince of Hwai.
瑞親王綿忻
V. Mien Yü, Prince of Hwai.
惠親王綿愉
隱智郡王奕緯
I. Yih Wei, Prince of Yin Che.
II. Yih ?
III. Yih ?
咸豐奕詝
IV.
Hien Fêng. (Yih Chu). 1851-1861.
(a) 惇親王奕誴
V. Yih Tsung, Prince of Tun, (adopted as heir to the 3rd son of Kia K'ing).
恭親王奕訢
VI. Yih Sin, Prince of Kung.
醇親王奕譞
VII. Yih Hwan, Prince of Ch'un.
鍾郡王奕詥
VIII. Yih Ho, Prince of Chung.
孚郡王奕譓
IX. Yih Hwei, Prince of Fu.
(a) 惇親王奕誴
Yih Tsung, Prince of Tun, 5th son of Tao Kwang
瑞敏郡王奕誌
奕詳
奕詢
奕謨
dead.
dead.
dead.
dead.
貝勒載中改名載治
Tsai Che, son of Yih Ki, adopted by decree of Hien Fêng in 1854 as posthumous heir.
同治載淳
T'ung Che. (Tsai Ch'un). 1862—
Has issue. See under 3rd son of Kia K'ing.
貝勒載澂
Tsai Ch'êng (born about 1856).
載瀅
Tsai Ying (adopted as heir to his deceased uncle, the Prince of Chung).
(c) 載湉
Tsai Tien.
Tsai Ying, (son of the Prince of Kung).
載瀅
載濂
載漪
Tsai I, (adopted as heir to the 4th son of KiaK'ing).
載瀾
載瀛
貝勒載漪
(b)
Tsai I, 2nd son of the Prince of Tun).
I. P'u ?
II. P'u ?
III. P'u ?
溥倫
IV. P'u Lun, (born Nov. 1874.
dead.
N.B.—The fact of adoption into one of the branches in the above Table is indicated by a triangle substituted for a circle. Adoption from a branch is indicated by the addition of the lozenge below the circle.

Adoption is, in fact, observed on an extensive scale among the members of the Imperial clan, whose family relationships are thus made not a little intricate. The fifth son of Tao Kwang, next brother to the emperor Hien Fêng, commonly known by his title of Prince of Tun, has been in this wise alienated from the closest to a collateral degree of kinship with the young emperor. He was given in adoption many years ago (in 1845) to his deceased uncle, the prince of Tun K'ih, third son of Kia K'ing; and one of his sons, again, the prince (*beileh*) Tsai I, has been made into his nephew through adoption as grandson to another of the sons of Kia K'ing (see Table). The alienation of Tsai I from the paternal stock is alleged to have been decreed as a punishment meted out to the Prince of Tun for a violation of self-restraint, prescribed by the ritual of mourning, at a period antecedent to the entry of the young prince into the world.

As the Table shews, the offspring of Tsai Che, who was himself by the decree of 1855 indicated as a possible heir to Hien Fêng, should be now the most direct claimants to the privilege of furnishing an heir by adoption to the reigning and childless emperor. Four sons have been born to this prince, of whom it is believed that only one, an infant, still survives. It seems possible, however, that in the deliberations of the Imperial Clan Court, the fact of Tsai Che being himself an adoptive son may militate, the case arising, against the eligibility of his children, and under such circumstances (provided also that the alienation of the Prince of Tun should bar the claim of his descendants) it appears probable that the offspring of the two uncles of his Majesty, next in order of seniority, would be the most available candidates. In any case, it is alleged by those who are versed in the principles of Chinese genealogy, the adoption of an heir not junior in the line of descent to the reigning Emperor could only be feasible by his being made heir to one of the earlier sovereigns (Hien Fêng or Tao Kwang). The Prince of Tun has several sons (eight in all have been born to him), of whom the eldest is married, but the probability of their alienation from the direct line of inheritance is, as has been remarked above, at least matter for consideration. If this be the case, the possible candidate next in order would be the elder son of the Prince of Kung, the *beileh* Tsai Ch'êng. This young prince is of about the same age with the emperor, and was married in the course of last year. The "seventh Prince," younger brother of the Prince of Kung, has likewise a son, a mere lad. The favour with which the "seventh Prince" has been looked upon by the Emperor might cause the choice to be directed here. The degradation of the *beileh* Tsai Ch'êng, together with his father, by the decrees of the 10th and 11th September last, have been matters of public notoriety.

It may be useful to note, in conclusion, that the titles conferred on members of the present imperial house are of twelve degrees. The sons of an emperor, before receiving a special title by patent, are known simply by the designation *Ako* (in Manchu *e.g.*), with the numeral indicating their seniority by birth prefixed. The twelve degrees of rank are as follows:

1.—和碩親王 *Ho-shih Ts'in Wang*—Prince of the 1st order. 2.—多羅郡王 *To-lo Kün Wang*—Prince of the 2nd order. 3.—多羅貝勒 *To-lo Beileh*—Prince of the 3rd order. 4.—固山貝子 *Ku-shan Bei-tsz*—Prince of the 4th order. 5 to 8.—公 *Kung* (with distinctive qualifications). 9 to 12—將軍 *Tsiang Kün* (with distinctive qualifications).

Imperial princes usually receive patents of the first or second order on reaching the age of manhood, and their sons are invested with the title *beileh*. A *beileh's* son becomes a *beitsz*, and rank is thus transmitted in a *diminuendo* scale, until the son of a titular *tsiang kün* of the lowest degree would be no longer the inheritor of a title.

(*Note.*—An apparent departure from the symmetry of the rule of nomenclature may be observed in the case of the Prince Yih Wei, the eldest of the sons of Tao Kwang. His name of Wei is written 緯 with the radical 糸 (*Silk*), whereas Hien Fêng and his brothers are distinguished by the radical 言 (*word*). The discrepancy arose, it is explained, after Yih Wei's decease, when the Emperor Tao Kwang ordained the abandonment of the radical 糸 *silk* and chose 言 *word* as its substitute. It is unnecessary here to dilate upon the changes which, according to Chinese ideas of reverential duty, have been made in the form of the characters employed successively for the personal name of each emperor. An instance may, however, be given in that of the present sovereign, since whose accession the character Ch'un 淳 has been altered into the form 湻.

The titles given to the princes of imperial descent are largely compounded of Manchu words. Thus *ho shih* (originally *banner*) signifies one of the four divisions of the army or State; and *beileh* has the meaning of *commander* or *leader*. The military origin of the dynasty is commemorated in these appellations.

N. B.—The above was written before the death of his late Majesty, the Emperor T'ung Chih, who died on the night of Jan. 12th, 1875.

莫將煩惱著詩篇（勿以憂詩言）百歲原如一覺眠（人生）

（若虛夢）夢短夢長同是夢（性靈聽即與死無異）獨留真氣滿

坤乾（不僅形骸尚有靈在）

天地生材總不虛（人生世上行走非虛生也總期有用）由來豹死

尚留皮（何謂死埋方至極處）縱然出土仍歸土（聖書所云人身原土）

（終當歸土）靈性常存無絕期（此言人身非謂靈也）

無端憂樂日相循（其樂其憂均不可專務）天命斯人自有

真（天之生人別有所命）人法天行強不息（所命者作為專圖日日長進）

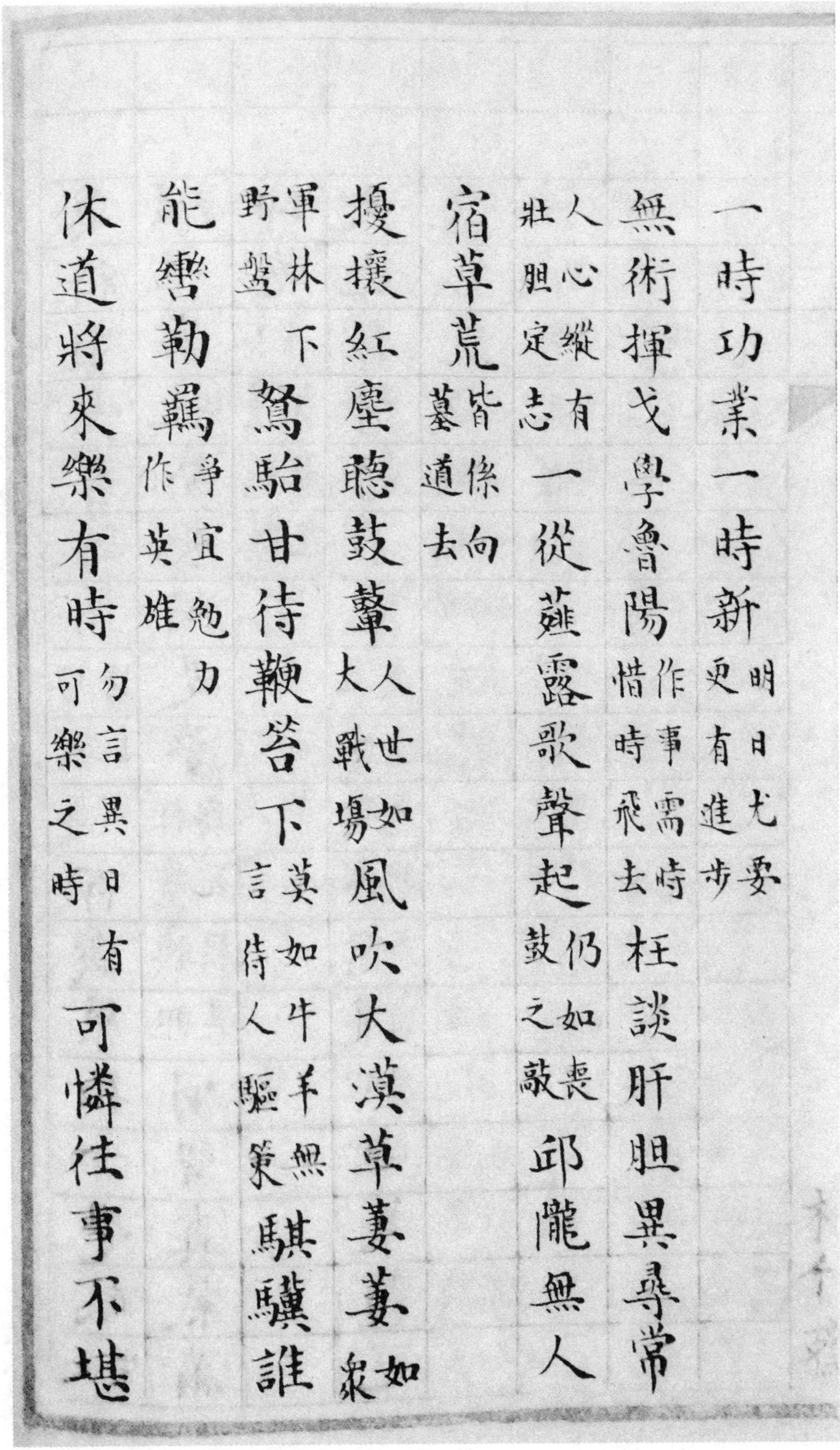
一時功業一時新明日尤要更有進步
無術揮戈學魯陽作事需時惜時飛去枉談肝胆異尋常
人心縱有壯胆定志一從薤露歌聲起仍如喪鼓之敲邱隴無人
宿草荒皆係向墓道去
擾攘紅塵聽鼓鼙人世如大戰場風吹大漠草萋萋如衆
軍林下野盤駑駘甘待鞭笞下莫如牛羊無言待人驅策騏驥誰
能轡勒羈爭宜勉力作英雄
休道將來樂有時勿言異日有可樂之時可憐往事不堪

思（既往日亦由已埋已）祇今有力均須努（目下努力切切）人力殫

時天祐之（中盡已心上賴天祐）

千秋萬代遠蜚聲（著名人傳看則繫念）學步金鼇頂上行

（想我們在世亦可置身高處）已去冥鴻猶有跡（去世時尚有痕跡）雪

泥爪印認分明（勢如留在海邊沙面）

茫茫塵世海中漚（蓋人世如同大海）絕過來舟又去舟

（果有他人過海）欲問失風誰挽救（船隻擱淺受難失望）沙洲遺跡

可採求（見海邊有跡繞知有可解免）

一鞭從此躍征鞍（謂此即應奮起動身），不到峰頭心不甘。
（心中預定無論如何總期有濟）日進日高還日上（日有成功愈求進功），肯教中道偶停驂（習其用工堅忍不可中止）。

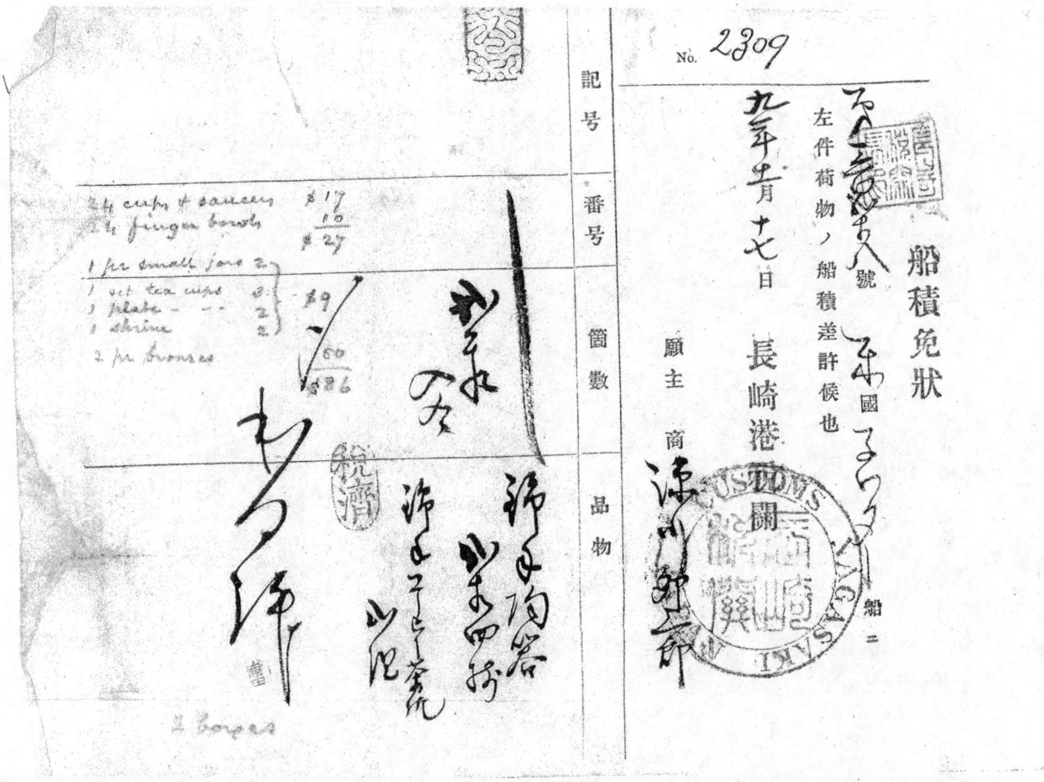
No. 2309

船積免狀

號 國 船

左件荷物ノ船積差許候也

九年十一月十七日

長崎港 關

願主 商

記号 番号 箇數 品物

24 cups & saucers $17
24 finger bowls 10
$27
1 pr small jars 2
1 set tea cups 2
1 plate 2
1 shrine 2
2 pr bronzes
$9
60
$86

2 boxes

CUSTOMS NAGASAKI

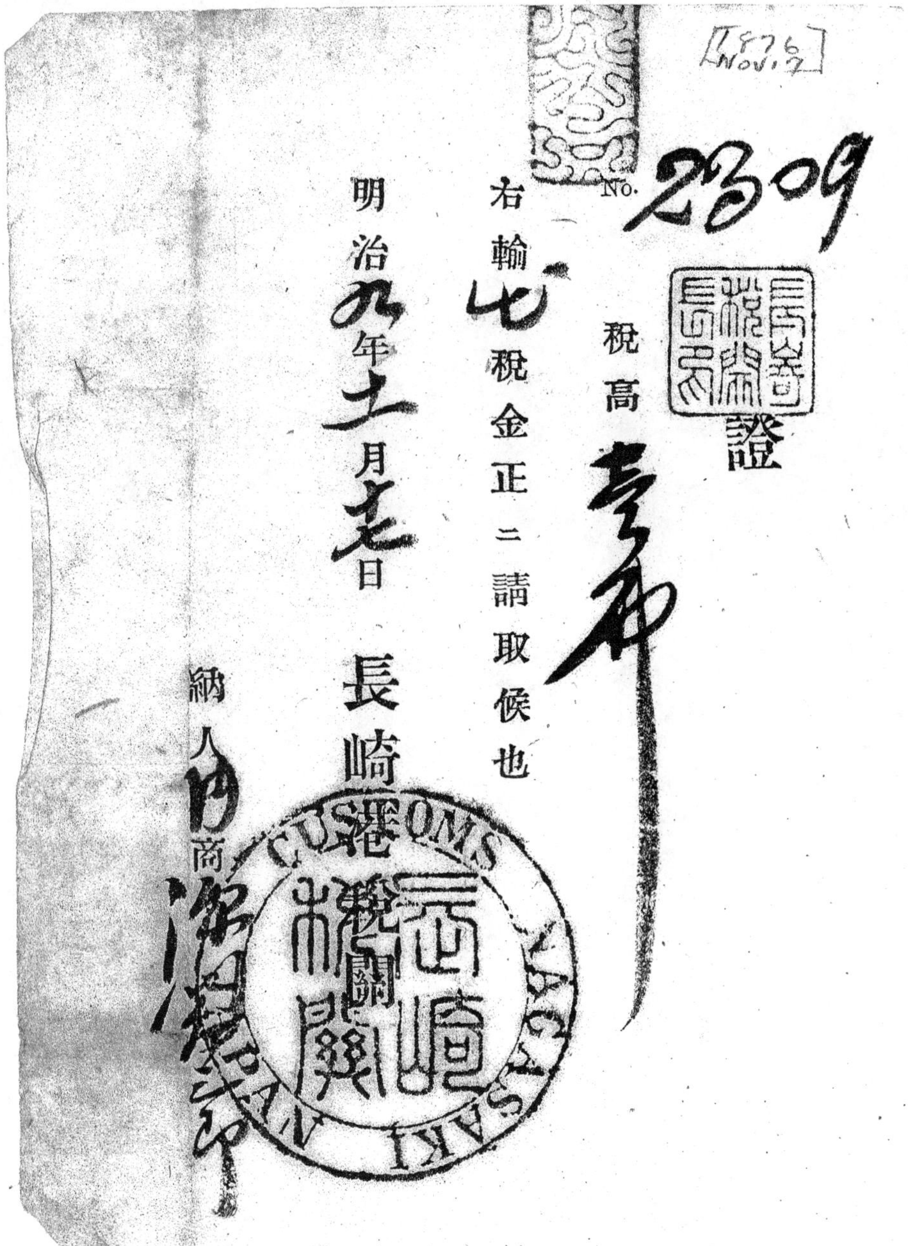
[1876 NOV 17]

No. 2309

證

税高 [illegible]

右輸出税金正ニ請取候也

明治九年十一月十七日 長崎港税関

納人 内商 [illegible]

第 5 部分

耶鲁执教及身后哀荣

中國總論
THE
MIDDLE
Kingdom,
西方之人有聖者也
仁者愛人由親及疏

書有六體曰篆曰隸曰楷曰行曰艸曰宋

書有六體曰篆曰隸曰楷曰行曰艸曰宋

書有六體曰篆曰隸曰楷曰行曰草曰宋

書有六體曰篆曰隸曰楷曰行曰草曰宋

書有六體曰篆曰隸曰楷曰行曰草曰宋

書有六體曰篆曰隸曰楷曰行曰草曰宋

Honored by Emp. Ping - AD 1 as Duke Ni, all Complete & Illustrious
In AD 492, as The Venerable Ni, the accomplished Sage -
Now it is, Kung the ancient Teacher, the perfect Sage -

In the 大成殿 Confucian Hall

聖集大成 Kiaking
The Holy One embodied in himself the Great Perfection

萬世師表 Kanghi
The Pattern and Leader of all Ages

生民未有 Yungching
Mankind never had another like him

與天地參 Kienlung
The Equal of Heaven and Earth

聖協時中 Taukwang
The Holy One who aids in harmonizing the seasons

德齊幬載 Hienfung
His Virtue equals that of the Empyrean and Demeter

聖神天縱 Tungchi
~~The Holy God whom Heaven cannot limit~~
His Holiness is like that of the Gods, Heaven cannot limit it

THE DEAD SHALL BE RAISED

IN GRATITUDE TO GOD
FOR THE LIFE OF
FREDERICK WELLS
WILLIAMS
MACAO, CHINA, OCTOBER 31, 1857
NEW HAVEN, JANUARY 22, 1928
AND HIS WIFE
FRANCES WAYLAND
PROVIDENCE, R.I. APRIL 12, 1864
NEW HAVEN, SEPTEMBER 16, 1948

Correspondence.

TREATY OBLIGATIONS TOWARDS THE CHINESE.

By S. Wells Williams, LL.D.

[The following noble appeal for justice to the Chinese, will come with force from one who has spent more than forty years of his life in China, and who is better acquainted with that country than any other living American.—ED. EVAN.]

The American flag was first seen in Chinese waters at Whampoa, the port of Canton, on the 28th of August, 1784, on board of the ship "Empress of China"; her captain, John Green, and her supercargo, Samuel Shaw, were both courteously received by the Chinese hong-merchants in their official capacity, and hopes expressed that the intercourse then begun between China and the *New People* (as they styled the United States) might be mutually agreeable and beneficial. Nearly a century has since elapsed, and considering the relative position and civilization of the two countries, their intercourse in China has gone on with very little jarring. The gradual enlargement of the privileges of the Americans in respect to trade and recognition by the Imperial Government, has been owing, in common with other nations, to the efforts of the British Government, backed by the fleets and armies sent to enforce its demands. All nations are now regarded as standing on a political equality with China, and the United States enjoys as much consideration at Peking as it has worked for. The British, French and Russians are, no doubt, more respected and feared, for they have demonstrated to the Chinese that they can employ force to obtain their demands, which was not likely ever to be resorted to by the Americans; for, with them as with all people, there is a hidden power in armaments which is not so plainly felt in arguments.

The Chinese officers began to have, however, a favorable opinion of the Americans, from their gradual understanding of the fact that they had nothing to fear from them as a nation; and the moral force of this opinion increased among the natives, as years went on, by the knowledge that Americans had nothing to do with the opium trade. In 1839, before hostilities had actually commenced with the British, in consequence of his seizure of opium, Commissioner Lin found that the Americans had this reputation at Canton, and he endeavored to enlist them on his side in his efforts to suppress it. On one occasion he sent a special agent to Macao, to request Rev. Mr. Bridgman, the American missionary, to come to him, supposing that he might have some influence in this direction. An interview was held, and although Lin was disappointed in his plan of intermediation, he learned many new ideas concerning the impending struggle, and the relative power of his own country and Great Britain, as well as the inefficiency of his attempt to prevent it. It was the first effort on the part of any Chinese official to open political relations with the Americans, and was in itself a tacit acknowledgment of the reputation which Mr. Bridgman had obtained among the people during his ten years' residence at Canton. At that time the American trade was second in value to the British. The Chinese Government sincerely desired to stop only the opium trade and develop all other branches; but the British Government, ruled as it is by the shortsighted selfishness of trade, refused to coöperate in this despairing effort to restrain an evil of which its victims knew the effects better than their destroyers. England then lost a golden opportunity to elevate moral above mercenary motives in the eyes of a heathen people, which she has never recovered; she showed no desire to stay the destroying agency so profitable to herself.

The proposal of the American Government in 1844, to open political relations with the Court of Peking, was more favorably received by it than a similar one from any other nation would have been at that moment, owing to this general opinion of its citizens; and the first article of Mr. Cushing's treaty of July, 1844, indicated the hopes of such a make-weight against the British. It read as follows: more satisfactory basis. The four treaties signed at Tientsin in June, 1858, brought China into the family of nations—much against her will, and smarting under a sense of injury, indeed, but doubtless for her good and her future safety. In the new treaty made with the United States on this occasion by Mr. Reed, the first article was enlarged as follows:

"There shall be, as there has always been, peace and friendship between the United States of America and the Ta Tsing Empire, and between their people respectively. They shall not insult and oppress each other for any trifling cause, so as to produce an estrangement between them; and if any other nation should act unjustly or oppressively, the United States will exert their good offices, on being informed of the case, to bring about an amicable arrangement of the question, thus showing their friendly feelings."

By this article the United States have bound themselves to treat the Chinese, as they ask them to treat American citizens, in a way which they have not bound themselves to do with any other nation. In China, its spirit and letter have, on the whole, been well carried out. In 1848, three men were executed for the murder of Rev. W. M. Lowrie, and six more banished; and in 1856 a man was executed at Fuhchau for killing Mr. Cunningham in a mob. This was by the Chinese authorities. On the other hand, one David Williams was sentenced to death at Shanghai in the United States Consular Court for piracy and murder in Chinese waters in 1863, and would have been executed if he had not committed suicide the night before the appointed day. Another man, named Thompson was subsequently tried and found guilty of murdering a Chinese, but he escaped from prison two or three days before the day set for his execution. These instances have sufficed to show the determination of the authorities of both countries to vindicate the laws of their lands in maintaining treaty stipulations. In the retrospect of the thirty-five years, since the treaty of Nanking, and considering the way in which foreign treaties were forced out of the Chinese, and their feeling that they seldom get redress when they are the plaintiffs, they deserve respect for the manner in which they have observed them.

During this period the Chinese have been made acquainted with the position, resources, and character of the United States, almost wholly through her missionaries. The official correspondence and interpreting between the Chinese and the Ministers, Admirals, and Consuls, who have successively represented her, has been, with slight exceptions, done by them or their sons; and they have themselves acted as the nation's representatives on many occasions. Not a dollar has ever been spent by the United States to train up a class of interpreters who could perform this necessary duty, as is done by every other country which has extensive political relations with China; even nations like Denmark and Austria deem it politic to educate their own official interpreters, though their trade is trifling and their subjects number only a few scores.

Two Americans have been in the service of the Chinese Government within the past twenty years, whose deeds are not likely to be soon forgotten. One of them was General Frederick Ward, who formed the Ever Victorious force. He led it against the Taiping rebels in several attacks, and was mortally wounded in 1862 near Ningpo, at the head of his men, whom he had inspirited with his own courage. The other has been more widely known, but in Anson Burlingame the Chinese had an equally useful servant. In his capacity as the first American Minister who lived in Peking, he made a good impression upon the Chinese officials; and at that time it was exceedingly desirable to remove the bizarre and erroneous ideas these men had been taught, in their seclusion from the world at large, to believe respecting the manners and policy of foreign nations. Mr. Burlingame and Sir Frederick Bruce were personally well fitted to remove their fears, and did combine to strengthen their hopes for the gradual adoption of better relations. When, therefore, they appointed Mr. Burlingame in 1867 to be their Envoy to son, by and with the advice and consent of the Senate, before it was sent out to Peking, and submitted to the consideration of the other contracting Power. The Chinese Government delayed to affix the Imperial seal for many months, simply because it wished to see whether its Envoys would make any more treaties with other nations, for the usage is that whatever is granted to one nation is free to all.

It is not likely that the Burlingame Treaty has ever had any perceptible effect on the emigration of the Chinese to this country. Few, very few of the people know that such an article as that now quoted exists. They do know that none of their countrymen go as contract laborers to the United States, and that when a man leaves Hongkong under the American flag for the Kau Kăm Shan or Old Gold Hills, there is a certainty of his friends hearing from him, and of his return home (if living) when he pleases. The treaty was made about twenty years after the emigratiom to California had set in, and myriads had gone out and returned home in the meantime. When Mr. Burlingame returned from San Francisco to Peking in 1866, he reported to the Chinese that a million of laborers could find employment on the Pacific Coast. The Pacific Railroad had not then been completed, and the prospect to the capitalists engaged in that and other public and private works of getting labor from China, at a cheaper rate than could elsewhere be obtained, was very tempting. The Chinese were likely to be well treated when they could be hired at half the price of Irish and German laborers.

The truth is, everything has been done on our side to encourage and regulate the immigration of Chinese into this country. They were useful at first, in humble labors, when the search for gold engrossed the attention of others; and became of real value when the construction of the great Railroad depended on their industry. The Burlingame Treaty only expressed its approval of what existed, and the Emperor of China had no power to prevent his subjects leaving their native soil, even if that compact had set itself against their landing on the shores of America. They have been emigrating for centuries, and have settled themselves in all the islands of the Indian Archipelago and Pacific Ocean, as well as the inviting countries nearer by. They go at their own risk, however, and the Son of Heaven used to care very little what became of them, if they were so unwise as to leave a civilized land for the barbarous, lawless regions beyond its pale.

It should be stated, too, that strictly speaking, none come to this country direct from China; from the very first, they have all sailed away to San Francisco from British territory, the ships have come under British rules and restrictions in relation to provisioning and numbers, and British officers at Hongkong have given clearances to ships with Chinese going to San Francisco, just as British officers have given them to ships with Irish going from Queenstown. The Burlingame Treaty would not have anyhow prevented Chinese going to Hongkong, and the Emperor of China cannot stop his subjects going abroad. The old and common ideas respecting the danger to a man who did so have been exaggerated, for no one was punished who returned home; on the contrary, in olden time he was regarded with curious interest if he had gone at first from places far in the interior. Probably not five per cent. ever did return; and far the greater part of those who have gone to Siam, India, and the Archipelago, and elsewhere, went of their own accord, and on the same conditions that they have gone to California and Australia, viz: by mortgaging their labor to pay for their passage.

The above is one side of the Chinese Question. That of treaties, of capital and labor, and of treatment of our citizens in China, where we have compelled their rulers to let us live under our own laws within their borders, is the other. This right of ex-territorial jurisdiction is a sore spot in the minds of those rulers, and they usually oppose any demands for further privileges on the part of American representatives, and even of all foreign nations, by comparing the legal position of the two peoples in each other's territories.

Comparing the civilization of one side with the other in this singular condition of things, what do we see? The first has been nurtured under the highest standards of moral principles, and claims to be guided by elevated sentiments and an intelligent public opinion; and yet all this has failed to secure the commonest rights of humanity to the second, who are weak, ignorant, poor, and unprotected. When the Chinese first arrived in California after the gold was discovered, they were not allowed to testify in the courts; and the consequences were such as were well known in the slave States, where the evidence of negroes was ruled out. Murders, robberies, oppressions, and assaults upon them became so common, and usually unpunishable for want of evidence, that the legislators of California, for their own protection, were induced to pass an act allowing the Chinese to testify. Discriminating laws were passed against them, and their labor was taxed without securing to them the protection and privileges they paid
these acts were committed in that State, and no Chinese consul is there to plead officially for redress? It is not implied by this that no murderer has ever been executed for taking their lives, or robber punished for his crimes, but every one knows that such criminals do escape punishment, and that the Chinese in that State feel their insecurity and weakness. Wo be to them if they should attempt to redress their own wrongs!

This point is quite a different question from the speculative ones,—Whether the immigration of the Chinese should be allowed? Whether their labor will not destroy our own?

Whether we can absorb and assimilate such a mass of ignorant, immoral, and degraded heathen? The point brought up in these remarks, refers to the treaty obligations the American people has voluntarily taken upon itself in reference to the Chinese. We may say that we are suffering these evils from that people, and are determined to prevent any more of them coming. If the balance of evils suffered by the parties to these treaties be drawn, the Chinese would be found to have had by far the worst of them. It is better far to show that the treaties have brought more good results in their train to both than evil, and that it is for our own highest welfare to treat those whom we have done so much to induce to come here, with at least as much justice as we demand of them. Some fear that this country will be swamped altogether by this flood of aliens, but the 125,000 or so of Chinese now in this land, with few exceptions, all came from a small portion, two prefectures, of Kwangtung province. There is no probability of other parts of the empire joining in this emigration, for several reasons, one of which is the great differences in their dialects. The labor question, also, is quite irrelevant to the one before us. The laws of supply and demand, wages and work, food and machinery, are among the most vital and difficult of solution among mankind, and will doubtless often come into collision until their complicated interests are better understood. But to allow one ignorant laborer to maltreat another with impunity, because the former is stronger, has a vote, and will not try to understand why he suffers just as myriads of other laborers do, who are not troubled with the *heathen Chinee*, is to sap and weaken all law and order. If they are an inferior race, as we roundly assert, there is no fear of their ever interfering with our supremacy here in any department, and policy alone would counsel us to treat them fairly; and on the other hand, if they can rise, in their own land, under the same democratic institutions and Christian training to be our equals, we cannot, as a nation living next to them just across the Pacific, well afford to treat them as enemies.

The Chinese were treated reasonably well in California as long as our citizens could make money out of their cheap labor, and when the hopes of getting a large portion of the China and East India trade were encour- to trade and recognition by the Imperial Government, has been owing, in common with other nations, to the efforts of the British Government, backed by the fleets and armies sent to enforce its demands. All nations are now regarded as standing on a political equality with China, and the United States enjoys as much consideration at Peking as it has worked for. The British, French and Russians are, no doubt, more respected and feared, for they have demonstrated to the Chinese that they can employ force to obtain their demands, which was not likely ever to be resorted to by the Americans; for, with them as with all people, there is a hidden power in armaments which is not so plainly felt in arguments.

The Chinese officers began to have, however, a favorable opinion of the Americans, from their gradual understanding of the fact that they had nothing to fear from them as a nation; and the moral force of this opinion increased among the natives, as years went on, by the knowledge that Americans had nothing to do with the opium trade. In 1839, before hostilities had actually commenced with the British, in consequence of his seizure of opium, Commissioner Lin found that the Americans had this reputation at Canton, and he endeavored to enlist them on his side in his efforts to suppress it. On one occasion he sent a special agent to Macao, to request Rev. Mr. Bridgman, the American missionary, to come to him, supposing that he might have some influence in this direction. An interview was held, and although Lin was disappointed in his plan of intermediation, he learned many new ideas concerning the impending struggle, and the relative power of his own country and Great Britain, as well as the inefficiency of his attempt to prevent it. It was the first effort on the part of any Chinese official to open political relations with the Americans, and was in itself a tacit acknowledgment of the reputation which Mr. Bridgman had obtained among the people during his ten years' residence at Canton. At that time the American trade was second in value to the British. The Chinese Government sincerely desired to stop only the opium trade and develop all other branches; but the British Government, ruled as it is by the shortsighted selfishness of trade, refused to coöperate in this despairing effort to restrain an evil of which its victims knew the effects better than their destroyers. England then lost a golden opportunity to elevate moral above mercenary motives in the eyes of a heathen people, which she has never recovered; she showed no desire to stay the destroying agency so profitable to herself.

The proposal of the American Government in 1844, to open political relations with the Court of Peking, was more favorably received by it than a similar one from any other nation would have been at that moment, owing to this general opinion of its citizens; and the first article of Mr. Cushing's treaty of July, 1844, indicated the hopes of such a makeweight against the British. It read as follows:

"There shall be a perfect, permanent, and universal peace, and a sincere and cordial amity between the United States of America on the one part, and the Ta Tsing Empire on the other part, and between their people respectively, without exception of persons or places."

The 33d Article of this treaty disallowed the citizens of the United States from trading "in opium, or any other contraband article of merchandise," under penalty of losing all countenance or protection from their own Government. The word was not mentioned either in the British treaty or tariff, though all parties fully understood that the trade was illegal, and the ships of both these nations engaged in it.

The next fourteen years showed a great increase of intercourse of every kind, commercial, religious and political; and the American Treaty, from its being the most minute and carefully arranged, under the skilful hand of Mr. Cushing, of any one of the four then existing, became, so to speak, the charter-party of that intercourse. The American Ministers who represented their country after its ratification, were courteously received by the deputy of the Emperor at Canton, who was the Governor-general of the province, and answers tne murder of Rev. W. M. Lowrie, and six more banished; and in 1856 a man was executed at Fuhchau for killing Mr. Cunningham in a mob. This was by the Chinese authorities. On the other hand, one David Williams was sentenced to death at Shanghai in the United States Consular Court for piracy and murder in Chinese waters in 1863, and would have been executed if he had not committed suicide the night before the appointed day. Another man, named Thompson was subsequently tried and found guilty of murdering a Chinese, but he escaped from prison two or three days before the day set for his execution. These instances have sufficed to show the determination of the authorities of both countries to vindicate the laws of their lands in maintaining treaty stipulations. In the retrospect of the thirty-five years, since the treaty of Nanking, and considering the way in which foreign treaties were forced out of the Chinese, and their feeling that they seldom get redress when they are the plaintiffs, they deserve respect for the manner in which they have observed them.

During this period the Chinese have been made acquainted with the position, resources, and character of the United States, almost wholly through her missionaries. The official correspondence and interpreting between the Chinese and the Ministers, Admirals, and Consuls, who have successively represented her, has been, with slight exceptions, done by them or their sons; and they have themselves acted as the nation's representatives on many occasions. Not a dollar has ever been spent by the United States to train up a class of interpreters who could perform this necessary duty, as is done by every other country which has extensive political relations with China; even nations like Denmark and Austria deem it politic to educate their own official interpreters, though their trade is trifling and their subjects number only a few scores.

Two Americans have been in the service of the Chinese Government within the past twenty years, whose deeds are not likely to be soon forgotten. One of them was General Frederick Ward, who formed the Ever Victorious force. He led it against the Taiping rebels in several attacks, and was mortally wounded in 1862 near Ningpo, at the head of his men, whom he had inspirited with his own courage. The other has been more widely known, but in Anson Burlingame the Chinese had an equally useful servant. In his capacity as the first American Minister who lived in Peking, he made a good impression upon the Chinese officials; and at that time it was exceedingly desirable to remove the bizarre and erroneous ideas these men had been taught, in their seclusion from the world at large, to believe respecting the manners and policy of foreign nations. Mr. Burlingame and Sir Frederick Bruce were personally well fitted to remove their fears, and did combine to strengthen their hopes for the gradual adoption of better relations. When, therefore, they appointed Mr. Burlingame in 1867 to be their Envoy to all the twelve Powers with whom they had negotiated treaties, it was in the full belief that he would serve them faithfully. He had already done them a good service in the matter of the Lay-Osborne Flotilla, and his after course upheld the favorable opinion which had led to his appointment. If he had been spared to return to Peking and confer with them, it is probable that his mission would have had more permanent effects. As a mark of their peculiar regard for these two men, they have both been deified by the Emperor, (the latter, we hear, quite recently,) and their names enrolled among the worthies whose influence in the unseen world will benefit the Middle Kingdom. They are the only two foreigners, so far as is known, who have ever had this distinction.

In considering the political relations between China and the United States, it is well to refer to the fifth article in the treaty negotiated at Washington, known as the Burlingame Treaty, as it is continually referred to in this country as bearing on the immigration of the Chinese. It is supposed by many that that article stimulated emigration to America, as its modification or abrogation will stop it. million of laborers could find employment on the Pacific Coast. The Pacific Railroad had not then been completed, and the prospect to the capitalists engaged in that and other public and private works of getting labor from China, at a cheaper rate than could elsewhere be obtained, was very tempting. The Chinese were likely to be well treated when they could be hired at half the price of Irish and German laborers.

The truth is, everything has been done on our side to encourage and regulate the immigration of Chinese into this country. They were useful at first, in humble labors, when the search for gold engrossed the attention of others; and became of real value when the construction of the great Railroad depended on their industry. The Burlingame Treaty only expressed its approval of what existed, and the Emperor of China had no power to prevent his subjects leaving their native soil, even if that compact had set itself against their landing on the shores of America. They have been emigrating for centuries, and have settled themselves in all the islands of the Indian Archipelago and Pacific Ocean, as well as the inviting countries nearer by. They go at their own risk, however, and the Son of Heaven used to care very little what became of them, if they were so unwise as to leave a civilized land for the barbarous, lawless regions beyond its pale.

It should be stated, too, that strictly speaking, none come to this country direct from China; from the very first, they have all sailed away to San Francisco from British territory, the ships have come under British rules and restrictions in relation to provisioning and numbers, and British officers at Hongkong have given clearances to ships with Chinese going to San Francisco, just as British officers have given them to ships with Irish going from Queenstown. The Burlingame Treaty would not have anyhow prevented Chinese going to Hongkong, and the Emperor of China cannot stop his subjects going abroad. The old and common ideas respecting the danger to a man who did so have been exaggerated, for no one was punished who returned home; on the contrary, in olden time he was regarded with curious interest if he had gone at first from places far in the interior. Probably not five per cent. ever did return; and far the greater part of those who have gone to Siam, India, and the Archipelago, and elsewhere, went of their own accord, and on the same conditions that they have gone to California and Australia, viz: by mortgaging their labor to pay for their passage.

The above is one side of the Chinese Question. That of treaties, of capital and labor, and of treatment of our citizens in China, where we have compelled their rulers to let us live under our own laws within their borders, is the other. This right of ex-territorial jurisdiction is a sore spot in the minds of those rulers, and they usually oppose any demands for further privileges on the part of American representatives, and even of all foreign nations, by comparing the legal position of the two peoples in each other's territories.

Comparing the civilization of one side with the other in this singular condition of things, what do we see? The first has been nurtured under the highest standards of moral principles, and claims to be guided by elevated sentiments and an intelligent public opinion; and yet all this has failed to secure the commonest rights of humanity to the second, who are weak, ignorant, poor, and unprotected. When the Chinese first arrived in California after the gold was discovered, they were not allowed to testify in the courts; and the consequences were such as were well known in the slave States, where the evidence of negroes was ruled out. Murders, robberies, oppressions, and assaults upon them became so common, and usually unpunishable for want of evidence, that the legislators of California, for their own protection, were induced to pass an act allowing the Chinese to testify. Discriminating laws were passed against them, and their labor was taxed without securing to them the protection and privileges they paid for. The fact that the treaties were made cuse itself for such a breach of faith because these acts were committed in that State, and no Chinese consul is there to plead officially for redress? It is not implied by this that no murderer has ever been executed for taking their lives, or robber punished for his crimes, but every one knows that such criminals do escape punishment, and that the Chinese in that State feel their insecurity and weakness. Wo be to them if they should attempt to redress their own wrongs!

This point is quite a different question from the speculative ones,—Whether the immigration of the Chinese should be allowed? Whether their labor will not destroy our own? Whether we can absorb and assimilate such a mass of ignorant, immoral, and degraded heathen? The point brought up in these remarks, refers to the treaty obligations the American people has voluntarily taken upon itself in reference to the Chinese. We may say that we are suffering these evils from that people, and are determined to prevent any more of them coming. If the balance of evils suffered by the parties to these treaties be drawn, the Chinese would be found to have had by far the worst of them. It is better far to show that the treaties have brought more good results in their train to both than evil, and that it is for our own highest welfare to treat those whom we have done so much to induce to come here, with at least as much justice as we demand of them. Some fear that this country will be swamped altogether by this flood of aliens, but the 125,000 or so of Chinese now in this land, with few exceptions, all came from a small portion, two prefectures, of Kwangtung province. There is no probability of other parts of the empire joining in this emigration, for several reasons, one of which is the great differences in their dialects. The labor question, also, is quite irrelevant to the one before us. The laws of supply and demand, wages and work, food and machinery, are among the most vital and difficult of solution among mankind, and will doubtless often come into collision until their complicated interests are better understood. But to allow one ignorant laborer to maltreat another with impunity, because the former is stronger, has a vote, and will not try to understand why he suffers just as myriads of other laborers do, who are not troubled with the *heathen Chinee*, is to sap and weaken all law and order. If they are an inferior race, as we roundly assert, there is no fear of their ever interfering with our supremacy here in any department, and policy alone would counsel us to treat them fairly; and on the other hand, if they can rise, in their own land, under the same democratic institutions and Christian training to be our equals, we cannot, as a nation living next to them just across the Pacific, well afford to treat them as enemies.

The Chinese were treated reasonably well in California as long as our citizens could make money out of their cheap labor, and when the hopes of getting a large portion of the China and East India trade were encouraging. They had not carefully studied the thrifty and economical habits of the laborers whom they invited in to compete with native workmen, and how soon the real power of those habits which have given the Chinese their superiority in Asia would be seen here. No measures were taken by the rulers of California or San Francisco to compel the immigrants to live with some regard to their own health and the public comfort, but when they became "nuisances" to others from their overcrowding, then the whole blame was put upon them, whereas the chief fault lay with the municipality for not teaching them how to live properly. Further, a wise policy would have led the city and State authorities to educate suitable men in the Chinese language, who could have acted as their interpreters and translators, and thus maintained an intelligent intercourse with these people.

This reasonable course would have shown them that their condition was understood, a way prepared for them to improve, and proper persons appointed to help them in all suitable ways. Nothing of the kind has ever been done, though measures are taken in several other States to aid Germans, Norwegians, &c., spectively, without exception of persons or places."

The 33d Article of this treaty disallowed the citizens of the United States from trading "in opium, or any other contraband article of merchandise," under penalty of losing all countenance or protection from their own Government. The word was not mentioned either in the British treaty or tariff, though all parties fully understood that the trade was illegal, and the ships of both these nations engaged in it.

The next fourteen years showed a great increase of intercourse of every kind, commercial, religious and political; and the American Treaty, from its being the most minute and carefully arranged, under the skilful hand of Mr. Cushing, of any one of the four then existing, became, so to speak, the charter-party of that intercourse. The American Ministers who represented their country after its ratification, were courteously received by the deputy of the Emperor at Canton, who was the Governor-general of the province, and answers were returned to the Letters of Credence delivered through him for transmission to his Majesty. The peculiar notions of etiquette on such points prevailing among the crowned heads of Europe, prevented their representatives sending in their credentials, since these could only be delivered in person to the Emperor. The American Government deemed it suitable to its position to communicate a Letter of Credence to the proper officers appointed by the Chinese Government, as it was intercourse between the governments which was desired, rather than between their chiefs.

These points might now be considered as trifling things, but thirty years ago they formed part of the influence at work in changing the ideas, and removing the ignorance of the Chinese rulers and people. Those wrong ideas were rather more the misfortune than the fault of both, but their conceit hindered their learning salutary truths. The next war between Great Britain and China incidentally grew out of the opium trade as the first did, though it was veiled by a reference to an insult alleged to have been given to the British flag by the Governor-general at Canton, who probably had no such intention. The consequences were favorable to permanent peace, course upheld the favorable opinion which had led to his appointment. If he had been spared to return to Peking and confer with them, it is probable that his mission would have had more permanent effects. As a mark of their peculiar regard for these two men, they have both been deified by the Emperor, (the latter, we hear, quite recently,) and their names enrolled among the worthies whose influence in the unseen world will benefit the Middle Kingdom. They are the only two foreigners, so far as is known, who have ever had this distinction.

In considering the political relations between China and the United States, it is well to refer to the fifth article in the treaty negotiated at Washington, known as the Burlingame Treaty, as it is continually referred to in this country as bearing on the immigration of the Chinese. It is supposed by many that that article stimulated emigration to America, as its modification or abrogation will stop it. Though Mr. Burlingame was invested with full powers, it was not expected that he would negotiate any new treaties, and his associate Envoys were very reluctant to affix their names to this one without express instructions from Peking. It is, as a whole, rather an amplification of the stipulations and spirit of the treaty of 1858, and does not grant any really new privileges. The fifth article reads as follows:

"The United States of America and the Emperor of China cordially recognize the inherent and inalienable right of man to change his home and his allegiance, and also the mutual advantages of the free migration and immigration of their citizens and subjects respectively from the one country to the other for the purposes of curiosity, trade, or as permanent residents. The high contracting parties, therefore, join in reprobating any other than an entirely voluntary immigration for these purposes. They consequently agree to pass laws, making it a penal offence for a citizen of the United States, or a Chinese subject, to take Chinese subjects, either to the United States or to any foreign country; or for a Chinese subject or a citizen of the United States, to take citizens of the United States to China, or to any other foreign country, without their free and voluntary consent respectively."

Comparing the civilization of one side with the other in this singular condition of things, what do we see? The first has been nurtured under the highest standards of moral principles, and claims to be guided by elevated sentiments and an intelligent public opinion; and yet all this has failed to secure the commonest rights of humanity to the second, who are weak, ignorant, poor, and unprotected. When the Chinese first arrived in California after the gold was discovered, they were not allowed to testify in the courts; and the consequences were such as were well known in the slave States, where the evidence of negroes was ruled out. Murders, robberies, oppressions, and assaults upon them became so common, and usually unpunishable for want of evidence, that the legislators of California, for their own protection, were induced to pass an act allowing the Chinese to testify. Discriminating laws were passed against them, and their labor was taxed without securing to them the protection and privileges they paid for. The fact that the treaties were made with the Government of the United States, seems to have had no weight with the rulers of the States where the Chinese suffered these things. They fell between two stools. They had neither opportunity to know their treaty rights, money to go into the proper courts, advocates to plead for them, or the least consular protection or cognizance from their own home Government in Peking. The high officers there were urged to appoint suitable men to go to San Francisco as Chinese consuls, but while they acknowledged its importance, they could not, rather than would not, see their way clear to do so.

To say that the great majority of Chinese now in our borders are fairly treated, and have been paid their wages, and that the cases of outrage and unredressed wrongs form the vast exception, is simply to evade the responsibility which rests on a Government to secure protection to every individual within its jurisdiction. The Government of the United States properly requires and expects that every American citizen visiting or residing in China, shall be treated justly by the Chinese Government, and its consuls dwelling at the ports would soon be recalled if they failed to do their utmost to redress wrongs suffered in life, limb; those habits which have given the Chinese their superiority in Asia would be seen here. No measures were taken by the rulers of California or San Francisco to compel the immigrants to live with some regard to their own health and the public comfort, but when they became "nuisances" to others from their overcrowding, then the whole blame was put upon them, whereas the chief fault lay with the municipality for not teaching them how to live properly. Further, a wise policy would have led the city and State authorities to educate suitable men in the Chinese language, who could have acted as their interpreters and translators, and thus maintained an intelligent intercourse with these people. This reasonable course would have shown them that their condition was understood, a way prepared for them to improve, and proper persons appointed to help them in all suitable ways. Nothing of the kind has ever been done, though measures are taken in several other States to aid Germans, Norwegians, &c., in understanding our laws in their own tongue, so that no mistakes may be made. Yet no class needed it so much as the Chinese, and none would have been more likely to have accepted the laws when they understood them.

One cannot but feel indignant and mortified at the contrast between the way in which the Chinese have treated us in their country into which we have forced ourselves; and the way we have treated them in this country, into which we have invited them. We have too often used them as if they had no rights which we were bound to respect, and refused that protection as men and laborers which the existing treaties guarantied to them. Is it necessary, in order that we should carry out our own treaty obligations, that we wait for a Chinese Minister at Washington to officially inform the Secretary of State how they have been violated; or for a Chinese Consul at San Francisco to complain to its Mayor that his countrymen are stoned, and robbed, and set upon, and no one punished, no one arrested for such deeds? Is not our Christian civilization strong enough to do right by them? Have we no remedy when we make mischief by a law, and then excuse ourselves for wrong-doing under the plea of law?

OUR RELATIONS

WITH

THE CHINESE EMPIRE.

BY

S. WELLS WILLIAMS, LL.D.,

Late Secretary of the American Legation, Peking, China, author of "The Chinese Empire and its Inhabitants," "Tonic Dictionary of the Canton Dialect," "A Dictionary of the Chinese Language, in the Mandarin Dialect," etc., etc.

SAN FRANCISCO:

1877.

INTRODUCTION.

In republishing the subjoined very able and important article from the pen of S. WELLS WILLIAMS, LL.D, the letter addressed to him by American citizens of Shanghai, China, is prefixed, as a suitable introduction, showing that no man living is so well qualified to speak on the subject of our relations with the Chinese Empire. We are much mistaken if his words will not have manifold more influence than all the utterances of time-serving politicians.—J. G. K.

S. WELLS WILLIAMS, LL.D.

SHANGHAI, CHINA, *November 14th*, 1876.

Dear Sir:—On the eve of your final departure from China, we beg to offer you the expression, not only of our regret that we can no longer have you in our midst, but also of our affection for yourself, our reverence for your personal character and influence, and of our high appreciation of your literary attainments and large contributions from your abundant stores in aid of the work of others.

Your kindly cheerfulness and patient industry and Christian consistency have won our hearts, commanded our admiration, and given us an example full of instruction and encouragement.

. Your labors as Editor, Author, and Lexicographer, have laid us and all students of Chinese history and the Chinese language, under great and lasting obligations to your extensive and accurate knowledge, and to your painstaking and generous efforts in giving it to others.

The high official position which you have so long occupied, as United States Secretary of Legation and Interpreter, and, nine several times, as United States Chargé d'Affaires, has given you many and important opportunities of turning your knowledge and experience to valuable account for the benefit of the Chinese, the good of your own country, and, above all, for the advancement of the cause of Christianity in China. And we would express our grateful sense of the conscientious faithfulness with which you have discharged the duties of this responsible post.

But especially shall we delight to remember, that in all your relations, literary, diplomatic, and social, towards natives and foreigners in China, for the unprecedented term of forty-three years, you have faithfully and consistently stood by your colors as a Christian man and missionary.

We congratulate you, that you may carry with you the true "wealth of the Indies," in the consciousness of a life well spent in them, to the glory of the living and trne God, and the highest good of your fellow-men.

Wishing you God-speed in your future work, and God's best blessings here and hereafter, we bid you an affectionate farewell!

Faithfully and truly yours.

OUR RELATIONS WITH THE CHINESE EMPIRE.

The American flag was first seen in Chinese waters at Whampoa, the port of Canton, on the 28th of August, 1784, on board of the ship "Empress of China." Her captain, John Green, and her supercargo, Samuel Shaw, were both courteously received by the Chinese hong-merchants in their official capacity, and hopes expressed that the intercourse then begun between China and the *New People* (as they styled the United States) might be mutually agreeable and beneficial. Nearly a century has since elapsed, and considering the relative position and civilization of the two countries, their intercourse in China has gone on with very little jarring. The gradual enlargement of the privileges of the Americans in respect to trade and recognition by the Imperial Government, has been owing, in common with other nations, to the efforts of the British Government, backed by the fleets and armies sent to enforce its demands. All nations are now regarded as standing on a political equality with China, and the United States enjoys as much consideration at Peking as it has worked for. The British, French, and Russians are, no doubt, more respected and feared, for they have demonstrated to the Chinese that they can employ force to obtain their demands, which was not likely ever to be resorted to by the Americans; for, with them as with all people, there is a hidden power in armaments which is not so plainly felt in arguments.

The Chinese officers began to have, however, a favorable opinion of the Americans, from their gradual understanding of the fact that they had nothing to fear from them as a nation; and the moral force of this opinion increased among the natives, as years went on, by the knowledge that Americans had nothing to do with the opium trade. In 1839, before hostilities had actually commenced with the British, in consequence of his seizure of opium, Commissioner Lin found that the Americans had this reputation at Canton, and he endeavored to enlist them on his side in his efforts to suppress it. On one occasion, he sent a special agent to Macao, to request Rev. Mr. Bridgman, the American missionary, to come to him, supposing that he might have some influence in this direction. An interview was held, and although Lin was disappointed in his plan of intermediation, he learned many new ideas concerning the impending struggle, and the relative power of his own country and Great Britain, as well as the inefficiency of his attempt to prevent it. It was the first effort on the part of any Chinese official to open political relations with the Americans, and was in itself a tacit acknowledgment of the reputation which Mr. Bridgman had obtained among the people during his ten years' residence at Canton. At that time, the American trade was second in value to the British. The Chinese Government sincerely desired to stop only the opium trade and develop all other branches; but the British Government, ruled as it is by the shortsighted selfishness of trade, refused to coöperate in this despairing effort to restrain an evil of which its victims knew the effects better than their destroyers. England then lost a golden opportunity to elevate moral above mercenary motives in the eyes of a heathen people, which she has never recovered. She showed no desire to stay the destroying agency so profitable to herself.

The proposal of the American Government in 1844, to open political relations with the Court of Peking, was mor favorably received by it than a similar one from any other nation would have been at that moment, owing to this general opinion of its citizens; and the first article of Mr. Cushing's treaty of July, 1844, indicated the hopes of such a makeweight against the British. It read as follows:

"There shall be a perfect, permanent, and universal peace, and a sincere and cordial amity between the United States of America on the one part, and the Ta Tsing Empire on the other part, and between their people respectively, without exception of persons or places."

The thirty-third article of this treaty disallowed the citizens of the United States from trading "in opium, or any other contraband article of merchandise," under penalty of losing all countenance or protection from their own Government. The word was not mentioned either in the British treaty or tariff, though all parties fully understood that the trade was illegal, and the ships of both these nations engaged in it.

The next fourteen years showed a great increase of intercourse of every kind, commercial, religious, and political; and the American Treaty, from its being the most minute and carefully arranged, under the skilful hand of Mr. Cushing, of any one of the four then existing, became, so to speak, the charter-party of that intercourse. The American Ministers who represented their country after its ratification, were courteously received by the deputy of the Emperor at Canton, who was the Governor-General of the Province, and answers were returned to the Letters of Credence delivered through him for transmission to his Majesty. The peculiar notions of etiquette on such points prevailing among the crowned heads of Europe, prevented their representatives sending in their credentials, since these could only be delivered in person to the Emperor. The American Government deemed it suitable to its position to communicate a Letter of Credence to the proper officers appointed by the Chinese Government, as it was intercourse between the Governments which was desired, rather than between their chiefs.

These points might now be considered as trifling things, but thirty years ago they formed part of the influence at work in changing the ideas, and removing the ignorance of the Chinese rulers and people. Those wrong ideas were rather more the misfortune than the fault of both, but their conceit hindered their learning salutary truths. The next war between Great Britain and China incidentally grew out of the opium trade as the first did, though it was veiled by a reference to an insult alleged to have been given to the British flag by the Governor-General at Canton, who probably had no such intention. The consequences were favorable to permanent peace, as they placed all international relations on a more satisfactory basis. The four treaties signed at Tientsin in June, 1858, brought China into the family of nations—much against her will, and smarting under a sense of injury, indeed, but doubtless for her good and her future safety. In the new treaty made with the United States on this occasion by Mr. Reed, the first article was enlarged as follows:

"There shall be, as there has always been, peace and friendship between the United States of America and the Ta Tsing Empire, and between their people respectively. They shall not insult and oppress each other for any trifling cause, so as to produce an estrangement between them; and if any other nation should act unjustly or oppressively, the United States will exert their good offices, on being informed of the case, to bring about an amicable arrangement of the question, thus showing their friendly feelings."

By this article, the United States have bound themselves to treat the Chinese, as they ask them to treat American citizens, in a way which they have not bound themselves to do with any other nation. In China, its spirit and letter have, on the whole, been well carried out. In 1848, three men were executed for the murder of Rev. W. M. Lowrie, and six more banished; and in 1856, a man was executed at Fuhchau for killing Mr. Cunningham in a mob. This was by the Chinese authorities. On the other hand, one David Williams was sentenced to death at Shanghai in the United States Consular Court for piracy and murder in Chinese waters in 1863, and would have been executed if he had not committed suicide the night before the appointed day. Another man, named Thompson, was subsequently tried and found guilty of murdering a Chinese, but he escaped from prison two or three days before the day set for his execution. These instances have sufficed to show the determination of the authorities of both countries to vindicate the laws of their lands in maintaining treaty stipulations. In the retrospect of the thirty-five years, since the treaty of Nanking, and considering the way in which foreign treaties were forced out of the Chinese, and their feeling that they seldom get redress when they are the plaintiffs, they deserve respect for the manner in which they have observed them.

During this period, the Chinese have been made acquainted with the position, resources, and character of the United States, almost wholly through her missionaries. The official correspondence and interpreting between the Chinese and the Ministers, Admirals, and Consuls, who have successively represented her, has been, with slight exceptions, done by them or their sons; and they have themselves acted as the nation's representatives on many occasions. Not a dollar has ever been spent by the United States to train up a class of interpreters who could perform this necessary duty, as is done by every other country which has extensive political relations with China; even nations like Denmark and Austria deem it politic to educate their own official interpreters, though their trade is trifling, and their subjects number only a few scores.

Two Americans have been in the service of the Chinese Government within the past twenty years, whose deeds are not likely to be soon forgotten. One of them was General Frederick Ward, who formed the Ever Victorious force. He led it against the Taiping rebels in several attacks, and was mortally wounded in 1862 near Ningpo, at the head of his men, whom he had inspirited with his own courage. The other has been more widely known, but in Anson Burlingame the Chinese had an equally useful servant. In his capacity as the first American Minister who lived in Peking, he made a good impression upon the Chinese officials; and at that time it was exceedingly desirable to remove the bizarre and erroneous ideas these men had been taught, in their seclusion from the world at large, to believe respecting the manners and policy of foreign nations. Mr. Burlingame and Sir Frederick Bruce were personally well fitted to remove their fears, and did combine to strengthen their hopes for the gradual adoption of better relations. When, therefore, they appointed Mr. Burlingame, in 1867, to be their Envoy to all the twelve Powers with whom they had negotiated treaties, it was in the full belief that he would serve them faithfully. He had already done them a good service in the matter of the Lay-Osborne Flotilla, and his aftercourse upheld the favorable opinion which had led to his appointment. If he hadbeen spared to return to Peking and confer with them, it is probable that his mission would have had more permanent effects. As a mark of their peculiar regard for these two men, they have both been deified by the Emperor, (the latter, we hear, quite recently,) and their names enrolled among the worthies whose influence in the unseen world will benefit the Middle Kingdom. They are the only two foreigners, so far as is known, who have ever had this distinction.

In considering the political relations between China and the United States, it is well to refer to the fifth article in the treaty negotiated at Washington, known as the Burlingame Treaty, as it is continually referred to in this country as bearing on the immigration of the Chinese. It is supposed by many that that article stimulated emigration to America, as its modification or abrogation will stop it. Though Mr. Burlingame was invested with full powers, it was not expected that he would negotiate any new treaties, and his associate Envoys were very reluctant to affix their names to this one without express instructions from Peking. It is, as a whole, rather an amplification of the stipulations and spirit of the treaty of 1858, and does not grant any really new privileges. The fifth article reads as follows:

"The United States of America and the Emperor of China cordially recognize the inherent and inalienable right of man to change his home and his allegiance, and also the mutual advantages of the free migration and immigration of their citizens and subjects respectively from the one country to the other for the purposes of curiosity, trade, or as permanent residents. The high contracting parties, therefore, join in reprobating any other than an entirely voluntary immigration for these purposes. They consequently agree to pass laws, making it a penal offence for a citizen of the United States, or a Chinese subject, to take Chinese subjects, either to the United States or to any foreign country; or for a Chinese subject or a citizen of the United States, to take citizens of the United States to China, or to any other foreign country, without their free and voluntary consent respectively."

This treaty was ratified by President Johnson, by and with the advice and consent of the Senate, before it was sent out to Peking, and submitted to the consideration of the other contracting Power. The Chinese Government delayed to affix the Imperial seal for many months, simply because it wished to see whether its Envoys would make any more treaties with other nations, for the usage is that whatever is granted to one nation is free to all.

It is not likely that the Burlingame Treaty has ever had any perceptible effect on the emigration of the Chinese to this country. Few, very few of the people know that such an article as that now quoted exists. They do know that none of their countrymen go as contract laborers to the United States, and that when a man leaves Hong Kong under the American flag for the Kau Kam Shan or Old Gold Hills, there is a certainty of his friends hearing from him, and of his return home (if living) when he pleases. This treaty was made about twenty years after the emigration to California had set in, and myriads had gone out and returned home in the meantime. When Mr. Burlingame returned from San Francisco to Peking in 1866, he reported to the Chinese that a million of laborers could find employment on the Pacific Coast. The Pacific Railroad had not then been completed, and the prospect to the capitalists engaged in that and other public and private works of getting labor from China, at a cheaper rate than could elsewhere be obtained, was very tempting. The Chinese were likely to be well treated when they could be hired at half the price of Irish and German laborers.

The truth is, everything has been done on our side to encourage and regulate the immigration of Chinese into this country. They were useful at first, in humble labors, when the search for gold engrossed the attention of others; and became of real value when the construction of the great Railroad depended on their industry. The Burlingame Treaty only expressed its approval of what existed, and the Emperor of China had no power to prevent his subjects leaving their native soil, even if that compact had set itself against their landing on the shores of America. They have been emigrating for centuries, and have settled themselves in all the islands of the Indian Archipelago and Pacific Ocean, as well as the inviting countries nearer by. They go at their own risk, however, and the Son of Heaven used to care very little what became of them, if they were so unwise as to leave a civilized land for the barbarous, lawless regions beyond its pale.

It should be stated, too, that strictly speaking, none come to this country direct from China; from the very first, they have all sailed away to San Francisco from British territory, the ships have come under British rules and restrictions in relation to provisioning and numbers, and British officers at Hong Kong have given clearances to ships with Chinese going to San Francisco, just as British officers have given them to ships with Irish going from Queenstown. The Burlingame Treaty would not have anyhow prevented Chinese going to Hong Kong, and the Emperor of China cannot stop his subjects going abroad. The old and common ideas respecting the danger to a man who did so have been exaggerated, for no one was punished who returned home; on the contrary, in olden time he was regarded with curious interest if he had gone at first from places far in the interior. Probably not five per cent. ever did return; and far the greater part of those who have gone to Siam, India, and the Archipelago, and elsewhere, went of their own accord, and on the same conditions that they have gone to California and Australia, viz., by mortgaging their lalor to pay for their passage.

The above is one side of the Chinese question. That of treaties, of capital and labor, and of treatment of our citizens in China, where we have compelled their rulers to let us live under our own laws within their borders, is the other. This right of ex-territorial jurisdiction is a sore spot in the minds of those rulers, and they usually oppose any demands for further privileges on the part of American representatives, and even of all foreign nations, by comparing the legal position of the two peoples in each other's territories.

Comparing the civilization of one side with the other in this singular condition of things, what do we see? The first has been nurtured under the highest standards of moral principles, and claims to be guided by elevated sentiments and an intelligent public opinion; and yet all this has failed to secure the commonest rights of humanity to the second, who are weak, ignorant, poor, and unprotected. When the Chinese first arrived in California after the gold was discovered, they were not allowed to testify in the courts; and the consequences were such as were well known in the slave States, where the evidence of negroes was ruled out. Murders, robberies, oppressions, and assaults upon them became so common, and usually unpunishable for want of evidence, that the legislators of California, for their own protection, were induced to pass an act allowing the Chinese to testify. Discriminating laws were passed against them, and their labor was taxed without securing to them the protection and privileges they paid for. The fact that the treaties were made with the Government of the United States, seems to have had no weight with the rulers of the States where the Chinese suffered these things. They fell between two stools. They had neither opportunity to know their treaty rights, money to go into the proper courts, advocates to plead for them, or the least consular protection or cognizance from their own home Government in Peking. The high officers there were urged to appoint suitable men to go to San Francisco as Chinese consuls, but while they acknowledged its importance, they could not, rather than would not, see their way clear to do so.

To say that the great majority of Chinese now in our borders are fairly treated, and have been paid their wages, and that the cases of outrage and unredressed wrongs form the vast exception, is simply to evade the responsibility which rests on a Government to secure protection to every individual within its jurisdiction. The Government of the United States properly requires and expects that every American citizen visiting or residing in China, shall be treated justly by the Chinese Government, and its consuls dwelling at the ports would soon be recalled if they failed to do their utmost to redress wrongs suffered in life, limb, or property by the poorest citizen. The Imperial Government has already paid out about $800,000 to indemnify the losses of our citizens within its territory. Some of these losses were incurred by the direct act of British forces setting fire to the houses of Americans, and in no case, almost, were they caused by direct attacks on them as such. Mission chapels have been destroyed, or pillaged by mobs at Tientsin, Shanghai, Fuhchau, and Canton, and indemnity made in every case.

How mortifying is the record of robberies, murders, arsons, and assaults, committed on peaceable Chinese living on the Pacific coast, not one of whom had any power to plead their case, and most of whom probably suffered in silence! Do we excuse ourselves from fulfilling treaty obligations, the most solemn obligations a nation can impose on itself, and whose infraction always ought to involve loss of character and moral power, because the Chinese Government is a pagan Government, and weak, too, as well? Can this nation look quietly on while Chinese are murdered, and their houses burned over their heads, in California, and no one is executed for such murders, or mulcted for such arsons; and then excuse itself for such a breach of faith because these acts were committed in that State, and no Chinese consul is there to plead officially for redress? It is not implied by this that no murderer has ever been executed for taking their lives, or robber punished for his crimes, but every one knows that such criminals do escape punishment, and that the Chinese in that State feel their insecurity and weakness. Wo be to them if they should attempt to redress their own wrongs!

This point is quite a different question from the speculative ones, Whether the immigration of the Chinese should be allowed? Whether their labor will not destroy our own? Whether we can absorb and assimilate such a mass of ignorant, immoral, and degraded heathens? The point brought up in these remarks, refers to the treaty obligations the American people has voluntarily taken upon itself in reference to the Chinese. We may say that we are suffering these evils from that people, and are determined to prevent any more of them coming. If the balance of evils suffered by the parties to these treaties be drawn, the Chinese would be found to have had by far the worst of them. It is better far to show that the treaties have brought more good results in their train to both than evil, and that it is for our own highest welfare to treat those whom we have done so much to induce to come here, with at least as much justice as we demand of them. Some fear that this country will be swamped altogether by this flood of aliens, but the 125,000 or so of Chinese now in this land, with few exceptions, all came from a small portion, two prefectures, of Kwangtung Province. There is no probability of other parts of the Empire joining in this emigration, for several reasons, one of which is the great differences in their dialects. The labor question, also, is quite irrelevant to the one before us. The laws of supply and demand, wages and work, food and machinery, are among the most vital and difficult of solution among mankind, and will doubtless often come into collision until their complicated interests are better understood. But to allow one ignorant laborer to maltreat another with impunity, because the former is stronger, has a vote, and will not try to understand why he suffers just as myriads of other laborers do, who are not troubled with the *heathen Chinee*, is to sap and weaken all law and order. If they are an inferior race, as we roundly assert, there is no fear of their ever interfering with our supremacy here in any department, and policy alone would counsel us to treat them fairly; and on the other hand, if they can rise, in their own land, under the same democratic institutions and Christian training to be our equals, we cannot, as a nation living next to them just across the Pacific, well afford to treat them as enemies.

The Chinese were treated reasonably well in California as long as our citizens could make money out of their cheap labor, and when the hopes of getting a large portion of the China and East India trade were encouraging. They had not carefully studied the thrifty and economical habits of the laborers whom they invited in to compete with native workmen, nor how soon the real power of those habits, which have given the Chinese their superiority in Asia, would be seen here. No measures were taken by the rulers of California or San Francisco to compel the immigrants to live with some regard to their own health and the public comfort, but when they became "nuisances" to others from their overcrowding, then the whole blame was put upon them, whereas the chief fault lay with the municipality for not teaching them how to live properly. Further, a wise policy would have led the city and State authorities to educate suitable men in the Chinese language, who could have acted as their interpreters and translators, and thus maintained an intelligent intercourse with these people. This reasonable course would have shown them that their condition was understood, a way prepared for them to improve, and proper persons appointed to help them in all suitable ways. Nothing of the kind has ever been done, though measures are taken in several other States to aid Germans, Norwegians, etc., in understanding our laws in their own tongue, so that no mistakes may be made. Yet no class needed it so much as the Chinese, and none would have been more likely to have accepted the laws when they understood them.

One cannot but feel indignant and mortified at the contrast between the way in which the Chinese have treated us in their country into which we have forced ourselves, and the way we have treated them in this country, into which we have invited them. We have too often used them as if they had no rights which we were bound to respect, and refused that protection as men and laborers which the existing treaties guaranteed to them. Is it necessary, in order that we should carry out our own treaty obligations, that we wait for a Chinese Minister at Washington to officially inform the Secretary of State how they have been violated; or for a Chinese Consul at San Francisco to complain to its Mayor that his countrymen are stoned and robbed, and set upon, and no one punished, no one arrested for such deeds? Is not our Christian civilization strong enough to do right by them? Have we no remedy when we make mischief by a law, and then excuse ourselves for wrongdoing under the plea of law?

CHINESE IMMIGRATION

BY

S. WELLS WILLIAMS LL.D.

A Paper Read before the Social Science Association, at Saratoga September 10 1879

NEW YORK
CHARLES SCRIBNER'S SONS
743 AND 745 BROADWAY
1879

CHINESE IMMIGRATION.

THE question of Chinese immigration has drawn to it a degree of attention since the immigrants began to land in this country thirty years ago, which can hardly be explained by their numbers, their conduct, or their capacity. The total arrivals from China during a quarter of a century have not equaled the number of persons which have landed at New York from Europe in six months during most of those same years. Their behavior, under great provocation, has excited no commotion; nor has their learning, power, skill, or bigotry been such as to give any reasonable ground for alarm. It is not easy to account for the excitement on rational grounds, or to explain the many unfounded statements against the Chinese which have passed current, even after their inaccuracy has been shown. A good deal of the discussion has arisen from the different views taken as to what might grow out of their presence or increase. Some, drawing on their fears for their facts, regard them as the first ripple of an overwhelming flood of ignorance, poverty, heathenism, and vice; while others, speaking from experience, after trying them in various capacities, assure us that the Chinese are docile, temperate, thrifty, and industrious, and have great capacity for improvement.

My present object is to describe the origin, kind, and prospects of this immigration, the conduct and the rights of the immigrants, with notices of their treatment, so as to come to an intelligent idea of the question. Few incidents in the last few months have had a more picturesque setting in regard to the actors, the place of meeting, and the subject talked of, than the interview held last April between General Grant and the Chinese merchants at Georgetown, in Pulo Penang. This island owes its commercial importance to the industry and skill of its twelve thousand Chinese settlers, who, under the care and control of the British Government, have made it a mart for the traffic of the neighboring islands and continent. They met the late President of the United States, in his journey around the globe. His position as a mere traveler offered to their minds, no doubt, something anomalous and almost inexplicable, but still invested with a scantling of its original power. They presented him with an address, whose subject was equally remarkable with the origin of the interlocutors, for they asked him to use his influence to secure a fair and liberal treatment for their countrymen in America, and to remove any restrictions which had been imposed on their freedom to come and go, the same as any other nation. He told them, in reply, "that the hostility of which they complained did not represent the real sentiment of America; but was the work of demagogues, who in that, as in other countries, pander to prejudice against race or nationality and favor any measure of oppression that might advance their political interests. He never doubted and no one could doubt that, in the end, no matter what effect the agitation for the time being might have, the American people would treat the Chinese with kindness and justice, and not deny to the free and deserving people of their country the asylum they offer to the rest of the world."

I believe that this witness spoke truly. The discussions in the West and the East, in the pulpit and in Congress, will all tend to bring out the truth and help to maintain our national character for fairness and justice in relation to the Chinese. China itself is one of the best misrepresented countries in the world, and her people have been subject to the most singular diversity of opinion from writers and travelers, whose books have shown that they had had no opportunity to revise first impressions, or correct errors, and yet have furnished most of the statements relied on for the estimate taken of Chinese civilization. Now that scholars have increased, our acquaintance with the arts, culture, government, and literature of the sons of Han will help us better to understand the causes which have operated to make them, under the blessing of God, as much of a nation as they are.

They form one of the purest of existing races, and have occupied the eastern confines of Asia from very early times. The people are so often called Mongols in this country that it is concluded that they are of the same race as the nomads of the steppes. We may call them Turanians, if it be necessary to indicate their early race affinities ; but it is unjust to apply a term which only dates from Genghis Khan, in the 13th century, fully 3,000 years after their history begins. His grandson, Kublai, conquered China, and his family held sway over the empire for 83 years, under eleven emperors. All of them learned the elements of regular government from their subjects, whose manners, language, laws, and religion were generally adopted. Their expulsion left the Chinese to themselves, and the Mongols or Tartars, as they are now usually called, have been since mostly under the control of their former subjects.

The present rulers of China belong to neither of these races; but to the Manchu, which has occupied the northeastern shores of Asia since the 10th century. This race ruled the northern provinces of China for about 120 years, till A.D. 1232, when Genghis Khan destroyed their power and drove them back into their original haunts. They again grew powerful, and by a fortunate stroke repossessed themselves of Peking, in 1644, and have since ruled the empire with great prudence and vigor.

It is, therefore, an entire misnomer to call the Chinese Mongols, and I am sure that many persons use it in ignorance of the facts of the case. I am well aware how the term Mongolian is used by writers to include Laplanders, Tartars, Chinese, Japanese, with the Esquimaux and other Indian tribes, under one race; but we wrongly use it to designate a people occupying the Chinese Empire only. The old Aztecs and Iroquois, in this continent, were more alike in most respects than the Chinese and their neighbors in Central Asia, and they feel chagrined to be thus designated. Not a Mongol, to my knowledge, has ever landed in this country, and none are likely to come, any more than are the Arabians or Brahmins.

The southern Chinese alone have immigrated to foreign lands; and until recently went only to the Indian Archipelago, Siam, and India. This portion of the people is less pure as a race than their countrymen north of the Yangtse River, having early mingled with old Malayan tribes living south of the Nanling range in the province of Kwangtung. This mixed race exhibits some physical differences from their northern countrymen, the results of amalgamation, climate, and food; but is now quite the same in language, institutions, and religion. The people are smaller and more swarthy, have more commercial enterprise, are better educated, and exhibit higher mechanical skill.

Only six departments or prefectures, lying along the coasts of the two provinces of Kwangtung and Fuhkien, from Hing-hwa near Fuhchau, to Shau-king, west of Canton, have furnished all the emigrants to other lands. The emigration into Malaysia and the Indian Islands has been going on for two centuries, and its results have been greatly to the advantage of the native states. Wherever the Chinese have come into actual conflict with Europeans it has been only with regard to trade and taxes, and never on account of their attempts to set up independent governments. The prosperity of Luconia, Siam, and Borneo has been largely owing to this element of their population; and even in Java, where the Dutch closed their ports against them in 1840, they have recently been invited to return, as mechanics and traders.

The custom of these Southern Chinese has been to pass to and fro; and, though most of the emigrants remained where they landed, thousands returned to their homes. This gradually diffused a knowledge of foreign countries and people throughout these coast regions, and made it easier for the natives to go to the Gold Hills when the report came in 1849 of the discoveries in California and Australia. A few went first to San Francisco, and their favorable reports spread through the towns around Canton, as they showed the dust they had brought. In 1854, the emigration began to assume larger proportions, and foreigners gave every facility to the emigration, as the business gave profitable employment to their ships.

The foreigners who flocked to California about 1849, and after, were desirous of getting Chinese labor, so that every immigrant soon found work. But about that year the Cubans, Peruvians, and English were also desirous of importing Chinese laborers into their colonies; and the ignorance of the latter of all foreign countries led them to readily infer that when once out of China they would at last reach the Gold Hills. This coolie trade, as it has been since called, was greatly aided by the free emigration to San Francisco and Melbourne; but the two were radically different.

During the ten or twelve years ending in 1874, a marked and well-known distinction between free and contract emigration was drawn by the natives around Canton simply by the port the ship sailed from. If she cleared from Hong-kong, everybody knew that her passengers were free; if from Macao, forty miles west of it, all knew that they were coolies—or as the native term, *chu-tsai*, *i. e.* pigs in baskets, described them—and would probably never come back. So marked had this distinction become that the Portuguese had made a term from this phrase, *chuchairo*, to denote a coolie broker. In 1873 the atrocities connected with this business had become so outrageous that the Portuguese Government, at the urgent remonstrance of the British Government, put a stop to the shipment of all contract Chinese from Macao, and brought the evils to an end. Their recital would be only a repetition of the modes in which reckless cupidity, irresponsible power, crafty misrepresentation and cunning, well-planned temptation, or outrageous violence and callousness, all united to get the advantage over ignorance, poverty, and want. The Chinese authorities at Canton issued stringent regulations to punish and restrain crimps and other agents; but the laws were mostly a dead letter. The native kidnappers were sometimes caught by their countrymen, and put to death, with excruciating tortures, crucifixion, and burning. Still, so long as the coolies could be shipped from Macao, the trade went on, to the terror of the community in which it thrived and the disgrace of that settlement, till it was confessed that it never could be conducted with both profit and honor.

These notices of the coolie trade are given because much has been said in the United States about the coolies brought here. It may be stated that this word *coolie* is not Chinese, but Bengalee. It was originally the name of a hill tribe in India, whose able-bodied men were wont to go down to the plains in harvest-time, just as Irish laborers cross to England at the same season and return home when it is over. The name gradually extended to all transient laborers, and in 1835 such people were hired at Calcutta (under contracts) to go to Mauritius, where laborers were needed. The application of the word to Chinese contract laborers was easy, for the term was already in use among foreigners in China for lower house servants and day laborers. These last, on their part, supposed it to be an English word, and probably the immigrants, on reaching San Francisco, ready to do any kind of labor, and not knowing many English words, so called themselves. There are three different terms in Chinese for house servants, for day laborers, and for contract coolies; and I think that a good deal of our misapprehension as to the character of those in California has arisen from this misuse of the word.

The regions to which the coolies were carried included Cuba and Peru (where most of them landed), Jamaica, Trinidad, Demerara, Surinam, Hawaii, Brazil, and Central America. The Panama Railroad was mostly built by them, taken there in American ships. The only attempt to bring them to this country, which I have heard of, was made by some persons in New Orleans; but

I am not aware how it succeeded. The total number of men thus carried away was probably over 300,000. of whom 142,422 landed at Havana between 1847 and 1874. Out of the whole, I do not think that 500 ever escaped or returned home; and I am inclined to believe that over two-thirds of them all went abroad willingly, though ignorantly.

During these same years, men were going and returning from San Francisco and Melborne, with stories of their success. The total arrivals at the former port between 1852 and 1878, according to the custom house records, was 230,430, of whom 133,491 returned home or died, leaving 96,939 in the country, not including births. "Spofforth's Almanac" for 1878 gives the arrivals in all the United States between 1855 and 1877 at 191,118. At this rate, it will probably take a century before half a million will find a footing in our wide domain, and that too against the competition of the owners and settlers of the soil and the skilled labor of our artisans. If two-fifths returned home when the land was open and calling for laborers, and the building of railroads gave work and wages to thousands of these hands, is it not as certain as a thing can be, on these facts, that the supply of workmen will be proportioned to the demand? On our eastern shores almost half a million of immigrants landed at New York in 1872 alone; while the total number of arrivals from Europe for 30 years, ending in 1878, was 8,200,000, or more than one-sixth of our present population.

Nearly all the Chinese have come here from a strip of territory not much larger than the State of Connecticut, lying south and southwest of the city of Canton. Some alarmists said last year that myriads from the famine-stricken provinces in Northern China were to be brought to our shores; but not an emigrant has ever sailed from

Shanghai or Tientsin for California. All have gone from Hongkong. The province of Kwangtung, of which Canton is the capital, measures 79,456 square miles, and its inhabitants speak many local dialects, which tends to crystallize them into separate communities, and has great influence on emigration, because it is only those who speak the same dialect who naturally go together. A man from Canton, meeting one from Amoy, Fuhchau, Ningpo, Tientsin, or Hankow, would be unintelligible to each of them, as they severally would be to each other; and this feature almost compels emigrants to follow the lead already opened. Thus Swatow furnishes those for Siam, Amoy does those for Manila, Kia-ying for Borneo, and five districts in the central and southwest parts of Kwangtung province were the homes of those now in Australia and the United States. Their names are Sin-hwui, Sin-ning, Kai-ping, Ngăn-ping and Hiang-shan. For those coming from each of these five districts, or counties, a company has been formed in San Francisco to look after their welfare and to help them while in America. A sixth company does the same for all the immigrants from other places. The inducements and help of friends and the reports of returning miners have had great influence in stimulating their departure. Fears are entertained by some persons, however, that, if the gap thus opened in the vast population of the Chinese Empire be not stopped by limiting the number in one vessel to fifteen, or by abrogating the Burlingame Treaty, it will continue to run like a leak in a mill-dam, till we are all swamped. These are as baseless as the fear that the Indians are going to unite in a league to regain their ancestral hunting-grounds. Men do not change their homes and allegiance without adequate inducements and rewards, which are all wanting in this case.

Two or three other causes, besides the different dialects, have much influence in hindering Chinese emigration. One is their pride of country, which leads them to look upon those who go out of it as most unfortunate, running great risks of their lives, and putting themselves in the power of cruel and ignorant barbarians. Though there is now no law in force forbidding emigration, public opinion strongly discourages it, and the love of home acts against it.

A second deterrent cause is a strong sectional antipathy between the natives of different provinces, and even parts of the same province, leading them to shun each other like the clans of Scotland in the olden time. In Kwangtung, constant strifes arise between *settlers* and *squatters*, called *pun-ti* and *hak-ka*, often resulting in much loss of life. This repugnance tends to confine the immigrants to our shores to the districts near Canton. Further strong influences are at work to detain those who are in office or belong to the gentry, and those who have property or are in business. Besides these, the ties of family and claims of infirm, needy, and sick dependants compel myriads to stay. The numbers, which seem to be great here, are not missed there. Their departure or return makes no impression nor stimulates other throngs to do likewise. The men we have are the common peasantry from country districts—young and healthy, thrifty and industrious, willing to work and make their way in the world. They are neither paupers nor lepers, and certainly not criminals, for such could not get away nor obtain the aid or security needed. China has not yet learned how to dispose of her criminals this way. Most of them can read a little. Hundreds get over by borrowing money on high interest, to be repaid as they earn it, the lenders risking it on their life and habits. One hears so much of the serfs, slaves, coolies, peons, Mongols, and such like poured on our shores, that very erroneous notions of their character prevail. One official document even described them as "voluntary slaves by the unalterable structure of their intelligent being." Complaint has been often made that the immigrants bring no families; but custom is too strong for the women to leave home to any extent. I think, when we consider how timid and ignorant they are—many of them crippled by cramping the feet—that, under the circumstances, it has been better as it is. Their sufferings would have probably been great, unable as most of them are to speak English, the objects of obloquy, and exposed to manifold temptations.

The new constitution of California gives us the intentions of the opponents of Chinese labor in Art. XIX., and shows the ignorance of its framers by the impossibility of carrying out its provisions. Some of them are in violation of the laws and constitution of the United States. "Asiatic coolieism" is prohibited; but is not defined. It was needless, however; for Asiatic coolieism had never existed in California, or any other State of the Union. It had already been declared to be illegal and piratical by Congress, and the law-makers might have fortified their position by referring to the Act approved February 19th, 1862, before inserting the following extraordinary section in the organic law of their State:

"SECT. 4. The presence of foreigners ineligible to become citizens of the United States is declared to be dangerous to the well-being of the State, and the legislature shall discourage their immigration by all the means within its power. Asiatic coolieism is a form of human slavery, and is forever prohibited in this State, and all contracts for coolie labor shall be void. All companies or corporations, whether formed in this country or any foreign country, for the importation of such labor shall be subject to such penalties as the legislature may prescribe. The legislature shall delegate all necessary power to the incorporated cities and towns of this State for the removal of Chinese without the limits of such cities and towns, or for their location within prescribed portions of those limits; and it shall also provide the necessary legislation to prohibit the introduction into the State of Chinese after the adoption of this constitution. This section shall be enforced by appropriate legislation."

If history repeats itself, legislation does so far more frequently; for here are the silly laws of China and mediæval Europe re-enacted in our Republic, and making new Ghettos for Chinamen near every town in California. This whole section reads more like the by-laws of a mining company, trying to keep its claim intact from the encroachments of other companies by erecting a fence around its land, than the deliberate result of a convention of wise men met to make a State constitution. It is not stated who are the foreigners ineligible to become citizens; nor is it defined how the company formed in a foreign country for the importation of coolie labor, even before it has done anything, is to be made subject to the penalties of a California legislature; nor how that State is going to execute laws prohibiting the introduction of Chinese into its borders, in face of a treaty between China and the United States. These points are left for the wisdom of a future legislature to attend to.

I have stated that an act of Congress is in existence prohibiting the introduction of contract laborers from China, or any other land, into the United States. In January, 1867, the following resolution unanimously passed both houses of Congress:

"*Whereas*, The traffic in laborers, transported from

China and other Eastern countries, known as the coolie trade, is odious to the people of the United States, as inhuman and immoral; and

"*Whereas*, It is abhorrent to the spirit of modern international law and policy, which have substantially extirpated the African slave-trade, to permit the establishment in its place of a mode of enslaving men differing from the former in little else than the employment of fraud, instead of force, to make its victims captive; be it, therefore,

"*Resolved*, That it is the duty of this Government to give effect to the moral sentiment of the nation, through all its agencies, for the purpose of preventing the further introduction of coolies into this hemisphere or the adjacent islands."

This resolution was a proper expression of public opinion; but it never prevented a single coolie afterward landing at Havana or Callao, any more than its tone would lead one to suppose that a hundred thousand coolies had already landed at San Francisco, through the agency of the six companies. The opponents of Chinese immigration have so persistently declared that those who land in this country are coolies, that the burden of proof, after what has been said, must rest with them. It is not a mere question of the meaning of terms. Even so distinguished a man as Senator Blaine seems to have got the idea that the men now arriving in San Francisco are the same class of people designated in this resolution. He certainly ought, for his own credit, to have learned the facts of the case, before he accused the Chinese Government, as he did, of violating the Treaty, by declaring from his seat in the Senate, that, "in the sense in which we get immigration from Europe, there never has one Chinese immigrant come to these shores. . . . The Chinese Government agreed to enforce the provision that there should be nothing else than voluntary emigration.

They have never done it. The Treaty stands broken and defied by China from the hour it was made to the present time. We had to legislate against it. We legislated against it in the Coolie Law. The Chinese were so palpably and so flagrantly violating it, that statutes of the United States were enacted to contravene the evil they were doing; and it has gone on, probably not so grossly as before, but in effect the same."

It is enough to say, in reply to this charge of breaking the Treaty, that the Chinese authorities, both central and provincial, had passed many laws to restrain and prevent the coolie trade, and that the last act against it passed by our Congress was on February 19th, 1862, more than six years before Mr. Burlingame signed the Treaty. When that Treaty was negotiating, in July, 1868, no one at Washington brought up the charge that the Chinese Government had been for years sending coolies to California, nor were the immigrants then so generally stigmatized as serfs, coolies, peons, slaves, and Mongol hordes, for their labor was needed. I crossed the Pacific in 1860 in a ship with three hundred and sixteen Chinamen, not one of whom had a contract, and three-fourths of them came from two villages. No Chinese ship has ever yet crossed the ocean; consequently no Chinese has ever brought coolies to this country, and the blame of violating the Treaty could not rightly rest on that Government. Certainly, if there is one matter in which the American and Chinese Governments have been of one mind, it is the restriction of the coolie trade; while all the difficulties, the responsibilities, and the sufferings, too, have been on the part of the latter.

The majority of members in the Congressional Committee sent to California in 1876 were against Chinese immigration. It obtained much evidence in support of their views; but none of the witnesses could produce a contract for bringing a single coolie from China. I have seen thousands and thousands of these contracts in Chinese and Spanish or English, containing the terms obliging the coolies to go abroad for so many years at such wages, and their stipulations are plain and explicit.

I come now to a consideration of the Treaty which exists between China and this country. The bill which passed Congress last February, intended to restrict Chinese immigration, had this undignified feature (a solitary instance in our national legislation), that it covertly abrogated this Treaty, without even referring to its existence; without citing an instance of its violation; and, what was worse, without first informing the other party. Its passage was quite unexpected; but it aroused quick remonstrances from State legislatures, from colleges, from missionary societies, from chambers of commerce, and from distinguished citizens, all alike presenting their reasons to the President against his approval.

In its Treaty with China, this nation has solemnly pledged its faith to firm, lasting, and sincere friendship with that empire; it has promised that the people of the United States should not, for any trifling cause, insult or oppress the people of China, so as to produce an estrangement between them; the Federal Government has covenanted that Chinese subjects in the United States should be exempt from all disability or persecution on account of their religious faith; it has asserted that there is mutual advantage from the free migration and emigration of the people of the United States and China respectively, from the one country to the other, for the purposes of curiosity, trade, or permanent residence; it has specifically pledged itself that Chinese subjects residing in the United States should enjoy the same privileges, immunities, and exemptions in respect to travel or residence as citizens of the most favored nation; and, finally, as if to place all stipulations in the Treaty on the highest moral basis, it invokes, in what is called the Toleration Article, as the standard of dealing between the two nations, the Christian sentiment that the principles of the Christian religion teach men to do good, to do to others as they would that others should do to them. In all these ways the Governor of Nations had beforehand placed the United States under peculiar liens toward this ancient kingdom to treat it with justice and patience. Some of the stipulations have a present application which could not have been anticipated when they were signed and ratified.

I would urge the maintenance of this Treaty, not alone on the high ground which the President takes in his veto—that it is not the function of Congress to make new treaties or modify existing ones, and "that the denunciation of a treaty by any government is confessedly justifiable only upon some reason, both of the highest justice and of the highest necessity"—but on the higher ground that we shall sin against right and justice if we do not. The highest expression of a nation's voice is in its treaties; they form almost the only declaration of its honor which other nations can appeal to. The denunciation of the conduct of the last king of Judah, for his violation of his covenant with the king of Babylon, stands on the sacred page as the highest attestation of the sacred character of such compacts. Says the prophet Ezekiel, speaking of king Zedekiah's conduct:

"Seeing he despised the oath by breaking the covenant, when, lo, he had given his hand, and hath done all these things, he shall not escape. Therefore, thus saith the Lord God, As I live, surely mine oath that he hath despised, and my covenant that he hath broken, even it will I recompense upon his own head."

I do not doubt that these words carry much weight with them still as a word of warning; and I believe that there is moral strength and principle in the people of this land quite sufficient to maintain what they have promised in the treaty with China.

The government of that empire has uniformly admitted its obligations; and, considering its great difficulties, has creditably fulfilled them. The four treaties signed at Tientsin in 1858 were, no doubt, obtained under great fear and pressure; but their stipulations placed international intercourse between the East and the West on a definite footing, and their operation has been to teach the secluded rulers of China both their own rights and their duties toward other nations. Great progress was shown, eleven years after, in sending Mr. Burlingame on a complimentary embassy to the powers with whom the Emperor had made treaties.

When the embassy reached Washington, it was received with great *eclat*. Among other things done during its stay was the negotiation of eight additional articles to the existing Treaty, by plenipotentiaries of the two governments, who signed them on the 28th of July, 1868. They were ratified by the Senate a few days afterward, and then forwarded to Peking, to be ratified by the Emperor, even before they had been submitted to his perusal. This was not done till the 23d of November, 1869.

Considering the circumstances under which the first or Reed Treaty was signed, those attending the second were indicative of great and real progress in the intervening ten years. Its fifth article relates to emigration from either country, and has drawn great attention in and out of Congress, as if it stood in the way of our ridding ourselves of an unbearable evil in the crowds of Chinese who had thereby been induced to come to this country. It reads:

"The United States of America and the Empire of China cordially recognize the inherent and inalienable right of man to change his home and allegiance, and also the mutual advantage of the free migration and emigration of their citizens and subjects respectively from one country to the other, for purposes of curiosity, of trade, or as permanent residents. The high contracting parties join, therefore, in reprobating any other than an entirely voluntary emigration for these purposes. They consequently agree to pass laws making it a penal offense for a citizen of the United States or Chinese subject to take Chinese subjects either to the United States or any other foreign country, or for a Chinese subject or citizen of the United States to take citizens of the United States to China or to any other foreign country without their free and voluntary consent, respectively."

The leading idea in this article is to discourage the coolie trade, and this public declaration of our Government as to the difference between it and voluntary emigration was not supposed to have any other meaning. It is hard to see, moreover, how the declaration of an inalienable right of all men should be supposed to encourage or hinder its exercise; it could not have incited emigration, for I am sure that not one in a hundred of the Chinese who have landed here ever saw it in their own country. Says Gov. Morton, the chairman of the Congressional Committee:

"When this Treaty was concluded with China, it was

regarded by the whole nation as a grand triumph of American diplomacy and principles; and Mr. Burlingame was regarded as a benefactor of his country by having secured to Americans the protection of the Chinese Government and the right to live there and trade, and for having secured from China a recognition of what may be called the great American doctrine of the inherent and inalienable right of man to change his home and his allegiance. For the recognition of this doctrine we had been struggling by negotiation ever since we had a national existence, and had succeeded with them one by one. Within the last eight years we have secured its recognition by Germany and other European states that had long held out against us."

I need not quote from the recorded views of Gov. Morton on the backward step this country has been urged to take in regard to Chinese immigration, by adopting the very policy China itself is forsaking. That opinion would have been even more decided if he had lived to join in the Congressional debate of last winter, and record his vote in the Senate against the bill.

The passage of this bill at that time drew public attention to the treaty rights of the Chinese, and the people sustained the veto of President Hayes, as a judicious, sound, and timely refusal to yield to a sectional demand to go back on a lifelong policy in regard to immigration. That veto saved this Republic from one of the most uncalled-for wrongs to its national reputation, in repudiating a solemn treaty, in fact, if not in form, without mentioning a single instance in the bill of the wrongdoing of the other party, as was done in 1798, when the treaty with France was abrogated by Congress, and without first stating to the Chinese our own case. It would have been hard for us to have made out a grievance. We would never have done so toward a strong nation, and it was entirely unnecessary to do it toward a weak one. The new constitution of California has, however, supplemented the bill by the following sections:

"No corporation now existing or hereafter formed under the laws of this State shall, after the adoption of this constitution, employ, directly or indirectly, in any capacity, any Chinese or Mongolian. The legislature will pass such laws as may be necessary to enforce this provision.

"No Chinese will be employed on any State, county, municipal, or other public work, except in punishment for crime."

The execution of these two sections is likely to cause some resistance on the part of corporations in that State, by their restrictions on the labor market—one of the chimerical objects of the majority of the Convention.

As another instance of unjust (if not impossible) legislation in the same direction, one where the object aimed at is almost forgotten in view of the manner in which it is to be reached, is a bill recently introduced in the Senate by Mr. Slater, of Oregon. This is what his bill forbids the hapless Chinaman to do:

"To engage in, carry on, or work at any manufacturing or mechanical business; or to own or lease, carry on or work any mine, or to own or lease any real estate for any purpose other than that of lawful commerce and for places of residence; or to conduct any farm, garden, vineyard, or orchard, for agricultural, horticultural, or other like purpose; or to own, have, or keep any herd of cattle, horses, sheep, goats, or swine, for the purpose of making profit by the increase, product, or use thereof; or to keep any hotel or restaurant for public entertainment (excepting for the use and accommodation of the citizens and subjects of

China); or to work or engage to work as mechanic, artisan, laborer, waiter, servant, cook, clerk, or messenger, or in any other kind of labor, skilled or unskilled, except for and in the employ of citizens and subjects of China lawfully engaged in commerce in the United States or traveling or residing therein."

The bill reads like an edict of Philip or Alva against heretics, for it declares that the penalty for every violation of these provisions is a fine of not less than $100, *and* an imprisonment for not more than six months. Conviction involves a "forfeiture of all property used or invested in the prohibited business." No person or corporation can employ a Chinese in prohibited work or business, under a penalty of $100 for each offense. Comment on such regulations could add nothing to their harshness, their impossibility, or their folly. It is true, indeed, that they have not yet the force of law, and I quote them only as an index of the kind of legislation which may be attempted at the next session in regulating the treatment of these people in the East as well as in the Pacific States.

I have endeavored to show that the Chinese are here under the strongest public sanctions of any race, and ought to be protected in their treaty rights by this nation. They began to come to the Pacific coast at the invitation of our own people, attracted there, as others were, by the search for gold. They took up the washed-out and abandoned diggings at first; but they have since continued to come and go, because there was a demand for their labor. We call them *Heathen Chinee*, and so, unhappily, they are; but they brought with them industrious and quiet habits, and during the past 27 years have added largely to the resources and wealth of this country. They have spread themselves over that and the neighboring States, wherever their labor was wanted, and have given general satisfaction in those branches of unskilled labor for which they were fit. It is impossible to estimate the money value of this industry ; but the evidence taken by the Morton Committee proves that, without their help, many enterprises now in full operation would not have been attempted when they were much needed. Among these enterprises the Pacific Railroad stands prominent, and one of its leading managers testified that Chinese laborers had given more employment to white laborers than they could otherwise have got, and that the road could not have been completed for many years if these Asiatics had not been available. Over a million acres of tule-lands have been reclaimed, which would otherwise have lain idle to this day. Irrigating canals for farms, with dams and sluices for the mines, all owe their existence to this source. One witness stated that without Chinese aid the population of California could not be maintained at more than one-half its present amount; and in regard to the cultivation of wheat, he assured the Committee that it could not be profitably raised at all if the cost of production were increased. I was told that in September, 1876, about 400,000 bushels were ready for the sickle, and that this crop could not have been moved unless Chinese laborers had been there to put it on board ship at a cheap rate. The only thing to be done with it was to let it rot or burn it. The ramifications of labor are so great that every one must see that it is nearly impossible to separate out one branch from all the others, and that to place the benefits of Chinese labor at a figure like $300,000,000 or $400,000,000 is to deceive one's self as to its true value. It is the way, however, that " we are ruined by cheap Chinese labor."

How fallacious, therefore, are the statements in the

California Senate Address by which its writers try to prove the loss to the country caused by this immigration. They roundly assert that the Chinese laborers make a draft upon the wealth of the nation, take from instead of adding to its substance, and have abstracted from California alone not less than $180,000,000 in gold, while they have contributed nothing to the State or national wealth, and prevent a more desirable class of settlers coming. An estimate is then made that 125,000 male European immigrants would have enriched the State at least $380,000,000, in which total is included the $180,000,000 carried home by the Chinese. In this singular sum in political economy, the capital value of so many European immigrants who had not yet landed in the State is set over against the actual earnings of as many Chinese, not one of whom could have got a cent to carry home until his labor made it and left its equivalent behind him. If, too, they carried it and themselves home, could not the writers see that just so many vacant places were left for the more desirable class? The very reason alleged against the Chinese carrying their earnings home is, therefore, incompatible with the fear expressed by the writers of the unarmed invasion impending from Asia. The impulse which led the immigrants to return should, in fairness, have been stated as a reason why there was little to fear as to their coming in vast numbers. But the one-sidedness of this Address is apparent throughout. If, however, the 125,000 European immigrants who, if the Chinese had never come, would have enriched the State nearly $400,000,000, have helped to enact the new constitution now in force, some of the American inhabitants may think that their presence has not been all clear gain.

The main arguments of those who have denounced the Chinese have been founded a good deal upon partial statements of facts which are not denied, and an exaggeration of evils which have been caused in a good measure by the bad treatment the Chinese have received. An instance of this mode of argument appears in this Address, where it describes the expected "unarmed invasion" which is to overwhelm the Pacific slope, and to resist which the Senatorial Committee calls upon this nation for help:

"Already, to the minds of many, this immigration begins to assume the nature and proportions of a dangerous, unarmed invasion of our soil. Twenty years of increasing Chinese immigration will occupy the entire Pacific coast, to the exclusion of the white population. Many of our people are confident that the whole coast is yet to become a mere colony of China. All the old empires have been conquered by armed invasions; but North and South America and Australia have been wrested from their native inhabitants by peaceable, unarmed invasions. Nor is this fear entirely groundless as to the Pacific coast, for it is in keeping with the principles which govern the changes of modern dynasties and the advance guard is already upon our shores. The immigration which is needed to offset and balance that from China is retarded by the condition of the labor question on this coast, and we have reason to expect that within ten years the Chinese will equal the whites. In view of these facts, thousands of our people are beginning to feel a settled exasperation—a profound sense of dissatisfaction with the situation. Hitherto this feeling has been restrained and the Chinese have had the full protection of our laws. It may be true that at rare intervals acts of violence have been committed towards them; but it is also true that punishment has swiftly followed. Our city criminal courts invariably inflict a severer punishment for offenses committed upon Chinese than for like offenses committed against whites. The people of this State have been more than patient. We are satisfied that the condition of affairs, as they exist in San Francisco, would not be tolerated without a resort to violence in any Eastern city. It is the part of wisdom to anticipate the day when patience may cease, and by wise legislation avert its evils. Impending difficulties of this character should not in this advanced age be left to the chance arbitrament of force. These are questions which ought to be solved by the statesman and philanthropist, and not by the soldier."

It has been by such a mixture of facts, fears, and assertions that much of the ill-will against the Chinese has been fostered. Its influence has probably been greater than that of any other document issued; for it is signed by the Chairman and Secretary of the Committee, and few of its readers have the means of verifying or examining its statements. The single fact, however, that less than 120,000 Chinese, at the highest estimate, even now remain in our borders, indicates the little depth and force of this unarmed invasion.

This Address was fully answered December 8th, 1877, by a Memorial from the Six Companies addressed to the Senate and House of Representatives, containing statements drawn from public documents, and proofs of its inaccuracy, which could not be denied. The amounts of poll and other taxes paid by the Chinese in the State were far beyond the proportion paid by other inhabitants, especially in the miner's tax. Every page of this Memorial bears evidence of the carefulness with which it was written, in view of the scrutiny which would assail its assertions. It has borne the examination; but in the Eastern States it has not been made known as widely as the Address. The contrast between the writers and the objects, arguments, and animus of the two documents is one of the most singular and instructive in the history of the American people. The charges brought against the British Crown by our fathers in the Revolution, detailing the bad treatment experienced by the colonists, did not compare with the injustice and wrongs which have been suffered by the Chinese under the laws of California.

In face of the assertion just quoted from the Address, as to the "severer punishment inflicted upon those who attacked the Chinese," I abridge a sentence or two of the argument of Mr. Bee, spoken before the Morton Committee, in 1876, about a year before the Address was issued :

"I regret exceedingly, Mr. Chairman and gentlemen, to bring to your notice scenes and acts which have transpired upon the streets of San Francisco, which are a disgrace to any and all civilization. No country, no government, I undertake to say, has ever permitted the indignities to be cast upon any race of people that the government and municipality of San Francisco and California have permitted upon this class. I have myself seen one of the Pacific Mail steamships hauled into dock in this city, loaded with 1,000 or 1,500 Chinese. They were put into express wagons, to be taken to the Chinese quarter ; and I have seen them stoned from the time they landed till they reached Kearney Street, leaning out of the wagons with their scalps cut open. I have seen them stoned when going afoot from the vessel. No arrests were made, no police interfered. I do not recollect of ever an arrest being made when the hoodlums and street Arabs attacked these immigrants. I say it with shame, that they have no privileges, and do not seem to have the protection of the laws extended to them in any particular."

This treatment by the hoodlums of that city was corroborated by a clergyman who was giving one reason for the few conversions among the Chinese, and there seems to have been no efforts made by the police to restrain such wrong-doers. The writers of the Memorial, in view of these facts, most justly ask the question:

"Where is your boasted independence, when an agrarian mob dictates what kind of labor you must employ? Where is your boasted freedom of speech, when a daily press dare not discuss both sides of a question or speak a word in favor of an abused and persecuted stranger? Where is that liberty your fathers fought for, that a mob, led by aliens, can undisturbed hold their daily gatherings, and threaten to hang your best citizens, burn their property, and denounce them as thieves? And where does this lawless element look for encouragement, but to that class which occupies a higher political plane, whose exaggerated opinions concerning the Chinese we have quoted."

This memorial also refers to Gov. Irwin's assertion in his message that the Chinaman has had his rights adjudicated in the courts with the same fairness that other immigrants have had theirs; and then asks, What justice was meted out at Antioch, at Truckee, at Rocklin, Penryn, and Secret Ravine, when the property of Chinese was destroyed, they shot down as they tried to escape, and all driven away? They ask if one of the actors in the July riots of 1877 in San Francisco, when their property was destroyed and a Chinese murdered for defending his domicile, and his body thrown into the flames, has ever been punished.

These accusations, charges, rejoinders, etc., all indicate the existence of serious antagonism in the society of the Pacific States. What are their causes? The strength and violence of this antagonism have been fostered by some peculiar circumstances; and, as evils never cure or weaken themselves, we do well to look at their workings in the light of such facts as are before us.

To my own mind, there is no fear of a great or irresistible immigration, and the reasons for its increase are less now than when the country was first opened. Thirty years have passed since the providence of God placed this region under the control of a Protestant nation, and, by disclosing its metallic treasures, after its sovereignty had been secured, attracted a population with such rapidity that California alone of all our States was never a colony or a territory, but arose at once from its military sway to be a fully organized State. That population was so ill assorted, too, that its reckless, lawless elements soon became too strong for the law-abiding portion, and the Vigilance Committee was the only remedy to save the State from anarchy. With hundreds of convicts, escaped from Australia, came hundreds of "moon-eyed Celestials," as the Chinese were called. A greater contrast was hardly ever seen between two classes of immigrants. No power was in the hands of the latter, and they were ere long exposed to discriminating legislation, the object of special laws which taxed away their property without their being allowed any voice in the matter. As soon as a law of the State had declared that a Chinese was an Indian, and its courts affirmed it, he was in reality outlawed. In 1852, Governor Bigler said there was no provision in the Treaty with China how Chinese immigrants should be treated, and that the Chinese Government would have no right to complain of any law excluding them from the country, by taxation or otherwise. This was before the date of the Burlingame Treaty; but while an act of the California legislature could not turn a Chinese into an Indian, any more than an act of Congress could turn a greenback into a piece of gold, it could prevent their evidence being taken in court; it could prevent their fishing or mining, their taking up land or settling on it ; it could prevent their becoming citizens ; and it did expose them, without remedy, to the most unjust treatment.

The summary manner in which the courts in California converted the Chinese into Indians, when it was desired to bring a law to bear against them, has a spice of the grotesque in it. The physiologist Charles Pickering, includes Chinese and Indians among the members of the Mongolian race ; but the Supreme Court there held "that the term Indian included the Chinese or Mongolian race." It thus upheld a wrong, while it enunciated a misconception. It placed the subjects of the oldest government now existing upon a parity with a race that has never risen above tribal relations. It included under one term a people whose literature dates its beginning before the Psalms or the Exodus, written in a languagewhich the judge would not have called Indian, if he had tried to learn it, and containing authors whose words have influenced more human beings than any other writings, with men whose highest attainments in writing have been a few pictures and totems drawn on a buffalo robe. It equalized all the qualities of industry, prudence, skill, learning, invention, and whatever gives security to life and property among mankind, with the instincts and habits of a hunter and a nomad. It stigmatized a people which has taught us how to make porcelain, silk, and gunpowder, given us the compass, shown us the use of tea, and offers us their system of selecting officials by competitive examinations, by classing them with a race which has despised labor, has had no arts, schools, or trade, and in the midst of the Californians themselves were content to dig roots for a living.

The anomalies growing out of our present laws relating to naturalization are such as to allow the authorities in one State of the Union to give the Chinese citizenship within its borders, while those of another State may refuse it. The first has been done in New York, the latter is the rule in California. In 1878, Judge Sawyer of the U. S. Circuit Court for the District of California, rendered a decision on this point, quoting Sect. 2169 of the Revised Statutes of the United States, "that the provisions of this title (33) shall apply to aliens being free white persons, and to aliens of African nativity and to persons of African descent." He decided that Chinese are not by law entitled to naturalization in this country because they are not white persons within the meaning of the statute, and that the intention of Congress was to exclude from naturalization "all but white persons and persons of African nativity and African descent." This decision would, therefore, properly exclude all Malays, Siamese, Burmese, Hindus, and Arabs, but it is an open and doubtful question whether it would exclude all Chinese and Japanese. The Chinese now in this country are more swarthy than their northern countrymen, for they come from just within the tropics; but that people occupy a million and more square miles lying in the temperate zone, and those living in the northern provinces are about as white as Europeans on the same latitude; both are more nearly olive than white. Three times has this question been decided in the courts of California in like manner "that the term *Indian included the Chinese or Mongolian race;*" but it is high time that a question in ethnology and national hue should be examined carefully and settled on some basis before a judicial sentence carries with it such consequences.

When all this was done by those in power, then they declare that the Chinese will not assimilate with us.

Senator Blaine describes the result, after the two races have been living side by side for more than thirty years, as not one step toward it; but he omits to mention the feelings which have flowed from thirty years' ill-treatment, as tending to strengthen the divergence.

Some might reply that this was only a fair return for the opprobrious epithets which their countrymen and rulers have given to all foreigners for hundreds of years and the ill-usage and the restrictions which these epithets indicated; but the times of that ignorance we can well afford to wink at, for they are passing away, and it is quite too late to use such arguments for our vindication. We are now mutually learning that there is far more of worth and promise in each other than either had supposed; and I believe, after forty-three years' intercourse with the lowest and highest classes, that only a wider knowledge is needed to cause a higher appreciation. It is reasonable, therefore, that a different status be given them, and now, that a Chinese legation has been received at Washington, and a Chinese consul accepted for San Francisco, it is suitable that the countrymen of Yung Wing and Seet Mingcook be no longer classed with Sioux and Pawnees.

Their helpless condition before the law in early times in California made them easy victims to violence. It stimulated the robberies, murders, ejections, and assaults which ere long became so barefaced that a member of the legislature at Sacramento used them as an argument for allowing the Chinese to testify in courts, because otherwise white persons would be exposed to similar violence.

"The wretches who committed these atrocities," as the Rev. Dr. Speer, in his valuable work, says, "felt secure under a threefold cover. First, comparatively few of the Chinese could speak English or knew how to obtain justice. In the next place, the officers of justice were too often under the control of the men who committed the offense, nominated and elected by them, and the villains let it be known that they would vote against any man who favored the Chinese. Lastly, these strangers have not been allowed to speak in an American court, and say: This was the man who shot down my brother in cold blood, and robbed his dying body of the gold for which he had been toiling for years, to send it home to make more happy the old age of our parents." Such things as these compelled a change.

One of these three disabilities still lies very much at the root of the whole question—viz., the inability to speak and read the English language. Its natural effect has been to drive the Chinese into closer compact amongst themselves, to strengthen the clannish feelings which would urge each aggrieved person to seek aid against his enemy from those who could hear his complaints, and to make him more thoroughly an alien by the feeling that he had been outraged without the hope of redress. This ignorance was insurmountable in the great portion of the immigrants, for they were too poor to spend their time in learning our language properly, and were too old to talk it intelligibly.

One result, too, was to throw great responsibility on the Six Companies, through whom the immigrants tried and did generally find counsel and aid. These companies have been the objects of more unjust charges, vituperation, and unfounded suspicion than any one can imagine who has not read what has been alleged against them. Yet I do not see how we could have got on, as the case has been, without them. What could have been done, otherwise, with thousands of active, young, and well-disposed men landing at San Francisco, not one of whom could read a word of English, and few of them talk it, yet each man eager to work as soon as he knew where? If the municipality of that city, seeing the facts of the case, had encouraged a few Americans to study the written language, and talk the Cantonese dialect, and had employed them as official interpreters and translators, to inform the immigrants of their duties, privileges, taxes, and other important points, the latter would have been ushered into their new condition with some idea of its requirements. Such a thing seems never to have been thought of as a practical end, and the Chinese were left to be looked after by the Six Companies alone. Whatever the managers of those companies might say respecting their organization, rules, and actual operations toward their countrymen, it seems as if it all went for nothing in the eyes of their detractors. The Address just referred to says, speaking of "our ignorance of the Chinese language," that "the great mass of the Chinese residents of California are not amenable to our laws; but are governed by secret tribunals, unrecognized by law, formed by the several Chinese companies, which are recognized as legitimate authorities by the Chinese population. They levy taxes, command masses of men, intimidate interpreters and witnesses, enforce perjury, regulate trade, punish the refractory, remove witnesses beyond the reach of our courts, control liberty of action, and prevent the return of the Chinese to China without their consent. In short, they exercise a despotic sway over one-seventh of the population of California."

If these allegations are true, it is no credit to a State to allow such things to go on, and plead "our ignorance of the Chinese language" as a reason for not breaking up companies who did them. The writers speak as if the Legislature, which they represented by their committee, had no voice or responsibility in the matter. When, therefore, the companies deny the charges, and assure us that they never had organized or secret tribunals to administer justice in this country, and that many misunderstandings and difficulties they have settled among themselves, in the way of arbitration, we are disposed to believe them. The Rev. Dr. Speer's account of their design, given in Chap. XIX. of his valuable work, called "China and the United States," would have shown these writers how they grew out of the necessities of the case and what has been their practical operation during the past twenty-eight years. He justly calls them "institutions which have no parallel for utility and philanthropy among the immigrants from any other nation or people to our wide shores." Since he wrote his work the wider dispersion of the immigrants and their greater knowledge of English has limited the action of the companies as it has lessened their need.

With all these sources of information open to him, it is somewhat mortifying to read the answer of Mr. Blaine to Senator Matthew's request for his proofs of the manner, degree, and extent to which the Chinese Government is responsible for the establishment of the Six Companies for the purposes of immigration. Mr. Blaine replies:

"That I do not know. The secrets of the Chinese empire are past finding out. I do not know what sort of agency they have from the government. They have some, undoubtedly, and they retain it. They are, in a certain sense, agents of the Chinese Government for the importation of this coolie population."

Mr. Sargent was equally loose in his assertions, and,

like his colleague from Maine, felt that the Treaty was in the way of passing the bill before the Senate. He said:

"The Burlingame Treaty ought to be cut up by the roots, in fact, as all these treaties should be. There is no reciprocity in them. We are allowed to enter but five ports in China. An American traveling in the interior of China has to do it upon a passport, and that is difficult to obtain. The Chinese come here by the hundred thousands, travel over this country, and do as they please. By the Chinese census only five hundred and forty-one Americans are in all China. Our citizens can only go in at certain ports and are impeded in their passage through the country."

A reply to one count in this singular charge, and this statesmanlike reason for cutting up a treaty by the roots, could have been found if he had read the Reed Treaty, where seven open ports are enumerated, and since it was signed in 1858 eleven more have been opened. The passport system was pressed upon the Chinese plenipotentiaries by foreign envoys, as the best means of protecting the natives against reckless foreigners, and the passports are all issued by their own ministers and consuls. I have myself issued many to Americans citizens, and they can go everywhere they please, though in many districts a lawless population makes travel sometimes dangerous to persons not knowing the language; not nearly so dangerous, however, as it used to be for Chinese traveling in California. Once more, the Chinese have never taken a census of foreigners, and why the fact (if it be one) that only five hundred and forty-one Americans are in all China is an argument for abrogating the Treaty needs some clearer explanation.

Honorable Senators who make such random statements do more than merely weaken the arguments deduced from them in support of their cause; and if they had inquired at the Chinese Legation in Washington they could have learned the truth. It may seem to many to be a trifling matter anyway; but the reputation of this Republic for honorable dealing is not a trifling matter to those who now hear me, and this aspersion of the Chinese Government recoils on ourselves if the charges cannot be sustained.

President Woolsey says, in section 18 of his "International Law:"

"The honor or reputation of a State is equally its right; and the injury done by violations of this right will seem very great when we consider the multitudes who suffer in their feelings from a national insult, and the influence of the loss of a good name upon intercourse with other states, as well as upon that self-respect which is an important element in national character."

The real reason why so much has been said about this Treaty, it seems to me, is because the opponents of the Chinese were unwilling to squarely propose a law contrary to all the declarations of the American people as to the asylum they offer to the people of other lands. But the Treaty really has had no perceptible effect on their coming. It merely quotes the inherent right of man to change his home and allegiance—as if it was properly higher than a Treaty stipulation—not so much to qualify it, as a reason for taking measures to prevent its notorious abuses in the coolie trade. The Emperor of China is as helpless to prevent his subjects leaving their native land as Congress and President Hayes together are to keep Americans at home. President Woolsey says: "The right of emigration is inalienable. Only self-imposed or unfulfilled obligations can restrict it." He also shows that a government is no more justified in prohibiting a subject from emigrating, than it would be in prohibiting a foreign sojourner from doing the same. It is an old right, too, for it was inserted in Magna Charta, and claimed then not only for natives, but foreign traders also; and if the Emperor of China is respectable enough among the potentates of the earth for this Government to make a treaty with, why should we hesitate to grant him the rights and courtesies involved in it?

It is plain that the struggle over the Chinese question on the Pacific Coast is only another form of the labor question; and that question is not to be adjusted by the puerile policy of limiting the number of immigrants in one ship from China to 15, while 1,500 may come from Japan, Siam, or any other country. The main features of this question were illustrated by an incident which was reported when I was in San Francisco. A patriotic American employed an Irishman to saw a load of wood for a dollar, and he was soon after seen quietly smoking, as he watched a Chinaman doing the job for twenty-five cents. In this epitome of labor and capital who would blame either of the three parties; or who could restrain them with any justice; or how long would it be before the intermediary smoker became a laborer or a capitalist?

The adoption of the new constitution of California has placed this great issue between capital and labor on a new ground, by making State laws against express treaty stipulations. Politics have also been mixed up with it, for the Chinese in that State are of no value in politics; but the Irish are worth much to those who please them. It is a very high compliment to the former that they have stood such tests during the past years. What other class can show so small a proportion of inmates of the prisons, alms-houses, and other reformatory places? What other class would have submitted to such taxation? The miner's tax, the laundry tax, the fishing tax, the school tax, the immigrant's poll tax, the 500-cubic-feet-of-air-law, the queue ordinance, and that regulating the removal of coffins, are the names of various discriminating State or local acts (probably most of them now repealed), by which the Chinese have been fleeced. It was once even proposed to vaccinate every immigrant, at a charge of $30, in order to protect the State against small-pox! Mr. Bee shows that before the miner's tax was repealed in 1862, it was estimated that it had taken over $31,000,000 out of the earnings of Chinese miners, from whom it had been mostly levied. A recent decision of the United States Supreme Court has awarded $10,000 damages for cutting off the queue of a Chinese by the sheriff, in accordance with the city ordinance. In delivering his opinion in the case, Mr. Justice Field characterizes it as special legislation against a class of persons, being intended only for the Chinese in San Francisco, and avowed to be so by the supervisors there, who urged its adoption and continuance as a means of inducing a Chinaman to pay his fine. He properly adds: "It is not creditable to the humanity and civilization of our people, much less to their Christianity, that an ordinance of this character was possible;" and says further: "It is legislation unworthy of a brave and manly people."

The conduct of these immigrants is, of course, to be judged by their early education and moral training in a heathen land; not absolutely, but in connection with their standards of morals and usages of society. I do not need to describe their personal habits, nor would I extenuate their moral character; their proneness to lying and gambling, or their destructive habit of opium smoking. No doubt hundreds of needy sharpers have landed with the intention of preying upon their thrifty countrymen and living by their wits; but, on the other hand, I can refer to the students now in New England to prove that some can appreciate our civilization and assimilate to our teachings. The reports of various reformatory and penal institutions in California furnish some data for a judgment. Out of 95,000 Chinese in California, 198 were in State-prison in 1877, while 347 whites were there. In twelve years 711 natives of Ireland were committed, and 750 natives of China; but the adult Irish population was only 35,000, or about one-third of the other. In the Industrial School were four Chinese, among 225 others in the year 1875. In the alms-house, out of 498 inmates that year, not one Chinese, but 197 Irish; while in 1878 one Chinese was admitted, and 175 Irish. In the hospital report for 1875, out of 3,918 inmates, only 11 were Chinese and 1,308 Irish; in 1878, out of 3,007 admissions, 948 were Irish and 6 were Chinese. In the pest-house there were 22, none of them Chinese. The arrests for drunkenness in San Francisco alone for the year ending June 30th, 1878, were 6,127, not one of whom was a Chinese. Out of 4,977 deaths in the same place and time, 496 Chinese and 693 Irish are enumerated.

Yet, in face of these figures and facts, which are drawn from public documents, the following conclusions respecting the immigrants are put forth in the Address:

"The evidence demonstrates beyond cavil that nearly the entire immigration consists of the lowest orders of the Chinese people, and mainly of those having no homes or occupations on the land, but living in boats on the rivers, especially those in the vicinity of Canton. It would seem to be a necessary consequence flowing from this class of immigration that a large proportion of criminals should be found among it; and this deduction is abundantly sustained by the facts before us, for of 545 foreign criminals in our State-prison 198 are Chinese, while the jails and reformatories swarm with the lower grade of malefactors."

The singular assertion here made as to the origin of the immigrants—that most of them have no homes or occupations on land, but live in boats near Canton, accounting for their criminality by their locality—is an entire mistake. The fact and the inference are equally out of the way. It would, however, be useless to indicate all such misstatements.

The conduct and condition of these people would, I am sure, have been far worse than these figures indicate, if it had not been for the untiring efforts of Christian men and women around them. These efforts have been going on for nearly thirty years, and only those who have lived in California can appreciate the perseverance, the patience, the care, and the faithfulness shown by many unpaid teachers in Sabbath and evening schools, as well as others belonging to and conducting more regular mission work. Statistics do not convey a just idea of the results of this benevolent work, which has largely been of that preventive and reformatory nature that helps men to be better, and keeps them out of jails and saloons, to the great advantage of society. Coming directly from their native hamlets in Kwangtung across the ocean, into a city where they were the objects of insults and obloquy; unable to talk an intelligible sentence of English, even if they could read their own tongue; not a law of the land translated into it to guide them, they naturally huddled together in their own quarter for safety and society. As they left San Francisco to seek work in the country, these kind friends of whom I speak found them out, and began to teach them English, by telling them the old, old story, which never wears out. They thus became acquainted with the highest truths and the best rules for conduct, while fitting themselves for such work as they could find, by learning to talk and read English. Their teachers felt that God in his providence had brought them to our shores for some other, higher end than merely to be our Gibeonites, and well have they performed their work. While the legislators of California seem to have exhausted their wisdom in divising, from time to time, all the contrivances to tax and fine these people which could be brought to bear on them, their real friends were opening schools and meetings, and showing them wherein the true glory of this land consisted.

Every person who learned even a little of the truths of our holy faith from these benevolent efforts would be all the more likely to prove a good member of society.

If that excellent man, Gov. Seymour, had seen these efforts to teach the Chinese, and their results of a preventive and elevating nature, he would not, I am sure, declare that there has been no assimilation, that the race is alien to our institutions, and that their presence here in small numbers is dangerous. He would have borne in mind that everything had been done to hinder their assimilation, preventing them by law from becoming citizens, and then making them ineligible to enter the schools which would fit them to be citizens, even though they paid taxes for those schools.

The record of these efforts is contained in many reports; but the best digest I have seen of their results is in Rev. Otis Gibson's recent publication issued in Cincinnati, called "Chinese in America," which I can recommend to all who are desirous to learn the truth on this subject. From this book and later sources the following figures have been gathered:

Total average attendance at evening schools for Chinese.....	825
Total roll-call....................................	2,750
In Sunday-schools, average..........................	1,100
Roll-call of Sunday-schools.........................	3,300
Chinese baptized in United States....................	400
Native churches in Presbyterian Mission................	2
Chinese pastors, teachers, and helpers.................	15

A Chinese Young Men's Christian Association exists in San Francisco, with members and branches over the country. The number which has openly ceased from idolatry is not known; but must be over 5,000. The contributions from members for maintaining these efforts are daily increasing. It is perhaps not irrelevant to the general question to add that $12,000 were sent last year by the Chinese on that coast to relieve the sufferers from yellow-fever in the Southern States.

Into the difficult subject of wages I will not enter. So far as I can learn, the unskilled Chinese laborer gets as much on the Pacific coast as his compeer gets on this side for the same work, and the prices of food and clothing there are less. In their cry against Chinese labor the workingmen in California unconsciously put themselves below their competitors in the race of endurance, skill, and value in the battle of progress; while all the advantages of position, power, language, machinery, and priority are on their side. Charges are made that this influx brings with it a flood of vice; but where can we find the laboring community in all that region which has been heathenized by their contact with the Chinese? Have the Mormons or the Irish been made any worse or different from the presence of these people?

Even the recent Congressional Committee, under Mr. Wright's chairmanship, in its visit to California, where it spent four days, found that the labor question was the prominent one connected with this subject. Farmers, tradesmen, mechanics, peddlers, miners, and workmen, all agreed that they could not hold their own against the Chinaman; and, without intending anything of the sort, they bore the strongest testimony in favor of the skill, business capacity, industry, patience, endurance, and frugality of the Chinese.

In fact, it is with their good qualities that most fault seems to be found. Whether these good qualities are so undesirable that immigrants possessing them ought to be excluded from the country is a question not for Congress and the Government alone, which so recently brought us to the doing of a national wrong, but for the common-sense and equity of the people at large. These qualities, therefore, should have their due prominence in our estimate of the bearings of the immigration.

If they find no demand for their labor, no remunera- for their outlay, they will not come. They are not held at home as serfs by feudal barons or great landholders; they are not oppressed there, nor compelled to work in mines, factories, or penitentiaries; they are in no particular danger of starving, from which and other evils they hope to escape by running away to America. China suffers much from the evils of ignorance, poverty, idolatry, licentiousness, cruelty, and unjust administration of laws, and I would not keep back any of their vices. Those now here have, on the whole, I believe, found no reason to regret their venture. In the ease with which they go and come lies one of the benefits they are to derive from mingling with us; and also one of the strong reasons for believing that the immigration will never become an invasion.

I prefer to see the hand of God in the way in which the millions of China and Japan are being gradually brought out of their long seclusion and ignorance into a knowledge of and participation of the benefits existing in Christian lands. Those two kingdoms and our own land cannot keep apart, and our intercourse will prove mutually beneficial, if we only treat their people in the same manner as we ask them to treat us. Mutual wants will beget the desires and means of growing exchanges, and, as we stand now in good relations, we have it in our power to do them lasting benefits.

The laws of California declare that the Chinese are Indians and aliens, and her legislators have treated them as if they had no rights which we were bound to respect. As I believe that the most complete way to settle our chronic difficulties with the Indians is no longer to regard them as aliens and treat them as wards or children, but in every legitimate way to induce and help them to become fit for citizens, so I would set this goal before the Chinese. As soon as they have an adequate knowledge of English and a certain amount of property, give them citizenship, if they desire it. An alien race is properly declared to be dangerous to the State, and the only way to remove or neutralize the danger, therefore, is by making such residents eligible for citizenship. The right to become citizens will stimulate great numbers of the Chinese to fit themselves for it, and there are now about 2,000 of them born in this land who ought not and cannot justly be debarred.

I close this paper by a quotation abridged from Senator Morton's views, written after he had returned from California. It expresses the deliberate opinion of a competent observer on this point:

"The limitation of the right to become naturalized to white persons was placed in the law when slavery was a controlling influence in our Government, was maintained by the power of that institution, and is now retained by the lingering prejudices growing out of it. After having abolished slavery and established equal political rights, without regard to race or color, it would be inconsistent and unsound policy to renew and reassert the prejudices against race by excluding the people of Asia from our shores. It would be to establish a new governmental policy upon the basis of color and a different form of civilization. In California the antipathy to the Mongolian race, though differing in its reasons and circumstances of its exhibition, belongs still to the class of antipathies springing from race and religion. As Americans, standing upon the great doctrines of our polity, and seeking to educate the masses into their belief, and extending equal rights and protection to all races and conditions, we cannot now safely take a new departure, which in another form shall resurrect the odious distinctions which brought upon us a civil war. If the Chinese were white people, though in all other respects what they are, I do not believe that the complaints and warfare made against them would have existed to any great extent. As the law stands, they cannot be naturalized, and I do not know that any proposition has been made to change it. The question is whether they shall be permitted to come here to work or trade, to acquire property or to follow any pursuit. I think they cannot be protected in the Pacific States while remaining in their alien condition. Without representation in the legislature or Congress, without a voice in the selection of officers, surrounded by fierce and in many respects unscrupulous enemies, the law will be found insufficient to screen them from persecution. Complete protection can be given them only by allowing them to become citizens and acquire the right of suffrage. Then their votes would become important and their persecutors in great part converted into kindly solicitors. In considering any proposition to prohibit Chinese immigration, we have to remember that they come entirely from the British port of Hongkong. Our refusal to permit a Chinaman to land, who had embarked at a British port upon a British vessel, would be a question with the British Government, and not the Chinese. The fact that he was a Chinaman, who had never sworn allegiance to that Government, would not change the question."

His short sojourn in California did not afford Senator Morton opportunity to study all the points in the Chinese question, and the underlying one of difference of language is quite left out in this view. Time alone can remove much of the trouble by raising up Chinese who can easily teach their countrymen English enough to get along, as they teach them other things. The question which asks for solution now is: How can we remove the present irritation? Considering how the Chinese have been treated, it is creditable to them that they have given so little provocation or resistance to law. The facts prove that they have been a benefit to the Pacific States, with all the drawbacks alleged against their presénce. I can see no more effectual way to remove strife than to remove legal disabilities, treat them as we do other immigrants, and defend them, if need be, in the possession of rights guaranteed them by treaty.

Yale College,

New Haven. February 21st, 1879.

To His Excellency RUTHERFORD B. HAYES,

President of the United States:

SIR,—The members of the Faculty of Yale College are induced to address you in consequence of the passage of a Bill by Congress limiting the number of Chinese who can legally land from any one vessel in the United States to fifteen persons. The bearings of this Bill upon the relations of this country to the Government of China and upon our national honor, and its results upon the position of hundreds of our countrymen living in China, are matters of the deepest moment.

We are not able to judge of the accuracy or pertinence of all the statements, and the arguments based on them by the speakers in support of their votes for the Bill, but the discrepancies are so wide that it is difficult for us to accept the conclusion that it is best thus to shut our doors, or annul a treaty. It is needless here to discuss the stipulations of the treaty of 1868. They not only permitted but encouraged the Chinese to come to our shores by declaring that it is an inalienable right of every man to change his home and allegiance, thus placing this permission to immigrate on a higher plane than a treaty right. This treaty is the only one in our national records containing such a declaration, and was negotiated when the number of Chinese in the country was probably two-thirds as many as at present. It did not cause those people to come, nor did it greatly stimulate them to leave their own land; for they come and go from their own shores just as freely as Americans do from theirs.

The total immigration during the past 25 years on the Pacific coast has, however, not left such a surplus as to make it evident that their number is now so great and threatening as to call for thus suddenly annulling this treaty stipulation to save ourselves from imminent danger arising from these immigrants. It was negotiated and signed by the respective Plenipotentiaries, and then ratified by the Senate before it was even submitted formally to the Government of China for consideration and ratification; but the Emperor affixed his seal without demur.

The evils of this influx of a few myriads of laborers to the Pacific States are said to be great, and the Report offered in the House of Representatives on the 14th of last month, enumerates many prospective calamities and disadvantages if they increase, but it is vague and reticent on the evils actually suffered. The recorded testimony proves, moreover, that the immigration has brought with it many real and acknowledged benefits to all that region, and that future evils are likely to be similarly balanced. We do not compare the harsh treatment sometimes experienced by these aliens in past years, with the different treatment of Americans living in China since the treaty of 1844, for the facts are open to all. That treaty contained the principle of ex-territoriality by which the right of governing our own citizens living in China was confirmed to their own Goverment, to be exercised entirely by its own officers also living there.

Cyrus Northrop
Simeon E Baldwin
Addison Van Name
Franklin B. Dexter
E. L. Richards
I. T. Beckwith
L. J. Sandford
E. S. Dana
D. C. Eaton
James K Thacher
Henry A Beers
John P. Peters
Theodore S. Woolsey
Frank B. Tarbell
William Beebe
A W Phillips
Henry W Farnam
Edward D Robbins
B. Perrin
Henry P Wright

Note. This letter was circulated in three separate copies by as many students, on the afternoon of the 21st; but every member of the Faculty could not be found, and three declined to sign it. The names were all copied on one printed sheet, & it was sent to Mr. Hayes in the evening. by

S W W

If this Bill becomes an Act, some results may ensue which should be considered. The privilege of self-government depends at present upon the sanctity and stipulations of the treaty of 1858. The Chinese Government has never shown any intention to abrogate those treaties forced from it by western nations, though its authorities chafe under the confessed disabilities it places them in regard to complete jurisdiction on their own soil. Therefore, if the first step be taken by our Government in changing treaty stipulations, we furnish the other party with all the example and argument needed, according to the usages of international law, to justify it in abrogating this principle of ex-territoriality. To do so will throw out our countrymen living in China from the protection of our laws, and neutralize consular interference in upholding them, thereby turning the residents over to the provisions of Chinese law, and the usages of Chinese Courts administered by ignorant or prejudiced officials.

Many of these our fellow-citizens live in districts remote from the open ports, and are engaged in benevolent works of various kinds among the people. Much of their success has been owing to the feeling of security which these treaty rights have thrown over them in their distant homes, and were recognized by the local rulers. Under ~~the operation of this treaty,~~ natives who have attacked our countrymen have been punished, some capitally, and indemnity made for property destroyed. To approve this Act will give them the excuse to cancel what irks them, though we do not presume to say how soon or how far those results will follow.

In addition to these reasons for withholding your approval, we add one which is local, and has had its influence in presenting this letter. The Chinese Educational Commission located in this State is an experiment of a graduate of this University. Its object is to extend, under the sanction and with the funds of his own Government, the knowledge which he obtained years ago. His enterprise has thus far proved successful, and he hopes that these students will return home qualified to become benefactors to their countrymen. Some have entered this college, and others are preparing to do so. We know that an amendment to the Bill makes an exception to others who may desire to gain a like education in this land. Yet to require that young persons from China, seeking to obtain those means of improvement here, shall be compelled to ask their own Emperor to grant them a certificate which has never been thought of in respect to any other nation or people, Christian or pagan, civilized or barbarous, is to place ourselves in a very humiliating and invidious position. Such Chinese as may wish to learn the science and polity of the West are not likely thus to lower themselves, when every other land is freely open to them.

We do not refer to other reasons for this request, derived from the repeated declarations of the American people respecting the freedom of their shores to all nationalities. We will not discuss the well-known laws of supply and demand, influencing labor and wages, which have already begun to show their power to restrain this inflow of laborers. Nor will we bring forward the adverse effects such a Bill may have upon the great and growing commerce and intercourse still to arise between the nations on the shores of the Pacific Ocean, for these points must in some measure be all familiar to you. But we do, in conclusion, adduce the highest considerations, drawn from the value of a nation's honor and good faith, and from the relative power, knowledge and civilization of the two countries now in question, giving the preponderance to the United States in all possible contingencies, for your thought in deciding this question.

In view of them all, we again earnestly and respectfully request you to withhold your approval of this Bill.

Signed by

Noah Porter

Theodore D Woolsey, Trustee of Yale College

James D Dana

Franklin Carter

James M Hoppin

Francis Wayland

Lewis R. Packard

Edward B. Coe

George P. Fisher

W. A. Norton

C. S. Lyman

Leonard Bacon

W. G. Sumner

Geo. J. Brush

Francis A Walker

S. W. Johnson

W H Carmalt

William M Barbour

George E Day

Samuel Harris

Sidney I. Smith

John F Weir

I R Lounsbury

J. J. Skinner

Johnson T Platt

Timothy Dwight

H. A. Newton

Thomas A Thacher

S. Wells Williams

G W Wright

送上書目開列

計　開

第壹箱
淵鑑類函　二十函一百四十本
全唐詩　十五函一百二十本
瀛寰誌畧　一函十本
同善錄　二函二十本
四庫簡明目錄　二函十二本
平定髮匪　一函十本
段氏說文　一函四本
春秋列國　二函二十四本
以上八套計三百四十本

第貳箱
四書五經　八函四十本
文選　三函十八本
知不足齋　二十五函二百本
佩文詩韻　一函四本
登壇必究　六函三十六本
欽定左傳　二函十本
日知錄　二函十六本
韓昌黎集　二函六本
隨園尺牘　一函四本
則古齋算學　一函六本
以上十套計三百四十本

第叁箱
水滸　二函二十本
晒書亭集　一函八本
古今詩選　兩函十六本
漢隸字源　一函六本
資治通鑑　十七函一百七十本
子史精華　四函四十本
小酉腴山房　一函四本
小學集解　一函四本
段氏說文　二函十六本
以上九套計三百八十四本

第肆箱
歷象考成　四函四十二本
十三經注疏　百二十二本
四書集註　一函四本
胡文忠集　一函八本
三國志　二函八本
前漢書　四函十六本
後漢書　四函十六本
以上七套計二百一十六本

合共一千二百八十本

經 1 周易詳註 十卷 魏王弼撰 係詳解易經文義（易係河圖理數發言消長之理進退存亡之道）

X 易圖說 三卷 宋吳仁傑撰 係說八卦圖象

書經 2 書經體註 六卷 国朝人撰 係註解書經文義（係唐虞夏殷周修己治人之事）

3 九州山水考 三卷 国朝孫承澤撰 係考據書經内九州山水原委

詩經 4 毛詩正義 四十卷 漢朝毛萇撰 係註明詩經文義（係周朝各国人所作以驗風俗人情之厚薄）

4 詩地理考 六卷 宋王應麟撰 係考究詩内之山河土名

4 毛詩鳥獸草木考 二十卷 明吳雨撰 係考據禽獸草木之名識

禮經 5 周禮詳解 四十卷 宋王昭禹撰 係詳解周公所作之禮文（係周朝周公所作以辨上下定民志者）

5 禮記集說 一百六十卷 宋衛湜撰 係說明孔子弟子所記曲禮之意義

春秋 6 春秋左傳杜林詳註 十二卷 国朝杜林撰 係詳註孔子所作之春秋左氏所作之傳（係孔子所作以正名定分寓褒貶忠奸）

孝經 7 孝經正義 三卷 唐元宗明皇帝御 係教人孝行

8 七經精義 十二卷 国朝人撰 係總撮詩書易周禮禮記春秋孝經之文義

9 四書撮言 十二卷 国朝人撰 係撮講孔孟教人傳世之書文義

10 孔子家語 十卷 魏王肅註 係記孔子平日居家雜事 訂

11 史記 一百三十卷 漢朝司馬遷撰 係唐虞夏殷周秦漢記事之書

12 國語 二十一卷 吳韋昭注 係周朝列国記事之書

13 十七史詳節 二百七十三卷 宋呂祖謙撰
綱鑑易知 一百一十二卷 国朝吳楚材等撰
二書係記歷代正統僭竊暨良奸侵廢與存亡事

14 大清一統志 五百卷 係中国地輿全書

15 文獻通考 三百四十八卷 元馬端臨撰 係考中外風土人情政刑要之書

17 大清律例 四十七卷 係國朝刑罰科條

18 駁案新編 十卷 係国朝翻駁各様詞訟案書
百條金鑑 十二卷 国朝牛天宿撰 係仕宦品秩立朝規矩書
19 武備志 三百八十四卷 係用兵戰守全書

20 性理大全 十七卷 係儒家說心性之學
朱子讀書法 四卷 係教人讀書之要法
21 農政全書 六十卷 明徐光啟撰 係教民耕種要書

22 本草綱目 約有四十餘卷 係醫家用藥治病書
新法算書 一百卷 明徐光啟及西洋人龍華民等撰 係推算天文書

欽定協紀 六十四卷 係擇日書
卜法詳考 四卷 国朝胡煦撰 係卜已往未來之書
樂曲 三十六卷 明黃佐撰 係作樂用
舞志 十二卷 明張敉撰 係誌干羽舞列之事

23 琴譜大全 十卷 明楊表正撰 係說彈琴調法

居家雜用

24 康熙字典 四十二卷 欽定 係每字審音較畫詳註典據
25 御定佩文韻府 四百四十四卷 係分韻詳註古典故事書
26 山海經廣註 十八卷 国朝吳任臣撰 係記中外山水人物書

御定全唐詩 九百卷 係唐朝詩人所吟之詩
歷代詩話 八十卷 国朝吳景旭撰 係編歷代名人詩
酒邊詞 二卷 宋向子諲撰 係詞曲
山中白雲詞 八卷 宋張炎撰 係詞曲書

古文分編 三十五卷 国朝人撰 係編註歷代名人文章
27 列國 三十卷 係周戰国征伐存亡事
三國志 三十五卷 晉陳壽撰 係記後漢三国爭戰書
說唐 十卷 係記唐朝本末書

30 今古奇觀 四卷 係說古今奇怪雜事
31 聊齋 三十四卷 係笑弄借虛雜說
西廂 二十六卷 係幽閒寄情雜說
致富奇書 四卷 陶朱公撰 係栽種畜養雜說

32 智囊 十卷 係編靈敏雜事

33 搜神記 二十卷 晉干寶撰 係註鬼神証據

朱子家訓 二卷 係說教訓家人之事

35 風俗通義 十卷附錄一卷 漢應劭撰 係編各風土世情事

飲食須知 八卷 元賈銘撰 係飲食雜說

茶經 三卷 唐陸羽撰 係說所飲的茶事

北山酒經 三卷 宋朱翼中撰 係說飲酒書

芥子園 四卷 係山水人物花卉畫圖

朝野僉載 六卷 唐張鷟撰 係說朝廷草野雜事

35 銘心寶鑑 二卷 係教人修行雜說

談徵 八卷 係說閒談俗語中之經義

36 故事尋源 四卷

37 爾雅

29 十才子 全

38 成語考註 二卷

42 55
206

三字經 千字文

41 狀元幼學詩

42 道德真經註 4

43 釋氏稽古略 4

39 大清會典

40 瀛環志畧 徐繼畬撰

45 神仙傳 十卷 晉葛洪撰

44 莊子解 三十卷 國朝吳世尚撰

46 耕織圖詩 一卷 宋樓璹撰

Memorandum of Agreement,

DATED, June 15th 1882

BETWEEN

S. Wells Williams LL.D.

AND

CHARLES SCRIBNER'S SONS,

FOR THE PUBLICATION OF

"The Middle Kingdom"

Memorandum of Agreement, *made this* Fifteenth *Day of* June 1882
between S. Wells Williams LLD.
of New Haven, Conn.
and CHARLES SCRIBNER'S SONS, *Publishers, of New York City.*

Said S. Wells Williams *being the author and proprietor of a work entitled:* "The Middle Kingdom" *in consideration of the covenants and stipulations hereinafter contained, agreed to be performed by said* CHARLES SCRIBNER'S SONS, *grants and guarantees to* CHARLES SCRIBNER'S SONS *the exclusive right to publish said work during the terms of copyright and renewals thereof, hereby covenanting with said* CHARLES SCRIBNER'S SONS *that he is the sole author and proprietor of said work.*

Said S. Wells Williams *further guarantees to said* CHARLES SCRIBNER'S SONS *that the said work is in no way whatever a violation of any copyright belonging to any other party, and that it contains nothing of a scandalous or libelous character; and that he and* his *legal representatives shall and will hold harmless the said* CHARLES SCRIBNER'S SONS *from all suits, and all manner of claims and proceedings which may be taken on the ground that said work is such violation or contains anything scandalous or libelous; and he further hereby authorizes said* CHARLES SCRIBNER'S SONS *to defend at law any and all suits and proceedings which may be taken or had against* CHARLES SCRIBNER'S SONS *for infringement of any other copyright or for libel, scandal, or any other injurious or hurtful matter or thing contained in or alleged or claimed to be contained in or caused by said work, and to pay to said* CHARLES SCRIBNER'S SONS *such reasonable costs, disbursements, expenses, and counsel fees as they may incur in such defense.*

Said CHARLES SCRIBNER'S SONS, *in consideration of the right herein granted and of the guarantees aforesaid, agree to publish said work at their own expense, in such style and manner as they shall deem most expedient, and to pay said* S. Wells Williams *or* his *legal representatives,* ten *per cent. on their Trade-List (retail) price, cloth style, for all copies of said work sold by them* ~~*after the sale of*~~ ~~*copies.*~~ Provided, *nevertheless, that no percentage whatever shall be paid on any copies destroyed by fire or water, or sold at or below cost, or given away for the purpose of aiding the sale of said work.*

Expenses incurred for alterations in type or plates, exceeding ten per cent. of cost of composition and stereotyping or electrotyping said work, are to be charged to the author's account.

Statements to be rendered semi-annually, on the author's application therefor, in the months of February and August, and settlements to be made in cash, four months after date of statement. The first statement shall not be rendered until six months after date of publication.

If, on the expiration of five *years from date of publication, or at any time thereafter, the demand for said work should not, in the opinion of said* CHARLES SCRIBNER'S SONS, *be sufficient to render its publication profitable, then this contract shall cease and determine; and thereupon said* S. Wells Williams *shall have the right, at his option, to take from said* CHARLES SCRIBNER'S SONS, *at cost, the stereotype plates and engravings (if any) of said work, and whatever copies they may then have on hand; or, failing to take said plates and copies at cost, then said* CHARLES SCRIBNER'S SONS *shall have the right to dispose of the copies on hand as they may see fit, free of any percentage or royalty, to melt up the plates, and to cancel this contract.*

Provided, *also, that if, at any time during the continuance of this agreement, said work shall become unsalable in the ordinary channels of trade, said* CHARLES SCRIBNER'S SONS *shall have the right to dispose of any copies on hand, paying to said* S. Wells Williams ten *per cent of the net amount received therefor, in lieu of the percentage hereinbefore prescribed.*

It is understood and agreed that the ownership of the illustrations and map used in the said work shall vest in the said Charles Scribner's Sons; but no construction of this clause shall permit said Charles Scribner's Sons to sell separate copies or impressions of the said map, except upon the payment to the said S. Wells Williams of a royalty of ten per cent. of the retail price of every copy or impression so separately sold.

In consideration of the mutuality of this contract, the aforesaid parties agree to all its provisions, and in testimony thereof affix their signatures and seals.

Witness to signature of S. Wells Williams
C. W. McIlvaine

S. Wells Williams

Witness to signature of Charles Scribner's Sons
E. L. Burlingame

Charles Scribner's Sons

ministered the affairs of his prefecture in one of the most civilized parts of the country, without he both spoke and read Chinese, as well as Mongolian. At the end of 24 years, they returned home by way of southern Asia, so completely altered that their friends and countrymen did not know them; and the three Poles had some difficulty to convince them, that though long absent, they had at last really returned. The story is commonly related that they determined, by a public display, to satisfy their countrymen as to the happy results of their journey. "All their relations and acquaintances were invited to a magnificent feast. They then presented themselves in splendid dresses, first of crimson satin, next of damask, and lastly of velvet, bearing the same color, which they successively threw off and distributed among the company. Returning in their ordinary attire, Marco produced the rags in which they had all been disguised, ripped them open, and exhibited such a profusion of diamonds, rubies, sapphires, and precious jewels, as completely dazzled the spectators. On the news of their wealth and adventures, persons of all ranks, ages, and professions, flocked to the house with congratulations and inquiries. Marco, whose society was courted by all the distinguished youths, stood forth as principal orator. Having often occasion, in his enumerations of people and treasure, to repeat the term *million*, then not common in Europe, the name of Messer Marco Milliono was applied to him, first in jest, but after in reality." His travels were translated into the languages of Europe soon after their appearance, and the various editions and versions contain many discrepancies, variations and additions, which have exercised the ingenuity of commentators to explain and compare. The title of Herodotus of the Middle Ages has been applied to him, and Ritter says, "if the name of Discoverer of Asia were to be assigned to any person, nobody would better deserve it."

On reaching Venice, by way of India & Persia, the long lost were so completely altered that their friends & countrymen did not know them. Their wealth & entertaining recitals, however, soon restored them to the highest ranks of society, & the industry of the recent editors has probably brought together all that can be learned of their subsequent history.

In 1254, Haitho or Hayton, king of Little Armenia, undertook a journey to the grand khan, Mangu, to petition for an abatement of the tribute which he had been obliged to pay the Mongols. He had no opportunity to see much of the Chinese, and gives the same account of the haughty [illegible] held by the court and camp of the khan, which Carpini does.

Having first sent forth his brother Sempad or Sinibald (in 1246) to Kuyuk Khan, Hayton himself set out upon the accession of his successor. Passing through Kars & Armenia Proper to the Volga he was there received by Batu & forwarded by a route, to the north of that passed by Carpini, to Karakorum & the Grand Khan. At the end of a six weeks' sojourn with the court, during which time he appears to have been kindly received, Hayton commenced his homeward journey via Bishbalig & Tsungaria, to Samarkand, Bokhara, Khorasan & thence to Tabriz. The accounts of these two embassies, wherein are described many wonderful things concerning the heathens of the east & barbarians upon the route, made up, doubtless, a large part of the *History* (written in 1307) by the king's relative Hayton of Gorigos.*

The different positions held by these men and the Polos, led them naturally to look upon the same people and events with very different feelings. The efforts of

(naturally led each of them)

---

* The chapter on Cathay appears in Yule's *Cathay* p. cxcv. A translation of the elder Hayton's narrative is given by Klaproth in the *Journal Asiatique*. II Series. tome XII. p. 273 ff.

speaking of the Portuguese, "was not calculated to impress the Chinese with any favorable idea of Europeans; and when, in the course of time, they came to be competitors with the Dutch and the English, the contests of mercantile avarice tended to place them all in a still worse point of view. To this day, the character of Europeans is represented as that of a race of men intent alone on the gains of commercial traffic, and regardless altogether of the means of attainment. Struck by the perpetual hostilities which existed among these foreign adventurers, assimilated in other respects by a close resemblance in their costumes and manners, the government of the country became disposed to treat them with a degree of jealousy and exclusion which it had not deemed necessary to be exercised towards the more peaceable and well ordered Arabs, their predecessors." ~~Medhurst~~ #

These characteristics of avarice and power have been the leading traits in the Chinese estimate of foreigners from their first acquaintance with them, and foreigners themselves have done nothing to effectually disabuse them. The following record of their first arrival, taken from a Chinese work, is still good authority, in the opinion of the natives. "During the reign of Chingtih (1506), foreigners from the west, called Fah-lan-ki (or Franks), who said they had tribute, abruptly entered the Bogue, and by their tremendously loud guns, shook the place far and near. This was reported at court, and an order returned to drive them away immediately, and stop the trade. At about this time also, the Hollanders, who in ancient times inhabited a wild territory, and had no intercourse with China, came to Macao in two or three large ships. Their clothes and their hair were red; their bodies tall; they had blue eyes, sunk deep in their head. Their feet were one cubit and two tenths long; and they frightened the people by their strange appearance." The term *Hung-mao* or "red-haired," then applied to the Dutch, has since been transferred to the English.

The Portuguese Rafael Perestrello sailed in a junk for China in 1516, five years after the conquest of Malacca, and was the first person who ever conducted a vessel to China, under a European flag. Ferdinand Andrade came the next year, in four Portuguese and four Malay vessels, and gave great satisfaction to the authorities at Canton by his fair dealings; his ships were allowed to anchor at Sanchuen, or St. John's Island. His brother Simon

The Chinese vol. i. p. 20.

Before entering upon what may be termed the modern period of our knowledge of China, it remains to notice the overland journey of the Jesuit Goës, "who in seeking Cathay found heaven." Born on one of the Azore Islands in 1561, Benedict Goës [lawlessness,] spent his youth in the profession of a soldier on board of the Portuguese fleet. Becoming suddenly converted, he entered the service of the Jesuits as a lay brother — which modest position he resolutely held during the rest of his career — and was sent to the court of Akbar. His residence in India gained him a high reputation for courage, judgement & skill in the Persian tongue — the *lingua franca* of Asia at that date. He was selected therefore, to undertake a journey to the Cathay of Marco [Rome] Polo, in the Capital of which Jerome Xavier thought he had hopes of finding the Christian ruler & descendant of Prester John. Goës set out from Agra in 1602, joined a company of merchants, and with them took a route passing Kabul, the Hindu Kush, along the river Oxus to its headwaters on the Pamir table-land & so to Yanghi-hissar, Yarkand, Aksu & Suchau, where he was detained seventeen months and finally died, shortly after assistance had been sent him from the mission in Peking. The journey was full of hard-ships but the information concerning the unknown regions of Central Asia must have been priceless could we have Goës's own narrative of his experience. His journals, however, were either [torn or] destroyed during his miserable detention in Suchau, & nothing remained save a few meagre notes & his faithful Armenian servant Isaac, whose language no one at Peking could understand. Such as it was an account was compiled [from these sources] ~~[illegible]~~ by Ricci himself, & published after his death in the work of Trigautius, *De Christ. Exped. apud Sinas.* A translation of this notice appears in Col. Yule's oft-quoted volume, "Cathay & the Way Thither."

THE MIDDLE KINGDOM

A SURVEY of the GEOGRAPHY, GOVERNMENT, LITERATURE. SOCIAL LIFE, ARTS, and HISTORY of the CHINESE EMPIRE and its INHABITANTS

By S. WELLS WILLIAMS, LL.D.

Two Vols. 8vo. With many Illustrations, and
A NEW MAP OF THE EMPIRE

Charles Scribner's Sons · New York

The opening of the Chinese ports and the entrance of foreign envoys have resulted in throwing the fullest light upon the history and condition of the Chinese, and Dr. Williams has availed himself of the information contained in the writings of all who have treated of China, but his own experience and the resources afforded by his vast and minute knowledge of Chinese literature, and his wide acquaintance with prominent Chinese officials and statesmen have enabled him to treat more fully and with greater accuracy the large variety of topics to which his book relates than anyone else could.

This new issue is practically a new book. The text of the old edition has been almost entirely rewritten and the work has been largely expanded so as to include the new material collected by Dr. Williams during the later years of his residence in China, as well as the most recent information respecting all the departments of the Empire. Many new illustrations have been added and the best of the old engravings have been retained. An important feature of the edition is a large map of the Chinese Empire from the best modern authorities, more complete and accurate than any map of the country hitherto published.

The wonderful advance in the arts of civilization and intellectual development made by China during the thirty-five years since this book was first written, and especially the new basis upon which its foreign relations have been established and the events that are even now occurring in this connection, together with the recent immigration of Chinese to this country, render the publication of this revised edition unusually important.

(*Specimen Page.*)

North of the Imperial City lies the extensive *yamun* of the *Ti-tuh,* who has the police and garrison of the city under his control, and exercises great authority in its civil administration. The Drum and Bell Towers stand north of the *Ti-ngan Măn* in the street leading to the city wall, each of them over a hundred feet high, and forming conspicuous objects; the drum and bell are sounded at night watches, and can be heard throughout the city; a clepsydra is still maintained to mark time—a good

Portal of Confucian Temple, Peking

instance of Chinese conservatism, for clocks are now in general use, and correct the errors of the clepsydra itself.

Outside of the south-western angle of the Imperial City stands the Mohammedan mosque, and a large number of Turks whose ancestors were brought from Turkestan about a century ago live in its vicinity; this quarter is consequently the chief resort of Moslems who come to the capital. South-west of the mosque, near the cross-wall, stands the *Nan Tang,* or old Por-

BOOKS TO BE PUBLISHED

Wednesday, October 3d, 1883,

BY

Charles Scribner's Sons, Publishers,

743 AND 745 BROADWAY, NEW YORK.

EARLY ORDERS SOLICITED.

Number of Copies Wanted.

The Middle Kingdom.

A SURVEY OF THE GEOGRAPHY, GOVERNMENT, LITERATURE, SOCIAL LIFE, ARTS AND HISTORY OF THE CHINESE EMPIRE AND ITS INHABITANTS. WITH ILLUSTRATIONS AND A NEW MAP OF THE EMPIRE. BY S. WELLS WILLIAMS, LL.D., PROFESSOR OF THE CHINESE LANGUAGE AND LITERATURE AT YALE COLLEGE; AUTHOR OF TONIC AND SYLLABIC DICTIONARIES OF THE CHINESE LANGUAGE. 2 vols., 8vo. $9.00.

The wonderful advance in the arts of civilization and intellectual development made by China during the thirty-five years since this book was first written, and especially the new basis upon which its foreign relations have been established and the events that are even now occurring in this connection, render the publication of this revised edition unusually important.

Dr. S. Wells Williams' "Middle Kingdom" has long occupied the position of a classic. It is not only the fullest and most authoritative account of the Chinese and their country that exists, but it is also the most readable and entertaining. This new issue is practically a new book. The text of the old edition has been largely rewritten and the work has been expanded so as to include a vast amount of new material collected by Dr. Williams during the later years of his residence in China, as well as the most recent information respecting all the departments of the Empire. Many new illustrations have been added and the best of the old engravings have been retained. An important feature of the edition is a large map of the Chinese Empire from the best modern authorities, more complete and accurate than any map of the country hitherto published.

We may well believe that in that last appalling experience, Margaret gave way to the apathy of despair. She had striven so long, so determinedly, against the trials and disappointments which were strangely frequent and poignant in her life, that now, when, with the shores of her native land in sight, and home, mother and friends so near, the horrors of shipwreck came upon her, she whispered to her soul in the awful agony, "It is enough. Let me depart with my loved ones, and be at peace."

We cannot do better in closing this fragmentary review of the latest tribute to the memory of a great genius, perhaps the greatest born among American women, than to repeat the paragraph with which Mrs. Howe concludes her portrayal of the final scene:

"Death gives an unexpected completeness to the view of individual character. The secret of a noble life is only fully unfolded when its outward envelope has met the fate of all things perishable. And so the mournful tragedy just recounted set a seal upon a career whose endeavor and achievement the world is bound to hold dear. When all that could be known of Margaret was known, it became evident that there was nothing of her which was not heroic in intention; nothing which, truly interpreted, could turn attention from a brilliant exterior to meaner traits allowed and concealed. That she had faults we need not deny; nor that, like other human beings, she needs must have said and done at times what she might afterwards have wished to have better said, better done. But as an example of one who, gifted with great powers, aspired only to their noblest use; who, able to rule, sought rather to counsel and to help,—she deserves a place in the highest niche of her country's affection. As a woman who believed in women, her word is still an evangel of hope and inspiration to her sex. Her heart belonged to all of God's creatures, and most to what is noblest in them. Gray-headed men of to-day, the happy companions of her youth, grow young again while they speak of her. One of these, James Freeman Clarke, who is also one of her earlier biographers, still recalls her as the greatest soul he ever knew. Such a word, spoken with the weight of ripe wisdom and long experience, may fitly indicate to posterity the honor and reverence which belong to the memory of Margaret Fuller."

SARA A. HUBBARD.

CHINA.*

China is the enigma of the world. Its language, its literature, its government, its religious vacuities, the manners and customs of its people in all the details of common and of special observances, in food, clothing, and labor, in agriculture and in arts, the whole fibre and texture of the Chinese brain, the nature and flavor of Chinese thought, and the sources, extent, and drift of Chinese development, all are entirely unlike and opposite to the corresponding items as found in western horizons. The western mind seems to comprehend and understand the conditions of life in the central flowery kingdom about as inadequately as the Chinaman understands the condition of life among the outside barbarians.

For this reason it is difficult to write about China, since the writer will find it hard to assure himself or to persuade others that his vision is free from subjective color. For the reader the same difficulty remains. The more perfect the picture, the farther is it removed from the experiences and the consequent appreciation of the western mind.

The first marvel appears in the antiquity and endurance of the Chinese nation. What is the nature of that vital force which has kept China a unified, consolidated, healthy, and, in its own slow way, a progressive people for more than forty centuries? Allowing for the uncertainties that are inseparable from history which dates to periods so remote, and setting entirely aside the accounts of earlier mythological ages that are doubtless fictions, the beginnings of Chinese chronology date to B.C. 2852, or possibly farther back. The date given is that of the accession of Fuh-hí, which is thus placed 4735 years before the present year of grace. Its relation to other chronologies will be better understood if we say that it makes this ruler a contemporary with Noah in his declining years, and antedates the confusion of tongues by about three centuries and the birth of Abraham by about seven hundred years. From that remote period to the present, China has maintained a continuous autonomy. Dynasties have changed. The Huns, Tartars, Mongols, and Manchus have, at different times, obtained power, and their dynasties have possessed the throne; but China has remained China through all. If conquered, she has still absorbed and assimilated her conquerors. Her life has not been simply a vegetation, but has been vigorous and active. Her long intervals of peaceful progress have been separated by sharp and sanguinary conflicts, wars with neighboring hordes, and struggles for supremacy between opposing factions. Contrasted with this perennial kingdom, recall the long line of empires that in the west arose, blazed with meteoric splendor, and vanished: Egypt, Greece, Media, Nineveh, Babylon, India, Rome, Carthage, the Saracens, and the Empires of Mahomet, Charlemagne, and Napoleon. During this epoch, western civilization

* THE MIDDLE KINGDOM. A Survey of the Geography, Government, Literature, Social Life, Arts, and History of the Chinese Empire and its Inhabitants. By S. Wells Williams, LL.D., Professor of the Chinese Language and Literature at Yale College. Revised Edition, with Illustrations, and a new Map of the Empire. In Two Volumes. New York: Charles Scribner's Sons.

has had its periods of magnificent development in Egypt, Greece, and Rome, and in Western Europe since the seventeenth century, interspersed with periods of long and sad depression and destruction. Chinese civilization, of a feebler type indeed, yet more equable in its growth and strength, has shown through all its centuries of life a continuous and persistent development.

Counting from the accession of Fuh-hí, the succession of Chinese monarchs includes two hundred and forty-six rulers in twenty-six dynasties. Prominent in the long line stands the Emperor Chi Hwangti, of the Tsin dynasty, which took its name from the province Tsin, whose prince had wrenched the throne from its rightful occupant. This emperor divided his realm into thirty-six provinces, in which he appointed governors for the better administration of justice; built and adorned a magnificent capital; opened roads and canals; drove out the marauding Huns, and to keep them out conceived the idea of uniting some short walls already built into the Great Wall along the northern frontier. For the work the various communities were required to furnish men, and to provide food and clothing until the quota of each was finished. The wall is of such material as the vicinity could afford, mostly earth cased with bricks. It is about twenty-five feet thick at the base, fifteen feet at the top, and from fifteen to thirty feet high. It stretches away over plains, gorges, streams, cliffs, and mountain summits—in one place surmounting a peak more than 5,000 feet high—a continuous rampart whose total length of nearly 1,500 miles would reach from Philadelphia to Topeka. Yet all this work occupied but ten years in building. It was finished B.C. 204, seven years after the death of its projector.

The government of China appears to be to a marked degree a government of law. The laws have been the development of the long succession of centuries. They came originally from the government of patriarchal chieftains, deriving their force at first from the good character of these rulers, and their intrinsic merit. Afterward this merit was attributed to a divine authority, believed to have descended from heaven upon the emperors, to whom they were accountable for its use. The political and social ethics of Confucius commended themselves to the judgment of both rulers and people, and after a time became themselves crystallized into laws, which with customs and institutions grew up gradually into a great social polity. Reverence for this polity, for the government of semi-divine origin, for ancestors and for all ancient and established things, came to be the inspiring principle of so much of religion as the people possessed, and the ruling thought in all their education, beginning with the youngest child and continuing through all the stages of competitive examinations to the officer highest in rank and nearest the person of the emperor. The Chinese system seems to be established by the instincts of heredity; by the teachings of a peculiarly intensified, though narrow, education; by conditions of complete individual and mutual responsibility, — visiting the sins of the offender upon his family, his kindred, and even his neighbors, so that personally or vicariously every offence must have its atonement; and by a system of strict surveillance, extending from the emperor through all classes to the lowest. Carried to its perfection, this order of government would insure that every act of every man should be known even to his idle words, and for every idle word the man should give account. If this government be judged by its fruits it will not be found utterly wanting. It has insured its own perpetuity, and the longest continuous national life known in the world's history. It has secured this without the costly array of a standing army or the expensive machinery of a state religion. It has fostered in its people the virtues of industry, frugality, temperance, and contented lives. It has given its people great security in the possession of things they have learned chiefly to value, the control of themselves, their lives, their homes, their children, and the graves of their ancestors. Its code is described by competent English authority as reasonable, clear, consistent, brief, direct, and moderate. Barbarous punishments, involving maiming or mutilation, though common elsewhere in Asia, are unknown in China, and if some offences meet presently condign punishment, it is that other evil-doers may be more surely deterred from the violations of law.

The system is nevertheless deficient in two important respects. It fails to develop the subtler and higher qualities of its people in whatever belongs to the humanities, as expressions of honor, or truthfulness, or charity. It cultivates no science worthy the name. It fosters no art but the extravagant and the grotesque. It knows no philosophy that reaches inwardly to the spiritual and the religious nature of man. It recognizes no conscience, exercises no faith. It takes little account of a future life as a reflex of this present life, a reason for its grander development or its holier conduct. While it cannot be true to say that China makes no progress, she is still an unprogressive nation. Her movements are like the slow metamorphoses of geologic epochs, rather than like the sturdy and constant growth which organic forces produce in living things.

Failing in these respects, it has failed to secure a strength which should serve its necessities when it has come into collision with other powers, particularly those which are the embodiment of the forces of western civilization. Though possessing in 1882 a population estimated at 380,000,000 of people—seven times that of the United States, twelve times that of the United Kingdom of Great Britain and Ireland—with every opportunity of strength in concentration and organization, with abundant material resources of every conceivable nature, it is pitiful to behold the government of the Chinese empire prostrate again and again at the feet of a few thousand English or Russians, giving to one vast areas of territory, with broad rivers as avenues of trade or power, and paying to another large sums of money for indemnity incurred in a strife wherein a heathen government contended to protect its people from the demoralization which a nation professing Christianity sought to impose upon it. It should be credited to the Chinese government as a grand moral triumph that it confiscated and *destroyed* in May, 1839, 20,291 chests of opium, weighing more than two and a half millions of pounds, costing nearly eleven millions of dollars, and worth at the time about nine millions of dollars,—"a solitary instance," remarks Dr. Williams, "in the history of the world, of a pagan [or Christian ?] monarch preferring to destroy what would injure his subjects, rather than to fill his own pockets with its sale." It must be charged against the English people as a crime devoid of excuse, and without palliation, that it wrung from the weakness of the Chinese emperor six millions of dollars as a ransom for this same opium. It is hardly surprising to learn that this same ransom, the price of national disgrace, was never fairly divided among the merchants who suffered as losers when the opium was confiscated.

It is interesting to observe the skill with which Dr. Williams, in spite of the condemnation which he is compelled to award to the English for their course in the "opium war," a condemnation which from the judgment-seat of a Christian missionary he could not help pronouncing, endeavors to make it appear that this war was after all, like the tornado and the earthquake, a needful infliction upon China, and one productive of great good to her, to other nations, and to the propagation of truth. The Emperor was apparently a bad boy who ought to have been shaken well and set down hard; it's a great pity that he would throw stones at our boys who stole his chickens, but then he needed chastisement on general principles, and doubtless feels better now that he has his deserts.

Dr. Williams has condensed into the two volumes of his work a vast amount of information, interesting and instructive, in the fields of geography and geology, ethnology and anthropology; the flora and fauna of the several provinces; the culture of fields and gardens, of silk and of fish; architecture, dress, and social life, with the customs pertaining to marriage, divorce, and death; public ceremonies, the administration of government, and the enforcement of the laws.

Like all other Chinese institutions, their education reaches to a hoary antiquity. Three thousand years ago it was written of those then called ancients that for the purposes of education "villages had their schools, districts their academies, departments their colleges, and principalities their universities." The early training of children requires them to know and to practice maxims of modest behavior, respect for parents, and veneration for ancestors. The minutest points of good breeding are insisted upon. The rules to be observed in the prosecution of studies are worthy of high commendation; advising firm resolution, the aiming at high attainments, and at thorough comprehension. "Better little and fine, than much and coarse." But the warp and the woof of instruction, from the day when the teacher sings,

"Jin chi tsu, sing pun shen:
Sing siang kin, sih siang yuen;"

which his pupils simultaneously chant in their turn, until they have learned both the words and their written signs, to the day when the last examination is finished, appears to be the development and application of the memory. The classic writings are committed in enormous bulk, and are reproduced in never ceasing compositions. The examinations set forth themes to be written upon, and the product is a multitude of essays, which are ranked in excellence according as they contain the maximum of classical lore, clearly written and tersely expressed, in rhyme and rhythm if required.

There are four literary degrees. The first is called *sin-tsai*, or "flowering talent." The candidates are examined first in their own districts. Of 4,000 competitors, twenty-seven won the first step, *hien ming*, "having a name in the village." These, again examined, may become *fu ming*, "having a name in the department." These meet at the provincial capital, and passing the third step obtain the first degree *sin-tsai;* of these there are about twelve thousand to nineteen millions of inhabitants. For these a triennial examination is held in the provincial capital, from which the successful emerge as *ku-jin*, or "promoted men." The candidates for *ku-jin* at Canton have been as many as 6,000 or 8,000 in a single examination, from which not more than eighty or a hundred were passed. These may enter a triennial examination at Peking for the third degree of *tsin-sz'*, "entered scholars" or doctors, from whom the fourth degree men, "*hanlin*," are selected.

The *siu-tsai* are students; the *ku-jin* may be appointed to office throughout the empire; the *tsin-sz'* fill offices of higher degree; while the *hanlin* are members of the Imperial Academy, and as such receive salaries. The system is marred by occasional departures from the strict rules provided, but it is admitted that the machinery is managed with "a degree of integrity, patriotism, and good order, which shows that the leading minds in it are well chosen."

A very intelligible account follows of the language of China, and of its literature, classical and polite.

The religion of China is described with as much difficulty as its law, its education, or its social life. There is no word expressing religion, but *kias*, as applied to all sects, means simply "doctrines taught." There are three principal sects, Confucianism, Buddhism, and Taoism, and yet these are not sects, since they are not separated; a man may accept the tenets of Confucius, and at the same time may worship at a shrine of Buddha, or join in a Taoist festival. The state worship is an adoration of the powers of nature, as the sky and the earth, and the ancestral Emperors, on set occasions, and with imposing ceremony.

"There is no deification of sensuality, which, in the name of religion, could shield and countenance the licentious rites and orgies that enervated the minds of worshippers and polluted their hearts in so many other pagan countries."

"The chains of caste woven in India, the fetters of the Inquisition forged in Spain, the silly rites practised by the augurs in old Rome, or the horrid cruelties and vile worship once seen in Egypt and Syria—in each case under the sanction of the State—have all been wanting along the Yellow River, and spread none of their evils to hamper the rule of law in China."

Confucianism is rather a system of ethics than a religion. Born in B.C. 551, Confucius gave his early years to the study of ancient learning and to public duties. In later years he gained influence at the court, gathered disciples, administered the affairs of an important office, passed various vicissitudes of good and bad fortune, and finally died after making a complete revision of all his writings, at the age of seventy-three. Worship of him consists in little more than raising a tablet to his memory.

"The leading features of the philosophy of Confucius are subordination to superiors and kind, upright dealing with our fellow men; destitute of all references to an unseen Power, to whom all men are accountable, they look only to this world for their sanctions, and make the monarch himself only partially amenable to a higher tribunal."

His one word for a constant rule of practice was *shu*, reciprocity. He said, "What you do not want done to yourself, do not do to others."

The sect of the Taoists dates to B.C. 604, its founder being Lan-tsz. His writings are meagre, consisting mostly of aphorisms, in which he teaches tenets not unlike those of the Greek Zeno; recommending retirement, contemplation, the annihilation of passion, and evanishment in *Tao*. *Tao* is a reaching after the unknown. *Teh* is sublime virtue, goodness, sincerity. His work is called the *Tao-Teh-King*. The votaries of *Tao* are few, and are mostly the priests who live a wandering life, or dwell in temples and sell charms and nostrums.

The religion of China which possesses most of the elements of a faith, in that it somehow connects man with the supernatural and the invisible, is that of Buddhism. Its followers are scattered throughout India, China, and Japan. Their master is Buddha, who dates about B.C. 623, and whose myths have been rehearsed by Edwin Arnold in his "Light of Asia." The central thought of Buddhism is the purification of the soul by its own efforts, earning joy in the future by austerities in the present, and eliminating by persistent toil all sin from the soul, with the assistance of a whole creation of invisible beings, but without either a God or an atoning Saviour. Buddhism flourishes in China, because it offers to the people some ideas of a future life, and some notion of supernatural beings and powers. It lacks much of the grandeur which glorifies other pagan beliefs, but it is free also from their vices and cruelties. It leads the way toward the worship of ancestors which forms so large a part of Chinese religion. In its rites and in its forms of worship, dresses, fastings, purgations, worship of relics, prayers for the dead, holy water, candles, incense, bells, and miracles, it has many points of resemblance to the Romish church.

Much space has necessarily been given to an account of the opening of China by the efforts of the Western nations, as well for purposes of trade and commerce, as for the introduction of the Christian religion. The wars with England, with their causes and results, are very clearly described. The good which has followed and which may be expected to follow is clearly set forth. If China and Japan could but assimilate such valuable elements from the western civilization that insists on opening their gates, without imbibing also the multitude of demoralizing agencies which are as fevers in the western constitutions but are like leprosy to the Asiatic, then might we be sure that these two peoples would come in early times to take prominent positions in the family of nations. They who have forced on these unwilling nations contact with so much that was distasteful to them and foreign to the long established habits of their national lives, have incurred responsibilities of overwhelming import, lest there should have been grafted upon these ancient trunks only such scions as will bring with their life blight, mildew, decay, and death.

SELIM H. PEABODY.

BRIEFS ON NEW BOOKS.

OF the three new volumes of verse by Whittier, Aldrich, and Story, issued in dissimilar but individually tasteful styles by Houghton, Mifflin & Co., the interest is chiefly divided between those of the two authors first named. Mr. Whittier's collection as a whole will not disappoint his old-time admirers, while many of the pieces will give sincere pleasure; Mr. Aldrich's achievement will doubtless entitle him to a distinct if moderate advancement in his rank as poet; while Mr. Story's somewhat uncertain poetic position is not likely to be materially affected by his latest production. Mr. Whittier's volume, "The Bay of Seven Islands, and Other Poems," contains the pieces he has written since the publication of "The King's Missive," in 1881, most of them having already appeared in magazine pages. In the title poem he has found material suited to his hand, and this piece is perhaps the most characteristic, as it is the longest, in the collection. "How the Women Went from Dover," recounts an incident of the Quaker-whipping period of Massachusetts. It is written, naturally enough, with strong feeling, and its partial lack of impressiveness as poetry is no doubt due to the unpoetic nature of its material. Several of the remaining pieces are personal; Longfellow, Fields, Henry Wilson, Mrs. Stowe, and Mrs. Spofford being each the subject of an affectionate tribute. Not the least interesting of the pieces are those revealing the poet's own personality; particularly the closing one, "An Autograph," in which he appears to have fashioned for himself an epitaph, beautiful in its simplicity and dignity.—Mr. Aldrich's volume, "Mercedes, and Later Lyrics," is spoken of as poetry; yet half of it is taken up by "Mercedes," which is not a poem, but a drama — or, as the author himself calls it, a sketch — with lyrical interludes. The story, an incident of one of Napoleon's Spanish campaigns, is a spirited one; its movement is dramatic, and the dialogue is managed with much beauty and grace. The latter half of the volume contains the lyrical productions of Mr. Aldrich for the last seven years. These have the daintiness of style and the exquisite polish that characterize his poetry. The "Intaglios" especially prove what can be done with trifles of fancy by painstaking art.— Mr. Story entitles his volume "He and She; A Poet's Portfolio," and in it he seems to have hit upon the device of permitting his poet to be persuaded by a lady friend to ransack his portfolio and read aloud the verses that are brought to light, each poem furnishing the subject of a free discussion between them. The device is, it must be confessed, somewhat lacking in brilliancy and novelty; the dialogue is scarcely witty enough to sustain the interest, and the poems, some of which have a fair lyrical quality, are really placed at a disadvantage by being made to bear the weight of the dull prose. Mr. Story has succeeded in being unconventional, and also in being tiresome.

CRITICISM upon the rather ambitious title, "A Bird's-Eye View of the Civil War," written by Theodore Ayrault Dodge, U. S. Army, and published by J. R. Osgood & Co., is partially disarmed by the statement, in an introductory letter addressed to the author's son, that no claim is made to originality, that errors have probably crept into the volume, and that the facts narrated and many of the opinions expressed have been gleaned from many authors. The perusal of the work makes it rather probable that the author's principal source of both fact and opinion has been the Scribner Campaign Series; indeed, wherever this series could be used its synopsis is given, more full, it is true, than its index, but certainly not so interesting as the original. The work contains errors of fact which a more accurate and prolonged study of the subject would have prevented. For example, in describing the action between the Merrimac and our vessels — the Cumberland, Minnesota, and Congress,— the author says (page 38) that the former vessel "destroyed the United States steamer Cumberland, and *disabled* the Congress and the Minnesota, before the Monitor came up." The truth is that the Congress was captured by the Merrimac, and that she was then set on fire by her captors and blown up. Besides the errors to which we refer, many typographical mistakes, liable in some instances to mislead the cursory reader, are also to be found in the work. It gives plain evidence of haste and want of care in its preparation; and this is to be regretted the more as the title selected for it is one which not only suggests many possibilities, but will induce many to read it who have not the time to study details and yet are anxious to have a full knowledge of facts. To write a bird's-eye view of our civil war — vast as the struggle was in its field of operations, in the important questions involved, in the large armies by which it was fought to its close — requires talent of the most varied character. An author of such a work should possess a thorough knowledge of the vexed political questions which had for many years

Nation March 9, 1871

The Middle Kingdom. By S. Wells Williams. Fourth edition. 2 vols. (New York: John Wiley & Son. 1871.)—The reissue of this standard work evinces the interest felt by Americans in all matters pertaining to China and the Chinese. Few publications of a similar nature have achieved a more merited and widespread popularity than "The Middle Kingdom," it being accepted, both in this country and in Europe as the best authority upon Chinese matters extant. The copy before us presents a marked improvement over previous editions in mechanical finish, both as regards letterpress and illustrations. We must, however, enter a protest against the words "fourth edition" on the title-page, as, however technically correct, they are calculated to mislead the public. The words "new edition" so generally imply a revision and emendation of previous issues, that one feels inclined to resent their application to a bare reprint, as is the case in this instance. How literally the old text has been adhered to may be easily seen. Thus (vol. ii., p. 594) we read: "From the close of the year 1844 to the present period, nothing has occurred to disturb the amicable relations existing, in general, between China and other nations except the opposition of the citizens of Canton, etc." And again, p. 599: "They (the Chinese) are afraid to act against the opium vessels on the coast, most of which sail under English colors, lest the Governor of Hong Kong demand reparation, etc." Nothing is said of the disturbances which have so lamentably signalized the history of foreign intercourse with China during the past decade, or of the treaties which legalized the opium traffic, and thereby added considerably to the income of the Chinese exchequer. We have taken these examples at random from pages which, accurate enough when first written, stand grievously in need of revision now that twenty-seven years have elapsed since their original publication. Had the retention of these pages been accompanied by an explanatory note, but little need have been said in the way of criticism. But the "preface to a new edition" only brings matters up to 1860, with the very briefest mention at that; leading the uninformed reader to infer that no event worth recording in the history of foreign intercourse had occurred since the signing of the Tientsing treaty.

It is to be hoped that Dr. Williams will, before long, undertake the revision of his second volume, and thus render the work under notice not merely our best authority on all that relates to Chinese geography, ethnology, manners, and customs, etc., but complete also as a history of foreign intercourse with that remarkable people. Meanwhile, despite the grave omission we deem it a duty to point out, "The Middle Kingdom" remains the most perfect compilation relating to China yet published in any European language.

李慈銘《越縵堂日記》光緒五年四月十日所記吳可讀事跡

吳吏部可讀（柳堂）自縊於蘇州野寺中，蓋以穆宗立嗣事為屍諫也。聞其人素慷慨，喜為詩歌，不飾邊幅，初以爭成祿事鐫秩歸舉蘭，左湘陰甚重之，延主書院。比再入都補官，年已將七十，人竊以其再出為疑，而閉門謝客，不復賦詩飲酒。前月大雪，忽戎車告其子，以獨遊盤山，如久不歸，當至山相迎也。蓋其再出時志已早定，欲俟山陵事畢，從殺皇於地下，孤忠獨行，二百年來所僅見者。然其書專為穆宗紹統，則不知帝王立後與臣庶異，凡嗣位者，皆為子道，豈若民間必別立後人承祧傳嗣乎？

一誤再誤而終歸於不誤者此也彼時罪臣即以此意擬成一摺由都察院轉進呈稿底奏稿底俱
已就草伏思罪臣業經降調不得越職言事且此何等事此何等語出之親臣重臣大臣則
為深謀遠慮出之疏臣遠臣小臣則為干進希名又思在諸臣中忠直最著者未必即以
此事為可緩言亦無益而置之故罪臣且留以有待及罪臣以查辦廢員內蒙　恩圈出引見
奏　旨以主事特用仍復選授吏　迴来又已五六年
及於此者今逢我　大行皇帝永遠奉安　山陵恐遂漸久漸忘則罪臣所昔日留以有
待者今則迫不及待矣仰　溯湖之　仙駕瞻戀　九重回望弓劍於橋山愧依尺帛謹以我
先皇帝所賜餘年為我　先皇帝上乞　懿旨數行於我　兩宮皇太后之前惟是臨命
之身神志昏亂摺中詞意未克詳明引用率多遺忘不及前此未上一摺一二繕寫又
不能莊正罪臣本無古人學問豈能似古人從容昔有赴死而行不復成步者人曰子懼
乎曰懼曰既懼何不歸曰懼吾私也死吾公也罪臣今日亦猶是鳥之將死其鳴也哀人之
將死其言也善罪臣豈敢比曾參之賢即死其言亦未必善惟望我　兩宮皇太后我
皇上憐其哀鳴勿以為無疾之呻吟不祥之舉動則罪臣雖死無憾宋臣有言凡事言於未然
誠為太過及其已然則又無所及言之何益可使朝廷受未然之言不可使臣等有不及之悔今
罪臣誠願異日臣言之不驗使天下後世笑臣愚不願異日臣言之或驗使天下後世謂臣明等杜
牧之罪言雖逾職分效史鰌之尸諫祇盡愚忠罪臣尤願我　兩宮皇太后我　皇上體
聖祖　世宗之心調劑寬猛養忠厚和平之福任用老成毋爭外國之所獨爭為中華留不
盡毋創　祖宗之所未創為子孫留有餘罪臣言畢於斯願畢於斯命畢於斯再罪臣曾任
御史故敢昧死具摺又以今職不能專達懇由臣部堂官代為上進罪臣前以臣衙門所派
行禮司員內未經派及罪臣是以罪臣再四面求臣部堂官大學士寶鋆始添派而來罪臣
之死為寶鋆所不及料想寶鋆並無不應派而誤派之咎時逢　盛世豈容有疑於古來
殉葬不情之事特以　先皇帝龍馭永歸天上普天同泣故不禁哀痛迫切謹以大統
所繫貪陳悽悽自稱罪臣以　聞謹具　奏

光緒五年閏三月初五日服毒自盡
在順天府薊州東門三義廟內
甘肅皋蘭縣人庚戌科進士蘭州府

吏部稽勳司主事前任河南道監察御史臣吳可讀跪　奏為以一死泣請　懿旨豫定將來大統
之歸以畢今生忠愛事竊罪臣聞治國不諱亂安國不忘危危亂而可諱可忘則進苦口於
堯舜為無疾之呻吟陳隱患於聖明為不祥之舉動罪臣前因言事忿激自甘或斬或囚經
王大臣會議奏　請傳臣質訊乃蒙我　先皇帝曲賜矜全既免臣於以斬而死復免臣
於以囚而死又復免臣於以傳訊而觸忌觸怒而死犯三死而未死不求生而再生則今日罪臣
未盡之餘年皆我　先皇帝數年前所賜也乃天崩地坼忽遭十三年十二月初五日之變即日
欽奉　兩宮皇太后懿旨大行皇帝龍馭上賓未有儲貳不得已以醇親王之子承繼為　文宗
顯皇帝為次子入承大統為嗣皇帝俟嗣皇帝生有皇子即承繼大行皇帝為嗣特諭罪臣
涕泣跪誦反覆思維竊以為　兩宮皇太后一誤再誤為　文宗顯皇帝立子不為我
大行皇帝立嗣既不為我　大行皇帝立嗣則今日　嗣皇帝所承大統乃奉我　兩宮
皇太后之命受之於　文宗顯皇帝非受之於我　大行皇帝也而將來大統之承亦未奉
有明文必歸之承繼之子即謂　懿旨內既有承繼為嗣一語則大統之仍歸繼子自不待言
罪臣竊以為未然自古擁立推戴之際為臣子所難言我　朝二百餘年　祖宗家法子以
傳子骨肉之間萬世應無間然況醇親王公忠體國中外翕然稱為賢王觀王當時一奏
令人忠義奮發之氣勃然而生言為心聲豈能偽為罪臣讀之至於歌泣不能自已倘王聞臣
有此奏未必不怒臣之妄而憐臣之愚必不以臣言為間離間之端且我　皇上仁孝性成承我
兩宮皇太后授以寶位將來千秋萬歲時均能以我　兩宮皇太后今日之心為心而在廷之
忠佞不齊即眾論之異同不一以宋初宰相趙普之賢猶有首背杜太后之事以前明大學士
王直之為國家舊人猶以黃竑請立景帝太子一疏出于蠻夷不出于我輩為愧賢者如此遑
問不肖舊人如此奚責新進名位已定者如此況在未定不得已於一誤再誤中而求一歸於不
誤之策惟有仰乞我　兩宮皇太后再行明白降一諭旨將來大統仍歸承繼　大行皇帝嗣
子　嗣皇帝雖百斯男中外及左右臣工始不得以異言進正名定分豫絕紛紜如此則猶是
本朝祖宗以來子以傳子之家法而我　大行皇帝未有子而有子即我　兩宮皇太后未有孫
而有孫異日繩繩揖揖相引於萬代者皆我　兩宮皇太后所自出而不可移易者也罪臣所謂

N.Y. Tribune 1884

OBITUARY.

PROFESSOR S. WELLS WILLIAMS.

NEW-HAVEN, Feb. 17.—Professor Samuel Wells Williams, LL.D., of Yale College, died yesterday after two weeks' illness. The funeral will be held at 4 o'clock on Tuesday afternoon.

Professor Williams was born in Utica, N. Y., on September 22, 1812, and was graduated at the Rensselaer Polytechnic Institute at Troy, in 1832. In 1833 he went to Canton, China, as printer to the American Board of Foreign Missions. He succeeded in placing the press of the mission on a good foundation. He applied himself to the study of Chinese and rapidly gained an extensive acquaintance with it and published a number of standard books that were useful to students who came after him. Soon after going to China Dr. Williams undertook the editorship of *The Chinese Repository*, in which he was assisted by many able contributors. After the lapse of many years *The Repository*, extending through twenty volumes, says *The Celestial Empire* (Shanghai), "is looked upon as of priceless worth, and the name of the editor will be long and honorably remembered by sinologues in connection with it." Professor Williams completed at Macao in 1835 the printing of Medhurst's "Hokkeen Dictionary." In 1837 he visited Japan to return some shipwrecked sailors, and soon after he learned the Japanese language, into which he translated the Book of Genesis and Matthew. He aided Dr. Bridgman in preparing the "Chinese Chrestomathy," and in 1842 he published his "Easy Lessons in Chinese." This was followed in 1844 by "The Chinese Commercial Guide" and "An English and Chinese Vocabulary in the Court Dialect." In 1845 Dr. Williams returned to the United States, remaining here for three years, and delivered a course of public lectures on Chinese subjects which delighted and instructed many audiences. In 1848 he published "The Middle Kingdom," a work which still considered to be the best of the kind in China. In 1848 he returned to China with a new font of Chinese type made in Berlin. In 1853-'54 he accompanied Commodore Perry to Japan as the interpreter for the expedition. He was appointed Secretary and interpreter for the United States Legation in Japan, of which he had charge until the arrival of the first Minister. In 1856 Dr. Williams published a "Tonic Dictionary of the Chinese Language in the Canton Dialect," but most of the copies were burned with the mission-press at Macao in December of that year. In 1858 he aided William B. Reed in negotiating the treaty of Tientsin, and in 1859 he accompanied Mr. Ward to Pekin to exchange the ratifications.

Dr. Williams revisited the United States in 1860–'61, but returned to China in 1862 as Secretary of the United States Legation, then first established at Pekin. In 1863 he published a fifth edition of his "Chinese Commercial Guide," which he had nearly rewritten. In 1874 he brought out at Shanghai the great work of his life, "The Syllabic Dictionary of the Chinese Language," and in 1876 he returned to the United States, having been appointed lecturer on Chinese at Yale College, where he remained until his death.

N.Y. Times Feb 17 '84

A YALE PROFESSOR'S DEATH.

NEW-HAVEN, Feb. 16.—Prof. Samuel Wells Williams, LL. D., the well-known Oriental scholar and Professor of Chinese Language and Literature in Yale College, died at 8:40 o'clock this evening at his residence, No. 39 College-street. Two years ago he received a fall that induced a slight shock of paralysis, and ever since then he had been losing strength. Since the 1st of January he had been confined to his house. On Friday night he had a serious relapse, and was for a long time unconscious. His inability to assimilate his food brought on enema. At his bedside were his family and his aged brother, A. Dwight Williams.

WILLIAMS—On Saturday evening, February 16, in New Haven, Conn., S. Wells Williams, in the seventy-second year of his age.
Funeral in Battell Chapel, Yale College, Tuesday, February 19, at 4 P. M.
Interment at Utica, N. Y. N.Y. Eve. Post

EW YORK, SATURDA]

YALE COLLEGE.

The Scholarly Influence of the Late Professor Williams—Satisfaction of the Students with Professor Richards's Letter on Athletics—Lecture Courses.

[Correspondence of the Evening Post.]

NEW HAVEN, Ct., February 22.

The funeral of Professor Williams was held on Wednesday afternoon in the Battell Chapel. Dr. Barbour conducted the service and President Porter delivered an address. There were present also representatives of the American Bible Society, of which he was President at the time of his death. Professor Williams has been connected with the College for only eight years, and although a regular university professor, has never given any instruction except in the form of lectures on Chinese history and literature. There have never been any candidates for the courses in the Chinese language which he was prepared to give. His great work, 'The Syllabic Dictionary of the Chinese Language,' was already completed and published before he came to New Haven. Since his residence here, in addition to the miscellaneous literary work for magazines and newspapers which his special knowledge brought him, he has been constantly engaged in the revision of his book on 'The Middle Kingdom.' His health failed him before he had completed the task, but he was fortunate in having the assistance of his son toward the end. Through his agency the work was completed and published before his father's death. Mr. Williams was already sixty-five years of age when he was elected to his professorship, but his interest in the College was very great, and he at once entered into sympathy with its policy and aspirations. He was a very busy man up to a few weeks before his death, and even after his strength began to give way his vigor and acuteness of mind maintained themselves. He had a very wide range of interests, and his information was of that encyclopædic character which one finds in men of his kind. Although the nature of his department isolated him from contact with the undergraduates, he counted very greatly in the university life by the inspiration of both his example and his reputation. A considerable body of young graduates, moreover, sought his society, for he was the most accessible of men, and got direction and stimulus from association with him. It is the presence of such men as he which gives its peculiar scholastic air to an old institution of learning. His last public work was to preside at the meeting of the American Oriental Society held here last fall.

N.Y. Post Feb 18. '84

—— Professor S. Wells Williams, LL.D., of Yale College, died on Saturday after an illness of two weeks. He was seventy-two years of age. After being graduated at the Troy Polytechnic Institute he went to Canton, China, as printer to the American Board of Foreign Missions. He studied Chinese, and published a number of standard books on the subject. He was the editor for many years of the *Chinese Repository*. In 1837 he visited Japan and studied that language, into which he translated the books of Genesis and Matthew. In 1842 he published 'Easy Lessons in Chinese.' He returned to the United States in 1845. In 1848 he published 'The Middle Kingdom,' a standard work on China, of which a new and carefully revised edition was published a few months ago. He returned to China in 1848. He resided there and in Japan for many following years, publishing valuable works. In 1874 he brought out at Shanghai the great work of his life, 'The Syllabic Dictionary of the Chinese Language,' and in 1876 he returned to the United States, having been appointed lecturer on Chinese at Yale College, where he remained until his death.

St. Albans Messenger Feb. 19 1884

The Late Professor Williams.

Prof. Samuel Wells Williams, LL. D., of Yale College, who died in New Haven, Feb. 16, was born in Utica, N. Y., in 1812, and was graduated at the Rensselaer Polytechnic Institute at Troy, in 1832. In 1833 he went to Canton, China, as printer to the American Board of Foreign Missions. He succeeded in placing the press of the mission on a good foundation. He applied himself to the study of Chinese and rapidly gained an extensive acquaintance with it and published a number of standard books that were useful to students who came after him. Soon after going to China Dr. Williams undertook the editorship of the Chinese Repository, in which he was assisted by many able contributors. After the lapse of many years the Repository, extending through twenty volumes, says the Celestial Empire (Shanghai), "is looked upon as of priceless worth, and the name of the editor will be long and honorably remembered by sinologues in connection with it." Professor Williams completed at Macao in 1835 the printing of Medhurst's "Hokkeen Dictionary."

In 1837 he visited Japan to return some shipwrecked sailors, and soon after he learned the Japanese language, into which he translated the Book of Genesis and Matthew. He aided Dr. Bridgman in preparing the "Chinese Chrestomathy," and in 1842 he published his "Easy Lessons in Chinese." This was followed in 1844 by "The Chinese Commercial Guide" and "An English and Chinese Vocabulary in the Court Dialect." In 1845 Dr. Williams returned to the United States, remaining here for three years, and delivered a course of public lectures on Chinese subjects which delighted and instructed many audiences. In 1848 he published "The Middle Kingdom," a work which is still considered to be the best of the kind in China. In 1848 he returned to China with a new font of Chinese type made in Berlin.

In 1853–'54 he accompanied Commodore Perry to Japan as the interpreter for the expedition. He was appointed secretary and interpreter for the U. S. legation in Japan, of which he had charge until the arrival of the first minister. In 1856 Dr. Williams published a "Tonic Dictionary of the Chinese Language in the Canton Dialect," but most of the copies were burned with the mission-press at Macao in December of that year. In 1858 he aided Wm. B. Reed in negotiating the treaty of Tientsin, and in 1859 he accompanied Mr. Ward to Pekin to exchange ratifications. Dr. Williams revisited the United States in 1860–'61, but returned to China in 1862 as secretary of the United States legation, then first established at Pekin. In 1863 he published a fifth edition of his "Chinese Commercial Guide," which he had nearly rewritten. In 1874 he brought out at Shanghai the great work of his life, "The Syllabic Dictionary of the Chinese Language," and in 1876 he returned to the United States, having been appointed lecturer on Chinese at Yale college, where he remained until his death.

N. H. Palladium (?) Feb. 18, '84

By the death of Professor S. Wells Williams, which occurred Saturday evening, American scholarship loses one of its most distinguished representatives. As a specialist in the line of oriental languages, and particularly as an authority in all matters pertaining to the Chinese dialect, Professor Williams had no superior. It has been said of him that he was the only American who could easily read, write and speak the Chinese language. A student of indomitable persistence, and an enthusiast in his particular line of study, he probably did more than any other man of his time to give the world a correct impression of the peculiarities of the great nation of the east with whose interests he was so long identified. His "Middle Kingdom," a revised edition of which was recently published, is unquestionably the most reliable authority concerning all matters touching China and the Chinese extant. It was as a linguist, however, that Professor Williams achieved his highest reputation, his "Syllabic Dictionary of the Chinese Language," published in 1874, being the most thorough, comprehensive and reliable work of the kind ever issued. The professor was not only a laborious scholar, but he possessed the happy faculty of turning his great acquirements to practical use.

N. H. ~~Register~~ + Journal

The Late S. Wells Williams.

Feb. 18 '84

A Sketch of His Life and Services—His Distinguished Career as an Oriental Scholar.

Professor Samuel Wells Williams, of Yale college, died at his residence, No. 39 College street, at 8:40 o'clock on Saturday evening. His age was 71. He had been in failing health for some months. On the last day of January, two years ago, he met with a severe fall on Chapel street and fractured his left arm near the shoulder. His health had been previously undermined by arduous and protracted mental labor, and a few months after his fall a partial paralysis of the brain ensued. He was not rendered unconscious, but was disabled from his literary work and for a time was bereft of his power of speech. He gained slowly, however, and the following summer improved much at Litchfield and last summer gained also during a stay at Holderness, in the White Mountain region, near Lake Winnipiseogee. Since December last he had been gradually weakening. He was last on the street during the week following New Year's. Inability to assimilate his food was the feature of the disease which terminated his useful and valuable life. His wife died about three years ago. She was from Plattsburg, New York. Her death was a great loss to the deceased and no doubt hastened the decline of his health. He leaves two children, one of whom is Mr. Frederick W. Williams, of this city, assistant librarian at Yale, the other the wife of Hon. Thomas Grosvenor, late of the English diplomatic service in China. They recently returned from that country and are visiting at the paternal residence, Moor Park, just out of London. Deceased leaves also two brothers, Mr. Robert Williams, of Utica, N. Y., and H. Dwight Williams, who for the past two years has resided with deceased, and who for twelve years resided in China, holding an important official position. The late Professor Williams had long since earned world-wide fame as an Oriental scholar. He was a native of Utica, N. Y., and a school mate of Professor Dana, the eminent geologist of Yale, who is a native of Utica. He graduated at the Polytechnic school at Troy and soon after embarked in his life long work in China. He went there in 1833 and joined the famous Dr. Morrison, the first English missionary to China, and Dr. Bridgman, the American missionary. With the latter he edited the Chinese Repository, and after preparing himself sufficiently in the Chinese language took entire charge of the magazine and continued its publication till 1832. During that time the entire charge of the mission printing devolved upon him and he was the author of many valuable works. In 1835 he removed to Macao to complete the printing of Medhurst's Hokkeen dictionary; and in July, 1837, he went to Japan in a vessel sent by C. W. King, of Canton, to return to their homes seven shipwrecked Japanese. The vessel was driven away from two ports by cannon balls, and the men were brought back to Macao. Mr. Williams obtained from some of them an acquaintance with their language, translated a treatise on smelting copper from the original, and made a version of the book of Genesis and the gospel of St. Matthew into the Japanese. After the publication of Dr. Bridgman's "Chinese Chrestomathy," to which Mr. Williams contributed about one-third, he printed in Chinese his "Easy Lessons in Chinese" in 1841, "English and Chinese Vocabulary" in 1843 and "Chinese Commercial Guide" in 1844. In November, 1844, he set out for America, passing through Egypt, Syria and Europe and reaching New York in October, 1845. The project of casting a font of movable Chinese type in Berlin had been started, and to obtain funds for the enterprise he delivered lectures on the condition of China, which were afterward enlarged and published under the title of "The Middle Kingdom" in 2 volumes, 12 mo., New York, 1848. Soon after the publication of this work the faculty of Union college conferred upon him the degree of LL.D. In 1853-4 he accompanied Commodore Perry's expedition to Japan as interpreter. In 1855 he was appointed secretary and interpreter to the United States legation and took charge of it until the arrival of the minister, Mr. Parker. He was charge d'affaires for a considerable period during the changes of ministers. He published in 1856 a "Tonic Dictionary of the Chinese Language," and in 1858 went with Mr. Reed to Tien-tsin to assist in the negotiations connected with the treaty, and the next year with Mr. Ward to Pekin to exchange the ratifications. In 1860 he revisited the United States and delivered lectures before the Smithsonian institute and elsewhere. Afterwards he returned to China and lived there until December, 1877, when he took up his residence in this city. His family had previously resided here for some years. In the same year he was elected professor of Chinese language and literature in Yale. He had this professorship at the time of his death. He was a frequent contributor to the New Englander and other magazines. A few years ago he delivered a course of lectures on China before the Yale Theological school.

He visited this country four times during his long residence of 43 years in China. Fourteen years he resided in Pekin. While there he issued his Syllabic Dictionary of the Chinese language, an important work. In the fall of 1883 he published a new and enlarged edition of the "Middle Kingdom," which is undoubtedly the most complete account of the condition and history of China at the present time. This was his second revision of this very valuable work which occupied a considerable part of his time for some years.

The funeral will take place to-morrow (Tuesday) afternoon at 4 o'clock from the College chapel. The remains will be taken to Utica, New York, for interment in the family lot.

GIFTS TO YALE.

What a Professor and a Dead Student's Mother Present.

By the terms of the will of the late Professor S. Wells Williams, $5,000 is left so that it will eventually revert to Yale college. During the lifetime of a widowed sister of the late professor, the interest of the sum will be paid to her, but at her death it will go to the Chinese Professorship fund, or, if there is no incumbent of that position the money will be applied toward paying the educational expenses of any Chinese student who may enter Yale college. The sum of $1,000 is left to Yale Theological seminary and that part of the late professor's collection of Chinese curios which consists of minerals and carved stones is also bequeathed to the college.

The gift of $50,000 to Yale college for the erection of a new dormitory comes from a Mrs. Lawrance, of New-York city, the mother of the late Thomas G. Lawrance, who was a member of the senior class and not from a Mrs. Lawrence, of Chicago, as has been reported in the New-York papers.

N.Y. Herald

OBITUARY.

Feb. 17. 1884

PROFESSOR SAMUEL WELLS WILLIAMS.

Professor S. Wells Williams, of Yale College, died last evening. Two years ago he fell and broke his collar bone. This was closely followed by a paralytic shock, from which, however, he recovered. About two weeks ago he began to fail, and he declined rapidly from that time.

The first professor of the Chinese language and literature at Yale College was, until a late period of his life, better known in China than in his own country. He was born in Utica, N. Y., September 22, 1812, and graduated at the Rensselaer Polytechnic Institute in Troy at the age of twenty. The next year, 1833, he went to Canton as printer for the American Board of Foreign Missions, but almost immediately after his arrival added to his duties the assistant editorship of the *Chinese Repository*. In 1835 he was transferred to Macao to complete the printing of Medhurst's Hokkeen Dictionary. Two years later he learned the Japanese language from some shipwrecked sailors of that nationality whom he had been appointed to return to their native island, and made the first use of his newly acquired knowledge by translating the book of Genesis and the Gospel of St. Matthew into Japanese. He rendered important assistance to Dr. Bridgman in his work intended to facilitate the study of the Chinese tongue, and himself prepared a little book of "Easy Lessons in Chinese." This he followed by an "English and Chinese Vocabulary of the Court Dialect," and by a "Chinese Commercial Guide," which has been almost invaluable to business men having transactions with that country, and of which the fifth edition, published in 1863, was nearly rewritten by him. The years 1845 to 1848 were spent by him in America in delivering lectures and otherwise obtaining funds to secure the casting of a font of Chinese type for the use of the mission press. The lectures were afterward enlarged and published under the title of "The Middle Kingdom," and secured in that shape a large circulation. At this time he was made an LL. D. by Union College. From 1848 to 1851 he resumed the charge of the *Chinese Repository*, which was then discontinued.

He served as interpreter to Commodore Perry in the expedition to Japan, and afterward as secretary and interpreter to the United States Legation in that country, of which he was in charge until the arrival of the United States Minister. In 1856 he published his "Tonic Dictionary of the Canton Dialect," which was republished twenty years later by the English authorities in that country. The years 1858 and 1859 were chiefly occupied in diplomatic service in China, the next two years in the United States in the service of the mission. The immense labor involved in the preparation of a "Syllabic Dictionary of the Chinese Language" occupied the greater portion of his time for several years. It appeared in 1874 and has lightened the labors of all persons who have occasion to study the language to an incalculable degree. In the next year he returned to America, having accepted the call to fill the newly created chair at Yale, to which he carried the same enthusiastic and indomitable persistence which had wrought successful achievement through the whole of his laborious career. He distinguished himself as an advocate of "spelling reform" on the ground of its affording substantial aid to foreigners, especially Orientals, in mastering our language. Besides his heavier work Professor Williams was a frequent contributor to the memoirs of the American Oriental Society.

DR. S. WELLS WILLIAMS. Feb. 18.

DR. S. WELLS WILLIAMS, so long a missionary printer and a United States-official in China, died Saturday evening, in New Haven, where he has lived since his appointment as professor of Chinese in Yale college. Measured by any proper scale, Mr. WILLIAMS was one of the most eminent men ever born in Utica or who has made this city his dwelling place. It fell to his lot to take important part in what all men now agree with him in considering "one of the greatest movements of this century—the introduction of China and Japan into the family of nations."

Dr. WILLIAMS was born in Utica, September 22, 1812. He was the son of WILLIAM WILLIAMS, the early Utica printer and bookseller, whom ASAHEL SEWARD taught to set type, and afterwards made his partner. The firm of SEWARD & WILLIAMS published various books and newspapers, their place of business being on part of the land now occupied by the HERALD office. Under his father, S. WELLS WILLIAMS learned to set type. At the age of twenty, he was graduated from the Rensselaer Polytechnic institute in Troy and the next year he went to China. He was sent there by the American board of commissioners for foreign missions, as a missionary printer. He arrived at Canton, October 25, 1833. He soon after became the assistant editor of the *Chinese Repository*, a serial publication in English, about the size of *Harper's Weekly*, which was continued many years. It was the medium thro' which foreign residents learned the news of the empire, and the government decrees which affected them. Mr. WILLIAMS spent forty-three years in China. The time was almost equally divided between his work as printer and publisher, and his more public service as secretary and interpreter of the United States legation in that country. The latter service continued until the growing importance of our relations with China justified the appointment of a minister resident. Such a representative was accredited in 1874. October 25, 1876, Dr. WILLIAMS left Pekin, forty-three years, to the day, after his arrival at Canton. A brief portion of this time had been spent in this country, tho' not even that in idleness, or forgetfulness of the welfare of the Chinese. At this time the degree of LL. D. was conferred upon him by Union college.

The published works of Dr. WILLIAMS are "Easy Lessons in Chinese," "English and Chinese Vocabulary of the Court Dialect," "Chinese Commercial Guide," "Tonic Dictionary of the Canton Dialect" (1856), "Syllabic Dictionary of the Chinese Language" (1874) and "The Middle Kingdom." Each of these works is a valuable one in its way. The most important is the "Syllabic Dictionary." Its title page is as follows: "Syllabic Dictionary of the Chinese Language, with the Pronunciation of the Characters as heard in Pekin, Canton, Amoy, and Shanghai, by S. WELLS WILLIAMS. Printed in Shanghai in 1874. Published by the American Presbyterian Mission Press." It is a mammoth work, about the size of WEBSTER'S Dictionary, showing an amount of labor which it would seem no one man could accomplish. "The Middle Kingdom," the work by which the author was most known in this country and in England, is a comprehensive account of China, and the characteristics of its people. It is an authority upon the subject, so cited, for example, by the Encyclopædia Brittanica, in its article on China. One of the last labors of Dr. WILLIAMS, has been its revisal and rewriting, with the aid of his son, for the new edition which has been brought out within a year. It is a work of great interest as well as value.

A striking thing about the career of S. WELLS WILLIAMS is the persistent industry which it shows. He made himself the best Chinese scholar in America. He had an excellent knowledge of Japanese. He began its study by communicating with some shipwrecked Japanese sailors, who were given work in his office. When Commodore PERRY made his expedition to Japan to seek better relations with that country, Dr. WILLIAMS was the interpreter. He studied these languages in a scientific way also, and knew much about general philology. These tongues have been considered the most difficult in the world for a foreigner to acquire. They are of a different family from our own, and, as we, at least, are pleased to think, they are in a more primitive stage. The work of Dr.

WILLIAMS has made it far easier thro' all time to come, to learn the Chinese language. Whatever the native energy, such labors could not have been accomplished except by a man inspired by a noble cause. Dr. WILLIAMS was a missionary, and in the most useful ways. He was beloved and trusted by the Chinese. With other men like himself, he gained the confidence of that people in this country. In spite of our recent miserable legislation, that linking continues. As long as memory of the opium wars lasts, we will have an advantage in China over other leading nations. Amicable feeling was established and cherished by Dr. WILLIAMS. His work in this direction was nearly as important as thro' his books. Few men have opportunities for such great and lasting usefulness to their country, and to humanity. Few are fitted to grasp them.

Since his appointment to Yale college to the newly established chair of Chinese, Dr. WILLIAMS has, so far as health allowed, shown the same energy which has characterized his life. He had a remarkable store of general information. Of recent years he has written review articles, and contributions to the publications of the American Oriental society. He was at his death president of the American Bible society, and of the Royal Geographical society of England. About two years ago, Professr WILLIAMS fell and dislocated the shoulder joint and breaking the arm very near to the joint. He had a stroke of paralysis soon after but recovered from that. Lately his health has not been good, and two weeks ago, his brother, ROBERT S. WILLIAMS, of this city, went to him. He was troubled with nausea and difficulty in assimilating food. He seemed to be improving, however, and death came at last quite unexpectedly. He will be buried in Utica. His wife died about two years ago. A son, FREDERICK W. WILLIAMS, and a daughter, Mrs. SOPHIA W. GROSVENOR, survive. His brother, H. DWIGHT WILLIAMS, formerly of New York, has lately lived with him and was present at the time of his death. ROBERT S. WILLIAMS of this city is another brother, and SOPHIA, Mrs. J. V. P. GARDNER, who has lately lived in Clinton, is a sister. Utica Herald.

Dr. S. Wells Williams' Work.

For the semi-centennial celebration of the granting of a charter to Utica and its becoming a city, among the best of the letters prepared and forwarded to the committee in charge, was the one by Professor S. Wells Williams of Yale college. In view of the death of Dr. Williams which occurred Saturday, the letter is printed. It shows indirectly the great importance of his work, tho' his intention was nothing of this kind, as he was a very modest man:

NEW HAVEN, Feb. 27, 1882.

Robert S. Williams, Chairman of Committee of the Oneida Historical Society:

Dear Sir: It seems to me to be a suitable manner of celebrating the semi-centennial anniversity of the city charter, and I can do no less than send a short reply to your kind invitation to join the symposium.

When the city charter was granted, I was at school in the Rensselaer institute at Troy, and never had the opportunity of voting at any municipal election. During the fifty years which have since passed, I have spent hardly one of them in Utica altogether, but the scattered visits have served to revive and strengthen the attachments of youth to the town and its citizens. I can be now personally known to comparatively few of the latter, but it has been a source of grateful surprise to me, on my return there at intervals of twelve or fifteen years, to find that I had been kept in memory by so many friends of my parents and brother.

Out of the fifty years now brought to their close, I have spent forty-three years in China or (with few exceptions,) away from Utica. During that period I have been permitted to see and aid in one of the greatest movements in this century—the introduction of China and Japan into the family of nations. Before this century those populous countries had been known rather as vast outlying regions where untold millions of our fellow-men lived and died in their own special spheres, irrespective of the rest of mankind—somewhat as the outlying planets Uranus and Neptune, which had traveled on for ages in their remote orbits quite unknown to us, until recently discovered.

I arrived in Canton, October 25, 1833, and was reported to the Chinese authorities (who took cognizance of all foreigners coming to dwell in their land,) as a *fan kwei*, or "foreign devil," who was to reside in the American, or *Kwang-yuen* hong. Kingqua, its owner, was the special Hong merchant, who had the oversight and responsibility of my good conduct. As it turned out, I never saw my guardian, and the American missionaries, four in number, all remained under his nominal cognizance as long as he lived.

The different state of things when last I left Peking, October 25, 1876, will indicate the great changes which had passed over the empire in the intervening years. Instead of one port where foreign ships of every flag were obliged to trade, thirteen were opened. Nine foreign ministers had their legations at the capital instead of their several mercantile consuls at Canton, who acted as go-betweens in behalf of their countrymen and the native officers; nor could these be induced to receive anything directly from the hands of the foreigners themselves, while the Hong merchants would accept nothing if not drawn up in the form of a petition.

In November, 1874, the United States minister, Mr. Avery, delivered his credentials to the Emperor Tunachi, and I interpreted them and his address to his imperial majesty. The last refuge of Chinese supremacy over other nations had been removed the year before by the emperor's peacefully yielding the point of prostration whenever plenipotentiaries from foreign lands came into his presence. The last and most important change during the period of my residence was the facility possessed for travel and missionary labor. At my arrival the land was shut up to foreign travelers for any purpose; while converts in the Protestant mission at Canton numbered only two or three, under the care of two missionaries. At my departure the work was spreading into each of the eighteen provinces, and its legality had been secured and guarded by the sanctions of treaty. In forty years from 1833 to 1873, China had been introduced into the fraternity of nations, where, I hope, she will be allowed to stay and exercise her rights. The other governments are likely to make her fulfill her duties.

PROFESSOR S. W. WILLIAMS. News

The Author of "The Middle Kingdom" Dies at his Home in this City.

Professor Samuel Wells Williams died at his residence, 30 College street, at 8:40 o'clock on Saturday night. He came to this city in 1877 when he was appointed professor of Chinese language and literature in Yale college. About two years ago he received a severe fall on the sidewalk and dislocated his shoulder. Paralysis followed and it was discovered that his strength was slowly leaving him. Since the first of January he has been confined to his home, and during the last two weeks he failed rapidly.

Professor Williams was born in Utica, N. Y., in September, 1812. He received his education at the Renselaer school in Troy, and in 1833 he went to Canton, China, as a printer. There he began the study of the Chinese language and assisted in editing the *Chinese Repository*, a monthly publication started the year before by Dr. Bridgman. He removed to Macao in 1835 to complete Medhurst's Hokkeen dictionary, and in July, 1837, he went to Japan in a vessel sent by C. W. King to return seven shipwrecked Japanese to their homes. The vesel was driven away from two ports and the men were brought back to Macao. Mr. Williams gained an acquaintance with the Japanese language on this voyage and subsequently translated a treatise on smelting copper, and made a version of the book of Genesis and the gospel of St. Matthew into the Japanese.

Following the publication of Dr. Bridgman's Chinese Chrestomathy," of which Mr. Williams contributed about one-third, he printed in Chinese his "Easy Lessons" in Chinese in 1841, an English and Chinese vocabulary in 1843, and "Chinese Commercial Guide" in 1844. In November of the last year he started for America, passing through Egypt, Syria and Europe, reaching New-York in 1845. To obtain funds for the project of casting a font of movable Chinese type in Berlin he delivered lectures on the condition of China, which were afterwards published under the title of "The Middle Kingdom."

Soon after the publication of this work the faculty of Union college conferred upon him the degree of LL.D. He went back to Canton in 1848 and took charge of the *Chinese Repository* which ceased publication in 1851. He was with Commodore Perry in the expedition to Japan as interpreter and in 1855 was appointed secretary and interpreter to the United States legation and took charge of it until the arrival of Mr.

Parker, the minister.

From 1861 to 1874 he was engaged in preparing a dictionary of the Chinese language. In 1877 he returned to this country and made New-Haven his home. In 1881 he was made president of the American Bible society and of the Oriental society. In the latter part of 1883 he published a new and enlarged edition of the "Middle Kingdom," which is a complete account of the condition and history of China at the present time.

Professor Williams leaves a rich collection of Chinese curiosties. He was a most interesting companion, and many friends all over the world will be grieved at his loss.

N.H. Palladium **OBITUARY.** Feb. 18. '84

S. Wells Williams.

Died on Saturday evening, February 16, Professor Samuel Wells Williams, LL. D., aged seventy-two. The funeral services will be held in the Battell chapel on Tuesday at 4 p. m. Dr. Williams was universally acknowledged to be one of the most eminent scholars in Chinese literature, geography and history, who was not of Chinese lineage. He was born in Utica, N. Y., September 22, 1812. He was graduated in 1832 at the Rensselaer Polytechnic institute in Troy. In 1833 he went to Canton as a printer in the mission of the American Board of Commissioners for Foreign Missions. He then assisted in editing the "Chinese Repository," a monthly periodical begun the year before by Dr. Bridgman. In 1835 he removed to Macao to complete the printing of Medhurst's Hokkein Dictionary. In 1837, while on a voyage to Japan to return home some shipwrecked mariners, he learned their language and translated the books of Genesis and Matthew into it. He contributed about one-third to Dr. Bridgman's "Chinese Christianity," and published "Easy Lessons in Chinese" (Macao, 1842), "Chinese Commercial Guide" (1844), "English and Chinese Vocabulary in the Court Dialect" (1844). He visited the United States in 1845, and to obtain funds for casting a font of Chinese type delivered lectures on China, which were enlarged and published under the title of "The Middle Kingdom" (two volumes, New York, 1848). Soon after he received the degree of LL.D. from Union college In 1848 he returned to Canton and took charge of the "Chinese Repository," which was discontinued in 1871 with its twentieth volume. He accompanied Commodore Perry's expedition to Japan in 1853-54 as interpreter and in 1855 was appointed secretary interpreter to the United States legation to Japan and took charge of it until the arrival of the minister. In 1856 he published a "Tonic dictionary of the Chinese language in the Canton dialect" and an enlarged edition of the "Commercial Guide," both printed at the mission press in Macao, which was burned with the most of the books in December 1856. In 1858 he assisted Mr. Reed at Tientsin in the negotiation connected with the treaty and the next year accompanied Mr. Ward to Pekin to exchange the ratifications. He visited the United States in 1860-61 and on his return to China in 1862 the legation was removed to Pekin. The next year he published the fifth edition of the "Commercial Guide" nearly new written. In 1874 he published the 'Syllabic dictionary of the of the Chinese language" (4to. Shangai) containing 12,527 characters with the pronunciati n as heard at Pekin, Canton, Amoy and Shangai. This has superseded all other Chinese-English dictionaries. A new edition of the Tonic dictionary, revised by Dr. Eitel, has been published by aid of the English authorities (Hong Kong, 1876.) Dr. Williams returned to the United States in 1875. In 1876 he came to New Haven to reside, and in 1877 was elected professor of the Chinese language and literature in Yale college. So far as he has been known by our citizens he has been esteemed and beloved. His modest demeanor, his loving spirit, his gentle manners and his glowing Christian faith have won the hearts of every one whom he has met, even for a brief interview. His accurate and varied knowledge of events and countries that are not easily accessible, his discriminating judgment and his sturdy common sense, have often elicited the wonder of those who have resorted to him for counsel and information. The kindly humor which beamed from his face seemed to impart to his presence perpetual sunshine, while his solid sense, his definite knowledge and his unswerving Christian faith commended the respectful homage of all who knew him. Two or three years ago he was called to part with the wife who had been the joy of his life—whom no one ever knew and could forget. Subsequently he was partially disabled by paralysis, but neither the clearness of his mind, nor the sweetness of his spirit, nor the steadfastness of his childlike faith were disturbed by his personal and domestic trials. A few months ago he finished the new edition of his "Middle Kingdom." Since that time he has quietly waited the Master's call, which should bid him come up higher. The many friends who loved and honored him cannot doub' that the call was welcome, and that w' him the earthly has gently passed into heavenly life.

FEBRUARY 17. 1884

N. H. Register.

THE DEATH RECORD.

Prof. S. Wells Williams—Career of a Distinguished Sinologue.

Samuel Wells Williams, the venerable and world-known Oriental scholar and professor of Chinese language and literature in Yale college, died at his residence, 39 College street, at 8:40 last evening. Two years ago Professor Williams received a severe fall ou the stairway in his residence. A slight paralytic stroke followed. He seemed to recover, but after awhile it was found that his strength was slowly leaving him. Since the first of January has been unable to leave the house. He has been failing fast for two weeks. His inability to assimilate his food brought on enemia. Ever since his fall he has been carefully attended by his brother, H. Dwight Williams. At his death he was surrounded by his family, who were not unprepared for the result.

Professor Williams was born in Utica, N. Y., in September, 1812. He was educated at the Rensselaer school in Troy. He went to China in 1833 as a printer in the newly established mission of the American board of commissioners for foreign missions at Canton. Here he began the study of the Chinese language and assisted in editing the *Chinese Repository*, a monthly publication started the year before by Dr. Bridgman. In 1835 he removed to Macao to complete the printing of Medhurst's Hokkeen dictionary; and in July, 1837, he went to Japan in a vessel sent by C. W. King, of Canton, to return to their homes seven shipwrecked Japanese. The vessel was driven away from two ports by cannon balls, and the men were brought back to Macao. Mr. Williams obtained from some of them an acquaintance with their language, translated a treatise on smelting copper from the original, and made a version of the book of Genesis and the gospel of St. Matthew into the Japanese. After the publication of Dr. Bridgman's "Chinese Chrestomathy," to which Mr. Williams contributed about one-third, he printed in Chinese his "Easy Lessons in Chinese" in 1841, "English and Chinese Vocabulary" in 1843, and "Chinese Commercial Guide" in 1844. In November, 1844, he set out for America, passing through Egypt, Syria and Europe, and reaching New York in October, 1845. The project of casting a font of movable Chinese type in Berlin had been started, and to obtain funds for the enterprise he delivered lectures on the condition of China, which were afterward enlarged and published under the title of "The Middle Kingdom" in 2 volumes, 12 mo., New York, 1848. Soon after the publication of this work the faculty of Union college conferred upon him the degree of LL.D. In 1848 he returned to Canton and took charge of the *Chinese Repository*, which was closed in 1851 with its twentieth volume. In 1853-4 he accompanied Commodore Perry's expedition to Japan as interpreter. In 1855 he was appointed secretary and interpreter to the United States legation and took charge of it until the arrival of the minister, Mr. Parker. He published in 1856 a "Tonic Dictionary of the Chinese Language," and in 1858 went with Mr. Reed to Tien-tsin to assist in the negotiations connected with the treaty, and the next year with Mr. Ward to Peking to exchange the ratifications. In 1860 he revisited the United States and delivered lectures before the Smithsonian institute and elsewhere. Afterwards he returned to China and lived there until 1876, when he took up his residence in this city. In the same year he was elected professor of Chinese language and literature in Yale. He held this professorship at the time of his death. He was a frequent contributor to the *New Englander* and other magazines. In the fall of 1883 he published a new and enlarged edition of the "Middle Kingdom," which is probably the most complete account of the condition and history of China at the present time.

Phila. Press.

EBRUARY 18, 1884.

OBITUARY.

Dr. S. Wells Williams, Chinese Scholar and Ex-Secretary of Legation.

NEW HAVEN, Feb. 16.—Professor Samuel Wells Williams, LL. D., the well-known

Dr. Williams, who died yesterday in the 71st year of his age, has been for fifty years identified with Oriental scholarship, and the greater part of this period in the front rank of Chinese scholars. For eight years past a professor of the Chinese languages and literature in Yale College, for seventeen years before the secretary and interpretor of the American legation in China, and for nearly twice this period in the service of the American Board: from his landing in China in 1833 until his final departure, in 1875, he bore his important share in the creation of a Christian literature for China, in unlocking Chinese literature to the West, and in aiding, by book tract and speech, by the labors of the closet, the despatches of the diplomat and the earnest work of the missionary, in the great labor of opening the Western ideas, and, above all, to the Christian religion the millions of China.

Born September, 1812, he had just been graduated from the Troy Polytechnic Institute in his 20th year, when the call of the American Board for a printer in China led him to abandon his scientific studies and make his way, in 1833, to the strip of seacoast to which European trade with China was restricted. Like his three classmates, Professor Dana, of Yale; Professor Gray, of Harvard, and Professor Hall, chief of the New York Geological Survey, he was looking forward to a life of scientific research from which he turned aside to a work apparently hopeless and long fruitless, but crowned at length with the abundant rewards of study and research which extended from his printing press and the Chinese language to the broad field of the Chinese Empire, its history, its literature, its commerce, its products and its society. In all, Dr. Williams was an original observer, on most he became an accepted authority, and nearly a hundred titles, extending from the "Middle Kingdom" to short papers, attest the scope of his remarks, the industry of his pen and the value of his labors. The first twelve years of his long residence in China were devoted to the patient preliminary studies which laid the broad foundation of his later attainments. A series of elementary works on the Chinese language appeared during these years, he added Japanese to his knowledge of Chinese, and in addition to contributions to the *Chinese Repository*, he prepared the lectures which in 1848 were enlarged and published as the "Middle Kingdom," a work which in its last revision issued in 1883, remains the standard authority upon China.

The publication of this work made him conspicuous among Chinese scholars and known to the general public. In 1851 he accompanied Commodore Perry's expedition to Japan and remained for twenty years after, associated with the diplomatic intercourse of China and the United States. Earlier he had aided in the preparation of the Cushing treaty, and until he retired from the service he was charged with the prolonged negotiations, always difficult, often delicate and sometimes dangerous, by which the United States, without firing a gun or clearing the deck of a single vessel, gained from China all the commercial and diplomatic privileges extorted on behalf of other nations by wars. He successfully piloted the American Legation to Pekin in 1859, when other embassies were excluded, and his personal influence upon the Chinese coast and in the Chinese Court came to among the most remarkable fruits of a life of patient devotion to the printing press and the printed page.

In 1875 he came to this country, and he has since lived in New Haven as professor of Chinese language and literature, continuing in retirement his Chinese studies. Before leaving China, he published the crowning work of his life, the "Syllabic Dictionary of the Chinese Language," a work which stands alone among Anglo-Chinese lexicons. Twenty years before, he had published a "Tonic Dictionary" of the Canton dialect. Besides these works, he had issued a number of lesser works, translated parts of the Bible into Japanese, and published through a long series of years successive editions of a "Chinese Commercial Guide" still employed as a manual of Chinese commercial usage. His later years were given to successive corrections of his Syllabic Dictionary and the preparation of a new edition of the "Middle Kingdom," in which he was assisted by his son, Wells Frederic Williams. Besides his son, he leaves a daughter, now married to Thomas Grosvenor, of the British diplomatic service. His remarkable scholarship was scarcely less remarkable than his simple devotion to duty, illustrated, as it was only likely to be, by a man of Puritan blood in providing a substitute during the war while resident abroad and punctiliously paying his income tax as a just contribution to the necessities of his government.

Death of Samuel Wells Williams.

Prof Samuel Wells Williams, probably the most accomplished Chinese scholar outside of China, whose labors as missionary, diplomat, linguist and civilizer have been of the highest importance to that country and the western nations, died at New Haven Saturday evening. He was at the time of his death professor of the Chinese language and literature in Yale college, to fill which he returned in 1875 from over 40 years work in China and Japan. Born at Utica, N. Y., September 12, 1812, he was graduated from the Rensselaer polytechnic institute in Troy at the age of 20, and the next year went to Canton as printer for the American board of foreign missions, becoming almost immediately after assistant editor of the Chinese Repository, a periodical of great interest and value, then in its third year. In 1835 he was transferred to Macao to complete the printing of Medhurst's Hokkeën dictionary. Two years later, being appointed to return some shipwrecked Japanese to their own land he learned their language, and proceeded to translate into it Genesis and Matthew's gospel. He contributed a third of Dr Bridgman's "Chinese Chrestomathy," a book designed to help in the study of Chinese; prepared a book of "Easy Lessons in Chinese," an English and Chinese vocabulary of the court or mandarin dialect, and a "Chinese Commer-'mercial Guide,"—which last has been of great value to men doing business in or with China, and reached a fifth edition in 1863, which was almost wholly rewritten by him. Mr Williams returned to America in 1845, in order to obtain funds for casting a font of Chinese type in Berlin for the use of the mission press; and to this end he delivered a series of lectures which were enlarged and in 1848 published under the title of "The Middle Kingdom." This book was immediately accepted as the best account up to that time given of China, and has never lost that authoritative place; its last edition, completed and issued last year, altogether surpassing every other for comprehensive, accurate and judicious presentation of the history, constitution, race characteristics, social economy, religion and literature of China. Mr Williams was in 1848 made an LL. D. by Union college; he went back to China in that year and resumed the charge of the Chinese Repository, which ran for three years and was then discontinued.

The next year the great event occurred of Commodore Perry's expedition to Japan, and Dr Williams went with it as interpreter, and remained as secretary and interpreter to the United States legation in that country, being in charge of the legation until the arrival of the United States minister. In 1856 he published his "Tonic Dictionary of the Canton dialect," which 20 years later was republished by the English authorities there. During 1858-9 he was attached to the United States embassy, assisting William B. Reed in the negotiation of the treaty of Tientsin, and accompanied Ward to Pekin to exchange the ratifications. Then, after two years spent in this country in the interest of this mission, Dr Williams devoted himself for years in China to the preparation of his "Syllabic Dictionary of the Chinese Language," which was published in 1874 and contains 12,527 characters with their pronunciation as heard at Pekin, Canton, Amoy, and Shanghai. This at once superseded all other dictionaries of Chinese.

In 1875, as before stated, Dr Williams returned to be the first occupant of the chair of Chinese language and literature at Yale, and there devoted himself to the thorough revision of his great work, "The Middle Kingdom." He fell and broke his collar-bone, two years ago, and shortly after had a paralytic shock, which disabled him from work, so that his son, Frederick Wells Williams was called upon to complete the labor. Prof Williams, however, recovered his health in such a degree that he was able to supervise the second volume. In the preface to the edition of 1883 he observes how the 43 years of his work in China compassed the entire history of the opening of the country. "On my arrival at Canton 'in 1833," he writes, "I was officially re'ported, with two other Americans, to 'the hong merchant Kingqua as *fankwai*, or "foreign devils,' who had come to live under his 'tutelage. In 1874 as secretary of the American 'embassy at Pekin, I accompanied B. P. Avery 'to the presence of the emperor Tungchi, when 'the minister of the United States presented his 'letters of credence on a footing of perfect equal'ity with the 'Son of Heaven.'"

Prof Williams's career indicates his marked traits,—enthusiasm, earnestness, indefatigable industry, a single devotion to purpose,—and that purpose, intelligently pursued from first to last, the elevation of his fellow-beings. He believed thoroughly in the paramount importance of Christian missions, and never failed on their advocacy. He never tolerated belittling views of the Chinese, and was prompt to correct any expression of such a view. His native abilities were considerable but his singular and devout energy made his achievements extraordinary. He has earned a secure and enviable fame among the most useful men of the age. Spr'field Republican

---

Hartford Courant Feb. 18. 1884

The death of Dr. S. Wells Williams the first professor of the Chinese language and literature in Yale college, is a loss to American scholarship. Two years ago he had a bad fall breaking his collar bone, and soon after suffered a shock of paralysis. He apparently recovered, but he was over 70. The end has now come, and it is an unusually busy and fruitful life that is ended. Just out of the Rensselaer Polytechnic school, a lad of 21 years, he went to China in the service of the A. B. C. F. M. and his missionary, diplomatic and philological labors in that country covered a stretch of over forty years. We owe to them his "Middle Kingdom," his "Easy Lessons in Chinese, "Vocabulary of the Court Dialect," "Chinese Commercial Guide" (now in its fifth edition)· "Dictionary of the Canton Dialect," and Syllabic of the Chinese Language." He accompanied the Perry expedition to Japan as interpreter, and translated two or three books of the Bible into Japanese. He has filled his chair in Yale college since 1875, and it will not be an easy thing to replace him.

Feby. 19 '84

THE LATE S. WELLS WILLIAMS.

Central New York has a melancholy interest in the death of Professor S. WELLS WILLIAMS, of Yale College, announced yesterday, less however, from personal association, although the region of his birth, than from knowledge of his lifework. Professor WILLIAMS was born at Utica, September 22, 1812, and immediately upon the completion of his collegiate education at the Rensselaer Polytechnic Institute at Troy, he, in 1833, went to Canton, China, as printer for the American Board of Foreign Missions, but almost immediately after his arrival added to his duties the assistant editorship of the *Chinese Repository*. In 1835 he was transferred to Macao to complete the printing of MEDHURST's Hokkeen Dictionary. Two years later he learned the Japanese language and immediately utilized it in translating into that language the book of Genesis and the Gospel of ST. MATTHEW. He rendered important assistance to Dr. BRIDGMAN in his work intended to facilitate the study of the Chinese tongue, and himself prepared a little book of "Easy Lessons in Chinese." This he followed by an "English and Chinese Vocabulary of the Court Dialect," and by a "Chinese Commercial Guide," which has been almost invaluable to business men having transactions with that country, and of which the fifth edition, published in 1853, was nearly rewritten by him. The years 1845 to 1848 were spent by him in America in delivering lectures and otherwise obtaining funds to secure the casting of a font of Chinese type for the use of the mission press. The lectures were afterward enlarged and published under the title of "The Middle Kingdom," and secured in that shape a large circulation. At this time he was made an LL. D. by Union College. From 1848 to 1851 he resumed the charge of the *Chinese Repository*, which was then discontinued. He served as interpreter to Commodore PERRY in the expedition to Japan, and afterward as secretary and interpreter to the United States Legation in that country, of which he was in charge until the arrival of the United States Minister. In 1856 he published his "Tonic Dictionary of the Canton Dialect," which was republished twenty years later by the English authorities in that country. The years 1858 and 1859 were chiefly occupied in diplomatic service in China, the next two years in the United States in the service of the mission. The immense labor involved in the preparation of a "Syllabic Dictionary of the Chinese Language" occupied the greater portion of his time for several years. It appeared in 1874 and has lightened the labors of all persons who have occasion to study the language to an incalculable degree. In 1875 he returned to the United States and accepted the position of Professor of the Chinese Language at Yale College, then just established, and to which he brought all the enthusiasm and energy which had ever been characteristic of him. He has also of late years been an ardent advocate of the "spelling reform," which gains ground very slowly, however. His argument in its behalf was chiefly the substantial aid it would afford foreigners, and particularly Orientals, in acquiring the English language. Professor WILLIAMS was stricken with paralysis about two years ago, but recovered. For the past two weeks he has rapidly failed, and finally succumbed to a mightier than human power, on Saturday evening.

Syracuse Journal

The American Stationer

OBITUARY.

N.Y. Feb. 21. 1884

S. WELLES WILLIAMS.

Professor Samuel Welles Williams, LL. D., died at New Haven, Conn., on Saturday evening, February 16, aged seventy-two.

Dr. Williams was acknowledged to be one of the most eminent scholars in Chinese literature, geography and history, who was not of Chinese lineage. He was born in Utica, N. Y., September 22, 1812. He was graduated in 1832 at the Rensselaer Polytechnic Institute in Troy. In 1833 he went to Canton as a printer in the mission of the American Board of Commissioners for Foreign Missions. He then assisted in editing the "Chinese Repository," a monthly periodical begun the year before by Dr. Bridgman. In 1835 he removed to Macao to complete the printing of Medhurst's Hokkein Dictionary. In 1837, while on a voyage to Japan to return home some shipwrecked mariners, he learned their language and translated the books of Genesis and Matthew into it. He contributed about one-third to Dr. Bridgman's "Chinese Christianity," and published "Easy Lessons in Chinese" (Macao, 1842), "Chinese Commercial Guide" (1844), "English and Chinese Vocabulary in the Court Dialect" (1844). He visited the United States in 1845, and, to obtain funds for casting a font of Chinese type, delivered lectures on China, which were enlarged and published under the title of "The Middle Kingdom," (two volumes, New York, 1848). Soon after he received the degree of LL D. from Union College. In 1848 he returned to Canton and took charge of the "Chinese Repository," which was discontinued in 1871 with its twentieth volume. He accompanied Commodore Perry's expedition to Japan in 1853–54 as interpreter and in 1855 was appointed secretary interpreter to the United States legation to Japan, and took charge of it until the arrival of the minister. In 1856 he published a "Tonic dictionary of the Chinese language in the Canton dialect" and an enlarged edition of the "Commercial Guide," both printed at the mission press in Macao, which was burned with the most of the books in December, 1856. In 1858 he assisted Mr. Reed at Tientsin in the negotiation connected with the treaty and the next year accompanied Mr. Ward to Pekin to exchange the ratifications. He visited the United States in 1860-61 and on his return to China in 1862 the legation was removed to Pekin. The next year he published the fifth edition of the "Commercial Guide" nearly new written. In 1874 he published the "Syllabic dictionary of the Chinese language" (4to. Shangai) containing 12,527 characters with the pronunciation as heard at Pekin, Canton, Amoy and Shangai. This has superseded all other Chinese-English dictionaries. A new edition of the Tonic dictionary, revised by Dr. Eitel, has been published by aid of the English authorities (Hong Kong, 1876) Dr. Williams returned to the United States in 1875. In 1876 he went to New Haven to reside, and in 1877 was elected professor of the Chinese language and literature in Yale college. His funeral took place on Tuesday last.

The Book Buyer (N.Y.) March 1884.

SAMUEL WELLS WILLIAMS.

DR. WILLIAMS, the author of important works relating to China and Chinese literature, died at his home in New Haven on Saturday evening, February 16th.

Principal among his works were a "Tonic Dictionary of the Chinese Language in the Canton Dialect," published in 1856; "The Middle Kingdom," the first edition of which was brought out in 1848; and "The Syllabic Dictionary of the Chinese Language," published in 1874. Dr. Williams was born in

In the opening of Japan I also had a share. In 1837 I was passenger in the American ship Morrison, which was bound to Yedo for the purpose of restoring seven shipwrecked Japanese to their homes. The vessel was repulsed by four cannon brought to bear upon us from the shore, but happily no serious damage was received during six hours of firing. After our return, three of the men were employed in my printing office, and I learned in a rather rude fashion, the use of their native tongue. In 1853 I was one of Commodore Perry's suite, which landed within a short distance of the spot where the four cannon had been placed 16 years before; here, on this occasion, we delivered President Fillmore's letter asking for better treatment for American ships than the Morrison had received. During this short visit, and the five months that the squadron was in those waters the next year, I was able to explain much of the purpose of the American expedition to the officials and people at the three ports and the Lewchew islands, and perhaps remove their fears that its real design was conquest or pillage.

During the half century of your charter, these two ancient nations have undergone the most rapid and thoro' changes which have ever happened to any nation recorded in history—changes involving their political, religious and social life, and which are likely to obliterate the action of their former ages. It was a great satisfaction to me to have been a close observer of and coworker in these mighty alterations. Most of them tended to the elevation and benefit of the two nations involved; and with the political and commercial relations established by the treaties of 1858, came also the toleration and teaching of the Holy Scriptures among the people in their own tongues, thereby giving them valid reasons for the changes proposed.

Few of the citizens of Utica who will join in this half century commemoration have gone farther than I have or stayed away longer; yet my love for the old homestead seems to grow with increasing years. Three of my former schoolmates visited me while abroad in the first twelve years—John T. K. Lothrop, Joab Brown and Lieutenant M. Hunt. Out of the whole period I spent twenty-two years in the employ of the American board of missions, and twenty-one in the service of the United States; but my sole aim in all of them was to promote the welfare of the Chinese.

Allow me, in conclusion, to thank you for this opportunity of joining in your civic celebration. As I can not tell you anything about Utica, I am constrained to say what I do about the land of my adoption—speaking with pleasure of the wonderful advances it has made within the past five decades; and I believe that during the next five, the Governor of the nations, whose wisdom and power are now seen as his promises to the land of Sinim are fulfilling, will show even ... things for the ancient race of Han.

Troy Times. Feby. 19 1884

Samuel Wells Williams.

Dr. S. Wells Williams, professor of Chinese language and literature in Yale college, died at New Haven on Saturday. He was a native of Utica, born in 1812, educated in the Rensselaer polytechnic institute, Troy, under Dr. Amos Eaton, went to Canton, China, as missionary printer in 1833, returned to the United States in 1845, lectured extensively on China to get a font of Chinese type, cast in Berlin, published "The Middle Kingdom," a most complete and exhaustive work in China, in 1848, married in 1849 a niece of Chancellor Walworth in Plattsburgh, was made doctor of laws by Union college, returned to China, made a dictionary of the Canton dialect, and in 1855 became secretary of legation to the United States government in China, a position which he held for twenty-one years, residing at the capital, Pekin. There he spent eleven years on a syllabic dictionary of the language, which has superseded all former vocabularies with learners of the language. A revised edition of his "Middle "Kingdom" was published last year. He spent forty-three years in China, returned in 1876, in 1877 was made professor of Chinese in Yale, and in 1880, on the death of President Allen ot Girard, was made president of the American bible society. He was a man of strong sense and unwearied application, a sample of the American "self-educated" man, enlisting in the missionary work at twenty years of age, and filling every hour of a long life with varied and useful labors.

S. Wells Williams.

—Class of '32 Utica

We gave in a late number of the INQUIRER a brief synopsis of the work of Rev. S. Wells Williams, the Chinese missionary and Christian Oriental scholar. We are glad to give a more detailed and interesting tribute to the memory of this distinguished man, read at the monthly meeting of the Oneida Historical Society, last Monday evening, Rev. Dr. Hartley presided at the up stairs meeting. He first called upon Thomas W. Seward, who, in an half hour's address, paid an admirable and characteristic tribute to the memory of the late S. Wells Williams. Mr R. S. Williams, of this city, is a brother of the missionary. The portion relating to Professor Williams' life-work is as follows:

It remains for me to give briefly an outline of his labors and the things he accom lished. On his arrival in China, in 1833, he began to assist Dr. Bridgman in editing and publishing the *Chinese Repository*. In 1835 he moved to Macao, and completed the printing of Medhurst's Dictionary. In 1837 there occurred an important episode in his life, the voyage to Japan, for the purpose of restoring to their home some shipwrecked seamen, the repulse of the ship from Japanese shores, its return to Macao, and the learning their language while the homeless mariners were inmates of his house. To Dr. Bridgman's "Chartomathy" he contributed about one-third. In 1842 he began writing and publishing his own works, viz: "Easy Lessons in Chinese," "Chinese Commercial Guide," a book which was repeatedly enlarged, and "English and Chinese Vocabulary in the Court Dialect." The first edition of his "Middle Kingdom" was published in this country in 1848. In 1856 he published "A Tonic Dictionary in the Chinese Language in the Canton Dialect.' In the same year the mission press in Macao was burned and most of his library. In 1874 he published, at Shanghai, "The Syllabic Dictionary of the Chinese Language," containing 12,527 characters, with their pronunciation, as heard at Pekin, Canton, Amoy and Shanghai. This dictionary has not only taken the place of all other Chinese and English dictionaries, but is an enduring witness to extraordinary learning and research.

In the services of the United States, Mr. Williams went as an interpreter with Commodore Perry's squadron to Japan in 1853, and in 1855 was put in charge of the legation until a member should arrive from the United States. In negotiating a treaty with China in 1858, he was of indispensable service, the great esteem in which he was held by the Chinese government enabling him to secure points of advantage not otherwise obtainable. During the twenty years of his connection with the United States embassy he was, in effect, the soul of it, most of the time doing the work of an embassador with the rank of a secretary. That he was not made minister by his government is its lasting opprobrium.

In 1857, Mr. Williams withdrew from the service of the American Board of Missions, to devote himself to the duties pertaining to the American embassy. Not long afterward, and as soon as his income would permit, he returned to the treasury of the board all the money he had ever received from it, together with some interest, which a less conscientious and more careless man might possibly have neglected to compute. His largest contribution to the board, however, was money paid him by the United States government for acting as interpreter, and which amounted to the considerable sum of $2,705. His benefactiyns were constant and widely spread. I know of his once sending $50 to the Episcopal Theological Seminary of Dakota, Wis., being prompted thereto by discovering that the school depended upon daily contributions for daily bread. He bequeathed the larger part of the property of the Chinese Dictionary to the American College in Peking, together with one important legacy to the American Bible Society, for the specific printing of the Bible in the Chinese language.

Analysis of Mr. Williams' character, after what I have here written, and others have written and will continue to write, is not needed. Analysis presupposes complexity of elements. In him there was no complexity. He was as open and genial as the sunlight, and wherever he went he took the light and warmth with him. He was sincere, modest, gracious, industrious, pains-taking, courageous, patient, charitable, tolerant, humane, spiritual. He went to China because he saw the path of duty, and was not afraid to walk therein. Established there, he determined to give the whole of a preparatively long life to finding out and appropriating everything that in any way pertained to the mysterious people he had come to enlighten and to help. Hence his exhaustive contributions to the world's knowledge of China and the East, contributions which have acted reflectively, and stimulated beyond computation the work of foreign Christian missions, of which he was a chief exemplar.

During his first visit to this country, and in the year 1847, Mr. Williams married Miss Sarah Walworth, of Plattsburg, N. Y. In saying that Mrs. Williams fully met all the requirements demanded of her by her husband's responsible employments and positions, as well as the far more important requirements of domestic, social and religious life, we add nothing to the glad testimony of those who enjoyed the great privilege of intimacy, friendship or acquaintance with her. She died January 26, 1881, in New Haven, and was buried in Forest Hill, by the side of three of her children who had preceded her in their childhood. Thither also, on the 20th of February, 1884, her husband was carried and there left in the company of kindred belonging to four generations of his family and name.

S. WELLS WILLIAMS, D.D., LL.D.—A "MAN GREATLY BELOVED."

By R. A. Sawyer, D.D.

The author of that English classic on China, "The Middle Kingdom," the intrepid mediator between the United States and the "Hermit Nations," the President of our own Bible Society, and member of several societies in England, with one of whose noble families he is allied through his daughter's marriage, has just "passed over" (in words often on his lips) "to the majority," and left a vacancy not soon to be filled or forgotten.

Though he was known to all the world in his public character and work, yet to comparatively few was his personal presence familiar, in which the quiet dignity of innate greatness was singularly blended with the gentle serenity of a goodness which seemed truly apostolic.

On a certain occasion he stood before the University and spoke of the missionary work in his quiet way from an experience of forty-seven years, and the impression made may be inferred from the remark of a student on retiring: "Did you mark Dr. Williams's face? He looked like St. John and St. Paul in one. The most eloquent face conceivable!" The instincts of youth are seldom truer than in this judgment. No one could look into Dr. Williams's eye as it lit with thought, glowed with fervid conviction, and twinkled with controlled humor, all at once, without the feeling that he was in the presence of something as rare as it was unique. The fulness of mind and heart were fused into a crystalline manliness, which won affection and exacted reverence. And when by a fall on a slippery sidewalk the shock was given which for nearly two years assaulted, and at length terminated his life, the serene strength of his character came out like a mighty fortress, from which obscuring forests had been cut away. To have heard him speak in terms of Scripture as he pointed to that disabled arm, was to learn something new, both of faith in God and of the meaning of His Word. To be led by him in prayer, was to go literally upward into the "secret place," when in solemn quiet one of the greatest men spoke in childlike terms, as he breathed his confidences into the ear of the Father Almighty.

Dr. Williams sympathized with the late Dr. Bacon in his oft-expressed opinion that "public prayer was fast becoming a lost art." A distinguished minister once used the following expressions in pulpit prayer: "We thank Thee that all men are Thy children, and that when we love men, we love Thee; when we think highly of human powers, we praise Thee; when we worship human genius, we are not idolaters, as our fathers thought." Coming out of the church, a Western man went swinging by, saying to his comrade "Great Scott, what praying!" "He probably means," said Dr. Williams, "John the Scot, who taught that every man was a theophany; and that is the way the new theology prays. Let us go in here," he added as we passed an Episcopal church, "and follow one of Cranmer's prayers, *to get the taste out of the mouth.*"

The scholarship of Dr. Williams was exact and searching, yet it covered a wide territory. His resources of information were as ready and sure as they were ample. His spirit was catholic and tolerant, yet he was jealous for the "ancient faith," and dealt vigorously with anything that tended to throw discredit on the work or belief of the great authorities of the reformed faith. Leaving the College chapel once, he exclaimed "Long life to our preacher! He does not hold up our fathers in the faith to be laughed at."

One who has come close enough to such a man to learn to value his companionship, can but feel lonely for his death. But he needed rest, and hath entered into it. "Thank God," he once said, "for the rest that remaineth!" With his dauntless, patient alertness, he tracked the tangled thickets of the Chinese phonetics till he once described himself as "Cooper's Pathfinder—a worn-out Leatherstocking!" Yet the last work of his life lacked nothing of finish or fidelity. How full-orbed his life was! How beautiful his old age! How like a translation, one thought of his death! How sweetly he spoke of the great sorrow of his last years, being comforted by the triumphant faith of the Christian wife who "moved on a little before"! How bravely he faced the "final solitude," which is more keenly bitter because the darkness deepens toward the night! Who can know these things save the few who were the nearest? But it is a legacy to those who loved him, more precious than his undying fame.

Two passages of Scripture, Dr. Williams once said, contained weightier truth, and more sublime, than any other words in human speech. The one was "The Word was made flesh"; the other, "We shall be like Him, for we shall see Him as He is." We may fittingly now say of him, as he spake of her who preceded him, "*His* eyes have seen the King in His beauty, and he is *satisfied.*"

N.Y. Observer Feb. 21 '84.

OBITUARY.

SAMUEL WELLS WILLIAMS, LL.D.

Prof. S. Wells Williams, of Yale College, who had spent most of his life in China, died at New Haven, on Saturday last, after an illness of two weeks. His health had been feeble for several years, and he had suffered from slight attacks of paralysis, but he continued active to the time of his death.

Prof. Williams was born in Utica, N. Y., Sept. 22, 1812. His father was in prosperous business at that place as a publisher, and the son while acquiring the art of printing devoted himself also to study, for which he had ample opportunities at his father's home. After being graduated at the Rensselaer Polytechnic Institute at Troy, in 1832, at the invitation of the American Board of Foreign Missions he went to Canton as a printer, where he succeeded in placing the press of the mission on a good foundation. He applied himself to the study of Chinese, and rapidly gained an extensive acquaintance with it and published a number of standard books that were useful to students who came after him. Soon after going to China Dr. Williams undertook the editorship of *The Chinese Repository*, in which he was assisted by many able contributors. After the lapse of many years *The Repository*, extending through twenty volumes, says *The Celestial Empire* (Shanghai), "is looked upon as of priceless worth, and the name of the editor will be long and honorably remembered by sinologues in connection with it." Prof. Williams completed at Macao in 1835 the printing of Medhurst's "Hokkeen Dictionary." In 1837 he was invited by the firm of Olyphant & Co. to visit Japan in their ship Morrison to return some shipwrecked sailors, and learned the Japanese language, into which he translated the Book of Genesis and Matthew. He aided Dr. Bridgman in preparing the "Chinese Chrestomathy," and in 1842 he published his "Easy Lessons in Chinese." This was followed in 1844 by "The Chinese Commercial Guide" and "An English and Chinese Vocabulary in the Court Dialect."

In 1845 Dr. Williams returned to the United States, remaining here for three years, and delivered a course of public lectures on Chinese subjects which delighted and instructed many audiences. In 1848 he published "The Middle Kingdom," which has been regarded as the most complete source of information on China and the highest authority on Chinese matters. A new and largely re-written edition has just been published. In 1848 he returned to China with a new font of Chinese type made in Berlin. In 1853-54 he accompanied Commodore Perry to Japan as the interpreter for the expedition, and was appointed Secretary and interpreter for the United States Legation in Japan, of which he had charge until the arrival of the first Minister. In 1856 Dr. Williams published a "Tonic Dictionary of the Chinese Language in the Canton Dialect," but most of the copies were burned with the mission-press at Macao in December of that year. In 1858 he aided William B. Reed in negotiating the treaty of Tientsin, and in 1859 he accompanied Mr. Ward to Pekin to exchange the ratifications.

Dr. Williams re-visited the United States in 1860-61, but returned to China in 1862 as Secretary of the United States Legation, then first established at Pekin. In 1863 he published a fifth edition of his "Chinese Commercial Guide," which he had nearly re-written. In 1874 he brought out at Shanghai the great work of his life, "The Syllabic Dictionary of the Chinese Language," and in 1876 he returned to the United States, having been appointed lecturer on Chinese at Yale College, where he remained until his death.

In March, 1881, Dr. Williams was chosen President of the American Bible Society, and presided at the monthly meetings of the Board of Managers when his health permitted. Dr. Williams was a man of strong and clear intellect, of profound learning, of the utmost simplicity of character, and with singleness of heart and mind devoted himself to the work of his divine Master.

Feby 21.

W-YORK EVANGELIST

DEATH OF S. WELLS WILLIAMS, LL.D.

This venerable missionary and scholar passed away at his home in New Haven on Saturday last, Feb. 16th. His confinement to his bed had been only of a few days, though for some time his health had been delicate and uncertain, once or twice, we believe, preventing, during the past year, the usually punctual and greatly interested discharge of his duties as President of the American Bible Society, here in New York. Dr. Williams succeeded to this post of honor on the death of James Lenox—and with peculiar fitness in the eyes of all the American Churches, and it might well be added, of evangelical Christendom. His life-long aims and labors were consonant in spirit and breadth with these later duties. First a printer, then a publisher and editor, then an author, later an interpreter and mediator for his own or his adopted country, and ever a herald of peace and good will, one whose very feet may be said to have been "beautiful upon the mountains," as surmounting great barriers of difficulty to the intercourse of nations, he was yet ever and always a simple missionary of the Cross in intent and spirit. We here copy a succinct account of his life and labors from Johnson's Cyclopædia:

Samuel Wells Williams, LL.D., was born at Utica, N. Y., Sept. 22, 1812; graduated at the Rensselaer Polytechnic Institute at Troy, N. Y., in 1832; went to Canton, China, as printer to the American Mission, in 1833; assisted in editing 'The Chinese Repository'; completed at Macao the printing of Medhurst's Dictionary; visited Japan to return some shipwrecked sailors in 1837; learned the Japanese language, into which he translated the books of Genesis and Matthew; aided Dr. Bridgman in preparing his 'Chinese Crestomathy'; published 'Easy Lessons in Chinese' (Macao, 1842), 'The Chinese Commercial Guide' (1844), and 'An English and Chinese Vocabulary in the Court Dialect' (1844); visited the United States in 1845, delivering lectures on China, and procuring from Berlin a new font of Chinese type; published 'The Middle Kingdom: A Survey of the Geography, Government, Education, Social Life, Arts, Religion, etc., of the Chinese Empire and its Inhabitants' (two volumes, 1848; third edition in 1857), which is still considered the best work of the kind on that country; returned to China in 1848; edited 'The Chinese Repository' until 1851, when it was discontinued; accompanied Commodore Perry as interpreter on his expedition to Japan in 1853–54; was appointed Secretary and Interpreter of the United States Legation in Japan, of which he had charge until the arrival of the first Minister; published a 'Tonic Dictionary of the Chinese Language in the Canton Dialect' (1856), of which most of the copies were burned in December of the same year, along with the Mission Press at Macao; aided Hon. William B. Reed in the negotiation of the Treaty of Tientsin in 1858; accompanied Mr. Ward to Peking to exchange the ratifications of 1859; revisited the United States in 1860–61; went to reside at Peking as Secretary of the United States Legation in 1862, then first established in the capital of China; published a fifth edition of 'The Commercial Guide' (1863), nearly rewritten; completed and brought out the great work of his life, 'The Syllabic Dictionary of the Chinese Language' (4to, Shanghai, 1874); returned to the United States in 1875, and settled at New Haven, Conn., where he was appointed Lecturer on Chinese at Yale College. A new edition of his 'Tonic Dictionary,' revised by Dr. Eitel, has been published by the English authorities (Hong Kong, 1876).

This bare mention of Dr. Williams' li
may possibly fail to interest here and
reader, but certainly no minister or
capable of estimating intellectual indus
achievement at its worth, will lightly
it. And setting out in life in the full s
consecration, he seems to have been f
by the Master whom he served to th
close. It is but a few months since h
pleted a thorough revision of the great li
monument of his life, "The Middle King
As now published by the Scribners, it
sentially a new book. But we need not
of it here, as quite recently a lengthy and
ful review of it, written by Dr. Erski
White, appeared in THE EVANGELIST.

Of all Europeans, Gen. Gordon is dou
China's most brilliant benefactor. B
served the Empire but as a soldier and
campaig[illegible]e Dr. Williams and such
whether [illegible]nt there or for a little h
America, de[illegible]ted long lives of assiduou
disinterested effort to the highest welf
all her people. The future will magnify
Culbertson and Bridgman and William
men of like devotion, have done, by illust
its far-reaching influence for good.

One more of them has gone. Professor Samuel Wells Williams, of Yale College, was one of the few boys closely linked together in the Sunday school of the First Presbyterian church, Utica, N.Y. He died on Saturday, the 16th inst., at New-Haven, after an illness of two weeks, in his 72nd year. We knew him as a thoughtful, modest, gentlemanly boy, and after a life of special usefulness as a missionary, author, civilian and professor, he died the Lecturer on Chinese in Yale College and the President of the American Bible Society. He became a missionary to China in 1832, and continued its service until 1876, when he entered upon his New-Haven Professorship. His contributions to literature, both in the Chinese and English languages, were of great value, and his influence everywhere was ennobling. Of the few boys to whom we have referred, Professor James D. Dana, of Yale College, Mr. Henry Ivison, of this city, and some others are still living, and so is at least one of the teachers, Mr. Frederick S. Winston, the President of the Mutual Life Insurance Company. Most of the others have gone to their last home, and those of us who remain will never cease to be thankful for the good Providence which brought us together through so many years, in what was then the only Sunday school of note in Utica, and practically a union school.

... Examiner, Feb. 28

Feb. 28.'84

—The late Dr. S. Wells Williams went out to China half a century ago as a printer in the service of the American Board of Commissioners for Foreign Missions. He afterward became Secretary of Legation for our Government at the Court of Peking. His influence was very great both with the American ministers and with the Chinese. A man of pure life, of eminent Christian character, and of devotional nature, he never failed to command the respect of his fellow-men. The news of his death will be received by many in China—both foreigners and natives—with sincere regret. Christian Advocate

Dr. S. Wells Williams.

WITH a feeling of sadness we mentioned three weeks ago the death of this great and good man. Sadness is the word, not because his life had not been well rounded out, or that dying was not gain to him. In these respects we may well congratulate our departed friend. But that we shall see his face no more, and here after miss his venerable and genial presence, and words of counsel and wisdom, this is a sore thing under the sun. Likewise the great void in the ranks of the living, who that knows how great and singular was the place he filled, can fail to appreciate it? It is true that the ranks of living men close up, as a brother man falls out, and to the casual observer no man seems to be of much account to the contemporary life of the world out of which he is taken, be he President or man of letters. But surely this is not all the truth. There is a deeper current of life and being that sensibly shrinks its volume when a great and good man is transferred to another sphere, not to recover itself till the advent of others of kindred spirit enlarges the stream of blessed tendency.

That a man with meagre early advantages should rise, step by step, to such an eminence, indicates first of all a good stock, and next the use of all those elements of success without which men never rise to greatness. He was what might be called "a born linguist," were it not that the impression given by this term is apt to be that the mastery of tongues comes to such an one without labor. Greater mistake could not be made. Dr. Williams reached his great eminence, left his impress upon Chinese letters, and became an authority in all matters pertaining to this greatest of Oriental peoples, only by the most persistent labor. His thoroughness in work, his urbanity of manner, his fine balance of intellectual powers, his deep sympathy with the Chinese, and faith in their future, as a great people to be brought under the sway of the Gospel beyond a peradventure, made him, at once, a scholar to be respected, a missionary to be heeded, a diplomatist to be trusted. His works in the Chinese tongue will make easier the path of every student of that difficult language. His "Middle Kingdom," as it now stands—two massive volumes of treasured wisdom, on all points of inquiry likely to be raised for a generation, from the press of the Scribner's—will do for the English-speaking world what needs so much to be done to set right our misguided notions and give us a juster estimate of a great people.

His interest in the Chinese continued to the last. We find him named among recent contributors to a new church edifice in Canton. A brother of brilliant parts, laid down his life in the valley of the Euphrates, as a missionary of the American Board. These noble spirits have gone to their reward, united now in the praise of Him whose kingdom they nobly served, in the faith that the kingdoms of this world were to become the kingdoms of their Lord. Mar. 13 ...

.... Not altogether unexpected but none the less irreparable, is the loss the Christian world has sustained in the death of S. Wells Williams at New Haven last Saturday, in the ripe beauty of his seventy-second year. Greeted on his arrival in China in 1833 as a "foreign devil," he has lived to do more for the history, the letters and the world's knowledge of that country than we have from any or all other sources. His great work, "The Middle Kingdom," published first in 1848, originated in lectures, whose proceeds purchased the font of Chinese type he carried back with him that year to the country. His labors in Chinese and Japanese grammar and linguistics have been abundant. He was permitted to complete the really new reproduction of his work before his death, and to see before he died its enthusiastic reception. His was the rare combination of the man perfected in all ways and who united high native powers with great simplicity and beauty of person, mind, life and character. Independent

New Haven Mch. 5, 1885

ORNING NEWS. THURSD

IN MEMORY OF PROF. WILLIAMS.

The New Window Put Up in the Battell Chapel.

A memorial window to the late Prof. S. Wells Williams has been put up during last Tuesday and yesterday in the Battell chapel. The glass which occupies the northwest corner window of the chapel, over the Elm street entrance, was made by Louis C. Tiffany & Co., of New-York., and is an uncommonly brilliant example of the rich color effects produced by this house. For the design a characteristic Chinese memorial monument has been selected—the tablet raised upon the back of a tortoise—such as may be found in all temple yards and about the burial enclosures throughout northern China. The tortoise in this case rests upon a great disc consisting of a rough piece of dark wine-colored glass. On the tablet are seven characters from the *Analects* of Confucius, "By his earnest activity his achievements were great; by his justice all were delighted," written 23 centuries ago concerning the Chinese philosopher and brought out to-day as the fittest tribute which Chinese classical literature can pay to the western scholar who made it his own. This tablet, of a pale, grayish green, stands out well against a pearl-white background, and occupies all the central portion of the window. Above is an interlaced pattern, conforming somewhat with the general motive of the other windows, and above this, in the pointed arch, a luminous rosette, where the principal coloring of the composition is massed in jewel glass of dark greens and part red. The prevailing color of the window is therefore green, relieved and offset by a broad, richly colored border and by the important features of the tablet, and tortoise and disc beneath. At the bottom the inscription reads:

SAMUEL WELLS WILLIAMS,
Missionary, Scholar, Diplomatist,
MDCCCXII—MDCCCLXXXIV,
Professor of Chinese in Yale College.

A very richly colored stained glass window was yesterday put in the college chapel in memory of the late Professor S. Wells Williams. The design, made by Tiffany, is a Chinese funeral memorial upon which in seven Chinese characters, is a quotation from Confucius: "By his earnest endeavor his achievements were great, by his justice all were delighted." The inscription under the window is as follows: "In memory of Samuel Wells Williams, LL. D. Mdcccxii—mdcclxxxiv. Missionary, scholar, diplomatist. Professor of the Chinese language in Yale college."

The Star in the East.

The Truth anyway——Peace if possible.
Charity . . . rejoiceth in the Truth.

FRIDAY, 11TH APRIL, 1884.

WE regret to announce the death of Samuel Wells Williams, L.L.D., which occurred on the 16th of February last at New Haven, U.S.A. The *Men of the Time* gives the following:—

Williams, Samuel Wells, L.L.D., born at Utica, New York, in September, 1812. He was educated at the Rensselaer Institute, Troy, learned printing, and in 1833 proceeded to China as a printer for the Missionary Board at Canton, and aided in editing *The Chinese Repository*. In 1837, while on a voyage to Japan, he obtained some knowledge of the Japanese language, in which he subsequently perfected himself and translated some Japanese books into English and portions of the Scriptures into Japanese. In 1841 he published "Easy Lessons in Chinese;" in 1843, an "English and Chinese Vocabulary;" in 1844, a "Chinese Commercial Guide." He returned to the United States in 1845, and published "The Middle Kingdom" (1848). Returning to China, he became editor of *The Chinese Repository*; in 1853-4 he was interpreter to Commodore Perry's Japan Expedition; and in 1855 was secretary and interpreter to the U.S. Legation. In 1856 he published "Ying Wá piu Wau, Ti üt I'u: a Tonic Dictionary of the Chinese Language in the Canton Dialect," a work of great value. In 1858 he assisted Mr. W. B. Reed, the American Envoy, in the negotiations at Tientsin, and in 1859 went with Mr. Ward to Peking to exchange the ratifications. In 1860 he returned to the United States, and spent nearly two years there; then went to China as Secretary of Legation, and rendered great service in the negotiations between the Western Powers and China.

THE United States Consular flag was at half-mast last Tuesday out of respect to the memory of the late Dr. S. W. Williams. Shanghai.

THE CELESTIAL EMPIRE.

April 9, 1884.

DEATH OF DR. SAMUEL WELLS WILLIAMS.

It is with regret that we learn news has been received in Shanghai of the death of Dr. Samuel Wells Williams, the author of the celebrated book on China and the Chinese called "The Middle Kingdom." The following sketch of his career appears in *Men of the Time*:—"Samuel Wells Williams, LL. D., was born at Utica, New York, in September, 1812. He was educated at the Rensselaer Institute, Troy, learned printing, and in 1833 proceeded to China as a printer for the Missionary Board at Canton, and aided in editing *The Chinese Repository*. In 1837, while on a voyage to Japan, he obtained some knowledge of the Japanese language, in which he subsequently perfected himself and translated some Japanese books into English and portions of the Scriptures into Japanese. In 1841 he published "Easy Lessons in Chinese;" in 1843, an English and Chinese Vocabulary;" in 1844, a "Chinese Commercial Guide." He returned to the United States in 1845, and published "The Middle Kingdom" (2 vols., 1848). Returning to China in 1848, he became editor of *The Chinese Repository*; in 1853-4 he was interpreter to Commodore Perry's Japan Expedition; and in 1855 was secretary and interpreter to the U.S. Legation. In 1856 he published "Ying Wá piu Wau, Ti üt I'u: a Tonic Dictionary of the Chinese Language in the Canton Dialect," a work of great value. In 1858 he assisted Mr. W. B. Reed, the American Envoy, in the negotiations at Tientsin, and in 1859 went with Mr. Ward to Peking to exchange the ratifications. In 1860 he returned to the United States, and spent nearly two years there; then went to China as Secretary of Legation, and rendered great service in the negotiations between the Western Powers and China." We may add to the above that Dr. Williams' name will ever be associated with those who have held high and honoured places in public estimation and regard in the history of foreign intercourse with China, having earned for himself a distinguished position in literature, diplomacy, scientific knowledge, and Christian work. The American Government did well to avail itself of his services on his return to China about the beginning of the last war with England, when everything was in a very unsettled state. He was called upon to act as Secretary of the Legation, when he performed important duties in making the treaty with the United States. He was also called upon frequently to act as *Chargé d'Affaires* for the United States, and it is not too much to say that the course he took in that position was marked by a high ability on the one hand and a uniform integrity and consistency on the other that gained for him the warm respect and esteem of all acquainted with him. He left China for home towards the end of 1876, having laboured for more than forty years in China. He carried with him the esteem of all with whom he was acquainted, and the well-earned consciousness that he had not lived and laboured in vain. Since he left China he has revised and added to his book of "The Middle Kingdom," and the new edition has only recently been very lengthily reviewed in our columns. This book alone will long preserve the name of Dr. S. Wells Williams, and his life throughout was well and most usefully spent. We hear that he died on the 16th February last, and having been born in 1812, he was 72 years of age.

The Temperance Union.

SATURDAY, 12TH APRIL, 1884.

The *Temperance Union* is published every Saturday by

THE TEMPERANCE UNION ASSOCIATION.

All letters for the Editorial and Business Departments should be addressed to the

OFFICE OF THE "TEMPERANCE UNION."

If any of our numerous subscribers fail to receive their copy of the "Temperance Union," we shall feel much obliged by their letting ur know as early as possible and also by theis notifying us of change of address.

THE LATE DR. S. W. WILLIAMS.

IT is with feelings of deep regret that we record the death of the HON. S. WELLS WILLIAMS, LL.D., on February 16th. The United States has lost an honoured citizen, China a true friend, the Church an earnest Christian worker, the world a philanthropist. Dr. WILLIAMS did honour to any cause entrusted to him. He was born in Utica, New York, on September 22nd, 1812. At the age of 21, before most young men have completed their college life, he had taken his diploma in the Troy (New York) Polytechnic Institute, and had come out to China to enter upon that career of energetic usefulness which did not terminate until his life was finished. He came to Canton in 1833 in connection with the American Board of Commissioners for Foreign Missions, and was put in charge of the Mission Press. He probably began the study of Chinese immediately, and the result of his studies is a Dictionary, the value of which is admitted to-day. It has been superseded, however, by his great work to which we shall soon refer. His literary labours are very varied. He edited the *Chinese Repository*, whose pages are replete with valuable information necessary for the student of to-day. He published "Easy Lessons in Chinese," An English and Chinese Vocabulary in the Court Dialect," A "Commercial Guide," "The Middle Kingdom," which first appeared in 1847, and was revised and republished in handsome form in 1883, and last and most important of all "a Syllabic Dictionary of the Chinese Language." The first edition issued from the American Presbyterian Mission Press in 1875. It is the crowning literary work of his life, an inestimable aid to all who seek to penetrate the labyrinth of this language, and it will be long before it will be displaced. It represents the study and work of forty years, and was put out at Dr. WILLIAMS' own cost at an expense amounting to $12,000. By it his reputation as one of the foremost Chinese scholars was fully established. But what was of greater importance to him, by it, those who come to China to help the Chinese are enabled to master the language more speedily and enter upon their philanthropic labours better furnished. Dr. WILLIAMS' name is linked with every step of progress which the Chinese have made. His familiarity with the whole country, his knowledge of the people, the confidence placed in him by the Chinese and by his own Government, all gave him great influence, and when the time for making treaties came, this in fluence was felt. His diplomatic career was honourable to himself, and profitable both to the Chinese and the United States. To-day we bring honour upon ourselves by this tribute to his memory as a scholar and diplomatist. But he deserves more honourable mention for a higher reason. He was more than a scholar, more than a diplomatist; he was always a Christian man. The motive power which kept him at work was the power of God's Spirit. His aim in all he did was not a name, but a service for God and humanity. He strove to help on Missionary work in China in every way within his power and means. He was not an ordained minister, but he was a minister of God's mercy, and a willing, happy, hopeful man. It has been the privilege of the writer to have correspondence with Dr. WILLIAMS for the past eight years, most of which time the Doctor spent at New Haven, in connection with his duties at Yale College, as Professor of the Chinese Language and Literature. His health was very feeble, a partial paralysis having compelled him to give up active work. But in the correspondence, alway written with his own hand, there has shone forth that deep, yet humble faith which filled his heart. As for this country in which he spent so many years, he had only the brightest hopes, but always in connection with the spread of Christianity. He recognized in the Gospel the only power which can renovote this land. A sentence in the Preface to the new edition of the "Middle Kingdom," shows what importance he attaches to this subject. He says "The stimulus which in this labour of my earlier and later years has ever been present to my mind is the hope that the cause of missions may be promoted. In the success of this cause lies the salvation of China as a people both in its moral and political aspects."

We must only touch upon one other element in Dr. WILLIAMS' character. He was a *thorough going teetotaller*. He had spent 40 years in China and he knew the evils which drink has produced, here and elsewhere, and spoke against the use of intoxicants. His last public appearance in China was upon the platform of the Temperance Hall, and his words were wise and moderate; he never ranted, but decisive against the use of wines and liquors. We venture to say he never found it necessary at Peking to maintain the honour of his Government by using or providing drink for his guests. Perfection is never seen among mortals, but we point to this man, now gone, as one who possessed a well rounded character, who lived a godly life, and whose life is a legacy of untold value to all who knew him.

THE LATE PROFESSOR SAMUEL WELLS WILLIAMS.

[FROM A PHOTOGRAPH BY PACH.]

PROFESSOR SAMUEL WELLS WILLIAMS.

This gentleman, the first Professor of the Chinese language and literature at Yale College, was, until a late period of his life, better known in China than in his own country. He was born in Utica, N. Y., September 22, 1812, and graduated at the Rensselaer Polytechnic Institute in Troy at the age of twenty. The next year, 1833, he went to Canton as printer for the American Board of Foreign Missions, but almost immediately after his arrival added to his duties the assistant editorship of the *Chinese Repository*. In 1835 he was transferred to Macao to complete the printing of Medhurst's Hokkeen Dictionary. Two years later he learned the Japanese language from some shipwrecked sailors of that nationality whom he had been appointed to return to their native island, and made the first use of his newly-acquired knowledge by translating the book of Genesis and the Gospel of St. Matthew into Japanese. He rendered important assistance to Dr. Bridgman in his work intended to facilitate the study of the Chinese tongue, and himself prepared a little book of "Easy Lessons in Chinese." This he followed by an "English and Chinese Vocabulary of the Court Dialect," and by a "Chinese Commercial Guide," which has been almost invaluable to business men having transactions with that country. He served as interpreter to Commodore Perry in the expedition to Japan, and afterwards as secretary and interpreter to the United States Legation in that country. In 1856 he published his "Tonic Dictionary of the Canton Dialect." The years 1858 and 1859 were chiefly occupied in diplomatic service in China, the next two years in the United States in the service of the mission. The immense labor involved in the preparation of a "Syllabic Dictionary of the Chinese Language" occupied the greater portion of his time for several years. In the next year he returned to America, having accepted the call to fill the newly created chair at Yale.

"The Gospel must first be Published among all Nations."—Mark xiii. 10.

VOL. XXIX. NEW YORK, MARCH 20, 1884. NO. 3.

S. Wells Williams, LL.D.,

Late President of the American Bible Society.

On the 25th of October, 1833, Samuel Wells Williams, a young man who had just passed his majority, landed in Canton, whither he had gone in the service of the American Board as a missionary printer. He was born in Utica, N. Y., Sept. 22d, 1812, and graduated in 1832 at the Rensselaer Institute in Troy. From his boyhood he had been familiar with the work done in the printing establishment of his father, who was a publisher of Bibles and other books, and for a year before his embarkation he had been making special preparation for his work in a distant land.

His appointment was a recognition on the part of the American Board of the fact that in all lands the oral preaching of the gospel needs to be supplemented by the printed page. He went not for conquest, or emolument, or personal distinction, or scientific research, but on an errand of philanthropy and good will. Other men have circumnavigated the globe in order to determine the contour of continents and the location of islands, or to observe and record the phenomena of the skies. He went as an *interpreter* of Christian truth and civilization to an empire embracing one-half of the heathen world: "the most populous and most inaccessible empire on the globe." His was the work of a herald, surmounting obstacles, penetrating a dense wall of prejudice and pride, bringing good tidings, publishing salvation, announcing a new kingdom as at hand; and it was his to build a viaduct by which the treasures of eighteen centuries of Christian thought might be poured into the Chinese mind.

In all this he was one of a small band of pioneers. Dr. Robert Morrison, the eminent British sinologue, who had preceded him by twenty-six years, was still in the service of the East India Company but was approaching the end of his useful career. Dr. Gutzlaff, a Prussian by birth, who had been sent out by the Netherlands Missionary Society, was employed in the same way. Two Americans had gone to China as chaplains for seamen, the Rev. David Abeel and the Rev. Edwin Stevens. The American Board had one single representative in the field, the Rev. E. C. Bridgman, a graduate of Andover Seminary, who arrived in Canton in February, 1830. Mr. Williams was accompanied by the Rev. Ira Tracy. Dr. Peter Parker followed in 1834.

The Chinese were reputed to be a nation of readers; but so profound was their conceit that instead of seeking light from all sources, and asking what new thing might possibly be learned from remote lands, they excluded all foreigners, repelled every advance, and even imposed severe penalties on any of their countrymen who should presume to teach their language to "outside barbarians." They had books indeed, and held a printed page in reverence; but their printing was done in the rudest style from wooden blocks, moveable types and printing-presses being unknown to them; and "it was not altogether safe for a Chinaman to be seen reading a tract which spoke of Jesus, much less for him to undertake to distribute them; and it was even dangerous for him to engage in printing them."

The empire was inaccessible, Canton being the only point where contact with the outside world was tolerated. The outlook for the work was discouraging in the extreme. After all Dr. Morrison's toil and faith and prayer, "he saw only three or four converts, with no churches or schools founded, and no congregations publicly assembled." These discouraging aspects were well understood in this country. In the formal instructions given to Mr. Bridgman he had been told, "even if you should live to old age, you may never witness so much advance as to be permitted to preach a sermon publicly within the empire." And three days before Mr. Williams sailed, a letter was received from Mr. Bridgman, lamenting that after three years of constant labour he was not able to report a single case of conversion. "To the eye of man, (says Dr. Williams), the prospect at that time was gloomy enough, that China would be rendered accessible to the efforts of Christians. It had been closed for about one hundred and fifty years, and it was likely to remain so."

There were other obstacles besides the stolidity of the Chinese character and their policy in respect to international affairs. One of the most serious of them had its historical foundation in the confusion of tongues. The Chinese language, in its written form, differs from the languages of the Occident in being without an alphabet. Each of its many thousand characters is the symbol of an abstract idea. They are not the signs of articulate speech. The sounds of the voice have nothing corresponding to them on the printed page. Moreover the speech of the people is polyglott. The words of the Cantonese are unintelligible in Shanghai, and a few miles of travel may carry one beyond the province where his utterance is understood; and so great is the disproportion between the numbers of ideas and of monosyllabic sounds, that a single word may have ten or more significations, which can be distinguished only by some peculiarity of *tone*. To become proficient in such a language, even with the best helps of the present day, is no easy matter. For the pioneers the task was almost insuperable.

"It *was* rather discouraging, (says Dr. Williams) in commencing the study of the Chinese language to sit down with a man utterly ignorant of any tongue but his own, and have no aid except Morrison's quarto dictionary in another dialect, and an imperfect Anglo-Chinese vocabulary; for these comprised all there was. And then if one attempted to use his acquisitions, his dialogist would express much surprise, and wish to know the name of the man who taught him; or he would ridicule his rude pronunciation, and try to exhibit his own better knowledge of English in every reply."

A visionary enthusiast might perhaps be willing to make brief experiment to try the temper of the Chinese and see what response to the gospel would come from within the gates. But the spirit which prompted Mr. Williams's mission, and which steadied his aim through the long periods marked by reverses rather than progress, was one of personal consecration to the service of Christ, and of unwavering confidence in the ultimate triumph of light over darkness. Surely he had heard some voice saying, "Who art thou, O great mountain? before Zerubbabel thou shalt become a plain."

A mere enthusiast, for lack of results, might exaggerate the details of effort; but when the press had become an institution and zealous men might suppose the problem of Chinese evangelization to be solved, Mr. Williams wrote to guard Americans against an exaggerated estimate of this agency; saying, in 1839: "This branch of missionary effort is worthy of all the attention it has received; but * * * hitherto we have had no proofs that the thousands of books thrown among this people have incited one mind to enquire concerning them; have induced one soul to try to find a teacher among the foreigners in China; or have been the means of converting an individual."

These were words of candor, but not of discouragement; and thirty years afterwards he said, "I thank God that no shade of doubt as to the triumphant result, or regret at having engaged in it, has ever arisen in my mind."

Years brought a change to China. Her massive gates, creaking on their hinges, slowly opened and gave entrance for an army of evangelists. In 1842 the treaty of Nanking opened five ports to traffic, and foreigners were allowed to bring their wives with them. Twelve years later, the three missionaries had increased to ninety; daily religious services were held in every open port; a million Testaments were in process of printing or circulation; and the whole Chinese mind had been cast into a ferment by a body of insurgents who rejected idolatry and professed to worship the true God.

In 1858 the treaties of Tientsin were signed, and the one dispatch which came over the newly laid Atlantic cable that autumn announced that the Chinese empire was open for all trade; that the Christian religion was to be allowed and recognized, and that foreign diplomatic agents were permitted to reside at the capital.

Now the door is open wide for the proclamation of the gospel. The Scriptures are circulated in nine of the different languages of China, at an average rate of more than a thousand copies daily. Travellers go on long tours into the interior without molestation. In 1880 two ladies of the China Inland Mission went without European escort a thousand miles to the west of Wuchang, in safety; and to-day five hundred foreigners are engaged in active missionary work, while more than 20,000 communicants stand enrolled as members in the Protestant churches of the empire.

The dawn of a better day has come; and in view of such facts, the herald who went fifty years ago to rouse the empire from its midnight slumber, and found nothing to dishearten him when his cry seemed to be uttered in vain, may well say as the closing prediction of his life:

"The future is full of promise, and the efforts of the Church with regard to China will not cease until every son and daughter of the race of Han has been taught the truths of the Bible, and has had them fairly propounded for reception or rejection. They will progress until all the cities, towns, villages, and hamlets of that vast empire have the teacher and professor of religion living in them; until their children are educated, their civil liberties understood, and political rights guaranteed; their poor cared for, their literature purified, their condition bettered in this world by the full revelation of another made known to them. The work of missions will go on until the government is modified, and religious and civil liberty granted to all, and China takes her rank among the Christian nations of the earth, reciprocating all the courtesies due from people professing the same faith."—*Middle Kingdom*, 2 : 371.

For fifty years the personal relations of Dr. Williams to this grand movement have been most intimate and varied. Before he went abroad funds had been provided by members of the Bleecker Street Presbyterian Church in New York, for the purchase of a printing-press for Canton, and he was sent to take charge of it. But however important the routine of a printing establishment, and the superintendence of its details, the work which eventually opened before him had a grander scope, and he became an editor, author, translator, interpreter, historian, and diplomatist, and at last, in serene old age, he became a University professor of the Chinese language and literature in his native land, and the honoured head of a Society whose sole aim is to encourage a wider circulation of the Holy Scriptures at home and in foreign lands.

A year or two after his arrival in Canton, Chinese interference with his native helpers compelled him to remove his press to Macao; thence at a later date it was transferred to Hongkong; and thence again to Canton, where in December, 1856, his own residence, and the entire establishment, comprising three presses and copious fonts of type, with 7,000 printed books, were destroyed by fire. He not only published the Chinese Repository but shared with Dr. Bridgman in its editorial management, and to its twenty volumes between 1832 and 1851, he contributed about one hundred and forty distinct articles. His more important publications were: "Easy Lessons in Chinese," (1842); "The Chinese Commercial Guide," (1844, reaching a 5th edition in 1863); "An English and Chinese Vocabulary in the Court Dialect," (1844); "A Tonic Dictionary of the Canton Dialect," (1856, which fortunately escaped the fire of that year, and passed through a new edition in 1876); and "A Syllabic Dictionary of the Chinese Language," (1874,) containing 12,527 characters with the pronunciation as heard at Peking, Canton, Amoy, and Shanghai. In 1845 he came to the United States, and during his visit delivered courses of lectures on China, with the proceeds of which he secured from Berlin a new font of Chinese type. He also before returning to China published, in 1848, "The Middle Kingdom," which at once became a standard book of reference, and which re-appeared in 1883 in a revised and greatly enlarged edition.

In 1857, having accepted the post of Secretary of Legation of the United States, he resigned his connection with the Mission, though he looked upon this as only a temporary interruption of the relation he had sustained for nearly a quarter of a century. His services, however, in this official position proved to be invaluable to the cause of missions as well as to the government, and after a long period of diplomatic life he did not return to the missionary work.

The world owes it to Dr. Williams, and to Dr. W. A. P. Martin who was associated with him as interpreter, that the treaty which was negotiated by Mr. Reed at Tientsin in June, 1858, contained an article providing for the toleration of Christianity throughout the empire and protection of Chinese converts. The day had come for signing the treaty, and the reluctance of the Chinese officials to make any concession to Protestant missions was so decided that all allusion to the matter was likely to be omitted, when at an opportune moment these gentlemen called on the commissioners, and presented a draft of the "toleration clause" so happily worded that it was at once accepted and incorporated in the treaty which was signed a few hours later. "If we had not gone that morning (says Dr. Williams) we had failed certainly to get anything inserted in the treaty, which was to be signed in the evening; but God moved Kwei-liang to say that it was excellent." The article was shown to Lord Elgin, and was incorporated in substance in the British treaty which was signed a few days afterwards.

Mr. Reed's official despatch on the 30th of June paid this high compliment to the American missionaries who had rendered him essential aid: "Without them as interpreters, the public business could not be transacted. I could not, but for their aid, have advanced one step in the discharge of my duties here, or written or understood one word of correspondence or treaty stipulations. With them there has been no difficulty or embarrassment."—*Chinese Recorder*, 10 : 226.

The wall of separation between the empire and other nations broke down sixteen years later, when the emperor consented to withdraw the veil that secluded him and to receive ambassadors from foreign lands with no sign on their part of inferiority. To two personal experiences Dr. Williams refers, as marking the greatest conceivable contrast and the changes which forty years had wrought. He says: "On my arrival at Canton in 1833, I was officially reported, with two other Americans, to the hong merchant, Kingqua, as *fan-kwai*, or 'foreign devils,' who had come to live under his tutelage. In 1874, as Secretary of the American Embassy at Peking, I accompanied the Hon. B. P. Avery to the presence of the emperor, Tungchi, when the Minister of the United States presented his letters of credence on a footing of perfect equality with the "Son of Heaven." —*Middle Kingdom*, 1 : 14.

Not less worthy of note is the relation which Dr. Williams sustained to the opening of Japan to Christianity. Long before that empire was accessible, the missionaries at Canton recognized the desirableness of being ready to enter with the gospel, and Dr. Williams undertook to learn the language and to prepare a font of Japanese type. His first voyage to Japan was in July, 1837, when he was one of a party sent by Messrs. Olyphant & Co. in the ship Morrison to restore seven shipwrecked seamen to their homes. None of the party were allowed to land; but first in the Bay of Yedo, and again in that of Kagosima, their peaceful mission was repelled by force, and after hours of exposure to a cannonading from batteries on shore, they escaped without serious harm and returned to Canton. A devout believer in divine providence, Mr. Williams recognized this repulse as perhaps the best thing that could have happened. "Because one attempt has failed (he said), shall all future endeavours cease? Let us not abandon this nation; but by making the best use of the men whom we have, get better prepared to do them permanent good; and by-and-by, if God permits, we will try again."

So he went back to China, took some of these shipwrecked mariners into his own house, learned their language, translated for them the Book of Genesis and the Gospel of Matthew, and had the pleasure of seeing them embrace Christianity, the first fruits of the harvest now being gathered in Japan. This knowledge of the language came in play fifteen years afterwards, when he was selected as interpreter for Commodore Perry, who went to Japan in 1852 to carry a letter from President Fillmore to the emperor, and on his second visit negotiated the first American treaty with a nation which up to that time had pursued a policy of non-intercourse.

After retiring from the service of the government in 1876, Dr. Williams returned to the United States, and took up his residence in New Haven, where he found congenial society and a pleasant home. His piety had not been dimmed by long isolation from Christian lands, by the study of Confucian literature, by protracted toil on dictionaries and grammars, or by the formalities and ceremonials of diplomatic life. The religion of Jesus Christ was central in all his thoughts, and his heart was quick to respond to Christian sentiments.

Many honours had come to him in the course of his life. As far back as 1848, Union College had recognized his abilities and conferred on him the degree of Doctor of Laws. Yale College honoured itself by admitting him to the ranks of its alumni and enrolling his name among its corps of instructors. The Oriental Society called him to preside in its councils; but no honour was more grateful, no office more welcome, than that which he has held for three years as President of the American Bible Society. For this office he was peculiarly fitted by his attainments in scholarship, his large acquaintance with the field of missions, his experience in diplomacy, and his abiding interest in the diffusion of the truth.

His encyclopedic knowledge, his retentive memory, his perfect equipoise, his quickness of appreciation and his discrimination made him a valued and trusted counsellor and friend, while his genial spirit, his loyalty to the truth, and his unshaken confidence in the final triumphs of the gospel, commanded the respect and admiration of all who knew him. E. W. G.

IN MEMORIAM.

At the monthly meeting of the Board of Managers of the American Bible Society, March 6th, the death of the Hon. S. Wells Williams, LL.D., late President of the Society, having been announced, remarks relating to his life and character were made by Mr. Winston and Mr. Tracy, who had known him in his early youth, and also by Mr. Randolph and Dr. Gilman.

A set of Dr. Williams's published works was also exhibited, including his great Dictionaries of the Chinese language, the "Middle Kingdom" in its earlier and later editions, his "Commercial Guide," and "Easy Lessons in Chinese," and twenty volumes of the "Chinese Repository," of which for many years he was publisher and co-editor.

The address of Mr. Winston was as follows:

Before I perform the duty of appointing a suitable committee to prepare such a memorial of Samuel Wells Williams, LL.D., your late President, as shall be fitting to place on the records of this Society, recounting his public character and services, will you allow me to revert to the early years of his personal and domestic history while his habits of thought and life were being formed and he himself prepared for the useful career he was to lead.

As I look back for sixty years my clearest and most distinct recollection of him is his visits to his father's printing-office whenever he could snatch an hour from his studies at school. Setting types and learning the printer's art were then his favourite recreations. He was a bright and modest boy, exceedingly amiable and obliging, with but little taste for the ordinary sports and pastimes of youth.

His father was William Williams, of Utica, and his mother was the daughter of Samuel Wells, of Oneida County. In that important village, then the residence of many persons of unusual intelligence and moral worth, Mr. Williams, though unassuming and unobtrusive, was the natural leader. He was an elder of the Presbyterian Church, at the head of the Union Sunday School (then the only one in the place), the head of the fire department and of the military organization of the neighbourhood. Whenever courage, coolness, and promptitude were demanded he was expected to be present fulfilling his duty.

His mother was a fitting companion, in Christian character, intelligence, and worth, for such a man. Our deceased friend grew up and was trained by such parents, under such influence. As his mind and character developed he seemed to have been called, like Samuel of old, in his youth to devote himself to preparing for that higher life in his Master's service upon which he voluntarily entered at an early age. While he was diligent in his studies, yet his mind and heart were in the printing office; and he attained such practical knowledge and skill that before his majority he was prepared to offer himself to the American Board of Commissioners for Foreign Missions as qualified to take charge of their important printing operations in China.

From this time forth his life and history belonged and were given to the Church, whose servant he was, and to his own country, which had frequent occasion to use his knowledge of Chinese and his personal services in important national negotiations with the millions in China, whose history he had prepared, and whose spiritual, intellectual, and temporal interests he strove, by his various books and his personal efforts, to promote.

But his public history will be more ably sketched and presented to you by the committee upon whom this duty will fall. I would not have presented this picture of his early years had I not recognized that "the boy was father to the man;" and that few if any of you could look back through the vista of sixty years and recall the events in his early history, which combined to mould, under divine guidance, the life and extraordinary labours of our deceased President.

Upon the report of a committee appointed to draft a suitable minute, the following paper was adopted:

S. WELLS WILLIAMS, LL.D.,

PRESIDENT OF THE AMERICAN BIBLE SOCIETY.

On Saturday, the 16th of February last, S. Wells Williams, LL.D., departed this life in the city of New Haven, Conn., in the seventy-second year of his age. He had been the President of the American Bible Society nearly three years, having been unanimously elected to this office on the third day of March, 1881.

Dr. Williams resided for most of his life in oriental lands, where he was actively and prominently identified with the sagacious movements which resulted in introducing China and Japan into the great brotherhood of nations. Acting, at times, under the auspices of the American Board of Commissioners for Foreign Missions, and again under the direction of the United States government, he filled many positions of trust and honour, commanding always the unqualified approval of intelligent Christians in both hemispheres. Returning to his native land in 1876, he devoted himself to oriental studies with unabated interest, and continued to manifest his wisely-tempered zeal in all the efforts of his countrymen to evangelize the world. When, therefore, the presidency of the American Bible Society became vacant by the resignation of Dr. Allen, the action of the Managers in calling Dr. Williams to succeed him was deemed on every hand most appropriate and felicitous.

The decease of President Williams, after so brief a term of service, not only conveys to all associated with him a solemn admonition to work while it is day, but it removes an honoured officer of this Society, whose peculiar culture and whose accurate information in many departments of thought and action rendered his counsels of inestimable value; while his rare simplicity and gentleness made him a most agreeable co-labourer in the great work of circulating the Holy Scriptures. He died, as he lived, with a calm personal trust in Christ, and with radiant anticipations of the early triumph of the Redeemer's kingdom in heathen lands.

The Managers hereby direct that this paper be placed upon the minutes of the Board, and that a copy of the same be forwarded to the family of President Williams.

COMMEMORATIVE NOTICES.

To the preceding sketch of Dr. Williams's life we append some appreciative notices from the daily and weekly newspapers.

The *New Haven Palladium* paid the following tribute:

So far as he has been known by our citizens he has been esteemed and beloved. His modest demeanor, his loving spirit, his gentle manners and his glowing Christian faith have won the hearts of every one whom he has met, even for a brief interview. His accurate and varied knowledge of events and countries that are not easily accessible, his discriminating judgment and his sturdy common sense, have often elicited the wonder of those who have resorted to him for counsel and information. The kindly humour which beamed from his face seemed to impart to his presence perpetual sunshine, while his solid sense, his definite knowledge, and his unswerving Christian faith commanded the respectful homage of all who knew him. Two or three years ago he was called to part with the wife who had been the joy of his life. Subsequently he was partially disabled by paralysis, but neither the clearness of his mind, nor the sweetness of his spirit, nor the steadfastness of his childlike faith were disturbed by his personal and domestic trials. A few months ago he finished the new edition of his "Middle Kingdom." Since that time he has quietly waited the Master's call, which should bid him come up higher. The many friends who loved and honoured him cannot doubt that the call was welcome, and that with him the earthly has gently passed into the heavenly life.

The *Utica Herald* said:

A striking thing about the career of S. Wells Williams is the persistent industry which it shows. He made himself the best Chinese scholar in America. He had an excellent knowledge of Japanese. He began its study by communicating with some shipwrecked Japanese sailors, who were given work in his office. When Commodore Perry made his expedition to Japan to seek better relations with that country, Dr. Williams was the interpreter. He studied these languages in a scientific way also, and knew much about general philology. Those tongues have been considered the most difficult in the world for a foreigner to acquire. They are of a different family from our own, and as we, at least, are pleased to think, they are in a more primitive stage. The work of Dr. Williams has made it far easier through all time to come to learn the Chinese language. Whatever the native energy, such labours could not have been accomplished except by a man inspired by a noble cause. Dr. Williams was a missionary, and in the most useful ways. He was beloved and trusted by the Chinese. With other men like himself he gained the confidence of that people in this country.

The *New York Evangelist* remarked:

His confinement to his bed had been only for a few days, though for some time his health had been delicate and uncertain, occasionally preventing the usually punctual and greatly interested discharge of his duties as President of the American Bible Society, here in New York. Dr. Williams succeeded to this post of honour on the resignation of Dr. Allen, and with peculiar fitness in the eyes of all the American Churches, and it might well be added, of evangelical Christendom. His life-long aims and labours were consonant in spirit and breadth with these later duties. First a printer, then a publisher and editor, then an author, later an interpreter and mediator for his own or his adopted country, and ever a herald of peace and good will, one whose very feet may be said to have been "beautiful upon the mountains," as surmounting great barriers of difficulty to the intercourse of nations, he was yet ever and always a simple missionary of the cross in intent and spirit.

The New Haven correspondent of the *Evening Post* wrote:

The funeral of Professor Williams was held on Tuesday afternoon in the Battell Chapel. Dr. Barbour conducted the service and President Porter delivered an address. There were present also representatives of the American Bible Society, of which he was President at the time of his death. Professor Williams has been connected with the college for only eight years, and although a regular university professor, has never given any instruction except in the form of lectures on Chinese history and literature. There have never been any candidates for the courses in the Chinese language which he was prepared to give. His great work, "The Syllabic Dictionary of the Chinese Language," was already completed and published before he came to New Haven. Since his residence here, in addition to the miscellaneous literary work for magazines and newspapers which his special knowledge brought him, he has been constantly engaged in the revision of his book on "The Middle Kingdom." His health failed him before he had completed the task, but he was fortunate in having the assistance of his son toward the end. Through his agency the work was completed and published before his father's death.

Mr. Williams was already sixty-five years of age when he was elected to his professorship, but his interest in the college was very great, and he at once entered into sympathy with its policy and aspirations. He was a very busy man up to a few weeks before his death, and even after his strength began to give way his vigour and acuteness of mind maintained themselves. He had a very wide range of interests, and his information was of that encyclopedic character which one finds in men of his kind. Although the nature of his department isolated him from contact with the undergraduates, a considerable body of young graduates sought his society, for he was the most accessible of men, and got direction and stimulus from association with him. It is the presence of such men as he which gives its peculiar scholastic air to an old institution of learning. His last public work was to preside at the meeting of the American Oriental Society held here last fall.

The *Christian Intelligencer* said:

He was one of the very few remaining links between the pioneers of Christianity in China and the present. Few men achieved as much in introducing and extending the knowledge of the gospel in that great empire, and a knowledge of a higher civilization, and few men commended general and religious knowledge so well by their lives. He was sent to China as a missionary printer, and from that position rose to be one of the highest authorities in the Chinese language and literature. Associating familiarly with men of all ranks he attained a knowledge of Chinese life and affairs excelled by no other foreigner. Chinamen of rank esteemed and trusted him, and the common people honoured and confided in him. His mind was inquisitive, active, and retentive. He was simple, pure, candid, sympathetic in nature. He had superior practical and administrative ability. His characteristics and attainments gave him great influence, and led men to seek his help in difficult and delicate negotiations.

Foreign Department.

BULGARIA.—Dr. Bliss reports that ten colporteurs employed in Bulgaria in connection with the Methodist Mission, during the last six months of 1883, sold eighty-nine Bibles, 1,449 Testaments, and 131 Portions—a total of 1,669 copies. The

In Memoriam.

S. WELLS WILLIAMS, LL. D.

IN MEMORIAM.

A SERMON

DELIVERED IN THE

FIRST PRESBYTERIAN CHURCH, UTICA, N.Y.

UPON THE LIFE AND LABORS OF

SAMUEL WELLS WILLIAMS, LL. D

BY REV. H. L. BACHMAN.

April 20, 1884.

UTICA, N. Y.
Press of Curtiss & Childs.
MDCCCLXXXIV.

SERMON.

Text—Ezekiel, 47:9

"Everything shall live whither the river cometh."

Standing on Mount Moriah and looking down into the eastern valley, the Prophet Ezekiel saw fountains sending forth pure, life-giving waters. As they threaded their way southward and eastward, he followed them for many miles with the natural eye, and when sight failed, his mind still traced their onward course. In imagination he saw them crossing the plains of Jericho, falling into the Jordan, and rapidly descending to the salt sea. So sweet and pure were these waters which had issued from the caverns of Mount Moriah, that the prophet never once seemed to think that it was possible for them to become bitter by coming in contact with the Dead Sea. But on the other hand, he so magnified their purity and power, as to believe that they would give life to that lake of death; that they would penetrate it, diffuse themselves through it, and eliminate from it all impurity, so that it would be healed, and become the home of teeming animal life. And so he says, "everything shall live whither the river cometh."

In this declaration, the mind of the prophet went far beyond the pure, flowing waters of Moriah, and their marvellous effect upon the Dead Sea. By means of them the Holy Ghost suggested or revealed to him grand spiritual facts which should take place in the history of this sinful world. For him, the curtain which veiled the future, was lifted. In looking down the ages he saw the origin, the onward flow and the blessed results of the river of salvation. In type, this river had its origin on Mount Moriah when Abraham sacrificed Isaac. In antitype, it had its origin in the sacrifice of Jesus Christ. In the shedding of His atoning blood, a fountain was opened for sin and uncleanness. His life, teachings, death and resurrection constitute the great reservoir of the waters of life, and from it countless streams have issued, flowing through various channels and all directions. And wherever they have touched the dead sea of a sinful world, they have touched it with life; they have refreshed and purified it. To this fact, all history bears witness. Notwithstanding all the knowledge and culture of ancient Athens, it was nevertheless morally and spiritually dead till it tasted the waters of life at the hands of the apostle. All the legal, political and military powers of Rome could not cleanse her of moral pollution. Notwithstanding them the mightiest empire of earth tottered to its fall and ruin. And its degraded and besotted people never experienced a regenerating and purifying power, until they felt the touch of the gospel of Christ.

And as we look over the map of the world to-day, where do we find the highest degree of general intelligence, the most liberal and stable governments, the largest number of benevolent and humane institutions, and the greatest material prosperity? We find them in those lands where the streams of the gospel have flowed in their greatest number, depth and fullness. And where in the moral and spiritual deserts of heathen lands will we find oases, if not in those places where the gospel has been planted, and exerted its legitimate influence? Wherever the story of the cross has gone, wherever the name of Jesus has been heard, temporal and spiritual blessings have been its fruit. And all this accords with the vision of the old prophet. As he saw the river of salvation flowing through this sinful world, he saw its course attended with the highest happiness and prosperity. In view of these beneficial results, he exclaims, "everything shall live whither the river cometh."

His vision of the living waters presents to us two chief characteristics of the gospel, namely, its purifying power, and its diffusiveness. He saw that it would not only elevate and bless those to whom it came, but he saw that by reason of its adaptation, and by reason of its diffusive character, it was destined in the providence of God, to reach all lands and people, to spread over the whole earth. And in this respect, we see how rapidly and how wonderfully the prophet's vision is being fulfilled; how the waters of life are flowing to earth's remotest bounds; and how the deserts of sin are being made to yield the abundant fruits of righteousness. But it should be remembered that the gospel, or the water of life, has never been diffused simply through miraculous agencies. In so far as it has reached men, it has reached them at the hands of men. They are the ordained channel of God through which his truth is to flow to perishing sinners. The proclamation of the gospel was never delegated to angels. Mortals alone have been commissioned to this great and glorious work. They are the instruments through which the divine truth and the divine Spirit manifest their power in saving sinners and blessing mankind. And oftentimes we have been filled with astonishment and admiration as we have seen marvellous results flowing from the life of one man, or one woman, wholly consecrated to the work of making known the truth as it is in Jesus Christ. As we look upon their labors and their far reaching and beneficent influence, we realize, as never before, the power of human agency and the grand possibilities which lie before us as co-laborers with God for the redemption of a sinful world.

In harmony with these general reflections, it is my purpose to turn your attention to the life and labors of one who, years ago, went out from this church as a misssionary of the Cross, and through whom God was pleased to pour the waters of life into the most populous heathen nation of earth, and through whose scholarly and literary labors those waters will continue to flow for coming ages, and for the salvation of millions yet unborn in the land of Sinim. The one to whom reference is here made is the late Samuel Wells Williams.

And in the first place, let us notice the influences which surrounded his youth, and which did much in giving direction to his after life. When we stand by a broad, deep river and see the countless blessings it dispenses to the lands through which it courses, in the way of green foliage, fertile fields and rich harvests, we little think of its origin; but if we follow it to its source, we will find it rising in some beautiful, crystal spring in the far-away mountains. And so it is with many a grand, useful life. We look upon its mature labors, and see how they have blessed mankind; how they have brought knowledge to the ignorant, freedom to the enslaved, relief to the oppressed, wealth to the poverty stricken, hope to the desponding, courage to the fearful, salvation to the lost. In our admiration of such results, we are prone to forget the origin of that life from which they flowed: but if we trace it to its source, we will find it springing up in some far-away moral and Christian influences. So it was with the noble life we this day consider. As we follow it up the stream of time, we find its origin in a beautiful Christian home. The infancy and youth of Wells Williams were fostered under the shadow of the family altar and under the moulding power of the divine word. Although his father was a man of great business activity, yet he always had time to honor God in his own home in the way of family worship. With great faithfulness and fidelity he maintained the Church in the house. Daily he committed and commended his household to the mercy of the covenant-keeping God.

While the character and example of the father did much in moulding and directing the life of the son, yet the training, the prayers, the influence of the mother did still more. She was a woman of gentle disposition, of cultured mind, of a loving Christian heart, and of great religious zeal and activity. While aiding and encouraging every good work, she especially devoted herself to the cares and the duties of her own home. Knowing as she did the impressibleness of youth, she was quick and constant in laying her mother's hand upon the rapidly forming character of her children. She would allow nothing to wrest this golden opportunity from her, for she well knew that when it was once gone it was gone forever. As a Christian woman she was especially interested in the great work of evangelizing the world. The spirit of missions dwelt richly within her, and this spirit not only manifested itself in earnest effort and in generous benevolence, but it breathed itself out in earnest prayer for her own children, that some of them might become heralds of the Cross to the perishing millions of heathendom. As proof of this, we have a beautiful incident in her life. Attending a Foreign Missionary meeting on one occasion, she found herself without any money for the collection. After the plates had been passed, a slip of paper was found among the donations with these words, "I give my two sons." Few, if any, richer missionary collections were ever taken than that. For under the influence and prayers of a Christian mother, and under the blessing of God, it contained the rich gift of W. Frederic Williams to Turkey, and Samuel Wells Williams to China. The mother of these noble sons felt that she could consecrate them to no nobler work than that of making known the riches of the gospel of Christ to the perishing millions of earth; and to-day, the history of Foreign Missions vindicates the correctness of her motherly judgment. And as we look upon the work of Wells Williams alone, and contemplate its far-reaching results, we are compelled to feel that mothers not only largely hold the destiny of their sons in their own hands, but that through their sons they hold the destiny of countless thousands. When Mrs. Sophia Williams laid her moulding hand upon the life of her boy and directed it in the channel of Christian missions, she unwittingly laid her hand upon the millions of China, and in so doing bestowed upon them innumerable temporal and spiritual blessings.

Aside from the Christian home and the Christian mother, there was another agent who did much in fashioning and directing the life of young Williams. This was his Sabbath School teacher. In a letter written from Peking, in 1866, he says, "The first desire I ever had to be a missionary arose from a remark of my Sunday School teacher about the destitution of the heathen." What a little thing, yet what momentous results. That Sabbath School teacher little thought that through the boy before him he was touching and blessing the far-off nations of earth. Nor do we wonder that the slight remark of the teacher made such an indellible impression upon the mind of the pupil, when we know that that pupil committed to memory the entire New Testament. The Word and the Spirit of God made him susceptible to the least good influence: and as his early life was surrounded by so many Christian influences, we do not wonder that that life flowed onward in the channel of Christian missions, and dispensed numerous blessings along its course. The stream that had such a high, full and pure source, could not but be refreshing, healthful and life-giving.

In the second place, let us notice the ambitions he laid aside and the obstacles he encountered for Christ. In the course of his education he developed a marked love for natural science and history; and doubtless if he had devoted his time and energies to these he would have attained as great eminence as did his two class-mates, Professor Gray of Harvard, and Professor Dana of Yale College. In these fields of investigation just as grand opportunities opened up to him for the achievement of success and fame as for them. In this direction his future was just as promising as theirs; and as he looked toward it, in all probability the vision of wealth, of position, of honor loomed up before him and beckoned him on. But while pursuing his studies in Rensselaer Institute, he received an invitation from the American Board to go to China as a missionary printer. If he accepted that invitation he would have to forego many of his life plans and cherished ambitions. The hopes which lured him on to position, usefulness and honor along the lines of his favorite studies, would all be blasted. He would have to turn to unknown and untried fields of investigation and toil. But in considering this invitation, seemingly only one question came before him for decision—the question of duty. Ought he to remain in his native land and pursue the calling which his natural tastes preferred and for which his natural talents so well fitted him? Or ought he to lay aside his own preferences and go to a distant land, in order that he might make known the story of Christ and his love to the ignorant and the dying? Between these questions he did not long hesitate. The prayers of his mother were about to be answered. The instructions of his Sabbath School teacher were about to bear fruit. Within twenty-four hours he decided the momentous question, and his decision was not for self or selfish interests; it was for God and for China. After some fifteen months of thorough preparation for the great work to which he had consecrated himself, a young man of twenty-one years, he bade farewell to his friends at the old Genesee street bridge in this city, and then on a packet-boat made his way to New York; thence he sailed on the 15th of June, 1833, and reached Canton on the 25th of October the same year.

But what obstacles confronted him! The only port of the great Empire which was accessible to foreigners was Canton; and those who landed here were called by the natives, "foreign devils." No Chinaman was allowed to read a tract which spoke of Jesus, much less to print one; and the acquisition of the native language was a herculean task. There was a perfect confusion of tongues. The language of one city was almost unintelligible to the inhabitants of another, and there were very few and imperfect helps to one acquiring the native tongue. Aside from all this, Christianity had made very little progress in Canton, notwithstanding the faithful labors of those who had toiled there for years. Dr. Morrison had labored most incessantly for twenty-six years, and yet "he saw only three or four converts, with no churches or schools founded, and no congregations publicly assembled." Dr. Bridgman had toiled and prayed for three years, and after all was unable to report one single conversion. These facts were known to Mr. Williams before he sailed for China, but notwithstanding them he gave himself to the then almost hopeless work of evangelizing that vast Empire. In after years, referring to these facts, he said: "To the eye of man, the prospect was at that time gloomy enough that China would be rendered accessible to the effort of Christians. It had been closed for about a hundred and fifty years, and it was likely to remain so." But in view of all these discouragements and obstacles, he heard the voice of God commanding him to go forward; and like the Christian soldier he was, he obeyed. He conferred not with flesh and blood. With Christian cheerfulness he layed aside the hopes and ambitions of life, and went into the darkest and most unpromising field of heathendom, to live and to labor for Christ.

In the third place, let us notice some of the beneficial changes which he was permitted to see, and which he was largely instrumental in effecting. Nine years after the arrival of Mr. Williams at Canton the treaty of Nanking took place—in 1842. By means of it, five ports were opened to trade, and foreigners, with their wives, were allowed to reside in them. In 1854, twelve years after the opening of these ports, there were found in them ninety Christian missionaries, holding daily religious services, and a million of New Testaments were being printed and circulated. The American missionary printer was now making his power felt as never before, by distributing in those five open ports, leaves from the tree of life, which were for the healing of China.

In 1858, the most important event in the history of Chinese civilization and evangelization took place. During that year the four great powers, England, France, Russia and the United States made treaties with the government which opened the whole Empire to trade and commerce. But in these treaties was found what is now known as the "toleration clause," a clause which gave freedom and protection to the Christian religion throughout the Empire. How did this article find a place in these governmental treaties? It found its place there solely through the agency of Dr. Wells Williams and Dr. W. A. Martin, who were the official interpreters of our Minister to China, Hon. William Reed. As the representative of our government, he had brought about the desired political treaty, and we are told, "the day had come for signing the treaty, and the reluctance of the Chinese officials to make any concessions to Protestant missions was so decided that all allusions to the matter was likely to be omitted, when at an opportune moment Drs. Williams and Martin called on the Commissioners, and presented a draft of the 'toleration clause' so happily worded that it was at once accepted and incorporated in the treaty which was signed a few hours later;" and through these gentlemen this clause was substantially incorporated in the treaties made by the other great powers. Since it has become so historic, and since such great things for China and for Christianity have been accomplished by means of it, and since it was one of the marked labors and events in the life of Dr. Williams, it will be of interest to quote it in this connection. It is as follows:

"The principles of the Christian religion as professed by the Protestant and Roman Catholic Churches, are recognized as teaching men to do good, and to do to others as they would have others do to them. Hereafter those who quietly profess and teach these doctrines shall not be harassed or persecuted on account of their faith; any person, whether citizen of the United States or Chinese convert, who, according to these tenets, peaceably teaches and practices the principles of Christianity, shall in no case be interfered with or molested."

When we speak of China being opened to the gospel, it is well to remember this clause through which religious truth and civil liberty gained access to her millions, and with whom this clause originated. In his providence, God used Samuel Wells Williams for swinging wide open the gates of China, which for ages had been bared against the truth as it is in Jesus.

And in this connection it is well to remember what invaluable services he and Dr. Martin rendered our government as interpreters. In one of his official despatches, Mr. Reed, our

Minister to China, says: "Without them as interpreters the public business could not be transacted. I could not have, but for their aid, advanced one step in the discharge of my duties here, or written or understood one word of correspondence or treaty stipulation. With them there has been no difficulty or embarrassment." Let those who have no sympathy with foreign missions, who think they are a useless waste of time, treasure and human life, who never give them one word of encouragement, or one dollar in the way of contribution, ponder this official statement, and then say, if they can, that missions, even from a secular standpoint, do not pay. Aside from what they have accomplished in the salvation of souls, their indirect benefits to science, history and human government have been of untold value. And of this fact we have a marked illustration in the labor of Dr. Williams as an interpreter in behalf of the purely secular affairs of China and America.

Nor was his work in relation to the opening of Japan any less important. He believed in the providence of God it would be opened; and this belief stimulated him to make preparation for entering it whenever the opportunity might come. Before the Empire was at all accessible, he began learning the Japanese language, and preparing a font of Japanese type. In 1837 he was sent to return seven shipwrecked Japanese seamen to their home, but the party was not suffered to land. Doubtless he hoped that in performing the errand of mercy he would be able to gain a foothold in that almost unknown land. But while disappointed, he did not lose hope. In speaking of the event he said, "Because our attempt has failed, shall all future endeavors cease? Let us not abandon this nation, but by making the best use of the men whom we have, get better prepared to do them permanent good; and by and by, if God permits, we will try again." How faithfully did he heed his own exhortation. When he returned to China with those shipwrecked sailors, he took some of them into his own home, learned from them their language, and translated for them a portion of the Scriptures. And his heart was cheered by seeing them embrace Christianity. As Christian converts they were the first fruits of that golden harvest which is now being gathered in Japan. Fifteen years rolled on before God's time had come for opening Japan to the reception of the Gospel, and one of his chief instruments in accomplishing that great work was Dr. Wells Williams. He accompanied Commodore Perry as interpreter, in 1852, in bearing the salutation of the President of the United States to the Emperor of Japan. And through his instrumentality America negotiated a treaty with that nation, which for centuries had no intercourse with the world, and which is now fast taking rank among the nations for enterprise, progress and education. Whoever shall write the faithful history of Japan's evangelization must incorporate the name and the labor of Samuel Wells Williams, in opening that Empire to the gospel of Christ.

And here it may be remarked, that whoever will carefully study the history of our diplomatic affairs, in relation to these two great Empires, China and Japan, will be compelled to wonder how and why it was, that one who was so eminently fitted as Dr. Williams for the honored and responsible position of foreign minister to these nations, was never appointed such by our own government. And whoever attempts to solve this mytery, will be compelled to acknowledge that Republics are ungrateful, and that political influence in high places rob many a worthy and faithful citizen of his just dues. Doubtless Dr. Willlams' views concerning the Burlingame Treaty, and concerning the rights of Chinamen in this country under that and previous treaties, had weight and influence at our seat of government in withholding from him the appointment of Minister to China, an appointment he well deserved, and one which would have reflected credit and honor upon our civil authorities at Washington. But let come what would to himself in the way of honor or the want of honor, in the way of position or the want of position, in the way of gratitude or ingratitude, on the part of his loved and native land, nothing could deter him from championing the cause of the poor Chinaman, from defending his treaty rights, from arraigning our own government for injustice toward the almond-eyed sons of the East, who had sought a temporary home in the famed Christian Republic of the West. He was not simply their friend upon Chinese soil. He was equally their friend upon American soil; and that, too, when he knew that such friendship was not pleasing to the civil powers at Washington, and that in all probability it would, as it did, stand in the way of his appointment of Minister to China.

In 1877, Dr. Williams published a most noble and earnest appeal for justice to Chinamen on the part of our government. After ably reviewing the whole history of treaties between the two nations, and after showing how the Imperial Government of China had always observed these treaties, and how it had paid eight hundred thousand dollars to indemnify the losses of our citizens within its territory, he says: "How mortifying is the record of robberies, murders, arsons, and assaults, committed on peaceable Chinese living on the Pacific Coast, not one of whom had any power to plead their cause, and most of whom probably suffered in silence. Do you excuse yourselves from fulfilling treaty obligations, the most solemn obligations a nation can impose on itself, and whose infraction always ought to involve loss of character and moral power, because the Chinese Government is a pagan Government, and weak, too, as well? Can this nation look quietly on while Chinese are murdered, and their houses burned over their heads, in California, and no one is executed for such murders or mulcted for such arsons; and then excuse itself for such a breach of faith because these acts were committed in that State, and no Chinese Consul is there to plead officially for redress? Is it not implied in this that no murderer has ever been executed for taking their lives, or robber punished for his crimes, but every one knows that such criminals do escape punishment, and that the Chinese in that State feel their insecurity and weakness. Woe be to them if they should attempt to redress their own wrongs. One cannot but feel indignant and mortified at the contrast between the way in which the Chinese have treated us in their country, into which we have forced ourselves, and the way we have treated them in this country, into which we have invited them. We have too often used them as if they had no rights which we were bound to respect, and refused that protection as men and laborers which the existing treaties guaranteed to them."

In these noble words, Dr. Williams has justly rebuked our government for its treatment of the Chinaman within our borders; and in these same words he has stood and still stands the faithful friend and brave defender of the homeless and friendless pagan in a Christian land. And the glory and honor which have come to him in consequence, and which will continue to bless and embalm his memory as the years roll by, are worth more than all the position and power our government might have conferred upon him, had he not stood the advocate of Chinese immigration, and the fearless champion of Chinese rights on American soil.

Aside from all his public and diplomatic services, he bestowed untold blessings upon the cause of missions by his constant and faithful labor in the quietude of his study. After listening to a most valuable historical paper prepared and read by Dr. Williams, recounting the condition of foreign society in Canton prior to 1840, Consul Medhurst made some remarks in which he said, "I would ask you to remember that Dr. Williams has been one of the ablest pioneers of our intercourse with China, alike as a missionary, a diplomatist and a scholar. In this last capacity he has left us the solid 'footprint on the sands of time,' the Chinese Repository, which I regard as still our best authority in matters Chinese." But the two books which stand, and which will continue to stand for coming ages as the monuments of his thorough scholarship, his wide knowledge and great perseverance, are his "Middle Kingdom," and his "Syllabic Dictionary of the Chinese Language." The first of these is acknowledged to be the highest authority in the English language upon the Empire of China; and the second work makes the future acquisition of the Chinese language merely a holiday pastime, in comparison with what it formerly was. By means of it, he has largely harmonized the different dialects, and thus removed one of the greatest obstacles in the progress of the gospel among four hundred millions of heathen. In scholarship and usefulness, this work, in all probability, will not be surpassed in a century.

As an interpreter, a publisher, a diplomatist, a scholar, an author and a missionary, he was efficient, under God, in bringing about changes which have wrought, and are still working for the political, social and religious reformation of both China and Japan, and which will continue to work onward and upward to the glorious consummation of the enlightenment and salvation of their teeming millions. Before his earthly labors closed, he was permitted to see marvellous revolutions in these vast Empires, both of a civil and religious character. In 1833, when he arrived in Canton, after a passage of one hundred and twenty-seven days, he was officially reported, with two other Americans, to the Hong merchant Kingqua as "foreign devils" who had come to live under his tutelage. But in 1874, as Secretary of the American Embassy at Pekin, he accompanied Mr. B. P. Avery to the presence of the Emperor Tungchi, when the Minister of the United States presented his letters of credence, on a footing of perfect equality with the "Son of Heaven."

In the fourth place, let us consider a few of the prominent characteristics of Dr. Williams.

He was a patriotic man. While he had consecrated himself to the Master's work in China, he did not lose his interest in, or his love for America, his native land. He closely noted her development and her danger, and when at length he saw her involved in civil war, the spirit of the soldier possessed him. He felt as if he must defend the old flag, and do what he could to preserve the Union. So while he stood at his post on a foreign field, he hired a substitute to fill his place in the Union army. Seldom do we find a higher and nobler exhibition of true patriotism.

He was an honest man. Although in a distant land, and although every opportunity offered for avoiding his financial obligation to his own government, yet, like the honest man he was, he conscientiously paid his yearly income tax. He felt that while he had protection beneath the American flag, it was his duty to support the American government. What an example here, for many in our land, who in various ways try to avoid the payment of their full and lawful taxes.

He was an unselfish man. This trait of his character is beautifully illustrated in his official and missionary life. When he withdrew from the American Board to render diplomatic service to the government, he returned to the Board all the money he had ever received from it in the way of salary, as rapidly as his income would admit. And not only this, but he computed and returned the lawful interest. He might honorably have retained all this and his integrity never been questioned, but his generous and unselfish spirit led him to gladly refund it. And for his services as interpreter in behalf of our government, while he was in the employ of the American

Board, he received remuneration to the amount of $2,705; and this handsome sum he returned to the Board. And for a number of years after our civil war, he gave two hundred dollars annually to the freedmen's cause. He frequently said, that neither the present nor coming generation could pay them their honest dues. These instances not only illustrate his honesty, but they also illustrate his generous, unselfish nature.

He was a hopeful man. He had witnessed marvellous changes, and he believed that coming generations would behold still greater ones. Listen to his own words. He says, "The future is full of promise, and the efforts of the Church with regard to China will not cease until every son and daughter of the race of Han has been taught the truths of the Bible, and has had them fairly propounded for reception or rejection. They will progress until all the cities, towns, villages and hamlets of that vast Empire have the teacher and professor of religion living in them; until their children are educated, their civil liberties understood, and political rights guaranteed; their poor cared for, their literature purified, their condition bettered in this world, by the full revelation of another made known to them. The work of missions will go on until the government is modified, and religious and civil liberty granted to all, and China takes her rank among the Christian nations of the earth, reciprocating all the courtesies due from people professing the same faith." * These grand and reasonable predictions fill us with hope, and nerve us to more earnest prayer and faithful effort. And in accord with them, Dr. Williams has made provision in his will, in so far as his means would allow, for carrying on the evangelization of China to its glorious completion.

He was a man who dearly loved his work. He did not engage in it simply out of a sense of duty. He regarded it the highest possible privilege to work for Christ and lost souls. In writing to the Sabbath School of this Church, in 1866, he said, "When I bade good-bye, with a sorrowing heart, to the friends standing around the packet-boat at Genesee street bridge, just thirty-three years ago to-day, I had a partial idea of the honor and joy attending the mission work; but I am now sure that I would make the same choice (if I could) again."

* Middle Kingdom, Vol. 2, pp. 371.

After his return to this country to spend his remaining and declining years, his undying spirit of activity constantly manifested itself. Under the elms of New Haven, within the classic walls of Yale College, he continued his scholarly and literary pursuits. He carefully revised and amended his "Middle Kingdom," only finishing the last volume a few weeks before his death. Having beautifully and faithfully rounded up his life-work, God called him to his heavenly and eternal reward, February 16, 1884.

He was an humble man. If any one had cause for spiritual pride he had, and if any one had reason to glory in his achievements, surely he had reason for so doing; yet he was wonderfully free from Pharisaism. Never did he boast of his greatness or superiority over others. Never did he seem to think of claiming any personal merit, or of resting upon his good works for salvation. His only glorying and his only confidence were in the Cross of Christ. In proof of this, listen to the preamble of his will, drawn by his own hand:

"Feeling the uncertainty of life, and the desirableness of making such distribution of the property intrusted to me that its disposition will be attended with as little trouble as possible to my heirs and executors, I, Samuel Wells Williams, residing in New Haven, Connecticut, United States of America, being of sound mind, do make this my last will and testament:

"First of all, I desire to record my unfeigned and devout thanks to Almighty God, that I have been permitted to assist in the great work of Christian Missions in the Empire of China, during the greater part of my life, and spared to see wonderful progress during the forty-three years of my residence there. I humbly trust the literary labors of those years may be blessed to aid the studies of those who may engage in the same work, and to the promotion of true religion among the Chinese. My only ground of acceptance with God is faith in the atoning blood of the Lord Jesus Christ, and that for his sake my transgressions are all forgiven, and my redeemed soul will be received to that everlasting peace promised to all believers."

Here is the photograph of the humble, sincere, child-like, Christian character of Samuel Wells Williams. Its nobleness and greatness are found in its true humility.

Like a broad, deep river, his life and labors have flowed in the channel of Christian missions, to the watering and refreshing of two mighty Empires; and while his mortal life has ended and his soul has entered into eternal rest, yet his works follow him. His labors and the never-dying influence of his life and character will flow on down the ages; and of them, we may say with the old prophet, "Everything shall live whither the river cometh." As his labors have been for the elevation of man and the glory of God, in the past, so they will continue to be in the future. They will be a rich legacy to all coming generations.

And what an honor has been conferred upon this church, in that it has been permitted to give such a noble son to the cause of Christian missions. In view of what he has accomplished, what great encouragement has this church to engage more and more earnestly in the evangelization of the world. May the spirit of Christ which dwelt so richly in the heart of Samuel Wells Williams, dwell more richly in all our hearts, and actuate us to greater and more self-denying efforts for the advancement of the world's redemption. And if it please God, may he yet choose from this church many noble sons and daughters, who shall consecrate themselves to the blessed work of making known the infinite love and the saving power of Christ to the ignorant and perishing millions of earth.

[Notice of S.W.W., p. iii.]

AMERICAN ORIENTAL SOCIETY.

Proceedings at Boston, May, 1884.

AMERICAN ORIENTAL SOCIETY.

Proceedings at Boston, May 7th, 1884.

THE Society met, as usual, in the Library of the American Academy, at ten o'clock. The meeting was called to order by the Vice-President, Dr. N. G. Clark, of Boston.

The minutes of last autumn's meeting were read and approved, and the order of business for the day was announced. The reports of the retiring officers were then presented.

The Treasurer's summary of accounts was referred to Messrs. Avery and Hall as a Committee of Audit, and found correct; it is as follows:

RECEIPTS.

Balance on hand, May 2d, 1883,		$984.47
Annual assessments paid in,	$95.00	
Sale of the Journal,	72.62	
Interest on deposit in Savings Bank,	39.25	
Total receipts for the year,		206.87
		$1,191.34

EXPENDITURES.

Printing of Proceedings,	$134.90	
Expenses of Library and Correspondence,	18.50	
Total expenditures of the year,		$153.40
Balance on hand, May 7th, 1884,		1,037.94
		$1,191.34

The Bradley type-fund now amounts to $955.53.

The Librarian reported the following additions to the Library: 50 whole volumes, 49 parts of volumes, 64 pamphlets, and one manuscript. The accessions were chiefly by exchange. The whole number of titles is now, of printed books, 4263, and of manuscripts, 141.

The Committee of Publication announced that the second half of volume xi. of the Journal was not yet in the printer's hands, but that there was a good prospect of completing it soon, by the issue of Professor Bloomfield's edition of the Kauçika Sûtra (which is now nearly ready for the press), or otherwise.

The Directors announced that, in response to an invitation from the Johns Hopkins University, they had appointed the autumn meeting to be held in Baltimore, and had made Messrs. Gilman and Bloomfield and the Corresponding Secretary a Committee of Arrangements. The date was to be Wednesday, October 29th, unless the Committee found reason to change it. They had reappointed the Committee of Publication of last year, substituting the name of Professor Toy for that of the late Dr. Abbot. The Committee now consists of Messrs. Salisbury, Toy, Van Name, Ward, and Whitney. The Directors proposed and recommended to the Society for election the following persons:

As Corporate Members—

Mr. Robert Arrowsmith, of New York;
Gen. Henry B. Carrington, of Boston;
Mr. Harry T. Peck, of New York;
Mr. Herbert W. Smyth, of Williamstown, Mass.;
Prof. John Phelps Taylor, of Andover, Mass.

The gentlemen thus proposed were elected without dissent.

The presiding officer appointed Messrs. Dickerman, Crane, and Lyon a committee to nominate officers for the ensuing year, and the following ticket, brought in and proposed by them, was elected without dissent:

President—Professor W. D. Whitney, Ph.D., LL.D., of New Haven.

Vice-Presidents—Rev. A. P. Peabody, D.D., of Cambridge; Professor E. E. Salisbury, LL.D., of New Haven; Rev. W. H. Ward, D.D., of New York.

Recording Secretary—Professor C. H. Toy, D.D., LL.D., of Cambridge.

Corresponding Secretary—Professor C. R. Lanman, Ph.D., of Cambridge.

Secretary of the Classical Section—Professor W. W. Goodwin, Ph.D., LL.D., of Cambridge.

Treasurer and Librarian—Mr. Addison Van Name, of New Haven.

Directors—Professor John Avery, of Brunswick, Maine; Professor Joseph H. Thayer, D.D., of Cambridge; Mr. A. I. Cotheal and Professor Charles Short, LL.D., of New York; Professor Isaac H. Hall, Ph.D., of Philadelphia; and President Daniel C. Gilman, LL.D., and Professor Maurice Bloomfield, Ph.D., of Baltimore.

The Corresponding Secretary (Prof. Whitney) read the names of the members who had died during the preceding year: namely, of the Corporate Members—

Prof. Ezra Abbot, of Cambridge;
Prof. Arnold Guyot, of Princeton;
Mr. Richard S. Fellowes, of New Haven;
Prof. S. Wells Williams, of New Haven.

and of the Honorary Member—

Safvet Pasha, of Constantinople.

Prof. Whitney remarked upon the unusually severe losses of the Society during the past year, and upon the life and work of the gentlemen just named, especially in their relations to the Society. In particular, he spoke of the character and achievements of the late President, Prof. Williams. He recounted the services of Dr. Williams in the conduct of the diplomatic intercourse between China and the United States, and his successful efforts to procure the insertion of the "toleration clause" in the Tientsin treaty of 1858, and spoke finally of the results of his persistent and well-directed literary activity. He also read a letter from Dr. D. B. McCartee, who spoke with deep feeling of his life-long intercourse and friendship with Dr. Williams, and of the latter's courage as a pioneer, his zeal in promoting the Christian religion, and his extraordinary productivity. Prof. Thayer paid a hearty and fitting tribute to the memory of his friend, Prof. Abbot, calling to mind his profound and varied learning, and the beauty and modesty of his character. He was followed by Prof. Hall, who spoke of Prof. Abbot's self-sacrificing devotion to his friends.

On motion, a Committee, consisting of Dr. Clark, Prof. Whitney, and Prof. Toy, was appointed to make some suitable expression of the feelings of the Society respecting its loss in the death of Messrs. Williams and Abbot. The following minutes were prepared by them and unanimously adopted:

The American Oriental Society desires to put on record its sense of the great loss sustained by the world of scholars and by this Society, in the death of its President, the Hon. Samuel Wells Williams, LL.D. He was a man of rare intellectual gifts, of singular industry, and of fidelity to all the trusts committed to him. He was of wide and varied learning, and without a superior in the knowledge of the country, the language, the literature, and the moral and religious systems of the Chinese. He was eminent for his services to his native land as Secretary of Legation of the United States in China, and for the aid which he rendered to commerce and to Christian missions by his executive labors, by his important contributions to periodical literature, and by his published works, especially *The Middle Kingdom*, *The Commercial Guide*, and *The Syllabic Dictionary of the Chinese Language*.

The Society desires in like manner to express its sense of the bereavement that it has suffered in the death of Ezra Abbot, D.D., LL.D., Professor of the Criticism and Interpretation of the New Testament in the Harvard Divinity School at Cambridge. He was for nearly thirty years the faithful Recording Secretary of the Society. As a student of the textual and historical criticism of the New Testament, he won for himself an enviable reputation for exact and broad scholarship, and made contributions of enduring value to the department of learning to which he was devoted.

A few of the facts respecting the lives of these two men may be mentioned here:

Samuel Wells Williams was born at Utica, New York, September 22nd, 1812. His father, a highly esteemed citizen of Utica, was a book-seller, and engaged also in the business of printing and binding. The son entered the Rensselaer Institute at Troy in 1831. The next year he was invited to go to China as a missionary printer of the American Board. He immediately accepted, but on condition that he be allowed a year to learn more thoroughly the printer's art, whose rudiments he had acquired as a school-boy. He sailed from New York, June 15th, 1833, reaching Canton in October. Here he was met by Dr. E. C. Bridgman, who had gone out in 1830, and had begun the publication of the *Chinese Repository* in 1832. Dr. Williams took charge of the printing-press which had been sent out from New York, and for more than twenty years he assisted in the publication of the *Repository*. In 1835, he went to Macao, and, working with his hands as a type-setter, he completed in seventeen months Medhurst's Dictionary. In 1837, he sailed to Japan to take home some shipwrecked mariners. He was not allowed to land them, and so, on returning, he learned from them their language, and made (1839–41) a translation into Japanese of Genesis and of Matthew's Gospel. In 1844, he returned to America. In 1853, when the American Government attempted to open Japan, he accompanied Commodore Perry as interpreter. The next year he resumed his missionary work in China, and in 1855 was made Secretary and Interpreter to the American Legation. In 1858, he accompanied Minister Reed to Shanghai and Tientsin, where England, France, Russia, and the United States made treaties for mutual intercourse with China. To Dr. Williams is due the insertion of Article xxix, which provides for the toleration of the Christian religion. In 1859 he went to Peking to aid in the ratification of the treaty of Tientsin. During 1860 and 1861, he was absent on leave at home for about a year. In 1862 Dr. Williams removed his family to Peking, and there he resided until October 25th, 1876, the forty-third anniversary of his arrival in China, when he bade farewell to the Flowery Land, the scene of his laborious and successful life. He established himself at New Haven, and was elected Professor of the Chinese language and literature in Yale College, in 1877. In 1881, he was made President of the American Bible Society and of the American Oriental Society. His last public duty was to preside at the meeting of the Oriental Society in October, 1883. His death occurred at New Haven, on the 16th of March, 1884.

To the twenty volumes of the *Chinese Repository* Dr. Williams contributed about 140 articles. These included twenty articles upon subjects connected with the Chinese government and people, sixteen relating to the natural history, and ten to the arts, sciences, and manufactures of China. The *Journal* and *Proceedings* of the American Oriental Society, the *Journal* of the North China Branch of the Royal Asiatic Society, and the volumes of the *United States Diplomatic Correspondence relating to China* contain many learned and important papers from his hand. His *Easy Lessons* (in the Canton Dialect), appearing in 1842, his *English and Chinese Vocabulary of the Court Dialect* (1844), his *Tonic Dictionary of the Canton Dialect* (1856 and 1876), and his three volumes of the *Anglo-Chinese Calendar*, were of inestimable value to students of the spoken dialects at a time when helps were few. His *Syllabic Dictionary of the Chinese Language* (1874) contains 12,527 characters, with the pronunciation as heard at Peking, Shanghai, Amoy, and Canton. In 1844 appeared *The Chinese Commercial Guide*, and this most useful work reached a fifth edition in 1863. The work by which Dr. Williams is best known to the general public is *The Middle Kingdom*, which first appeared in 1848; and it was with feelings of devout thankfulness that he alluded to the completion of the beautiful new edition of this work toward the close of his serene and happy life at New Haven.

Dr. Abbot was born in 1819 at Jackson, Maine, and, after studying at Phillips Exeter Academy, entered Bowdoin College and graduated in 1840. After teaching several years in Maine, he went to Cambridge in 1847, taught there in the High School in 1852, was appointed Assistant Librarian of Harvard College in 1856, and Bussey Professor of New Testament Criticism and Interpretation in the Harvard Divinity School in 1872, which last position he held till his death. His first publication was a catalogue of the Cambridge High School Library. In 1869 appeared his *Literature of the Doctrine of a Future Life*. The American edition of Smith's *Dictionary of the Bible* is greatly enriched by valuable bibliographical contributions from Dr. Abbot. As an example of the minuteness and breadth of his exegetical study may be cited his article on Romans ix. 5, in the *Journal* of the Society of Biblical Literature and Exegesis. On textual criticism, the subject to which he devoted most of his time, he has unfortunately published comparatively little in his own name. To Dr. F. H. A. Scrivener he sent a long and important list of corrections to his *Plain Introduction to the Criticism of the New Testament*. As member of the American Committee of Revision of the New Testament, he had opportunity to make a worthy use of his text-critical learning; but, beyond such results as may exist in the revised translation and a few newspaper articles, he has left no record of his researches. The first volume of the Prolegomena to Tischendorf's eighth edition of the Greek New Testament contains textual and grammatical contributions by Dr. Abbot, prepared with minute accuracy and careful discrimination. His only historical-critical work is *The Authorship of the Fourth Gospel* (1880), an examination of the external evidence in the case, a work remarkable for scholarly precision and close reasoning. An account of his printed works gives no idea of his unceasing activity, and only his pupils and friends know the inspiration given by the high character of his scholarship, and the purity, faithfulness, and self-sacrificing devotion of his daily life.

The *Missionary Herald* for April, 1884, contains a notice of the life of Dr. Williams by Pres. Porter, and the *Bible Society Record* for March 20th has another, by Mr. E. W. Gilman. Professor Thayer's commemorative notice of Dr. Abbot appeared in the *Independent* for March 27th and Apr. 3rd, 1884 (reprinted in the *Christian Register* for Apr. 3rd), and another notice, from which the above is excerpted, appeared in the *Nation* of March 27th.

The Corresponding Secretary further gave some account of the life and labors of the distinguished scientist, Prof. Guyot, during many years an interested, though for the most part not an active, member of the Society; and of Mr. Fellowes, an eminent citizen of New Haven, whose liberal hand and efficient helpfulness in every good work make his loss keenly felt there. He also stated what particulars were known to him of the enlightened and scholarly Turkish gentleman, who, elected at the instance of our late member, Hon. J. P. Brown, had since 1850 graced our List of Members with his name. Safvet Pasha was at one time Grand Vizier of the Ottoman Empire. His death occurred on the 17th of Nov. 1883.

The correspondence of the half-year was presented, and some parts of it were read.

The following communications were presented at the meeting:

1. On a Cippus from Tarsus, bearing a Greek Inscription with the name of Paul, by Prof. Isaac H. Hall, of Philadelphia.

In the late spring of 1877, the U. S. ship "Alliance" brought down from Mersine, the port of Tarsus, a round marble cippus from the site of the latter city; which was given by the American consul (or vice-consul) there to the Hon. John T. Edgar, then U. S. Consul at Beirût. Mr. Edgar gave it to the museum of the Union Theological Seminary in New York city, through the Rev. Dr. Philip Schaff, who was then returning from his tour in the East. The stone is now in the Seminary Museum in New York, labeled: "Inscription from Tarsus, with the name of Paul." This label is true enough, but the inscription has no reference to the great apostle who was once Saul of Tarsus.

The inscription is in uncial letters, rather late, plainly and deeply cut, and reads as follows:

ΤΟΠΟϹ ΠΑΥΛΟΥ	Or, Τόπος Παύλου
ΜΑΓΙΡΟΥΤΟΥЄΠΙϹ	Μαγίρου τοῦ 'Επισ-
ΚΟΠΙΟΥΚΑΙΒΟ	κοπιου καὶ Βο-
ΑϹΙΑΟΥΤΟϹΤΗϹ	ασιαοῦτος τῆς
ΑΤΟΥΓΑΜЄΤΗϹ	α[ὐ]τοῦ γαμετῆς.

Or, in English, "Tomb of Paulus Magirus the [son] of Episcopius, and of Boasious his wife."

The chief interest in this inscription lies in the feminine proper name, which shows that in certain Cilician inscriptions in C. I. G., where the editor has ventured corrections, the stone is probably right and the editor wrong.

Examples of the genitive feminine ending in *-ουτος* (nominative probably—sometimes certainly— *-ους*) are to be seen in C. I. G. 4822 (*μητρος Φιλουτος*). 4826 (*μητρος Σαραπουτος*, where the editor has corrected the *η* to *π*), 4927 (*Πετοσουτος μητρος*, where the editor has corrected the second *ε* to *σ*), 4403 and 4404 (where the editor has ventured similar corrections).

If this Tarsus inscription were treated in the same way, we should probably change the *Βοασιαουτος* to *Βοασισουτος* or *-πουτος*; but the better opinion would be that the stone-cutter was right in all the instances.

2. On a Shapira Roll in Philadelphia, by Prof. I. H. Hall.

In the Ridgway Branch of the Philadelphia Library is deposited a leather roll, composed of pieces of Synagogue-rolls of different hands and ages, each full-sized

1884. No. 2.

BULLETIN

OF THE

American Geographical Society.

No. 11 West 29th Street.

SAMUEL WELLS WILLIAMS, LL.D.

Late Corresponding Member of the Society.

[Chief Justice Daly, LL.D., brought to the notice of the Council, at its meeting held March 1st, 1884, the decease in New Haven of the eminent missionary and Chinese scholar, Prof. S. Wells Williams, a corresponding member of the Society, and on his motion the Council resolved "that an appropriate entry on the minutes be made by Mr. Jas. Mühlenberg Bailey, Domestic Corresponding Secretary." In compliance therewith, Mr. Bailey submits the following minute for publication in the Society's Bulletin.]

Samuel Wells Williams was born in Utica, N. Y., September 22d, 1812. His early education was carefully conducted, at home and in the neighboring village of Paris Hill. Horatio Seymour, Judge Bacon, James D. Dana and Justice Ward Hunt were his schoolmates, and there they obtained such primary education as was in those days possible. As a boy he was of an exceptionally inquiring as well as studious nature, and also thoroughly explored Oneida County, with his especial friend Dana, in search after minerals and botanical specimens, with the original intent of fitting himself for a professional life in one or the other of these sciences. He next attended the Rensselaer Institute in Troy, then in its infancy, under the management of Professor Amos Eaton, the botanist. However interested and eager his mind may have been upon the various branches of natural history in the school curriculum, his was even more a devout than a zealously scientific taste; and doubtless to it, with the fervent religious example and training given him by his pious mother, was due his ready consent, so soon as a proposal came to him from the American Board of Foreign Missions to, take in charge the printing press of that society in China.

His dreams of a life of study and pleasant retirement in a professor's chair were at once resigned, and he accepted the call as promptly as it had been given, with a condition that he might be allowed time to complete his year at school, and afterwards acquire the details of the printing, binding and publishing business at his father's printing office in Utica.

On the 25th October, 1833, Mr. Williams arrived at Canton, and was nominally consigned to the charge of one of the Chinese Hong-merchants, and was at once buried in the difficult study of a language without dictionary or grammar, in which he could expect little assistance from the great merchant engrossed in commerce. Extended travel through any part of the empire, largely unknown, was impossible at that period. The entire foreign population of China—perhaps 150 in all—were congregated in a batch of houses covering a space not larger than that occupied by the Great Pyramid (8 acres), out of which they walked or were rowed on the river only at personal risk. Admittance within the city walls was utterly denied, and permits to travel as far as the Portuguese settlement of Macao were charily furnished through the Hong-merchants.

Under such conditions and surroundings, the early missionaries in China pursued their studies, gathering whatever information they could concerning the closely guarded country. With but one or two exceptions, the missionaries comprised all the foreigners who could in any way be called students of the Chinese, and into their monthly periodical, the *Chinese Repository*—edited first by Bridgman, afterwards by Bridgman and Williams, and lastly, from 1850 to 1853, by the latter alone—were gathered those early papers on the language, geography, social customs, religions and government of China, which have during half a century served as an invaluable authority and source of reference for subsequent writers upon these topics. Here, among other contributions, Mr. Williams furnished a series of articles on the geography of the empire, based, of course, upon native works, and the information gathered from personal intercourse with Chinese travellers and scholars; a part of these articles were published separately from his press at Macao in 1844, under the title of *Chinese Topography, an Alphabetical List of the Provinces, Departments and Districts in the Chinese Empire . . . &c., &c.*, and received more than twenty years later that rarely honest testimony to the practical worth of a book—a pirated second edition. Five years after his arrival in Canton, his interest in the outlying countries of the empire, joined to a lively spirit of charity, induced Mr. Williams, with some others, to undertake the return of seven ship-wrecked Japanese mariners, in an American ship, to their native shores. The expedition proved unsuccessful, was driven back by violent cannonading from Japan, and returned at the close of the second month to replace the missionaries and refugees in their contracted quarters at Canton. It cannot, however, be called a failure, were even its only result the fixing a closer interest upon Japan and inducing the young printer, who had already charge of Chinese and Portuguese hands, to add these sailors to the number of his employees, and to get from them their language while teaching them his trade. About the end of 1844 he returned *via* Egypt and Europe to his native land, where the enthusiasm of his interest in missions was devoted to preparing and delivering lectures upon China throughout the more important cities of the Eastern States.

These lectures, extempore in the first place, were elaborated during the winter of 1847–8, and published in the form of the "*Middle* Kingdom," now sufficiently well known to be accepted as the Hand-Book and History of the Celestial Empire. One's sense of the contented ignorance of the last generation upon this country is quickened by learning that no publisher in New York could be found who would print such a work without a considerable advance in the first place, and a guarantee against loss in the future. Of hardly less importance than the book in those days was the map of all China which accompanied it. This was founded upon the famous chart of the Empire, made under the Emperor Yungching, in 1708–18, by the Jesuit missionaries, whose full surveys were afterwards engraved on copper in Paris, and made the basis of subsequent maps in China. Upon a native reduction of this, together with some assistance from the Admiralty coast surveys then being conducted by the British Government, Mr. Williams constructed the first practical map of China proper and its outlying colonies. A second plate, with the names in Chinese characters, was engraved and found a ready circulation among educated Chinamen. In this connection it may not be without interest to mention another attempt at the geography of his adopted country, a map of the eighteen provinces, on a considerably enlarged scale, for which he collected an important mass of authorities in native local topographies, surveys of French and English engineers, &c. The vessel which carried these materials, the result of a dozen years of labor to the map-maker and engraver in America, went down with all on board and fairly discouraged the amateur cartographer from further efforts in this direction. The task has not since been undertaken.

Mr. Williams received the degree of LL.D. from Union

College as recognition of his work on China. Soon after the issue of this book, likely to become the *magnum opus* of his life, he returned with Mrs. Williams to his position as Superintendent of the Press at Canton. The tardy outcome of his study of their language with the shipwrecked mariners in 1837 was made manifest in 1853, when he received the appointment of Interpreter to the American expedition to Japan, as the only foreigner alive who could read or converse in the language of that land. The mission was to look into whatever might prove interesting in its way, and for this purpose the squadron made a rendezvous at the Loo Choo islands, from whence they visited the Bonin Isles before proceeding to Japan (July 2).

To the lover of natural history, the student of Oriental literature and the languages, the ethnologist, the geographer, the missionary all in one, this opportunity of a glimpse at wholly unknown peoples and their homes was a rare occasion for instructive adventure as well as the most serious of trusts.

What indeed could call him from plucking a herbarium from the strange and gorgeous flora about Hakodate and Yedo, where every specimen might prove an unknown species, save the weightier importance of communicating to a hermit nation the message of the New World? or from his enthusiasm as a naturalist over the yet unknown creations of Providence in the islands and from the adjacent sea, save the grave reflection that his was the only tongue present which could tell a heathen people of the priceless boon of Christianity? and record their progress and development for Christendom. The negotiations of this visit were purposely of a tentatory character. Only in the following year (1854), when Dr. Williams again accompanied Commodore Perry as an interpreter to Japan, was a treaty obtained arranging future intercourse in a manner now appreciated. "In taking my departure from China," writes Commodore Perry to Mr. Williams in September of this year, "I feel myself called upon to bear the most ample testimony to the talents, zeal and fidelity with which you conducted the important duties intrusted to your management. I say little when I declare that your services were almost indispensable to me in the successful progress of the delicate business which had been intrusted to my charge." In 1856, Dr. Williams received the appointment of Secretary of Legation for the United States, and resigned his connection with the Missionary Society the following year. Soon after he found himself again employed in diplomatic services, when, in 1858, he accompanied the Hon. William B. Reed and the Legation to Shanghai, Japan and Tientsin, and was present at the negotiation of the second treaty between China and the United States. The story of his relations with this and a second expedition, when, with Mr. Ward, he proceeded to Peking, of his subsequent negotiations with the Imperial Commissioners concerning the audience question, of his presence at the storming of the Taku Forts, of his eventual establishment with the American Embassy (1862) in the capital of China, and of his multiplied experience with officers of the Chinese Government, during a residence of fourteen years—these belonged to a more comprehensive sketch than this claims to be. Immediately after his return from a third visit to the United States, in 1860–61, Dr. Williams entered upon a project, the need of which had long been recognized among foreigners in China, and which in a manner presented itself as a duty devolving upon his long residence and ripe scholarship in the various dialects and written language of that empire. A comprehensive and authoritative dictionary of Chinese and English, with the character sounds in two or three principal dialects as well as the court tongue, remained to be written; a substitute for Dr. Morrison's cumbrous lexicon published in 1822, and now scarce and costly as well as untrustworthy, appeared to be the chiefest need of both missionaries and laymen. The phrase books and "Tonic Dictionary in the Canton Dialect," published by Dr. Williams, served him as admirable stepping-stones to the undertaking of the more important work. His constant habit of uniting business drudgery with intellectual labor; of turning from the printing press, the bindery, the official preparing of his diplomatic despatches to book-writing; his untiring energy, which brought him back to the Chinese teacher and the articulation of half-defined characters, even after interruptions continuing for months, involved uncommon labor. Most of all, his ardent trust in a Divine Ruler, whose protection would never fail this earnest effort in behalf of the spread of Christianity—a trust which sustained and cheered him through failing health and failing eyesight—these were the helps and hindrances under which he employed the spare moments of fourteen years in writing and editing the "Syllabic Dictionary of the Chinese Language"—a quarto volume about the size of Johnson's English Dictionary, and of not unlike influence upon the foreign students of Chinese. These works, it is just to say, we may recognize with pride as achievements of American scholarship in the contribution of the ripe fruits of his erudition while his heart was yet among the "laborers in the vineyard," though his feet were planted amid the ways and dwellings of men.

Among Dr. Williams's writings of more local or temporary interest may be mentioned the "Commercial Guide," a *vade mecum* for merchants and mariners about the sea-board of China, the fifth edition of which, issued soon after his residence at Peking, contains 650 pages, including treaties, tariffs, regulations, trade tables, and an appendix of sailing directions.

From 1849 to 1859 he also issued yearly "Anglo-Chinese Almanacks"—a continuation of Morrison's idea—designed to cover as much information as could be legitimately crowded into a pamphlet of convenient dimensions. His contributions to the *Chinese Repository*, about 150 in all, and extending over sixteen years, might fill, perhaps, three or four volumes.

In 1876 he resigned his post of Secretary of Legation in China, and took up a residence in New Haven, where, in the summer of 1877, he became the first incumbent of the Chair of Chinese Language and Literature in Yale College, with a nominal compensation.

Dr. Williams to his last hours devoted his leisure to the delivery of lectures, to occasional articles in magazines, and to the thorough revision of his "Middle Kingdom," a work which was near to his heart, and remained upon his desk during the better portion of five years, and appeared from Scribner's press rewritten but a few months before his death.

Dr. Williams, in the course of his labors, practically developed much in the geography of the East. His extended chart of China, entitled "Map of the Chinese Empire, 1872; by S. W. Williams," added by him as a valuable contribution to the Society's cartography, in itself founds a claim to our recognition. His lecture, entitled "China: the Country and People," and published in Vol. VIII. of the Society's Journal, delivered at Chickering Hall, January 11th, 1876, strengthens that claim to its recorded recognition and praise.

THE

NEW ENGLANDER.

MARCH, 1885.

(By Rev. H. Blodget, D.D.)

ARTICLE II.—A SKETCH OF THE LIFE AND SERVICES OF THE LATE S. WELLS WILLIAMS, LL.D.,

PROFESSOR OF THE CHINESE LANGUAGE AND LITERATURE IN YALE COLLEGE.

WHEN one who has been widely known and highly honored, and has drawn to himself a large share of the respect and affection of his fellow men is removed from his earthly labors it is prescribed alike by regard for the dead, and by what is due to the living, that some record of the chief incidents of his life and services be presented to the public, and some expression given to the just estimate and affection in which he was held. The only fitness the writer can claim for undertaking such a task in regard to the distinguished author and missionary, the late S. Wells Williams, LL.D., tidings of whose death have been recently received in China, is a sincere respect and affection for the deceased, and a friendship extending over almost thirty years.

Samuel Wells Williams was born in Utica, in the State of New York, Sept. 22, 1812. His father, William Williams, was in a prosperous business as a publisher and bookseller of that city. The family, after having come from England among the earliest settlers of New England, took up its residence in Massachusetts, in the town of Roxbury, now a part of Boston, from whence his father removed to New York. Dr. Williams was the eldest of thirteen brothers, three of whom engaged in business, while one, the late W. Frederic Williams, became a missionary to Turkey. While a lad he acquired the art of printing in the office of his father, and he also improved his ample opportunities for study. Subsequently he went to the Rensselaer Polytechnic Institute in Troy, N. Y., to complete his education.

In his boyhood he was an associate and school-fellow of James D. Dana; and the two, who had always been warm friends, were brought together again in later years as Professors in Yale College, the one of Geology and Mineralogy, which chair he had long and honorably filled, and the other of the Chinese Language and Literature.

His coming to China was a sudden movement. The invitation to take the charge of the mission press at Canton was answered in the affirmative within twenty-four hours from the time of its reception. Although the decision was so hastily made, it was never repented of during his forty-three years of labor in China. On the contrary, he often spoke of it as a cause of rejoicing and thanksgiving to God. He reached China on the day before he was twenty-one years of age, and landed in the city of Canton with his fellow voyager, the Rev. Ira Tracy, on the 26th of October, 1833. The name of the ship on which they came, the Morrison, and their gratuitous passage, given by Messrs. Oliphant & Co., indicated the attachment of that firm to the cause of missions in China.

On his arrival Mr. Williams found but three Protestant missionaries in China proper, the Rev. Dr. Morrison, who with unwearied diligence had pursued his solitary labors since 1807; also Messrs. Bridgman and Abeel, who arrived in 1830. The Rev. Edwin Stevens, who afterwards became a missionary to the Chinese, was then Seaman's Chaplain at Canton; and Mr. Charles Gützlaff had already excited great interest by his voyages along the coast of China. Besides these there were six missionaries to the Chinese scattered in different places in the Indian Archipelago.

Mr. Williams' work was ready to his hand. A press, sent from America in 1831, had been put into operation early in 1832 under the direction of Mr. Bridgman, who then commenced the publication of the *Chinese Repository*, of which he was also the editor. The superintendence of this press devolved upon Mr. Williams from the time of his arrival in 1833 to the time of its destruction by fire in 1856. He also assisted Mr. Bridgman in editing the *Repository*, which in its last three volumes fell entirely under his care.

The object of this journal, issued monthly, was to make Europeans acquainted with the great empire of China, its dominions, government, language, literature, religions, social customs, and all that pertained to the Chinese people; to promote also in every way the spread of the Christian faith among all the multitudes of Eastern Asia. With such an object Mr. Williams was heartily in sympathy, and he entered with avidity into the necessary studies and researches, so that we find no less than eighty articles from his pen scattered through the twenty volumes of the *Repository*, besides many shorter paragraphs, notices of books, and passing events.

Mr. Williams also assisted in the preparation of Bridgman's *Chinese Chrestomathy*, furnishing about one-third of the 700 pages of this volume (royal 8vo), which was published in the year 1841. In the year 1842 he published his *Easy Lessons*, 304 pages, 8vo, a work intended for beginners in the study of the Chinese language, which was followed in 1844 by an *English and Chinese Vocabulary in the Court Dialect*, also an octavo volume of 440 pages. This effort shows that his mind was early directed to the study of lexicography, and was a preparation for his later and more complete works in the same direction.

In the same year appeared from his pen a small manual of *Chinese Topography*, of 103 pages, 8vo, being an alphabetical list of all the Provinces, Departments, and Districts of the Chinese Empire, with the latitude and longitude of each; also his *Commercial Guide*, consisting of a collection of important facts in regard to trade with China, a description of the open ports, sailing directions, etc., etc. This work he re-wrote repeatedly, and enlarged as trade expanded, new ports were opened, and new treaties formed, until in its fifth edition, printed at Hongkong in the year 1863, and containing 653 pages, 8vo, it has become a most valuable source of information in all business transactions with the Chinese.

During this early period of his life he availed himself of the opportunity, afforded by the presence of several shipwrecked Japanese sailors in Macao to gain some knowledge of the Japanese language, into which he translated the book of Genesis, and the gospel of Matthew. The Japanese referred to, after a great variety of misfortunes had been brought to Macao by the humane efforts of Europeans to have them restored to their native country. To carry out this purpose the ship Morrison, belonging to Messrs. Oliphant & Co., and fitted out by them, had made an unsuccessful attempt in 1837 to land them on their own shores. Mr. Williams accompanied this expedition, which was not without peril, owing to the unaccustomed navigation, and to the hostile fire from Japanese batteries upon their ship, and he subsequently published in the *Chinese Repository* an account of the various events of this early visit to the Loo Choo Islands and Japan.

Although the intended kindness was so rudely repulsed, yet he was not discouraged thereby. The expedition incited him to the study of the Japanese language, and to put forth efforts for their good. "We hope," he writes, "that the day of their admission into the family of nations is not far distant; when the preacher of peace and truth shall be allowed access to their hamlets and towns. When the arts of western lands shall be known, and commerce, knowledge, and Christianity, with their multiplied blessings shall have full scope." . . . . "Bye and bye, if God permits, we will try again." These hopes of his earlier years he lived to see realized in his later visits to that country; and he himself bore a part in the transactions by which that nation was opened to western intercourse.

In the year 1844 Mr. Williams left China on his first visit to the United States, being then thirty-two years of age. He had spent eleven years in his mission field, years filled with important events in the history of foreign intercourse with China. The control of the East India Company over British trade with this empire ceased in 1834, the year after his arrival. He had seen the last of that remarkable adjustment of trade between the West and the East in the "Thirteen Factories" of "Old Canton." Here, in this little settlement on the north bank of the Pearl river, in the western suburb of Canton, the wealth, pride, culture, power, unscrupulousness, greed of gain, benevolence, learning, Christian piety, of the West had met the timidity, ignorance, weakness, duplicity, pride, contempt, politeness, acuteness, business sagacity, and probity, of the Chinese. Here the Hoppo and Cohong had met the trading companies and merchants of the English, Americans, Dutch, Prussians, Austrians, Swedes, Danes, French, Spaniards, and Italians. Here had commenced that system of trade and intercourse with China, which has in our day assumed such vast proportions. Here had been nursed and fostered the opium traffic, which now spreads its baleful influence all over the land. Here had been initiated those efforts for the enlightenment, healing, and Christianization of the Chinese, which now extend to all the provinces, and constitute the only hope for the future of this great nation. Canton was no longer to be the focus of influence and power. What had there been commenced during two centuries of foreign intercourse was to be extended and diffused throughout the empire.

The unsettled state of trade after the withdrawal of the East India Company, the adjustment of terms of direct intercourse between China and other nations, the protests of the Chinese government against the opium traffic, the seizure and confiscation of the opium, the war with China, the forming of treaties, and the opening of the five ports, all had occurred during these early years of the residence of Mr. Williams in Canton.

Returning to the United States at this time (a journey which he accomplished by way of Egypt, Syria, and Europe), it was natural that his mind should be filled with those events of absorbing interest, which had so recently transpired in China. A general interest had been excited in this far-off land, and Mr. Williams soon commenced a course of public lectures on various subjects connected with China, its geography, history, government, religions, literature, education, intercourse with other nations, and such topics, by which he delighted and instructed many audiences. These lectures attracted general attention, and became the basis of his first edition of the *Middle Kingdom*, which was published in 1848, the year of his return to China. This work, which had an extensive sale, and reached its fourth edition in 1857, did much to enlighten the public mind, and substitute accuracy and veracity for romance and fiction in western views of the celestial empire. By it the author was brought prominently before the public, and he received the honorary degree of Doctor of Laws from Union College, New York.

It was during this visit to the United States that the Secretaries of his Society and other friends urged him to receive ordination as a minister of the gospel. This he steadily declined. While he had always held religious services with the men in his office, and had preached to the Chinese on the Sabbath and other days, yet he did not feel himself called to the work of the ministry. Another line of effort had opened out before him which he conceived it his duty to pursue, and he chose to return to China in the same capacity in which he had gone there at the first.

During the period before the war of 1842, the missionaries to China were unmarried. Foreigners were not allowed to bring their wives to Canton. But now, owing to the recent treaties, the conditions of life had become very different, and Dr. Williams, having been united in marriage to Miss Sarah Walworth, embarked with Mrs. Williams in June, 1848, for Canton. Here he resumed his duties as superintendent of the press, being also the editor and publisher of the *Chinese Repository* until it was discontinued in 1851.

In the year 1853 Commodore Perry, under commission of the U. S. government to negotiate a treaty with Japan, came with his fleet into Chinese waters, and invited Dr. Williams, as the American best qualified to act as interpreter, to accompany the expedition in that capacity. For this office he was eminently fitted by his knowledge, both of the Chinese and Japanese languages, as well as by his experience in the voyage to Japan in the year 1837. In the discharge of its duties he won high commendation for his skill, tact, and fidelity. The expedition, having successfully completed its negotiations, returned to Hongkong after an absence of less than four months, and Dr. Williams then resumed his usual duties at Canton. In January, 1854, he again accompanied the squadron to Japan, and returned again to Canton in the latter part of the summer, the treaty having been secured, and all things arranged in a satisfactory manner. He has given an interesting account of these voyages to Japan, and of the negotiation of the treaty, which is published in Journal of the North China Branch of the Royal Asiatic Society.

Excepting these periods of absence Dr. Williams remained at his post, engaged in his usual employments, after his return from the United States in 1848 until the year 1856. During these years he published annually an *Anglo-Chinese Calendar* of about 130 pages, 8vo, containing much valuable information for residents in China. His principal work however was the preparation and publishing of his *Tonic Dictionary of the Canton Dialect*, an octavo volume of 832 pages, which has proved a valuable aid to students of that dialect, and has been recently republished in an edition carefully revised by Dr. Eitel of Hongkong. Dr. Williams' services in the expedition to Japan had attracted the attention of officials of the United States government, who so represented the value of his skill and attainments at Washington that he was invited to become Secretary of the Legation of the United States in China. In the providence of God, while his decision in regard to this offer was pending, the mission press of which he had been superintendent, was consumed by fire, together with many copies of the *Chinese Repository* and his *Tonic Dictionary*, besides other valuable works; while his copious fonts of Roman, Chinese, Manchu, and Japanese type were entirely ruined. There was little prospect that the press would ever be restored. Under these circumstances his way seemed plain to accept the offer of the government. In his letter resigning his connection with the American Board, which had then continued twenty-three years, he writes: "I do not however regard this as a final separation from your body, far less a dissolution of my connection with Christian missions in China, and therefore desire you to look upon it as only a temporary interruption of a relation which has many probabilities of being resumed."

Dr. Williams held the office of Secretary of Legation for twenty years, during which period, in intervals of the absence of any resident minister, he acted as *Chargé d'Affaires* nine times. When he resigned his position in 1876 he held the oldest commission in the diplomatic corps of the government. Having so extensive an acquaintance with the language and usages of the Chinese, with all that pertained to foreign trade, and also an accurate knowledge of the history of American intercourse with China from the first, he was always the intelligent adviser and assistant of the Minister for the time, and was abundantly capable of directing the affairs of the Legation in his absence. His services were of the greatest value to the government during his whole term of office, but especially so during the negotiation of the treaties at Tientsin, in 1858, and in the adjustment of subsequent difficulties. The securing of the clause regarding the toleration of Christianity in the American treaty with China was almost entirely due to his exertions. The writer well remembers with what satisfaction and gratitude to God his report of those negotiations was made at a united meeting of missionaries in Shanghai after his return to that city.*

After the destruction of the foreign residences at Canton by fire in 1856, Dr. Williams removed his family to Macao, where they remained during the unsettled state of political

* Dr. Martin, of Peking, who was interpreter to the Legation when the treaty was formed at Tientsin in 1858, gives the following account of the insertion of this article in the treaty. The Russians and the French had arranged articles in reference to the toleration of the Christian religion in the Greek and Latin forms; which they were to have inserted in their respective treaties. Dr. Williams was very desirous to have a similar article in the American treaty, in which Protestant Christians might also be recognized by the Chinese government, and claim equal protection of the laws. The United States Minister, Mr. William B. Reed, did not object to such an article, but was not inclined to take active measures in its favor. He had fixed on a certain day for the signing of the treaty, and if the article on toleration could be gained prior to that day he offered no objection; but he would not consent to delay the signing of the treaty in order to secure it. Dr. Williams proposed an article to the Chinese commissioners, but it was so modified by them as to destroy its virtue. Another form was sent to them with no better success. The day before the signing of the treaty, a form which had been proposed by Dr. Williams was returned to him, with such changes, made by the Chinese, that it could not be accepted. Failure seemed inevitable. The next morning Dr. Williams, as he rose from his bed, said to Dr. Martin that he had slept but little during the night on account of the danger of a failure of inserting any article on the toleration of Christianity in the treaty, which was to be signed that day. He had now a form to propose which he had thought over during the night, and which he believed would be satisfactory to both parties. The form was stated to Dr. Martin, who also approved it, and urged that both of them should go in person at once to secure its adoption, instead of sending by messengers as heretofore. This suggestion was approved, and they went accordingly to the headquarters of the Chinese officials, where they were kindly received, and in no very long time, to their great joy, had attained their object. The article was approved, and inserted in the treaty. The article on the toleration of Christianity in the British treaty, which was signed subsequently to the American, was due, it is believed, to this successful effort.

affairs in China, until their return to the United States in 1858. The treaty, formed in 1858, having been ratified in 1859, Dr. Williams the next year followed his family to the United States to make his second visit to his native land, and was there during the war of England and France with China, in 1860, as also during the exciting scenes of the opening of the late war in the United States. Returning to China in 1862 he left his family in Macao, and came to Peking in July of the same year to make preparation for the residences of the American Legation. The following year he brought his family to Peking, and this city continued to be his residence so long as he remained in China.

Having waded through the necessary delays, vexations, and interruptions incident to the negotiating for and putting in order residences for the families of the Legation, the same to be repeated at a later day, he gave himself in the intervals of relief from official duties to that, which after all must be regarded as the great work of his life, the preparation of his Syllabic Dictionary of the Chinese language. For this work his earlier efforts in the Easy Lessons, the Chrestomathy, the Vocabulary, and the Tonic Dictionary proved helpful in the way of preparation. Of course he availed himself of these, and also, as far as possible, of the labors of all his predecessors in the work of lexicography. He well knew that a complete dictionary of the Chinese language, which should satisfy permanently the demands of students, must be the work of a company of men, many of them specialists, each laboring in his own department; but he judged that, with the blessing of God, he might embody with the results of his own labors those also of his predecessors in this department, and thus produce a dictionary which would supply a manifest need for the current years, and be very useful to those engaged in Chinese studies. To this undertaking he now gave himself with unwearied diligence. His eyes and ears were ever open to catch some new form of expression of thought in the Chinese language, whether from books, or the speech of men. With his own pen he wrote out in Chinese every character, and every example to illustrate its meaning, throughout his dictionary.

What with the materials already accumulated, and his fresh acquisitions, his work progressed so rapidly that he was able to commence the printing in Shanghai in 1871, and to give his dictionary to the public in 1874. It is in the form of a quarto volume of 1336 pages, containing articles on 12,527 characters of the Chinese language, besides his lengthened introduction on the structure of the language, its tones, dialects, and primitives, and systems of spelling its sounds. In the conclusion of his preface he writes: "I have the satisfaction of feeling that the labor spent upon this work during the past eleven years in the intervals of official duties will now be available for students in acquiring the Chinese language. Its deficiencies will be hereafter supplied by others, who will build upon their predecessors, as I have done; for the field is too vast to be explored or exhausted, even by many laborers. The stimulus to past effort and the hope that it would not be in vain, both sprung from the desire to aid the labors of those who are imparting truth in any branch to the sons of Han, especially those religious and scientific truths whose acquisition and practice can alone christianize and elevate them. At the end of forty years spent in this country in these pursuits I humbly thank the good Lord for all the progress I have been permitted to see in this direction, and implore his blessing upon this effort to aid their greater extension."

It was characteristic of the author that he gave, in reduced prices of his dictionary as sold to missionaries, the sum of $1,200 as a thank-offering to God for having enabled him to bring this work to a conclusion; and it must have been a gratifying testimony to the value of his work that a new edition of 750 copies was required in 1882, every copy of the first edition of 1000 copies having been already sold.

Dr. Williams returned to Peking from Shanghai in 1873. His health had now become seriously impaired. The strain upon his powers in preparing and publishing his dictionary had proved too great. Doubtless his days were shortened thereby. While at Shanghai in 1872 he was obliged for a time to suspend all work, and seek relief in a voyage to Japan. The respite from care after the completion of his dictionary in 1874 did something in the way of restoring his health, and in the year 1875 he made his third visit to America, which gave him an additional period of rest. It is worthy of remark that however much of care and labor Dr. Williams had in hand, he never seemed burdened by it, but always appeared sprightly and cheerful, ready for every good work, and not annoyed by frequent interruptions.

His last return to Peking was in the year 1876, his family remaining in the United States. He spent some months in the city and at his usual summer resort at the western hills. He seemed more tenderly attached than ever to the places in which he had labored, to the people for whom he had given his life of toil, and to the friends who had been his co-workers in efforts for their good. It was difficult for him to break off so many tender associations and leave finally the land of his adoption.

However at his period of life, and with his impaired health, he judged that his work in China was done. For years he had been urged to take a place among the faculty of Yale College, who thought that the language and literature of China should have some representative in this institution of learning, and earnestly desired that Dr. Williams should accept such a position. This he consented to do, after some deliberation, and accordingly in 1877 commenced a residence in New Haven, where he remained until his death.

The revision and enlargement of his *Middle Kingdom* had been long in contemplation, and the materials for it accumulating. Indeed he had already begun the work before leaving China in 1876. This revision, with occasional articles for various reviews, attendance upon the meetings of societies, and public gatherings where matters relating to China were in discussion, seem to have occupied his time during these later years of his life. Among other things he entered very warmly into the question of Chinese immigration, protesting against the injustice done to the Chinese in raising this wall of separation to keep them out of the United States, and writing long articles in favor of unrestricted immigration. In the year 1881 he was chosen President of the American Bible Society; and he was always present at its monthly meetings when his health would allow it. He was also chosen President of the

American Oriental Society, and held both these offices at the time of his death.

His health at this time was far from being robust, and his eyesight was very imperfect. In 1882 he had a serious fall upon the ice. This was followed by an attack of paralysis, from which he gained only a partial recovery. Happily at this time he had completed his revision of the *Middle Kingdom*, and made arrangements for its publication. In the latter part of his work, and in carrying it through the press he was greatly assisted by his son, Mr. Frederick Wells Williams. "By the blessing of God most manifestly," he wrote to a friend about this time, "do I see the probable completion of this work, and I praise the God of all grace." After its completion he wrote again, "I have made my last effort, and implore the blessing of God on this work which has for its object to further Christ's kingdom. That is all I want." Still later, about seven months before his death, he wrote, "I am glad to say that the last proof sheet of the *Middle Kingdom* went last week to the publishers. If it has the blessing which the first edition had I shall be content. I had great difficulty in writing the preface. . . . I did not realize how weak my brain was. . . . I must decrease, others must increase; and God be praised that the work, in which he has promised that the kingdoms of this world shall be given to his Son, will never lack his ministers and servants."

Of the work thus completed it is safe to say, that as it was his last, so it will probably be the most widely read and of the greatest permanent usefulness. It has been well received, both in the United States and in England. Among the many favorable notices of the book we find the following. "Written by a thorough scholar forty-three years resident in China, it seems to us unlikely that for fulness of information, fairness of statement, and freshness of style, this work will be excelled as a comprehensive statement of the whole subject. One may expect, rather, to see the most attractive portions of this immense territory apportioned among the specialists." This is a just estimate of the value of the work.

Dr. Williams did not long survive its completion. Still later in September, after the work was published, he wrote,

"On every side I see men and women active in the affairs of life, but I have no part in their activities. I feel that the brain is crippled, and continuous labor or thought impossible. I do not repine. My heart is resigned to that will which is my happiness, so far as I know, and he will provide. I have all that I want for this life, more would be a trouble, and perhaps would be a temptation. The outer world must be henceforth to be seen by me, as if I were in a gallery, looking down on the arena. Happily the mercy seat is ever open, and there are family, missions, China especially, and many objects nearer by, to implore divine blessings upon. How we are bound to one another through and by that mercy seat, and up to the Head of the One Fold." This was written only five months before his death. During the interval his condition remained much the same.

One who was present at his funeral writes, "Dr. Williams died on Saturday, the 16th of February, in the evening. He had been failing fast since the first of the month, but his mind was clear until a few hours before his death. On the last day he fell into a comatose condition and died without pain. The evening of his life was very peaceful and happy. He was held in high honor at New Haven, and had great influence there. He took great pleasure in the completion of the new edition of his *Middle Kingdom*, and in its favorable reception. His son read him flattering notices of it from the English press only four days before his death. His funeral took place in the Battell Chapel, all the faculty and the college attending. Dr. Barbour the college pastor, President Porter, and Dr. Clark, Secretary of the American Board, spoke of his life and services with discrimination and feeling. He was buried in the family cemetery in Utica, New York."

In reflecting upon such a life one is impressed with its completeness. Many of those who have entered the race in China with the fairest prospects have been cut down in early manhood; others in riper years. It was not thus with Dr. Williams. He was spared to complete that which he had purposed. His life was well rounded out. His usefulness commenced early and continued late. This was owing on the one hand to his patient, industrious, well-directed efforts, and on the other to the protection and blessing of God amid the dangers incident to so long and eventful a course. Dr. Parker, his early friend and medical adviser at Canton, said of him: "His health was such in the first part of his life in China that I feared we should lose him." Yet he survived and was able to perform a great amount of diligent labor until the end of his days.

The life of Dr. Williams covered an eventful period in the history of foreign intercourse with China. Mention has already been made of the cessation of the monopoly of the East India Company in 1834, the war with England in 1841, 1842, the withdrawal of power from the Hong merchants, the opening of the five ports, also of the opening of Japan to western nations. Later followed the capture of the city of Canton in 1857, the new treaties of 1858, the war of England and France with China in 1860, and the supplementary treaties; the opening of new ports of trade in different parts of China and her dependencies; the establishment of the Legations in Peking, and the peaceful settlement of the question as to the audience with the Chinese Emperor. The new order of things thus inaugurated was followed by a vast expansion of trade and evangelistic effort. Dr. Williams in his own person formed a connecting link between the old and the new, between the trade confined and shackled at Canton and the now unrestricted commerce with all important parts of China; between Dr. Morrison, the first Protestant missionary to China, who in order to secure a permanent residence in the land became interpreter to the East India Company, and the present generation of missionaries scattered all over the empire.

It must be evident to any one who knew Dr. Williams that he was a man of quick parts, active intellect, retentive memory, and patient industry. He took a sensible, comprehensive view of subjects brought before him, and adhered to it consistently. What he saw, he saw clearly, and at once. He did not dwell too long in elaborating his views or in modifying what he had written. Content with that degree of excellence which he was able easily and naturally to attain, he passed on to other subjects and fresh labors.

Dr. Williams was known by all to be a man of humble, consistent Christian piety. He received the gospel in its simplicity. His mind seems never to have been exercised by skeptical doubts although he was familiar with the objections of scientific men, and had lived long among unbelievers. Religion was to him altogether true and a very practical concern. His Christian character adorned his domestic and social intercourse and gave inspiration and direction to his whole course in life. His bible lessons with his children and his sabbath forenoon exercises with his Chinese servants were faithfully maintained. In all society, and among all classes of men he won respect as a follower of Christ.

A part of his religion consisted in giving of his substance to charitable purposes. One-tenth of his income was the rule Dr. Williams followed in such bestowals. It is believed that in one way or another he quite repaid to the Board which sent him to China all the expense they had been at on his account; and many other missionary societies, as well as a great variety of objects, shared his benefactions.

If he had a large measure of prosperity he had also no small measure of adversity, and in both he bore himself with Christian equanimity. His eldest three children, two sons, Olyphant and Walworth, and a daughter were stricken down by death in the United States while he was absent from them. He bore their loss not only with resignation, but with the cheerfulness of Christian hope.

His Christian principles and kindly feelings were conspicuous in all his intercourse with the Chinese, both of a public and private nature, as also in his writings. This is very observable in his *Middle Kingdom*, one object of which he declares to be, "To divest the Chinese people and civilization of that peculiar and indefinable impression of ridicule which has so generally been given them by foreign authors," and "to show the better traits of their national character." In reading these volumes one can but feel that the Chinese are in the hands of a friend. The underlying principles of the writer are kindness, benevolence, justice. The faults of the people do not excite his hatred or derision, but rather move him to greater efforts to impart to them knowledge and truth. He speaks plainly and boldly of the wrongs done them by Christian nations, while he acknowledges also the necessity of decided measures at times for their own good.

In the preface to this work, at the close, he writes: "The stimulus, which in this labor of my earlier and later years has been ever present to my mind, is the hope that the cause of missions may be promoted. In the success of this cause lies the salvation of China as a people, both in its moral and political aspects." . . . . "The promise of that Spirit will fulfill the prophecy of Isaiah, delivered before the era of Confucius, and God's people will come from the land of Sinim and join in the anthem of praise with every tribe under the sun." These were the last words he ever wrote for the press, and they form a fitting close to the life work of the writer; a close also to this imperfect tribute to his life and services.

SCRIPTURE UNION MONTHLY.

THY WORD IS A LAMP UNTO MY FEET.

HOLY BIBLE

聖書之友月報

汝の聖言は吾が足の燈なり

No. 10. Vol. I.
Tôkyô, Friday,
November 9th 1888.

明治二十一年十一月九日(金曜日)第十號

故ドクトル、ウイリヤムス。

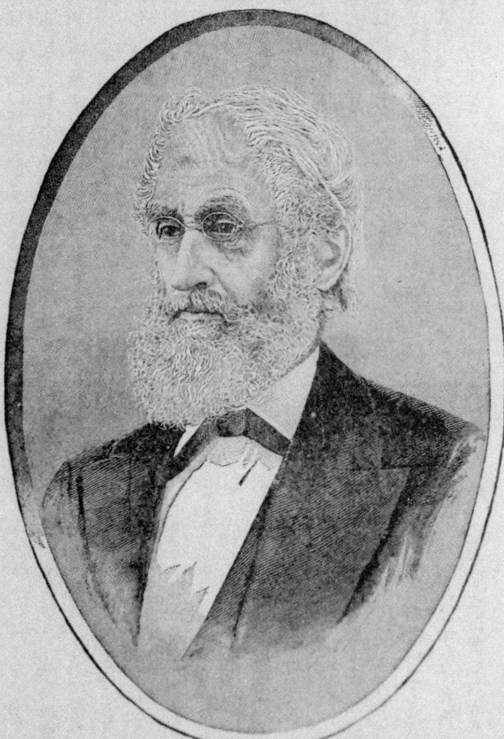

The Late Dr. Williams of China.

金六錢を送る人は十二月分月報及び二十二年日課表を同時に受るを得べしソハ日課表を月報の附錄としたればなり

目次

CONTENTS.

兒童のため。 FOR CHILDREN.

ドクトル、ウヰリヤムスの傳

The Life of Dr. Williams.

ドクトル、ウヰリヤムスの名と傳とは常に支那の大帝國か開化に進みたると親密の關係あり其帝國にクリスト敎の入りしとも付ては尚ほ〱深き關係あり氏は其溫和にして沈着にして練磨せる人なりき氏は其絕へざる勉强に依て種々なる國語に通じ其歷史を暗んじ世人より見認めて東洋の一大帝國の社會政治宗敎に關したる事柄に於ては尤も信用すべき記者と知られたり抑其門地は甚だ善して其父は勇氣と世に盡その精神に充ちたる有名の人にして其母は高尚なる氣慨を有し敎育ある婦人にして其近邊の慈善其他クリスト敎主義の善行の中心となれり恰も此婦人の死する前に或る宗敎の集りに出席したりしが其席に外國傳道の爲めに寄附を募るとありしに婦人は自ら紙をとり予は我が二人の子を寄附すと記したり斯て此婦人の死したる後二人の息子は名高き傳道師となつてアメリカンボードに屬したりしが其一人なるドクトルウヰリヤム氏は千八百三十三年支那の廣東に到着せり其より四十三年を經て本國に歸りしが其四十三年間は非常なる勉勵を顯はせり抑も氏が支那語に通したると且つ勉勵の精神あるとは氏をして有益なる多くの書籍を發行せしめたり其尤も必要なるものは支那國語字典にして氏が耐忍と勉勵の記念碑として永く存す可きものたり

千八百卅七年に氏は日本に來りて或る日本人を伴ひ支那に歸り之れに活版術を敎へ己れは是より日本語を學び頓て創世記と馬太傳を日本語に譯したりしが千八百五十三年に水師提督ペルリ氏が日本へ來りし時氏を擧げて譯官とせしかは氏の知りたる日本語は大ひなる助けとなりたり

千八百七十七年亞米利國に歸りてエィル大學の支那語の敎授となり千八百八十一年の三月米國聖書會社の社長に撰擧せられ七十一才にして死去せり氏は死去せり去れ共氏が殘したる事業と勉勵は朽ちずして其善事の爲めには熱心にして且寛大なるとたりしとを證明せり

乞ふ是より支那に於てキリストの爲に青春妙齡の時期を過たる所の他の一人を說かん即ちマセマチックに於て第一等賞を得ユークリットに於て第一等賞を得勉勵と善事とに於て第一賞を得たるはロォドスコッフヰルドにして氏が學校の賞與を取らんと初めたるはクリストを信じたる後にしてスコッフヰルドのキリスト敎は勉强の中にも遊技の中にも入り來り讀書に於ても人に優り夜會の遊びに於ても人に優り自轉車の競走に於ては第一等なりき斯て其大學にあるや淸潔と正義の空氣を吐き出し種々なる不潔の談話もスコッフヰルドの入り來るを見ては直ちに休み惡しき行もスコッフヰルドの室に入り來るを見ては休みたり彼は小學にありし節自らキリストの僕なりと云ふを恥ぢざるが如く大學にありても亦キリストの僕なりと云ひ顯はし信仰のよき戰を戰ひり（提摩太ノ六ノ十二）其大學よりロンドンの一大病院に赴きしが多くの患者に接して驚く可き神の大ひなる力を知り神の爲めに務めたりしが小兒の時に己れの一身を神にさゝげしが如く此時も全く身を神に捧げたり（羅馬十二ノ一）

其後久しからずして尙は一段神につかへ得べき神の召を被れり己れは今迄の能き位置に居るとを忘れ己れが安樂を忘れてスコッフヰルドは宣敎師として派遣せられんと決心せりそれ支那の大なる暗夜より頻りに光を求め（路加一ノ七、十八）又救主も其耳に私語て我誰をか遣はさん誰か我の爲めに遣はさんと云ひ給ければ悅びて我玆にあり請ふ我を遣はし給ひと云へり（以塞亞六ノ八）以上の有樣なるより此の能力ある若きドクトルは異敎國の民を敎へて世界の救主の前に出しめんか爲に己れの一身を捧げたり故に子供の時より彼と共に在ませし神は青年の時も大人の時も亦終りに至る迄も彼れと共に在したり（馬太廿八ノ廿）斯猛き心を出して支那の爲め活潑なる働きをなすと數年にして其

の能力を有する者は少かるべし讀書に於て一等の譽を得難かるべし男らしき遊びに於て先驅けなるとを得ざる可し去れ共我汝に謂ん汝等はスコッフヲルドとウヰリヤム氏とを以て汝の正義の手本と爲すとを得べし彼等を見は跡を追ふの法を知る可し已に救主に從へバ家に於ても學校に於ても商賣に於ても人は汝がヱスと共にあるとを知るを得可し(使徒行傳四ノ十三)汝等心に記憶するゥ汝は汝の汝に非ずしてヱスの尊き血を以て償はれしものなるとを(哥林多前書五ノ十九廿)

婦人のため。 FOR WOMEN.

尊む可き婦人の傳

The Lives of Noble Women, Mary W. Thomas.

第一 米國バルチモール、なるメリー・ダブルユー・トーマス婦人

此の愛す可きキリスト教徒の婦人はつひ此頃此れ世の務めを離れて見ぬ世に移りしものなるが此の人の行ひを若し婦人が己れの身も魂も悉く神に捧ぐるならバ如何なる事業も爲し得べしと云ふとを身に顯はせり此婦人ハ結婚して間もなく悔ひ改め直ちに主の爲めに働んと決心し己が家族のとにハ彼是と心配せねバならず且つ人の妻として人の母として爲さねバならぬ務め多きにも關はらず多くの宗教上の企に力を盡したり、或る集りの折に此婦人謂ける樣は家族の務を怠る勿れ然れ共かてゝ加へて働きをも爲すべし若し神に忠實ならバ日々人の魂を救ふとを得べし或ハ子ゝ賜なしと云ふもあらん然らば何故に求めざるや求よさらば神ハ與ひ玉ハん此婦人ハ友愛協會或ハタヒカーと呼ばれたるキリスト教の仲間にて生れ又其仲間にて育て擧けられたるものなるが故に深く神の前にハ男女共に同樣なる可しと信じ斯く信するが故に神の爲めには男の如く演説をもなを可しと思ひ殊に如何にして婦人の地位を高む可きか如何にして婦人の受くる不法を除き去るとを得るかと云ふとに思慮を費やせり

此婦人ハ深く聖書に通じてあるが故に友愛會の內に此婦人が受持つ聖書の組にハ毎週多くの出席者ありて他の教派の人々も好て出席せり其教會を治むると十二年にして常に人の記憶する所なりしが外國傳道の事業に於ては尤も力を盡し其他日曜學校クリスト教婦人靑年會禁酒等の事にも大ひに力を費せり然し其尤も愛したるとハ家族の生活なりき八人の子供あり四人ハ男にして四人ハ女なるが皆淸らかに樂しくも成長し其外二人ハ幼なくして早く天に昇れり此婦人ハ家を以て樂き塲所となし凡ての家族をして互〱に思やり互に熱心を以て善をなさしめ已れが心に思ふ高尙淸潔なる理想を書き出して彼等に示し又家の外の事業に依て決して家族に對するの責任を亂させしめぬ樣にせり去れ共若し家族の一人にして病氣に罹るものあらば萬事を擲て其病人の看護に力を盡せり詰る處此婦人ハ全く己れと云ふとを知らす己れの時と云ふとを考ひす斯くて知らず〱己れの心の美麗なるとを發表せりと云ふ可し其着物ハ甚奇麗さっぱりとして飾なく如何なる流行ありとて決して此婦人を心配せしむるに足らざりし何となれバ此婦人の飾ハ外形に非ず金銀を鏤にあらず髮を組み金をかけ又衣を着るが如き外面の飾に非ず唯心の內に隱れたる柔和靜かなる靈を以て飾としたればなり(彼得前三ノ三) 此の婦人の用ゆる飾ハ唯一つの黃金なる婚姻の時用ひたる指輪而已なり去れど我々ハ最早此婦人のかゝる行の點ハ說かざる可し數ヶ月の病ハ此婦人をして事業を廢せしめ神と親しく交はるの暇を得せしめ斯くて去ル六月安らかに天に入れり其質性ハ美麗なる其行の役に立ちし其死したる時に勝利を得たる誠に尊むへき婦人と云ふ可し思ふに其生命は甚だ短かりしなり去れ共其事業ハ甚だ永かりし玉既に全く成りたれど神は其冠の上に置かんとて之れを取り上げ玉へり此婦人は多くの經驗に依りてこの全き玉となれり故に神は之れを取り上げ玉ひるなり

此婦人の傳を見ても知るべし神もし我と共にあり玉ふを知れば我等ハ弱きを憂ふるに及ばざるなり(以塞亞廿六ノ四)此婦と口にこそ云はね神は正しきものゝ助けと成り玉ふとを敎ゆ神は我等を救はんか爲め救ひ主を下し玉へるものなる事を行を以て我等に敎へたり(希伯來七ノ廿五)クリストは我等を自由に爲んと待ちつゝ居玉へど何人も躊躇に及バずと敎ひたり(加拉太五ノ一)神我等の周圍に居る故に我等ハ苦を耐ひ悩に忍ぶゞ勝利ハ我等の日の信徒も亦神の約束を深くも之れを味ハへしならばヨヱアと同一なる言葉を發し得べけれ何となれば此約束ハ汝等及び汝等の子孫又凡ての遠き人即ち主たる我等の神に目醒むる人に屬けバなり(使徒行二ノ卅九)然して多くの約束の中今日馬太傳十一章の廿節にあるが如く凡て勞れたる者又重

REVIEW.

有弗學學之弗能弗措也

人一能之己百之人十能之己千之

The Life and Letters of Samuel Wells Williams, L.L.D., Missionary, Diplomatist, Sinologue. By his son, Frederick Wells Williams. New York & London, G. P. Putnam's Sons, the Knickerbocker Press. 1889.

The superior man, while there is anything he has not studied, or while in what he has studied there is anything he cannot understand, will not intermit his labour.

If another man succeed by one effort, he will use a hundred efforts. If another man succeed by ten efforts, he will use a thousand. (Doctrine of the Mean, ch. XX. V. 20. Legge's Translation.)

The 'Life and letters' of Dr. Wells Williams, by his son, is an 'honest tale plainly told' with little bias of filial affection. In writing thus we would be understood to commend highly the handsome volume just issued by G. P. Putnam's Sons. It is said there are persons whom to know is to love; there certainly are some whom to write about is to praise. Of these latter was Dr. Samuel Wells Williams. The barest register of facts and incidents in his unique career would be full of suggestion. This book is more than a bare record. Mr. Frederick Wells Williams had access to just the kind of material needed for the filling in of well-known outlines. He has used this to good purpose so that friends and admirers of his father will, we think, have no reason to be dissatisfied with the results.

Missionary, diplomatist, sinologue—this is the true order. To reverse or change it would be to do grave injustice to the honoured subject of this memoir. Dr. Williams was first and foremost and beyond all else a Missionary. At the outset to recognize this fact is to begin by understanding the man and his life work in China.

Samuel Wells Williams came from a Puritan stock and he inherited the best traits of Puritan character. Resistless energy, invincible patience, dogged determination to surmount obstacles and carry to successful issues 'labours more abundant,' were marks of a Puritan ancestry. So was an unmistakeable elevation of feeling which he exhibited constantly and which commanded the respect of the best men among his contemporaries. Sir Thomas Wade says, 'he (Dr. Williams) was one of the very few whom I have known whose mind never seemed to lose sight of the precept "Seek ye first the Kingdom of God."' Sir Thomas thinks it was the recognition of Arnold's principle, 'depend upon it, unless your life be part of your religion, your religion can be no part of your life,' that made Samuel Wells Williams really great in the greatest sense. In these days few persons are found to believe in the Puritans, the chief reason being that few give themselves the trouble to ascertain what manner of men they were. These Puritans were made of sound if stern stuff. They were indefatigable workers and they accomplished much. Looking at the multitude and magnitude of the tasks Dr. Williams attempted and performed, we judge him to have been a not unworthy descendant of Puritan forefathers.

The China to which the young Missionary printer came, in 1833, is well described in these letters. They give a graphic and striking picture of life in the Co-hong at Canton. Relations between Chinese and foreigners half a century ago were in what the author calls 'a state of nature.' It is not easy for us to realize what is meant by the Co-hong system. One never ceases to wonder at the patience of the 'barbarian' traders who bore with quiet dignity so much galling restraint and degrading surveillance. Some of the incidents narrated by Dr. Williams will be new to the reader and most of them have a partly ludicrous aspect. Thus Mr. Jardine of Jardine Matheson & Co. acquired among the native Chinese of Canton the nickname of 'the iron headed old rat,' because being struck on the head 'he never stirred or gave any indication that the blow had hurt him.' Mr. Jardine was then at the Oil Gate where, following the custom of that day when as yet Consuls in China were not, he had gone with a petition to the Chinese Authorities.

To succeed in China, one must be hard-headed. The Chief of Jardine's was eminently hard-headed and eminently successful. There can be little doubt that the men of a former day understood well the native they had to deal with and made the best of the trying situation. Witness the following story. Mr Innes, a Scotchman, having gone to the Gate of petitions with a paper of grievances, waited at the Gate long and in vain. The purport of his petition was known and the word had gone forth not to receive the document. Nothing daunted, Mr. Innes ordered his boy to bring a bed to the Oil Gate and intimated a fixed intention to take up permanent residence on that spot. 'When the Hong-merchants came to know that, they received his petition.' To play a waiting game was and is the true way to conquer, and quiet persistency in dealing with native Chinese is a lesson which foreigners may still learn with no small advantage to themselves.

In the Co-hong at Canton, Mr. Williams found Dr. Robert Morrison, the first Protestant Missionary to China, and his son Mr. John Robert Morrison. Of his meeting with the Morrisons, it is said in one of Williams' early letters, 'I was introduced to Dr. Morrison and his good son John.' Dr. Morrison was naturally looked upon with esteem and affection by the younger Missionaries who considered him the great representative of their common cause, a chief adviser in 'their undertakings.' Morrison died in the following year 1834, and the newly-arrived Missionary was thus deprived of the assistance which this veteran Sinologue might have rendered. For the son of Dr. Morrison, Dr. Williams always had a high esteem.

The fellow worker with whom Williams was assciated most intimately in those early days, was Dr. Bridgman of Chrestomathy and Repository fame. They were co-adjutors, serving together the cause of missions and sinology. Williams collected half the subject matter for the chrestomathy. Bridgman assisted and directed the studies of Williams. How strong and healthful was the influence of the elder on the younger man, may be gathered from this statement in the letters. 'What a difference it would have made to me if I had been joined in the first years of my residence with a freaky impulsive man! I should probably have gone away from the country. Blessed be God for Bridgman's example and influence!'

The conditions under which the Missionary printer lived and laboured, while in the service of the American Board, are described by Mr. Robert Thom, a contemporary. Mr. Thom was one of the five residents who studied Chinese in Canton during the time that Lin was Commissioner. In the preface to his translation of a story taken from the 今古奇觀 he thus writes of the obstacles that barred the way of the ardent student. 'Our Chinese associates are Hong merchants, linguists, compradores and coolies, people who make no pretensions to literary merit; people who cannot if they would and who dare not if they could convey to us any literary instruction and who, while they eat our bread, most commonly hate and despise us: such is the case more or less with every foreigner who sets his foot in China.' To the above extract from Mr. Thom's preface, written in 1839, we may add two statements from the Life and Letters to throw light on the position in which those Chinese placed themselves who consented to help foreigners in learning the language of China. Dr. Morrison's teacher carried poison about his person, ready to use on himself at the moment of arrest by the Authorities. Dr. Williams' teacher adopted the device of carrying to and fro a foreign boot, so that on an emergency he might transform himself into a shoemaker.

The American Board do not appear to have understood the situation or to have appreciated fully the untiring zeal and the good work of their Missionary printer. From the time of the establishment of its press in 1832, the year before Dr. Williams arrived in China, to the date of its destruction in 1856, about 38,000 volumes were issued from the press under his charge and $12,0 0 were earned when all expenses had been paid. During these years were published Williams' Easy Lessons in Chinese (1842), his Topography of China (1844) and his Tonic Dictionary in the Canton dialect (1856), besides a Vocabulary, various editions of a Commercial Guide, an Anglo-Chinese Calendar and an almost constant succession of articles in the Chinese Repository. This 'tale of work' done under desperately unpromising conditions, betokens an industry, pluck and perseverance, little short of marvellous.

Concerning the adequate motive which carried him through these manifold labours, we will let Dr. Williams speak for himself. 'The stimulus which in this work of my earlier and later years has been present to my mind is the hope that the cause of missions may be promoted. In the success of this cause lies the salvation of China, as a people, both in its moral and political aspects.' These are the closing sentences of his preface to the new edition of the Middle Kingdom. We are bound to admit the impelling and inspiring force of Christianity exhibited in this man of undaunted purpose and indomitable energy. Throughout the Life and Letters it is plain that, no matter what the task Mr. Williams was engaged in, the end which he intended his life work to subserve was the cause of Christianity. Other things were viewed as subsidiary, as means only. There was even present to him the sense of a divine call to do all that lay in his power to christianize. This animating principle remained with Dr. Williams to the last. The Missionary spirit brought him to China, kept him in China during many years of toilsome up-hill struggles, moulded and shaped his entire career, and had for him the force of a ruling passion. Well does Dr. Porter say, 'he was a speaking witness of the dignity and inspiration of the Missionary calling when it becomes an inspiration.' He had a profound realization of a higher life and a habit of bringing it to mind even in the busiest moments. This was for him the real meaning of religion and the moving spring of his whole career.

II. DIPLOMATIST.

The period of American diplomacy in China, with which the name of Wells Williams is associated, was the age of transition from 'a state of nature,' above described, to a state of law. The treaty of Tientsin and the Burlinghame 'co-operative policy' would alone suffice to render the period noteworthy. Burlinghame's policy substituted fair diplomatic action for violence, and guaranteed to China her autonomy. At Tientsin, Dr. Williams was solicitous to secure the insertion in the Treaty of what are known as the 'Toleration clauses' and by the exercise of his usual energy and determination this end was accomplished. That no better man could be found for the post of Secretary and Interpreter to the American Legation in China and for the post of Acting Minister, is in this instance no figure of speech. No other person could pretend to equal qualifications. In Dr. Wells Williams the American Embassy had a man who understood the Chinese language and the native mind, and one prepared to carry into the discharge of his official duties, zeal, patriotism, conscientiousness, breadth of view and not a little political insight. The longer the period of association with him in diplomatic service, the more cordial and appreciative the language of colleagues and of American high officials for the assistance rendered.

When Dr. Williams joined the Legation, the object of America was not to fight China, but to obtain without conflict the same privileges which England and France were bent on getting by force of arms. America sought to 'impress' China as she had already 'impressed' Japan. All the nations of the West were interested in forcing China out of her isolation and compelling her to enter upon new relations with them. With all that is most honourable in the negociations during the twenty years, the name of Dr. Williams is connected. Few have served the State with more fidelity or truer foresight. When, in 1855, Dr. Williams was led to sever his connection with the American Board of Foreign Missions and accept office under the Government, he took the step after careful self-examination and a good deal of hesitation. There can, however, be no doubt he was then adopting the best means in his power of serving the cause of Christianity and civilization in China. Mission work he had always regarded broadly as embracing all those beneficent influences which 'made for righteousness' and aid the progress of the Kingdom of God on earth. He held that in a valley of dry bones like China, subsidiary means to teach and practice the principles of Christianity are worthy of not a little care. That the views of the American Board did not agree with his own on this point, does not prove him to have been in the wrong. Nothing is plainer than the fact that in his new sphere Dr. Williams brought to bear the same qualities of mind and disposition which distinguished his Missionary life.

III. SINOLOGUE.

The life and letters of Dr. Williams have a peculiar interest for the student of the Chinese language and literature. Here he finds a noble example of what may be accomplished by zealous and continuous application. We have heard the acquisition of Chinese compared to the picking up of scattered coins. A pile may be made little by little. This representation is not however entirely just to the language in question. The gold of Chinese lies in heaps. This one may see by a glance at the pages of a dictionary in which the classification is according to phonetics. To know all that can be known of these phonetics, which includes of course a true idea of structure, drawn from the best sources, the Shüt-man 說文 and the phonetic dictionaries (these books are now made available for the foreign student), and to have the sound, tone and meaning for each phonetic, means to have the key to a great treasure house wherein the riches of Chinese lore are stored. In fact the characters on top of the pages in Dr. Chalmers' Compendium of K'ang-hi are the true 'open sesame' to the language and through the language to the literature of China. These once learned, the way is opened into the treasure house and all else is a mere question of storage and carrying capacity. 'Verbum sap.'

This was not the method of Dr. Wells Williams, and therefore on this ground, if on no other, we must dissent from the view that his magnum opus, the Syllabic Dictionary, is the book of most practical use in the study of the language. Touching the faults and errors of the Syllabic Dictionary quite enough has been written. Three hundred 'translations and mis-translations' were discovered and pointed out by one critic. Perhaps the worst minor fault of the work is the unsound etymology.

This much, however, can be said of all Dr. Williams' books, not excepting the large Dictionary. They were an immense advance on everything that preceded. They marked a new era in the study of the language and the people of China. All his works are monuments of extensive research, unflagging industry, and above all good sense. The true order of merit in Williams' best known and most widely used books is, we think, to place them thus:—

1 The Middle Kingdom
2 The Tonic Dictionary
3 The Syllabic Dictionary.

When about to issue the new Middle Kingdom, the author wrote, 'after all one cannot do much in such a line of research that will endure, for it is constantly changing and developing and needs frequent delineation.' Now it seems to us that Dr. Williams had special capacity and a quite extraordinary aptitude for this particular 'line of research.' On Chinese subjects there is no book to compare for one moment with the Middle Kingdom. Like a certain famous hand-book on one of the natural sciences, the language of Dr. Williams' book on China admits of expansion but not of condensation. We only know things by their opposites and the value of the Middle Kingdom as a work of authority may be known by contrast. Of books on China there is no lack. With a few noteworthy exceptions, it cannot be said that the material in them is well selected, well digested, well assorted or well arranged. Dickens did not caricature so much as prophesy, when he introduced the critic on the staff of the Eatonsville Gazette writing a copious review of a work on Chinese metaphysics. The sagacious newspaper man read for metaphysics under the letter M, and for China under the letter C, and combined his information. Much information drawn from foreign sources is still read into things Chinese. A reviewer once suggested disagreeably but not inappropriately that the reading of a certain learned work on China was like cutting open a shark. Both processes brought to light a motley collection of objects seemingly as much out of place as the specks in the human system which it is the wont of doctors to designate 'foreign bodies.'

Dr. Williams excelled in the faculty of seeing all round Chinese questions and leaving no point unnoticed or undetermined. He went beneath the surface to discover reasons and principles. Like the superior man praised by Confucius, he did not intermit his labour if there was anything he had not inquired about, or if there was anything in what he had inquired about which he did not understand, he did not intermit his labour. His efforts as compared with those used by others were as one hundred* to one or one thousand to ten. Whereas it is the practice of many writers on China to make a little knowledge go a long way, Williams' practice was to get much information into a small space. He never tried to spread his facts thinly or cover sins of ignorance with the mantle of pretension. For accuracy and fairness of statement, for careful research and for sound judgment, the author of the Middle Kingdom is without a compeer. Till the time arrives when fuller use can be made of the great topographical descriptions of each province, the large editions of Chinese classics and laws and the immense mass of material in the native encyclopaedias, it is likely that the Middle Kingdom will continue to hold the first place as a work of authority.

As regards the Tonic Dictionary of the Canton dialect, every person who has used the book will join Dr. Eitel in his 'tribute of unfeigned admiration for its undoubted excellencies.' Till Dr. Eitel's Dictionary in the Canton Dialect was issued, Williams' was the great book of reference for all students of Cantonese. The merits of Dr. Williams' Tonic Dictionary were its correctness, the variety and usefulness of the illustrative phrases and its conciseness. Nothing was more astonishing to a Chinese teacher than to see a foreign pupil on the first day of Chinese study turn up in the Tonic Dictionary the characters for which the pedagogue gave the sounds.

Native Cantonese teachers were ready to decide off-hand that Wai-lam-sz deserved a place among the sages. This opinion was strengthened when the pupil proceeded to read out Canton colloquial phrases from the Dictionary illustrations of the use of characters. My own teacher, a Canton man whose strong point was colloquial, often affirmed that it was not possible to improve to any great extent Williams' selection of colloquial phrases, those in the Dictionary being the most common and typical. The correctness of the tonal marks was not the least merit of the book. We mention this because the utility of some works in this dialect is lessened by the unfortunate circumstance that a beginner cannot depend on the tone marks. Dr. Williams was nothing if not thorough. Assiduous attention to the trifles which make perfection was a mark of the man. The result was that he came nearer than others to the perfection which is no trifle. We have heard persons fond of good living express gratified surprise that a Chinese cook, in a Chinese kitchen with Chinese cooking pots, can send up a dinner fit for a prince. Something analogous is the surprise which Williams' Dictionary is likely to awaken when the circumstances of its preparation are considered fairly. The sources and facilities at the author's disposal for collecting, arranging and printing seem inadequate, but Dr. Williams was a man of resources, and, as his son tells us, the passion for collecting was part of his father's nature.

The Syllabic Dictionary, based on the Wu fang yuen yin 五方元音 and intended to strike the general average of the spoken language of China, is, we think, a mistake in principle. There is, as we have pointed out, a method in the madness of studying Chinese, by following which this language becomes 'a thing of beauty and joy.' This is not the method of the Syllabic Dictionary.

In China all men and all things run in groups or classes. Shops devoted to the sale of the same kind of goods are found in the same street. 'None but shoe buyers,' says the proverb, 'come to Willow-lane Canton.' The Chinese human animal too is gregarious. It is almost impossible to segregate a man and deal with the individual apart from his 'cousins, his sisters and his aunts.' Kinsfolk and acquaintance, family and clan, interpose at every turn, and the strength of the social system, like the bundle of sticks, lies in the parts being bound up together. And herein is a parable which he who runs may read. As are all men and all things in China, so is the written language. Let the student learn characters, not singly but as parts of groups. Let him submit to be introduced through the individual character to its true connections and relations, and he has the clue out of the maze. To master the phonetics, then derivations, sounds and meanings, with their order under the radicals, is the first step to the learning of Chinese in a scientific and satisfactory way. Whether in the end the student succeed or not in mastering the language, he will, by thus mastering the phonetics, acquire a hold on Chinese. This principle in dictionary-writing Dr. Chalmers recognized and Dr. Williams did not. Its omission is to our way of thinking a radical defect of far greater consequence than the faults and errors, 'translations and mistranslations,' dwelt on by the critics of Dr. Williams' Dictionary.

Space will not permit further remarks on the various contributions made by Dr. Williams to the Chinese language and literature. His first articles on Chinese weights and measures and on the imports and exports of Canton, in the February number of the Recorder for 1834, evince the same thoroughness of method and terse comprehensiveness of statement, so characteristic of the man. In these early articles the reader will find a clear description of the abacus and the native mode of reckoning, an account of the values attaching at different times to the Chinese 里 mile, the quantity of alloy in the common copper cash, a note on the circulation of silver in China, and other unmistakable signs of industrious research. From the time of writing these early articles in the 1834 Repository, to the re-issue of the Middle Kingdom in 1883, there is an interval of nearly half a century, filled with literary work of high value to all persons interested in China, its language and its people.

The lesson of Wells Williams' career as a sinologue is conveyed in the word 'persevere.' The language is learned by keeping on. There is a stage of dismal tone practice, a stage of incoherent sentence forming, followed by a stage in which there is a hopeless mixing up of sounds and characters, succeeded by a stage of doubtful renderings, but the light will dawn if the student has patience. The superior man will not intermit his labours.

Mr. Robert Lowe once remarked, in the course of a parliamentary debate on the comparative merits of certain classes of studies pursued in England, 'If a man wants mere mental athletics, let him learn Chinese,' meaning that this study has the most remote bearing on practical life. With residents in China it is far otherwise. There are few foreigners at the coast ports who could not turn a knowledge of the language and customs of the natives to practical account. A better understanding on both sides, closer contact and truer touch would then be possible. The opening up of China must be through the minds and hearts of the Chinese, and to these the indefatigable labours of Williams and other great sinologues have already pointed the way.

The life depicted in the pages of this book was one of great beauty as well as great fruitfulness. Strong and steady and sturdy, the character of Dr. Williams was rounded off, mellowed and softened by the noble character of a Christian spirit. He made many friends and, what is better, kept them. There recently passed away one of the oldest and worthiest of these friends, Mr. Gideon Nye of Canton. To Mr. Nye, Dr. Williams was indebted for a 'multitude of kindnesses.' It was characteristic of Mr. Nye to recall the bye-gone Co-hong days and review in his old age many scenes and incidents that occurred in the 'morning of his life in China.' In these scenes Dr. Williams played a prominent part. He held the chief place among Mr. Nye's 'Heroes of the olden time.' So it was with other kindred minds who understood and sympathized with Dr. Williams. There was no withholding the tribute of kindly esteem and true affection. Few better examples could be found to show that genuine force of character, joined with the gentler virtues, form together the highest and most useful type of manhood. Writing of Confucianism in 'Present-day Tracts,' Dr. Legge affirms that 'the Chinese measure foreigners from their own standpoint, weighing them as well as they can in the balances of benevolence, righteousness, propriety, wisdom, and sincerity.' The remark is just. Furthermore it is the statement of a fact which foreigners are slow to realize. Weighed and measured from the Chinese standpoint, Samuel Wells Williams would not have been found wanting. In him was preserved the balance of the virtues on which Confucianism sets store. In the task he had before him as Missionary, Diplomatist and Sinologue, much depended on the good-will of the Chinese. In having this, he had the best guarantee of success. His virtues were in accord with their own highest and purest standards. The secret of his character and actions lay, says his son, in 'perfect humility and an absolute faith.'

Rev. THOMAS W. PEARCE

London Mission
Canton
China

“19世纪的东亚与美国
——纪念卫三畏诞生200周年”
国际学术研讨会

An International Symposium in Memory of S. W. Williams

Relations between East Asia and the United States in the 19th Century

会议手册
Program

14-18/12/2012　北京 · Beijing

THINK × ACT
関西大学
KANSAI UNIVERSITY

主办单位 Organizers

北京外国语大学中国海外汉学研究中心

Research Center of Overseas Sinology, Beijing Foreign Studies University

日本关西大学亚洲文化研究中心

Center for the Study of Asian Cultures, Kansai University

北京外国语大学世界亚洲研究信息中心

Information Centre for Worldwide Asia Research, Beijing Foreign Studies University

卫三畏（Samuel Wells Williams, 1812--1884）是近代东亚与美国关系史上的重要人物。他是美国最早来华的传教士之一，也是美国大学史上的第一位汉学教授，同时又是日本开国的见证人和新教赴日传教的推动者。他在广州、澳门、北京以及日本工作和生活了43年之久，是同光新政时期美国对华理性外交的代表人物之一。2012年是卫三畏诞生200周年，为了重新检讨这位活跃于十九世纪亚洲太平洋舞台的历史人物，总结中美之间、日美之间以及东西方之间相互学习、平等对话和建设性互动的历史经验，特召开此次学术研讨会。

“中国文化海外传播动态数据库”工作会议系列

会议背景

卫三畏（Samuel Wells Williams, 1812--1884） 是近代东亚与美国关系史上的重要人物。他是美国最早来华的传教士之一，也是美国大学史上的第一位汉学教授，同时又是日本开国的见证人和新教赴日传教的推动者。他在广州、澳门、北京以及日本工作和生活了 43 年之久，是同光新政时期美国对华理性外交的代表人物之一。2012 年是卫三畏诞生 200 周年，为了重新检讨这位活跃于十九世纪亚洲太平洋舞台的历史人物，总结中美之间、日美之间以及东西方之间相互学习、平等对话和建设性互动的历史经验，特召开此次学术研讨会。

Samuel Wells Williams (1812 – 1884) is an important figure in the relations between East Asia and the United States in the 19th century. He is one of the earliest missionaries to China, and the first university professor of sinology in US. He is also an eye-witness to the opening of Japan and a promoter of Protestant missions in Japan. He worked in Canton, Macau, Beijing and Japan for 43 years, and was one of the initiators of American rational diplomacy during the Tongzhi and Guangxu reign periods. In memory of the 200th anniversary of S. W. Williams' birth, this conference aims to re-examine his life and work and the relations between East Asia and US in the modern era.

议题：

1. 19 世纪及 20 世纪初美国与东亚的关系
2. 美国传教士在近代东亚的活动
3. 美国早期汉学史（包括语言、文学和历史等）
4. 澳门在 19 世纪中、日、美关系中的地位
5. 近代东西方之间相互学习和建设性互动的历史经验

Themes

1. Relations between East Asia and US in the 19th and Early 20th Centuries
2. American Missionaries in Modern East Asia
3. Early American Sinology and Japanology (language, literature, history, etc.)
4. The Status of Macao in the Relations between East Asia and US in the 19th Century
5. Historical Experience of Mutual Learning and Constructive Interaction between East and West

附录一

禅治文相关资料

AND THE LEAVES OF THE TREE WERE FOR THE HEALING OF THE NATIONS. Rev. C 22 V 2

This is to Certify That

Reverend Elijah C. Bridgman

by virtue of a contribution of Fifty Dollars,

made by his friends in

Belchertown Massachusetts

is a Director for Life, of the

AMERICAN TRACT SOCIETY.

Boston July 1833

Attest William Reed President.

Seth Bliss Cor. Secy

Pendleton's Lithogy Boston.

Answered May 27th 184[illegible]

Boston, October 25th

Sir:

I have the honor to inform you that at a m

The American Oriental Societ

held in this City on the thirteenth day of Oct

you were elected ——— a member, in consid

for valuable researches in the Chinese Language

A copy of the Constitution and By-Law

Society is annexed.

I am very respectfully,

Your Obedient Servant,

Wm. W. Greenou

Corresponding S

Rev. Eli Bridgman

D.D. &c. &c.

Amer O. Soc.
Diploma
Oct. 25 - 1842

Rev. E. C. Bridgman D.D.
Canton

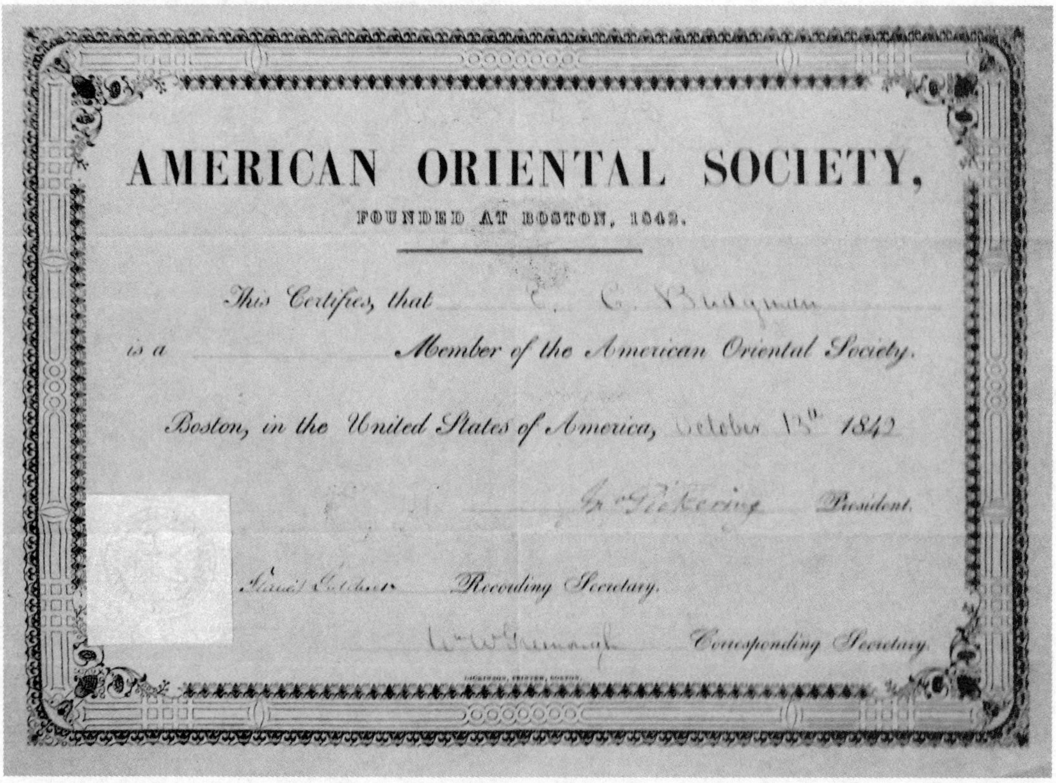

AMERICAN ORIENTAL SOCIETY,

FOUNDED AT BOSTON, 1842.

This Certifies, that E. C. Bridgman

is a Member of the American Oriental Society.

Boston, in the United States of America, October 13th 1842

Pickering President.

Recording Secretary.

Wm W. Greenough Corresponding Secretary.

CONSTITUTION

OF THE

AMERICAN ORIENTAL SOCIETY.

ADOPTED OCTOBER 13, 1842.

ARTICLE I. This Society shall be called the AMERICAN ORIENTAL SOCIETY.

ARTICLE II. The objects contemplated by this Society shall be—

1. The cultivation of learning in the Asiatic, African, and Polynesian Languages.
2. The publication of Memoirs, Translations, Vocabularies, and other works relating to the Asiatic, African and Polynesian nations.
3. The collection of a Library.

ARTICLE III. To become a member of the Society, a candidate must be proposed by the Directors, and must receive the votes of three fourths of the members present at an annual or stated meeting.

ARTICLE IV. Foreigners shall be eligible as Honorary Members, on being proposed by the Directors. The votes of three fourths of the members present, at an annual or stated meeting, shall be necessary to their election. Foreigners, however, having a permanent residence in the United States, shall be eligible as members.

ARTICLE V. The Government of the Society shall consist of a *President, three Vice Presidents, a Corresponding Secretary, a Recording Secretary, a Treasurer, a Librarian,* and *five Directors,* who shall be annually elected, and such elections shall be made at the annual meeting.

ARTICLE VI. The President and Vice Presidents shall perform the customary duties of such officers, and shall be *ex-officio* members of the Board of Directors.

ARTICLE VII. The Secretaries and Librarian shall perform their duties under the superintendence of the Board of Directors.

ARTICLE VIII. It shall be the duty of the Board of Directors to regulate the financial concerns of the Society, to superintend its publications, to carry into effect the resolutions and orders of the Society, and to exercise a general superintendence over its affairs. Three Directors at any regular meeting shall be a quorum for doing business.

ARTICLE IX. The annual meeting of the Society shall be held in Boston, on the Tuesday before the last Wednesday in May; the place and hour of the meeting to be determined by the Directors.

ARTICLE X. The Constitution may be amended on recommendation of the Directors, by a vote of three fourths of the members present at an annual meeting.

BY-LAWS.

I. THE Corresponding Secretary shall conduct the correspondence of the Society; and it shall be his duty to keep in a book provided for the purpose, a copy of his letters.

II. The Recording Secretary shall keep a record of the proceedings in a book provided for the purpose, and shall notify the meetings in such manner as the President or the Board of Directors shall direct.

III. The Treasurer shall have charge of the funds of the Society; and his investments, deposits, and payments, shall be made under the superintendence of the Board of Directors. At the annual meeting he shall report the state of the finances, with a brief summary of the receipts and payments of the previous year.

IV. The Librarian shall keep a catalogue of all books belonging to the Society, and shall be governed in the discharge of his duties by such rules as the Directors shall prescribe.

V. All MSS. deposited by authors for publication, or for other purposes, shall be at the disposal of the Board of Directors.

VI. The admission fee shall be five dollars, and the annual assessment two dollars; but on the payment at one time of fifty dollars, a member shall be exempted from both of these assessments.

VII. Stated meetings of the Society shall be held on the first Thursday of January, July, and October; the place and hour of the meeting to be determined by the Directors. The Directors may call special meetings.

VIII. SIX members shall form a quorum for transacting business, and THREE to adjourn.

IX. The Society shall appoint some member to pronounce a discourse at the annual meeting.

OFFICERS

OF THE

AMERICAN ORIENTAL SOCIETY.

1842.

PRESIDENT.

JOHN PICKERING, *of Boston, Massachusetts.*

VICE PRESIDENTS.

WM. JENKS, *of Boston, Massachusetts.*
MOSES STUART, *of Andover,* "
EDWARD ROBINSON, *of New York.*

CORRESPONDING SECRETARY.

WM. W. GREENOUGH, *of Boston.*

RECORDING SECRETARY.

FRANCIS GARDNER, *of Boston.*

TREASURER.

JOHN JAMES DIXWELL, *of Boston.*

LIBRARIAN.

FRANCIS GARDNER, *of Boston.*

DIRECTORS.

RUFUS ANDERSON, *of Boston.*
BARNAS SEARS, *of Newton.*
C. C. FELTON, *of Cambridge.*
SIDNEY WILLARD, *of Cambridge.*
JOSEPH WM. JENKS, *of Boston.*

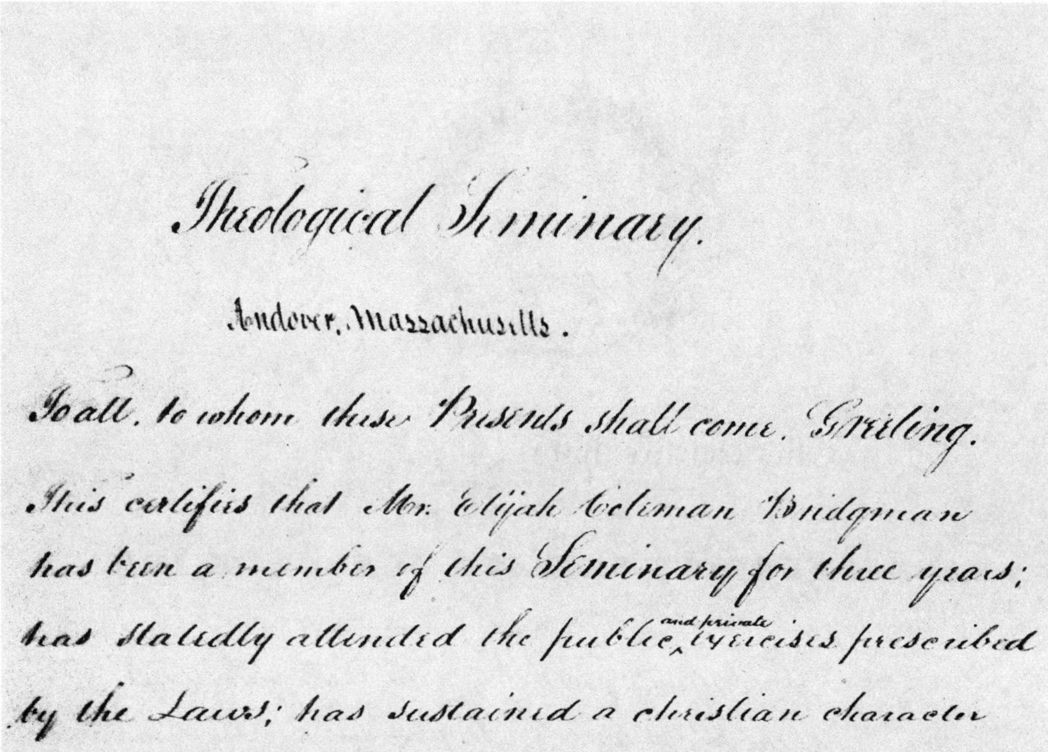

Theological Seminary.

Andover, Massachusetts.

To all, to whom these Presents shall come, Greeting.

This certifies that Mr. Elijah Coleman Bridgman has been a member of this Seminary for three years; has statedly attended the public and private exercises prescribed by the Laws; has sustained a christian character and honorably completed the regular course of Theological Study.

Given at Andover this 23 day of Sept. 1829.

In behalf of the Faculty.

E. Porter —— President

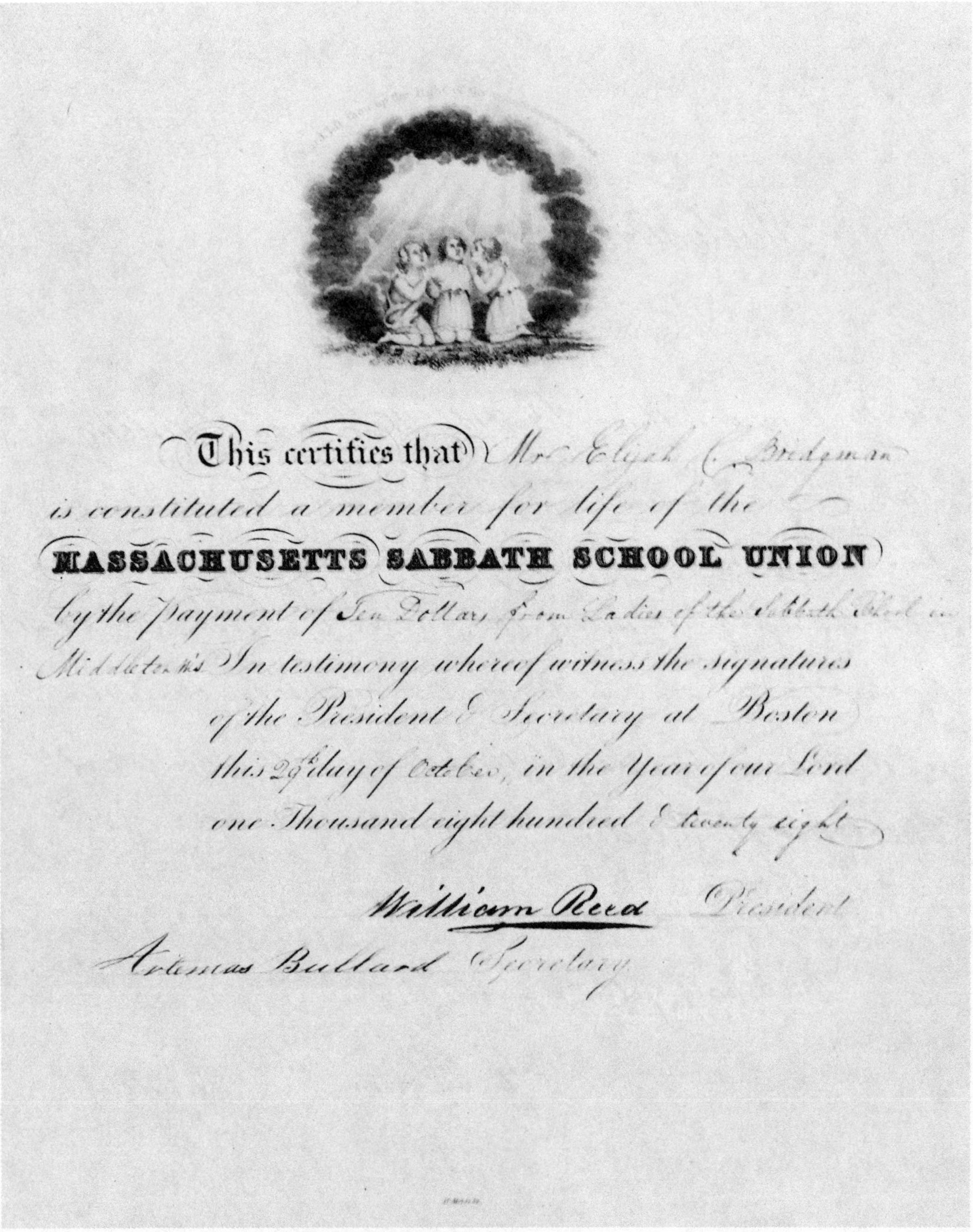

This certifies that Mr. Elijah C. Bridgman
is constituted a member for life of the
MASSACHUSETTS SABBATH SCHOOL UNION
by the payment of Ten Dollars from Ladies of the Sabbath School in
Middletown. In testimony whereof witness the signatures
of the President & Secretary at Boston
this 29th day of October, in the Year of our Lord
one Thousand eight hundred & twenty eight

William Reed President
Artemas Bullard Secretary

[1839 Aug 21]

Consulate of the United States of America at Macao. —

To all to whom these presents shall come — Greeting —

No 2

I the undersigned, Consul of the United States of America, hereby request all whom it may concern, to permit safely and freely to pass, Elijah Coleman Bridgman a citizen of the United States; and, in case of need, to give him all lawful aid and protection.

Age. 38 years
Stature 5 feet 4½ inches
Eyes Hazle
Forehead high
Nose Aquiline
Mouth Mid. size
Chin Round
Hair Brown
Complexion Light
Face Oval

Signature of the bearer
E. C. Bridgman.

Given under my hand and the Seal of my Consulate in China the Twenty first day of August One Thousand Eight hundred and thirty nine

P. W. Snow
U. S. Consul

THE LATE REV. DR BRIDGMAN.

The announcement of the death of the Rev. Dr Bridgman at Shanghae has saddened the hearts of all who have known him ; for to know him was to esteem him, and his decease is at the same time a public loss and a personal misfortune. We are not prepared to give anything like a proper biographical notice of him at this time, and therefore only offer such a sketch of his character and labours as memory can furnish.

Elijah C. Bridgman was born in Belchertown, in the State of Massachusetts, in 1801. His parents were farmers, and he lived with them until he entered college at Amherst in the same state. He was early the subject of deep religious impressions, and joined himself to the Congregational Church in Belchertown when about twelve years old. Having decided to enter the ministry, as soon as he had graduated at Amherst College, he went to the Theological Seminary at Andover, in 1826, then under the superintendence of Drs Porter, Woods, and Stuart, those fathers in the American Church, whose renown has increased as years have proved their merits. Under their guidance, Mr Bridgman became well grounded in those studies connected with the languages, customs, and interpretation of the Holy Scriptures, which fitted him for his future course.

It was at Andover that his attention was directed to the work of Foreign Missions, and the existence of a society among the students, whose object was the acquisition and diffusion of information upon this particular subject, deepened his interest in it, and led him to offer himself to the Committee of the American Board of Foreign Missions in Boston. He was examined and readily accepted ; and the Secretaries, one of whom was Jeremiah Evarts, were so much impressed with his sober and just views of mission work, that they decided to send him as their missionary to Canton, where they were then encouraged to commence the first American Mission in China.

He embarked at New York in October, 1829, in the ship *Roman*, whose philanthropic owners, Messrs Talbot, Olyphant & Co., gave him and his fellow-passenger, the Rev. David Abeel, free passages to Canton. This House took such an interest in the enterprise, that they had agreed to provide a house, and support both these gentlemen for at least a year after their arrival, one as a missionary to the Chinese, the other as chaplain to the seamen at Whampoa. When he reached Canton, in February, 1830, he found Dr Robert Morrison, and began the study of the Chinese language under his direction. He also opened a small school in his own rooms, which was continued for three years, and broken up by the proceedings of the Chinese officials in relation to Lord Napier, in 1834.

Encouraged by the advice of his friends, especially the Doctor, and his son John Robert Morrison, Mr Bridgman made arrangements for commencing the publication of the *Chinese Repository* ; and the arrival of a small printing establishment, contributed by one of the leading churches in New York, facilitated the early issue of the work, which was warmly commended by the Mission Board. The partners of the House of Olyphant & Co. in China agreed, too, to bear the pecuniary responsibility of the enterprise, so that no portion of funds sacred to mission purposes should be diverted to this end.

Mr Bridgman briefly stated the motives and objects he had in view in commencing the *Repository* in its introduction, but we have room for only a sentence or two :—

> "We enter on our work unbiased," he remarks, "and influenced rather by considerations of duty than of reward. Every man has his purposes, the accomplishment of which is the highest object of his heart's desire. To spend and be spent in publishing glad tidings to those who had never heard the joyful sound, and to bear the lamp of life to those who were perishing for lack of vision, a Greater than the wisest of the sons of men took an earthly tabernacle ; and now, having ascended up on high, He commands man to go and teach his fellow—to publish the gospel to *every* creature. . . . There is a most lamentable lack of knowledge among the millions inhabiting eastern Asia, yet we do anticipate the day (may it come quickly !) when all that is most valuable to man, and now so richly enjoyed by the nations of the West, elevating and still more to elevate them, shall be equally enjoyed, and produce the same results among the nations of the East. The efforts to accomplish a work so vast must be various, well directed, and long continued ; requiring patience, self-denial, meekness, gentleness, and the sterner qualities which can cheerfully endure hardness, stripes, and death. To bear some humble part in such efforts, we regard as not less our happiness than our bounden duty."

These purposes actuated our departed friend during his whole residence of thirty-one years in China, and one strong wish on his dying bed was, that he might live ten years longer to do more in furthering them. He was sole or chief Editor of the *Repository* for more than half of its existence from 1832 to 1851 ; and we think every one who examines its pages will agree with us that the purposes aimed at were continually kept in view, and in a great measure accomplished. The list of his articles shows the variety of subjects which engaged his attention ; and his own feelings prompted him to issue the work anonymously from the very first.

While conducting the *Repository*, Mr Bridgman was engaged, in connection with the late Dr Medhurst, in revising the translation of the New Testament, which was issued in 1836. He also issued a History of the United States, and several tracts in Chinese. In 1837, he commenced the preparation of the Chinese Chrestomathy under the patronage of the Society for the Diffusion of Useful Knowledge in China, and completed it in 1840. It has proved to be a useful aid in learning the Canton dialect, but its plan was too extensive to be carried out in the prescribed space. He also promoted the formation and establishment of the Morrison Education Society, designed as an honourable memorial of the labours of him whose name it bore, while carrying on those labours more thoroughly than he could himself alone have done. In everything that related to this Society, Dr Bridgman took a warm interest, and after the retirement of Mr Lancelot Dent from China in 1843, he was chosen its President, and retained that place till the time of his death. The Medical Missionary Society in China, and the Society for the Diffusion of Useful Knowledge in China, also owed much of their usefulness to his aid ; the latter in fact depended at the last on him alone.

Until the dispersion of the foreign community at Canton in 1839, by the proceedings of Commissioner Lin, our departed friend had the conduct of their public religious services, and supplied the pulpit himself a large portion of the time. It was not deemed safe to have religious services for the natives there in public, but this portion of his missionary work was by no means neglected. On the occupation of Hongkong, he removed there for a while, opening a Chinese chapel in Queen's Road, and continuing, more publicly and regularly than he had before been able to do, religious services in that language. The liberty to hold meeting now enjoyed in this region shows the advance that has been made in this direction, and newcomers into the mission field can hardly understand the apprehension and suspicion then felt by natives, when asked to join in Christian worship.

In 1843, the New York University conferred the honorary degree of Doctor of Divinity upon both Mr Bridgman and the Rev. James Legge, fellow labourers in the mission field. In April, 1845, Dr Bridgman was married to Miss Eliza J. Gillett, of New York, who now survives him. After the settlement of affairs at Canton, Dr and Mrs Bridgman returned there ; the printing of the *Repository* was also resumed there, and measures initiated to open schools and chapels. In 1847, their labours at this port were brought to a close by the choice of Dr Bridgiman B. as the delegate from all the Protestant Missionaries at Canton in the Committee on translating the New Testament into Chinese. This Committee decided to meet at Shanghae, and there was his residence during the rest of his life.

The preparation of an accurate and idiomatic version of the Holy Scriptures in Chinese was one of the great objects of Dr Bridgman's life, and he heartily joined in this plan of united efforts to accomplish it. Before the meeting of the committee at Shanghae, however, no small discussion had arisen among all Protestant Missionaries respecting the best term for *God* in Chinese ; and the argument was resumed by its members with vigour, Bishop Boone appearing as the advocate of *Shin*, and Dr Medhurst maintaining the reasons for the use of *Shang-ti*. While Dr Bridgman coincided with the Bishop, he admitted all papers on both sides into the pages of the *Repository*, which therefore contains nearly all that is worth knowing on the question. The controversy waxed warm, until, owing to this disagreement and other causes, the advocates of *Shang-ti* retired from the committee, which was then engaged upon the Old Testament, and finished their labours upon it as a separate body. As soon as arrangements could be made with societies in the United States, Dr Bridgman, Bishop Boone, and the Rev. M. S. Culbertson, were selected as suitable persons to complete the Old Testament, and they have since been employed upon it, though the Bishop has never been able to do more than review and revise the work of his coadjutors. This labour of translation was congenial to Dr Bridgman's tastes, and he has worked at it unremittingly and diligently during the last fourteen years, suspended only for about eighteen months in 1852-3, while he made a trip to America. This visit was owing to a severe fever, the only serious illness he had during his residence in China, and which had left him so weak, a voyage was the only remedy apparently left to preserve his life.

During his residence at Shanghae he aided in the formation of the North-China Branch, of the Asiatic Society, to whose transactions he contributed several papers, and of whose meetings he was elected the presiding officer for one or two years. Mrs Bridgman had opened a girls' school in her house, and the Doctor had the happiness of baptizing several of the scholars, who, with a few other converts, formed a mission church, over whom he watched with paternal care. Within a few months he enjoyed so much strength of body and mind that he had begun to mark out plans for other kinds of labour, after his translations were finished, and hoped to commence a mission somewhere along the Yangtsz'. Aided by the liberality of his countrymen in Shanghae, he had recently republished a new edition of the History of the United States 大美聯那志畧 in one small folio of 200 pages, the maps of which were painted by Mrs Bridgman's scholars.

Thus quietly pursuing his useful labours, he was found ready for the call when the messenger came, as Bunyan beautifully emblematizes, to say to him, "Thy Master hath need of thee, and that in a very little time thou must behold his face in brightness." While Mrs Bridgman was absent on a trip to Hankau, he was ailing a little, and a few days after her return, on Tuesday the 29th ultimo, he was taken with a violent dysentery, which yielded to no remedies ; and on Saturday at noon, as one present expressed it, "he quietly and peacefully, without a motion but of his lips, breathed out his life, and fell asleep on the bosom of the precious Saviour, whom he loved and served and trusted."

If the sorrowful promptings of private friendship at his death should be followed, this notice would be prolonged too much. He was a constant and warm-hearted friend, one to whom all who knew him could go in confidence, and be sure of sympathy and good advice. He had given his life to the cause of missions among the Chinese, in the full conviction that in its progress and final success was to be found the *only* remedy for the misgovernment and ignorance which afflicted them. His impression of the evils caused by the use of opium was strong, chiefly derived from observation among its victims ; and the pages of the *Repository* exhibit his efforts make known these evils. We remember once hearing him say, with great earnestness, "If I could remove these evils from the Chinese, or greatly reduce them, by the sacrifice of my life in any way, I would willingly lay it down."

His talents were not brilliant nor remarkable, but his industry, system, and perseverance, enabled him to accomplish much. He never became a ready or fluent speaker in Chinese, and did not attempt to open a chapel after settling at Shanghae ; but the scholars in his own house formed an attentive audience. He attained a good proficiency as a translator and writer of Chinese, and the version of the New Testament in which he bore a chief part is his best and greatest work. The general respect and esteem with which he was regarded in China, especially at Shanghae, where he was latterly best known, was the appropriate meed of a consistent and useful life, the reward of a Christian Minister and Missionary.

The Chinese always found him their friend, and several instances of their confidence could be mentioned. Two will suffice :—in 1839, Commissioner Lin dispatched a special agent, desiring him to visit him at the Bogue, to confer upon public affairs ; he went up from Macao, and had a long conference with the Commissioner, then engaged in destroying the opium ; but finding that he wished to make him a mere messenger to the English officers, he declined to act. On another occasion, in 1844, the real owners of some land in Hongkong came down to that colony to assert their claim, and engaged him to return with them across to the main, to the district town of Sin-ngan, to examine the title-deeds of their property in the record-office, in order that the proofs of ownership might be clearly drawn up.

—China Mail, November 28.

附录二

卫三畏家族文书目录

Manuscripts and Archives

Guide to the Samuel Wells Williams Family Papers

MS 547

compiled by John Espy, Carol King, and staff of Manuscripts and Archives

April 1980
Revised: September 2016

Yale University Library
P.O. Box 208240
New Haven, CT 06520-8240
mssa.assist@yale.edu
URL: http://www.library.yale.edu/mssa/

Table of Contents

Paging Instructions

To request items from this collection for use in the Manuscripts and Archives reading room, please use the request links in the HTML version of this finding aid, available at http://hdl.handle.net/10079/fa/mssa.ms.0547.

To order reproductions from this collection, please go to http://www.library.yale.edu/mssa/ifr_copy_order.html. The information you will need to submit an order includes: the collection call number, collection title, series or accession number, box number, and folder number or name.

Overview

REPOSITORY: Manuscripts and Archives
Sterling Memorial Library
128 Wall Street
P.O. Box 208240
New Haven, CT 06520
Web: http://web.library.yale.edu/mssa
Email: mssa.assist@yale.edu
Phone: (203) 432-1735
Fax: (203) 432-7441

CALL NUMBER: MS 547

CREATOR: Williams, S. Wells (Samuel Wells)

TITLE: Samuel Wells Williams family papers

DATES: 1809–1983

BULK DATES: 1809–1941

PHYSICAL DESCRIPTION: 23.83 Linear Feet (36 boxes)

LANGUAGE(S): The materials are in English .

SUMMARY: The papers include correspondence (comprising over half of the collection), manuscripts of Samuel Wells Williams's Syllabic Dictionary of the Chinese Language, themes and lecture notes by Frederick Wells Williams, diaries, newspaper clippings, articles on China, maps, and pictures. The bulk of the correspondence relates to S. W. Williams, missionary, diplomat, and sinologue. The period between 1845 and 1855 has extensive correspondence with missionaries and with James Dwight Dana and Matthew C. Perry, whom Williams accompanied on his mission to open Japan and on his return visit in 1854. Williams's letters to friends and family comment on progress made and their reception in Japan. In 1856 Williams became secretary and interpreter to the American Legation in China and many of the letters refer to Chinese problems of the following 20 years. His correspondents include, in addition to Dana and Perry, Anson Burlingame, Hamilton Fish, Asa Gray, Frederick Low, William Bradford Reed, and William Henry Seward. The remaining correspondence covers the period 1885 to 1939, encompassing the correspondence of F.W. Williams, Yale professor, and Wayland Wells Williams, writer.

FINDING AID LINK: To cite or bookmark this finding aid, use the following address: http://hdl.handle.net/10079/fa/mssa.ms.0547.

Administrative Information

Provenance

Gift of Yale-in-China from the library of Frederick Wells Williams and of Mrs. Dalton V. Garstin, 1945-1946; and Cynthia G. Blackwell, 1980 (Accession 1981-M-002). Transfer from East Asian Curator, 2004 (Accession 2005-M-014). Gift of Huntington Williams III, 2009 (Accession 2010-M-027), 2012 (Accession 2013-M-006).

Information about Access

The collection is open for research.

Series I. Correspondence, 1824-1939, is available on microfilm. Patrons must use FILM HM 277 instead of the originals.

Series II. Samuel Wells Williams, Journal: trip to Japan with Commadore Perry, is available in digital form. Patrons must use digital use copies instead of the originals.

Cite As

Samuel Wells Williams Family Papers (MS 547). Manuscripts and Archives, Yale University Library.

Alternative Formats

Correspondence and related papers, 1853-1854, of Samuel Wells Williams regarding his services as an interpreter of Commodore Matthew Perry's expedition to Japan is available on microfilm (96 frames on 1 reel, 35 mm.) from Manuscripts and Archives, Yale University Library, at cost. Order no. HM22.

Series I. Correspondence, 1824-1939 is available on microfilm (10 reels, 35 mm.) from Manuscripts and Archives, Yale University Library, at cost. Order no. HM277.

Series II. Samuel Wells Williams, Journal: trip to Japan with Commadore Perry (Box 29A, Folders 1 and 2), is available in digital form from Manuscripts and Archives, Yale University Library.

Associated Materials

Williams Family Letters (GEN MSS 761). General Collection, Beinecke Rare Book and Manuscript Library, Yale University.

Biographical Sketch

Samuel Wells Williams (1812-1884): missionary to China, 1833-1845; printer and author; helped prepare Chinese dictionary; accompanied Perry expedition to Japan as interpreter in 1853-1854; in 1856 became secretary and interpreter of the American Legation to China, and remained until 1876; in 1877 became professor of Chinese at Yale University.

Description of the Papers

The collection covers three generations of the Williams Family: Samuel Wells Williams, 1812-1884, and his brother Robert Stanton Williams; Frederick Wells Williams, 1857-1928; and Wayland Wells Williams, 1888-1945. The correspondence covers the years 1824-1939, nearly two-thirds of which (10 boxes) relates to Samuel Wells Williams and his life in China and the U. S. In addition to its being the largest part of the collection, the Samuel Wells Williams's correspondence, is by far the richest part.

Throughout this collection there is a great deal of family correspondence. However, Samuel Wells Williams also corresponded with James Dwight Dana, Asa Gray, Anson Burlingame, Commodore Matthew C. Perry, Hamilton Fish, Frederick Low, William Bradford Reed, and William Henry Seward. The collection contains few Frederick Wells Williams's letters and none from Wayland Wells Williams. In the later period there is one Pearl Buck letter and a few William Henry Brewer letters.

Samuel Wells Williams, missionary, diplomat, and sinologue sailed for China in 1833 and for nearly forty years this was his home. He first began his work in Macao with the missionary press and repository. He aided others in translating Chinese texts and himself compiled one of the first comprehensive Chinese-English dictionaries, A Syllabic Dictionary of the Chinese Language.

The very early years of the correspondence - 1824 to 1844 - represent a small part of the collection. However there are several letters to and from James Dwight Dana and Peter Parker. The next period which is quite extensive is 1845 to 1855. This part includes correspondence with Elijah Coleman Bridgman, James Dwight Dana and other members of the missionary family in China. An important part of the correspondence falls within the years 1853 and 1854, for it was in this period that Matthew C. Perry and Samuel Wells Williams met. Numerous letters pass between the two. Samuel Wells Williams accompanied Perry on his mission to open Japan and on his return visit in 1854. This trip resulted in some exceedingly interesting letters to friends and family on the progress made and the reception received. In addition, there are copies in Chinese of letters from Perry to the Chinese on Okinawa.

In 1856 Samuel Wells Williams became secretary and interpreter to the American Legation in China. He held this post until he left China in 1876. During this time he corresponded with Anson Burlingame, William Bradford Reed and William Henry Seward. The letters in this section make reference to the following events: 1858-revolution and riot in China and the struggle of foreign powers seeking greater freedom and toleration of missionaries; 1859-English, French and Chinese diplomatic conflict, new treaties with the U. S. and Claims; and 1862-rebel activity and destruction.

During the years 1871 to 1874 a great deal of the correspondence relates to Samuel Wells Williams's dictionary and the inadequacy of the American Legation in China.

The last eight years of Samuel Wells Williams's life were spent in the U. S. where he became the first professor of Chinese languages at Yale and president of the American Bible Society. He also revised his book, The Middle Kingdom. In this final stage there are many letters from missionaries remaining in China, the American Bible Society and voluminous correspondence from Scribners concerning the publishing of The Middle Kingdom.

The remaining correspondence (four boxes) covers the period 1885 to 1939. Personal Correspondence composes 90% or more of this section of the collection. The period from 1885 to 1890 contains more correspondence from Scribners and letters praising Frederick Wells Williams's book about his father. From 1903 the correspondence consists of letters from Wayland Wells Williams's mother, sister and friends. Frederick Wells Williams, the son of Samuel Wells Williams, was a professor at Yale and his son Wayland Wells Williams was a writer.

The collection also includes an annotated copy of the 1848 edition of Williams's The Middle Kingdom, along with a variety of letters, bills, clippings, and illustrations that were interleaved in the two volumes. There are also two journals, which appear to have been written by Williams after the events discussed. One chronicles Williams's trip to Japan with Commodore Matthew Perry, while the other records a trip to Peking in 1858-1859 and seems to be a compilation of extracts from his letters.

Arrangement

The collection is arranged in five series and two additions; all accessions received prior to August 2009 have been incorporated into this arrangement: I. Correspondence, 1824-1939. II. Samuel Wells Williams papers, 1828-1905. III. Frederick Wells Williams papers, 1876-1927. IV. Papers of others, 1831-1941. V. Oversize folios, 1826-1886.

Collection Contents

Series I. Correspondence

Box	Folder	Description	Date(s)
		Series I. Correspondence	1824-1939
1	1-19	1824-1846	1824-1846
18	20-43	1847-1853	1847-1853
2	44-92	1854-1861 May	1854-1861 May
3	93-137	1861 June-1868	1861 June-1868
4	138-184	1869-1873 February	1869-1873 February
5	185-233	1873 March-1878 February	1873 March-1878 February
6	234-284	1878 March-1881 April	1878 March-1881 April
7	285-334	1881 May-1897	1881 May-1897
8	335-368	1898-1929 April	1898-1929 April
9	369-395	1929 May-1938 May	1929 May-1938 May
10	396-398	1938 June-1939	1938 June-1939
10	399-402	Undated	
10	403-404	Unidentified	

Series II. Samuel Wells Williams papers

Box	Folder	Description	Date(s)
		Series II. Samuel Wells Williams papers	1828–1905
		Note: It has not been possible to distinguish the papers of S.W. Williams from those of his son, F.W. Williams, with perfect certainty. In particular, some items filed under SWW may pertain to FWW.	
		Writings	
		A Syllabic Dictionary of the Chinese Language...	
11	1-4	Vol. 1: manuscript	1874
11	5-8	Vol. 2: manuscript	1874
12	9-11	Vol. 2: manuscript	1874
12	12-15	Vol. 3: manuscript	1874
12	16	Tables	1874
12	17	List of missionaries who received copies at $6.00	1874–1875
		The Middle Kingdom	
29	1	Volumes I and II	1848
29	2	Loose material found in Volumes I and II	1844-1891
12	18	Part of printed copy, with manuscript corrections	1883
12	19	Lithographs and proofs of illustrations	1883
12	20	Publicity	1883
13	21	"List of Articles by S. Wells Williams in the Chinese Repository"	Undated
13	21	List of letters to W.F. Williams	Undated
13	21	Other bibliographical notes	Undated
13	22	Autobiographical sketch: manuscript, reprint	1878-1889
13	23	Letters to editors: clippings	1858–1884
13	24	"Canton Prior to 1840": clipping	1873 January 23
13	25	"Description of the town of Hakodadi, in Japan": reprint	Circa 1854
13	26	"The Great Famine": clipping	1879 December 11
13	27	Letter to President Hayes by the Faculty of Yale College, on Chinese immigration: reprint, with annotations	1879 February 21
13	28	"Notes of remarks to Linonians," on Chinese immigration: manuscript	1879 February 24
13	29	Draft of letter to the editor of the New York Tribune on Chinese immigration to and rights in America	1880 April 19
13	30	Note and extracts from letters on the application of treaty provisions to Americans residing in China and Japan	Circa 1880 April
13	31	"Our Treaties with China": manuscript	Undated

Box	Folder	Description	Date(s)
13	32	"Treaty Obligations Towards the Chinese": clipping	1877 November 8
13	33	Article on the Lewchew Islands: manuscript	Circa 1879-1880
13	34	Article on exterritoriality: manuscript	Undated
13	35	Draft and translations on the place of women in Chinese culture	Undated
13	36	"Female education and authors in China, with a translation of a primer for girls": manuscript	Undated
13	37	"Tea Culture": manuscript	Undated
13	38	Draft of general article on the Chinese language	Undated
13	39	Draft of article on learning the Chinese language	Undated
13	40	Article on the development of Chinese writing: manuscript	Undated
13	41	Draft of North American Review article on historical value of early Chinese records	Undated
13	42	"A Chinese Historical Novel Lieh Kwoh Chi, or The Records of the Feudal Kingdoms: with a translation of Chapters I and II": reprint, with manuscript translation of chapters I-IX	1880
13	43	Translation of Lieh Kwoh Chi chapters IX-XIX: manuscript	Circa 1880
13	44	Princeton lectures on Chinese religion and philosophy: manuscript	1882
13	45	"Nature of the Chinese religious and political institutions and reasons for their perpetuity": manuscript	Undated
13	46	"Mission Work in Japan": draft	Undated
13	47	Review of two books on Christian merchants' missionary work in China: manuscript	Undated
13	48	"The Controversy among the Protestant Missionaries on the Proper Translation of the Words God and Spirit into Chinese, Bibliotheca Sacra" : manuscript	1878 October
13	49	"Shin: Does it mean God or Spirit?": manuscript	Undated
13	50	Article on Mormonism: manuscript	Undated
13	51	Circulars	1869-1875
		Notes	
13	52	Miscellaneous lists of, and notes on, Chinese orthography	Undated
13	53	"Lists of plants in the treatise on grains and planting," in Chinese and English	Undated
13	54	"System of Orthography commonly used in writing the Amoy Dialect,"	Undated
14	55	Gazetteer of Chinese districts and cities	Undated

Box	Folder	Description	Date(s)
14	56	Chronology and survey of Chinese history; lists of Chinese emperors and reigns, and Japanese diaries; Chinese historical survey by states	Undated
14	57	Miscellaneous	Undated
		Diaries and account books	Undated
14	58	Expense account of his trip from China through the Near East and Europe to the United States and of his sojourn in the United States; calling card and papers laid in	1844–1848
14	59	Account book, mostly of personal accounts, kept in Shanghai, Macao, and Hong Kong, during mission work, and at Legation in Peking; calling card and note laid in	1858–1865
14	60	Account book and diary of his trip from China through the Near East and Europe to the United States	1875–1876
14	61	The National Diary, 1881, with manuscript entries, including a few by Sarah (Walworth) Williams	1881
15	62	Statements of account for Williams's books	1852-1884
15	63	Accounts, correspondence, and circulars re: payments for Williams's work for the Japan Expedition and for the Legation at Peking	1854–1863
15	64	Register of receipts from an auction of Williams's belongings, with buyers' names written in	1876 October 18-19
15	65	Miscellaneous accounts, receipts, and bills of sale	Circa 1863-1883
29A	1-2	Journal: trip to Japan with Commodore Perry	1853-1854
		The journal is digitized. Researchers must use the digital use copies instead of the originals.	
29A	3	Loose material found in journal	1852-1936
		The material is digitized. Researchers must use the digital use copies instead of the originals. See also: box 26, folder 2 (p. 16).	
30	3	Journal: trip to Peking	1858-1859
30	4	Loose material found in journal	1858-1859
		Legal papers	
15	66	Claim against the Chinese Government for losses suffered, and proposal re: surplus paid to U.S. authorities	Circa 1856-1859
15	67	Agreement between the British and Foreign Bible Society and the American Bible Society re: editions of translations of the Bible	1861
15	68	Agreements with printers and publishers	1874-1882
15	69	Power of attorney, and memorandum concerning lease of Legation at Peking	1875-1876

Box	Folder	Description	Date(s)
15	70	Copies of petition to Congress for reimbursement of salary, with reply	1878 January-February
15	71	Outline of will	Undated
		Writings of others	
15	72	Writings about Williams, some by family members, and a resolution adopted by the Peking Missionary Association at his death	Circa 1877-1888
15	73	Williams family genealogies, one with a preface by Williams	1880-1882
		Elijah Coleman Bridgman	
15	74	Papers regarding ordination, minutes of a meeting of The Congregational Association of China, certificates and licenses, expense account, account of Robert Morrison's estate, and obituary clipping	1828-1861
15	75	Manuscript copy of an English translation of Lao Tse, The Book of the Way and of Virtue; prepared for Bridgman by a student	1859
15	76	Thomas George Grosvenor: "Yun-Nan Inquiry": private accounts while at British Legation at Peking (in same volume with following item)	1875–1878
15	76	Sophia Gardiner (Williams) Grosvenor Gray: household accounts while at The Hague	1877–1878
15	77	Ko Kun Hua: Chinese and English poetry dedicated to Williams; correspondence, calling cards, and clippings laid in	1881–1882
15	78	Susan Schereschewsky: birthday poem to Williams, with his reply	1870 September 21
15	79	Tung Ta-jin: "Stanzas on the departure of Anson Burlingame"	1867 November 22
15	80	U.S. Legation at Peking: Centennial observance: printed poem and programs, and manuscript poems by Chauncey Goodrich, George Frederick Seward, and [Chester Holcombe?]; also another patriotic poem	1870-1876
15	81	T.F. Wade and Tung Siun: Chinese translation of Longfellow's "Psalm of Life"	Undated
15	82	Unidentified: "A few lines on the occasion of Dr. Williams's leaving China"	Undated
		Printed matter	
15	83	Biographical notices and obituaries of Williams, and reviews of Life and Letters of SWW	1875–1905
15	84	Scrapbook of obituary clippings on Williams	1884
15	85	Reviews of A Syllabic Dictionary of the Chinese Language...	1874–1876
16	86	Reviews of The Middle Kingdom	1848-1884

Box	Folder	Description	Date(s)
16	87	Miscellaneous	Circa 1835-1883
		Photographs	
16	88	Samuel Wells Williams, with illustration	Circa 1876
16	89	Members of the North China Mission	1874
		Memorabilia	
16	90	Lock of Williams's hair	1884 February 16
16A	91	Scrapbook of calling cards, correspondence, and printed memorabilia The scrapbook is digitized. Researchers must use the digital use copies instead of the originals.	Circa 1854-1874
16	92	Certificates and notices from organizations	1864–1881
17	93	Chinese documents, some with Williams's annotations	Circa 1843-1874
17	94	Chinese documents, some with Williams's translations or annotations, and one with silk envelope	Circa 1866-1876
17	95	Miscellaneous Chinese documents and printed matter, including a document with postage stamps enclosed	Circa 1871
17	96	Chinese books, including translations of English works	Undated
17	97	Miscellaneous: rubbing, mat, kitchen god	Undated
17	98	Two Chinese dolls	Undated
17	99	Lithographs by W. Heine for Matthew C. Perry's Narrative of the Expedition of an American Squadron to the China Seas and Japan	1856
17	100	Manuscript maps of China, in Chinese	Undated
17	100	Printed maps of China, in English	Undated

Series III. Frederick Wells Williams papers

Box	Folder	Description	Date(s)
		Series III. Frederick Wells Williams papers	1874–1927
		Note: It has not been possible to distinguish the papers of S.W. Williams from those of his son, F.W. Williams, with perfect certainty. In particular, some items filed under SWW may pertain to FWW.	
		College compositions: manuscripts	
19	1	"The Life and Poems of Shelley"	1876 June 28
19	2	"The Fool in 'King Lear'"	1876 October 14
19	3	"Charles II and James II compared"	1876 November 7
19	4	"Tito Melenia as a Study of Character"	1876 December 16
19	5	"The Poet Cowper"	1877 February 16
19	6	"The War of 1812--Its causes and consequences"	1877 March 9
19	7	"Tennyson and Longfellow compared"	1877 April 13
19	8	"British Relations with Afghanistan"	1878 November 7
19	9	"Mr. Gladstone and Lord Beaconsfield"	1879 February 7
19	10	"Scholasticism and Confucianism--the Civilization of the Middle Ages and of the Chinese"	1879 March 29
		Notes taken in Berlin	
19	11	Hermann Grimm, "The History of German Art"	1880 May-August
19	12	Miscellaneous, with registration book	Circa 1880
		Books	
19	13	Anson Burlingame and the First Chinese Mission to Foreign Powers: notes, draft of preface, printed matter, agreement with publishers	1912
		Lectures, articles, and notes	
19	14	"Robert Stanton Williams": reprint	1892
19	15	"A Pioneer of German Art: Asmus Jakob Carstens": reprint	1889 May
19	16	German art: manuscript, program	Undated
19	17	"Australian Problems": manuscript	1890
19	18	"Saladin": typescript	1917
19	19	China: physical aspects: manuscript	Undated
19	20	"English relations with China": manuscript	Undated
19	21	"France and China": manuscript	Undated
19	22	"The Historical Development of the Relations between the United States and China": typescript	Undated
19	23	China: history: manuscript	Undated

Box	Folder	Description	Date(s)
19	24	"The Chino-Japanese War": manuscript	1895
20	25	"Chinese Emigrants in the Far East," American Historical Association: manuscript, program	1899 December
20	26	"The Inauguration of Representative Government in China": typescript	1910
20	27	"Recent Administrative Changes in China": reprint	Circa 1910
20	28	"Yuan and China's Struggle for Freedom": typescript	Undated
20	29	China: history and politics: manuscripts, printed matter	Circa 1895-1906
20	30	Asian architecture, and Chinese and Japanese literature: manuscripts	Circa 1898
20	31	"Chinese Art": typescript, programs	1914
20	32	China: history and culture: manuscript, typescript	Undated
20	33	China: miscellaneous	Undated
20	34	China: religion (originally in envelope labelled "(Cambridge) 1912," apparently sent (back?) to Williams by Prof. Irving Fisher): manuscripts	Undated
20	35	Miscellaneous	
		Course lectures and notes: manuscripts	
20	36	"European Colonies in Asia and Africa"	1901–1905
		"History of the Ancient World" (originally "Ancient Oriental Nations from the Earliest Times")	
21	37	Greece and Rome	Circa 1905-1921
21	38	Babylonia and Assyria	Circa 1905-1921
21	39	Egypt	Circa 1905-1921
		Asiatic history (various courses)	
21	40	China and India	Circa 1899-1923
21	41	Japan and Korea	Circa 1899-1923
22	42-43	Miscellaneous	Circa 1899-1923
		Teaching materials	
22	44	Syllabi and bibliographies, some by other professors	1914-1927
22	45	Grade books	1894–1923
22	46-50	Papers of students: ancient history, colonization, the Philippines, and the Hawaiian Islands	1900-1917
		Includes a petition for the elimination of Williams's June examination.	
		Miscellaneous papers	
23	51	Diary kept in New Haven, New York, and Utica, with calling cards laid in	1881–1882
23	52	Hunan-Yale College of Medicine: correspondence	1910–1916

Box	Folder	Description	Date(s)
23	53	Statements of account from stay in Germany	1886
23	54	Statements of account, bills, receipts, stock-holders' report, including tax receipts for Martha Wayland	1889–1926
23	55	Copies of publishers' agreement with H.L. Wayland re: Francis Wayland as an Educator	1895 June 15
23	56	Photographs: Macao Protestant Cemetery; interior of study	Circa 1888
		Printed matter	
23	57	Miscellaneous Yale memoranda	Circa 1914-1915
23	58	Biographical notices and reviews	1891-1912
23	59	China: opium	1881-1895
23	60	China: rebellion	1906-1912
23	61	China: miscellaneous	Circa 1911
23	62	Current events: miscellaneous	1892–1894
23	63	Reviews of others' writings	1887–1891
24	64	Alfred Thayer Mahan, "The War on the Sea and its Lessons"	1898–1899
24	65	The Holiness Baptist, later The Evangel: incomplete run of issues, with 2 reports	1908–1915
24	66	Miscellaneous	1885-1926
		Memorabilia	
24	67	Receipt from Japanese priest, on the occasion of the presentation of two Ryokai Mandala scrolls to Williams (possibly those in folio 27)	1908 July 16
24	68	Pieces of tree bark, with lettering on them	Undated
24	69	Miscellaneous sketches	1874-1902
24	70	Maps	Undated
24	71	Calling cards	Undated

Series IV. Papers of others

Box	Folder	Description	Date(s)
		Series IV. Papers of others	1831–1941
25	1	Williams, William, journal	1831-1837
		Williams, Sarah (Walworth)	
25	2	"Translations of the Bible into Chinese": manuscript	Undated
25	3	Expense account kept in China, Europe, and America	1869-1874
25	3	Printed diary with manuscript entries and accounts, kept chiefly in New Haven	1872
25	4	Editions of Letts's Pocket Diary, and an Almanac, with manuscript entries and accounts, kept in China, Europe, and America	1874–1875
31	1	Williams, H. Dwight, scrapbook	1874–1875
		"Scraps-China" contains primarily newspaper clippings relating to Chinese and Japanese culture and history.	
25	5	Williams, Cornelius Wade, miscellaneous volume of notes, letters, mounted clippings, accounts, and scribblings; kept at Milford, Conn.	Circa 1869-1877
25	6	Williams, Fanny Hapgood (Wayland), memorabilia	1932-1936
		Williams, Wayland Wells	
		New Haven Colony Historical Society	
25	7-8	Correspondence	Circa 1933-1941
25	9	Memoranda, minutes, treasurer's reports, and budgets	Circa 1933-1941
		Printed matter	
25	10	Reviews and program of "Second Choice"	1928
25	11	Stock certificate	1918

Series V. Oversize Folios

Box	Folder	Description	Date(s)
		Series V. Oversize Folios	1826-1886
		Samuel Wells Williams Papers	
26	1	Statement of Acheen's claim for indemnity for losses	1856
26	1	Bill of sale for a girl, Macao	1857 May
26	1	Good-bye letter of appreciation	1876 November
26	1	Illustrations for The Middle Kingdom	1883
26	1	Catalogue, in Chinese, of books read by SWW	Undated
26	1	Official letter from the military governor Li at Fu P'ing (Kuangsi) to a group of foreigners	Undated
26	1	Letter from the governor of a High Commissioner sent by the king asking for a reply to his previous letter	Undated
26	1	Photographs of the interior of the study of Frederick Wells Williams	Undated
26	1	Passports, appointments, and college diploma of Samuel Wells Williams and Frederick Wells Williams	1826–1886
26	2	Loose material found in journal of trip to Japan with Commodore Perry	
27		Two Japanese wall scrolls	Undated
		Manuscript maps mounted on Chinese scrolls, captioned as follows by SWW or FWW	
28		"Karafto, and Eastern part of Manchuria"	Undated
28		"Manchuria, Corea, and Russian possessions"	Undated
28		"West Manchuria, Liantung, Chihli, Shantung south to Fuhkien"	Undated
28		"Mongolia, Shansi, Shensi, Honan, Hukwang, Kwangtung"	Undated
28		"Mongolia, Kansuh, Sz'chuen, Yunnan"	Undated
28		"East of Tibet, Mongolia, and Barkoul"	Undated
28		"Ili and West of Tibet"	Undated
28		"West end of Tibet"	Undated

Accession 2010-M-027. Additional material

Box	Folder	Description	Date(s)
		Accession 2010-M-027. Additional material	1809-1983
1	1-13	Correspondence	1809-1889
		Correspondence is primarily from Robert Stanton Williams of Utica, New York, to his brother Samuel Wells Williams regarding family matters and finances. There are several 1853-1854 typed transcriptions of letters from William Frederic Williams to Rev. Leonard Bacon, of New Haven, written from Mosul. Also included are a letter from Matthew C. Perry to Mr. Lao Shumming regarding his employment as a translator, and a letter from Perry addressed to Samuel Wells Williams in Canton.	
1	14	Financial records	1817-1884
1	15	Floor plans	Circa 1882-1883
1	16	Genealogical material	Circa 1880s
1	17	Printed pamphlets and articles by and about Samuel Wells Williams	1841-1884
		Gilman, Rev. E. W., American Heroes on Mission Field, No. 8, S. Wells Williams, LL.D.; Williams, Samuel Wells: Notices of Fu-Sang, and Other Countries Laying East of China (1880), Education of Woman in China, The First and Second Reports of the Medical Missionary Society in China (1841), and Bulletin of the American Geographical Society (1884, No. 2).	
1	18	Williams, Huntington, Huntington Williams, M.D., published for family and friends, Baltimore	1983
2	1	"Answer Respecting Limits," Japanese (written in Chinese characters) text on onion skin paper (1 sheet), accompanied by photostatic copy	1854 May 22
		Document relating to the treaty with the United States that opened Japan to foreign trade, and described by Samuel Wells Williams in his "Journal of the Perry Expedition to Japan," Transactions of the Asiatic Society of Japan (1910), pages 191-192.	

Accession 2013-M-006. Additional material

Box	Folder	Description	Date(s)
		Accession 2013-M-006. Additional material	1848-1853
		Correspondence	
1	1	Williams, Catherine Huntington	1848 July 4, 1852 October 1, 1853 December 11
1	2	Williams, Robert S. (brother of Samuel Wells Williams)	1848 April 22, 1853 February 14
1	3	Genealogical material relating to Thomas Williams (grandfather of Samuel Wells Williams)	Undated

Access Terms

Diaries.
Historians.
Clergy.
New Haven (Conn.)
Missionaries.
China.
Educators.
Family.
Missionaries -- Correspondence.
Missions -- China.
English language -- Dictionaries -- Chinese.
Missionaries -- Biography.
Account books.
Chinese language -- Dictionaries -- English.
Asia.
Japan -- Foreign relations -- United States.
United States -- Foreign relations -- Japan.
China -- History -- 19th century.
China -- History -- Opium War, 1840-1842.
Curtis, George William
Speer, William
Stanley, Charles Alfred
Smith, Arthur Henderson
Townsend, William K. (William Kneeland)
Treat, Selah Burr
Syle, Edward W.
Tattnall, Josiah
Seelye, Julius H. (Julius Hawley)
Seward, Frederick William
Rondot, Natalis
Scribner, Charles
Seyffarth, Gustav
Sheffield, Devello Z.
Seward, George F. (George Frederick)
Eaton, Daniel Cady
Williams, Robert Stanton.
Williams, Henry Dwight
Williams, Frederick Wells
Williams, Fanny Hapgood Wayland.
Williams, Talcott
Williams, Sarah Walworth
Dana, James Dwight
Ward, William Hayes
Wade, T. F. (Thomas Francis)
United States Naval Expedition to Japan(1852-1854)
Twichell, Joseph Hopkins
Williams, Charles Augustus
Whitney, William Dwight
Watson, James C. (James Craig)
Yung, Wing
Hoar, George Frisbie
Gilman, Daniel Coit
Williams, Wayland Wells
Williams, William Perkins
Woolsey, Theodore Dwight
Yale University. Curricula.

Yale University. Faculty.
Yale University. Students.
Yale-China Association.
Yates, M. T. (Matthew Tyson)
Brewer, William Henry
Deĭch, G. M. (Genrikh Markovich)
Gray, Asa
Buck, Pearl S. (Pearl Sydenstricker)
Parkes, Harry, Sir
Perry, Matthew Calbraith
Parker, Peter
Rensselaer College.
Riggs, T. Lawrason (Thomas Lawrason)
Reed, Thomas B. (Thomas Brackett)
Williams family.
Reed, William B. (William Bradford)
Martin, W. A. P. (William Alexander Parsons)
Mateer, C. W. (Calvin Wilson)
Mabie, Hamilton Wright
Marcy, William L. (William Learned)
Nye, Gideon
Olyphant, George Talbot.
Morrison, John Robert
Muirhead, William
Judson, Adoniram
Jessup, Henry Harris
Jackson, A. V. Williams (Abraham Valentine Williams)
Ivison, Henry
Lowell, Josephine Shaw
Low, Frederick Ferdinand
Lockhart, William
Kerr, J. G. (John Glasgow)
Silliman, Benjamin
Dwight, Timothy
Hepburn, J. C. (James Curtis)
Haupt, Paul
House, Samuel Reynolds
Palmer, Ray
Hopson, William Fowler
Holt, William S.
Holcombe, Chester
Foster, John Watson
Garstin, Elizabeth Williams.
Goodrich, Chauncey
Gray, Sophia Gardner Williams Grosvenor
Hance, Henry Fletcher
Happer, A. P. (Andrew Patton)
Fenollosa, Ernest Francisco
Fisher, George Park
Seward, William Henry
Folds, Thomas McKey
Canaday, John.
Coward, Tim.
Cushing, Caleb
Denby, James.
Dean, William
Bowring, John, Sir
Brown, Samuel Robbins
Bridgman, E. C. (Elijah Coleman)
Cass, Lewis
Browne, J. Ross (John Ross)

Burlingame, Edward L. (Edward Livermore)
Burlingame, Anson
Bloomfield, Maurice
Boone, William Jones, bp.
Bird, Howard S.
Evarts, William Maxwell
Blodget, H. (Henry)
Bartlett, John Russell
Bender, Clifford.
Avery, Benjamin Parke.
Avery, Samuel Putnam
Angell, James Burrill
Ashmore, William
Anderson, Rufus
Henry, Joseph
Fish, Hamilton
Williams, S. Wells (Samuel Wells)

附录三

编者相关论文及《每日新闻》报道

国益と人権 揺れる米外交

幕末の思想家、吉田松陰が1854（安政元）年、ペリー率いる「黒船」艦隊に密航を求めて失敗し、静岡・下田の獄に監禁された際、米艦の医師に心境を訴えた漢文の写しを、関西大の陶徳民教授（東西文化交流史）が見つけ、学芸総合誌『環』（藤原書店）第14号に発表した。1853年のペリー来航から今年で150年。この漢文と米側資料を併せ読むと、開国を迫る強圧的な米外交の陰に人道主義の源流があったことが浮かび上がる。【岸俊光】

吉田松陰 監禁中の心境伝える漢文の写し

関西大・陶教授が米大学で発見

写しは今年3月、米エール大スターリング記念図書館古文書部のS・W・ウィリアムズ家文書の中から発見された。ウィリアムズはペリーの首席通訳官で、晩年同大教授を務めた人物。その自筆の日記『ペリー日本遠征随行記』に挟み込まれていた。

漢文は獄を訪れた外科医に松陰が板切れに書いて渡したとされ、板切れ自体は現存していない。文書の存在は知られていたが英訳や日本語への重訳で、写しは原文をより正確に伝えていると見られる。

陶 徳民さん

とう・とくみん　1951年、中国生まれ。上海復旦大で修士号、大阪大で博士号を取得。米プリンストン大・ハーバード大研究員を経て現職。著書に『日本漢学思想史論考』など。

松陰が乗船を求めた「投夷（とうい）書」と呼ばれる手紙に対し、陶教授は今回の漢文を「第二の投夷書」と名づけ、筆跡からウィリアムズの中国人助手羅森（らしん）の筆写と推定している。

初期の日米交渉で、漢文が重要な役割を果たしたことは余り知られていない。米側に日本語を十分解する者が見当たらず、幕府の担当者が漢文に堪能なためだった。そこで重要な役割を果たした中国人通訳に陶教授は着目し、偶然文書に出会うことになった。

「日本の役人には英語が分からず、英語を用いた国交交渉はできなかった。蘭学の伝統があるオランダ語で口頭の交渉を進め、漢文の文書で一字一句を確認したと思う」と陶教授は説明する。

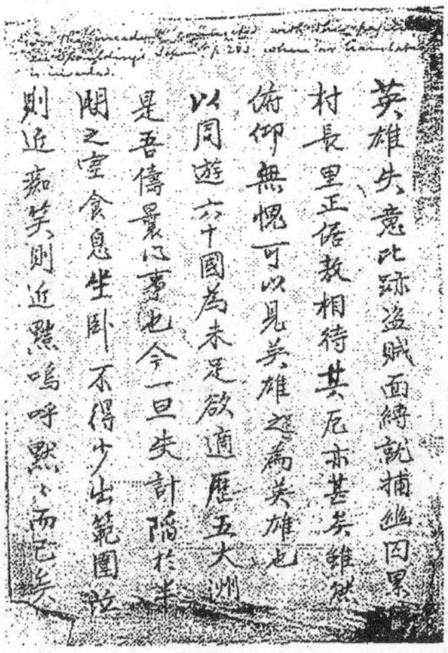

英雄失意此跡盗賊面縛就捕幽囚累
村長里正倨教相待其厄亦甚矣雖然
俯仰無愧可以見英雄之為英雄也
以周遊六十國為未足欲適歷五大洲
是吾儕素心也今一旦失計陥於半
間之室食息坐臥不得少出範圍泣
則近痴笑則近黠嗚呼黙黙而已矣

米エール大図書館に保存されていた、松陰が心境をつづった漢文の写し＝陶徳民教授提供

見つかった写しは、縦約19㌢、横約14㌢。全部で103文字、2段落からなる白文で、密航に失敗して捕まり、盗賊のような扱いを受けていることを嘆きながらも、海外への強い思いを伝えている。

この漢文によって、英訳や日本語訳に誤りがあることも分かった。〈面縛就捕〉の中の〈面縛〉とは、〈両手を後ろに縛り面を前に向ける〉という意味だが、ウィリアムズは〈公衆の面前で捕縛され〉という趣旨に英訳している。

また、〈可以見英雄之為英雄也〉は本来、既に自分を英雄視する松陰の豪まいな気概を伝えているのに、これまでは、今や英雄たりうるかどうかが立証されるべき時と未来形で訳されているという。

悲惨な監禁状態と斬首の可能性を知った米側は松陰の処分に積極的に関与し始め、極刑はしないという幕府側の約束を取り付けた。その際、この漢文はペリー側を動かす一因になったと陶教授は見る。

捕まってなお〈5大陸を渡り歩くことを望む〉と書いた松陰の知的好奇心に感銘し、公式記録の『日本遠征記』に次のように記している。

〈日本人は……探究心のある国民であり、道徳的、知的能力を広げる機会を歓迎するだろう。あの不運な二人の行動は、同国人の特質であると思うし、……好奇心をこれほどよく表しているものはない〉

加えて〈半間の室に陥り、食・息・坐・臥、少しも範囲を出づるを得ず〉という訴えは、米側にアメリカ・インディアンの監禁法を連想させるものだった。ウィリアムズにより、松陰と従者の金子重輔が閉じ込められていたのは長さ約1・8㍍、幅0・9㍍、高さ約1・4㍍の狭い空間だったことが実測されている。

陶教授は「和親条約の締結に悪影響を与えないよう密航を拒否した国益中心の考え方と、囚人の扱いで人権を重視する側面があった。現在につながる米外交のジレンマが読み取れる」と話している。

「自らを英雄視」は疑問

田中彰・北大名誉教授（日本近代史）の話　人権について、米国側と幕府の考え方に大きな落差があったのは間違いない。国に対して権力外交を展開しても、日本側の罪人の扱いには米国の基準に照らして不満があったのだろう。これはペリー来航時に限った話でなく、面白いテーマだと思う。従来の翻訳に問題があったという指摘もうなずけるが、松陰が自らを英雄視していたという解釈には疑問がある。松陰のヒューマニズムには身障者など弱者へのまなざしが感じられ、それを念頭に置くべきだと思うからだ。

2003年8月8日付毎日新聞

米艦日誌に記載

吉田松陰「下田密航」

事件の時間経過詳細に

「回顧録と矛盾なし」

関大教授発見

幕末の思想家、吉田松陰＝写真＝が1854年、静岡・下田沖に停泊していたペリー提督の黒船に乗り外国へ密航しようとした事件の詳しい時間経過が、陶徳民・関西大教授（東西文化交流史）が米国立公文書館で発見した資料から分かった。松陰が事件の7カ月後に著した回顧録「三月廿七夜記」の記述と矛盾がなく、その現代的な時間感覚が浮かぶ。この「下田密航」から25日で155年。【岸俊光】

きょう155年

記録が見つかったのはペリー提督が率いる艦隊の旗艦、ポウハタン号の航海日誌で、記載責任者はマクルーニー艦長。1854年4月25日の欄に「(午前)2時45分、2人の日本人が小さいボートで乗艦してきて、約45分間滞留した。乗艦した際、彼らのボートが漂失したため、提督の指示で本艦の小艇で岸辺へ送還された」と書かれていた。「2人の日本人」は、吉田と従者の金子重之助を指す。

事件はペリーが再来航し、日米和親条約の締結後に起きた。2人はポウハタン号より前にミシシッピ号へ乗艦を試みた。公式記録「ペリー艦隊日本遠征記」は、それを「午前2時ごろ」と記す。

今回の資料を合わせて陶教授は、松陰らは25日午前2時ごろミシシッピ号にたどり着き、2時45分ごろポウハタン号に乗艦、約45分滞留し、3時半ごろ送還へ——と結論づけた。2人はその後自首し獄につながれた。

陶教授は「事件の貴重なデータであり、松陰の厳格な時間観念と驚異的記憶力も裏づけられる」と話している。

梅渓昇・大阪大名誉教授（日本近現代史）の話　松陰が時間を大事にすることで時代を正しく認識していたのは重要だ。のちの岩倉使節団などにつながる日本近代化の先駆けとなった松陰の向学心を知ってもらいたい。

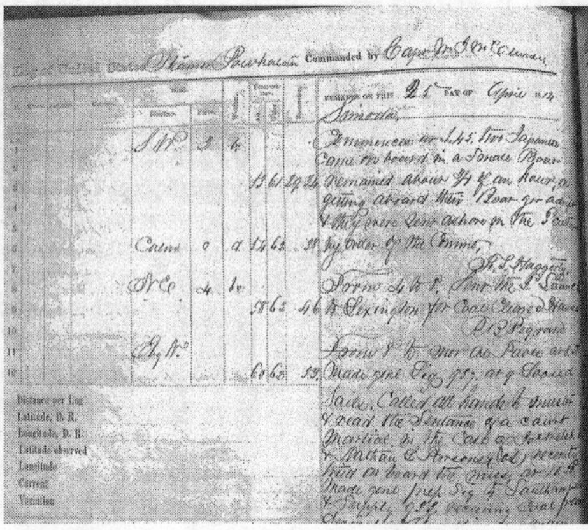

下田密航事件の記録が見つかったポウハタン号の航海日誌＝陶徳民教授提供

2009年４月25日付毎日新聞

A Charitable Man from Afar:

A Reappraisal of S. W. Williams' (1812–1884) Involvement in East Asia

De-min TAO

Trans-Pacific Relations
December 2015

III. Section 1: Early Ties Made by Missionaries, Diplomats, and Students

A Charitable Man from Afar:
A Reappraisal of S. W. Williams' (1812–1884) Involvement in East Asia

De-min TAO

Outline

I. Introduction

When Frederic Wells Williams[1] was compiling his father's biography, *The Life and Letters of Samuel Wells Williams,* in 1889, he used the three words "Missionary, Diplomatist, and Sinologue" in the subtitle. As a missionary printer sent to China in 1833 for the Canton press of the American Board of Commissioners for Foreign Missions (ABCFM), Williams worked enthusiastically for two decades for the opening of China and Japan to the West and to Christianity until he accepted an invitation to become secretary and interpreter for the American legation in China in 1856. His contribution in securing the Kanagawa Treaty of 1854 was so impressive that Commodore Perry wrote the following letter to him from Hong Kong on September 6, 1854:

1 Born in Macao, F.W. Williams (1857–1928) spent his boyhood in Peking and graduated from Yale in 1879. He joined the Yale faculty as a historian of the Orient in 1893 and played a leading role in Yale-in-China, the Yale foreign missionary society that developed educational and medical institutions in Changsha, Hunan Province after 1901. The spirit and tradition of the society, known as the Yale-China Association today, has been revitalized by Yale's President Richard C. Levin through his initiatives in promoting collaborative research programs with China's top universities, such as Peking University and Fudan University.

> In taking my departure from China I feel myself called upon by every sense of propriety and justice to bear the most ample testimony to the talents, zeal, and fidelity with which you conducted the important duties entrusted to your management as Chief Interpreter of the Mission to Japan. I say little when I declare that your services were almost indispensable to me in the successful progress of the delicate business which had been entrusted to my charge.
>
> With high abilities, untiring industry, and a conciliating disposition, you are the very man to be employed in such business.
>
> With my best respects to Mrs. Williams, I am, dear sir, very truly yours, M. C. Perry.[2]

For the next two decades after 1856, Williams served as a diplomat in China. He helped negotiate the Tientsin Treaty of 1858, and was responsible for the successful insertion into the treaty of the clause granting toleration of Christianity.[3] He was several times in charge of the American legation in Peking in the intervals when there were no resident ministers. When he decided to resign in 1876, the State Department sent him the following notification in recognition of his outstanding accomplishments:

> Your knowledge of the character and habits of the Chinese and of the wants and necessities of the people and the government, and your familiarity with their language, added to your devotion to the cause of

---

2 F. W. Williams, *The Life and Letters of Samuel Wells Williams, LL.D.: Missionary, Diplomatist, Sinologue* (New York and London: G.P. Putnam's Sons, 1889), pp. 229–30. Perry also eagerly tried to secure Williams' help in compiling the narrative of the Japan expedition after returning to the US and wrote to the latter on March 13, 1855 in New York as follows: "I shall be impatient until I hear from you, and hope you will write by return of mail, and write fully. I should be greatly disappointed not to have your assistance.... The truth is, every incident connected with the Japanese expedition is looked upon with great interest, and there is one universal demonstration of applause at every event which has occurred, and I feel a nervous desire to make the report alike creditable; in doing so I depend confidently on your services in the way I have suggested. You write with so much care and so graphically that it will not give you half the trouble it would many others.
Do not forget to send me some translations of Japanese poetry, as also Chinese done into English, if you have any; these scraps can be appropriately introduced. The specimens furnished to the *Hongkong Register* by your Chinese clerk are quite interesting." Ibid, p. 231.

3 For details about the drafts and revisions of the "toleration clause" based on an archival discovery at Yale, see De-min Tao, "The Chinese-American Negotiations on Relaxing the Prohibition of Christianity in 1858 as seen from *S. W. Williams Family Papers*" (in Chinese) in *Wakumon* (Journal of Association for the Study of Cultural and Linguistic Exchanges between China and the West, Kansai University), No. 9, pp. 57–65.

Christianity and the advancement of civilization, have made for you a record of which you have every reason to be proud. Your unrivalled Dictionary of the Chinese Language and various works on China have gained for you a deservedly high position in scientific and literary circles. Above all the Christian world will not forget that to you more than to any other is due the insertion in our treaty with China of the liberal provision for the toleration of the Christian religion.[4]

Returning home, Williams became the first professor of Chinese language and literature at Yale in 1877, and the president of the American Bible Society and the American Oriental Society in 1881. With the help of his son, F.W. Williams, he spent almost two years from 1881 revising and enlarging his monumental work, *The Middle Kingdom*, first published in 1848 and based significantly on the *Chinese Repository* (1832–51). He was fortunate to see publication of the new version in October 1883, just a few days before the celebration of the half-century anniversary of his first landing at Canton in 1833, and about four months before his passing away in February 1884.

It is obvious that Williams' experiences as a missionary, diplomat, and Sinologist were unusually rich and extraordinary.[5] The present paper focuses on Williams' personal thoughts in relation to these accomplishments, especially his less well-known contributions as a humanitarian activist. The author hopes to shed some new light on his attitudes toward East Asia as well as on American involvement in the region during the mid-19th century.[6]

4 *The Life and Letters,* p. 412.

5 There have been differing views over Williams' character as a missionary. For example, Murray A. Rubinstein points out in his book, *The Origins of the Anglo-American Missionary Enterprise in China, 1807–1840* (The Scarecrow Press, 1996, p. 256), that Williams "was not a typical missionary candidate nor did he become a typical missionary." As a printer, a China watcher, and a Sinologist, he "would serve his nation and its people better than he served his God." Although Williams was not a preacher, he was still a qualified missionary in the real sense. From my study of Williams' hand-written journal of the 1853 and 1854 Japan expedition kept at Yale, I identified the over thirty places where Williams indicated his missionary zeal; these were omitted by F. W. Williams when he was editing the journal for publication in the early 20th century.

6 Tyler Dennett compiled the pioneer work, *Americans in Eastern Asia: A Critical Study of United States' Policy in the Far East in the Nineteenth Century* (MacMillan Company), based on the theory of power politics current in 1922 when the Washington Naval Conference had just ended. Contrary to that approach, there is a need to reexamine the history in terms of the humanitarian concerns of our age. The availability of *S. W. Williams Family Papers* at Yale and relevant publications in the post-WWII period has made this study possible.

II. Disseminating Christianity through Intellectual and Medical Aid

From its very beginning, the American Protestant mission to China tended to use intellectual and medical aid to disseminate Christianity, and thus had a uniquely pragmatic character.

After the arrival of Elijah C. Bridgman (1801–1861) with David Abeel in 1830 in Canton as America's first missionaries, Bridgman immediately started learning Cantonese at the suggestion of Robert Morrison (1782–1834). Gradually, he became aware that "during the long intercourse which has existed between the nations of Christendom and eastern Asia, there has been little commerce in intellectual and moral commodities," and that "this whole nation [of China] is in a profound sleep." As exemplified by the modern Western experience, the most important means of improvement of China would be an "increase of knowledge."[7] He also pointed out that because "the Chinese government will not tolerate the public preaching of the gospel, the great means of introducing a knowledge of Christianity will be tracts and books."[8] Fortunately, the joint proposal of Bridgman and Morrison to establish a mission press at Canton was approved by the American Board and supported by the American merchant D.W.C. Olyphant with the generous arrangement of a donation. The prominent monthly, *Chinese Repository,* was thus commenced in May 1832.

Williams arrived in China in 1833 to manage the printing office and to assist Bridgman in editing the journal. From time to time, printing and distribution of the journal, tracts, and books was interrupted by the Chinese authorities. In August 1834, Williams reported to Secretary Rufus Anderson of the American Board:

> We are much hampered on account of a recent search which was instituted by the provincial authorities at command of the emperor, in order to find any natives who had been engaged in the manufacture of two Christian books which had been sent to Peking by the governor of Fukkeen. This edict caused some alarm and our teachers instantly left us. Search has also been made at Macao for traitorous natives, but we do not hear of any who have thus far been apprehended.... Thus are we hindered more at present than ever before. We cannot get a book printed, and those now printed can neither be sent away nor distributed prudently in Canton; and we cannot procure a teacher with whom to study the language.... [The situation] induces us to think of prosecuting

7 Michael C. Lazich, *E.C. Bridgman (1801–1860): America's First Missionary in China*, The Edwin Mellen Press, 2000, pp. 86, 112.

8 Ibid., p. 82.

our operations out of reach of the officers of this government. Whether such an establishment cannot be organized nearer China than Singapore, is a point not yet settled.[9]

The arrival of Dr. Peter Parker in October 1834 in Canton seemed to be a turning point. On the advice of the American Board, he had studied theology and medicine at Yale in order to be prepared to minister to both the physical and spiritual needs of the Chinese people.[10] His arrival in China

> … introduce[d] a new factor that has performed a service of the highest importance between foreigners and Chinese by removing their mutual misunderstandings. This was the establishment at Canton of a dispensary and hospital for the free treatment of natives. No branch of mission work in the East is now better known or more universally successful than this of medicine; its direct use in spreading the Gospel among all classes of the people has been inestimable; but at this time the experiment was considered hazardous by the foreign community in China, and was looked upon with suspicion by local authorities. At the end of its first year, however, when thousands of impatient Chinese were clamoring for admission to the crowded dispensary, the residents of the factories cordially agreed to pay back the sum advanced to Dr. Parker by the mission, and formed the "Medical Missionary Society" by subscribing sufficient funds to carry on the benevolent work. The hong-merchant Howqua, as soon as he understood the object, gave the free use of a large house during twenty years for hospital purposes.[11]

Because of such successful experiences, when the American Board tried to change its policy in 1852, Williams expressed his dissatisfaction in a letter to his brother, W. F. Williams, a missionary in the Near East, complaining that:

> The worthy secretaries in Boston have nearly concluded to bring my printing-office to a conclusion and get all our printing done by other offices at such rates as we can arrange by the job. Dr. Anderson seems disposed to subordinate and surcease all printing-offices, schools, and hospitals, and turn all the energies of the missions hereabouts into preaching…. Amid such a valley of dry bones as China, subsidiary means, like schools and hospitals, in which to teach and practice the principles of Christianity, are worthy of not a little care. Dr. Parker's

9 *The Life and Letters,* p. 76.
10 *The Origins,* p. 270.
11 *The Life and Letters,* pp. 76–77.

hospital still goes on, supported by the charity of foreigners, and the Gospel is constantly made known there; so also at other hospitals. I will not deny that too much stress and time may be given to these departments, but it is difficult to tell beforehand what will prove the most promising path. Blessed is the work of doing good in any line; all finally run into the same Sea of Glass where its earthly agents will one day be so happy in casting their crowns of glory before Jesus, that they will quite forget the discussions as to whose rill was straightest, and deepest, and had the purest water. My vocation seems to be rather hereditary, and I think I should be dissatisfied if I had no printing-office to look after, though belike I am not now well able to judge.[12]

Given the fact that the monthly journal *Chinese Repository* had been earning a good reputation for the American Protestant mission for about twenty years, it is understandable that Williams was unwilling to give up his jobs as both editor and printer. But more importantly, he expressed here his belief in pragmatism that every kind of good action would eventually lead to the dissemination of Christianity.

It is interesting to see that in the same letter, Williams told his brother that "A large fleet of United States ships of war is here at present, and Com. Perry" will soon "visit Japan and tell the Siogoun that he must treat our whalers more civilly."[13] It was fortunate for Perry that he secured the service of Williams, a missionary who had been in China for about twenty years and acquired profound knowledge of East Asian languages and cultures, and who was then in a transitional period and thus available to assume a new responsibility.

III. A "Cooperative Policy" toward China and Japan

During the mid-19th century America's diplomacy toward China and Japan appeared less aggressive and more patient when compared with the European powers, although gunboat diplomacy was used at times.

Concerning the peaceful conclusion of the Kanagawa Treaty,[14] Williams wrote proudly when he was about to leave Japan in June 1854 that

> … now, not a shot has been fired, not a man wounded, not a piece of property destroyed, not a boat sunk or a single Japanese found who is the

---

12 *The Life and Letters,* pp. 180–181.

13 Ibid., 181.

14 Perry did not try to force the Japanese to conclude a treaty by just one visit in 1853, but gave the Japanese government several months to think about its options in responding to the American request and then came back again in 1854.

> worse off, so far as we know, for the visit of the American expedition.... By permission of the Commodore, I drew up a paper of a general character which was sent to Lin [the Japanese chief commissioner Hayashi] last evening by Moriyama. In it I endeavored to show how Japan could learn much which would be of enduring benefit to her by adopting the improvements of western lands, and allowing her people to visit them and see for themselves; adding that it was to set before them the most useful and curious specimens of Western art that the President had sent out to them, such things as a steam engine, a telegraph apparatus, a daguerreotype, all sorts of agricultural implements, books and drawings explaining these and other things....[15]

This kind of attitude can also be found in the diplomatic efforts of Townsend Harris (1804–1878), the American consul in Ningbo, China, who went to Japan as the first American Consul General in 1856 and succeeded in persuading the Japanese negotiators to conclude the 1858 Treaty of Amity and Commerce by guaranteeing them a higher importation tariff rate and a ban on the opium trade.[16]

Williams was also known for his criticism of England's opium trade. While he was supportive of English war against China in 1840 for its commercial and diplomatic aims, he thought that:

> The whole expedition is an unjust one in my mind on account of the intimate connection its sending here had with the opium trade, but we shall find very few expeditions that have not had a good deal to find fault with in them. There is a way some have of saying that 'it will all work well, and that good will come out of evil,' which is only a sheer excuse for leaving themselves in indolence. For my part, I am far from being sure that this turn up is going to advance the cause of the Gospel half so much as we think it is. England has taken the opium trade upon herself nationally, and can that be a cause to bless? for the success of her arms here would extend that wicked traffic ten thousand times more than

15 S. W. Williams, *A Journal of the Perry Expedition to Japan, 1853–1854*. Edited by F. W. Williams. Kelly & Walsh, 1910, pp. 224–225.

16 See Mario E. Cosenza, *The Complete Journal of Townsend Harris: First American Consul General and Minister to Japan*. Japan Society, New York, 1930. As Dennett has commented, the treaty "was not only more liberal in its provisions than the Cushing treaty with China (of 1844), but even more liberal than the treaties of Tientsin which had followed the occupation of Canton and the destruction of the Taku forts." He even quotes the following comment by the British historian Longford: Harris's service in Japan would not be "exceeded by any in the entire history of international relations." *Americans in Eastern Asia*, pp. 362–364.

the Church is ready to extend her stakes here.[17]

In 1850, in view of rising tensions between the Chinese and English, Williams pointed out again that "The poverty induced by the opium trade is pressing harder and harder upon them [the Chinese people], and the lower classes are devoting themselves to robbing, piracy, and emigration in order to procure food and work."[18] Because of his consistent stance on the issue, when the new version of his *Middle Kingdom* was released in October 1883, almost all the reviews by English readers condemned his "opium intolerance"—his settled conviction that England, by reason of her opium policy, was at the bottom of much of the present misery in China."[19]

Williams was also critical of French consul Henri-Victor Fontanier's excessive intervention in the cases of controversies and conflicts between missionaries, converts, and anti-Christian Chinese. In November 1870, with great effort by China's leading officer, Tseng Kuo-fan (1811–1872), it seemed to the Chinese as well as Williams that the "Tientsin Catastrophe"[20] was almost settled, and

> the French Chargé has received 460,000 Tls. ($657,000), of which 250,000 Tls. are for the families of the victims and the rest for the buildings destroyed. The acceptance of this sum seems to me to close all warlike action on the part of France, but I hear that Rochechouart [the French Chargé] says that he has left his country free either to fight or make up. The American mission chapels are paid for—4,500 taels—and the English soon will be.... What a pest France is in this world! She never learns to treat others justly, nor is she content to mind her own affairs, while the mass of people are almost as ignorant as heathen, and quite as superstitious. She has made more wars, more trouble, more tyranny, more persecution, than any other Christian (so-called) nation.[21]

During Williams' twenty-year diplomatic career as secretary and interpreter in Peking, the most respected American minister he worked with was Mr. Anson Burlingame (1820–1870), who served as minister from 1861 to 1867. Early in 1860, the U.S. Congress decided to return to China the surplus and accumulated interest of the indemnity money (claimed originally

17 *The Life and Letters,* p. 122.
18 Ibid., p. 175.
19 Ibid., p. 460.
20 For details of the incident, see Paul A. Cohen, *China and Christianity: The Missionary Movement and Growth of Chinese Anti-foreignism 1860–1870.* Harvard University Press, 1967, pp. 229–261.
21 *The Life and Letters,* pp. 386–387.

by the Americans who had suffered property losses during the wars in China) to China. Williams proposed to use the money for establishing "an American-Chinese College in China, in which Chinese students should be instructed in Western learning and American students could receive such instruction as would fit them for positions in the consular, diplomatic, customs and commercial life in China. Anson Burlingame supported this proposal, and it seemed to have met with the approval of President Lincoln." However, it was not realized because "Congress took no action on it." Dennett praised Williams' proposal as the "most notable one" because "in it was clearly foreshadowed the system of 'Indemnity Students' for which provision was made at the time of the return of the Boxer Indemnity surplus nearly 50 years later."[22]

Burlingame was known for his "cooperative policy" toward China. As defined by Burlingame, "that policy is briefly this: an agreement on the part of the Treaty Powers to act together upon all material questions; to stand together in defense of their treaty rights, but determined to maintain the foreign system of customs, and to support it in a pure administration and upon a cosmopolitan basis; to menace the territorial integrity of China."[23] The policy was seconded by Sir Frederic Bruce, the British Minister in China, for the majority in the Parliament and the Foreign Ministry had come to realize, after two so-called "opium wars," that it was in the best interest of Britain to maintain the autonomy of China so as to avoid the responsibility of managing a colony, which would be unstable and costly. Williams commented:

> Despite the opposition of the foreign trading communities along the coast (the bitterness and arrogance of whose bearing towards the natives can be measured and understood only by those who are familiar with the principles and conduct of foreign adventurers in the East), the Burlingame policy succeeded before long in establishing an equitable friendship with the leading statesmen in China, and in preserving their country from the inevitable effects of a doctrine which if persisted in would have resulted in the disruption of the empire.[24]

On the other hand, after the upheaval of the Taiping Rebellion and the

---

22 *Americans in Eastern Asia,* p. 330.

23 *The Life and Letters*, p. 359. For a discussion of the context of Burlingame's cooperative policy and his relations with Secretary William H. Seward of the State Department, see *Americans in Eastern Asia,* pp. 367–390.

24 *The Life and Letters,* pp. 359. Burlingame was also known for his introduction to Prince Kun and the Tsungli Yamen of W.A.P. Martin and his translation of *Laws of All Countries*. See Ssu-yu Teng and John K. Fairbank, eds., *China's Response to the West*: *A Documentary Survey 1839–1923*. Harvard University Press, 1954, p. 98.

Arrow War (the so-called "Second Opium War"), leading Chinese statesmen such as Prince Kun, Tseng Kuo-fan, and Li Hung-chang (1823–1901) launched a number of reform programs for self-strengthening. The Tsungli Yamen, the newly-founded foreign affairs department, went so far as to entrust Burlingame with China's first mission to the West for revision of the Tientsin Treaties when it learned that Burlingame was going to retire in late 1867.[25] The Chinese Emperor's rescript on the appointment ran as follows:

> The envoy, Anson Burlingame, manages affairs in a friendly and peaceful manner, and is fully acquainted with the general relations between this and other countries; let him, therefore, now be sent to all the treaty powers as high minister." This was apparently a recognition of the "cooperative policy" promoted by Burlingame, and as evaluated by F.W. Williams, the author of *Anson Burlingame and the First Chinese Mission to the Foreign Powers*, "the greatest compliment ever paid by one great nation to another.[26]

IV. The Fight for Exiles, Coolies, and Immigrants

Williams joined the 1837 "Morrison" adventure from Macao to open communication with Japan's authorities in the hope of repatriating seven shipwrecked Japanese. But the American ship was fired on in both Edo Bay and Kagoshima Bay due to Japan's seclusion policy. Upon leaving Japan, Williams realized that:

> There was little prospect of being received at any other port; moreover our men [the shipwrecked Japanese] declared that their lives would be in jeopardy if they should now be received anywhere, or if they should attempt to steal ashore under cover of night.... Their disappointment was great for their expectations had been raised to the highest pitch; and three of them shaved their heads like Buddhist priests, in order that the hair might grow equally, thereby showing their determination to live among foreigners. All of them agreed to go quietly back and become perpetual exiles.[27]

Eventually, the seven men were taken back and employed by the missionaries. As Williams recalled some forty years later:

---

25 While there has been a preliminary comparison of the Burlingame mission and the Iwakura mission by Professor Tanaka Akira, this interesting topic deserves more careful study in the future. See Tanaka Akira, *Meiji Ishin to seiyō bunmei: Iwakura shisetsudan wa nani o mita ka*. Tokyo: Iwanami Shoten, pp. 166–170.

26 *The Life and Letters*, p. 371.

27 *The Life and Letters*, p. 98.

Two remained with Mr. Gutzlaff for many years; and two worked in my printing office at Macao.... Rikimats[u], the youngest man, went to Nagasaki with [British] Admiral Stirling in 1855 as his interpreter. He and Otosan, who lived at Shanghai, both showed in their correct lives that the faith which they had professed was a living principle. They were the first-fruits of the church of Christ in Japan, whose numbers are now flocking in like doves to their windows."[28]

Williams not only fought for the Japanese exiles, who had been deprived of their rights, to return home, but also fought for Chinese coolies and immigrants. In early 1860, he stayed for a few weeks in Macao before taking a leave of absence from his position as diplomat. There he learned that some American ships had been participating in the coolie trade and had carried off kidnapped men to Peru. He got so angry at his fellow countrymen's wrongdoings that he caused "the arrest of one vessel charged with having such unwilling freight on board, and presided at the examination of more than three hundred men, all of whom were released and sent home."[29] It was in this connection that he wrote and circulated 6,000 copies of his only Chinese tract in just two weeks, entitled "Words to Startle Those Who Are Selling Their Bodies [to go] Abroad."[30] He exposed the means employed by the Portuguese to beguile natives into accepting contracts for coolie labor.

> The Chinese have been dreadfully misused by these coolie dealers; in Macao, the Portuguese are not able to get workmen to come either to their houses and ships, so great a dread have the natives of being stolen and packed off to the barracoons. Over ten thousand Chinamen have been sent away in 1858, and half this number are already gone this year from here. The Portuguese are ruthless and reckless, and they get hold of natives ten times more the children of hell than themselves, and make these to act for them.[31]

Williams fought for the Chinese immigrants in California during his tenure as Professor of Chinese language and literature at Yale. Some ten years earlier, when the US-China Treaty of 1868 was signed between Anson Burlingame, who was envoy to China, and Secretary of State William Seward, the latter was very much "concerned about the delays in the completion of the Pacific railroad due to the inability of the contractors to secure labor." As Burlingame explained later to Otto von Bismarck in Berlin, the treaty there-

28 Ibid., p.99.
29 *The Life and Letters*, pp.325–6.
30 Ibid., p.326.
31 Ibid, p.326.

fore offered "substantial protection to the Chinese in California," because "a treaty being the supreme law of the land overrides obnoxious local legislation against the Chinese immigrants."[32] As a result, "there were large importations of coolies to work on the Pacific railroads and in 1869, out of a total of 10,000 railroad laborers, nine tenths of them were Chinese.... By 1875 the number of Chinese on the Pacific coast, notwithstanding the large numbers who had returned to China, had risen to 100,000."[33]

Since Williams was quite familiar with the course of the treaty revision, he strove to stem the tide of anti-immigrant hostility that arose in the Pacific coast states in the late 1870s. He succeeded to some extent. He drafted a detailed paper entitled "Chinese Immigration" to fight against popular prejudices, reading it before the Social Science Association at Saratoga in September 1879. He had it published afterwards in a brochure. He also drew up a petition, which was signed by the entire faculty of Yale College, to urge President Hayes to veto Congress's Chinese Immigration Bill of 1879. He stated in it:

> If this Bill becomes an Act some results may ensue which should be considered. The privilege of self-government depends at present upon the sanctity and stipulations of the treaty of 1858. The Chinese Government has never shown any intention to abrogate those treaties forced from it by Western nations, though its authorities chafe under the confessed disabilities it places them in regard to complete jurisdiction on their own soil. Therefore, if the first step be taken by our government in changing treaty stipulations, we furnish the other party with all the example and argument needed, according to the uses of international law, to justify it in abrogating this principle of extra-territoriality. To do so will throw out our countrymen living in China from the protection of our laws, and neutralize consular interference in upholding them, thereby turning the residents over to the provisions of Chinese law, and the usages of Chinese courts administered by ignorant or prejudiced officials.[34]

As Williams had hoped, President Hayes vetoed the Bill in question, and then sent a mission to Peking to modify the treaty and have the issue solved.

As a retired diplomat and professor at Yale, Williams was still deeply concerned about what was happening in China:

32 *Americans in Eastern Asia,* p.540.
33 Ibid., p.538.
34 *The Life and Letters*, pp.430–431.

The suffering caused by the great famine of 1878 in northern China elicited his keenest sympathies and inspired him to pour all the energy at his command into its alleviation. Whatever public notices and private appeals could influence those about him, Williams tried ardently and often. His knowledge of the afflicted provinces and his personal acquaintance with the missionaries of all denominations who were engaged upon the spot in organizing means of relief, combined to make him a useful associate in circulating information and receiving contributions in America.[35]

Williams even tried to induce the Congress to return a portion of the indemnity surplus of 1859 in order to relieve the famine district.[36] The suggestion was not adopted, however, because some Senators were not in favor of it due to their prejudice against the Chinese.

V. Appreciation of East Asian Traditions and Progressive Minds

In a sense, it could be said that Williams' appreciation of Chinese cultural tradition was best manifested by the above-mentioned tract, *Chinese Immigration*, which aimed at rebutting misunderstanding of and prejudice against the Chinese. One of the passages in his paper on Chinese immigration stated:

> The summary manner in which the courts in California converted the Chinese into Indians, when it was desired to bring a law to bear against them, has a spice of the grotesque in it. The physiologist Charles Pickering, includes Chinese and Indians among the members of the Mongolian race; but the Supreme Court [of California] there held "that the term Indian included the Chinese or Mongolian race.
>
> It thus upheld a wrong, while it enunciated a misconception. It placed the subjects of the oldest government now existing upon a parity with a race that has never risen above tribal relations. It included under one term a people whose literature dates its beginning before the Psalms or the Exodus, written in a language which the judge would not have called Indian, if he had tried to learn it, and containing authors whose words have influenced more human beings than any other writings, with men whose highest attainments in writing have been a few pictures and totems drawn on a buffalo robe. It equalized all the qualities of industry, prudence, skill, learning, invention, and whatever gives security to life

35 Ibid., pp. 431–432.
36 Ibid., p. 433.

> and property among mankind, with the instincts and habits of a hunter and a nomad. It stigmatized a people which has taught us how to make porcelain, silk, and gunpowder, given us the compass, shown us the use of tea, and offers us their system of selecting officials by competitive examination, by classing them with a race which has despised labor, has had no arts, schools, or trade, and in the midst of the Californians themselves were content to dig roots for a living.[37]

Here Williams enumerated with admiration almost all the major contributions to world civilization made by traditional China, from literary accomplishments and technical innovations, to the civil service examination system. Needless to say, China also had many social and cultural shortcomings, and had fallen behind Western nations significantly in the process of industrialization. Williams chose not just to expose China's "dark side" but to understand it as a whole objectively and to introduce China's merits with profound empathy.

In July, 1883, after revision and enlargement of his monumental work, *The Middle Kingdom: A Survey of the Geography, Government, Literature, Social Life, Arts, and History or The Chinese Empire and Its Inhabitants*, he restated in the preface his motivations for writing the book:

> In this revision the same object has been kept in view that is stated in the Preface to the first edition—to divest the Chinese people and civilization of that peculiar and indefinable impression of ridicule which has been so generally given them by foreign authors. I have endeavored to show the better traits of their national character, and that they have had up to this time no opportunity of learning many things with which they are now rapidly becoming acquainted.... They will become fitted for taking up the work themselves and joining in the multiform operations of foreign civilizations. Soon railroads, telegraphs, and manufactures will be introduced, and these must be followed by whatsoever may conduce to enlightening the millions of the people of China in every department of religious, political, and domestic life.[38]

There were good grounds for Williams' optimism about China, for he had had more than forty years of experience there during which he witnessed a number of great changes. He recalled:

> On my arrival at Canton in 1833 I was officially reported, with two

37 *The Life and Letters*, pp.428–429.

38 S.W. Williams, *The Middle Kingdom*. London: W.H. Allen & Co., 1883, Preface in vol.I, pp.XIV–XV.

> other Americans, to the hong merchant Kingqua as *fan-kwai*, or 'foreign devils,' who had come to live under his tutelage. In 1874, as Secretary of the American Embassy at Peking, I accompanied the Hon. B. P. Avery to the presence of the Emperor Tungchi, when the Minister of the United States presented his letters of credence on a footing of perfect equality with the 'Son of Heaven.' With two such experiences in a lifetime...it is not strange that I am assured of a great future for the sons of Han.[39]

Williams' experiences also included contact with several of the progressive minds of China. For example:

> One of the members of the Foreign Office [the Tsungli Yamen], now dead, was the governor, in 1849, of the province of Fuhkien, and published a geographical and historical account of other lands, the matter for which he had collected mostly from personal inquiries of Rev. David Abeel and of the son of Dr. Morrison. Being too favorable in his remarks on foreign lands, he was degraded for its publication and returned to his native village, about 1851, where he engaged in school-teaching. Fourteen years afterward, this man, Seu Ki-yu 徐繼畬 (1795–1873),was recalled to the service of his sovereign for the same reason which had wrought his degradation, viz., his superior knowledge of foreigners, then more than ever needed in dealing with them at the capital. Our own government, at my suggestion, sent him a fine portrait of Washington, whom he had eulogized in his *Ying Wan Chi Lioh* (瀛環志略), or 'Survey of What is within the Islands and Seas.' The last act of Mr. Burlingame as Minister to China was to present it to him in Peking. His infirmities erelong compelled him to resign and return home, where he lingered a few years.[40]

The ups and downs of Seu Ki-yu's political life, as illustrated in the two instances that Williams mentions above, symbolized the transition in China's attitude toward the outside world during the mid-19th century.

It is worth noting that Williams's appreciation of Chinese culture developed to a large extent from his close relations with his Chinese tutors and assistants. Of these, the Cantonese Lo Sun, who participated in the second expedition to Japan in 1854, was the most reliable and welcome partner he had ever hired. As chief interpreter, Williams had confidence in himself in reading and speaking Chinese. But he still needed a Chinese assistant to help polish his translations and copy them into elegant calligraphy that would

---

39 Ibid., p. XIV.
40 *The Life and Letters*, pp. 417–418.

impress the Japanese officials, headed by Hayashi Fukusai (林復斎;1800–1859), *Daigaku no kami*, with whom Perry would negotiate. It had been the practice in Tokugawa Japan for the master of the Hayashi house (serving as the president of the shogunal college as well as foreign affairs advisor to the Tokugawa shogun) to handle diplomatic correspondence in Chinese. In addition, Williams also planned to use his free time during the lengthy voyage to continue his study of Chinese and to work on translation projects. These two reasons justified the employment of a Chinese assistant.

In a letter to his wife from "Hakodadi, Island of Yesso" on May 21, 1854, Williams praised Lo as follows:

> The non-arrival of the envoy and Dutch interpreter from the capital has thrown the whole business of interpreting upon me, and I can assure you I've business enough for twenty tongues to be kept up at trip-hammer rate the livelong day...so I bring Lo into considerable service to make one language help the other, and thereby avoid many mistakes. He takes a lively interest in all our operations and gets on admirably with the natives [Japanese]; he is, indeed, the most learned Chinaman they have ever seen, and their delight in showing off to him their attainments in Chinese is increased when he turns a graceful verse or two for them upon a fan; of these he has written, I should think, more than half a thousand since coming to Japan, and nothing pleases him like being asked to do so.[41]

It was during this expedition that led to the conclusion of the Treaty of Kanagawa that Williams got to know the Japanese commissioners and to appreciate their open-mindedness. He wrote in his journal:

> In reviewing the proceedings of the last few months, it is fair to give the Japanese officers the credit of showing none of that hauteur and supercilious conduct, which the perusal of books might have reasonably led one to infer formed a part of their character. Compare the conduct of the Burmese when Crawford went to see them at Ava, or of the Chinese when Amherst went to Peking, with that of Hayashi and his colleagues, and down, too, in the subordinate ranks of officials, a class who are noted in China for their contemptuous treatment of foreigners, and everyone must admit their superiority in point of courtesy, their decorum, their willingness to receive suggestions, and their general good sense in discussing the matters brought forward for their acceptance.

41 *The Life and Letters*, p. 219. For details about Lo, see De-min Tao, "Negotiating Language in the Opening of Japan: Luo Sen's Journal of Perry's 1854 Expedition," *Japan Review*, No. 17 (2005), pp. 91–119.

> Perhaps more impracticable men could easily have been found, and these seven [commissioners] were probably chosen for their views being favorable for a change in the national policy, but the other qualities referred to may fairly be taken as part of the national character, since we have seen them among all classes to some extent. In no country could more agreeable and kind-hearted men be found than old Yedo and Fuzhiwara at Hakodadi, and if one could converse with all he would find some traits to please him.[42]

VI. Conclusion

The prominent Yale professor of Christian missions and Oriental history, Kenneth C. Latourette (1884–1968), pointed out in the 1920s that he himself "does not cease to be impartial when he declares that the presence and the labors of the missionary were most fortunate for China. Defects the missionary enterprise undoubtedly had. Sometimes it did evil. On the whole, however, it was the one great agency whose primary function was to bring China into contact with the best in the Occident and to make the expansion of the West a means to the greater welfare of the Chinese people."[43]

The welfare mentioned here does not only include the training of Chinese leaders in diplomacy, administration, education, and the medical profession, or the introduction of Chinese culture and language into the Occident, but also the re-enforcement of Chinese ethical standards, the quickening of the Chinese public conscience, and a heightened regard for the individual.

> The missionary was active in fighting opium, gambling, and prostitution. He attacked whatever he believed cramped or harmed the best development of the individual—famine, poor labor conditions, concubinage, the custom of foot-binding, the exposure of infants." "No person was too lowly to have, in the judgment of the missionary, an immortal soul of infinite value. No outcast girl infant, no beggar boy, no work-broken coolie, no opium sot, no leper, no bandit or prodigal son, but worth saving. Jesus' followers must, as did he, 'seek and save that which was lost.[44]

This kind of concern for the unfortunate may be called "Christian humanitarianism," and it was well exemplified by Williams' thought and actions in the mid-19th century, as described above. It seems to me, however, that

42 *A Journal of the Perry Expedition to Japan*, p. 226.

43 K. C. Latourette, *A History of Christian Missions in China*. London: Society for Promoting Christian Knowledge, 1929, p. 843.

44 *A History of Christian Missions in China*, p. 837.

Williams' humanism was in a sense closely associated with, and enhanced by, his profound love for botany, an interest and hobby developed in his boyhood, which lasted through his later years. As one of his close friends in Peking recalled, Williams' "fondness for botany became almost a passion; the beauty and wonder of growing things being ever a joy to him." "And, if we followed him with his flowers [gathered on an evening stroll] to his cheerful home, he seemed in inviting us to his table to possess the happy art of making these visits appear as favors conferred upon himself, rather than as obligations imposed upon his guests. Nor was he unobservant of the simple country people whom he met in the streets or country lanes [in Peking]. He loved to give them kindly salutations, adding at times some question as to the welfare of those whom he knew, and bit of friendly help to those in need. His name and those of his children became in time well known to these poor peasants, and to this day its fragrance lingers in their comfortless homes."[45]

45 *The Life and Letters*, pp. 367–368.

Opinion Forum

Turning Stone into Gold:
Some Reflections on My Research about the 1854 Shōin-Perry Encounter

De-min TAO*

When Yoshikawa Kōjirō 吉川幸次郎 (1904–1980), a prominent scholar of Kyoto University known for teaching Chinese literature in spoken Mandarin, was writing a critical biography of the Sinologue Ogyū Sorai 荻生徂徠 (1666–1728), he commented that Sorai was a linguist when he was young, a literary man in his middle ages, and a philosopher in his later years. After three decades of research, I found the comment to be a great inspiration, reminding me that I should now try to be a bit more philosophical so as to refine and sublimate my scholarship and share my experience with students in an memorable way. In this spirit, I developed the following four-line instruction set that I call "Shihai shibei" 史海拾貝 (Collecting shells from the sea of history), based mainly on my research about the 1854 Shōin-Perry encounter at Yale, the National Archives and Records Administration (NARA), based in Washington, D.C., and Tokyo. This instruction set incorporates several well-known Chinese and Japanese proverbs:

(1) 就著碎影拼月亮, 自圓其說。
(2) 大海撈針何處尋, 巧思引路。
(3) 兩個兔子輪番追, 有心插柳。
(4) 問題意識勤磨練, 點石成金。

The following is a brief translation:
(1) Make your moon whole from partial fragments; justify your claims.
(2) It is hard to fish a needle out of the ocean; use creative thinking to lead the way.
(3) Chase two rabbits in turn; plant a willow with purpose.
(4) Refine your awareness of the question itself; touch a stone and turn it into gold.

---

* Professor, Kansai University; Founding President of the Society.

For the story I am going to tell today, I will change the sequence to (3), (2), (4), and (1).

1 Taking the Second Rabbit Seriously: Shōin's Petitions kept at Yale

There is a Japanese proverb 二兎を追う者は一兎を得ず, meaning "One who chases two rabbits at the same time catches neither." But my experience tells me that you should chase two rabbits in turn—the first rabbit being the research topic planned at the outset, and the second rabbit being the interesting materials that you unexpectedly encounter when doing the actual research—so as not to discount the accidental discoveries that you make in pursuing your original topic.

In a sense, my discovery of Shōin's petitions at Yale was accidental. I came to Yale in the spring of 2003 to find the original diary of Luo Sen 羅森 (1821–1899), Chinese assistant to Samuel Wells Williams (1812–1884).[1] As you may know, *kanbun* (classical Chinese), the Latin of East Asia, was the language of negotiation in the days of Japan's opening, both for the U.S.-Japan treaty and for Shōin's attempted stowaway.[2] Although by 1853 Williams had been in Hong Kong and Macau for 20 years and was familiar with the Chinese language, as the first interpreter, he still needed Chinese assistants to help him polish diplomatic documents and copy them into elegant calligraphy. Luo was recruited shortly before Perry's second visit in 1854 and kept a diary during the encounters. He published his *Riben riji* 日本

1 The Asian Center of Kansai University and Sinology Center of Beijing Foreign Studies University cohosted an international conference in Beijing in December 2012 to honor the bicentennial of Samuel Wells William's birth. The proceedings of the conference will be published by Hong Kong University Press.

2 De-min Tao, "Negotiating Language in the Opening of Japan: Luo Sen's Journal of Perry's 1854 Expedition," *Japan Review*, no. 17 (March 2005). Luo was quite popular in Yokohama, Shimoda, and Hakodate in the Spring of 1854. In response to overwhelming demand from Japanese officers and commoners, he inscribed his extempore verse in elegant calligraphy on hundreds of blank paper fans. Four of Luo's fans survive in the Municipal Museum of Hakodate and the Local Museum of Matsumae in Hokkaido. Williams told his wife in Macau that Luo "takes a lively interest in all our operations and gets on admirably with the natives; he is, indeed, the most learned Chinaman they have ever seen, and their delight in showing off to him their attainments in Chinese is increased when he turns a graceful verse or two for them upon a fan; of these he has written, I should think, more than half a thousand since coming to Japan, and nothing pleases him like being asked to do so" (F. W. Williams, ed., *The Life and Letters of Samuel Wells Williams, LL.D.: Missionary, Diplomatist, Sinologue* [1889], p. 219). See also Tao De-min 陶徳民, "Kurofune no motarashita Kanton-jin senpū: Ra Shin no kyozō to jitsuzō" 黒船のもたらした広東人旋風：羅森の虚像と実像 (The Cantonese Whirlwind Brought by the Black Ships: Luo Sen, Fiction and Fact), in *Image and Identity: Rethinking Japanese Cultural History*, edited by Jeffrey Hanes and Hidetoshi Yamaji (2004).

日記 in the earliest Chinese journal, the *Xiaer guanzhen* 遐邇貫珍 (Chinese Serial), shortly after returning to Hong Kong, and its English translation, *Journal of a Visit to Japan* by Williams, was included in the second volume of *Narrative of the Expedition of an American Squadron to the China Seas and Japan: Performed in the Years 1852, 1853, and 1854, under the Command of Commodore M. C. Perry, United States Navy, by Order of the Government of the United States*, edited by Francis L. Hawks.

Through a close comparison, I found an important difference between the two published versions of the diary. Many Japanese then were wondering why a Chinese man joined the American expedition to Japan. Luo had a long written conversation 筆談 with Hirayama Kenjirō 平山謙二郎, a *metsuke* 目付 (surveillance officer), in which Hirayama shared Confucian knowledge and contemporary concerns with Luo. In this conversation, Luo made it clear that although he had organized a militia group to fight against the British soldiers during the Opium Wars of 1839 to 1842, his efforts were not rewarded afterwards by the Qing government.[3] He was so angry about this that he left his hometown in Nanhai county, Guangdong Province, to go to Hong Kong and serve as a Chinese teacher and secretary in the new British colony. But this story, which was included in Williams's translation, was missing in Luo's *Riben riji*, and the reason for this was apparently that Luo would occasionally visit his hometown and relatives there, and was cautious about possible trouble that the Qing government might give him if the Chinese version included the truth, and so he decided to cut it out before submitting the diary to the publisher of *Xiaer guanzhen*.

This discovery made me wonder if there were other differences between the English and Chinese versions, and I tried to find Luo's original handwritten diary or a copy in the S. W. Williams Family Papers at Yale. Although I did not find what I was looking for, I did find Shōin's *kanbun* petitions, "Tōisho" 投夷書 (Letters to Foreigners), including the well-prepared first letter submitted to the American side seeking to stow away (accompanied by a *sōrōbun* 候文 note beginning with the famous sentence "We two want to see the world"), and the second letter written in the Shimoda jail.[4]

3 In March 2016, Kansai University Press will publish a volume that includes Hirayama's collected works in Chinese (held by Hokkaido University Library), the written information he got from Luo, *Manshin kiji* 満清紀事 (held by Kansai University Library), his 1854 diary kept during the investigation of Ezochi 蝦夷地 (Hokkaido) and Sōya Strait 宗谷海峡, and a diary kept by two prison guards who escorted Shōin from Shimoda jail to Edo in 1854 (both part of the materials on the aftermath of the Meiji Restoration, held by the Historiographical Institute of the University of Tokyo). I will begin editing and annotating them in the coming summer.

4 I have made a thorough textual examination of the two petitions in the following

(See the appendix of this paper.) The first petition was discovered forty years ago by Yamaguchi Eitetsu 山口栄鉄, a Japanese instructor at Yale, and the second one was discovered by me on my 2003 visit to Yale.[5] The interesting fact here is that although the petition was carefully pasted on the inside of the back cover of S. W. Williams's journal to keep a record of the unusual incident, the importance of this document was unknown to his son, Yale Professor of East Asian History Frederic Wells Williams, who did not include it in *A Journal of the Perry Expedition to Japan (1853–1854)* (1889) or in his father's biography, *The Life and Letters of Samuel Wells Williams, LL.D.: Missionary, Diplomatist, Sinologue* (1910).

According to my examination of their calligraphic and prose styles, the *sōrōbun* note was in Shōin's own handwriting, whereas the two *kanbun* petitions were fair copies made by Luo Sen at Williams's direction, and in this sense, my discovery at Yale was not completely accidental. The second petition was originally written on a wooden board when Shōin and his fellow stowaway Kaneko were confined in the Shimoda jail in a small cage.[6] Its

---

articles: "Shimoda mikkō zengo ni okeru Shōin no Seiyō ninshiki: Beikoku ni nokoru 'Tōisho' o megutte" 下田密航前後における松陰の西洋認識：米国に残る「投夷書」をめぐって (Shōin's Understanding of the West around the Time of His Stowaway: The 'Letters to Foreigners' in the United States), *Kan* 環 13 (May 2003); "Shimoda goku ni okeru daini no 'Tōisho' ni tsuite: Shōin no kakugo ni taisuru Perī no kyōkan" 下田獄における第二の「投夷書」について：松陰の覚悟に対するペリーの共感 (The Second 'Letter to Foreigners' from the Shimoda Jail: Perry's Sympathy toward Shōin's Determination), *Kan* 環 14 (July 2003); "Ri-Mei jianjiao zhi chuyi zhuang toudu gongan de xin jiedu: Jitian Songyin 'Touyishu' zai Yelu Daxue danganguan faxian" 日美建交之初一樁偷渡公案的新解読：吉田松陰〈投夷書〉在耶魯大学檔案館発現 (A New Interpretation of the First Stowaway Case at the Dawn of Japan-U.S. Relations: The Discovery of Yoshida Shōin's "Letter to Foreigners" in the Yale University Archives), *Dongya Wenming Yanjiu Zhongxin tongxun* (National Taiwan University), no. 6 (January 2005).

5 An Okinawa-born leading scholar in the history of Ryūkyū's foreign relations, Professor Yamaguchi introduced the petition under the title "Nemutteita Shōin no missho" 眠っていた松陰の密書 (Shōin's Sleeping Secret Letter) (*Rekishi to jinbutsu* 1975, no. 10). Recently he supervised the publication of a complete reprint of the 3-volume *Narrative*.

6 The petition was considered "a remarkable specimen of philosophical resignation under circumstances which would have tried the stoicism of Cato, [and] deserves a record" (Hawkes, *Narrative*, 1: 422). From the comparison made with Cato Minor (95–46 BCE), the tragic hero who committed suicide in Utica, Africa, rather than falling alive into Caesar's hands, it seems that the Americans were deeply affected by Shōin's "letter on the board" and deeply concerned about his fate. The size of the cage, as Williams measured it, "was about six feet long by three wide and four and a half high, quite large enough to sit and sleep in, and entered by crawling through a low door; it is probably just such a cage as McCoy and his fellows were at last shut up in" (*Journal* 1: 181–182). Isaac McCoy (1784–1846) was a Baptist missionary, surveyor and U.S. Indian agent, and the association by similarity made

English translation by Williams was included in the first volume of the *Narrative*, and there have been seven Japanese translations based on the English without any knowledge of the *kanbun* original, from Tokutomi Sohō's 1908 biography of Shōin to the 2002 Japanese translation of J. Willett Spalding's *Japan Expedition: Japan and around the World*). After discovering the *kanbun* original, I found a critical mistake made by Williams that was inherited by all the Japanese versions.

2 Fishing a Needle Out of the Ocean: The Logbook of Perry's Flagship at NARA

A Chinese proverb 大海撈針 compares the difficulty of a situation by comparing it to fishing a needle out of the ocean. The mistranslation by Williams was in the sentence "In public have we been seized and pinioned and caged for many days." Here the original word 面縛 (*mianfu* in Chinese and *menbaku* in Japanese) is short for 面縛輿櫬 *mianfu yuchen*, meaning "to tie one's hands at the back and cart along one's coffin before the victor" and implying "to submit." Williams translated 面縛 as "in public have we been seized," as if Shōin and his fellow were caught during the daytime.

Shōin's *Kaikoroku* 回顧録 (Memoirs), written in the Noyama jail of the Hagi domain, made it clear, however, that after being sent ashore, Shōin and Hirayama, unable to find the boat they used to access the flagship, which contained some incriminating evidence, decided to turn themselves in to the village head of Kakizaki and were brought to the Shimoda police box shortly after the crack of dawn. The word 面縛 was used exactly in this sense, to turn oneself in.

But one problem still remained unresolved: When did Shōin actually climb aboard Perry's flagship, and how long did he remain on board? Shōin recalled that it was around 4 a.m. ("七つ時"), whereas Williams, who was present at the interview with Shōin, noted "2 a.m." in his journal. When I was traveling to NARA in Washington, D.C., in the spring of 2009 to find Williams's original letter to the Secretary of State suggesting using the surplus of the indemnity paid by the Qing government for the property loss of American citizens in China during the Arrow War to establish an American-Chinese college in China, an idea occurred to me: Why don't I use this chance to take a look at the logbook of Perry's flagship, the USS *Powhatan*, to see if there are any relevant records in it?[7] Fortunately, I was

by Williams here was apparently a criticism of the inhuman treatment of prisoners in Japan then. On McCoy, see George A. Schultz, *An Indian Canaan: Isaac McCoy and the Vision of an Indian State* (Norman: University of Oklahoma Press, 1972).

7 Williams's suggestion was aimed at training interpreters, diplomats, and businessmen to foster American-Chinese relations, and it was approved by the State Department

able to find Captain William J. McCluney's brief note, as follows:

> Remarks of This 25th Day of April, 1854
> Commences at 2:45 two Japanese came on board by a small boat, remained about 3/4 of an hour, on getting aboard their boat got drifted & they were sent ashore by the S' [steamer's] cutter by order of the Commo. [Commodore].[8]

Shōin's attempt at stowaway was thus identified with a specific duration of time: forty-five minutes on board the flagship. His self-submission and asking for punishment can thus be reasonably explained as occurring in this sequence of time. Some may discount the importance of discoveries of this kind. Isn't this merely a trivial pursuit of Shōin's time on board? However, imagine the huge difference in time systems between Japan and West then. Thus, since Shōin had no way to make an appointment with the American officers due to the difference, he even wrote in another *sōrōbun* note, "Please come to rescue us when you see the fire we light as a sign at midnight tomorrow." Such drama gives one a better sense of the turbulence of the times when the West came into contact with the East. Salvaging an important lost historical record conveys the feeling of real history to today's digitized generation and helps us relive some exciting events that happened in the past.

Line (2) thus acknowledges the difficulty that researchers may encounter when trying to sift through a sea of information to find the most useful pieces of evidence, but at the same time, it gives hope that improving one's linguistic abilities, one's ability to use sources, and one's creative imagination will help to break through this formidable barrier.

3 Turning Stone into Gold: Humanitarian Concerns Mattered in the Age of Gunboat Diplomacy

The Chinese proverb 點石成金 means "To touch a stone and turn it into gold." If we look back at the history of research in certain areas or fields, we find that a major change in perspective can bring about a totally different view of the same historic figure, incident, or time period.

In two articles I published in Hong Kong and Tokyo, in 2003 and 2009

---

and President Lincoln, but was denied by Congress.

8 Tao De-min 陶徳民, "Perī no kikan ni nobotta Shōin no 'jikan' ni semaru: Pouhatan-gō no kōkai nisshi ni mita Shimoda mikkō kanren kiji ni tsuite" ペリーの旗艦に登った松陰の「時間」に迫る：ポウハタン号の航海日誌に見た下田密航関連記事について (Closing in on Shōin's Time on Board Perry's Flagship: An Entry in the Logbook of the *Powhatan* Related to the Shimoda Stowaway), *Higashi Ajia bunka kōshō kenkyū* (Institute for Cultural Interaction Studies, Kansai University), no. 3 (March 2010).

respectively, marking the 150th anniversary of Perry's first visit to Japan and the opening of Yokohama as a treaty port, I tried to break with existing nationalistic thinking and interpretations of the first U.S.-Japan encounter, as revealed in the alleged white-flag 白旗 incident and the view of the petition as a ruse for attack. Supposedly, Perry, in anticipation of possible hostilities, passed two white flags to the Japanese side for them to surrender with. He thus, insultingly, sought to teach the Japanese to act in a civilized manner. In the view of the petition as a ruse for attack 墨夷膺懲, Shōin's alleged real purpose in pretending to be a stowaway was to kill Perry and punish the Americans. Shōin is here portrayed as a patriotic terrorist.[9]

But what I found, on the contrary, was a story that exemplified the fact that humanitarian concerns did matter in the age of imperialism and nationalism. The evidence for this view can be found in three interrelated documents.

- In the *kanbun* version of the first petition copied by Luo, I found a Confucian term 仁厚愛物之意, meaning "kindness, generosity, and love of other beings," which could be compared to the concepts of humanism and tolerance in modern Western thought. The term appeared twice, first in the sentence "We are fully assured of *the kindness and liberality of your excellencies, and your regard for others*," and later in the sentence "If this matter should become known, we should uselessly see ourselves pursued and brought back for immediate execution without fail, and such a result would greatly grieve *the deep humanity and kindness you all bear towards others*."
- Shōin was then a twenty-five-year-old young man, and his petition had been polished by his mentor Sakuma Shōzan 佐久間象山 (1811–1864), a leading scholar of Chinese and Dutch learning who strongly encouraged Shōin to go abroad to study advanced Western military technology. It seemed that the appeal to the humanity of Perry and his team was both strategic and effective. When Perry got to know the miserable situation of Shōin and his companion in the cage, he sent his Flag Lieutenant Silas Bent and

9 Tao De-min 陶德民, "Shijiu shiji zhongye Meiguo dui Ri renquan waijiao de qishi: Xie zai Mei-Ri jianjiao 150 zhou nian zhi ji" 十九世紀中葉美國對日人權外交的啟示：寫在美日建交150周年之際 (Mid-Nineteenth-Century U.S. Human-Rights Diplomacy towards Japan: On the 150th Anniversary of the Dawn of U.S.-Japan Relations), *Ershiyi shiji* (Chinese University of Hong Kong), no. 82 (April 2004). De-min Tao, "The Stowaway's Dilemma: Yoshida Shōin's Encounter with Commodore Perry," in *Japan and Its Worlds: Marius B. Jansen and the Internationalization of Japanese Studies*, edited by Martin Collcutt, Katō Mikio, and Ronald Toby (Tokyo: International House Press, 2007).

Williams the following morning, only to find that the two had just been transferred to a jail in Edo. Out of serious concern over the possible beheading that Shōin had warned him of in the first petition, Perry decided to exert his influence. The *Narrative* describes his intervention as follows. "The fate of the poor fellows was never ascertained, but it is hoped that the authorities were more merciful than to have awarded the severest penalty, which was the loss of their heads, for what appears to us only liberal and a highly commendable curiosity, however great the crime according to the eccentric and sanguinary code of Japanese law. It is a comfort to be able to add, that the Commodore received an assurance from the authorities, upon questioning them, that he need not apprehend a serious termination."[10] The assurance was apparently a relief to Perry, who faced a difficult choice between national interest and human rights.

- According to *Bokui ōsetsu roku* 墨夷應接録 (Record of Negotiations with the Americans), compiled by the Bakufu's diplomatic team, Perry proudly boasted that respect for and rescuing the lives of people had been the major concern and policy of the American government.[11] He severely criticized the Bakufu for its inhumane treatment of American shipwrecked whalers and Japanese sailors who drifted abroad owing to storms. (In the 1840s and 1850s there were hundreds of American whalers operating in Japanese waters. Once a whaler was shipwrecked, the surviving castaways would be brought by the current to southern Ezochi. From there they were escorted by foot to Nagasaki, where they awaited ships of the Dutch East India Company, arriving on the monsoon current, to transport them to Batavia [present-day Jakarta]. There they would be picked up by American rescue ships. Also, surprisingly, Japanese sailors who drifted abroad because of storms were denied rights of repatriation to prevent any possible Christian influence.[12])

---

10 Hawkes, *Narrative*, 1: 423.

11 Tōkyō Teikoku Daigaku Bunka Daigaku Shiryō Hensan-gakari 東京帝國大學文科大學史料編纂掛. *Bakumatsu gaikoku kankei monjo* 幕末外國關係文書 (Sources of Late Tokugawa Foreign Diplomacy), appendix 1. In *Dai Nihon komonjo* 大日本古文書. Tokyo: Tōkyō Teikoku Daigaku, 1913.

12 During the eighteenth century, there developed a system of mutual aid between Tokugawa Japan, Qing China, Yi Korea, and Vietnam, in which each country agreed to help shipwrecked fishermen repair their boats, to provide them with food and other necessities, and to send them home. However, this arrangement did not apply to Westerners. In 1837 Williams and several other American missionaries headed to Japan from Canton on the American merchant ship *Morrison* in an attempt to repatriate seven Japanese shipwrecked sailors. However, they were driven away by cannon fire, first at Uraga Bay, and later at Kagoshima Bay, in accordance with the Edict to Repel Foreign Vessels 無二念打拂令 of 1825.

When I was investigating these sources, I was surprised to find stones that could be turned to gold, that is, important lines and critical facts, overlooked by scholars, that could be evaluated in the new light of humanitarianism. Line (4) thus recognizes the importance of refining one's awareness of the question itself by approaching the object from different angles and perspectives.

4 Make Your Moon Whole by Making Sense of the Rays and Shadows

To sum up, as the Chinese proverb 自圓其說 implies, the task of a researcher is to discern a path from all the possible sources of information and shape it into some sort of argument. This task is similar to piecing together the fragmented light that shines through the leaves to re-create a full moon, much like solving a jigsaw puzzle. Line 1 thus points out our limited capabilities in the face of the grandness of nature and the universe. Yet it also fully recognizes the possibility that we can deepen our understanding of both the external and internal worlds.

Many proverbs, taken literally, invite pessimism. But it is important to maintain a positive attitude toward what is admittedly a difficult field. For example, 二兎を追う者は一兎を得ず (One who chases two rabbits at the same time catches neither) instills a negative lesson, but in line (3) I change this negative lesson into a positive suggestion: 兩個兔子輪番追 (Chase two rabbits in turn). The line ends with 有心插柳 (Plant a willow with purpose). This derives from the Chinese proverb 有意栽花，花不开；无心插柳，柳成蔭 (A watched flower never blooms, but an untended willow thrives). Here too I made a positive change to remind scholars of the importance of always being attentive in their research, as the second rabbit they encounter might be a decisive clue that helps them develop their second or third areas of interest. A scholar needs three or more areas of expertise to establish scholarly credentials and research style, as suggested by the Chinese proverb 三足鼎立 (The Chinese cauldron stands on three legs).

Appendixes

The First Petition (translated by S. W. Williams)

Two scholars from Yedo, in Japan, present this letter for the inspection of the "high officers and those who manage affairs." Our attainments are few and trifling, as we ourselves are small and unimportant, so that we are abashed in coming before you; we are neither skilled in the use of arms, nor are we able to discourse upon the rules of strategy and military discipline; in trifling pursuits and idle pastimes our years and months have slipped away. We have, however, read in [Chinese] books, and learned a little by hearsay, what are the customs and education in Europe and America, and we have been for many years desirous of going over the "five great continents," but the laws of our country in all maritime points are very strict; for foreigners to come into the country, and for natives to go abroad, are both immutably forbidden. Our wish to visit other regions has consequently only "gone to and fro in our own breasts in continual agitation," like one's breathing being impeded or his walking cramped. Happily, the arrival of so many of your ships in these waters, and stay for so many days, which has given us opportunity to make a pleasing acquaintance and careful examination, so that we are fully assured of the kindness and liberality of your excellencies, and your regard for others, has also revived the thoughts of many years, and they are urgent for an exit.

This, then, is the time to carry the plan into execution, and we now secretly send you this private request, that you will take us on board your ships as they go out to sea; we can thus visit around in the five great continents, even if we do in this, slight the prohibitions of our own country. Lest those who have the management of affairs may feel some chagrin at this, in order to effect our desire, we are willing to serve in any way we can on board of the ships, and obey the orders given us. For doubtless it is, that when a lame man sees others walking he wishes to walk too; but how shall the pedestrian gratify his desires when he sees another one riding? We have all our lives been going hither to you, unable to get more than thirty degrees east and west, or twenty-five degrees north and south; but now when we see how you sail on the tempests and cleave the huge billows, going lightning speed thousands and myriads of miles, skirting along the five great continents, can it not be likened to the lame finding a plan for walking, and the pedestrian seeing a mode by which he can ride? If you who manage affairs will give our request your consideration, we will retain the sense of the favor; but the prohibitions of our country are still existent, and if this matter should become known we should uselessly see ourselves pursued and brought back for immediate execution without fail, and such a result would greatly grieve the deep humanity and kindness you all bear towards others. If you are willing to accede to this request, keep "wrapped in silence our error in making it" until you are about to leave, in order to avoid all risk of such serious danger to life; for when, bye-and-bye, we come back, our countrymen will never think it worthwhile to investigate bygone doings. Although our words have only loosely let our thoughts leak out, yet truly they are sincere; and if your excellencies are pleased to regard them kindly, do not doubt them nor oppose our wishes. We together pay our respects in handing this in. April 11 [1854]. (Hawkes, *Narrative*, 1: 420.)

The *sōrōbun* note (translated by the author)
We two want to see the world. Please allow us to board your ship in secrecy. Going to foreign countries, however, is strictly prohibited in Japan. We would be in deep trouble if you tell the Japanese officers about this. If your admiral were to consent to our intention, we hope that you will send a barge at midnight tomorrow to the shore of Kakizaki village to meet us. April 19 [1854]. Ichigi Kōda, Kwanouchi Manji

The Second Petition (translated by S. W. Williams)
When a hero fails in his purpose, his acts are then regarded as those of a villain and robber. In public have we been seized and pinioned and caged for many days. The village elders and head men treat us disdainfully, their oppressions being grievous indeed. Therefore, looking up while yet we have nothing wherewith to reproach ourselves, it must now be seen whether a hero will prove himself to be one indeed. Regarding the liberty of going through the sixty States [of Japan] as not enough for our desires, we wished to make the circuit of the five great continents. This was our hearts' wish for a long time. Suddenly our plans are defeated, and we find ourselves in a half sized house, where eating, resting, sitting, and sleeping are difficult; how can we find our exit from this place? Weeping, we seem as fools; laughing, as rogues. Alas! for us; silent we can only be. (Hawkes, *Narrative*, 1: 422ff.)

Illustrations

(1) Yoshida Shōin in Shimoda

(2) First Interpreter
S. W. Williams

(3) Luo Sen

(4) Hirayama Kenjirō

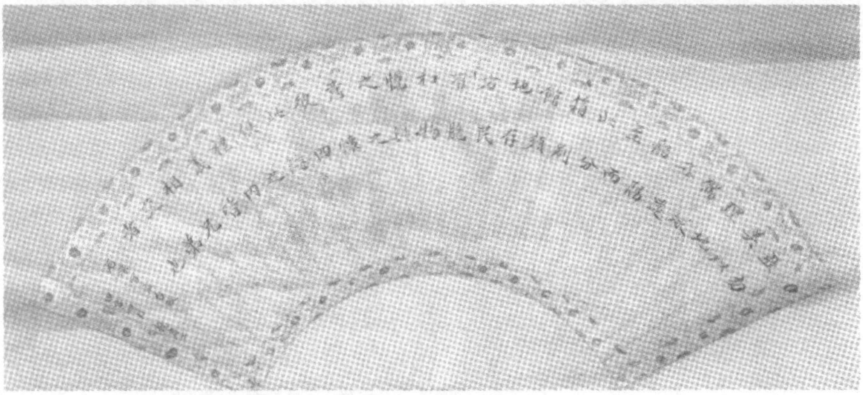

(5) A fan inscribed with friendly words including Confucian world view by Luo Sen and S. W. Williams

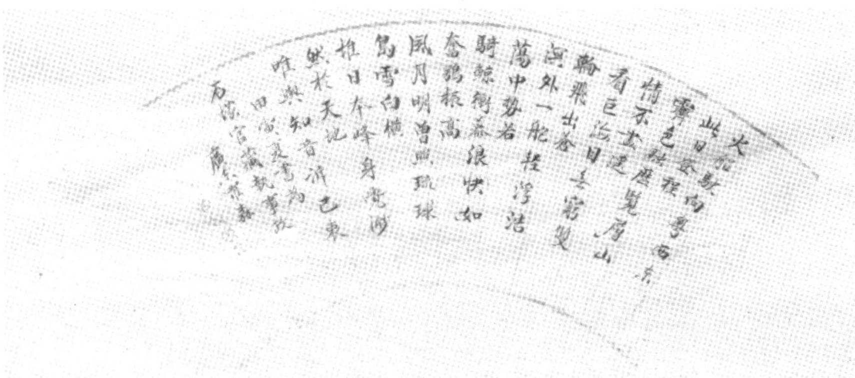

(6) Luo Sen's poem describes the powerful black ships and the beautiful landscape of Ryūkyū and Japan.

(7) Yoshida Shōin

(8) Commodore M. C. Perry

(9) Perry's flagship, the USS *Powhatan*

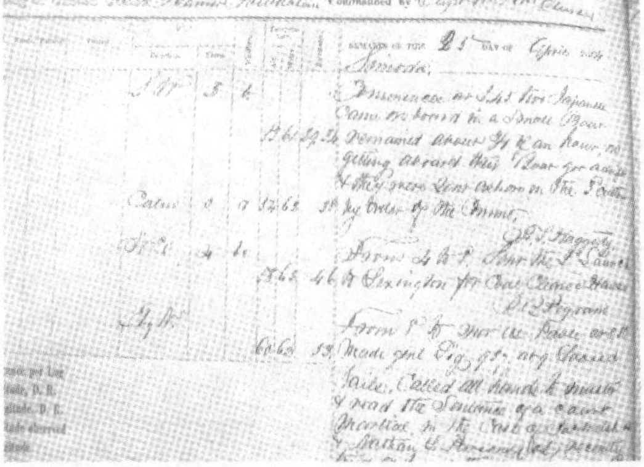

(10) Record of Shōin's time onboard in the logbook of the *Powhatan*

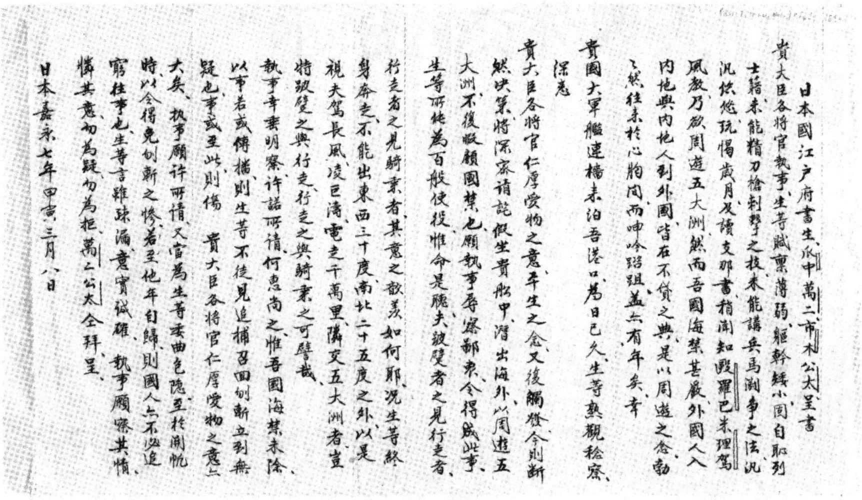

日本國江戸府書生瓜中萬二、市木公太呈書
貴大臣各將官執事。生等賦稟薄弱，軀幹矮小，固自恥列士籍。未能精刀槍刺擊之技，未能講兵馬鬪爭之法。汎汎然玩愒歲月。及讀支那書，稍聞知歐羅巴、米理駕風教，乃欲周遊五大洲。然而吾國海禁甚嚴，外國人入內地與內地人到外國，皆在不貸之典。是以周遊之念勃勃然往來於心胸間而呻吟蹉跎，蓋亦有年矣。幸
貴國大軍艦連檣來泊吾港口，為日已久。生等熟觀稔察，深悉
貴大臣各將官仁厚愛物之意，平生之念又復觸發，今則斷然決策，將深密請託，假坐貴船中，潜出海外，以周遊五大洲，不復暇顧國禁也。願執事辱察鄙衷，令得成此事。生等所能為，百般使役，惟命是聽。夫跛躄者之見行走者，行走者之見騎乘者，其意之歆羨，如何耶。況生等終身奔走，不能出東西三十度、南北二十五度之外，以是視夫駕長風，凌巨濤，電走千萬里，隣交五大洲者，豈特跛躄之與行走，行走之與騎乘之可譬哉。執事幸垂明察，許諾所請，何恵尚之。惟吾國海禁未除，此事若或傳播，則生等不徒見追捕，召回，刎斷立到，無疑也。事或至此，則傷 貴大臣各將官仁厚愛物之意亦大矣。執事願許所請，又宜為生等委曲隱蔽，至於開帆時，以令得免刎斬之慘。若至他年自歸，則國人亦不必追窮往事也。生等言雖疎漏，意實誠確。執事願察其情，憐其意，勿為疑，勿為拒。萬二、公太全拜呈。
日本嘉永七年甲寅三月八日

(11) The First Petition

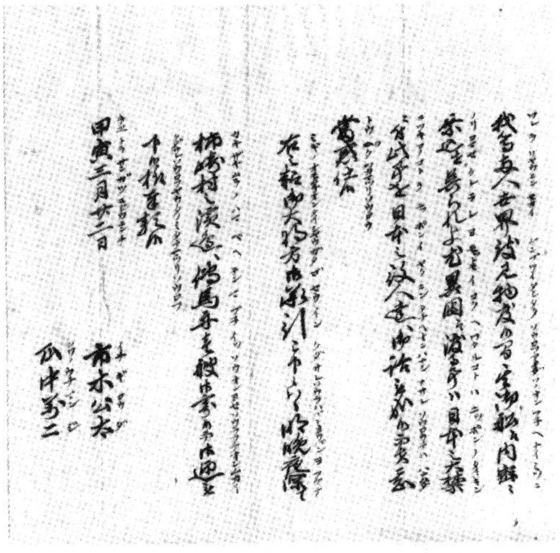

甲寅三月廿七日
市木公太
瓜中萬二

(12) The *sōrōbun* note

英雄失意兮蹤跡盜賊，面縛就捕兮幽囚累
村長里正倨傲相待，其厄亦甚矣。雖然
俯仰無愧，可以見英雄之為英雄也。
以周遊六十國為未足，欲遍歷五大洲。
是吾儕素心事也。今一旦失計，陷於半
間之室，食息坐臥不得少出範圍。泣
則近痴，笑則近黠。嗚呼，默默而已矣。

(13) The Second Petition

Note: The paper was given at "Treasures from Japan: An International Conference on Pre-modern Books and Manuscripts in the Yale University Library," on March 5–6, 2015, sponsored by the Council on East Asian Studies, the Beinecke Rare Book & Manuscript Library, and the East Asian Library, in cooperation with the Historiographical Institute (University of Tokyo) and the National Institutes for the Humanities (Japan).

Illustrations (5) & (6): Courtesy of Hakodate City Museum.

十九世紀中葉美國對日人權外交的啟示

——寫在日本開國150周年之際

● 陶德民

前言

今年3月31日，是標誌着幕末日本由「鎖國」轉向對外開放的《日美親善條約》簽訂150周年的日子。4月25日，是明治維新的先驅吉田松陰潛入來訪的美國旗艦偷渡被拒150周年的日子。近幾年來，日美兩國均有學者出書和召開學會，博物館舉辦展覽，電視台播放特別節目以紀念這些歷史性的事件。最近日本小泉政府在美國總統布什 (George W. Bush) 敦促下派兵伊拉克，也引起了各方面對近代以來日美關係種種演變的重新思考①。

筆者在前年秋天和去年春天兩度訪問耶魯大學斯德林紀念圖書館的檔案部，並有幸在《衛三畏家族文書》中找到《日美親善條約》談判的一些原始記錄以及吉田松陰遞交美方的〈投夷書〉②。對我來說非常有趣的是，這些文件竟有不少是用東亞的「拉丁語」即漢語寫的。因為當時美方沒有懂日語的翻譯，日方也沒有懂英語的翻譯，結果，談判是以漢語和荷蘭語為媒介來進行的。美國東印度艦隊司令官培理 (Matthew C. Perry, 1794-1858) 將軍在1853、54年兩次遠征日本之前，先在澳門僱用了通曉漢語並略通日語的衛三畏 (Samuel W. Williams, 1812-84) 為首席翻譯，然後在上海僱用了一名荷蘭語翻譯。而日本已有千年以上的漢學傳統和近兩百年的蘭學傳統，自然不乏漢語和荷蘭語的人才。加之近世外交文書一直由所謂「林大學頭」，即世襲最高學府昌平黌之校長職位的林家當家人以漢文作成，故1853年第十代大學頭林健便受命翻譯漢文版的美國總統國書，死後則由第十一代大學頭林韑擔任1854年談判的日方首席代表。

衛三畏隨同培理訪問日本之前，已在澳門經辦一家教會印刷所達二十年，參與編輯《中國叢報》(*The Chinese Repository*) 並出版了《中國總論》(*The Middle Kingdom*)，是一個中國通。不過，他雖然可以閱讀漢文，卻無法以漢語作文，對書法也無自信，所以在1853年隨訪時僱用了他的中文老師謝某為秘書。不料謝某這個鴉片鬼本來身體虛弱，在航海途中仍然偷食鴉

今年是標誌着幕末日本由「鎖國」轉向對外開放的150周年，也是明治維新的先驅吉田松陰潛入來訪的美國旗艦偷渡被拒150周年的日子。筆者在前年秋天和去年春天兩度訪問耶魯大學斯德林紀念圖書館，有幸找到《日美親善條約》談判的一些原始記錄以及吉田松陰遞交美方的〈投夷書〉。有趣的是，這些文件竟有不少是用東亞的「拉丁語」即漢語寫的。

片，故在逗留琉球之後、抵達日本之前便去世了，把培理急得要命③。幸好謝某死去之前已經把美國總統的國書譯完了，所以還不算是誤了大事。因為培理的對日外交原本打算分兩步走：1853年先遞交國書，促使日本考慮放棄鎖國政策，並相約次年再來，以正式締交條約。1854年再訪時，衛三畏僱用了廣東南海人羅森（字向喬）為秘書。羅森在鴉片戰爭中組織過平英團，因清政府未給他記功褒獎，憤而出走香港。他曾為英國當局做秘書和翻譯，在中環一帶得了地產，並做些生意。由於他善於吟詩作文並長於書法，在日本大受歡迎，經其題辭的扇面達一千多柄，至今猶有遺存。衛三畏對他的翻譯工作以及緩解美日間緊張氣氛的親和作用也大加讚賞，倚為左右手④。羅森訪日歸來以後，其《日本日記》英文版（衛三畏所譯）於1854年9月11日在《香港記錄周報》(*Overland Register and Price Current*)刊出，引起西方人士的極大關注，因為其中收錄了日本官員平山謙二郎致羅森的信件，透露出日本採取鎖國政策的一個原因是德川幕府恪守孔孟的「義利之辨」，認為「萬國交際之道，宜首講此義」，即「有無相通，患難相救」，而不願捲入西方的「貿易競利」，以致「人欲爭狠」而成「虎狼之交」⑤。同年11月，日記的中文版在香港英華書院出版的月刊《遐邇貫珍》分三期連載，也備受各方矚目，因為它頗為細緻地描繪了日本開國的過程⑥。培理在讀了日記的英文版後，認為這反映了一個有教養的中國人對其使命的理解，並把它作為附錄收入美國國會文件《培理艦隊日本遠征記》⑦。

關於以上這些事情，筆者已另有專文討論。這裏想以《日美親善條約》的簽訂及「吉田松陰偷渡事件」的處理為例，對當時美國的對日人權外交作一分析，以便對近代以來東西方交涉的一個重要方面重新加以認識⑧。

一 導致《日美親善條約》的人權問題因素

美國派遣艦隊率先打開日本國門，主要是出於以下幾項經濟因素。第一，為了和英國等列強爭奪亞洲市場。第二，西進運動抵達加州以後，建立太平洋航線以通向中國大陸已成為趨勢，而日本正是理想的中途站。第三，美國在太平洋上的捕鯨船不僅需要從日本補給煤炭和淡水，而且希望在發生海難事故時在日本海岸得到救援。

十九世紀中葉是美國對外膨脹節節勝利的時期，也是美國人篤信所謂「擴張乃天命」(Manifest Destiny)的時期。一般認為，美國派遣艦隊率先打開日本國門，主要是出於以下幾項經濟上的因素。第一，鴉片戰爭以後，美國為了和英國等列強爭奪亞洲市場，企圖把美中《望廈條約》適用於日本以拓展通商範圍。第二，西進運動隨着美墨戰爭和淘金熱潮在1840年代後期抵達加州以後，建立太平洋航線以通向中國大陸已成為趨勢，而藏有煤炭的日本正是理想的中途站。第三，美國在太平洋上的捕鯨業1840年代中期達到鼎盛階段，單是在日本近海作業的捕鯨船每年不下三百艘。這些船隻不僅需要從日本補給煤炭和淡水，而且希望在發生海難事故時在日本海岸得到救援。

這些經濟上的因素當然是推動美國遠征日本的主要動機。然而不可忽視的是，與第三項因素中的海難救助相關的人權問題，以及人權問題所隱含的東西方之間宗教文化的差異問題等，在美國對日外交中也佔有相當重要的地位，並形成打開日本國門的一個突破口。1853年7月16日，在培理將軍初訪日本、遞交美國總統國書的一周之後，衛三畏曾從江戶灣給其在土耳其傳教的弟弟衛廉士(William F. Williams)寫了一封長信，其中毫不隱晦地指出⑨：

培理告訴〔日方〕官員，他將在次年率領一支更大的艦隊，以求得到他們對所提要求的回答，即所有前來訪問或遇難流落日本海岸的美國人應得到善待，美國汽船在一個〔日本〕港口得到煤炭以及有關物資的補給。這些是我們花費巨大開支和派出強大艦隊到日本水域的表面上的理由，而真正的理由是為了提高我們民族的名譽和得到稱揚我們自己的材料。在這些理由的背後並通過這些理由，存有上帝的目的，即將福音傳布給所有國家，並將神旨和責任送達這個至今為止只是在拙劣地模仿耶穌之真的民族。我十分確信，東亞各民族的鎖國政策決非根據上帝的善意安排，其政府必須在恐怖和強制之下將之改變，爾後其人民或可自由。朝鮮、中國、琉球和日本必須承認這唯一活着的和真實的上帝，他們的鎖國之牆必將為我們所撤除，而我們西方的太平洋沿岸城市正開始派出船隊前往大洋的彼岸。

應該指出，衛三畏的這一見解固然與其傳教士的立場有關，但在西方人中間決非是一種奇特的看法。近代西方人前來東亞通商貿易的物質欲求，往往是與將東亞各民族加以「改宗」和「文明化」的精神衝動交織在一起的，因為他們認為基督教是高等宗教，工業文明是高等文明，代表着真善美。而通商貿易不僅可以推銷工業產品和採購原材料，還可藉以輸出西方的生活方式、社會制度以及精神文化。

衛三畏在此提到的日本鎖國政策，具體說來，是指十七世紀中葉至十九世紀中葉德川幕府為杜絕基督教影響和獨佔對外貿易利益而採取的海禁政策。在此期間，僅允許荷蘭和中國的民間商人來長崎一口通商，僅允許朝鮮國王和琉球國王在德川將軍換代時派遣使節來日本續修睦鄰友好關係，不許任何其他國家的人進入日本，也不許日本人渡海出國。更奇怪的是，即使是因漁船失事等漂流海外的日本人，也不問其情由而一律不許回國。從西方的人權觀念看來，這顯然是不近情理和非人道的。

1837年7月4日，美國奧立芬商社(即同孚洋行)的船隻「馬禮遜」號從澳門啟航駛向日本，試圖將七名日本難民送還他們的祖國。他們是因漁船失事分別漂流到加拿大和菲律賓之後轉來澳門的，衛三畏和郭實臘(Karl Friedrich A. Gützlaff)等在僱用他們的同時向其學習日語，並將《聖經》的有關章節譯成日語。伯駕(Peter Parker)帶了大批藥物和儀器，衛三畏為謹慎起見未帶聖經和書籍，而郭實臘則先期抵達琉球以待匯合。在衛三畏看來，這是藉以開始與日本友好交往的一個機會，不過最終目的仍在於「擴大文明和基督教」的影響。不過，他們的運氣並不好，在江戶灣以及鹿兒島灣分別遭到了炮擊，徒勞而返⑩。這是因為德川幕府早先發布的「異國船驅逐令」仍然有效，沿海藩主對國籍不明的船隻可以進行炮擊而無須半點猶豫(這一「驅逐令」要到1842年才取消)。衛三畏等把事件真相在倫敦、紐約和廣東的報紙上揭露出來後，引起了極大的國際反響。這一事件在日本國內也引起了震動，蘭學家渡邊華山和高野長英等著書立說，批判幕府的鎖國排外政策，因而分別遭到軟禁和終身徒刑的處分。

遭遇海難流亡海外的日本漂流民命運如此，遭遇海難流落日本海岸的美國漂流民命運又如何呢？如上所

近代西方人前來東亞通商貿易的物質欲求，往往是與將東亞各民族加以「改宗」和「文明化」的精神衝動交織在一起的，因為他們認為基督教是高等宗教，工業文明是高等文明，代表着真善美。而通商貿易不僅可以推銷工業產品和採購原材料，還可藉以輸出西方的生活方式、社會制度以及精神文化。

説，到十九世紀中期為止，捕鯨業是美國的重要產業，因為當時美國照明用的蠟燭和燈盞使用鯨油，大量工業機械的潤滑也靠鯨油，鯨油和鯨骨還是銷路很好的出口原料。由於十九世紀中期美國捕鯨業的主要漁場轉至太平洋北部，光是在日本近海地區作業的捕鯨船每年就有數百艘。當時美國海軍海洋調查船的一名軍官曾形容説，「今天和此時此刻，我國捕鯨船的白帆正把太平洋染成一片白色」⑪。如此眾多的捕鯨船，其中難免有失事的。由於海流的關係，在北太平洋遇難的捕鯨船往往漂流至當時稱為「蝦夷地」的北海道及其相鄰的千島列島南部一帶。「蝦夷地」當時還未開發，與日本本土的聯絡極不方便。而幕府堅持長崎一口通商的外交體制，漂流到日本最北邊的「蝦夷地」和千島的美國捕鯨船員，必須經過長途跋涉移送到最南邊的長崎交給荷蘭商館，等候定期來此的荷蘭商船帶到荷屬東印度的首府巴達維亞（今印度尼西亞首都雅加達）。途中遭到監視不説，飲食起居極不方便，加上言語不通和為期漫長，很少美國人能夠經受得住這番煎熬。

培理將軍在美國被稱為「汽艦之父」。在接受對日外交使命前不久，他已下定「畢其功於一役」的決心。他指揮的美國東印度艦隊在1853年遠征日本時是由四艘軍艦組成，將士近一千人。次年，艦隊由九艘軍艦組成，將士近兩千人。運轉自如的巨大「黑船」兩次出現時，都對日本官民的心理造成極大衝擊。

比如，1846年在堪察加遇難的「羅倫斯」號的捕鯨船員七人漂流到千島南部以後，經過十七個月才被帶到巴達維亞。又比如，1848年「拉格達」號的十五名船員集體脱逃至箱館（今北海道南部的函館），美國得知這一消息後，當即派東印度艦隊的「普列布」號駛往長崎，經過嚴厲交涉，終於由當地的荷蘭商館作為中介接回了這批船員。不過，這也費了整整十個月時間。因為兩次事件中均有人在拘留和移送途中死亡，在《紐約先驅論壇報》（*The New York Herald*）等加以渲染報導以後，美國公眾均認為日本是野蠻國家。國會和政府也十分重視保護捕鯨船員的生命財產，企圖尋求永久解決辦法，即與日本簽訂一個友好條約，免得每次海難發生以後興師動眾派軍艦去日本接回難民。

培理將軍在美國與墨西哥的戰爭中軍功赫赫，並因為把當時世界上最新式的蒸汽動力軍艦導入美國海軍，而被稱為「汽艦之父」。在接受對日外交使命前不久，他已下定「畢其功於一役」的決心：一支足以對日本示威的強大艦隊是完成這一使命的必須條件，如果因武力不足而「計劃歸於失敗的話，我自身的屈辱且不説，開始與日本及其附屬島嶼的友好關係、解放那些苦於殘酷和絕望的監禁生活的不幸人們（指遇難的美國捕鯨船員）這一最終目標的達成將被決定性地推遲」⑫。結果，他指揮的美國東印度艦隊經過大西洋和印度洋進入太平洋，在1853年遠征日本時是由四艘軍艦組成，將士近一千人。次年，艦隊由九艘軍艦組成，將士近兩千人。運轉自如的巨大「黑船」兩次出現時，都對日本官民的心理造成極大衝擊。

1854年3月上旬雙方在橫濱舉行會談，培理在標榜美國的人道主義的同時，歷數了日本的「罪狀」：「我國向來以尊重人命為第一來進行國政，所以，自己的國民且不論，即使是其他國家或向無交往的國家，見到其人民因漂流而遭遇困難時，亦竭力營救，予以厚待。而貴國則似乎從來不尊重人命，他國船隻在日本近海遇難，決不營救，靠近海岸時則炮擊防之。又有漂流至日本國者時，被像犯人一般對待，嚴加禁錮。且日本國人民漂流者，為我國人所救而企圖向（貴國）港口送還時，也決不接受，似乎要將自己的國民拋棄一般」，簡直是「不仁之至」。若不改弦易轍，便是「寇仇之國」，美國將集結戰艦與之「決一雌雄」⑬。日方首席代表林韑大學頭則竭力為日本的政策辯解，並表示願意就海難救助進行磋商時，培理則指出：「茲若能成此約，則本國亦無庸別臣奉急命，坐師船而到此矣」，意即條約若能談成，美國就不必在捕鯨船出事時派軍艦千里迢迢來日本救援自己的同胞了⑭。

培理隨後遞交了以美中《望厦條約》為藍本而加以簡化了的漢文條約草案，得寸進尺地要日本同意與美國通商，林大學頭則表示，日本物產豐富，無須交易也可以自足。「交易雖為國家利益，與人命則不相關，請勿再勉強提起交易一事。」⑮後來，在互換禮物時，美方把火車模型等贈送給日方，並邀請日方上旗艦赴宴，緩和了緊張氣氛。在3月31日簽訂的《日美親善條約》中，日本終於同意開放箱館和下田為避難港，分擔救助漂流民的費用，並給美國以最惠國待遇和十八個月後開設領事館的許可。

二 「吉田松陰偷渡事件」及其人權問題

《日美親善條約》標誌着日本與美國官方交往的開始，但並不意味着兩國人民可以自由往來。日本鎖國政策的改變，主要限於對美國船隻和遇難人員的照應。至於日本人渡海出國，當時仍屬大禁。因此，條約簽訂後不到一個月，年僅二十五歲的吉田松陰(名矩方，1830-59)及其同伴金子重輔(1831-55)趁美國艦隊仍在下田港逗留，於夜深人靜時爬上旗艦，企圖犯禁偷渡美國，成為震驚日本全國的一樁公案。

吉田為何要偷渡美國，事件又是如何展開的呢？其實，清末維新派的黃遵憲早在《日本國志》和〈近世愛國志士歌〉中就介紹過這個有名的故事。而戊戌政變時的梁啟超搭乘日本軍艦東渡亡命後，曾作〈去國行〉，又從吉田松陰及其弟子高杉晉作的經歷中看到自己的影子，一度改名「吉田晉」以示效法⑯。

黃遵憲〈近世愛國志士歌〉自註中的一節如下⑰：

吉田矩方，字松陰，長門人。受兵學於佐久間象山。象山每言今日要務，當周航四海，庶不致觀人國於雲霧中。會幕府託和蘭購兵艦，象山又曰：仰給於外，不如遣人往學之為愈也。幕府不納。矩方聞之感憤。時墨艦泊浦賀港，象山實司警衛事，乃密謀夜以小舟出港近墨船，偽為漁人墜水者，墨人救之，乃固請於墨將披理，求附載。披理奇其才，以犯禁故，仍送致幕府，請勿罪。幕府錮之其藩，密書寄象山曰：知時務如先生，今之俊傑也。今之諸侯，何者可恃？神州恢復，如何下手？茫茫八洲，置身無處，丈夫死所，何處為宜？乞告我。矩方卒被刑。維新以來，長門藩士之以尊王立功者，多其門人。

《日本國志》的有關介紹中還提到，「嘗觀陂理紀行書，謂矩方聰明，識天下大勢。日本罪斯人真為可惜。」⑱由此可知，黃遵憲等在當時的條件下對「吉田松陰偷渡事件」的來龍去脈已有大體上的把握。但是百年之後的今天，日美雙方有關檔案史料的發掘和研究大有進展，加之時代感覺

在1854年簽訂的《日美親善條約》中，日本同意開放箱館和下田為避難港，分擔救助漂流民的費用，並給美國以最惠國待遇和十八個月後開設領事館的許可。這標誌着日本與美國官方交往的開始，但並不意味着兩國人民可以自由往來。日本鎖國政策的改變，主要限於對美國船隻和遇難人員的照應。至於日本人渡海出國，當時仍屬大禁。

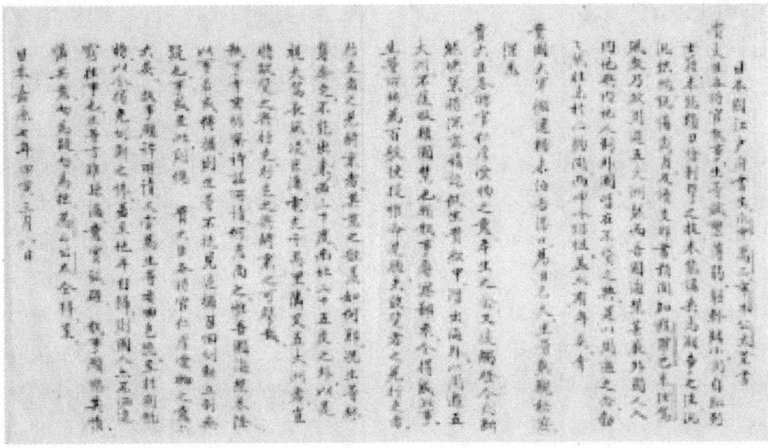

吉田松陰〈投夷書〉(45×24 cm)。此為羅森抄件，收藏於耶魯大學斯德林紀念圖書館檔案部《衛三畏家族文書》中。

和歷史觀的不同，再讀以上介紹就頗感不足了。

以下擬分兩點着重加以分析。

第一，吉田松陰的偷渡目的在於前赴美國學習先進軍事技術，標誌着日本的西學開始由蘭學轉向英美學，這一轉變的歷史意義不可忽視。1854年4月25日偷渡的前一天，吉田已將〈投夷書〉遞交在下田海岸散步的美國軍官。出身長州藩武士階層的吉田和金子在書中自稱「日本國江戶府書生」，並分別使用「瓜中萬二」和「市木公太」的化名，故作謙恭地表示，「生等賦稟薄弱，軀幹矮小，固自恥列士籍，未能精刀槍刺擊之技，未能講兵馬鬥爭之法，汎汎悠悠，玩愒歲月。及讀支那書，稍聞知歐羅巴米理駕風教，乃欲周遊五大洲。」可見其意在赴歐美學習先進的軍事技術。書中又對風馳電掣的「貴國大軍艦連檣來泊」表示讚嘆，並對自己困於鎖國制度無法出洋表示悲哀：

> 夫跛躄者之見行走者，行走者之見騎乘者，其意之歆羨如何耶。況生等終身奔走，不能出東西三十度南北二十五度之外（指日本列島的經緯度，意思是國土範圍狹小）。以是視夫駕長風，凌巨濤，電走千萬里，鄰交五大洲者，豈特跛躄之與行走，行走之與騎乘之可譬哉。

吉田松陰的偷渡目的在於前赴美國學習先進軍事技術，標誌着日本的西學開始由蘭學轉向英美學。《海國圖志》於1851年傳入日本後，吉田和他的老師佐久間象山都讀過，對魏源「師夷之長技以制夷」的戰略深表贊同。他們已經認識到蘭學本身的局限，以及借助荷蘭語譯著來了解英國、美國和俄國最新動態的局限性。

書中所謂「及讀支那書，稍聞知歐羅巴米理駕風教，乃欲周遊五大洲」，並非虛言。例如，《海國圖志》於1851年傳入日本後，其中的〈籌海篇〉和美國部分在1854年便得到翻刻，廣為傳布。吉田和他的老師佐久間象山都讀過，對魏源「師夷之長技以制夷」的戰略深表贊同。佐久間不僅有深厚的漢學功底，也是當時日本最有名望的蘭學家。他讀了《聖武記》序言後，曾引魏源為「海外同志」，因為《聖武記》作於1842年7月，而同年11月，他自己也曾向藩主上書建議加強海防。不過，同時也應該承認，近兩百年的蘭學傳統使得日本在順應西潮衝擊時表現較為敏捷。佐久間對當時的世界形勢有深刻認識，謂「露西亞先主彼得（大帝）以荷蘭為師，遂不見劣於荷蘭。而北美人以英吉利為師，終於戰勝英吉利」[19]。因而激勵吉田偷渡美國，並為之修改〈投夷書〉。

吉田登上美國軍艦後在紙條上寫到：「吾等欲往米利堅，君幸請之大將。」[20]失敗後在獄中據佐久間建議寫作《幽囚錄》，以記錄這一歷史性的倫渡事件。其中指出㉑：

荷蘭之學雖大行於世，至於露西亞、米利堅、英吉利的書，未聞有善讀者。現今諸國舶交至吾邦，吾邦人乃可不詳其方言乎。且技藝之流、器械之制，諸國各有新法妙思，經過荷蘭譯撰亦可以覩其概，然何若各就其國之書求之矣。今宜派遣俊才赴各國，購其國之書，求其學術，因立其人(留學歸國者)為學校師員。

這段論述表明，吉田和他的蘭學老師佐久間一樣，已經認識到蘭學本身的局限，以及借助荷蘭語譯著來了解英國、美國和俄國最新動態的局限性。

以往的研究只把1859年福澤諭吉(1835-1901)訪問横濱時所發的一番感慨作為日本由蘭學轉向英美學的象徵。即當時横濱開港伊始，上海和香港的英美商社紛紛來此開設分公司，掛出英語招牌。而傑出的青年蘭學家福澤來此參觀，目不識丁，大為震驚，因此下定決心轉學英語，終於成為近代日本提倡西化的主要思想家。因為有蘭學的底子，日本的英美學發展速度很快。據傳，1862年福澤在倫敦見到一位中國學者，兩人在交談中問起對方國家有多少人懂英語。當福澤告知日本有五百人左右時，那位中國學者慚愧地說，中國大約只有十一人會英語㉒。1868年明治維新以後，日本的英美學更有突飛猛進之勢。1872年中國派出第一批留美幼童共三十人，而日本已於前一年向歐美派出龐大的政府考察團，由岩倉具視、大久保利通、木戶孝允以及吉田松陰的學生伊藤博文等大臣率領。隨行人員中包括五十八名留學生，其中五位是去美國留學的少女。到1873年，光是東京府一地就在公立學校之外開設了1,130所私立英語學校㉓。

吉田松陰提倡學習英美要比福澤諭吉早四五年，為甚麼他上述重要主張竟然被人們忘卻了呢？這主要是由於「因人廢言」的緣故。吉田在幕末的政治鬥爭中為反對幕府而鼓吹「尊王攘夷」，而在太平洋戰爭中又被當時的日本軍國主義政府描繪成反對英美的先驅，因為他鑑於鴉片戰爭和「黑船」衝擊的教訓，確實策劃過先奪取近鄰各國、然後逐個擊破列強的長遠戰略。加上他蘭學造詣尚淺，他的跨越蘭學而轉學英美的主張就不如蘭學家福澤的現身說法來得有說服力。而他在偷渡失敗後所說的一些意氣用事和文過飾非的話，至今還有人用來證明他的目的不是要偷渡美國，而是要謀刺培理將軍。其實，只要看一下他偷渡時行囊中的書籍——《孝經》、《唐詩選掌故》、《和蘭文典》和《譯鍵》——便可知道，作為一個自小接受漢學訓練，長大後擔任兵學師範、有着戰略頭腦的人，他是決不會和目光短淺的「恐怖份子」一般見識的。

吉田松陰提倡學習英美要比福澤早四五年，他的重要主張竟然被人們忘卻，是由於吉田在幕末的政治鬥爭中為反對幕府而鼓吹「尊王攘夷」，而在太平洋戰爭中又被當時的日本軍國主義政府描繪成反對英美的先驅，加上他蘭學造詣尚淺，他的跨越蘭學而轉學英美的主張就不如蘭學家福澤的現身說法來得有説服力。

第二，吉田松陰的偷渡事件給培理出了一個難題，使之在美國的「國家利益」優先還是日本偷渡者的「人權」優先的問題上大傷腦筋，前後一共經歷了三次波折。

第一次波折是關於是否收留吉田和金子兩人的問題。其實，在兩人偷渡之前，培理已從衛三畏處得知在海岸散步的軍官轉交上來的〈投夷書〉的內容，其中有如下懇切的請求：

然而吾國海禁甚嚴，外國人入內地與內地人到外國，皆在不貸之典。是以周遊之念，勃勃然往來於心胸間，而呻吟踣跙，蓋亦有年矣。……生等熟覩稔察，深悉貴大臣各將官仁厚愛物之意，平生之念，又復觸發。今則斷然決策，將深密請詑(託)假坐貴船中，潛出海外，以周遊五大洲，不復暇顧國禁也。願執事辱察鄙衷，令得成此事。生等所能，為百般使役，惟命是聽。……執事幸垂明察，許諾所請，何惠尚之。惟吾國海禁未除，以事若或傳播，則生等不徒見追捕召回，刎斬立到無疑也。事或至此，則傷貴大臣各將官仁厚愛物之意亦大矣。執事願許所請，又當為生等委曲包隱，至於開帆時，以令得免刎斬之慘。若至他年自歸，則國人亦不必追窮往事也。生等言雖疏漏，意實誠確。執事願察其情，憐其意，勿為疑，勿為拒。

吉田松陰的偷渡事件給培理出了一個難題。由於《日美親善條約》剛剛簽訂，有關細則和具體辦法還有待交涉，若因收留日本的偷渡者而造成與幕府的矛盾，對培理來說會是很大的麻煩，所以他事先就已決定不予收留。吉田再三訴諸美方的「仁厚愛物之意」即人道主義，想藉此達到偷渡美國的目的，結果歸於失敗了。

不過，由於《日美親善條約》剛剛簽訂，有關細則和具體辦法還有待交涉，若因收留日本的偷渡者而造成與幕府的矛盾，對培理來說會是很大的麻煩，甚至有前功盡棄的危險。所以他事先就已決定不予收留，當然也就未照吉田在〈投夷書〉附件中所指示的那樣，在夜裏派小船去岸邊的柿崎村一帶迎接兩人。待吉田等爬上旗艦後，培理本人也未露面，而是讓衛三畏去作盤問。

盤問過程中雙方時而用漢語筆談，時而用日語會話。吉田按要求在紙上寫下兩人的化名即「瓜中萬二」和「市木公太」後，衛三畏當即回到艙內拿出〈投夷書〉加以對照，確認了其身份。據吉田回顧，衛三畏告訴他們：「此事只有大將和我知道，不讓他人知曉。大將和我心誠喜歡。但是在橫濱，米利堅大將和林大學頭已就米利堅天下和日本天下之事互相約束，故難以私下承諾君之請求。應稍等待，不久以後，米利堅人來日本，日本人來米利堅，兩國往來如同在國內一樣，其道路必將開通，其時機必將到來。且吾等在此逗留尚要三個月，並非馬上返回」，爾等可以在此期間向政府申請出國許可。吉田聽後，再次告知自己是犯禁而來，回去必受誅殺。衛三畏則回答說，現在仍是深夜，趁早回去，應當無人發現。吉田見無法說服，便要求退回〈投夷書〉，衛三畏也不許，曰「留置可也，皆讀得懂」。吉田轉而在紙條上寫下「廣東人羅森」一行字，要求與之見面。衛三畏則說，見他有何用，且現在臥牀睡覺。吉田仍不死心，以爬上旗艦後所乘小船已被風浪帶走，行囊中的文書會被扣留作為罪證，繼續苦苦相求。衛三畏勸說，已決定派小艇將你們送回岸邊，並指示艇長到各處幫助尋找你們的小船。如此周旋近兩小時後，吉田和金子兩人才在無奈和絕望之下離開了旗艦，被遣返岸邊。之後主動向當地的村長自首，隨之被政府拘捕㉔。吉田再三訴諸美方的「仁厚愛物之意」即人道主義，想藉此達到偷渡美國的目的，結果歸於失敗了。

第二次波折發生在吉田偷渡的次日下午。據美國國會文件《培理艦隊日本遠征記》記載，日方派翻譯前來詢問：昨日有兩個發狂的日本人到了美國艦隊的一艘船上，到的是否旗艦，有何不軌行動？美方司令副官為包涵起見，表示並無任何事端發生，同時還向日方翻譯確認了那兩個人平安回到岸上，這才放心。培理為了將大事化小，還特意派了一個士官前去會見日方官員，在對日方的關心表示感謝的同時，指出這樣的小事並不值得調查，因為美方不會作出任何有損互信和違反條約精神的事，沒有日本政府的同意，美方不會把任何一個日本人帶走。其實，培理心裏是同情這兩個可憐的日本人(指吉田等)的，因為他們只是想滿足自己對海外的好奇心而已，而這種好奇心又是受到美國人來訪的刺激而形成的。儘管從日本的法律來看他們的行動是有罪的，但美國人並不認為如此。這兩個有教養的日本人為增進知識而敢於冒生命危險，表明日本這個民族是前途有望的。不過，比起這種曖昧的人道主義，培理感到更重要的是，日本政府已經對美國作了許多重大讓步，所以盡可能遵從日本國內的諸多規定是唯一實在的政策。何況這兩個日本人的偷渡動機未必如其所說，他們也有可能是日方派來試探美方的間諜㉕。總之，在培理的心目中，佔據着優先地位的始終是對美國「國家利益」的考慮。

第三次波折發生在吉田被拘留在下田監獄時，大約在偷渡後十天左右。隨軍外科醫生等幾個美國軍官在當地散步，偶然看到吉田和金子被關在一個狹窄的木檻裏。吉田見到他們，便在一塊木板上寫了以下一段話來抒發自己的感慨。

> 英雄失意，比迹盜賊。面縛就捕，幽囚累日。村長里正，倨敖相待，其厄亦甚矣。雖然，俯仰無愧，可以見英雄之為英雄也。以周遊六十國為未足，欲適歷五大洲，是吾儕曩心事也。今一旦失計，陷於半間之室，食息坐臥，不得少出範圍。泣則近痴，笑則近黠。嗚呼，默默而已矣。

這裏的「六十國」是指日本的六十個州。吉田於此再度表明了擺脱鎖國體制、「周遊五大洲」的雄心壯志，並對「未敢翻身已碰頭」的監禁生活表示哀嘆。木板交給隨軍外科醫生後，轉

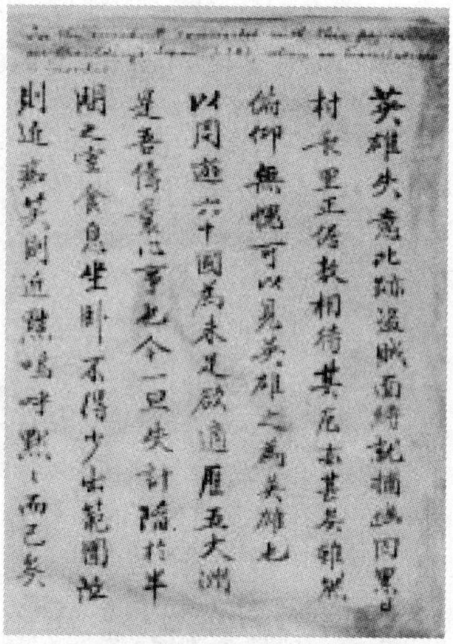

吉田松陰〈第二次投夷書〉(14×19cm)。此為羅森抄件，收藏於耶魯大學斯德林紀念圖書館檔案部《衛三畏家族文書》中。

到了首席翻譯衛三畏手中。培理在夜間得知這一消息以後，第二天早晨便派衛三畏和他的副官前去確認。然而不巧的是，吉田二人在那天一早已被從江戶來的官員帶走了。獄卒證實他們正是犯禁偷渡的罪人，可能會被嚴加處罰。衛三畏對木檻作了測量，其長約一點八米，寬約零點九米，高約一點四米，兩個成人關在其中不能動彈，難受程度可想而知。衛三畏由此聯想到美國印第安人用以囚禁罪人的木檻㉖。得到這一調查報告的培理最後終於動了憐憫心，向日方交涉，希望不要處以極刑，即吉田在〈投夷書〉中和旗艦上再三説起的斬首。在得到日方關於不會導致嚴重後果的保證以後，培理心裏才稍感安慰㉗。

吉田松陰手書的木板現在似乎已不復存在，我所發現的羅森的抄件，是被衛三畏小心翼翼地黏貼在自己的親筆日記《培理日本遠征隨行記》的封底內側，可見其十分珍視這一文書。美國國會文件《培理艦隊日本遠征記》收錄了這一文書的英譯，並視其為表現了臨難不懼和安心立命的哲人氣概的一個標本㉘。

結　語

1960年代初期擔任過肯尼迪(John F. Kennedy)總統特別助理的美國著名歷史學家小施萊辛格(Arthur M. Schlesinger, Jr.)曾經指出，美國人權外交的衝動始於1849年12月。當時，參議員卡斯(Lewis Cass)向參議院外交委員會提出一項動議：中止與奧地利的外交關係，以抗議其對1848年匈牙利革命的血腥鎮壓。雖然這項動議未能成功，它卻標誌着美國試圖在世界各地推進人權事業的開端。顯然，美國的人權外交在本質上是與獨立戰爭所孕育、其後又不斷完善的人權觀念密切相關的，同時也是與移民美國的各國人士為改善其出身國人權狀況所作的游説活動分不開的㉙。不過，小施萊辛格的視野並不包涵當時即十九世紀中葉的東亞地區。

1853、54年培理的對日交涉可以説是當時美國人權外交的典型例子。不過，美國對其國民之人權和利益的重視程度一貫高於對其他國家人民之人權和利益的重視程度，當美國要在其「國家利益」和其他國家人民的「人權」之間作出選擇時，往往以前者為優先。吉田松陰偷渡被拒事件就是明顯例子。

其實，1853、54年培理的對日交涉可以説是當時美國人權外交的典型例子，它不僅涉及保護遭遇海難的美國捕鯨船員的生命財產和避免其在滯留日本期間受到非人道待遇的問題，而且涉及漂流海外的日本漁民的歸國權利問題，以及吉田松陰這樣的偷渡未遂者在監禁期間的非人道待遇和所犯罪行的量刑等問題。其結果，不但藉此成功打開了日本國門，也促使日本反省其對內政策以及對外政策中的非人道因素。由此可見，美國在對外交往中標榜人道主義並實行「人權外交」，對改善其他國家的人權狀況是起到一定作用的。去年美國在對伊拉克進行轟炸並實施佔領體制之後，特意邀請各國記者參觀拘禁條件改善之後的巴格達監獄，以展示其人道主義，雖有粉飾其戰爭目的之嫌，卻也可以説是這種事例的一個最新版本。

不過，美國對其國民之人權和利益的重視程度一貫高於對其他國家人民之人權和利益的重視程度，當美國要在其「國家利益」和其他國家人民的「人權」之間作出選擇時，往往有以前者為優先考慮的傾向，這在吉田松陰一再告知犯禁出國有殺頭危險而其偷渡要求仍然被拒一事中有明顯的反映。況且，當美國在對日伸張其國民之人權(包括捕鯨船員、商人、傳教士及外交官等的權利)時，其國內仍然存在着奴隸制，即使在南北戰爭以後，猶有嚴重的種族隔離和種族歧視，可見美國本身亦有其歷史所形成的參差不齊的人權狀況，要到二十世紀中葉的民權運動(Civil Rights Movement)之後才得到大幅度改善。

註釋

① John H. Schroeder, *Matthew Calbraith Perry: Antebellum Sailor and Diplomat* (Maryland: Naval Institute Press, 2001). 大江志乃夫：《ペリー艦隊大航海記》(東京：朝日新聞社，2000)；岸俊光：《ペリーの白旗——150年目の真實》(東京：每日新聞社，2002)；井上勝生：《開國と幕末變革》(東京：講談社，2002)；三谷博：《ペリー來航》(東京：吉川弘文館，2003)；加藤祐三：《幕末外交と開國》(東京：筑摩書房，2004)。

② 見《每日新聞》，2003年1月11日及8月8日有關報導。陶德民：〈下田密航前後における松陰の西洋認識——米國に殘る「投夷書」をめぐつて〉，《環》第13號(2003春季)，頁164-84；陶德民：〈下田獄における第二の「投夷書」について——松陰の覺悟に對するペリー側の共感〉，《環》第14號(2003夏季)，頁423-30。

③ Roger Pineau編，金井圓譯：《ペリー日本遠征日記》(東京：雄松堂，1985)，頁132。

④ 王曉秋：〈近代中日文化交流的先驅者羅森〉，載《近代中日關係史研究》（北京：中國社會科學出版社，1997），頁263-74；陶德民：〈黒船のもたらした広東人旋風〉，載 *Image and Identity*（神戶：神戶大學經濟經營研究所，待出版）。

⑤⑦ Francis L. Hawks, ed, *Narrative of the Expedition of an American Squadron to the China Seas and Japan, Performed in the Years 1852, 1853, and 1854, Under the Command of Commodore M. C. Perry, United States Navy, by Order of the Government of the United States*, vol. II (Washington: Beverley Tucker, Senate Printer, 1857), 398-99; 395.

⑥ 最近，我的同事松浦章、內田慶市和沈國威出版了《遐邇貫珍の研究》（大阪：關西大學出版部，2004），其中包括該雜誌的完整影印、解説和索引，使用十分方便。

⑧ De-min Tao, "Reading Early U.S.-Japan Relations via a Fatal Stowaway: The Dilemmas of Yoshida Shoin's Request and Commodore Perry's Response", forthcoming in *A Symposium in Memory of the Late Marius B. Jansen* (Tokyo: The International House of Japan, 2004).

⑨⑩ Frederick W. Williams, *The Life and Letters of Samuel Wells Williams, LL.D.: Missionary, Diplomatist, Sinologue* (New York and London: G. P. Putnam's Sons, 1889), 197; 93-100.

⑪⑫ 平尾信子：《黑船前夜の出會い——捕鯨船長クーパーの來航》（東京：日本放送出版協會，1994），頁148；174。

⑬⑮ 〈墨夷応接録〉，《大日本古文書．幕末外國關係文書付錄之一》（東京帝國大學史料編纂掛，1913），頁538；541。

⑭ Samuel W. Williams著，Frederick W. Williams編，洞富雄譯：《ペリー日本遠征隨行記》（東京：雄松堂，1970），頁215註。

⑯ 郭連友：〈近代中國の吉田松陰認識〉，玉懸博之編：《日本思想史——その普遍と特殊》（東京：ぺりかん社，1997），頁437。

⑰ 黃遵憲：〈近世愛國志士歌〉，載錢仲聯箋註：《人境廬詩草箋註》，上冊（上海：上海古籍出版社，1981），頁287。

⑱ 黃遵憲：《日本國志》（上海：上海古籍出版社，2001），頁83下。

⑲ 佐久間象山：〈小寺常之助に贈る〉，載信濃教育會編：《象山全集》，下卷（東京：尚文館，1913），頁545。

⑳㉔ 吉田松陰：《回顧錄》，載《吉田松陰全集》，第七卷（東京：岩波書店，1935），頁414；415-16。

㉑ 吉田松陰：《幽囚錄》，載《吉田松陰全集》，第二卷（東京：大和書房，1973），頁49-50。

㉒ 井上清：《日本現代史》，第一卷（東京：東京大學出版會，1951），頁215。

㉓ 山本博文：《ペリー來航——歴史を動かした男たち》（東京：小學館，2003），頁195。

㉕㉘ 同註⑤，vol. I，頁421-22；422。

㉖ Samuel W. Williams, *A Journal of the Perry Expedition to Japan (1853-1854)*, ed. Frederick W. Williams (Yokohama: Kelly & Walsh, 1910)（即註⑭日譯本的英文原版），181-82.

㉗ 同註⑤，vol. I，頁422-23。另參註②陶德民：〈下田獄における第二の「投夷書」について〉。

㉙ Arthur M. Schlesinger, Jr., "Human Rights and the American Tradition", chap. 5 in *The Cycles of American History* (Boston: Houghton Mifflin Company, 1986).

陶德民 日本關西大學文學院教授。著有《懷德堂朱子學的研究》（大阪大學出版會，1994）和《日本漢學思想史論考》（關西大學出版部，1999）。

或問 WAKUMON 57
No.9, (2005) pp.57-65

从卫三畏档案看1858年中美之间的基督教弛禁交涉
——写在《基督教传教士传记丛书》问世之际

陶 德民

最近，复旦大学周振鹤教授主编的《基督教传教士传记丛书》由广西师范大学出版社陆续出版，可以说是近代中西文化交流史学界的一件大事，值得重视。已经问世的《马礼逊回忆录》、《卫三畏生平及书信》和丁韪良的《花甲忆记》等三本英文传记的中译本，恰巧皆与笔者近年所留意的人物有关，故更有如鱼得水之感。

记得以往在查阅王铁崖《中外旧约章汇编》时，对其中一些条款的内容颇觉费解。例如，1844年中美望厦条约有如下一条：

> 准合衆國官民延請中國各方士民人等教習各方語音，並幫辦文墨事件，不論所延請者係何等樣人，中國地方官民等均不得稍有阻撓、陷害等情；並准其採買中國各項書籍。[1]

又同年中法黄埔条约第二十四款如下：

> 佛蘭西人在五口地方，聽其任便僱買辦、通事、書記、工匠、水手、工人，亦可以延請士民人等教習中國語音，繕寫中國文字，與各方土語，又可以請人幫辦筆墨，作文學、文藝等功課。各等工價、束脩，或自行商議，或領事官代爲酌量。佛蘭西人亦可以教習中國人願學本國及外國語者，亦可以發賣佛蘭西書籍，及採買中國各樣書籍。[2]

学习外语、聘用教习以及购买书籍等，在今日正常的国际交往来看，应该说是天经地义之事，也是为增进相互理解所不可或缺之事，竟然必须以条约形式作硬性规定来保障这些基本权利，足见晚清的中外关系实在是異乎寻常。

不过，通读以上传记便不难发现，两国外交官坚持在1844年对华条约中加入此款，并在1858年天津条约中予以重申，决非无事生非。

比如，马礼逊在1814年因在中国印制和散发基督教书籍而引起清朝政府的注意，并被生怕影

---

[1] 王铁崖《中外旧约章汇编》第一册，三联书店1957:54页。
[2] 同上, 62页。

响对华贸易的澳门东印度公司解除其中文译员的职位时，曾向该公司董事会主席提出如下培训新手的建议：

> 中国老师因为要冒生命危险才敢来教中文，来了之后他们不敢进出英国商行，所以，中国学生部［马氏建议公司设立的中文译员培训部的名称］必须供给中文老师的食宿，并要有合理的、独特的应变办法，必要时可以帮助中国老师逃脱，以能躲过中国官府的缉捕和杀头，不致有生命危险。如果公司不作出这些安排，我想是没有办法可以找到好的中文老师的。[3]

次年即1815年，马礼逊为《华英字典》所制作的刻版被清朝政府抄走，圣经刻版虽然幸存下来，但为避免被发现作为罪证，也加以自行销毁。这种状况在马礼逊1834年8月于广州去世以后也没有改变。1835年8月，来华后将近两年的卫三畏在给波士顿美部会负责人安德森牧师的信中报告说：

> 修改［马礼逊《圣经》漢译本的］工作进展迅速，麦都思和郭士力几乎一直在从事这一工作，但眼下在广州我们的工作受阻，因为省政府根据皇帝的命令正在调查，是否有当地人参与了两本基督教书籍的制作，这两本书被福建巡抚送到了北京。这道命令引起了恐慌，我们的中文老师立刻离开了我们。[4]

总之，若是对当时中西交往中从语言、宗教到社会体制方面的重重障碍有所了解，才会对用条约的形式将这两个迥然不同的世界联结起来的必要性有所理解。

本文旨在对1858年中美《天津条约》谈判时的基督教弛禁交涉作一个考据性的探讨。这一方面是因为笔者正在从事题为“卫三畏与幕末日本的开国”的科研项目，打算将《卫三畏生平及书信》之有关部分从英文译成日文，并根据耶鲁大学斯德林记念图书馆档案部所藏《卫三畏家族文书》等详加注释，以便从近代东西方关系和东亚国际形势的全局来揭示1850年代美国打开日本国门的精神冲动亦即宗教动机；另一方面也可以说是拜《基督教传教士传记丛书》出版之赐，因为《卫三畏生平及书信》和《花甲忆记》的传主卫三畏和丁韪良是当时中美交涉的两个当事人，故将这两本传记对照来看时，极有参考价值。虽然这两本传记在中国史学会编《第二次鸦片战争》（中国近代史资料丛刊，1979年）的第六部分中被选译过一些片段，但是，人们现在终于可以见到它们的全貌了。

---

[3] 顾长声译《马礼逊回忆录》广西师范大学出版社 2004:106 页。

[4] 顾钧，江莉合译《卫三畏生平及书信》广西师范大学出版社 2004:31 页。

（一） 卫三畏的谈判对手“张大人”是谁？

众所周知，1858年担任美国驻华使团的正式秘书兼翻译的卫三畏在中美《天津条约》中写进基督教弛禁条款一事上贡献最大，以致1876年当他提出辞呈时，美国国务卿在回函中还专门就此事赞扬了他：“基督教世界将不能忘记，基督教弛禁这一宽大条款所以能列进我们的对华条约中，得力于你的地方，比其他任何人都要多些。”[5]。这是因为1858年6月中旬中美双方进行交涉时，美国驻华公使列卫廉对借此机会一举解决基督教的传教自由问题并不热心，问题的最终解决全靠卫三畏和丁韪良（因擅长北方话而被临时雇用为翻译）这两位传教士出身的外交人员的坚持和努力。关于这一点，《花甲忆记》可以作证：

> 6 月 18 日即将来临，列卫廉先生通知我们他希望在该天签署条约，希望后代能够把他的名字和威灵顿将军联系起来。在宗教宽容条款的措辞上仍存在一些分歧。那份现在成为条约荣耀之处的条款是卫三畏博士提出的。列卫廉先生对它感兴趣的程度可以从他的话语中表现出来：“现在，先生们（指卫三畏和丁韪良），如果你们能够加入该款，很好！但不管有没有该款，我都会在 6 月 18 号签署条约！”
>
> 决定命运的那天早上，卫三畏博士告诉我他一夜未眠，一直在考虑这份宽容条款。现在他想到了一种新的形式，可能会被对方接受。他写了下来，我建议我们应当马上坐轿子直接奔赴中方官邸解决这个问题。尽管我们除了前次发生的偶然事件外还没有到过那里，但我们还是这样做了。
>
> 中方代表接见了我们，他们当中的负责人稍作修改,就接受了卫三畏博士的措辞。[6]

由《花甲忆记》还可知道，这位中方代表的尊姓为“张”，在咸丰皇帝（1831-1861）的两个钦差大臣桂良（1785-1862）和花沙纳（1806-1859）于天津近郊的海光寺初次会见列卫廉时曾经作陪：

> ［列卫廉］出示了自己的委任状，并将翻译文本递给中方。他进而提议，由于必须长途跋涉交换意见，最好在双方使节的指导下，由各自指定的代表来进行新条约的文书工作，而双方使节只需在文件完成后签名并封印。这个建议获得认可，列卫廉先生指派卫三畏博士为他的代表，并询问中方准备派什么人来见他。［在试图指派官阶较低的卞先生一事被美方拒绝后］桂良又提出，高官花沙纳的随从里有个合适的人选。列卫廉先生则要求见见面。那人被叫了出来。他是一个矮小的、看起来很平庸的鞑靼人。他从中国官员队伍里走出来，却有些羞涩，像一个学生。这就是中国人的介绍礼节了，我们甚至对他的姓名和职务还一无所知。

---

[5] 转引自马士《中华帝国对外关系史》第一卷上海书店出版社重版 2000:592 页。

[6] 沈弘，恽文捷，郝田虎合译，丁韪良著《花甲忆记》广西师范大学出版社 2004:120 页。

"您贵姓？"我替列卫廉先生问道。"张。"他生硬地回答道。"您的官职是......"为了避免客套，另外一个人替他回答道："他是汉奎（Hankuin）的副官，世袭贵族——子爵。"尽管帽顶闪耀的红宝石映衬着他木然的神情，这高贵的身份也足够弥补他智力的不足了。列卫廉先生满意了，只是暗示卞先生可以跟随子爵参与会谈，充当幕僚。[7]

可是，这位代表中方与卫三畏谈判以确定条约文案的张姓子爵究竟是为何人，在笔者所见到的各种有关史书中均无详细记载。法国史学家科尔迪埃的《一八五七—一八五八年中国之征》一书中也只是提到"列威廉把这件事交给卫三畏先生，桂良则指定在场的官阶很高的张"而已。[8]

所幸者，笔者在上述《卫三畏家族文书》中找到署名为"张廷岳"的一张回条，似为其与卫三畏在基督教弛禁条款问题上讨价还价时亲笔所书［内容见下文］，故可加以断定。

据商务印书馆《中国人名大辞典》（1921年）：

張廷岳，漢軍鑲藍旗人。道光中襲三等子，同治間任庫倫辦事大臣。甘回竄入蒙古，廷岳防剿有功。官至正白旗蒙古都統。卒謚威勤。

由此可见，张廷岳尽管其貌不扬，后年却立了军功，死后还受了謚号，非同小可。虽然一时难以考定其生卒年份，但既在道光年中袭为三等子爵，到了咸丰八年（1858年）又以副官身份伴随担任吏部尚书·镶蓝旗汉军都统的花沙纳参与中美谈判，可见当时他已经有一定资历和岁数了。

从《卫三畏生平及书信》所引用的卫三畏日记来看，张廷岳是一个旗鼓相当的对手，在6月18日签约的前夜和当天上午，两人就基督教弛禁条款的内容和措词往复争议了好几回。为便于和第二节中列出的档案资料互相挂钩，特在以下所引日记中逐段加以编号。

6月17日

（1）晚上 9 点左右，当我们正为条约中加上了与基督教传播有关的条款而兴奋不已的时候，我和丁韪良先生收到了中方代表送来的便条，明确表示他们拒绝接受我们最希望他们接受的新条款。和便条一起送来的还有他们拟定的一项条款。根据这一条款，美国传教士只能在通商口岸活动，他们的传教活动由当地的美国领事和中国官员共同监管，这一条款也同样允许人们享有信仰基督教的自由。列卫廉先生既不坚持我们原先拟定的那一条，也不采纳中国人修改的这一条，而是主张干脆把这一内容从条约中去掉。这让我非常失望。

6月18日

（2）昨天晚上，我想，既然使节先生已经给了中国人这样一个答复，那么我也不必再白费力气重拟条款了。但是，经过一夜的考虑，我决定再试一试，并且这一次我只字

[7] 同注 6，《花甲忆记》112-113 页。
[8] 中国史学会编《第二次鸦片战争（六）》中国近代史资料丛刊 1979:157 页。

不提外国传教士。我以最快的速度写好了新的条款，并在早饭之前让信使送了过去。这是最后的机会，我在心中一遍又一遍地祈祷这次能成功。

（3）九点半，对方送来了回复。他们删去了允许进行宗教集会和散发宗教书籍的内容，同时还增加了一条：在通商口岸以外的地区，不论是当地人还是外地人，宣称信仰基督教者一律以违法论处。他们这样做的目的是为了将传教士的活动范围限制在通商口岸，但实际上更多的是损害了中国人的利益。我决定马上去见常大人，和他当面商讨解决这个问题。

（4）我和丁韪良先生立刻喊来了轿夫，风急火燎地赶到了常大人的住处。就在上个星期，杜邦上校还带着他的海军陆战队士兵到过这里。常大人看了我们再次修改的条款后开始挑剔起来。我告诉他，这是我们经过再三考虑后才确定下来的，要他马上拿去给钦差大人过目并请他们批准。不久，他回来了，说桂良大人同意了。我们的一番辛劳终于得到了回报。[9]

以上引文的第（3）、第（4）段中的“常大人”，英文原文为“Chang”。查卫三畏《汉英韵府》，“Chang”应读为“张”而不为“常”，故此人很可能就是张廷岳，和第（1）段中提到的“中方代表”为同一人。

（二）　《卫三畏日记》手稿本所含的条款草案

和《卫三畏生平及书信》一样，第二次鸦片战争期间的《卫三畏日记》的片段也被收入上述中国近代史资料丛刊的〈外文资料选译〉里。可是，这本日记和卫三畏在1853、1854年作为首席翻译官随佩理将军访日期间写下的日记同样，是由其儿子卫斐列在其去世二十多年后整理出版的，手稿本所附录的珍贵中文原件均未收入。比如，关于手稿本中夹着的基督教弛禁条款的几种草案，他不仅在每种草案上都尽可能用英文小字说明其性质和作者，而且在一处还有以下总体注释。

These slips of Chinese refer to the discussion respecting toleration of Christianity.

正如卫三畏自己所承认的那样，“最先在拟定条约时提出这方面要求的是俄国使节”普提雅廷，其于6月13日所签订的中俄《天津条约》第八条为：

天主教原爲行善，嗣後中國於安分傳教之人，當一體矜恤保護，不可欺侮凌虐，亦不可於安分之人禁其傳習。若俄國人有由通商處所進內地傳教者，領事官與內地沿邊地方官按照定額，查驗執照，果係良民，即行畫押放行，以便稽查。[10]

---

[9] 同注4，《卫三畏生平及书信》176-177页。

[10] 同注1，《中外旧约章汇编》第一册 88页。

卫三畏“弄到一本中俄条约的中文本，找到允许传教士行动自由的条款，依样为中美条约也定了这样一条。”他回忆说：“中俄条约中规定有允许‘一定数量的传教士’在中国生活，我把这一限制性的内容去掉了。我在新拟的条款中提到了‘新教’和‘罗马天主教’两个概念，并说明新教无论是在名称上还是在实质上都是有别于罗马和希腊的教会组织的。”[11] 过去我们无从了解经过改动后的条款是怎样的，现在根据手稿本可以知道，其草案如下：

> 耶稣基督聖教，亦名天主教，原爲勸人行善。嗣後中國於安分傳教之人，當一體矜恤保護，不可欺侮凌虐，亦不可於安分之人禁其傳習。若大美國人由通商處所進內地傳教者，領事官與內地沿海地方官酌定額數，查驗執照，果係良民，蓋用圖記放行，以便稽查。

两相比较，除卫三畏自己记得的改动以外，他还将“沿邊”改为“沿海”，以适应美英等国的需要。其最感兴趣者，是中俄条约中的“由通商處所進內地”一句，因为可以籍此扩大传教范围。

但是，正如第一节所引日记的第（1）段所示，6月17日晚上9点左右，“我和丁韪良先生收到了中方代表送来的便条，明确表示他们拒绝接受我们最希望他们接受的新条款。和便条一起送来的还有他们拟定的一项条款。根据这一条款，美国传教士只能在通商口岸活动。”

现据手稿本可以知道，中方的便条的内容如下：

> 基督教向來攙替貿易，與他國傳教者迥不相同。若入內地，断不准攙替貿易。況俄國內地二字亦必另改，否則又須會議，有误定期矣。專此佈達。即候
> 晚佳　　　　立候回音以便繕寫
> 衛・丁 二位大人閣下

同时送来的中方所拟条款，其内容如下（“Toleration article form proposed by the Chinese Commis <commissioners 之略>”）：

> 耶穌基督聖教，原爲行善。嗣後中國於安分傳教習教之人，當一體矜恤保護，不可欺侮凌虐。若大合眾國人，只須在通商處所行道，領事官與該處地方官酌定額數，查驗執照，以便稽查。

可见中方在回应中尽量防卫，甚至有撤回在中俄条约中给予天主教传教士进入内地的特权一语，以求防止基督教借以一体均沾而深入内地合法传教，并将其影响限制在通商口岸。

第一节所引日记的第（1）段还提到，“列卫廉先生既不坚持我们原先拟定的那一条，也不采

---

[11] 同注4，《卫三畏生平及书信》175页。

纳中国人修改的这一条，而是主张干脆把这一内容从条约中去掉。”而丁韪良秉承列卫廉的这一旨意当场起草的回函（Note to hasten copying of treaty so as not to miss their signing at the time appointed），也存于手稿本中，其行文如下（参照图1）。

逕覆者、頃閱
華翰、當經稟明、現奉
列大人面諭、倘除進內地三字、則不若將此款不列條約之內、全行刪去、免阻翌午互易、務希覆函、俾得發繕、至
尊處將條約謄正後、請即攜來敝寓、先行校對、致下午六點鐘可以互換、專此覆達、並頌晚安、

知名恕具　初七日

阴历初七日即阳历6月17日，这一天的交锋直到夜深时方告终结。但是，第一节所引日记的第（2）段所示，卫三畏“经过一夜的考虑”，“决定再试一试”，把新拟的条款在早饭之前让信使送了过去。这送去的新条款乃丁韪良所抄，甚至有可能是他按照卫三畏的意思所拟，因为手稿本中的草案说明为：“Alek’s draft of toleration article, first form.”（Alek 即丁氏英文全名 Williams Alexander Persons Martin 中 Alexander 的略称。）

第二十九款

耶穌基督聖教，又名天主教。原爲勸人行善，凡欲施諸已者亦如是施於人。嗣後所有安分習教之人，當一體矜恤保護，不可欺侮凌虐。凡有遵照教規聚眾祈禱分散聖書者，他人毋得騷擾。

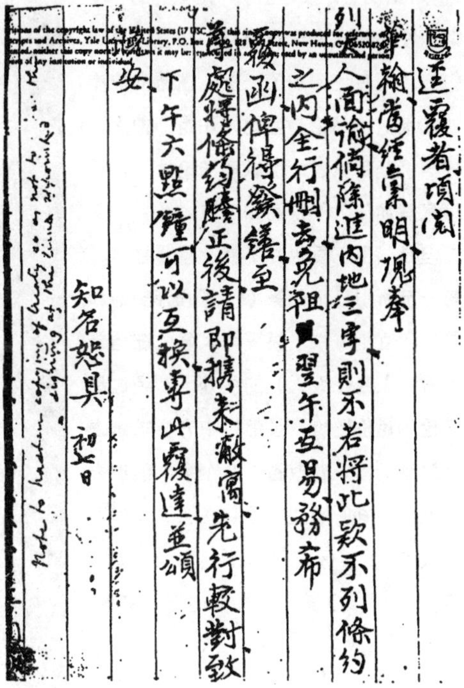
逕覆者頃閱
華翰當經稟明現奉
列大人面諭倘除進內地三字則不若將此欵不列條約之內全行刪去免阻翌午互易務希
覆函俾得發繕至
尊處將條約謄正後請即攜來敝寓先行較對致
下午六點鐘可以互換專此覆達並頌
晚安
知名恕具　初七日

图1　丁韪良的回函

可是，卫三畏岂曾料到，中方的回函是即迅速又严厉。如第一节所引日记的第（3）段所示，“9点半，对方送来了回复。他们删去了允许进行宗教集会和散发宗教书籍的内容，同时还增加了

一条；在通商口岸以外的地区，不论是当地人还是外地人，宣称信仰基督教者一律以违法论处。”这封写于“初八日辰刻”即6月18日上午8点左右、具上“张廷岳”大名并有其画押的回函如下（参见图2）：

逕啓者。頃接來

函。當即呈明

中堂大人 裁奪。秉

諭聚集祈禱分散聖書八字酌改通商處所安分傳習八字。令即繕寫，不可再改。專此覆

知。希即呈明

列大人定議。俾不误今日約期矣。原稿附呈。統希原諒。

此候　　刻佳　　　　　　　　　　張廷岳（画押）

可惜的是，張廷岳所“附呈”的“原稿”，在手稿本中未有留存，故卫三畏所谓中方“同时还增加了一条：在通商口岸以外的地区，不论是当地人还是外地人，宣称信仰基督教者一律以违法论处”，其措辞究竟如何，不得而知之也。

但是，卫三畏也并不就此善罢甘休，如第一节所引日记的第（4）段所示，他和丁韪良“立刻喊来了轿夫，风急火燎地赶到了常大人（张大人）的住处。”经过最后一轮的讨价还价，虽然按中方要求删去了“聚集祈禱分散聖書”八个字，但也去掉了上述中方所增加的限制在通商口岸以外传教的一条，从而形成下述当天签署的中美《天津条约》第二十九款的正式文案。

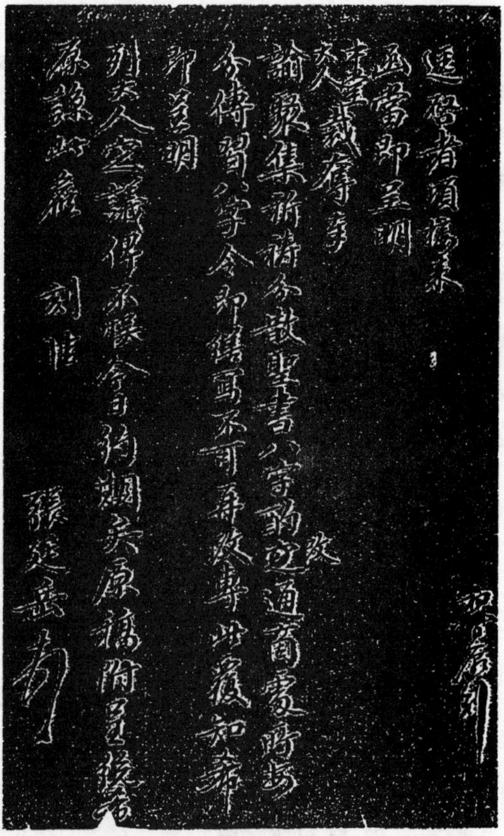

图2　张廷岳的回函

耶穌基督聖教，又名天主教，原爲勸人行善，凡欲人施諸己者亦如是施於人。嗣後所有安分傳教習教之人，當一體矜恤保護，不可欺侮凌虐。凡有遵照教規安分傳習者，他人毋得騷擾。[12]

[12]同注1，《中外旧约章汇编》第一册95页。

通观这一条款，中方固有得手处，但是总的说来，是美方更胜数筹。首先，基督教传教与天主教传教相并列而明文弛禁，显然是破天荒的收获。其次，为避免争议，条文中干脆不提在通商口岸和在内地传教的权利之分，这反而给美方的自由解释留下了很大的空间。再次，将基督教的“凡欲人施諸己者，亦如是施於人”这一与孔子的“己所不欲，勿施於人”具有互补性的处世哲学写入中美两国间的外交条款，不啻是基督教东传史上的一个特例。这一方案，很可能是出于著有《天道溯源》的丁韪良的灵机一动，而得到了同为传教士出身的卫三畏的赞同。

查同年6月26日签署的中英《天津条约》第八款中仅有“耶稣聖教暨天主教原係為善之道，待人如己”之语，6月27日签署的中法《天津条约》第十三款中仅有“天主教原以勸人行善為本”之语，而并无“凡欲人施諸己者，亦如是施於人”一句，则中美《天津条约》中的基督教弛禁条款的特异性可以说是昭然若揭也。

Japan Review, 2005, **17**:91-119

Negotiating Language in the Opening of Japan: Luo Sen's Journal of Perry's 1854 Expedition

De-min TAO
Kansai University, Suita, Osaka

In the negotiations between the United States and Japan that resulted in the treaty that marked the end of Japan's policy of seclusion (1854), not only the Japanese and English languages but also Chinese and Dutch were recognized for official communications. The chief U.S. interpreter, S. Wells Williams, had long experience in China and expertise in the Chinese language but not in Japanese. For preparation of written documents and participation in "brush conversations," he required the assistance of an educated Chinese assistant, and for Perry's second voyage to Japan in 1854 he engaged the service of Luo Sen. Luo kept a journal of his visit to Japan and the Ryukyus that was published soon after his return to Hong Kong in both Chinese and English; the English version was included in the official record of Perry's mission, published in 1856-57. Since then almost forgotten in the West, Luo's journal merits rediscovery for the insight it affords into cultural relations between Japan and China in the bakumatsu period, mutual understanding and misunderstanding among Japanese, Americans, and Chinese, and the status of Chinese as a negotiating language in the communications of two non-Chinese speaking nations.

Keywords: MATTHEW C. PERRY, U.S.-JAPAN TREATY OF PEACE AND AMITY, LUO SEN (RA SHIN), *JOURNAL OF A VISIT TO JAPAN*, S. WELLS WILLIAMS, CHINESE LANGUAGE, MEDIUM LANGUAGE, NEGOTIATION, BRUSH CONVERSATION (*HITSUDAN*), *NARRATIVE OF THE EXPEDITION OF AN AMERICAN SQUADRON TO THE CHINA SEAS AND JAPAN*

In early April 1854, having learned that the Kanagawa Treaty (U.S.-Japan Treaty of Peace and Amity) had been signed by Commodore Matthew Calbraith Perry and Hayashi Daigaku no kami 林大学頭, Yoshida Shōin 吉田松陰 (1830-59) and his fellow Chōshū samurai Kaneko Shigenosuke 金子重輔 (1831-55) began to make all-out efforts to evade bakufu restrictions on foreign travel and to smuggle themselves to the Western world aboard an American "black ship." They prepared a well-written petition in literary Chinese and brief notes in both Chinese and Japanese,[1] and selected a few books to take with them, including the *Book of Filial Piety* (*Xiaojing* 孝経), *References to the Selected Tang Poems* (*Tangshi-xuan zhanggu* 唐詩選掌故), and two Dutch-Japanese dictionaries.[2] Following Perry's squadron all the way from Yokohama to Shimoda, they finally got a chance to pass the petition and the notes to an American officer who happened to come ashore on 24 April.[3] Around two o'clock the next morning, they succeeded in reaching the deck of Perry's flagship, the *Powhatan*, where they repeatedly appealed to the humanity of the Americans. They were not allowed to remain on board, however, without obtaining permission from the shogunate. Perry was predictably loath to risk undermining the newly established official relations between Japan and the United States for the sake of accommodating a couple of unknown young men. In a last attempt to get the Americans to reconsider, Shōin passed a note to Perry's chief interpreter, Samuel Wells Williams (1812-84), asking for an interview with the Kantonjin Ra Shin 広東人羅森 (the Cantonese Luo Sen). Williams refused this request, saying that Luo was still sleeping. He had Shōin and Kaneko sent back ashore before dawn.[4]

Figure 1. Kantonjin Ra Shin. Source: Hibata Ōsuke, *Beikoku shisetsu Perī teitoku raichō zue* (Yoshida Ichirō, 1931).

Who was Luo Sen? How did Shōin get to know of him? Why was he involved in Perry's expedition, and what kind of views did he hold regarding the opening of Japan? Based largely on contemporary sources that include the journals of Luo, Williams, and Perry, this article attempts to answer these questions and thereby to shed new light on little-explored language problems in Perry's diplomacy toward Japan in the early 1850s.

I. Chinese as a Medium in U.S.-Japan Negotiations

When talking about the opening of Japan in 1853-54, many people simply assume that the negotiations were carried on with the assistance of English and Japanese interpreters, as bilateral talks between the two nations would be today. Few give any attention to the question of what languages were actually used. As a matter of fact, Chinese and Dutch were the principal languages employed.

In the first formal meeting between the

Americans and bakufu officials at Kurihama 久里浜 on 14 July 1853, Perry presented President Millard Fillmore's letters and letter of his own to the Japanese. With the English originals of these, he provided Chinese and Dutch translations.[5] When he came back the next year and presented the Japanese a draft of a U.S.-Japan Treaty of Peace and Amity, that document was essentially an abridged version of the Wangxia Treaty 望厦条約 signed by China and the United States, and he gave the bakufu representatives Chinese and English copies of that treaty, which had been executed in 1844.[6] At this time—March 1854—the Americans apparently suggested that bilateral communication should be carried on in Chinese and Dutch. Dutch should be used for oral communication, and Chinese for documentation and so-called "brush conversation" (筆談 Jp. *hitsudan*, Ch. *bitan*).

This "suggestion" made sense to the Japanese because they had a long tradition of Chinese studies extending back to ancient times, and they had been developing expertise in Dutch learning from the mid-eighteenth century. Throughout the two centuries of *sakoku* 鎖国 (seclusion), they still maintained trade relations with the Dutch and Chinese, and this contact had given them incentive to keep up skills in these two languages. In addition, it had since the time of Tokugawa Ieyasu been the practice for the master of the Hayashi house to handle diplomatic correspondence (in Chinese) with the Korean envoys 朝鮮通信使 and to act as a foreign affairs advisor to the Tokugawa shogun. From the third generation, that is, from the time of Razan's 羅山 grandson Hōkō 鳳岡, the master served as Daigaku no kami, the head of the Shōheikō 昌平黌, the shogunal college where Confucian studies (concentrating mainly on writings in Chinese) were paramount. It was the tenth generation, Hayashi Sōken 林壮軒, who translated Fillmore's letter from its Chinese version in 1853, and the eleventh generation, Hayashi Fukusai 林復斎 (1800-59), who was the bakufu's chief commissioner in the treaty negotiations with Perry in 1854.[7]

The American suggestion of use of Chinese and Dutch was conditioned by a choice that Perry made before coming to Japan. He could have hired Philipp Franz von Siebold (1796-1866), the German doctor and scholar who had served at the Dutch factory in Nagasaki in the 1820s and had written several books about Japan. As Perry was preparing his expedition, Siebold was known to be drafting diplomatic documents for renewed Dutch and Russian efforts to open Japan. Perry was determined, however, to break out of the mold of the traditional Dutch type of restrained and humble diplomacy toward Japan. Thus, although he made use of Siebold's published information about Japan, the naval officer-diplomat refused to employ Siebold as interpreter, and hired his fellow American Williams instead. Williams himself regarded this decision as questionable "so far as obtaining efficient intercourse with the Japanese goes."[8] Beyond the issue of efficiency of communication, however, there was a consideration that Williams overlooked. His very lack of past exposure to Japan meant that he came to Perry's mission with a clean slate. The German doctor, on the other hand, had gotten into trouble with shogunal authorities in 1828 when he tried to take maps of Japan out of the country, in violation of prohibitions. Siebold's direct involvement would not necessarily have been an advantage to, and might have jeopardized, Perry's negotiations with the Japanese.

Williams was hired as the chief interpreter despite having told Perry clearly at their

Figure 2. Williams, "who knows some Japanese."
Source: Same as for Figure 1.

initial meeting in 1853 that "I had never learned much more Japanese than was necessary to speak with ignorant sailors who were unable to read even their own books, and that practice in even this imperfect medium had been suspended for nearly nine years." He considered himself "ill prepared upon the duties of this position."[9]

In reading and speaking Chinese, by contrast, Williams did have confidence in himself. He had been in China since 1833 as printer for the Canton press of the American Board of Commissioners for Foreign Missions, and he made contributions to and became an editor of the *Chinese Repository* (1832-51), a journal initiated by Elijah C. Bridgman. By the time Perry was looking for an interpreter, Williams had composed several books on the Chinese language, and his *The Middle Kingdom: A Survey of the Geography, Government, Literature, Social Life, Arts, and History of the Chinese Empire and Its Inhabitants* (1848) was the standard book on China for the English-speaking world (and would remain so for the rest of the century).[10] He was an experienced translator and writer. Yet Williams still needed a Chinese assistant to help him polish his translations and copy them in elegant calligraphy that would impress the Japanese officials with whom Perry would be conducting diplomacy. Williams also planned to use his free time during the lengthy voyage to continue his study of Chinese and to work on translation projects. This justified the employment of a Chinese assistant.

For the first expedition, Williams hired his Chinese tutor, an old man named Sieh 薛.[11] It would seem that the choice was not carefully made, for Sieh was actually an incurable opium addict. Smoking heavily during the voyage, he eventually died a month before the Kurihama meeting, when the fleet was still anchoring in Ryukyu. Perry's deep concern about the incident and its negative consequences on the mission can be seen in his diary of 11 June:

> At one o'clock this morning the old Chinaman, who had been employed by Mr. Williams as interpreter, breathed his last, aged as he said 55 years. He was an educated man, and had been employed to teach the Chinese language to foreigners,

among others to Mr. Williams. He had for many years of his life been an inveterate opium smoker, and his frame had become so weak and attenuated in consequence, that when he came on board this ship, everyone predicted that he could not long survive. Thus we are left without a Chinese interpreter, for though Mr. Williams can convey the meaning of English words into the Mandarin dialect, and thus dictate, he cannot himself write the Mandarin language.[12]

Acting quickly, the Americans obtained a replacement for Sieh in Shanghai, from which the fleet was getting supplies on a regular basis. The new man was brought to Naha and presented to Williams. Speaking different dialects of Chinese, they had trouble understanding one another. Williams complained that he found his new assistant "a mere office copyist" who was unable to suggest alternative wording in the process of translation, but with patient effort they managed to put the letters of Fillmore and Perry into Chinese, and the primary purpose of Perry's first voyage—to hand these letters to the Japanese government at a place in Edo Bay so as to force it to consider abandoning its seclusion policy—could be accomplished.[13]

In contrast to the unhappy experiences with old Sieh and the man from Shanghai, Luo Sen's participation in the 1854 voyage was a big help to Williams. Shortly before departure for Japan, on 11 January, Williams confided his hopes about Luo to his journal: "I have secured the assistance of Lo, a teacher of good attainments and no opium smoker, so that I hope to do more study than I had before."[14]

Luo Sen (Xiangqiao 向乔, ca. 1821-ca. 1899) was from Nanhai 南海 county in Guangdong province. At the time Williams employed him, he was doing business in Hong Kong, and his occupation brought him into contact with Englishmen and Americans.[15] Asked by a friendly Japanese official why he had accepted a position with Perry's expedition, Luo frankly confessed that his dissatisfaction with Qing officialdom had entered into his decision:

During the war with the English [the Opium War], I led a body of braves, and put forth all my strength in the service of my country. Yet afterwards the officers of the government, bent on nothing but gain, made no account of my devotion and efforts. It was this neglect which set my mind on traveling abroad, and led me to my present position on board this steamer.[16]

It was Williams' good fortune to retain the services of an educated Chinese man with an open-minded attitude about the world outside China at a time when most Chinese scholar-gentlemen concentrated their attention and energies on the civil service examinations, the tried and true path to career advancement, and few were willing to cooperate with Westerners.[17] On 11 March, at "Bay of Yedo, off Kanagawa," Williams wrote a long letter to his wife. In it he detailed the initial meetings between Perry and the Japanese chief commissioner (whose name, he said, "is Lin in Chinese and Hayashi in Japanese"). He remarked also on his pleasant relations with Luo. The Chinese translator, he noted, seemed to have taken an interest in the nature of relations between the sexes in the West, for one thing, and he was getting along well with the Japanese, for another.

> My Chinese clerk, Lo, inquires for news, and I wish he had a line from his family. I tell him all the news from your note which would interest him, and he seems to think in hearing it, that a wife may, after all, be made of some use. He is an excellent man and is making friends among the Japanese by writing poetry on their fans for them; they often communicate with him on paper, there being many who can read and write Chinese readily, though no one talks it. Both of us have plenty to do, so time passes quickly and pleasantly.[18]

Two months later, in a letter from "Hakodadi, Island of Yesso" dated 21 May, Williams told his wife that the unexpected appearance of five American ships—come to survey the port—had frightened the native people, but that Luo was playing an important role in reducing tension, as well as sharing the heavy burden of translation.

> I have tried to allay their fears, which in the absence of all special instructions from Yedo were not surprising, and I hope they will soon resume their occupations, seeing that we are friends and may do them good. The non-arrival of the envoy and Dutch interpreter from the capital has thrown the whole business of interpreting upon me, and I can assure you I have business enough for twenty tongues to be kept up at trip-hammer rate of livelong day. . . . Heretofore, most of my talking has been in a small way and on unimportant matters, if I bungled it was not of so much consequence; but now the affair is serious, so I bring Lo into considerable service to make one language help the other, and thereby avoid many mistakes. He takes a lively interest in all our operations and gets on admirably with the natives; he is, indeed, the most learned Chinaman they have ever seen and their delight in showing off to him their attainments in Chinese is increased when he turns a graceful verse or two for them upon a fan; of these he has written, I should think, more than half a thousand since coming to Japan, and nothing pleases him like being asked to do so.[19]

With Luo's reliable and active assistance, Williams was able to perform his duty as chief interpreter to the satisfaction of his superior. Before leaving Hong Kong for the United States, Commodore Perry addressed Williams in an appreciative letter dated 6 September 1854:

> In taking my departure from China I feel myself called upon every sense of propriety and justice to bear the most ample testimony to the talents, zeal, and fidelity with which you conducted the important duties entrusted to your management as Chief Interpreter to the Mission to Japan. I say little when I declare that your services were almost indispensable to me in the successful progress of the delicate business which had been entrusted to my charge. With high abilities, untiring industry, and a conciliating disposition, you are the very man to be employed in such business.[20]

Luo himself was appreciated not only by the American side, but also by the Japanese side, who valued his cultivation and his graceful writing. In Shimoda, he reported, "both men and women are fond of carrying fans. While I was at this place I am sure I inscribed more than a thousand fans. The governor and the various officers conducting the intercourse with the Americans, all requested my services in this matter."[21] He was complimented several times by the Japanese officials, one of whom conveyed his appreciation in a poem.

> Say not our meeting here was all of chance;
> To you we owe the treaty and our peace.
> From far the strangers came, their language strange,
> 'Twas well we had your pencil and your tongue.[22]

In Yokohama and Hakodate as well as Shimoda, Luo quickly became popular and received hundreds of requests, from commoners as well as samurai officials, for samples of his poetry written on fans. In Yokohama early in April 1854, he had been sought out by a scholar of the Sendai domain named Ōtsuki Bankei 大槻磐渓 (1801-78), who had gotten a fishing boat to bring him to the American ship, and the men exchanged poems. Upon learning of this,

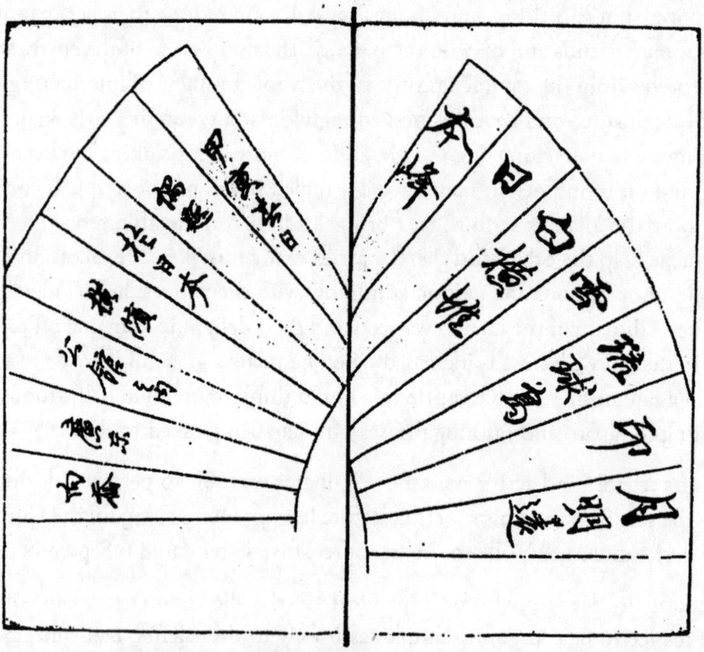

Figure 3. Ra Shin sensu-zu 羅森扇子図. Source: *Ebisu no uwasa* 恵比すのうわさ, in the collection of the National Diet Library.

Yoshida Shōin, who had already conceived his scheme to go abroad and hoped to get concrete advice about how to meet the Americans, invited Ōtsuki to dine with him.[23] It was because of his meeting with Ōtsuki that Shōin asked for an interview with Luo when he was aboard the *Powhatan*—he thought that Luo might be someone who could help him, because Luo previously had been friendly in communicating with the Japanese.

In Ryukyu, also, Luo was welcomed. An example of his receipt of special favor was a gesture by Ryukyu's prime minister Shang-hwang-heun (尚宏勳 pinyin Shang Hongxun, Jp. Shō Kōkun), who, after concluding his negotiations with Perry, presented a scroll to the Chinese interpreter. On it the high Ryukyuan official had copied in his own hand a poem by the prominent neo-Confucian scholar of the Song dynasty Cheng Mingdao 程明道.[24]

II. Luo's Journal of Perry's 1854 Expedition

On 11 September 1854, about a month after Luo's return to Hong Kong from Japan, the English version of his journal was published under the title "Journal of a Visit to Japan" in *Overland Register and Price Current*, a supplement to the *Hong Kong Register and Government Gazette*. The first time his observations were put into print and made available for public consumption, that is to say, it was in translation—a translation done by Williams.[25] The Chinese edition, *Riben riji* 日本日記 (Japan Journal), appeared later, in three installments of the monthly *Xiaer guanzhen* 遐邇貫珍 (China Serial); the first part came out in November 1854. I call *Riben riji* the "Chinese edition" rather than the "Chinese original" advisedly. The Chinese manuscript handwritten by Luo, which we might call the "actual original," has regrettably been lost. There are important differences in content between the *Riben riji* account and the one rendered in English by Williams. Almost certainly those differences reflected the diverse concerns of the author, the translator, and the editors of the two publications that put the work into print.[26] But the fact that the journal came out almost immediately in two languages is evidence that both Westerners and Chinese were eager to get firsthand information about Japan and American activity there. And Luo delivered quickly: his was the first personal account of the expedition to be published.[27]

In its English version, under the more precise title "Journal of the Second Visit of Commodore Perry to Japan," it was included in the appendixes to the second volume of Perry's official report, the *Narrative of the Expedition of an American Squadron to the China Seas and Japan, Performed in the Years 1852, 1853, and 1854, under the Command of Commodore M. C. Perry, United States Navy, by Order of the Government of the United States*. The brief introduction of Luo's account pays him a patronizing compliment:

> As it is a specimen of the intelligence of an educated Chinaman, and as, besides, it presents briefly the views of an Oriental, uninfluenced by the prevalent opinions of our countrymen around him, (for difference of language prevented much interchange of thought,) it has been supposed that it would not be without interest to the American reader, and a place has, therefore, been reserved for it in the appendix to this volume.[28]

The identity of the author of these lines remains a puzzle. Was it the editor of the *Narrative*, Francis Hawks, or was it Perry himself? Undoubtedly, however, this comment represents Perry's viewpoint. When the *Narrative* was in preparation, he had written to Williams from New York on 13 March 1855, urging the former chief interpreter to write "some forty or fifty pages or more" that "would reflect high credit on yourself and furnish a valuable acquisition to my report." Perry continued, "Do not forget to send to me some translations of Japanese poetry, as also Chinese done into English, if you have any; these scraps can be appropriately introduced. The specimens furnished to the *Hongkong Register* by your Chinese clerk are quite interesting."[29] Interesting, to be sure, but not to be incorporated into the *Narrative* without a qualifying comment. On the last page of Luo's "Journal of the Second Visit," Perry added a note expressing some reservations: "Although there are some errors in the descriptions of the Chinese writer, his paper has been faithfully copied."[30]

1) Explaining the Reasoning behind Japan's Seclusion Policy

As the editor of the *Overland Register and Price Current* pointed out, a letter addressed to Luo by "Ping-saw-heem-arh-lang" (Hirayama Kenjirō 平山謙二郎, 1815-90; not knowing the Japanese reading of the name of the bakufu foreign affairs official, Williams had romanized it according to its Cantonese pronunciation) is "especially worthy of attention."[31] Hirayama's letter takes up nearly two of the total twelve printed pages in the *Narrative* edition. Luo characterized the writer as "a gentleman [of] an ingenious nature and great learning"; Hirayama had been one of the shogunal officials who had supplied food and fuel to the American vessels when they were in Edo Bay, and he had played a key part in settling a number of issues, including the limits of ramble by American officers and crew members when they called at a treaty port. Apart from U.S.-Japan matters immediately at hand, he was also deeply concerned, Luo noted, about "the troubles which are at present distracting my native country," that is, about the Taiping rebellion.[32] At Hirayama's request, Luo showed two items he had written, one on the Nanking-centered Taiping rebellion (*Nanjing jishi* 南京紀事), and the other on government policies for maintaining public order (*zhi'an ce* 治安策). The bakufu official read these overnight and returned them with a long letter, a major topic of which was the relations between profit and righteousness, a classic Confucian debate. Hirayama wrote:

> The essential evil of such a state [of disorder and decay] may be described in a single phrase—it is the desire of gain. Now the desire of gain is common to all men, and is the pregnant womb of all evil. Confucius seldom spoke of gain, wishing to check the lust of it in its source. This, also, was the reason why my ancestors cut off all intercourse of foreign nations with Japan, because the desire of gain led astray the ignorant people, and wonderful arts in the investigation of principles deceived the perverse, so that they got striving together, seeking gain and hurrying after what was wonderful, till filial duty, modesty, and the sense of shame were all forgotten. To a man who has reached this stage of evil, neither his father nor his sovereign is anything.[33]

> If, on the contrary [of good faith and righteousness, which are the principles for mutual intercourse], commerce is conducted merely with a view to gain, quarrels and litigations will spring from it, and it will prove a curse instead of a blessing.

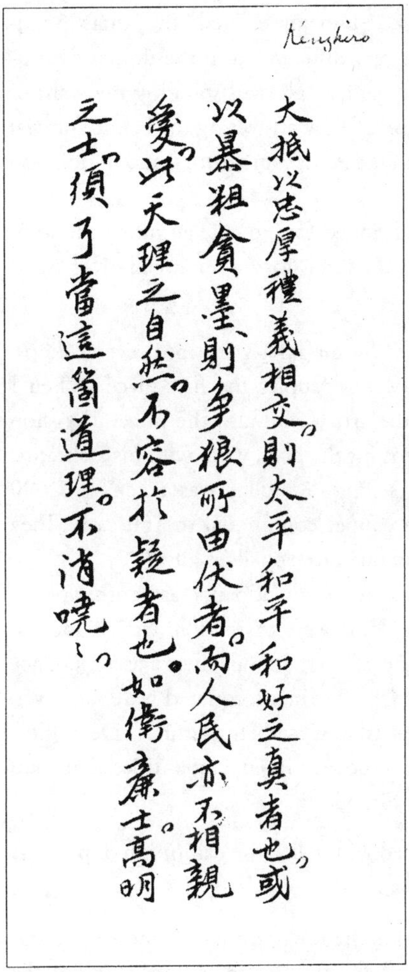

大抵以忠厚禮義相交，則太平和平和好之真者也。或以暴粗貪墨，則争根所由伏者，而人民亦不相親愛，此天理之自然，不容於疑者也。如衛康士高明之士，須了當這箇道理，不消嘵嘵。

Figure 4. Hirayama to Williams on what is proper in international relations: "Honesty and courteousness bring about peace, but wantonness and greed give rise to conflicts." Source: Williams Family Papers, Yale University.

Against such a result my ancestors were profoundly anxious.... It is but a hair's breadth which separates those different results; for, give selfishness the reins, and the righteousness is instantly merged in the desire of gain.[34]

A footnote to this passage, very likely written by Williams, remarked that this "Japanese gentleman writes Chinese with great freedom. Few, if any, Sinologues from the West could compete with him. Yet his composition might be plainer in some parts than it is. It is not easy to make out his meaning here, where he is touching on an interesting topic—the reason which induced the exclusion of foreigners from Japan"[35]

For most nineteenth-century Westerners, it was hard to understand the Confucian idea that to maintain social order and morality it was desirable to keep common people from gaining profit and seeking the *qiji yinqiao* 奇技淫巧, wonderful arts and excessive dexterity. This idea was a product of the premodern East Asian agricultural society and conservative mentality, which valued a self-sufficient life style and was satisfied with the status quo. Hirayama erred, however, when he adduced this single idea as the explanation for the decision of the Tokugawa "ancestors" to "cut off all intercourse of foreign nations with Japan." The fundamental concern of the shogun Tokugawa Iemitsu 徳川家光, in whose reign the seclusion policies reached their fully elaborated form, was that Western nations would use trade and missionary work as a means for seeking territorial aggrandizement.[36] It was only from around the turn of the eighteenth century, after Confucian ideology had gained its footing in Japan, that its reasoning came to provide a kind of official explanation for the policy of seclusion.[37]

Hirayama criticized profit-oriented Western expansion from the Confucian standpoint, pointing out that "all over the globe the strong destroy the weak, and the great swallow the small, as if the societies of men were like collections of tigers and wolves." He urged Luo to use his position on the American steamship to travel around the world spreading the ideas and "the wishes of Confucius and Mencius 孔孟之志."[38] Luo appreciated Hirayama's morality, but tried to persuade him that the "present age is very different from the times of antiquity; but who, with a conscience, can altogether disregard it? Notwithstanding my want of talent, for years I gave myself to the business of the world."[39] By answering the bakufu official in this manner, Luo helped the Japanese to understand the American visitors, and in doing so went beyond the limits of his duty as a translator.[40]

His practical business experience may have conditioned Luo to take an interest in local products, prices of commodities, and currency exchange rates, for he remarked on these as follows.

> Returning to the town [from the seashore of Shimoda] I went into several shops. Among articles for sale in these, laquered-ware occupies the first place. When I made any purchase, I wrote my name on the article and also the price. The shop keeper then carried it to the officer of customs for the port, who, with his assistants, superintended all matters of buying and selling. A dollar was taken as 1,600 cash. The Japanese themselves have a large copper coin, equal to 100 cash. They have also several coins of gold and silver, and one piece of silver gilt.[41]
>
> [On the streets of Hakodate:] The windows were mostly of paper, as in other places where we had been, and upon many of the doors were pasted Chinese characters, signifying "Wilderness House," "Tortoise House." In the shops there was abundance of silks, but of a quality inferior to those of China. Their lacquered ware, however, was admirable, and the shops were soon emptied of it by their visitors. Deer skins, the roach fish, and medicinal sea-weed were to be seen in large quantities. The food of the people was of a better quality than at Simoda.[42]

He was also fond of the *qiji yinqiao*, and described with relish the exhibition of presents brought by Perry to Japan:

> A circular railroad had been laid down outside the town, on which the engine and carriage swept round and round with great rapidity, to the astonishment of the beholders. The use of the electric telegraph was by means of copper wires to convey intelligence instantaneously from one place to another. By the daguerreotype apparatus pictures were taken by the reflection of the sun's light from the object on plates of metal. There is no need for pencils or drawing, and the pictures last long without fading. The lifeboat was fitted with air-boxes, by means of which it was kept from sinking. On occasions of shipwreck, parties may be saved by means of this invention. The implements of agriculture were the most ingenious contrivances for purpose of husbandry used in the United States.[43]

These lines show plainly that the writer was impressed, and it is no wonder that he disagreed with Hirayama's opinions about economic exchanges and technological advances, although he could show sympathy for the Japanese functionary's point of view, having held a similar view himself before being exposed to Westerners and Western material culture.

2) An Eyewitness Report on the U.S.-Japan Settlement

Luo stated his understanding of Perry's mission at the beginning of his journal: it was to open Japan in order to use it as a steppingstone for establishment of a cross-Pacific passage connecting America and Asia.

> Of late years, the intercourse between China and the State of California, in America, has greatly increased in extent and frequency. In consequence, the government of the United States was anxious that steam vessels should run between the two countries, and it became necessary to have an arrangement by which they could purchase coal at the Japanese islands, which lie between America and Asia. To obtain this, several steamers belonging to the Unite States visited Japan, in the third month of last year, (April or May,) and it was attempted to negotiate a treaty of peace and commerce, but the Japanese could not at once conclude the matter.[44]

On one occasion, wishing to convey his excitement about embarking on a black ship, Luo rhapsodized in poetry:

> Eastward my course, the ship of fire I joined,
> On travel bent, new scenes absorb my mind.
> What mountains rise to bless my wandering sight!
> O'er ocean's fields I gaze with vast delight;
> Our wheels! like wings whose power the eagle wields;
> Our helm ! t' its lightest touch the vessel yields;
> We dash along, a car whose steeds are whales;
> Like osprey strong, we sport with furious gales;
> By moonlight calm I saw Lew Chew's fair isle;
> I've marked of Japan's hills the snowy pile. [45]

Having accepted employment by the Americans in their expedition to Japan, what the Chinese scholar wished for was a peaceful settlement between the two nations. He had painful memories of the Opium War and a feeling that China and Japan shared a common cultural tradition. He was always sensitive to the development of tensions, and made efforts to mitigate them and create a peaceful and friendly atmosphere. Of the time when Yokohama was being selected as the meeting place for the negotiations, for instance, he wrote:

> On both sides, this being the commencement of intercourse between their respective countries, there seemed at first to be some suspicions. I observed a fleet of more than a hundred Japanese vessels, all with cloth sails, drawn up some distance off, near the shore, and on the land was a camp full of soldiers and their accoutrements, all in preparation for any hostilities which might arise. Next day two or three government boats came off to see the steamers, carrying at their stern a blue and white flag, with the words "Imperial Service" 御用 [*goyō*] on it. The American officers received the parties very courteously, and showed them the guns, trains, and everything on board

> their vessel. The visitors were greatly delighted. …Notwithstanding the difference of their language, I could introduce myself to them by means of the pencil, as they understood the Chinese character, and they responded to me in the same way, expressing their admiration of my country, and their pleasure at making my acquaintance. Many of them wrote down for me their names and titles, and a friendship was thus established between us.[46]

Not privy to the top secrets and perhaps a little naïve, Luo sometimes viewed demonstrations of might by both Americans and Japanese as a kind of entertainment. For example he described in these terms the transport of bags of grain by sumō wrestlers:

> In the first decade of the third month (March or April) the commodore had a conference on shore with the Japanese commissioners, on which occasion rows of *japonicas*, in full flower, were arranged outside the building. Lin, the chief commissioner, had several hundred bags of grain, each weighing more than two hundred catties, set down close by, and soon after, there appeared eighty or ninety burly fellows 肥人 [Ch. *feiren*], naked, excepting a cummerbund, though the weather was extremely cold, and taking up the bags, one man two, or three sacks at a time, they removed them, in a twinkling, to the shore. These men were not of uncommon height, but very stout, and immensely muscular. After they had removed the sacks of grain, they were made to exhibit their strength in wrestling and fighting in an open space in front of the reception hall--the victor being rewarded with three cups of wine.[47]

Fortunately Luo was able to see the U.S.-Japan Treaty of Peace and Amity settled on 31 March 1854 without a single exchange of fire, the best result he could have hoped for. There were four versions of the settlement, written in four languages, and Chinese was one of those. Luo composed a poem at the banquet held to celebrate the conclusion of the treaty, and he recorded the event in his journal.

> On the same day on which the exhibition of athletes took place, the articles of treaty were settled, and it was arranged that the two ports of Seang-Kwan 箱館 and Hea-teen下田, called by the Japanese, Hakodadi and Simoda, should be open to vessels from the United States, which should there be supplied with firewood, water, provisions, and coal. The most friendly feeling was displayed by both the contracting parties, and there seemed to be an end of their suspicions. A few days after, Commodore Perry gave an entertainment to Commissioner Lin on board his flagship, the *Powhatan*, which was decked out for the occasion. I made the following lines upon it:
>
> Two nations' representatives at Yokuhama met;
> To show their human brotherhood, the feast of joy was set.
> Here were the chiefs who doff the hat and friendly greetings pay.

And there the heroes with two swords, in proud and bold array.
They raised the sparkling cup to prove their words of peace sincere,
While roll of drums and clash of bells came thundering on the ear.
Love spake from every lip, strained every eye with pleasure,
Ever may the treaty last, a good securing measure![48]

3) Chinese Impressions of Social Life in Japan and Ryukyu

Luo's experiences in Japan and Ryukyu were testimony to the enduring power of the common literary culture in East Asia, which enabled him to make friends with the Japanese. His wide acquaintance then was revealed in the following lines.

> As the Japanese for two hundred years have had no intercourse with foreigners, and have seen none, excepting the few Chinese and Dutch who carry on the trade at Naga-saki, I found myself quite an object of interest; and as they set a great value on Chinese characters and compositions, whenever I went to the hall of reception many of them were sure to ask me to write on fans for them. The fans I inscribed during a month while we were at Yokohama could not be fewer than five hundred. The applications were, indeed, troublesome, and the writing took up much of my time, but it was difficult to decline acceding to their pressing requests. [49]

By making Japanese friends and appreciating the Japanese kanbun writings and ink painting, Luo was able to observe things about Japan that Westerners ignorant of Chinese culture could not see.

3.1) Samurai

At first Luo found the appearance of Japanese samurai a little strange. "Their dress was wide and loose, with large sleeves. Each man had a couple of swords at his girdle. Their hair was tied up in a knot, a small space over the *pia mater* in front being shaven. They wore shoes made of straw, and their trowsers were of gay and very various colors."[50]

But as a man of literary attainment, Luo was particularly drawn to Japanese persons with some sort of talent, and not surprisingly many of those he liked were samurai, since people of that status were well educated and acquainted with Chinese culture. He noted that when he was leaving Hakodate, he received from high-ranking officers of the Matsumae domain two ink paintings in rolls which were "not to be distinguished from those common in China", and several volumes of books which were "superior in terms of printing quality."[51] He also mentioned that upon his departure from Japan, he exchanged writings with several officials. The above-mentioned Hirayama, for example, gave him a fan on which he had copied the famous poem by Wang Wei 王維 written on the occasion of the Tang poet's seeing a friend off on a journey westward on the Silk Road.[52] Luo was also taken with "a young gentleman named Kwei-ching-min" 桂正敏, the attendant of a commissioner, whom he described as "of much intelligence and liveliness. All the visitors were very fond of him, and he had a great knack of drawing their likenesses."[53]

In a conversation with "Hop-yuen-tsaon-chwang" 合原操蔵, an official serving at Uraga, Luo learned that "both in the civil and military departments, officers were appointed after examination, only importance was not attached, as in China, to the making of verses; that the books of which they studied were those of Confucius and Mencius, and the writers of their school, and that after passing the examinations, and being approved as competent for office, parties were privileged to wear two swords."[54] This information reflected the fact that in the late Tokugawa era, the shogunal academy Shōheikō adopted certain procedures from the Chinese civil service examination system, which became the "ladder of success" for some students from hatamoto 旗本 families.[55]

3.2) Shimoda

Among the places Luo visited in Japan, Shimoda appealed to him most. He spent several days there visiting various sites. One thing that made a strong impression on him—and that was no doubt of great interest also to Williams and other Western readers of his journal—was that "the people are all Buddhists. All about, on the hill sides and by the seashore, are images of Buddha."[56] He went on,

> On the day after our arrival, the commodore went on shore, and took up his quarters in the Leaou-seen temple [Ryōsenji 了仙寺], on Fae-shun hill. There was a priest in charge of the temple called Yis-tsang, and two neophytes with him. Inside was a large hall for the worship of Buddha, and along the sides of it were many tombs-small structures made of stones-which it was the duty of the priests to sweep and keep clean, and where they presented daily offerings of flowers. The parties buried in them had, during their lifetime, made contributions to the temple. Behind the temple was a small pillared dome, built of stone, a small fish-pond, and many flowers and fruits.... Most of them [the women visiting the temple] were good looking, and before marriage their teeth are beautifully white. After they have children, however, they stain the teeth black with gall-nut powder.[57]

He touched on women's practice of teeth-blackening (*ohaguro* お歯黒), then continued with observations about one traditional type of house, the *nagaya* 長屋, and about *kon'yoku* 混浴 (mixed bathing).

> On another day I walked through the streets, and looked at the shops and houses. Some of them were built of bricks and covered with tiles, while others were merely huts of straw. They were mostly connected together, so that one could walk a long way, just passing from one house to another....Many of the men go about without any covering but the cummerbund, and the women think nothing of looking at obscene pictures [淫画 Ch. *yanhua*, Jp. *inga*]. There are bathing houses, to which both the sexes resort without distinction. The women came always in crowds to see a foreigner, but ran off when any of the two-sworded gentry [双刀人 Ch. *shuangdaoren*] made their appearance.[58]

Viewing these peaceful scenes in Shimoda, Luo could not help but contrast them with the chaos in contemporary China, where the Taiping rebellion was intensifying. He attributed the order that he saw in Japan to the effectiveness of the government there.

> Now every village (country) has that which is good in its order and government. Though Japan is a smaller country than China, yet robbing and oppression are unknown in it. The doors of the houses are for the most part but thin boards, or frames with paper pasted over them; yet a case of theft is hardly ever heard of. Surely these things are sufficient to prove the excellence and ability of its rulers.[59]

3.3) Ryukyu

If Shimoda seemed somewhat exotic to Luo, Ryukyu was more familiar. He discovered many similarities with Ming China:

> On the first day of our new year, (January 29,) I went on shore for a ramble, and finding a lot of boys on the street, gave them a few cash, which greatly delighted them. The people were very humble. Outside the doors of some of the houses congratulatory sentences [新春聯 Ch. *xinchunlian*] were posted up, as in China at the new year, but there was no excitement and no other sign of rejoicing. At Napa [Naha 那覇] I found a temple, and in the garden attached to it the burying place of the families of distinction. The surnames and names of the dead, and the time when they lived, were engraven on tombstones....The tombs of the common people are like those which obtained in China during the time of the Ming dynasty.[60]

Luo also remarked that "From the time of the Ming dynasty, its chief has received investiture from our emperor, having the title of king [世封王爵 Ch. *shifeng wangjue*]," [61] and mentioned that the dishes served at a Ryukyuan court banquet were nearly identical to those routinely used by the gentry class (to which he belonged) in China.[62]

III. Epilogue

Until the conclusion of the Kanagawa Treaty, and for a short time afterward, both the Americans and the Japanese were comfortable and confident in using the Chinese language as an official medium of communication. Williams preferred to use Chinese for documentation as well as for "brush conversation" on occasions when a Dutch interpreter was not available. Such a case occurred at Hakodate on 18 May 1854, when treaty privileges including the liberty to ramble had to be explained to the local officials. Williams noted in his journal, "The interview was rather tedious by reason of its having mostly to be written in Chinese, for I did not like to trust to talking."[63] He did realize later, however, that some confusion and misunderstanding might be attendant on interpretations when "the medium of communication is imperfect."[64]

On 13 June 1854, when Perry and Hayashi Fukusai were exchanging accusations at a meeting held in Shimoda—of spying and giving away obscene books on the part of the

Japanese, and of drunken frenzy and giving away Bibles on the part of the Americans—the "confusion and misunderstanding" caused by the imperfect medium of communication that Williams had realized unexpectedly became a serious political problem:

> A letter was brought in just received from Hokkaido via Yedo, inclosing some of our written conversations held there, and stating that Perry had declared that, if he could not have ten *ri* 里 about Hakodadi as limits [for ramble], he would make the Japanese to pay 10,000 cobans [***koban*** 小判, the gold coin of Edo period] as damages [caused by the delay in making the promised arrangements and the wasted sailing cost form Kanagawa to Hakodate]. The matter was placed in its true relations, but I could understand enough to hear them charge Lo and me with misinterpreting on these matters, and making trouble.[65]

According to Japanese records, Perry was perplexed at Hayashi's cross-questioning, trying to deny that he had made such a threat and to shift the blame for the misunderstanding to Luo alone. It seems doubtful that this was justified, however, when we think about Luo's function; he should have been taking Williams' dictation, and we can almost surely assume that he was. It is hard to believe that Perry's words could have been misunderstood by Williams and turned into a threat when written down by Luo. Precisely where the misunderstanding lay is not clear today, but it is not unreasonable to suppose that by blaming the Chinese translator, Perry was just attempting to save face.[66]

Shortly after this acrimonious diplomatic game was played to its end, the "Additional Regulations" concerning the limits of ramble in Hakodate and Shimoda were signed, on 20 June 1854. These Additional Regulations included a clause stipulating that U.S.-Japanese communications would henceforth be carried on in Japanese, English, and Dutch only, and Chinese would *not* be used in documentation. This provision was inserted at the insistence of Moriyama Einosuke 森山栄之助 (1820-71), the capable and vigorous chief Dutch interpreter for the bakufu.[67]

Unsatisfied with this clause and believing that Moriyama's ulterior motive in "discarding entirely the use of Chinese in all official communications" was "to keep the whole intercourse in his [own] hands," Williams persuaded the Japanese to accept a compromise on the language problem. No Chinese would be allowed "*when there was a Dutch interpreter*" on the scene (emphasis added). But this wording was largely symbolic; as a practical matter, Chinese was no longer recognized. Williams could only lament that "the Japanese hardly know how to behave towards foreigners; . . . the mutual ignorance of each other's language further opposes much intercourse."[68]

Chinese, the East Asian "Latin" and *lingua franca,* thus disappeared from official U.S.-Japan communications as a medium language in the last phase of Perry's expedition, after it had played a pivotal role in the major negotiations earlier on. Luo Sen did not record in his journal the incident of 13 June in which Perry had blamed him nor did he mention the suspension of use of Chinese as an official medium. We have no way to know his thoughts about these matters. The late historian Hora Tomio 洞富雄, who published a Japanese

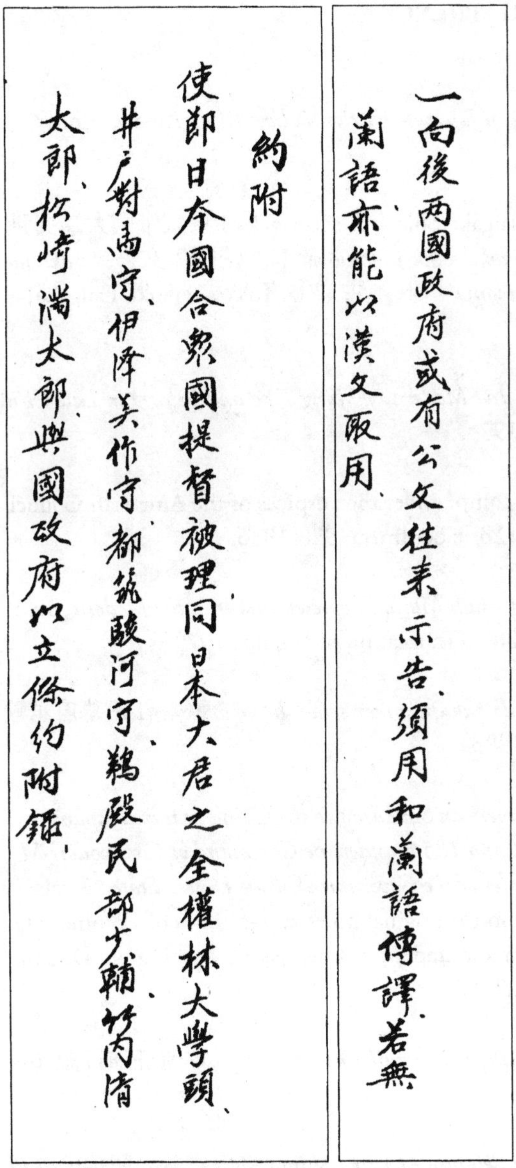
約附
使節日本國合衆國提督被理同日本大君之全權林大學頭、井戶對馬守、伊澤美作守、都筑駿河守、鵜殿民部少輔、竹内清太郎、松崎滿太郎、與國政府以立條約附錄、

一向後兩國政府或有公文往来示告、須用和蘭語傳譯、若無蘭語亦能以漢文取用、

Figures 5a (left) and 5b (right). Luo Sen's copy of the "Additional Regulations" specifying the role of the Dutch and Chinese languages. In the original, the passage in 5a appears before 5b. Source: Williams Family Papers, Yale University.

translation of Williams' journal in 1970, speculated that both Williams and Luo—especially Luo—must have felt relieved (*kiraku* 気楽) upon being released from the troublesome job (*mendō na shigoto* 面倒な仕事) of composing the Chinese documents.[69] But this is only Hora's guess.

Whatever Luo Sen's true feelings, it is clear that the Perry negotiations defined a pivotal point in the history of language use in diplomatic communication. Until the mid-nineteenth century, Japan was generally perceived by the West as closely related to China, as an integral part of the Chinese cultural sphere. This was one of Perry's primary reasons for his decision to choose Williams and to use Chinese as a medium for his approach to Japan. It was why, moreover, the British Foreign Office at the time sent diplomats and interpreters who had been appointed to positions in the British legation in Edo first to China; the assumption was that knowledge and experiences gained in China would be directly relevant and beneficial in performing duties in Japan. It was only after Japan's opening that the Westerners learned to appreciate the significance of the differences between the Chinese and Japanese languages.[70]

REFERENCES

Beasley 1955

W. G. Beasley. *Selected Documents on Japanese Foreign Policy, 1853-1868*. Oxford University Press, 1955.

BGKM

Tōkyō Teikoku Daigaku Bunka Daigaku Shiryō Hensan-gakari 東京帝國大學文科大學史料編纂掛. *Bakumatsu gaikoku kankei monjo* 幕末外國關係文書, *furoku no ichi* 附録之一. In *Dai Nihon komonjo* 大日本古文書. Tōkyō Teikoku Daigaku, 1913.

Cohen 1974

Paul A. Cohen. *Between Tradition and Modernity: Wang T'ao and Reform in Late Ch'ing China*. Harvard University Press, 1974.

Dictionary of American Biography

Dictionary of American Biography, comp. under the auspices of the American Council of Learned Societies. 20 vols. New York: Scribner, 1928-1936.

Fogel 2000

Joshua A. Fogel, trans. *Japan and China: Mutual Representations in the Modern Era*. Richmond, U.K.: Curzon Press, 2000. (Translation of Masuda 1979.)

Hashimoto 1993

Hashimoto Akihiko 橋本昭彦. *Edo bakufu shiken seido shi no kenkyū* 江戸幕府試験制度史の研究. Kazama Shobō, 1993.

Hawks 1856-57

Narrative of the Expedition of an American Squadron to the China Seas and Japan: Performed in the Years 1852, 1853, and 1854, under the Command of Commodore M. C. Perry, United States Navy, by Order of the Government of the United States. 3 vols. Compiled by Francis L. Hawks from the original notes and journals of Commodore Perry and his officers, at his request and under his supervision. Washington, D.C.: Beverley Tucker, Senate Printer, 1856-57.

Hora 1970

Hora Tomio 洞富雄, trans. *Perī Nihon ensei zuikō-ki* ペリー日本遠征随行記 (see Williams 1910). Yūshōdō, 1970.

Kamata 2002

Kamata Tōji 鎌田東二, *Hirayama Seisai to Meiji no Shintō* 平山省斎と明治の神道. Shunjūsha, 2002.

Kanai 1985

Kanai Madoka 金井圓, trans. *Perī Nihon ensei nikki* ペリー日本遠征日記 (see Pineau 1968). Yūshōdō, 1985.

Katō 1988

Katō Yūzō 加藤祐三. *Kurofune ihen: Perī no chōsen* 黒船異変：ペリーの挑戦. Iwanami Shoten, 1988.

Katō 1991

———. "Nichi-Bei washin jōyaku no shiyō gengo" 日米和親条約の使用言語. In *Geppō* 月報 20, included in NKST, vol. 1, *Kaikoku* 開国.

Katō 1993

———. "Bakumatsu ishin no kokusai seiji: Fukuzawa Yukichi no yakukō o tōshite" 幕末維新の国際政治：福沢諭吉の訳稿を通して. In *Fukuzawa Yukichi nenkan* 福沢諭吉年鑑 20 (1993).

Katō 1994

———. *Kurofune zengo no sekai* 黒船前後の世界. Chikuma Shobō, 1994; rev. and expanded from original Iwanami Shoten edition, 1985.

Kawasumi 1990

Kawasumi Tetsuo川澄哲夫, ed. *Nakahama Manjirō shūsei* 中浜万次郎集成. Shōgakukan, 1990.

Kitayama 1997

Kitayama Masashi 北山雅史, ed; Kabushiki Gaisha Ofisu Miyazaki 株式会社オフィス宮崎, trans. *Perī kantai Nihon ensei ki* ペリー艦隊日本遠征記. Eikō Kyōiku Bunka Kenkyūsho, 1997. (See Hawks 1856-57.)

Luo 1854

Luo Sen 羅森. "Journal of the Second Visit of Commodore Perry to Japan." In Hawks 1856-57, vol. 2. Trans. by S. Wells Williams from Luo's handwritten dairy and first published on 11 September 1854 in the *Overland Register and Price Current* of Hong Kong.

Luo 1854-55

———. *Riben riji*日本日記. In *Xiaer guanzhen* (published in the three issues of November and December 1854 and January 1855); also included in BGKM; Okada 1961 (Japanese translation by Nohara Shirō 野原四郎); Wang 1983; and Matsuura et al. 2004.

Luo 1971

Luo Xianglin 羅香林. "Xianggang kaibu chuqi wenjiao gongzuozhe Luo Xiangqiao shiji shushi" 香港開埠初期文教工作者羅向喬事蹟述釋. In *Bao Zunpeng xiansheng jinian lunwenji* 包遵彭先生紀念論文集. Taipei: Guoli lishi bowuguan, 1971.

Maehira 1991

Maehira Fusaaki 真栄平房昭. "Perī raikō-ji no kokusai kōryū to Chūgokujin Ra Shin: *Nihon nikki* no Ryūkyū kenbunroku o chūshin ni" ペリー来航時の国際交流と中国人羅森：日本日記の琉球見聞録を中心に, *Gengo* 言語 20:7 (1991).

Masuda 1979

Masuda Wataru 增田涉. *Seigaku tōzen to Chūgoku jijō* 西学東漸と中国事情. Iwanami Shoten, 1979.

Matsuura 2001

Matsuura Akira 松浦章 "*Kaji kanchin* [*Xiaer guanzhen*] ni miru Perī Nihon raikō: Ra Shin *Nihon nikki* zenshi" 「遐邇貫珍」に見るペリー日本来航：羅森「日

本日記」前史. In *Tōzai gakujutsu kenkyūsho sōritsu gojū-shūnen kinen ronbunshū* 関西大学東西学術研究所創立50周年論文集. Osaka: Kansai Daigaku Shuppanbu, 2001.

Matsuura et al. 2004

———, Uchida Keiichi 内田慶市, and Shen Guowei 沈国威. *Kaji kanchin [Xiaer guanzhen] no kenkyū: 1853-1856 Chinese Serial* 遐邇貫珍の研究. Osaka: Kansai Daigaku Shuppanbu, 2004.

Nakahama 1991

Nakahama Hiroshi 中浜博, ed. *Watakushi no Jon Manjirō; Shison ga akasu hyōryū hyakugojūnen-me no shinjitsu* 私のジョン万次郎：子孫が明かす漂流150年目の真実. Shōgakukan, 1991.

NKST

Nihon kindai shisō taikei 日本近代思想大系, ed. Katō Shūichi 加藤周一 et al. Iwanami Shoten, 1988-92.

Okada 1961

Okada Akio 岡田章雄, ed. *Gaikokujin no mita Nihon, dai-2 kan: Bakumatsu ishin* 外国人の見た日本・第二巻: 幕末維新. Chikuma Shobō, 1961.

Pineau 1968

Roger Pineau, ed. *The Japan Expedition 1852-1854: The Personal Journal of Commodore Matthew C. Perry*. Washington, D.C.: Smithsonian Institution Press, 1968.

Satow 1921

Ernest Satow. *A Diplomat in Japan*. London: Seeley, Service & Company, 1921.

Satō 1991

Satō Shin'ichi 佐藤慎一. "Aru hon'yakusha no shōgai" ある翻訳者の生涯. In *Geppō* 月報 22, included in NKST, vol. 15, *Hon'yaku no shisō* 翻訳の思想.

Spalding 1855

J. W. Spalding. *The Japan Expedition: Japan and around the World, an Account of Three Visits to the Japanese Empire*. New York: Redfield, 1855.

Statler 1963

Oliver Statler. *The Black Ship Scroll*. Rutland, Vt.: C. E. Tuttle, 1963.

Tao 2003a

Tao De-min 陶徳民. "Rashin ni yoseru Shōin no omoi" 羅森に寄せる松陰の想い. *Kansai Daigaku tsūshin* 関西大学通信308 (15 May 2003).

Tao 2003b

———. "Shimoda mikkō zengo ni okeru Shōin no Seiyō ninshiki: Beikoku ni nokoru 'Tōisho' o megutte" 下田密航前後における松陰の西洋認識: 米国に残る「投夷書」をめぐって, *Kan* 環 13 (May 2003).

Tao 2003c

———. "Shimoda goku ni okeru daini no 'Tōisho' ni tsuite; Shōin no kakugo ni taisuru Perī no kyōkan" 下田獄における第二の「投夷書」について: 松陰の覚

悟に対するペリーの共感, *Kan* 環14 (July 2003).

Tao 2004a

———. "Yoshida Shōin 'Tōisho' to no kaikō" 吉田松陰「投夷書」との邂逅, *Senryō (Kansai Daigaku Hakubutsukan ihō)* 阡陵 (関西大学博物館彙報) 48 (31 March 2004).

Tao 2004b

———. "Shijiu shiji zhongye Meiguo dui-Ri renquan waijiao de qishi: Xie zai Riben kaiguo 150 zhounian zhi ji" 十九世紀中葉美國對日人權外交的啟示: 寫在日本開國150周年之際, *Ershiyi shiji* 二十一世紀（香港中文大学中國文化研究所）82 (April 2004).

Teruya 2004

Teruya Yoshihiko 照屋善彦, *Ei senkyōi Betteruhaimu: Ryūkyū dendō no kunenkan* 英宣教医ベッテルハイム: 琉球伝道の九年間. Trans. by Yamaguchi Eitetsu 山口栄鉄 and Arakawa Yūkō 新川右好. Kyōto: Jinbun Shoin, 2004.

Wang 1983

Wang Xiaoqiu 王暁秋, ed. *Zaoqi Riben youji wuzhong* 早期日本游記五種. Changsha: Hunan renmin chubanshe, 1983.

Wang 1997

———. "Jindai Zhong-Ri wenhua jiaoliu de xianquzhe Luo Sen" 近代中日文化交流的先驅者羅森. In Wang, *Jindai Zhong-Ri guanxi-shi yanjiu* 近代中日關係史研究. Beijing: Zhongguo shehui kexue chubanshe, 1997

Wiley 1990

Peter B. Wiley. *Yankees in the Land of Gods: Commodore Perry and the Opening of Japan*. New York: Viking, 1990.

Williams 1856

S. Wells Williams. *A Tonic Dictionary of the Chinese Language in the Canton Dialect*. Canton: Office of the *Chinese Repository*, 1856.

Williams 1874

———. *A Syllabic Dictionary of the Chinese Language; Arranged According to the Wu-Fang Yuen Yin, with the Pronunciation of the Characters as Heard in Peking, Canton, Amoy, and Shanghai* 漢英韻府. Shanghai: American Presbyterian Mission Press, 1874.

Williams 1889

F. W. Williams, ed. *The Life and Letters of Samuel Wells Williams, LL.D.: Missionary, Diplomatist, Sinologue*. New York & London: G. P. Putnam's Sons, 1889.

Williams 1910

S. Wells Williams. *A Journal of the Perry Expedition to Japan (1853-1854) by S. Wells Williams*, ed. F. W. Williams. Yokohama: Kelly and Walsh, 1910. Also published as "A Journal of the Perry Expedition to Japan (1844-1854) by S. Wells Williams," ed. F. W. Williams. *Transactions of the Asiatic Society of Japan*, vol. 37, part 2 (1910).

Williams Family Papers

"Samuel Wells Williams Family Papers, 1824-1936." Manuscripts and Archives,

Sterling Memorial Library, Yale University.
Xiaer guanzhen
Xiaer guanzhen 遐邇貫珍 (Chinese Serial). Ed. W. H. Medhurst, C. B. Hillier, and J. Legge (successively). Anglo-Chinese College, Hong Kong (August 1853-May 1856).
Yoshida Shōin zenshū
Yoshida Shōin zenshū 吉田松陰全集. Ed. Yamaguchi-ken Kyōiku Kai 山口縣教育會. 10 vols. Iwanami Shoten, 1934-36.

Acknowledgments: An earlier version of this article was presented at the conference on "Misapprehensions and Prejudiced Views: Past and Present," co-organized by the International Research Center for Japanese Studies in Kyoto and the Center for Japanese Studies of the University of Hawai'i, held in Hawai'i in November 2000. I am grateful to Professors James Baxter, Martin Collcutt, Joshua Fogel, James McMullen, Saitō Makoto, and Sonoda Hidehiro in that conference for their kind comments and suggestions on the article. I also want to thank Professors Katō Yūzō, Shiba Yoshinobu, Oishi Keiichi, Wang Xiaoqiu, Umetani Noboru, Tanaka Akira, Miyaji Masato, Sasaki Suguru, Inoue Katsuo, Mitani Hiroshi, Maehira Fusaaki, Yokoyama Yoshinori, Hakoishi Hiroshi, Kirihara Kenshin, Yamaguchi Eitetsu, Kevin M. Doak, and John H. Schroeder, as well as Professor William W. Kelly of Yale and Messrs. Sasaki Tadao and Murakami Fumiki of Shimoda-shi, Tojima Akira and Muro Kenji of Yamaguchi-shi, Kondō Takahiko and Matsuda Teruo of Hagi-shi, Hoshina Tomoharu and Tominaga Ryūichi of Hakodate-shi, and Kubo Yasushi of Matsumae-chō for their kind advice and assistance during the course of my research on the topic.

NOTES

[1] The petition copied by Luo and the attached note written by Shoin himself are preserved in the Williams Family Papers at the Sterling Memorial Library, Yale University. See Tao 2003b and 2004a.
[2] Yoshida Shōin, "Kaikoroku" 回顧録, *Yoshida Shōin zenshū*, vol. 7, p. 388.
[3] J. W. Spalding was the officer who received Yoshida Shōin's petition at Shimoda. See chapter five of Spalding 1855.
[4] Yoshida Shōin, "Sangatsu nijūshichiya no ki" 三月二十七夜の記, *Yoshida Shōin zenshū*, vol. 7, pp. 413-18. In most of the English writing that mentions him, Luo Sen is called "Lo," following the Cantonese pronunciation of his name. His given name is generally omitted. I have decided to use the pinyin romanization of the *putonghua* pronunciation of his full name. This is the spelling used in the catalogues of, for example, the Library of Congress, the Harvard University Library, and the Yale University Library.
[5] Hawks 1856-57, vol. 1, p. 260.
[6] Ibid., p. 350. Katō Yūzō, emeritus professor of East Asian history and former president of Yokohama City University, has studied the issue of language usage in the U.S.-Japanese negotiations of the 1850s, particularly the use of kanbun as a medium for negotiation, for many years. See Katō 1988, pp. 126-27; Katō 1991; Katō 1993; and Katō 1994, pp. 399-406..
[7] Katō 1988, pp. 57, 66, 124-25. The bakufu could have used a Japanese who spoke English as interpreter in communicating directly with the Americans. Nakahama Manjirō 中浜万次郎 (1827-98),

a fisherman from the Tosa domain, had been saved by an American ship after an accident at sea in 1841. He was taken to the United States and received an education there before returning to Japan in 1851. Shortly after Perry's first visit, the bakufu had given him a post, and Egawa Hidetatsu 江川英竜 (1801-55; *kaibō gakari*, officer for maritime defense in 1853) had recommended that Nakahama should be assigned as interpreter for the negotiations with Perry's mission. Both the lord of Mito Tokugawa Nariaki 徳川斉昭 (1800-60) and the chief bakufu senior council member Abe Masahiro 阿部正弘 (1819-57) objected, however, having doubts about the loyalty of someone who had returned from overseas. They were afraid Nakahama might defect to the American side. See Nakahama 1991, pp. 106-107; Kawasumi 1990, p. 1100. For information on an interview conducted immediately before Nakahama Manjirō's employment by the bakufu, see Katō 1988, pp. 77-86.

[8] Williams 1889, p. 186.

[9] Ibid. Williams had joined the party on the *Morrison* in 1837 when that American commercial ship sailed to Japan in an attempt to repatriate several shipwrecked Japanese. He had learned some Japanese from one of them, and managed to prepare a translation of the Gospel of Matthew. In a pamphlet published in 1849, *Independent Oriental Nations and a Plan for Opening, Extending, and Protecting American Commerce in the East*, the American trader Aaron H. Palmer enthusiastically endorsed Williams as an American missionary and Sinologist who knew the Japanese language and collected Japan-related books and maps. Palmer also petitioned the president, through the secretary of state, about the potential of the Asian market. It might have been because of Palmer's mentioning his name that Williams was approached by Perry immediately after the latter arrived in Hong Kong in early April 1853. See Hora 1970, p. 531; Williams 1889, pp. 99-100.

[10] *Dictionary of American Biography*, vol. 20, p. 290. Perry indicated his appreciation of Williams' achievements by including him in a list of authorities: "Upon those subjects [China's commercial and social conditions] volumes have been recently published by persons whose long residence in the country has qualified them to impart information upon every topic connected with this singular empire. I may refer to the *Chinese Repository*; Martin's *China*; *China* by Davis; *Middle Kingdom* by S. Wells Williams; *Lettres edifiance et curieuses*; *A Visit to the Five Consular Ports*, by G. Smith, Lord Bishop of Victoria; *An American's Sojourn in Canton*; etc." See Pineau 1968, p. 55. Two of Williams' works on Chinese language were published before the Perry expedition: *Easy Lessons in Chinese, or Progressive Exercises to Facilitate the Study of that Language, Especially Adapted to the Canton Dialect* (Macao: Office of the Chinese Repository, 1842) and *Ying Hwá Yun-fú Lih-kiái* 英華韻府歷階 (An English and Chinese Vocabulary in the Court Dialect) (Macao: Office of the Chinese Repository, 1844). Within two years of his return from Japan he showed his mastery of Cantonese in *Ying wá fan wan tsüt iú* 英華分韻撮要 (A Tonic Dictionary of the Chinese Language in the Canton Dialect) (Canton: Office of the Chinese Repository, 1856).

[11] According to Williams' spelling, "Sieh" was for the Chinese character 薛. See Williams 1874, p. 798.

[12] Pineau 1968, p. 71.

[13] Williams 1910, p. 42. Also aboard the *Caprice*, the ship that brought Sieh's replacement, was another Chinese interpreter, a man named Qian Wen-qi 錢文琦, hired to aid B. Bettelheim, mentioned below in note 26. Bettelheim was as disappointed as Williams with his new assistant's Shanghai dialect. See Teruya 2004, p. 265.

[14] Williams 1910, p. 83.

[15] Luo 1971, pp. 289-293.

[16] Luo 1854, p. 400.

[17] It was not easy for Williams to secure a qualified Chinese assistant. Most Chinese scholars at that time concentrated their attention and effort on the civil service examinations, the tried and true path to career advancement. Few were willing to cooperate with Christian missionaries, partly because they held fast to traditional Sino-centric views and partly because anti-foreignism was strong and widespread following the Opium War. Yet there were some, if not many, candidates who had failed in their attempts to climb the "ladder of success" and had grown frustrated with the traditional examination system; they were ready to explore new opportunities at this unprecedented moment of Western impact. Men of learning of this mindset were exemplified by Hong Xiuquan 洪秀全, the leader of the Taiping rebellion, who claimed a personal (indeed genetic) relationship with the Christian God and Christ, and Wang Tao 王韜, the Shanghai "treaty-port intellectual" who helped a British missionary to translate the Bible and assisted the great missionary-scholar James Legge in his project of translating the Confucian classics. See Cohen 1974, p. 57; Satō 1991; and Katō 1994, pp. 356-57.

[18] Williams 1889, p. 212. For example, Luo thought that Williams's interest in botany had something to do with the teachings of Confucius: "The azalea is very abundant on the hills about, nor are other flowers rare. My friend made large collections of them, which he afterwards dried and preserved for future study, showing himself worthy to be a disciple of Confucius, who advised his followers to read the book of Odes, that they might become acquainted with the names of birds and animals, plants and trees." Luo 1854, p. 404.

[19] Williams 1889, p. 219.

[20] Williams 1889, pp. 229-30. Later in 1856, Perry further recommended Williams for the position of secretary and interpreter of the American legation in China. William remained in that post for two decades. In 1876, he returned to the U.S., where he served as a professor of Chinese language and literature at Yale and as president of the American Bible Society and the American Oriental Society.

[21] Luo 1854, pp. 404-5. I was told by the local historian Sasaki Tadao that a great earthquake occurred in late 1854, putting the whole town of Shimoda under water. This could explain why the fans that Luo inscribed cannot be found today.

[22] Luo 1854, p. 402.

[23] Yoshida Shōin, "Kaikoroku" 回顧録, *Yoshida Shōin zenshū*, vol. 7, p. 390.

[24] Luo 1854-55, See Wang 1983, p. 43.

[25] It was F. W. Williams who identified his father S. Wells Williams as the translator of Luo's journal for the *Hongkong Register*. Williams 1889, p. 218.

[26] *Xiaer guanzhen*, the earliest Chinese monthly in Hong Kong, was published by the Ying-Hua shuyuan 英華書院 (Anglo-Chinese College) between 1853 and 1856. A total of thirty-four issues appeared. See Matsuura 2001, pp. 393-411; Matsuura et al. 2004. The Chinese edition of Luo's journal included some information that was omitted from the English version, such as the purchases of commodities by the Americans according to the U.S.-Ryūkyū treaty and Luo's visit to the residence of Bernard Bettelheim (1811-1870), the British naval missionary and medical doctor in Ryūkyū whom Williams disliked. (The mutual distrust of the two missionaries was partly due to their different expertise in Chinese language ability: Williams could only speak Cantonese then, but Bettelheim could speak both Mandarin and the Ryukyu dialect and thus was able to serve as the interpreter for Perry in his negotiations with the prime minister of the Ryukyu Kingdom [see Teruya 2004, pp. 254-59].) Vice versa, the English version contained information that was missing in the Chinese edition, such that as Luo's discontent with the Qing government had led to his departure from Guangdong and moves to Hong Kong and Macao. We can speculate on the reasons for the differences; probably Luo needed to

return home to see his relatives from time to time, for example, and if the *Xiaer guanzhen* edition had included that information, it might have gotten him into trouble—Qing officials would have been far more likely to read the Chinese version than the English. I have searched for but not been able to find Luo's "actual original" manuscript diary in the Williams Family Papers. But whatever might have happened to the "actual original," Luo's account has yet to be thoroughly explored, at least in the English literature. One reason for the neglect was that its English version was marginalized early on; although it was included in Perry's official report (see Hawks 1856-57), it was relegated to a relatively obscure placement, in the appendix to the second volume. A Japanese translation of the English version was not published until quite recently (see Kitayama 1997). Among the few English studies that have mentioned Luo, Peter Wiley depicted him playing the role of fortune-teller, and cited his prediction of the future according to his reading of the movement of the clouds—symbols of great cosmic forces. Luo forecast that "the heavens prognosticate that our expedition will finally be successful, but difficulties will have to be overcome in the first." (Wiley 1990, pp. 377-378). Unlike the English version, the Chinese edition of Luo's journal has been known to the Japanese since the mid-nineteenth century. As Maehira Fusaaki noted, Yoshida Shōin had read Luo's journal when he was in jail, and Shimazu Nariakira 島津斉彬 (1809-58), the Lord of the Satsuma domain, had been an avid reader of *Xiaer guanzhen*, the periodical in which the journal was published (see Maehira 1991). The journal was included under the title of *Beikoku shisetsu zuikō Shinkokujin Ra Shin Nihon nikki* 米国使節随行清国人羅森日本日記 in the official compilation of late-Tokugawa foreign relations documents published in the early Taishō period (BGKM, pp. 633-647). In the 1960s Nohara Shirō completed a modern Japanese translation (see Okada 1961), and Hora Tomio examined the Japanese documents relevant to Luo and Perry's visits to Japan and Ryukyu when he was translating Williams's journal (Hora 1970). Concerning Japanese responses to the news about the Taiping rebellion brought by Luo Sen, Masuda Wataru made use of the Chinese interpreter's journal in 1972 (see "*Manshin kiji* to sono hissha; Wagakuni ni tsutaerareta Taihei tengoku ni tsuite" 『満清紀事』とその筆者：我が国に伝えられた「太平天国」について in Masuda 1979, pp. 280-320; Fogel 2000). Following Masuda's work, Wang Xiaoqiu republished the Chinese version in China and made a detailed study of it (see Wang 1983; Wang 1997). Recently, my colleagues at Kansai University Professors Matsuura Akira, Uchida Keiichi, and Shen Guowei published *Kaji kanchin* [*Xiaer guanzhen*] no kenkyû*: 1853-1856 Chinese Serial.* This includes a complete set of the periodical based on copies of the original edition in the collection of SOAS (property of the Council for World Mission), a newly-made index, and detailed explanations of the background and contents. This fine work will greatly facilitate future study of Luo Sen's journal, making it possible to place his observations in a broader contemporary context (see Shen Guowei, "*Kaji kanchin* kaidai" 『遐邇貫珍』解題, in Matsuura et al. 2004, pp. 91-128).

[27]Although a few private journals kept by the participants in the expedition began to appear from early 1855 on, Luo's was published prior to all the others. For a list of those publications, see Hora 1970, pp. 536-538.

[28] Luo 1854, p. 395.

[29] Williams 1889, p. 231.

[30] Luo 1854, p. 406.

[31] Ibid., p. 395. Hirayama's position at that time was known as *kachi metsuke* 徒目付. An able functionary and a faithful Confucianist, he was promoted in the 1867 to *wakadoshiyori* 若年寄 (bakufu junior councilor) and *gaikoku sōbugyō* 外国総奉行 (superintendent of foreign affairs). For a biographical sketch, see Kamata 2002, pp. 15-25, 247-52.

[32] Luo 1854, p. 398. For a Chinese poem by Hirayama composed in early 1854 when Perry had just returned to Japan, see Hora 1970, p. 252.
[33] Luo 1854, p. 398.
[34] Ibid., p. 399.
[35] Ibid., p. 398. It was the phrase "wonderful arts in the investigation of principles deceived the perverse" that the writer of the footnote singled out when he remarked that "it is not easy to make out [Hirayama's] meaning here."
[36] Beasley 1955, "The Background of Ideas" in his "Introduction," pp. 3-18.
[37] For example, to Perry's request for opening of trade relations, Hayashi Fukusai replied, "Although trade could contribute to the national interests through exchange of commodities, our Japanese nation has been self-sufficient with our own products and has no problems at all even though there are no foreign goods....You have stated earlier that the purpose of your visit was for salvage with concerns about [American] lives and ships. If that wish is obtained, your main purpose should be achieved. As for trade, it is an issue of profits but has nothing to do with people's lives" (see *Boku-I ōsetsu-roku* 墨夷応接録, BGKM, p. 541).
[38] Luo 1854, p. 399. It is said that when Hirayama was still in his late teens, he read *Yi-Luo yuanyuan-lu* 伊洛淵源録, a compilation by Zhu Xi 朱熹 of the words and deeds of such rigorous Neo-Confucian thinkers as Zhou Dunyi 周敦頤, Cheng Mingdao 程明道, and Cheng Yichuan 程伊川; by this study, Hirayama became a *dōgakusha* 道学者, that is, a faithful Confucian scholar. See Kamata 2002, p. 15.
[39] Ibid., p. 400.
[40] Luo even gave an introductory explanation of Christianity as a monotheism, using Confucian terminology (其所奉者獨一神，神即造化之主宰。所謂昭事上帝, 聿懷多福，其明徵歟), when he responded to a Japanese priest's question about the Americans' spiritual life. See Wang 1983, p. 38.
[41] Luo 1854, p. 404. Oliver Statler included a Japanese portrait of Luo in his book *The Black Ship Scroll*. Statler translated the Japanese description of the portrait: "A Chinese man from Canton, called Rasen, who came with the American ships. This man's duty was to translate documents on shipboard. He is also said to have served as interpreter in Chinese. This picture shows him as he strolled about Shimoda town checking prices on things and buying anything he thought cheap." He then explained that "Lo was an assistant to Williams," and observed that "Some of his shopping might have been to help Williams's friend Dr. Morrow. Morrow was collecting textiles and simple tools, and trying to find their true prices, rather than the inflated prices charged the Americans" (Statler 1963, p. 54).
[42] Luo 1854, pp. 405-6.
[43] Ibid., p. 401.
[44] Ibid., p. 395.
[45] Ibid., p. 405.
[46] Ibid., p. 397.
[47] Ibid., p. 400.
[48] Ibid., p. 401.
[49] Ibid.
[50] Ibid., p. 397.
[51] Wang 1983, p. 41; Luo 1854, p. 406.
[52] Wang 1983, p. 41. Entitled "Song Yuan Er shi An'xi" 送元二使安西, this famous Tang poem contains only four lines, of which two are very frequently cited (*quan jun geng jin yibei jiu, xi chu yangguan wu guren* 勸君更進一杯酒, 西出陽關無故人). For some reason, however, Williams did not

include it in the English version.
[53] Ibid., p. 42; Luo 1854, p. 406.
[54] Luo 1854, p. 400-1.
[55] For a detailed study of the examination systems, see Hashimoto 1993. Hashimoto writes that there had been some preliminary attempts to use examinations to select capable men for official appointment during Tokugawa Yoshimune's reign, but the real experiments were undertaken with the support of Matsudaira Sadanobu in the period of Kansei reforms, and the use of examinations continued to grow in the bakumatsu period.
[56] Luo 1854, p. 403.
[57] Ibid., p. 403.
[58] Ibid., p. 403.
[59] Ibid., p. 404.
[60] Ibid., p. 396.
[61] Ibid., p. 396.
[62] Ibid., p. 397.
[63] Williams 1910, p. 187.
[64] Williams' full comment on the disputes of 10 June concerning the limits of ramble in Shimoda was: "The incident was a good illustration of the ease with which a confusion of purposes may arise where the medium of communication is imperfect, and little pains taken to state the intention of each side. Isaboro accused me of misinterpreting and lying; so [the Flag Lieutenant] Mr. Bent was addressed in a long speech in Japanese and, to make the matter plainer, [Hori] Tatsunosuke [堀達之助] tried in vain to put it into English." Ibid., pp. 206-7.
[65] Ibid., pp. 208-10.
[66] For the background information, see Hora 1970, pp. 345-350.
[67] Moriyama had learned English from the American whaler and adventurer Ranald McDonald during the latter's exile in Nagasaki from 1848 to 1849, and had subsequently compiled an elementary English-Japanese dictionary. He also had experience in negotiating with Commander James Glynn, captain of the American battleship *Preble*, which sailed to Nagasaki in 1849 in an effort to take back fifteen American whalers who had become captives in Hokkaido. For commentary on Western diplomats' impressions of Moriyama, see Hora 1970, p. 197. If the proximate cause for the disappearance of Chinese was Moriyama's suggestion, there were some other reasons as well. The inefficiency of "brush conversation" was an apparent fact, and the problem became much more serious as the negotiations went into details. As for the Japanese side, the dramatically increased awareness of the importance of English as a diplomatic and international language must had been a major impulse for them to make such a move.
[68] Williams 1910, pp. 211.
[69] Hora 1970, p. 343.
[70] As the prominent British diplomat Ernest Satow (1843-1929) explained in his reminiscences, "Owing to the prevalence of a belief among those who then had the direction of our affairs in Japan that a knowledge of Chinese was a necessary primary to the study of Japanese, my fellow-student, R. A. Jamieson, and myself were joined early in 1862 by Russell Robertson, who also belonged to the Japan establishment. I pass over our sojourn there, which, though not without its own interest, was not long enough for me to gain any useful knowledge of China. But I learnt a few hundred Chinese characters which were of great help to me afterwards, and I even began the study of Manchu. . . . Our stay at the

Chinese capital was suddenly cut short by the arrival of a dispatch from Yedo, containing the original text of a Note from the Japanese Ministers, which it was found no Chinaman could decipher, much less understand. This was decisive of the question whether the short cut to Japanese lay through the Chinese language. I thought then, and still think, that though an acquaintance with Chinese characters may be found useful by the students of Japanese, it is no more indispensable than Latin is to a person who wish to acquire Italian and Spanish. We were consequently bundled off to Japan with the least possible delay" (Satow 1921, p. 18). Satow's opinion represented the younger generation in the West who formed balanced views of the relationship between Japanese and Chinese languages and cultures based on their own personal observations and experiences.

要旨

日米和親条約交渉における中国語の役割
ー羅森『日本日記』等に関する再考ー

陶徳民

徳川日本の鎖国政策の終焉をもたらした米日交渉において、日本語と英語だけでなく、中国語とオランダ語も公式な交渉用語であった。アメリカ側の首席通訳官Ｓ．Ｗ．ウィリアムズは中国における長期滞在の経験があり、日本語よりも中国語の専門家であった。外交文書や筆談記録の作成のため、彼は教養のある中国人助手の協力を必要とし、１８５４年ペリーの二回目の来航時に羅森を雇った。羅森は日本と琉球を訪問する時、日記をつけていたが、その日記の中国語版と英語版は香港帰着後まもなく出版された。英語版はのちにアメリカ議会の公式文書『ペリー艦隊日本遠征記』（１８５６－５７）にも収録された。羅森の日記は幕末期における日中文化関係に対する洞察や、日・中・米三国間の相互理解と誤解の諸相、および日米間の意思疎通における第三国の言語である中国語の介在の実態を披露した。

YOSHIDA SHŌIN'S ENCOUNTER WITH COMMODORE PERRY:

A REVIEW OF CULTURAL INTERACTION IN THE DAYS OF JAPAN'S OPENING*

De-min Tao**

The 150th anniversary of Commodore Matthew C. Perry's 1853 visit to Japan, commemorated on both sides of the Pacific with conferences, symposia and museum exhibitions, was a signal moment for reflection on the complex bonds between Japan and the United States over a century and a half. NHK, the public broadcasting giant, produced a special television program on Perry; the Constitution Memorial Museum,[1] as well as a number of local museums, mounted special exhibitions; several municipalities held special festivals, and scholars such as Mitani Hiroshi published new books to commemorate this historical event.[2] Quite coincidentally, reports of the (re) discovery of secret letters from Yoshida Shōin (1830–1859) , focused new attention on his failed attempt to steal out of Japan through Perry's flagship during the Commodore's return visit in 1854. A dozen of newspapers across Japan reported the find.[3]

I. Shōin's Letters to Perry

Yoshida Shōin was among the most charismatic figures in mid-19th century Japan, "a serious scholar of Confucianism," as Marius Jansen wrote, "a splendid teacher, and an impetuous

---

* A slightly different version of this paper was originally included in Martin Collcutt, Katō Mikio, and Ronald Toby, eds., *Japan and Its Worlds: Marius B. Jansen and the Internationalizatioin of Japanese Studies* (Tokyo: I-House Press, 2007). The author would like to express his gratitude to the editors for their kind advice for refining the paper.

** 陶徳民　関西大学文学部教授　関西大学ICISリーダー

1) The Kensei Kinenkan, operated by the Secretariat of Japan's House of Representatives.

2) Mitani Hiroshi, *Peri raikō* (Yoshikawa Kōbunkan, 2003).

3) For example, *Mainichi shinbun*, January 11 & August 8; *Yomiuri shinbun*, January 17; *Asahi shinbun*, April 5; *Kōbe shinbun*, July 16; *Ehime shinbun*, July 16; *Shizuoka shinbun*, July 19; *Kanagawa shinbun*, July 22; *Mutsu shinbun*, July 22; *Daily Tōhoku*, July 23; *Kushiro shinbun*, July 26.

activist,"[4] many of whose students went on to play leading roles in the military and political drama that brought down the Tokugawa regime.[5]

Shoin's letters to Perry made their way to Yale University as part of the Samuel Wells Williams Family Papers. Williams (1812–1884), First Interpreter for the Perry expedition, was an inveterate record keeper throughout his life. In his later years, he served Professor of Chinese language and literature at Yale, a position newly created to turn his decades-long experience in China as a missionary journalist and diplomat to advantage. I had encountered Shoin's letter, written in literary Chinese, and an attached note in Japanese epistolary style (*sōrōbun*), during a research trip to Yale in the fall of 2002.[6] Extremely interested in the fact that the initial U.S.-Japan negotiations were carried out in the two medium languages of Dutch and Chinese, I was

4) Marius B. Jansen, *the Making of Modern Japan* (Harvard University Press, 2000), p. 291. For a portrait of Shōin as teacher, see Richard Rubinger, *Private Academies of Tokugawa Japan* (Princeton University Press, 1989), pp. 191-207.

5) Classic biographies include Tokutomi Sohō, *Yoshida Shōin* (Min'yūsha, 1908; repr., Iwanami Shoten [*Iwanami bunko*, 33-154-1], 1980), and Kumura Toshio, *Yoshida Shōin* (Iwanami Shoten, 1936); for a more recent view, see Umihara Tōru, *Yoshida Shōin to Shōkason-juku* (Minerva Shobō, 1990). In English, perhaps the first biographical sketch was Robert Louis Stevenson's "Yoshida-Torajiro," in *Familiar Studies of Men and Books* (Chatto and Windus, 1882), pp. 172-191; H. J. J. M. van Straelen. *Yoshida Shōin, Forerunner of the Meiji Restoration: A Biographical Study* (Leiden: E.J. Brill, 1952), and Thomas M. Huber, *The Revolutionary Origins of Modern Japan* (Stanford University Press, 1981), pp. 7-91. Hirakawa Sukehiro discusses Shōin's "encounter with the West," and with the Perry expedition, in "Japan's Turn to the West," in Marius B. Jansen, ed., *The Cambridge History of Japan, Volume 5, The Nineteenth Century* (Cambridge University Press, 1989), pp. 449-452. This brief sketch of Shōin's life before he attempted to go abroad is drawn from these accounts.

6) The letter and the note had first been discovered by Yamaguchi Eitetsu, a Japanese Lecturer then at Yale, and introduced in *Rekishi to jinbutsu* in 1975 (No. 10), under the title, "Nemutte ita Shōin no missho"). An Okinawa-born leading scholar in the history of Ryūkyū's foreign relations, Yamaguchi had recently supervised the publication of a complete reprint of the 3-volume *Peri kantai Nihon ensei ki*, a translation of the original, official account of the expedition presented to the United States Congress, Francis L. Hawkes, ed. *Narrative of the Expedition of an American Squadron to the China Seas and Japan, Performed in the Years 1852, 1853, and 1854, under the Command of Commodore M. C. Perry, United States Navy, by Order of the Government of the United States* (3 v., A.O.P. Nicholson, 1856; below, "Hawkes, *Narrative*"). Hawkes compiled the *Narrative* "from the original notes and journals of Commodore Perry and his officers, at his request, and under his supervision." After finding the letter and the note at Yale, I traveled to Hagi, Yamaguchi, Hakodate, Matsumae, Tokyo, Yokohama, and Shimoda to visit local shrines, temples, museums, and libraries, and was able to find some new materials about the background of the letters and the incident. A detailed study entitled "Shimoda mikkō zengo ni okeru Shōin no Seiyō ninshiki: Beikoku ni nokoru Tō-i sho o megutte" was published in the special issue on the Meiji Revolution of the journal *Kan*, (No. 13, May 2003).

then searching for the Chinese documents generated during that process.[7] The letter in Chinese set forth Shōin's reasons for wanting to go abroad; while he was in prison, Shōin titled the letter "Tō-i sho," "A Letter to the Barbarians." The text follows, as it appears in Francis Hawkes's *Narrative of the Expedition*:[8]

Two scholars from Yedo, in Japan, present this letter for the inspection of the "high officers and those who manage affairs." Our attainments are few and trifling, as we ourselves are small and unimportant, so that we are abashed in coming before you; we are neither skilled in the use of arms, nor are we able to discourse upon the rules of strategy and military discipline; in trifling pursuits and idle pastimes our years and months have slipped away. We have, however, read in [Chinese] books, and learned a little by hearsay, what are the customs and education in Europe and America, and we have been for many years desirous of going over the "five great continents," but the laws of our country in all maritime points are very strict; for foreigners to come into the country, and for natives to go abroad, are both immutably forbidden. Our wish to visit other regions has consequently only "gone to and fro in our own breasts in continual agitation," like one's breathing being impeded or his walking cramped. Happily, the arrival of so many of your ships in these waters, and stay for so many days, which has given us opportunity to make a pleasing acquaintance and careful examination, so that we are fully assured of the kindness and liberality of your excellencies, and your regard for others, has also revived the thoughts of many years, and they are urgent for an exit.

This, then, is the time to carry the plan into execution, and we now secretly send you this private request, that you will take us on board your ships as they go out to sea; we can thus visit around in the five great continents, even if we do in this, slight the prohibitions of our own country. Lest those who have the management of affairs may feel some chagrin at this, in order to effect our desire, we are willing to serve in any way we can on board of the

7) Kato Yūzō, Emeritus Professor in East Asian history and the ex-president of Yokohama Municipal University, has explored the issue of using *Kanbun* (literary Chinese) as a medium in the negotiations. See his *Kurofune zengo no sekai* (Iwanami Shoten, 1985), pp. 354–360. *Kurofane lhen: Perī no chōsen* (Iwanami Shoten, 1988), , pp. 126-7; "Nichi-Bei washin jōyaku no shiyō gengo," *Geppō* no. 20, insert in *Nihon kindai shisō taikei*, vol. 1, *Kaikoku* (Iwanami Shoten, 1991); "Bakumatsu ishin no kokusai seiji: Fukuzawa Yukichi no yakkō o tsūjite," *Fukuzawa nenkan*, 20 (1993).

8) *Narrative*, 1: 420. The bracketed word "Chinese" before the word "books" in this English translation. But it has to be pointed out that the Chinese books introducing West world here meant the books published then in Chinese, including not only those compiled by Chinese editors, but also the those translated into Chinese by joint efforts of Chinese and Western scholars.

ships, and obey the orders given us. For doubtless it is, that when a lame man sees others walking he wishes to walk too; but how shall the pedestrian gratify his desires when he sees another one riding? We have all our lives been going hither to you, unable to get more than thirty degrees east and west, or twenty-five degrees north and south; but now when we see how you sail on the tempests and cleave the huge billows, going lightning speed thousands and myriads of miles, skirting along the five great continents, can it not be likened to the lame finding a plan for walking, and the pedestrian seeing a mode by which he can ride? If you who manage affairs will give our request your consideration, we will retain the sense of the favor; but the prohibitions of our country are still existent, and if this matter should become known we should uselessly see ourselves pursued and brought back for immediate execution without fail, and such a result would greatly grieve the deep humanity and kindness you all bear towards others. If you are willing to accede to this request, keep "wrapped in silence our error in making it" until you are about to leave, in order to avoid all risk of such serious danger to life; for when, by-and-bye, we come back, our countrymen will never think it worth while to investigate bygone doings. Although our words have only loosely let our thoughts leak out, yet truly they are sincere; and if your excellencies are pleased to regard them kindly, do not doubt them nor oppose our wishes. We together pay our respects in handing this in. April 11. (March 8, 1854 for the lunar calendar).

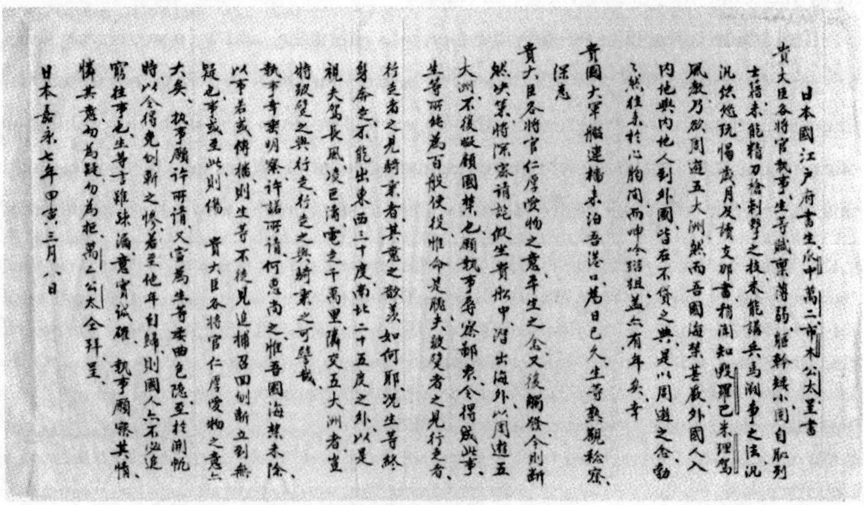
日本國江戶府書生、瓜中萬二、市木公太呈書
貴大臣各將官執事、生等賦稟薄弱、軀幹矮小、固自恥列
士籍、未能精刀槍擊刺之技、未能講兵馬鬬爭之法、汎
汎悠悠、玩愒歲月、及讀支那書、稍聞知歐羅巴米理駕
風教、乃欲周遊五大洲、然而吾國海禁甚嚴、外國人入
内地、與内地人到外國、皆在不貸之典、是以周遊之念勃
勃然往來於心胸間、而呻吟躡躋、蓋亦有年矣、幸
貴國大軍艦連檣來泊吾港口、為日已久、生等熟視稔察、
深感
貴大臣各將官仁厚愛物之意、平生之念又復觸發、今則斷
然決策、將深密請託、假坐貴船中、潛出海外、以周遊五
大洲、不復顧國禁也、願執事辱察鄙衷、令得成此事、
生等所能為百般使役、惟命是聽、夫跛躄者之見行走者、
行走者之見騎乘者、其意之欲羨、如何耶、況生等終
身奔走、不能出東西三十度、南北二十五度之外、以是
視夫駕長風、凌巨濤、電走千萬里、隣交五大洲者、豈
特跛躄之與行走、行走之與騎乘之可譬哉、
執事幸垂明察、許諾所請、何恩尚之、惟吾國海禁未除、
此事若或傳播、則生等不徒見追捕、召回、斬立刻無
疑也、事或至此、則傷　貴大臣各將官仁厚愛物之意亦
大矣、執事願許所請、又當為生等委曲包隱、至於開帆
時、以全得免斬刑之慘、若至他年歸、則國人亦不必追
窮往事也、生等言雖疏漏、意實誠確、執事願察其情、
憐其意、勿為疑、勿為拒、萬二、公太仝拜呈、
日本嘉永七年甲寅三月八日

漢文「投夷書」

My analysis of the handwriting shows that the letter in the Sterling Library was actually a fair copy made by Williams' Chinese assistant Luo Sen (1821–1899), a learned gentleman who had fought as a militia leader in Canton during the Opium War and escaped afterward to Hong Kong, where he pursued business opportunities. Luo was quite popular in Yokohama, Shimoda, and Hakodate in Spring 1854 for inscribing his extempore verse with elegant calligraphy on hundreds of blank paper fans, in response overwhelming demand from Japanese officers and commoners. Four of Luo's fans survive in the Municipal Museum of Hakodate and the Local Museum of Matsumae in Hokkaidō.[9] I have not yet gone Perry's own expedition-related documents at the National Archives in Washington, D.C.; I hope that Shōin's original letter may still remain there along with an attached Chinese note indicating how he planned to meet the Americans,[10] for both of them were translated into English and included in Williams's personal diary.[11]

By contrast, the attached note in Japanese laying out way Shōin planned to meet the Americans was very likely in Shōin's own hand; it was in a style unusual in *bakumatsu* documents, in that that each line had a phonetic transcription in *katakana* at the right side. Apparently Williams was not able to fully understand the note and therefore decided to keep it in his own folder, for there was no English translation of it. But he made use of it to get the pronunciation of the two aliases in the note: Yoshida went by 'Kawanouchi Manji,' based the Yoshida family crest, a 卍 (*manji*) against a gourd shape, while his follower Kaneko Shigenosuke (1831–1855) went by 'Ichigi Kōda.' Williams used the same technique in the English translation of the Chinese letter. But in a slip of the brush, when Shōin wrote the *katakana* for Kaneko's alias surname, the *katakana* "chi" looked like a "sa," so it appears in the English translation as

---

9) Williams wrote that Luo "takes a lively interest in all our operations and gets on admirably with the natives; he is, indeed, the most learned Chinaman they have ever seen, and their delight in showing off to him their attainments in Chinese is increased when he turns a graceful verse or two for them upon a fan; of these he has written, I should think, more than half a thousand since coming to Japan, and nothing pleases him like being asked to do so." F. W. Williams, ed., *The Life and Letters of Samuel Wells Williams, LL.D.: Missionary, Diplomatist, Sinologue*. G.P. Putnam's Sons, 1889, p. 219.

10) The note in the *Narrative* (vol. 1 , p. 420) reads, "The enclosed letter contains the earnest request we have had for many days, and which we tried in many ways to get off to you at Yoku-hama, in a fishing boat, by night; but the cruisers were too thick, and none others were allowed to come alongside, so that we were in great uncertainty how to act. Hearing that the ships were coming to S[h]imoda we have come to take our chance, intending to get a small boat and go off to the ships, but have not succeeded. Trusting your worships will agree, we will, tomorrow night, after all is quiet, be at Kakizaki in a small boat, near the shore, where there are no houses. There we greatly hope you to meet us and take us away, and thus bring our hopes to fruition. April 25."

11) S.W. Williams, *A Journal of the Perry Expedition to Japan, 1853–1854*, ed. F.W. Williams (Kelly & Walsh, 1910). Below '*Journal*.' See also the version in the congressional report, Hawkes, *Narrative*.

"Isagi" instead of "Ichigi."

My translation of the note follows:[12)]

> We two want to see the world. Please allow us to board your ship in secret. Going to foreign countries, however, is strictly prohibited in Japan. We would be in deep trouble if you tell the Japanese officers about this. If your admiral were to consent to our intention, we hope that you will send a barge at midnight tomorrow to the shore of the Kakizaki village to meet us.
>
> April 19, 1854 (Kinoetora, March 22) Ichigi Kōda, Kwanouchi Manji

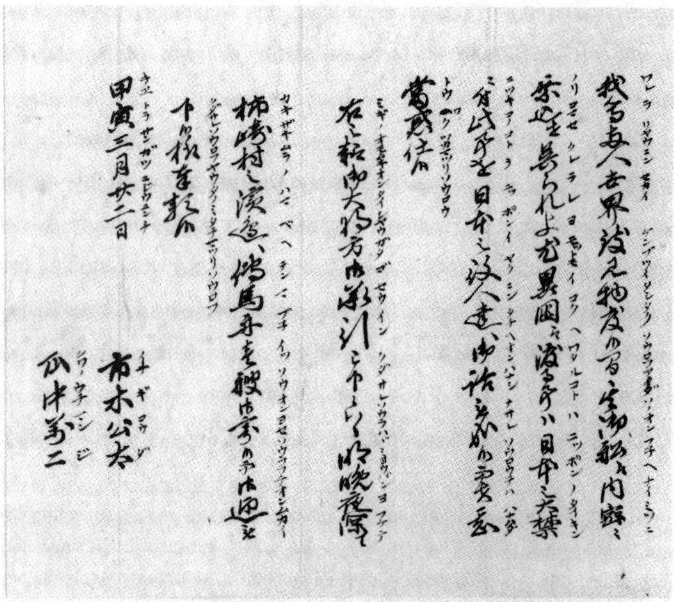

候文（和文）依頼書

Shōin's second letter in Chinese, also a fair copy by Luo Sun, was discovered during my research of the *Samuel Wells Williams Family Papers* in the spring of 2003.[13)] It seems to me that Williams prized it so much as to paste it carefully on the inner side of the back cover of his own handwritten Journal. According to the *Narrative*, the original letter, written on a piece of board was received from Shōin when he and Kaneko were imprisoned in Shimoda. They were

12) See my detailed study of this letter, "Shimoda goku ni okeru dai-ni no To-i sho ni tsuite: Shōin no kakugo ni taisuru Perī-gawa no kyōkan," in *Kan*, 14 (July 2003).

13) Ibid.

"immured in one of the usual places of confinement, a kind of cage, barred in front and very restricted in capacity....They seemed to bear their misfortune with great equanimity, and were greatly pleased apparently with the visit of the American officers, in whose eyes they evidently were desirous of appearing to advantage. On one of the visitors approaching the cage, the Japanese wrote on a piece of board that was handed to them the following, which, as a remarkable specimen of philosophical resignation under circumstances which would have tried the stoicism of Cato, deserves a record."[14)]

Williams' English translation of the letter, included in the *Journal*, the *Narrative*, and the memoirs of other expedition participants (there were at least eight versions of Japanese translation of the letter based on them, from Tokutomi Sohō's biography of Shōin, in 1908 to the 2002 Japanese translation of J. Willett Spalding's *The Japan Expedition: Japan and around the World*),[15)] but none of the translators were aware of the existence of a fair copy of this Chinese original), ran as follows.

When a hero fails in his purpose, his acts are then regarded as those of a villain and robber. In public have we been seized and pinioned and caged for many days. The village elders and head men treat us disdainfully, their oppressions being grievous indeed. Therefore, looking up while yet we have nothing wherewith to reproach ourselves, it must now be seen whether a hero will prove himself to be one indeed. Regarding the liberty of going through the sixty States as not enough for our desires, we wished to make the circuit of the five great continents. This was our hearts' wish for a long time. Suddenly our plans are defeated, and we find ourselves in a half sized house, where eating, resting, sitting, and sleeping are difficult; how can we find our exit from this place? Weeping, we seem as fools;

---

14) Hawkes, *Narrative*, 1: 422. From the comparison made with Cato Minor (95–46 BC), the tragic hero who committed suicide in Utica, Africa rather than falling alive into the hands of Caesar, it seemed that the Americans were deeply affected by Shōin's "letter on the board"and deeply concerned about his fate. The size of the cage, as Williams measured it, "was about six feet long by three wide and four and a half high, quite large enough to sit and sleep in, and entered by crawling through a low door; it is probably just such a cage as McCoy and his fellows were at last shut up in." *Journal*, 1: 181–2. Isaac McCoy (1784–1846) was a Baptist missionary, surveyor and U.S. Indian agent, and the association by similarity made by Williams here was apparently a criticism of the inhuman treatment of prisoners in Japan then. On McCoy, see George A. Schultz, *An Indian Canaan: Isaac McCoy and the Vision of an Indian State* (University of Oklahoma Press, 1972).

15) Tokutomi Sohō, *Yoshida Shōin* (Min'yūsha, 1908); J. Willett Spalding's *The Japan Expedition: Japan and around the World* (London: Sampson Low, 1856); Shimada Yuriko, tr., *Suporudingu Nihon ensei-ki*, in *Shin-ikoku sōsho* (36 v., Yūshōdō Shuppan, 1968-2005), pt. 3, v. 4.

laughing, as rogues. Alas ! for us; silent we can only be. [16)]

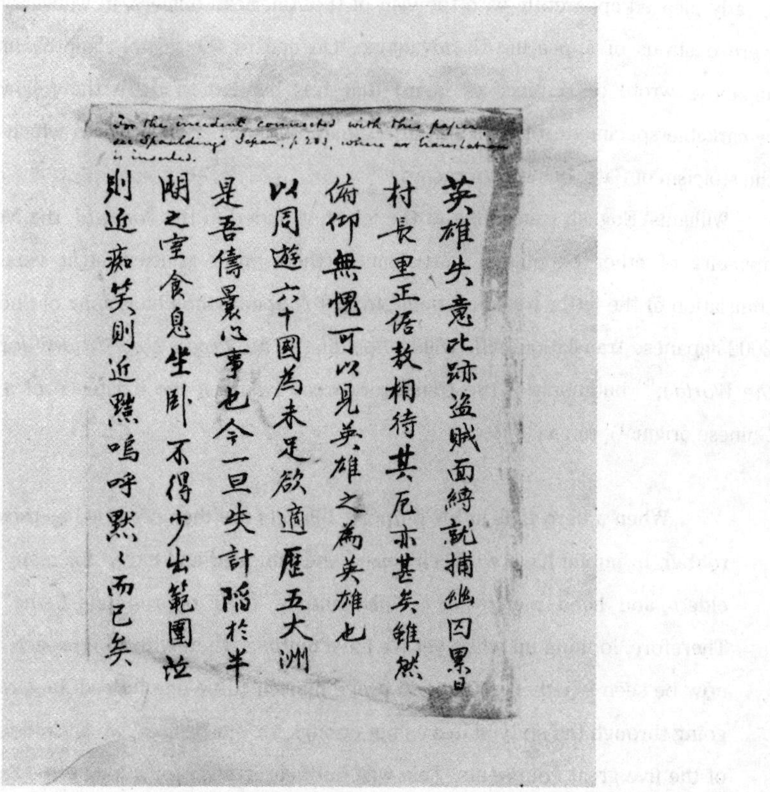
For the incident connected with this paper see Spalding's Japan, p. 283, where a translation is inserted.

英雄失意兮跡盜賊面縛就捕幽囚累日
村長里正倨傲相待其厄亦甚矣雖然
俯仰無愧可以見英雄之為英雄也
以周遊六十國為未足欲適歷五大洲
是吾儕曩昔之事也今一旦失計陷於半
閉之室食息坐臥不得少出範圍泣
則近痴笑則近黠嗚呼默々而已矣

第二の投夷書

But since Shōin's autograph original is no longer extant, this fair copy made by Luo Sen in the *Journal* became the only evidence to trace its original text. By a close examination of the text, however, I found that there were two mistakes in Williams's translation. First, the classical Chinese word *mianfu* (面縛, J. *menbaku*) means one's two hands are roped in the back while his face is toward the front, but it was translated into "in public have we been seized and pinioned." This mistranslation was associated with such assumed description in the Narrative that "the poor fellows had been immediately pursued upon its being discovered that they had visited the ships, and after a few days they were pounced upon and lodged in prison."[17)] But the truth was that Shōin and Kaneko, after being sent back ashore, immediately surrendered

16) Hawkes, *Narrative*, 1: 422f.

17) Ibid., 1: 422.

themselves to the nanushi, the village head, and were then transferred to the local authority and imprisoned.[18)]

Another error in Williams's translation leads to a misunderstanding of Shōin's self-image. The conditional clause, "looking while yet we have nothing where with to reproach ourselves" should have been followed by a conclusive clause in the present perfect tense, but Williams used the future tense saying that "it must now be seen whether a hero will prove himself to be one indeed." In other words, while Williams seemed to think that Shōin's greatest test still lay ahead, it is clear that Shōin already regarded himself a hero.

II. Shōin: A Terrorist or a Strategist?

Recently, Kawaguchi Masaaki has, based on a selective reading of some of Shōin's remarks made after his failed attempt to leave Japan with Perry's fleet, that Shōin's real purpose in seeking to board the Black Ship was to kill Perry.[19)] It is true that as a historical figure, Shōin had a fairly ambivalent attitude toward America during his short life, but at the time of Perry's second visit, he was by no means the kind of simple-minded terrorist Kawaguchi seems to envision.

First and foremost, Shōin was a military strategist. From early childhood he had absorbed the intensive education expected of a future military instructor for the Hagi domain. When he was appointed an instructor of military science in 1848, at the age of nineteen *sai*, he was entrusted by the domain to make a strategic defense plan and started an annual series of lectures for his lord on military strategy. It was, after all, only a few years since China's defeat in the Opium War, and the expanding Western presence in East Asia was then a major concern of Japan's leaders, as well as of intellectuals across the country.

By the time of Perry's second expedition, Shōin was among the most well-informed in Japan about domestic and international conditions, through extensive reading, travel around the country, and personal encounters with fellow intellectuals nationwide. By this time, his study with Sakuma Shōzan, a leading scholar of the Dutch and Chinese learning, as well as a military strategist and gunnery engineer in Edo, proved especially important to his rapidly evolving world-view. After Perry's first visit, Shōzan had tried to persuade the high-ranking bakufu officer Kawaji Toshiakira to send a mission overseas to purchase Western warships. As one of Shōzan's leading disciples, Shōin was supposed to join that mission. But since the bakufu later abandoned the

---

18) Yoshida, *Kaikoroku*, in *Yoshida Shōin Zenshu (YSZ)*, 7: 397.

19) Kawaguchi Masaaki, "Shimoda tokai kō," in Tanaka Akira, ed., *Bakumatsu Ishin no shakai to shisō*, pp. 126–51. Tokyo: Yoshikawa Kōbunkan, 1999.

mission, Shōzan encouraged Shōin to steal out of the country via the Russian or American steamers then visiting Japan, so that he could study the military technology of the West at first hand.

Both men knew well that both the bakufu and the domains urgently needed talented men to direct defense projects. The bakufu was saw the danger as so great it resorted to the unprecedented employment of commoner, Nakahama Manjirō (a.k.a. "John Manjirō," 1827–1898), a Tosa fisherman who had been shipwrecked, and later received an elementary education in America before returning Japan. Moreover, Shōin was then a rōnin, having lost both status and stipend because he had gone absent without the domain's permission. With no formal ties to the domain, he was determined to adventure to the outside world to acquire new knowledge and skills, believing that this was the path to recover his status. Given these greater motivations, it is hard to believe that he could simultaneously commit himself to the impractical plan of murdering Perry, his hoped-for path out of Japan.

While the seriousness of Shōin's purpose—and Shōin was nothing if not a serious man—can be inferred from a glance at the short list of books he had prepared to take with him overseas, including the *Classic of Filial Piety*, *References to the Selected Tang Poems* and two Dutch-Japanese dictionaries, they are articulated much more clearly in Shōin's *Yūshūroku*, his "confessional account of the events during the years of 1853 and 1854" written in the Hagi prison at the suggestion of Shōzan.

> Although the Dutch learning has prevailed, no one can read the books from Russia, America, and England. Now that the ships of foreign countries came to our country, how can we remain without knowing their languages? Moreover, different countries have different ideas on technical styles and instrumental systems. Though their outlines could be known through the Dutch translations, it can't be better than searching for each country's situation through its own books. Excellent students should be now dispatched to foreign countries to buy their books and learn their arts, and having those returned students to serve as school teachers.[20)]

Here, Shōin actually spells out the important message that "Dutch learning" (*Rangaku*) was no long sufficient to cope with the new challenges from Russia, America and England, and that therefore brilliant students must be sent directly to those countries and be employed as school teachers upon their return in order to absorb and master the latest in Western systems and technology.

20) Yūshūroku, in *YSZ*, 3: 49-50.

As is well known, Fukuzawa Yukichi credited his puzzlement at the signs in English on shops in the newly opened trading port Yokohama in 1859, as the reason he decided to study English. Fukuzawa's resolution has been repeatedly cited as an early symbol of Japan's shift of focus from Dutch to Anglo-American learning[21). Compared with the Shōin's argument in *Yūshūroku*, not to mention his action in attempting to go to America, however, it would not be an exaggeration to say that it was Shōin, rather than Fukuzawa, who first exemplified this new direction in Japan's Western learning.

It should be kept in mind, at the same time, that Shōin's thoughts regarding Western learning were basically derived form Shōzan, who viewed the West as a world of constant competition, and frequent changes of leadership, and believed that the only way to hold the barbariansat bay was to learn the barbarians' advanced military technology, a strategy earlier proposed by China's Wei Yuan in his *Haiguo tuzhi* (Illustrated Gazetteer of the Maritime Kingdoms), written immediately after China's defeat in the Opium War.[22)] For example, in his letter to an artillery specialist written on April 26, 1854, a day after Shōin's failure, Shōzan made the following analysis.

> You must know that Russia's former ruler Peter the Great learned from the Dutch, and eventually became no inferior to the Dutch; and the Northern Americans learned from the Englishmen, and finally defeated the Englishmen. Anyway, it is my opinion that there is no option but to use the barbarians' technology to hold the barbarians. If they have big battleships, we have to make big battleships too. If they have big canons, we have to make big canons, too.[23)]

What differentiated mentor and disciple, however, was that Shōin suggested in early 1855 a long-term strategy for Japan's survival and future supremacy.

---

21) "I had been striving with all my powers for many years to learn the Dutch language. And now when I had reason to believe myself one of the best in the country, I found that I could not even read the signs of merchants who had come to trade with us from foreign lands. It was a bitter disappointment, but I knew it was no time to be downhearted. Those signs must have been either in English or in French—probably English, for I had had inklings that English was the most widely used language. A treaty with the two English-speaking countries had just been concluded. As certain as day, English was to be the most useful language of the future. I realized that a man would lave to be able to read and converse in English to be recognized as a scholar in Western subjects in the coming time. In my disappointment my spirit was low, but I knew that it was not the time to be sitting still." Eiichi Kiyooka, trans., *The Autobiography of Yukichi Fukuzawa* (Columbia University Press, 1960), p. 98.

22) Shōzan had read Wei Yuan's *Haiguo tuzhi* and *Shengwu ji*, copies of which were circulating in Japan. Knowing that Wei was also a military strategist, Shōzan called him "a comrade overseas." *Seikenroku*, in *Nihon shisō taikei*, vol. 55, *Watanabe Kazan, Takano Chōei, Sakuma Shōzan, Yokoi Shōnan, Hashimoto Sanai* (Iwanami Shoten, 1971), pp. 251–2.

23) "Letter to Kotera Jōnosuke," in *Shōzan zenshū*, (2 v., Shōbunkan, 1913), 2: 545.

Now that the treaties with Russia and America have been settled, we should never violate them, which would cause the barbarians to lose faith in us. Rather, we should firmly observe them and treasure the faithfulness. In the meantime, try to strengthen our national power and control Korea, Manchuria, and China, which are easy to conquer, so as to cover the losses [we will incur] in trade with Russia and America with the land taken from Korea and Manchuria.

Although we had a big chance in 1853 and 1854, we have lost it without any accomplishments. But that is already in the past. To form a strategy for today, we should keep friendship with America and Russia in order to hold them, and seize this opportunity to enrich our nation and strengthen our military force, to tap Ezo, take away Manchuria, and incorporate Korea into southern Japan, then crush America and defeat Europe, so as to be invincible. It should not be a deep regret that we lost the chance in 1853 and 1854.[24)]

Here, Shōin showed a perfect roadmap to be followed by modern Japan. If taking both of Shōin's strategic suggestions of learning from America now and defeating America in the future into account, one may be easily aware that his first Chinese letter was written in an extreme dilemmatic situation: though he wished to go abroad for learning advanced military technology to defend his motherland, his government prohibited him from going; in order to defeat the Americans who intruded into Japan by gunboats, he had to first bow before Commodore Perry so as to get a passage to travel overseas. So, as a Japanese scholar has analyzed, Shōin's remarks on killing Perry made after his failed action might well have been a reveal of his grievance against Perry who treated him mercilessly regardless of his sincere expression of admiration for American military power and his repeated appeal to the humanity of the Americans.[25)]

III. Perry's Dilemma: National Interest vs. Human Rights

It was on April 25th, 1854, at around two o'clock a.m., that Shōin and Kaneko finally clambered onto the deck of the Powhatan after an exhausting struggle with wind, waves, and the American guards who tried to stop them from climbing aboard. Coming less than a month after the US-Japan Treaty of Peace and Amity was signed on March 31st, this incident put Perry in a dilemma of making a choice between the American national interest and human rights. And the

24) Quoted in Tokutomi, *Yoshida Shōin*, reprint of 1893 edition, with commentary by Uete Michiari (Tokyo: Iwanami Shoten, 2001), pp. 115–6.

25) Koyano Atsushi, "Bakumatsu no seiji shisō bunsho: Yoshida Shōin no To-i sho," in Ōsawa Yoshihiro, ed., *Tekisuto no hakken*, v. 6 of *Sōsho hikaku bungaku hikaku bunka* (6 v., Chuō Kōronsha, 1994).

incident did not end immediately, but evolved into a drama in three acts: importuning, investigation, and imprisonment.

The first act, according to the *Narrative*, was as follows.

> On their reaching the deck, the officer informed the Commodore of their presence, who sent his interpreter to confer with them and learn the purpose of their untimely visit. They frankly confessed that their object was to be taken to the United States, where they might gratify their desire of travelling, and seeing the world. They were now recognised as the two men who had met the officers on shore and given one of them the letter. . . . They were educated men, and wrote the mandarin Chinese with fluency and apparent elegance, and their manners were courteous and highly refined. The Commodore, on learning the purpose of their visit, sent word that he regretted that he was unable to receive them, as he would like very much to take some Japanese to America with him. He, however, was compelled to refuse them until they received permission from their government, for seeking which they would have ample opportunity, as the squadron would remain in the harbor of Simoda for some time longer. They were greatly disturbed by this answer of the Commodore, and declaring that if they returned to the land they would lose their heads, earnestly implored to be allowed to remain. The prayer was firmly but kindly refused. A long discussion ensued, in the course of which they urged every possible argument in their favor, and continued to appeal to the humanity of the Americans. A boat was now lowered, and after some mild resistance on their part to being sent off, they descended the gangway piteously deploring their fate, and were landed at a spot near where it was supposed their boat might have drifted.[26)]

Hawkes's description of the two-hour interview was basically identical to Shōin's account in the *Kaikoroku*, recording his negotiations with Williams, and the key message from Williams that, since the Commodore Perry and Hayashi Daigaku no kami had made a treaty between the two countries at Yokohama, so he and Kaneko could not be received here privately.[27)] However, Shōin did not know that Perry was not in bed then but in active charge of the interview, because he was facing Williams alone. Sometimes by speaking Japanese words, sometimes by writing Chinese words, the conversation was an uneasy one. During the interview, Shōin asked to meet with Luo

---

26) Hawkes, *Narrative*, 1: 421.

27) Kaikoroku, in *YSZ*, 7: 415. Hayashi Fukusai (1800-59) was the shogun's chief Confucian lecturer, and head of the bakufu-sponsored Confucian academy. More to the point, even before the first Perry expedition he had prepared for the bakufu a compilation of its diplomatic precedents from Ieyasu to the present day, *Tsūkō ichiran* (8 v., Kokusho Kankōkai, 1914).

Sen in order to obtain a more smooth and effective communication in writing Chinese, and also asked to get back the letter and notes now that his appeal had been denied, but both requests were gently refused. Needless to say, there were some suspicions on the American side about the real purpose of Shōin and Kaneko. As Williams noted in his *Journal*, they "were probably just what they said they were, eagerly wishing to go to the United States, though some said they were thieves, others spies sent by officers to see how far we would keep the Treaty, and others that they were refugees from justice."[28] But after all it was apparent that in Perry's mind about the national interest had a prior claim over the concern about human right, even though Shōin had expressed the fear that he would lose his head if he was sent back ashore.

The second act began the following day, when a Japanese official interpreter came out to Perry's ship to investigate the commotion Shōin and Kaneko had stirred up. Williams recorded the scene in his *Journal*:

> The Commodore, upon hearing of the visit of the interpreter and apparent anxiety of Japanese authorities in regard to the conduct of the two strange visitors to the ships, sent an officer on shore in order to quiet the excitement which had been created, and to interpose as far as possible in behalf of the poor fellows, who it was certain would be pursued with the utmost rigor of Japanese law. The authorities were thanked for the solicitude they had expressed lest the Americans should have been inconvenienced by any of their people, and assured that they need not trouble themselves for a moment with the thought that so slight a matter had been considered otherwise than a mere trivial occurrence unworthy of any investigation. The Japanese were further informed that they need give themselves no anxiety for the future, as none of their countrymen should be received on board the American ships without the consent of the authorities, as the Commodore and his officers were not disposed to take advantage of their confidence or act in any way that would be inconsistent with the spirit of the treaty. If the Commodore had felt himself at liberty to indulge his feelings, he would have gladly given a refuge on board his ship to the poor Japanese, who apparently sought to escape from the country from the desire of gratifying a liberal curiosity, which had

28) Williams, *Journal*, p. 175.

been stimulated by the presence of the Americans in Japan.[29)]

Perry recognized how serious the situation had become, even though, despite their warning about the unavoidable persecution they faced, he had decided to send Shōin and Kaneko back. Therefore, he saw to it that the two men reached shore in safety, and tried to persuade the Japanese authorities to play the things down, "hop[ing] to mitigate the punishment to which it was amenable." In the meantime, Perry reassured the Japanese authorities that he would not violate the spirit of the new treaty by giving refuge to any Japanese stowaways. Because, after all, "there were other considerations which, however, had higher claims than an equivocal humanity. To connive at the flight of one of the people was to disobey the laws of the Empire, and it was the only true policy to conform, in all possible regards, to the institutions of a country by which so many important concessions had already been reluctantly granted."[30)] Again, Perry's concern about the national interests gained up hands here over his compassion about the human rights.

The curtain rose on the third and final act when Perry received Shōin's letter on the wooden tablet, along with the report from the officers who had witnessed Shōin and Kaneko in their cage.

The Commodore, on being informed of the imprisonment of the two Japanese, sent his flag lieutenant ashore to ascertain unofficially whether they were the same two who had visited the ships. The cage was found as described, but empty, and the guards declared that the men had been sent that morning to Edo, on orders from the capital. They had been confined, it was stated, for going off to the American ships, and as the prefect had no authority to act in the matter, he had at once reported the case to the imperial government, which had sent for the prisoners, and then held them under its jurisdiction.[31)]

This time, Perry seemed to be quite concerned for the fate of the two men, and began to take serious measures to intervene with the Japanese authorities to ameliorate the penalties they

---

29) *Narrative*, vol. 1, p. 421–2. Shoin's brave and resolute action, gave Perry and the Americans expectations of a bright future for Japan. "The Empire of Japan forbids the departure of any of its subjects for a foreign country under the penalty of death, and the two men who had fled on board the ships were criminals in the eye of their own laws, however innocent they might have appeared to the Americans. . . . The event was full of interest, as indicative of the intense desire for information on the part of two educated Japanese, who were ready to brave the rigid laws of the country, and to risk even death for the sake of adding to their knowledge. The Japanese are undoubtedly an inquiring people, and would gladly welcome an opportunity for the expansion of their moral and intellectual faculties. The conduct of the unfortunate two was, it is believed, characteristic of their countrymen, and nothing can better represent the intense curiosity of the people, while its exercise is only prevented by the most rigid laws and ceaseless watchfulness lest they should be disobeyed. In this disposition of the people of Japan, what a field of speculation, and, it may be added, what a prospect full of hope opens for the future of that interesting country!"

30) *Narrative*, 1: 422.

31) *Narrative*, 1: 423.

might face. The *Narrative* describes Perry's intervention:

> The fate of the poor fellows was never ascertained, but it is hoped that the authorities were more merciful than have awarded the severest penalty, which was the loss of their heads, for what appears to us only liberal and a highly commendable curiosity, however great the crime according to the eccentric and sanguinary code of Japanese law. It is a comfort to be able to add, that the Commodore received an assurance from the authorities, upon questioning them, that he need not apprehend a serious termination.[32)]

It remains unclear whether "the assurance from the authorities" that Perry obtained government had come from the local authorities in Shimoda, or from Edo itself. But the assurance was apparently a relief to Perry, who had been in the dilemma of making a difficult choice between the national interest and human rights.

IV. Concluding Remarks

Yoshida Shōin's attempt to escape from Japan with Perry in 1854 has been a subject of both scholarly and popular attention for more than a century. By examining the text of the "original" letters kept at Yale and analyzing the dilemmas of both the addressor and the addressee, however, I have tried to rediscover its meaning in the context of Japanese dawning relations with the United States and other western nations.

I see no foundation for the assertion that Shōin was a terrorist trying to kill Perry. To the contrary, I have confirmed that he was a trained military strategist with lofty goals for himself and his country, and have argued that both his motives for going to American to study the advanced military technology, and his actions in attempting to do so, symbolized a new direction in Japan's Western learning. In this, Shōin had recognized the importance of learning about—and from—the English-speaking world fully five years before Fukuzawa Yukichi began to advocate shifting from "Dutch learning" to Anglo-American learning. At the same time, I noted that the unusual difficulties that Perry had experienced in choosing between the American national interest, and his concern for the human rights issues he recognized in dealing with Shōin's request for passage abroad—the fact that Shōin would be handled as a criminal.

Japanese scholarship has not, to date, seen the encounter between Shōin and Perry in terms of human rights, largely because Shōin was regarded a national hero making extraordinary contributions to the Meiji Restoration, and his role as mentor of such leading Chōshū politicians

32) *Narrative*, 1: 423.

as Itō Hirobumi and Yamagata Aritomo. Therefore, his attempt to stow away has been considered as motivated solely for the national cause, without interrogating his personal motivations, as I have done here. By "reducing" a hero to an average person and simply looking on Shōin as an ordinary stowaway, however, it has become possible to read the complexities of this historic event and the dilemmas on the both sides.

Chapter 7

黒船のもたらした「広東人」旋風
―羅森の虚像と実像―

The “Cantonese” Whirlwind Brought by the Black Ships

陶　徳民（De-min Tao）

I　「風雲児」の羅森

1854（安政元）年の春、横浜・下田および箱館など黒船の行った先々で羅森（字は向喬、約1821－1899）という広東人の名前が噂になっている。作詩が上手で、書道も得意だということで、空白の扇面をもって彼の題辞を求める日本の役人や庶民は殺到した。

図1　ポーハタン号〔「金海奇観」より早稲田大学図書館所蔵〕

図2　鍬形赤子画「米利堅人応接之図」より

横浜で書かれた羅森の日記によれば、

日本人はこれまでの200年間、外国人との交流を断ち切ってきた。そのため、長崎での交易が許されている少数の中国人やオランダ人を除いては外国人を見たことがなかったのである。私も珍しそうに見られているのを感じた。日本人は漢字や漢文を非常に尊重しているため、私は行く先々で、自分の扇子になにか書いてくれと頼まれた。横浜滞在中の１ヵ月の間に、私は少なくとも500本の扇子に漢文を書いた。実際のところ、このような依頼には困惑したし、書くにも時間がかかったが、彼らの熱心な頼みを断るのはむずかしかった[1]。

とある。そして、下田での様子については次のように述べられている。

下田の周辺７里四方には、羊、山羊、豚は１匹も見当たらなかった。しか

図３ 羅森が松前勘解由に送った扇面、松前町郷土資料館所蔵

図４ 羅森扇子図『恵比すのうわさ』より、国立国会図書館所蔵

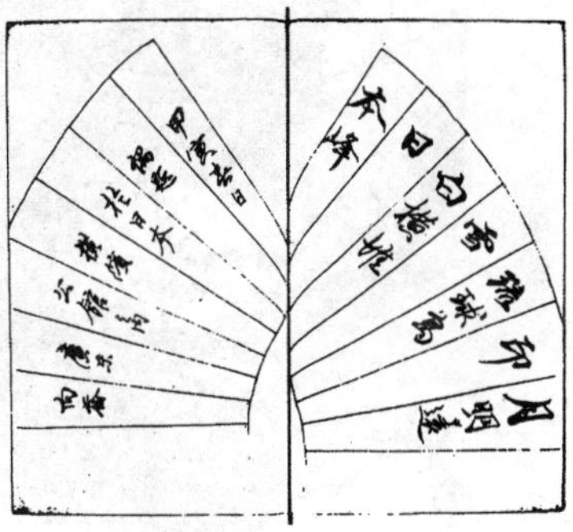

1 「ペリー提督の第２回日本訪問―ある中国人が記した日誌―」、株式会社オフィス宮崎訳『ペリー艦隊日本遠征記』Vol. II（栄光教育文化研究所、1997年）所収、400頁。これは、羅森の日記に対するウィリアムズの英訳文から日本語に訳されたものである。羅森自身が中国語で綴った『日本日記』の原本における関係記載は次のようになっている。（横浜にて）「予或到公館、毎々多人請予録扇、一月之間、従其所請、不下五百余柄」。王暁秋訓点『羅森等早期日本游記五種』（湖南人民出版社、1983年）、34頁。ここにいう「公館」は、幕府がペリーとの会談のために横浜で設けた「応接所」のことである。

なお、増田渉「『満清紀事』とその筆者－わが国に伝えられた「太平天国」について」（『西学東漸と中国事情』所収、岩波書店、1979年）、大石圭一「ペリー提督の通訳・羅森の子孫を香港に訪ねて」（『ニューフレーバー』第17巻４号、1983年４月）、王暁秋「近代中日文化交流的先駆者羅森」（同『近代中日関係史研究』所収、中国社会科学出版社、1997年）を参照されたい。

し牛はよく見られ、荷物の運搬に使われていた。牛はまた田畑を耕すのにも使われていた。女たちは中国と同様に機を織っていた。鍛冶屋や大工もわれわれの国と同じように働いていた。しかし、女たちが刺繍をしている姿は見られなかった。また男も女も好んで扇子を持ち歩くようである。ここに滞在している間、私は頼まれて少なくとも1,000本の扇子に漢文を書いた。奉行やアメリカ人との交渉を担当するいろいろな役人、誰もが私に同じことを頼むのである[2]。

自分の題辞した扇子の数に関する羅森の記述が決して自己顕示するための誇張ではなかったことは、後述に引用するペリーの首席通訳官S.W.ウィリアムズ（1812－1884、中国名は衛三畏）の私信でも分かる。要するに、羅森は開国当時の日本人の間でかなりの人気者になっていたことは確かである。

図5　萩市にある松陰（左）と金子重輔（右）の銅像

羅森の雷名は、当時海外脱出を図っている吉田松陰と同伴の金子重輔の耳にも入った。密航失敗後に書かれた松陰の『回顧録』によれば、

4月4日（旧暦3月7日）大槻平治時神奈川に留まる故、是れを訪ふ。平治漁舟に乗じ夷舶に至り、詩を賦し、羅森に贈りたる事を聞きし故、奇策はなきかと思ひ訪ひたるなり。かくて酒楼に登り酒を置き、舟を招き恣に酔飽せしめ、微言を以て之を動かす[3]。

---

2 同上、『ペリー艦隊日本遠征記』Vol. II、404頁。これに対応する羅森の中国語日記における関係部分は、（下田にて）「予于下田、一月之間、所写其扇不下千余柄矣」となっている。『羅森等早期日本游記五種』、39頁。

3 『吉田松陰全集』第九巻（大和書房、1974年）、363－364頁。

とある。すなわち横浜にいた松陰は、この日にすでに大槻平治（磐渓）を通じて羅森のことを知っていたわけである。したがって、4月25日（旧暦3月28日）午前2時ごろ下田でペリーの旗艦ポーハタン号に乗り込んだのち、ウィリアムズに「広東人羅森」と書いた一枚の紙を見せて、羅森との面会を求めた[4]。羅森に会えば、漢文による筆談でお互いの意思疎通がよりスムーズにできるだろうと想定していたのであろう[5]。

Ⅱ　「羅旋風」の正体

では、この羅森はいったいどのような人物であろうか。広東人である彼はなぜ、黒船に乗って来日したのだろうか。

いわゆる「黒船来航」、すなわちペリー提督の率いるアメリカ艦隊の日本来訪は2003年で150周年になった。そして、日本の開国を象徴する「日米和親条約」の締結も2004年で150周年になる。しかし、当時の日米交渉は日本語と英語ではなく、漢文とオランダ語という二つの媒介言語をもって行われていたということを知っている人は意外に少ないようである。

実際、先にふれたペリーの首席通訳官ウィリアムズも漢文の通訳に当っていた。ペリー来航までの20年間マカオ・香港などに滞在し、教会の印刷所を経営する傍らE.C.ブリッジマンの英字誌『中国叢

図6　ウィリアムズ肖像〔高川文筌筆「金海奇観」より、早稲田大学図書館所蔵〕

4 『回顧録』には、ウィリアムズとの問答における関連部分は次のようである。「江戸を発すること何日ぞ」。曰く、「三月五日」。「曾て予を知るか」。曰く、「知る」。「横浜にて知るか、下田にて知るか」。曰く、「横浜にても下田にても知る」。ウリヤムス怪しみて曰く、「吾れは知らず。米利堅へ往き何をする」。曰く、「学問をする」。（中略）吾れ等云はく、「君吾が請をきかずんば其の書翰は返すべし」。ウリヤムス云はく、「置きてみる、皆読み得たり」。予広東人羅森と書き、「此の人に遇はせよ」と云ふ。ウリヤムス云はく、「遇ひて何の用かある。且つ今臥して牀にあり」。同上、393－394頁。この中の「書翰」というのは、松陰の「投夷書」、すなわちペリー側に渡した海外密航のための嘆願書のことである。詳細は、拙稿「下田密航前後における松陰の西洋認識－米国に残る「投夷書」をめぐって－」（『環』第13号、藤原書店、2003年5月）、「下田獄における第二の「投夷書」について—松陰の覚悟に対するペリー側の共感—」（『環』第14号、藤原書店、2003年7月）、「羅森に寄せた松陰の想い」（『関西大学通信』第308号、2003年5月15日）を参照されたい。

5 事実上、松陰の供述にもとづいてまとめられた「下田一件調査報告書」に、「右アメリカ人之内ニ清国人も居候ニ付、於于時ハ筆談ニ而、何歟応答様之事仕候事共ハ無之哉」という記載もあるので、筆談による意思疎通の意図がはっきりしていると言える（「下田事件関係文書」、『吉田松陰全集』第9巻、岩波書店、1935年、382頁）。

報』の編集を手伝っていた彼は、漢語についてかなりの自信をもっていた。日本人漂流民を送還する1837年の「モリソン号事件」にかかわったので、日本語にも多少通じていた。(ちなみに、ペリー来航後、1856年からの約20年間は清国駐在米国公使館の書記官兼通訳として活躍し、晩年はエール大学の初代中国言語文学教授をつとめた。『中国総論』(The Middle Kingdom),『漢英韻府』(A Syllabic Dictionary of the Chinese Language) などの名著と辞書を残している。)

しかし、ウィリアムズの漢文能力は主に読解や会話の方にあったようで、漢文による作文はできず、外交文書を飾る流麗な書道も勿論上手ではなかった。したがって、外交文書や会談記録の作成は無理であった。そして、ウィリアムズはなかなかの勉強家で、航海途中でも中国人を助手とする語学研鑽や漢書英訳の計画を立てていた。このような二つの理由から中国人雇用の必要性が生まれたが、しかし、1853年一回目の来航時に広東で雇った中国人助手は阿片吸引者で病弱であったため、琉球滞在中の6月11日に亡くなってしまった。この意外な出来事で対日交渉に支障を来たすのではないかと憂慮したペリーは、日記に次のように書いている。

> けさ一時に、ウィリアムズ氏が通訳として雇っていた老シナ人が息を引きとった。五五歳だといっていた。彼は教育のある人で、外国人、とりわけウィリアムズ氏にシナ語を教えるために雇われていた。その生涯の長い間、彼は阿片吸飲常習者であって、全身は非常に弱化し、その結果やせ細っていたため、本艦にやってきた時には、誰もが彼は長生きできまいと予言した。こうしてわれわれはシナ語の通訳をもたぬ状態におかれた。というのは、ウィリアムズ氏は英語の意味を北京官話にして伝えることができ、またこうして口述することもできるが、北京官話を書くことはできないからである[6]。

半月後、上海で新期雇用した中国人助手が琉球に到着したが、しかし、彼の教養はあまり高くなかった。それに、彼の上海弁とウィリアムズの広東弁との違いもお互いの意思疎通の障碍となっていた。幸いに、二人が協力してアメリカ大統領の国書などを漢文に訳すことができたので、7月14日、久里浜でそれらを日本側に渡すことには影響が出なかったようである。

一方、羅森は広東省南海県の郷紳出身のもので、詩文に長じ書道も上手かった。アヘン戦争(1840−42)中、イギリス軍に抵抗する民兵を組織して戦ったが、戦争終結後、自分の功績を政府に評価されなかったことに憤慨し、香港・マカオに出かけていった。そこで英米人に中国語を教える傍ら、実業を営んでいたが、ペリーの二回目の来航時にウィリアムズに雇われ、日本に連れられてきた[7]。

---

6 金井圓訳『ペリー日本遠征日記』(雄松堂出版、1985年)、132頁。

7 羅香林「香港開埠初期文教工作者羅向喬事蹟述釈」、『包遵彭先生紀念論文集』(国立歴史博物館ほか編印、1971年)、289−293頁。

この香港・マカオ移住や日本来訪の理由について、羅森は平山謙次郎（名は敬忠、号は省斎、1815－1890）という日本の役人に宛てた書簡のなかで、次のように打ち明けている。

凡才の私ではありますが、何年も世界の出来事に関わってまいりました。イギリスとの戦いにおいても、勇敢な者たちを率いて、全力を尽くして故国のために戦ってまいりました。しかし、私腹を肥やすことだけに熱心な政府の役人は、私の貢献や努力を一顧だにしませんでした。このため私の心は外国に旅することに向けられ、この蒸気船に乗ってここまでやってきたのです[8]。

日本にやってきた羅森は、扇面題辞で莫大な人気を博したと同時に、対日交渉の文書作成や筆談記録などでも大活躍し、アメリカ側だけでなく日本側にも高く評価されていた。

たとえばウィリアムズは、箱館からマカオにいる妻へ送った私信のなかで次のように羅森を称えている。

首都からは使節もオランダ語の通訳も到着しないので、通訳の仕事が全部私にふりかかってきました。まるで二十枚の舌を終日、はねハンマーのように動かし続けるほどの仕事があるといっても過言ではありません。（中略）ところが、今や事柄は深刻になりましたので、私は羅にかなり手伝わせ、もう一つの言葉〔中国語〕の助けを借りて、あまり誤りをしでかさないようにしています。彼は、われわれの計画のすべてに強い関心を示し、住民ともうまくやっております。たしかに、彼らは彼ほど学のある中国人に会ったことがなかったし、彼が扇子に優美な詩を一、二行書いてでもやると、彼らはいっそう喜んで中国語の学識を彼に披露するのです。日本へ来てから五百本以上もの扇子に書いてやったのではないかと思いますが、これを頼まれるほど、彼を喜ばせることはないのです[9]。

一方、羅森は日本人からは次のような賛美の漢詩も受けた[10]。

横浜相遇豈無因
和議皆安仰頼君
遠方鴃舌今朝会
幸観同文対語人

---

[8] 同注（1）、『ペリー艦隊日本遠征記』Vol. II、399頁。しかし、書簡のこの部分は英訳された日記に載っているものの、公刊された羅森の中国語版『日本日記』には載っていない。その理由は次のように考えられる。すなわち中国語版『日本日記』は広東の清政府の役人も入手可能で、しかも読んで分かるのである。時々広東の故郷に帰省する必要のある羅森はその反政府言論のもたらすかもしれないトラブルを避けるために、書簡のこの部分を中国版から削除したのであろう。

[9] ウィリアムズ著・洞富雄訳『ペリー日本遠征随行記』（雄松堂出版、1970年）、446頁。

[10] 同注（1）、『ペリー艦隊日本遠征記』Vol. II、402頁。

私たちがここで出会ったことはまったくの偶然でしょうか、
条約と平和が得られたのはあなたのおかげです。
遠くから見知らぬ人々がやってきて、言葉も分からない私たちは、
あなたの筆と舌がなければどうなっていたことでしょう。

Ⅲ 誤解と理解の諸相

図7 羅森肖像、樋畑翁輔筆。『米国使節彼理提督来朝図絵』より

このように、日米交渉にかかわる羅森の仕事はおおむね双方の好評を得ていた。しかし、当時の一部の風評に現れているように、羅森に対する誤解がなかったわけではない。

たとえば、幕府応接掛の首班である林大学頭の了解を得て横浜応接所で写生を行っていた松代藩の医師兼画師・高川文筌が、羅森との会話を次のように記している。

席末に広東の羅森、字は向喬たる者あり、頗る書画を（善くす）。文、書を以て試問して曰く、何故此船に在るや。曰く、朱氏の乱を避くる。顧みるに、彼或いは罪科有り、潜亡して身を此船に寄る歟。屡に之を詰る。遂に他を言う。聞くことに、前年夏、国書を齎ふ時、漢文を作る者、彼の手に出ると云ふ[11]。

これによってみれば、羅森は知らない者には自分の来歴を安易に披露しない態度を取っていたようである。したがって、高川の質問に対して、太平天国の乱（実情とは違いこれを朱氏の乱と呼んだのは、清王朝に反旗を掲げた太平天国の乱の目的が、朱氏を皇族とした明朝の復活にあるといえば、一般の日本人でも分かると思ったからだろう）を避けるために日本にやって来たのだとごまかして答えた。繰り返し問い詰めても本当のことを聞き出せなかった高川は、結局、羅森は犯した罪を逃れるためにアメリカの軍艦に乗り込んだのだろうと推測したわけである。そして、前年ペリーから渡されたアメリカ大統領の国書の漢文版の作成者は謝氏であったにもかかわらず、ここでは羅森と誤認されてしまったのである。

そして、箱館の名主小嶋又次郎の目に映っている羅森の姿は次のようなものである。

此図広東人羅森ト申（ス）モノナリ。姿柔和ニ見セテ内心左ニアラザルヨ

---

[11] 高川文筌「横浜紀事」、樋畑雪湖編『米国使節彼理提督来朝図絵』（吉田一郎発行、1931年）所収。

シ。此モノ外（ノ）広東人ト違ヒ、筆法可也。依テ扇面モ諸方ニ書タルヨシ也。又気量モ相応ナルベシ。何ユイニ亜墨利加舟へ乗タルモノヤ、近頃彼等ガ国ニ於（テ）モ一戦（阿片戦争）有之候ヨシ。定テヘロリ（ペリー）ガ威勢ヲ恐（レ）、随心ト見得タリ。餓死テモ何トカノ水ヲ喰ハザルノ語ヲシラザルユイカ。又深キ謀ト有テノ所為カ。是ヲ謀トモ明白ニイワズ。此モノ、買求ル品ハ字引、墨之類、外品トモアメリカ人トチガイ、貧乏ナルカ金銭不足。買物至而直（値）切テ買モノ高不足、此モノ同ジ漢土ニテモ頭高ク[12]。

図8　羅森肖像、『亜墨利加一条写』より、市立函館博物館所蔵

図9　羅森（〔スタットラー『黒船絵巻』より〕）

要するに、正義感の高い小嶋はアヘン戦争の敗北から教訓を汲まず、強いアメリカに荷担する羅森を「無節操」のものと見ていたのであった。また、羅森の文才を買っているものの、その買い物時の貧相と値引き上手には好感を持っていなかった。

このほか、たとえば羅森を通訳という賤業（「鴃舌之門」）に陥った士人と見ている日本人もいた[13]。

種種の誤解を受けながらも、羅森は終始前向きの姿勢を変えなかった。

---

[12] 市立函館図書館所蔵『亜墨利加一条写』。本文での引用は、田中彰編『開国』（日本近代思想大系１、岩波書店）のそれによる（175頁）。分かりやすくするために、文中に適宜、括弧のなかに説明や語尾などを補足する片仮名を入れた。

[13] 同注（１）、『羅森等早期日本游記五種』、42頁。

図10　４分の１大のノリス社製機関車モデル（炭水車及び客車つき）
樋畑翁輔筆。（東京大学史料編纂所所蔵模本）

たとえば、和親条約締結後に行われたアメリカ側の近代的贈り物の展示や実演について、彼は次のような興奮した口ぶりで紹介している。

翌日、合衆国政府から日本の皇帝への贈り物が披露された。模型の機関車と客車、救命ボート、電信機、銀板写真機、さまざまな農機具などである。町はずれに模型機関車用のレールを円形に敷き、そこで機関車と客車をかなりの速度で走らせたところ、見物人は非常に驚いた。電信機は、銅線を使ってある場所からほかの場所に瞬時に情報を伝える装置である。銀板写真機は、太陽光線の反射を金属板に投影して写真を撮るものである。筆や写生は必要なく、写真は薄れることなく長持ちする。救命ボートは、空気ボックスがついており、沈まないようになっている。この発明品により、船の難破の際に乗組員の命を救うことができる。農機具は、合衆国の農業のために考案された便利な機具ばかりであった。日本の皇帝はこれらの品々を受け取り、返礼として漆器、陶磁器、絹などを贈った[14]。

そして、羅森のもっとも感動的事例はやはり、先にも触れた平山謙次郎との腹を割った交流であろう。開国当時は徒目付であった平山は学問はすぐれているものの、思想はやや保守的であった（幕末は外国総奉行に昇進し、明治維新以後は儒教・心学などをもとり入れた「神道大成教」を創立した。）羅森の『南京紀事』と『治安策』という二著を読んだ平山は、孔孟の「王道主義」にも

図11　平山謙次郎の書跡、『ウィリアムズ家文書』所収。エール大学スターリング記念図書館古文書部所蔵。

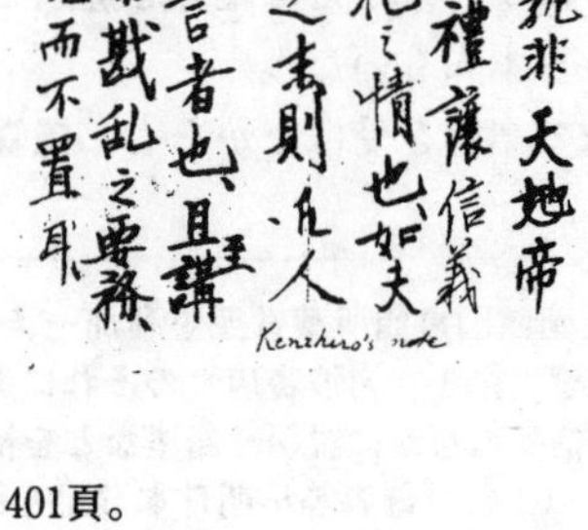

14 同注（1）、『ペリー艦隊日本遠征記』Vol. II、401頁。

とづいて次のような西洋批判を行っている。

相互交流という原則は、世界のどこでも共通です。大切なのは礼儀、親切、誠意、正義です。これを守るならば尊い調和が広がり、天地の心があますところなく現われるのです。これとは逆に、利益だけを求めて商売を行なえば、争いや訴訟が起こり、喜びではなく呪いとなります。（中略）人間の社会はあたかも虎や狼の群れのようになり、世界中のいたるところで強者が弱者を破滅させ、大が小を飲み込むことになるでしょう（中略）。

あなたはいま、合衆国の船に乗って海を旅していらっしゃいます。私が述べたような人物にお会いになったことがおありでしょうか。もしいまだお会いになっていないならば、あなたの行く先々で、その国と統治者にこの原則を説いてくださるようお願いいたします。そうすれば、孔子と孟子の願いが、何世紀も経過してやっと世界全体を明るく照らすようになるでしょう[15]。

平山のこの書翰を受け取った羅森は次のような返事を出した。

すばらしいお手紙をいただき、大変感動いたしました。私たちは水面を流れる葉のように出会い、あなたのご教示は私に光をなげかけてくれました。世界中のすべての人間は天地の子供であり、天理、礼儀、誠意、正義の原理にしたがって互いを遇するべきだというあなたの言葉はすばらしく、その通りだと思います。また、宇宙の寛大な心とわれわれの賢人の教えにある平等の慈悲心を十分に表わしていると思います。お手紙の一語一語に感謝しております。お言葉を常に心に刻みつけて忘れぬようにいたします[16]。

このように謙虚に平山の意見を傾聴した羅森は、一方、平山に対する婉曲な説得も試みたのであった。「現代は古代とは非常に異なった時代です。それを知りながら心ある者が見て見ぬふりをすることができるでしょうか[17]」という羅森の冷徹な現実主義的姿勢は、おそらく理想主義者の平山に一定のショックを与えただろう。

以上の対話も収録した羅森の『日本日記』は、一中国人による日本開国事情の証言として貴重なもので、早くも1854年の11月から『遐邇貫珍』という香港英華

図12　松浦章ほか編著『遐邇貫珍の研究』（関西大学出版部）より

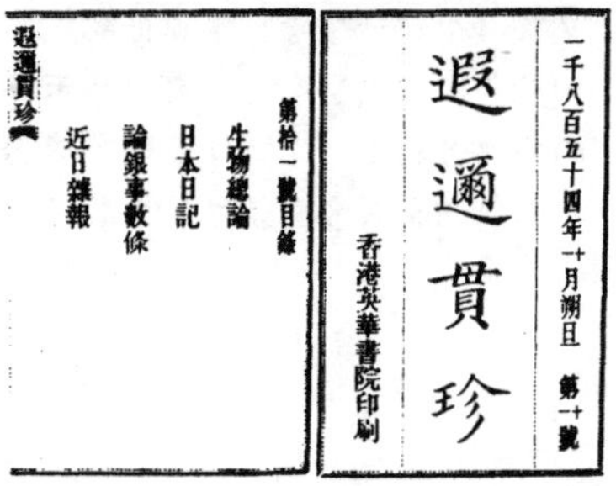
一千八百五十四年十一月朔旦　第十一號

遐邇貫珍

香港英華書院印刷

第拾一號目錄

生物總論

日本日記

論銀事數條

近日雜報

遐邇貫珍

15 同注（1）、『ペリー艦隊日本遠征記』Vol. II、398−399頁。
16 同注（1）、『ペリー艦隊日本遠征記』Vol. II、399頁。
17 同注（1）、『ペリー艦隊日本遠征記』Vol. II、399頁。

図13

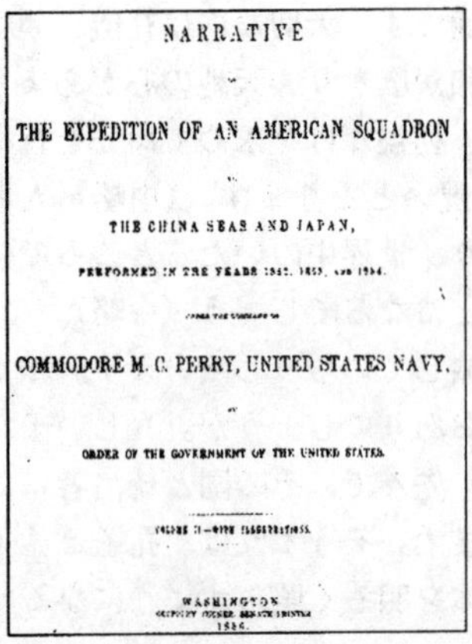
NARRATIVE

THE EXPEDITION OF AN AMERICAN SQUADRON

THE CHINA SEAS AND JAPAN,

COMMODORE M. C. PERRY, UNITED STATES NAVY,

ORDER OF THE GOVERNMENT OF THE UNITED STATES.

WASHINGTON

図14

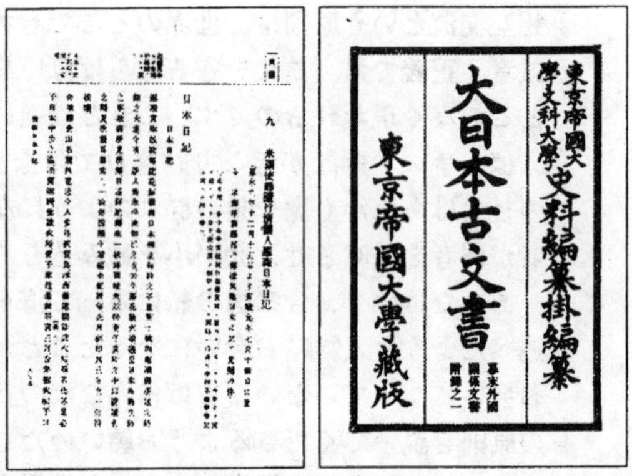

図15　羅森の名刺、『青窓紀聞』より、国立国会図書館所蔵

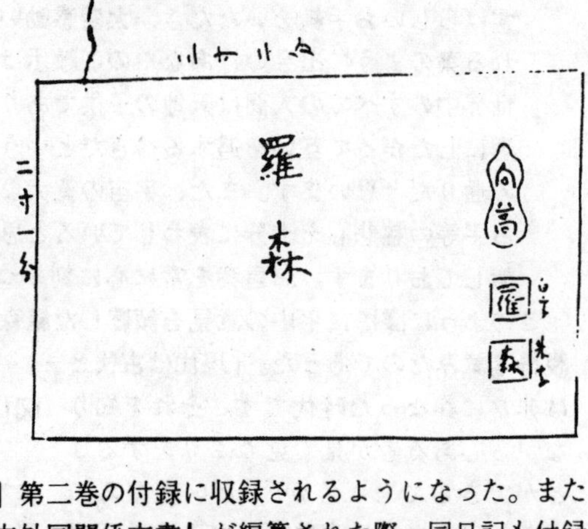

書院の漢文月刊に三回にわたって連載され、松陰を含む幕末の日本人有志の目に留まった。そして、ウィリアムズによって英訳された同日記は1854年９月『香港記録報』という英字商業週刊誌の増刊（*Overland Register and Price Current*）に掲載され、その価値はペリーに認められ、２年後に出版のアメリカ議会の公式文書『ペリー艦隊日本遠征記』第二巻の付録に収録されるようになった。また、1913年に『大日本古文書・幕末外国関係文書』が編纂された際、同日記も付録の一つとして「米国使節随行清国人羅森日本日記」というタイトルで収録され、その価値を再度確認されたわけである。

ペリーの旗艦に登った松陰の「時間」に迫る

― ポウハタン号の航海日誌に見た下田密航関連記事について

陶　徳　民

How Long Did Yoshida Shoin Remain on Commodore Perry's Flagship in Shimoda on April 25, 1854: Records found from a Log Book of the Powhatan Kept at NARA

TAO Demin

During the author's recent investigation at NARA (the National Archives and Records Administration) in Washington, D.C. of the log books of the Powhatan, the flagship that Commodore Perry used in his 1854 expedition to Japan, Captain William J. McCluney's notes on the "two Japanese" stowaways were found in the Remarks on the Day of April 25th, and the time of getting aboard and being sent ashore recorded here corresponds to what Yoshida Shoin had recalled later in his reminiscence. The discovery of the face will certainly generates further interest among researches and general readers in this well-known "Shimoda story."

キーワード：ペリー、ポウハタン号、マクルーニー、航海日誌、吉田松陰、
下田密航

2009年2月9日、ワシントン D.C.にあるアメリカ国立公文書館で海軍省関係のアーカイブに関する調査を行った。その結果、ペリーの旗艦、ポウハタン号（Steamer Powhatan）のLog Bookすなわち航海日誌の第二巻[1]（1853年9月11日—1854年9月7日）1854年4月25日のページ[2]から、吉田松陰の下田密航に関係する記事を見つけた。

記載責任者はポウハタン号の艦長、W. J. マクルーニー（Captain William J. McCluney）大佐であり、記載内容は次の通りである。

1）写真1参照。

2）写真2参照。

Remarks of This 25 Day of April 1854
Shimoda
Commences at 2.45 two Japanese came on board by a small boat, remained about 3/4 of an hour, on getting aboard their boat got adrift & they were sent ashore in the S' (Steamer' s) cutter by order of the Commo. (Commodore).[3)]

筆者なりの訳によれば、次のようになる。

下田
(午前) 2時45分、二人の日本人が小さいボートで乗艦してきて、約45分間滞留した。乗艦した際、彼らのボートが漂失したため、提督の指示で本艦の小艇で岸辺へ送還された。

ここにいう「二人の日本人」とはいうまでもなく、吉田松陰とその従者、金子重之助のことである。密航準備の一環として事前に米艦側に渡された「投夷書」に記した松陰の偽名は「瓜中万二」、金子重之助の偽名は「市木公太」であり、しかも書中において長州藩出身の兵学師範(軍事教官)と足軽であったという真実の身分を隠し、「江戸府の書生」と自称していた。なお、金子重之助は「渋木松太郎」という変名も有していたため、松陰は「三月廿七夜記」という密航の回顧録で金子のことを「澁木生」·「渋生」と呼んでいた。

では、この記事の発見は松陰の下田密航の全容解明、および新しい松陰像の形成にとってどのような意味を有するのだろうか。

第一に、松陰と金子がペリーの旗艦に登った時間、および二人の艦上滞留時間に関する確実なデータを入手できた、と言えるだろう。

私は、近著においてエール大学図書館古文書部で吉田松陰の「投夷書」と邂逅した経験にもとづき、「歴史学の使命と生命の一部はまさに重要な史実の細部をできるだけリアルに再現することにあり、それによってはじめて現代の読者に歴史劇場の臨場感を与えることができるのである」と述べたことがある[4)]。今回の発見も、松陰の下田密航の全容解明につながる重要な一歩である。というのは、密航に踏み切った松陰の行動に対処したペリー艦隊の重要な当事者として、ミシシッピー号の艦長、S. S. リー(Commander S. S. Lee)中佐がその航海日誌において、ポウハタン号乗艦に先立ち、同艦に乗艦しようとしたその事実に全然触れておらず[5)]、ポウハタン号の司令室で指揮を執っていたM. C. ペリー提督の日記も松陰来艦一件に触れていない。松陰を訊問した首席通訳官S. W. ウィリアムズの日記は松陰の密航および「投夷書」を記載しているが、時間関係については触れていなかった。したがって、ポウハタン号のマクルーニー艦長が航海日誌に記した「時間」、すなわち1854年4月25日午前2時45分に同艦搭

3) 写真3参照。上記の括弧中の内容は括弧直前の略式表現に対する筆者の解読結果である。
4)『明治の漢学者と中国』(関西大学出版部、2007年3月初版、2008年2月第二刷)、20頁、注25参照。
5) 写真4、写真5を参照。

乗、約45分間滞留というデータは、貴重で信憑性の高い史料に違いない[6]。

第二に、少年時代から兵学師範として養成された松陰の厳格な時間観念と驚異的記憶力が今回の発見によって裏付けられた、といえる。

密航７ヵ月後の松陰は、「三月廿七夜記」を著した。そのなかで、「八ツ時社ヲ出テ舟ノ所へ往ク、潮進ミ舟泛ヘリ、因テ押出サントテ舟に上ル」と、身を隠した弁天社から出て、伝馬船を使って密航に踏み切った時間を「八ツ時」であるとし、そして「時ニ鐘ヲ打ツ、凡ソ夷舶中、夜ハ時ノ鐘ヲ打ツ、余曰、日本ノ何時ゾ、ウリヤムス指ヲ屈シテ此を計ル、然レドモ答詞詳ナラズ、〔此鐘ハ七ツ時ナルヘシ〕」と、ウィリアムズの訊問を受け、やりとりが最終段階に達した時間を「七ツ時」であるとした[7]。

これは約155年前のことであったが、太陽暦自体のズレはさほど大きなものではないであろうから、下田における今年４月25日の「日の出」（六つ時）が午前５時１分であることを踏まえると、おおよそ「八つ時」は午前１時40分、「七つ時」は３時20分になることを推定できる[8]。

この推定結果によれば、松陰と金子は1854年４月25日午前１時40分に密航開始、２時ごろにミシシッピー号に辿り着き、２時45分ごろにポウハタン号に乗艦、約45分間滞留して３時30分ごろに同艦の小艇で岸辺に向かって送還され始めた、というシナリオが成り立つであろう。とすれば、訊問最中、艦上の鐘が鳴った時を「七ツ時」、すなわち「３時20分」とした松陰の推定が、送還されはじめる時間を「３時30分」としたマクルーニー艦長の記載とうまく合致していることが判明できよう。

上記で触れた拙著の同じ箇所のつづきで、筆者は「場合によっていままで隠され、あるいは見逃されてきた重大な史実の発見が従来の歴史理論や概括への修正を迫るというようなこともありうるのである。私はこのような史実と史論との対話と相互補完を促進しようとする立場で研究を続け、そこに自分の研究の存在意義を求めたのであった」とも述べておいた[9]。今回の発見は、「国益と人権」の間に揺れる米外交の先駆的事例として分析した下田獄における「第二の投夷書」ほど重要なものではないかもしれないが[10]、松陰の厳格な時間観念と驚異的記憶力の証拠として重視されるべきであろう。

筆者はこのポウハタン号航海日誌における関連記事が、時間観念・空間観念などをめぐる異文化交渉の視点から松陰の下田密航および幕末対外交渉史を再検討する新しい研究のきっかけとなれば、と期待している。

付記：今回、ワシントン D.C.にあるアメリカ国立公文書館での調査について、日本を出発する前NHK

6）二次的史料として、ミシシッピ号の艦長付書記であるW. スポルディングの『日本遠征記』には、松陰が岸辺に送還されたのは「ほとんど午前二時頃」となっているが、誤記であろう。一方、W. ホークスによる公式記録『ペリー艦隊日本遠征記』はミシシッピ号に乗艦しようとした松陰の行動は「午前二時頃」と記しているが、ポウハタン号への乗艦と滞留時間については触れていない。

7）『吉田松陰全集』第７巻（岩波書店、1935年）、413頁、416頁。

8）この推定は、東北大学大学院文学研究科助教で新進気鋭な松陰研究者でもある桐原健真氏のご教示によるものである。

9）同注４。

10）拙稿「下田獄における第二の「投夷書」について―松陰の覚悟に対するペリー側の共感」、藤原書店『環』第14号、2003年７月。なお、拙稿を評した岸俊光記者の文章（2003年８月８日『毎日新聞』夕刊２版掲載）を参照。

のキャスターで立教大学21世紀社会デザイン研究科教授である松平定知氏および渋沢栄一記念財団実業史研究情報センター長の小出いずみ氏の助言をいただき、現地では同公文書館Special Access and FOIA Staff 部門のChiefであるDavid Mengel氏、Textual Archives Service 部門のCynthia G. Fox氏(Deputy Director)、Jane Fitzgerald氏およびChris Killillay氏のお世話になりました。記して御礼を申し上げます。

付録　下田密航に関する松陰、ウィリアムズおよびホークスの記録

付録 ①

『吉田松陰全集』(岩波書店、1935年、第7巻413-417頁)における「三月廿七夜記」[11)]

三月廿七日、夕方、柿崎ノ海濱ヲ巡見スルニ、弁天社下ニ漁舟二隻泛ヘリ、是究竟ナリト大ニ喜ヒ、蓮臺寺村ノ宿ヘ帰リ、湯ヘ入、夜食ヲ認メ、下田ノヤトヘ往クトテ立出、〔下田ニテ名主夜行ヲ禁スル故、一里隔テ蓮臺寺村ノ湯入場ヘモ、ヤトヲトリ、下田ヘハ蓮臺寺ヘ宿スト云ヒ、蓮臺寺ヘハ下田ヘ宿スト云テ、夜行シテ夷船ノ様子彼是見廻リ、多ク野宿ヲナス〕、武山ノ下海岸ニ夜五ツ過マテ臥ス、五ツ過此ヲ去、弁天社下ニ至ル、然ルニ潮頭退キテ漁舟二隻トモニ沙上ニアリ、故ニ弁天社中ニ入リ安寢ス、八ツ時社ヲ出テ舟ノ所ヘ往ク、潮進ミ舟泛ヘリ、因テ押出サントテ舟に上ル、然ルニ櫓グイナシ、因テカイヲ犢鼻褌ニテ縛リ、船ノ両旁ヘ縛付、澁木生ト力ヲ極テ押出ス、褌タユ、帯ヲ解キカイヲ縛リ、又押ユク、岸ヲ離ルヽコト一町許、ミシッヒー船ヘ押付、是マテニ舟幾度カ廻リ廻リテユク、腕脱セント欲ス、ミシッヒー船ヘ押付レハ船上ヨリ怪ミテ燈籠ヲ卸ス、〔燈籠ハキ(ギ)ヤマンニテ作ル、形圓キ手行燈ノ如シ、蠟燭ハ我邦ニ異ナラズ、但シ色甚白ク心甚細シ〕、火光ニ就テ漢字ニテ吾等欲往米利堅、君幸請之大將、ト認メ、手ニ持チテ船ニ登ル、[船ニハ梯子アリテ甚上リヤスシ]夷人二三人出來リ、甚怪ム氣色ナリ、認メタル書付ヲ予與フ、一夷携テ内ニ入ル、老夷出テ燭ヲ把リ、蟹文字ヲカキ、此方ノ書付ト共ニ返ス、蟹文字ハ何事ヤラン讀メズ、夷人頻ニ手眞似ニテポウパタン船ヘユケト示ス、〔ポウパタン船ハ大將ヘルリ乘ル所ナリ〕、吾等頻ニ手眞似ニテバッテイラニテ連レ往ケト云、夷又手眞似ニテ其舟ニテ往ケト示ス、巳ムコトヲ得ズ、又舟ニ還リ、力ヲ極メテ押行コト又一丁許リ、ポウパタン船ノ外面ニ押付、此時澁生頻ニ云、外面ニ付テハ風強シ、内面ニ付ベシト、然レドモカイ自由ナラズ、舟浪ニ隨テ外面ニツク、船ノ梯子段ノ下ヘ我舟入リ、浪ニ因テ浮沈ス、浮フ毎ニ梯子段ヘ激スルコト甚シ、夷人驚キ怒リ、木棒ヲ携ヘ梯子段ヲ下リ、我舟ヲ衝出ス、此時予帯ヲ解キ立カケヲ着居タリ、舟ヲ衝出サレテハタマラズト夷船ノ梯子段ヘ飛渡リ、澁生ニ纜ヲトレト云、澁生纜ヲトリ未タ予ニ渡サヌ内、夷人又木棒ニテ我舟ヲ衝退ケントス、澁生タマリ兼、纜ヲ棄テ飛渡ル、巳ニシテ夷人遂ニ我舟ヲ衝退ク、時ニ刀及雜物ハ皆舟ニアリ、夷人吾二人ノ手ヲトリ梯子段ヲ上ル、此時謂ラク、船ニ入リ夷人(ト)語ル上ハ、我舟ハ如何様ニモナルベシト、我舟ヲハ顧ミズ夷船中ニ入ル、船中ニ夜番ノ夷人五六名アリ、

11) 原文中の略字、くり返し符号、挿入語句などについては適宜処置し、割注の部分は〔 〕で表示した。

皆或ハ立（チ）或ハ歩ヲ習ハス、一モ尻居ニ坐スル者ナシ、夷人謂ラク、吾等見物ニ來レリト、故ニ羅針等ヲ指シ示ス、予筆ヲ借セト云手眞似スレドモ、一向通セズ、頗ル困ル、其内日本語ヲシルモノウリヤムス出來ル、因テ筆ヲカリ、米利堅ニユカント欲スルノ意ヲ漢語ニテ認メカク、ウリヤムス云ク、何国ノ字ゾ、予曰、日本字ナリ、ウリヤムス哄曰、モロコシノ字デコソ、又云、名ヲカケ、名ヲカケト、因テ此日ノ朝上陸（ノ）夷人ニ渡シタル書中ニ記シ置ツル僞名、余ハ瓜中万二、澁生ハ市木公太ト記シヌ、ウリヤムス携テ内ニ入リ、朝ノ書翰ヲ持出、此事ナルベシト云、吾等ウナツク、ウリヤムス云、此事大將ト余ト知ルノミ、他人ニハ知ラセズ、大將モ余モ心誠ニ喜フ、但横濱ニテ米利堅大將ト林大學頭ト、米利堅ノ天下ト日本ノ天下トノ事ヲ約束ス、故ニ私ニ君ノ請ヲ諾シ難シ、少シク待ツヘシ、遠カラズシテ米利堅人ハ日本ニ來リ、日本人ハ米利堅ニ來リ、両国往來スルコト同国ノ如クナルノ道ヲ開クヘシ、其時來ルベシ、且吾等此ニ留ルコト尚三月スベシ、只今還ルニ非ズト、余因テ問、三月トハ今月ヨリカ來月ヨリカ、ウリヤムス指ヲ屈シ對曰、來月ヨリナリ、吾等云、吾夜間貴船ニ來ルコトハ国法ノ禁スル所ナリ、今還ラハ国人必吾ヲ誅セン、勢還ルベカラズ、ウリヤムス云、夜ニ乘シテ還ラハ国人誰カ知ルモノアラン、早ク還ルベシ、此事ヲ下田ノ大將黑川嘉兵知ルカ、嘉兵許ス、米利堅大將連テユク、嘉兵許サヌ、米利堅大將連テユカヌ、余云、然ラハ吾等舶中ニ留ルベシ、大將ヨリ黑川嘉兵ヘカケヤイ呉ルベシ、ウリヤムス云、左樣ニハナリ難シ、ウリヤムス反覆初ノイフ所ヲ云テ、吾カ帰ヲ促ス、吾等計已ニ違イ、前ニ乘棄タル舟ハ心ニカヽリ、遂ニ帰ルニ決ス、ウリヤムス曰、君両刀ヲ帯ルカ、曰、然リ、官ニ居ルカ、曰、書生ナリ、書生トハ何ソヤ、曰、書物ヲ讀ム人ナリ、人ニ学問ヲ教ユルカ、曰、教ユ、両親アルカ、曰、両人共ニ父母ナシ、〔此僞言少シク意アリ〕、江戸ヲ発スルコト何日ソ、曰、三月五日、曾テ予ヲ知ルカ、曰、知ル、横濱ニテ知ルカ、下田ニテ知ルカ、曰、横濱ニテモ下田ニテモ知ル、ウリヤムス怪ミテ曰、吾ハ知ラズ、米利堅ヘ往キ何ヲスル、曰、学問ヲスル、時ニ鐘ヲ打ツ、凡ソ夷舶中、夜ハ時ノ鐘ヲ打ツ、余曰、日本ノ何時ゾ、ウリヤムス指ヲ屈シテ此を計ル、然レドモ荅詞詳ナラズ、〔此鐘ハ七ツ時ナルヘシ〕、吾等云、君吾請ヲキカスンバ其書翰ハ返スベシ、ウリヤムス云、置テミル、皆讀得タリ、予廣東人羅森トカキ、此人ニ遇（ハ）セヨト云、ウリヤムス云、遇テ何ノ用カアル、且今臥テ牀ニアリ、予曰、來年モ來ルカ、曰、此ヨリハ年々來ルナリ、予曰、此船又來ルカ、曰、他ノ舶來ルナリト、帰ニ臨ミ、我等船ヲ失タリ、舟中要具ヲ置ク、棄置ケハ事発覚セン、如何セン、ウリヤムス云、我カ傳馬ニテ君等ヲ送ルベシ、船頭ニ命シ置ケリ、所々乘行テ君カ舟ヲ尋ネヨ、因テ一拜シテ去ル、然ルニバッテイラノ船頭直ニ海岸ニ押付、我等ヲ上陸セシム、因テ舟ヲ尋ルコトヲ得ズ、上陸セシ所ハ嵓石茂樹ノ中ナリ、夜ハ暗シ、道ハ知レズ、大ニ困迫スル間ニ夜ハ明ケヌ、海岸ヲ見廻レドモ我舟ミヘズ、因テ相謀テ曰、事已ニ至此、奈何トモスヘカラズ、ウロツク間ニ縛セラレテ見苦シトテ、直ニ柿崎村ノ名主ヘ往テ事ヲ告ク、遂ニ下田番所ニ往、吏（ニ）對シ囚奴トナル、ウリヤムス日本語ヲ使、誠ニ早口ニテ一語モ誤ラズ、而テ吾等ノ云所ハ解セサル如キコト多シ、蓋シ渠狡黠ナラン、是ヲ以テ云ント欲スルコト多ク言得ズ、

（後略）

甲寅十一月十三日、野山獄中録之、時天寒雪飛、研池屢凍

付録 ②

S. W.ウィリアムズ著・洞富雄訳『ペリー日本遠征随行記』(雄松堂出版、1970年、284頁、288頁)における関連記載

一八五四年 四月二十五日〔嘉永七年、三月二十八日〕、木曜日

昨夜〔当日午前二時〕、二人の日本人〔吉田松陰、金子重之助〕がわが艦船で合衆国に渡ろうとして艦上〔パウアタン号〕にやって来たが、提督は幕府から許可を得たものでなければ応じられぬとして、彼らの乗艦を断わった。彼らからは、前もって〔前日〕渡航したいと希望し、また艦内ではどんな仕事にも喜んで従事する、としたためた達筆の手紙を受け取っていた。この手紙の趣旨はつぎの通りであった。

[略　投夷書および別啓]

操舵下士官の助けを借りて彼らはタラップを登ったが、彼らが乗って来た小船は運悪く彼らが本船に移るときに離れて漂い去ってしまった。提督は彼らの用向きと上記の書翰についての報告を受けたが、条約の精神に違反して連れて行くことはできぬと断わった。これは彼らをひどく失望させた。だが、私は、便乗する機会もあるだろう他の船舶が追々ここへやって来るに違いないから、今回拒絶されたからといって、そう残念がることもない、といって聞かせた。彼らはボートで陸へ送り帰されることになり、できることなら彼らの小船を見つけようとすぐ風下に向ったが、それを探し出すには海面はあまりにも暗かった。彼らは予期していたよりはずっと平凡な顔つきであったが、明らかに教養のある人物で、二十三歳と二十五歳の青年——日本には扶養すべき両親も子供もない——であった。おそらく、みずから語った通りに、彼らは渡米を熱望している青年であったろう。しかし、われわれのある者は彼らを盗賊と断じ、ある者はいかに条約を履行するかを確かめようとして役人が放った密偵だとし、また、ある者は彼らを亡命者だと考えた。私には、流失した小船に残した刀やその他の持物が彼らを面倒な事件に巻き込むのではなかろうかと気がかりであった。果して、それが港の巡邏船の一隻に発見されたのだ。(後略)

付録 ③

F. L. ホークス編・オフィス宮崎訳『ペリー艦隊日本遠征記』(栄光教育文化研究所、1997年、第1巻421頁)における関連記載

翌日の夜、午前2時ごろ(4月25日)、蒸気艦ミシシッピ号の艦上で夜間当直をしていた士官は、舷側についた小舟から聞こえてくる人声に呼び起こされた。舷門にいって見ると、2人の日本人がすでに舷側の梯子を登ったところだった。話しかけると、乗艦させてほしいと身振りで示した。

彼らはなんとしても艦上にとどまることを許可してほしいと願っているらしく、乗ってきた小舟を惜し気もなく放棄する意思を表わして、海岸には戻らないとの決意をはっきりと示した。ミシシッピ号の艦長が旗艦に行くよう指示すると、彼らは小舟に引き返して、すぐさま旗艦に漕いでいった。港内の波が高かったため、いくぶん苦労しながら旗艦に達し、梯子にすがって舷門に登るやいなや、故意か偶然か、小舟は舷側を離れて漂い去った。甲板に着くと、士官が提督に2人の日本人が現われたことを報告した。提督は通訳を送り、2人と話し合い、不意の訪問の目的を聞き出させた。彼らは率直に、自分た

ちの目的は合衆国に連れていってもらうことであり、そこで世界を旅して、見聞したいという願望を果たしたいのだと打ち明けた。こうして、士官たちと陸上で出会い、そのひとりに手紙を渡したのは、この２人の人物だったことが分かった。舟を漕いできたため、２人ともひどく疲れているようだった。彼らが立派な地位にある日本の紳士であることは明らかだったが、その衣服はくたびれていた。２人とも２本の刀を帯びる資格があり、ひとりはまだ１本をさしていたが、残りの３本はすべて小舟の中に置いてきたので、舟とともに流されてしまっていた。彼らは教養ある人物であり、標準中国語を流暢かつ端麗に書き、物腰も丁重で非常に洗練されていた。提督は彼らの来艦の目的を知ると、自分としても何人かの日本人をアメリカに連れていきたいのはやまやまだが、残念ながら２人を迎え入れることはできない、と答えさせた。そして、２人が日本政府から許可を受けるまでは、受け入れを拒絶せざるをえないが、艦隊は下田港にしばらく滞在する予定だから、許可を求める機会は十分にあるだろうと言って聞かせた。提督の回答に２人は大変動揺して、陸に戻れば首を斬られることになると断言し、とどまることを許してもらいたいと熱心に懇願した。この願いはきっぱりと、しかし思いやりを込めて拒絶された。長い話し合いが続いた。彼らは自分たちを支持してくれるようあらん限りの議論をつくし、アメリカ人の人道心に訴え続けた。結局、１艘のボートが降ろされ、送り帰されることになった。２人は穏やかながら多少抵抗したあと、運命を嘆きながら悄然と舷門を下り、小舟が流れ着いたと思われる場所の近くに上陸させられた。

写真1　ポウハタン号の航海日誌第二巻

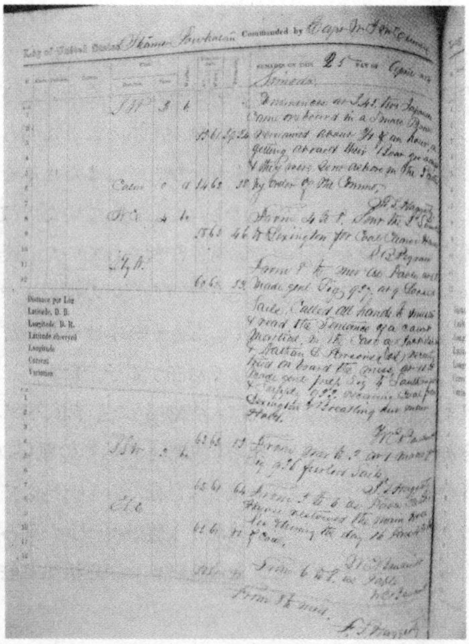

写真2　ポウハタン号の航海日誌第二巻1854年4月25日のページ全体

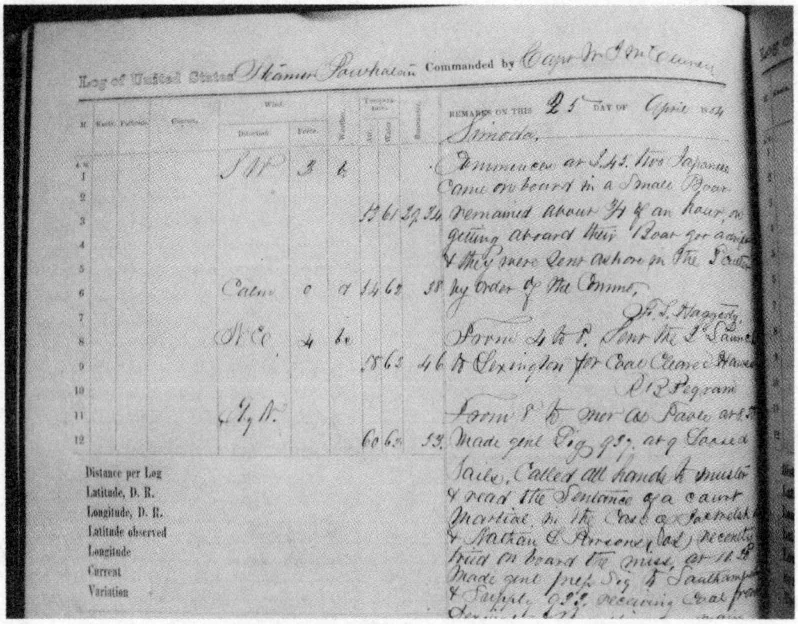

写真3　ポウハタン号の航海日誌第二巻1854年4月25日における密航関連記事（右側）

写真 4　ミシシッピー号の航海日誌第八巻

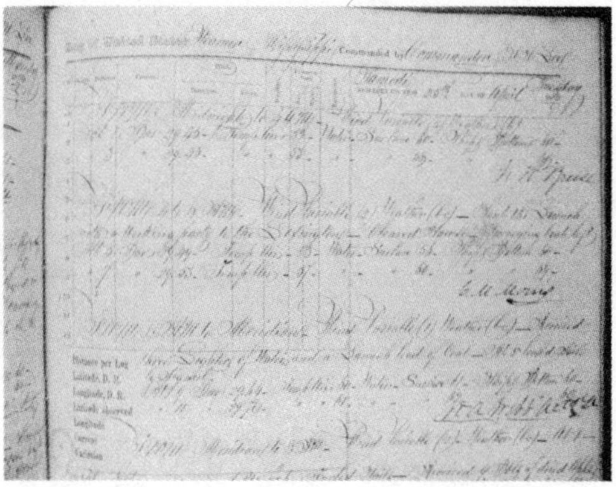

写真 5　ミシシッピー号の航海日誌第八巻1854年 4 月25日

写真 6　David Mengel氏との記念写真

写真 7　Jane Fitzgerald氏との記念写真

后　记

本书得以编辑成功，要感谢许多师长和友人。没有他们的指点和支持，这本书从形式到内容，可能都会是另外一种样子。

我在复旦大学攻读硕士学位时的指导教授吴杰先生，和期间作为交换研究生到关西大学搜集资料时的指导教授大庭脩先生；我在大阪大学攻读博士学位时的指导教授脇田修先生，后由大阪大学转去东京大学、现为东洋文库长的斯波义信先生，以及最近以九十五岁高龄故世、以研究明治政府所雇外国专家著称的梅溪升先生；我在普林斯顿大学作访问研究时的指导教授简森（Marius Jansen）先生，我在哈佛大学赖肖尔日本研究所做博士后时的指导教授入江昭先生等，都曾在挖掘处理史料和磨练问题意识方面给我以示范，令我终生难忘。

近二十年来在关于本专题的研究之中，我先后得到以下各位师友的帮助和激励，如以研究黑船来航著名的原横滨市立大学校长加藤祐三先生和东京大学名誉教授三谷博先生，以研究明治维新著称、曾先后担任东京大学史料编纂所所长和日本国立历史民俗博物馆馆长的宫地正人先生，以研究岩仓使节团著称的已故北海道大学教授田中彰先生，以及该校以研究幕府的开明派官僚著称的井上胜生教授，以研究幕末京都新撰组著名的京都灵山历史馆副馆长木村幸比古先生，以研究吉田松阴国际秩序观之转变著称的名古屋金城学院大学教授桐原健真教授，以研究吉田松阴偷渡故事和欧美日本学著名的耶鲁大学日语教授山口荣铁先生，以及现在活跃于耶鲁东亚研究团队的日本近代史教授勃茨曼（Daniel Botsman）先生，以研究罗森故事和近代中日交往史著称的北京大学历史系教授王晓秋先生，北京外国语大学的张西平、姚小平和李雪涛等教授和以研究卫三畏著名的顾钧教授，以及研究西人来华和西学东渐有名的复旦大学周振鹤教授及周振环教授等。尤其需要一提的是我们关西大学东亚研究团队中的几位同事，即松浦章、内田庆市和沈国威等教授，其旺盛而扎实的研究出版活动时时在提醒我不能松懈，其编辑的《遐迩贯珍的研究》以及《或问》杂志在东西言语文化接触研究界颇有影响，使以研究日本汉学为主的我也经常有机会关注和涉猎东西交涉的研究。还有一起去美国实地调查近代日本女子教育先驱津田梅子在美足迹的日本史教授薮田贯先生和大谷渡先生，正是那次调查，使我有机会顺便接触到耶鲁大学档案馆所藏的《卫三畏家族文书》，以后又追踪到首都华盛顿的美国国立档案馆，从而做出见于2003年及2009年日本每日新闻以及日本广播协会（NHK）2015 年大河剧《花燃》的预告节目“走向世界－幕末长州全知晓”的重要发现。是的，关西大学有创办于 1951 年的东西学术研究所，又有成立于 2007 年的文化交涉学研究中心，这两个卓越机构和连续执行了两个五年研究计划的亚洲文化研究中心，为我们的对外交流提供了极好的平台。身处其中，感到十分幸运。

构成本书主体部分的是耶鲁大学图书馆档案部所藏的《卫三畏家族文书》，这是需要特别感谢的（本书附录二特别收入了《卫三畏家族文书目录》，有需要查对者，可以加以利用）。此外，关西大学图书馆，日本国立国会图书馆和外交史料馆，东京大学史料编纂所，美国国立档案館的 Jane Fitzgerald，オフィス宫崎的宫崎寿子，冲绳县教育厅文化财课史料编集班的小野まさ子，山口县萩市松阴神社宝物馆的島本貴，长野县长野市松代町真田宝物館的溝部いずみ，京都市灵山历史馆的木村武仁，下田市了仙寺的松井大英，市立函馆博物馆的保科智治，每日新闻社的岸俊光，神户大学经济经营研究所的山地秀俊，日本英学史学会的塩崎智会長以及该学会的奥村紀子先生，湖南怀化学院金卫婷老师等，也都分别提供了宝贵的相关资料和论文，谨此一并致谢。

大象出版社李光洁编辑的耐心，和我的博士生苏浩的细心，都对本书的最后成形做出了贡献。由于种种原因，本书的出版迟延了不少时间，应该向作为《卫三畏文集》共同主编的澳门基金会吴志良先生和北外的张西平和顾钧两位教授致歉。

最后，想把本书中收入的一篇题为“Turning Stone into Gold: Some Reflections on My Research about the 1854 Shoin-Perry Encounter”的英文论文（原为 2015 年 3 月耶鲁大学图书馆与东京大学史料编纂所合办、在耶鲁大学著名的贝内克珍本书与手稿图书馆召开的国际讨论会上的报告）开头的四言诗之中英对照再录于此，作为结尾与大家分享，因为它概括了我几十年来的学术求索亦即“史海拾贝”的一些体会和感悟。顺便提到，英译者是我在哈佛大学做博士后时互教外语（language exchange）的好友、著名的翻译家 Alan Thwaits。当时他是麻省理工学院出版社的编辑，后来独立开业为中日英三语翻译的专家，我们至今保持着密切的业务往来。

（1）就著碎影拼月亮，自圆其说。（2）大海捞针何处寻，巧思引路。

（3）两个兔子轮番追，有心插柳。（4）问题意识勤磨练，点石成金。

（1）Make your moon whole from partial fragments；justify your claims.

（2）It is hard to fish a needle out of the ocean；use creative thinking to lead the way.

（3）Chase two rabbits in turn；plant a willow with purpose.

（4）Refine your awareness of the question itself；touch a stone and turn it into gold.

最后一句英译的前半部分，是我在大阪大学留学时的好友、现任美国塔夫茨大学日本史教授的 Gary Leupp 先生提示的译法，据说是得自他在新干线上与一位素不相识的日本禅僧讨论时受到的启发，即问题是层出不穷的，研究者需要不断更新其对问题的认知。

陶德民

2017 年 2 月 23 日

于日本大阪古江台书房